Y0-CDD-905

Visions of Women

CONTEMPORARY ISSUES IN BIOMEDICINE, ETHICS, AND SOCIETY

Visions of Women, edited by **Linda A. Bell,** *1983*

Ethics and Animals, edited by **Harlan B. Miller** and **William H. Williams,** *1983*

Profits and Professions, edited by **Wade L. Robison, Michael S. Pritchard,** and **Joseph Ellin,** *1983*

Medical Genetics Casebook, by **Colleen Clements,** *1982*

Who Decides? edited by **Nora K. Bell,** *1982*

The Custom-Made Child?, edited by **Helen B. Holmes, Betty B. Hoskins,** and **Michael Gross,** *1981*

Birth Control and Controlling Birth, edited by **Helen B. Holmes, Betty B. Hoskins,** and **Michael Gross,** *1980*

Medical Responsibility, edited by **Wade L. Robison** and **Michael S. Pritchard,** *1979*

Contemporary Issues in Biomedical Ethics, edited by **John W. Davis, Barry Hoffmaster,** and **Sarah Shorten,** *1979*

Visions
of
Women

Edited and with
an Introduction by

Linda A. Bell

*Being a Fascinating Anthology
with Analysis of Philosophers'
Views of Women
from Ancient to Modern Times*

Humana Press · Clifton, New Jersey

Dedication

To my sister Mary

Library of Congress Cataloging in Publication Data

Main entry under title:

Visions of women.

(Contemporary issues in biomedicine, ethics, and society)
   Includes index.
   1. Women—Addresses, essays, lectures.   2. Philosophical anthropology—Addresses, essays, lectures.
I. Bell, Linda A.   II. Series.
HQ1206.V58   1983   305.4   82-48866
ISBN 0-89603-044-X

©1983 The HUMANA Press Inc.
Crescent Manor
PO Box 2148
Clifton, NJ 07015

All rights reserved

No part of this book may be reproduced, stored in a retrieval system,
or transmitted, in any form or by any means, electronic, mechanical, photo-
copying, microfilming, recording, or otherwise without written
permission from the Publisher.

Printed in the United States of America.

Contents

Introduction   1

Plato

Meno   48
The Republic   50
Timaeus   56
Laws   58

Xenophon

Economics   59

Aristotle

Generation of Animals   63
History of Animals   65
Nichomachean Ethics   66
Politics   66
On Poetics   68

C. Musonius Rufus

"That Women Too Should Study Philosophy"   69
"Should Daughters Receive the Same Education as Sons?"   71
"On Sexual Indulgence"   73
"What Is the Chief End of Marriage?"   75
"Is Marriage a Handicap for the Pursuit of Philosophy?"   75

Quintus Septimus Florens Tertullian

The Apparel of Women   78

Jerome (Eusebius Hieronymus)

Letters   82
Against Jovinianus   83

Aurelius Augustine

The City of God   87
"Adultrous Marriages"   90

Peter Abelard

"Touching the Origin of Nuns"   91

Maimonides (Moses ben Maimon)

The Book of Women   94

Thomas Aquinas

The Summa Theologica   102

Thomas More

Utopia   116
Letters   119

Desiderius Erasmus

In Praise of Folly   125
"The Abbot and the Learned Woman"   126

Luis Vives

Instruction of a Christian Woman   131
The Learning of Women   135

Michel de Montaigne

"Of Friendship"   137
"Of the Affection of Fathers for Their Children"   138
"Of Three Kinds of Association"   139
"On Some Verses of Virgil"   139

Thomas Hobbes

Philosophical Elements of a True Citizen   145
The Elements of Law   145

Baruch Spinoza

Tractatus Politicus   148

John Locke

*Essay Concerning the True Original, Extent, and End of Civil
Government*   150

David Hume

A Treatise of Human Nature   153
"Of the Rise and Progress of the Arts and Sciences"   155
"Of Essay Writing"   156
"Of Love and Marriage"   157
"Of The Study of History"   159

Charles-Louis de Secondat, Baron de Montisquieu

Persian Letters   160
The Spirit of Laws   164

François-Marie Arouet Voltaire

"Women"   171

CONTENTS

Denis Diderot

"On Women" 177
"Woman" 181
Letter to his Daughter 191

Jean-Jacques Rousseau

"On Women" 194
A Discourse on the Origin of Inequality 195
A Discourse on Political Economy 196
Emile 196

Marie-Jean-Antoine-Nicolas Caritat, Marquis de Condorcet

On the Admission of Women to the Rights of Citizenship 209
Letters from a Dweller in New Heaven to a Citizen of Virginia 214

Mary Wollstonecraft

Vindication of the Rights of Woman 218

Immanuel Kant

The Philosophy of Law 239
Observations on the Feeling of the Beautiful and the Sublime 241
Anthropology from a Pragmatic Point of View 247

J. G. Fichte

The Science of Rights 253

G. W. F. Hegel

The Phenomenology of Mind 265
Philosophy of Right 268

Arthur Schopenhauer

"On Women" 270
"Position, or a Man's Place in the Estimation of Others" 277
"Ideas Concerning the Intellect" 278
"On Jurisprudence and Politics" 278
"Psychological Remarks" 279
The World as Will and Idea 279

Auguste Comte

The Positive Philosophy 281
System of Positive Philosophy 282

John Stuart Mill

The Subjection of Women 288

Frederick Engels

The Origin of the Family, Private Property and the State 299

Søren Kierkegaard
Stages of Life's Way   302
Works of Love   312
Journals and Papers   313

Margaret Fuller Ossoli
Woman in the Nineteenth Century   317

Lucretia Mott
''Discourse on Woman''   323

Friedrich Nietzsche
''The Greek Woman''   328
Beyond Good and Evil   330
Human, all-too-Human   334
The Joyful Wisdom   339
Thus Spake Zarathustra   341
The Twilight of the Idols   342
The Antichrist   343
Ecce Homo   343
The Will to Power   344

V. I. Lenin
''The Tasks of the Working Women's Movement in the Soviet
   Republic''   347

Josiah Royce
Letter   352
*On Certain Limitations of the Thoughtful Public in
   America*   353

William James
The Principles of Psychology   354
Review: Bushnell's *Women's Suffrage* and Mill's *Subjection of
   Women*   355

Emily James Putnam
The Lady   365

Emma Goldman
''Victims of Morality''   370
''The Tragedy of Woman's Emancipation''   372
''The Traffic in Women''   376
''Marriage and Love''   377

Anna Garlin Spencer
Woman's Share in Social Culture   381

Charlotte Perkins Gilman

Women in Economics   391
The Home   394
The Man-Made World   396
His Religion and Hers   404

George Santayana

The Life of Reason   405

Otto Weininger

Sex and Character   407

Bertrand Russell

Marriage and Morals   417

Max Scheler

"Toward an Idea of Man"   424
"On the Meaning of the Women's Movement"   425

C. S. Lewis

Letter to Eddison   437
Mere Christianity   437

Simone de Beauvoir

The Ethics of Ambiguity   439
The Second Sex   440

José Ortega y Gasset

Man and People   449
On Love   454

Julián Marías

Metaphysical Anthropology   460

Appendix

Maryellen MacGuigan: "Is Woman a Question?"   468

Index   481

Preface

People of Socrates' time were frequently aghast at the questions he would ask. Their responses were of the sort elicited by very dumb or extremely obvious questions: "Don't you know? Everyone else does."

Socrates was hardly alone in his knack for asking such questions. Philosophers have always asked peculiar questions most other people would never dream of asking, convinced as the latter are that the answers were settled long ago in the collective "wisdom" of society, including questions about woman: should women be educated? should they rule societies? should they be subordinate in marriage? do women and men have the same virtues, or are there separate virtues for each? which of the differences between women and men are conventional, and which are natural? is there a woman's work? do women and men have different types or degrees of rationality? Philosophers of the most diverse periods have raised these questions and their answers were often quite creative, not merely reflecting the conventions and mores of their societies.

With the publication of this anthology, their writings will be brought together in a single volume for the first time. This anthology differs from others not just in its inclusiveness. It also contains several translations of material previously unavailable in English. Moreover, it recovers for today's readers some pieces that, though previously published in English, were virtually lost because they were long out of print and relatively few copies seem to have endured. In addition, this anthology uncovers discussions of woman unfamiliar to many because they have essentially been buried in philosophical works on other subjects.

Although many philosophers have written about woman, relatively little is known about this aspect of the history of philosophy. Even less is known about the more feminist treatments of the various questions, and a remarkable number of philosophers were, at least by the standards of their own times, raging feminists. Questions about woman appear to have been generally regarded as not serious philosophical questions, and feminist answers to such questions have received the worst treatment.

For example, Plato proposed that women be educated in the same way as men, those capable becoming rulers. Plato was not always so favorably disposed toward women, and he hastens to add his conviction that no matter what the capabilities of a woman, there will always be some man who can best her. What is revealing is not Plato's apparent ambivalence about women and their abilities, but rather the derision that has greeted his suggestion that women be educated and perhaps even become rulers. Some noted scholars have even argued that the absurdity of this proposal indicated that Plato himself was not serious about the allegedly ideal society which he developed in *The Republic*.

Another philosopher, Erasmus, is well-known for his work *In Praise of Folly* where women are singled out for their folly. But Erasmus also wrote a short and delightful play, "The Abbot and the Learned Woman." It is virtually unknown and in fact is rather difficult to find today, printed in a slightly garbled version in a single volume of Erasmus' work. Yet in it, a "learned woman," believed to have been modeled after Margaret More Roper, Thomas More's eldest daughter, wins an intellectual joust with a not-so-learned abbot.

Condorcet's feminist writings have fared even worse. An essay arguing for the admission of women to the rights of citizenship was translated and published in the early 1900s and as far as I know has not been reprinted. A longer work in which Condorcet develops a similarly feminist stance with respect to women vis-à-vis government never has been translated into English; at least, such a translation has never been published.

John Stuart Mill may at first appear to be the exception in this list since his feminist work, *The Subjection of Women*, admittedly is quite well-known. The sense in which it is well-known, however, belies Mill's apparent status as an exception. Though most who study philosophy are familiar with the fact that Mill wrote this book, few references are seen to the arguments developed therein. There is little evidence to indicate that the book is widely read, much less discussed.

It is bad enough that the more feminist works and arguments have been generally ignored. The problem is compounded when we stop to recall the attention paid the antifeminist claims, even the most outlandish. For example, few philosophy majors make it through graduate school, perhaps even through college, without hearing several references, most snickering but some rather solemn, to Aristotle's view of the female as a deformed male, conceived when there is not sufficient heat to generate the superior product—a male. During my student days, philosophy instructors and fellow (male) students were quite fond of citing antifeminist and even misogynist arguments from Rousseau's *Emile* and from Schopenhauer's essay "On Women." It is not just in departments of philosophy that these antifeminist and misogynist arguments have continued to so seize attention as to exclude any serious discussion of counterarguments. These arguments have also exerted an extraordinary influence on our whole culture, although the original sources have long since been obscured by the causal chain that carries their effects into our day.

To understand these unenlightened, antifeminist arguments and to evaluate their impact on our society it is helpful to see the arguments at their origin and to examine the counterattacks that were developed against them then and later. In the following pages of this anthology, these arguments and counterarguments are presented as they were developed historically. This format will prove most useful to students of philosophy and history who wish to examine the views of certain philosophers or of particular periods. For those who are more interested in specific questions about women, the Introduction delineates a number of different questions, indicates readings in which the individual questions are discussed, and gives a brief synopsis of the alternative answers to each question.

This anthology reflects the expertise, willing assistance, and psychological support of many people. Diane L. Fowlkes, Thomas Fox, Janelle L. McCammon, R. Barton Palmer, and Irene B. Seay were especially generous in their willlingness to translate or to offer their translations for this volume. I am most grateful for the time and energy they have devoted to making this book possible.

Others who deserve special mention and thanks are Linda Alcoff, John Beversluis, Susan Fox Beversluis, Christine W. Sizemore, and Albert C. Skaggs for hours spent reading, rereading, and critiquing my introduction and much besides; Elizabeth Beardsley and Robert Fogelin for their helpful critiques and useful evaluations of my earlier proposals of this book; John B. Bell, III, Barbara Conner, Barbara Cornelius, Tony Edmunds, Paul G. Kuntz, C. G. Luckhardt, Helen North, Charlotte S. McClure, Anthony and Marcella Quinton, Jack Rice, and Jane F. Schneider for their suggestions of philosophers and works that should be included; Michael B. Brown for his painstaking transcription of a work unavailable to me, Jane G. Hobson for tracing and securing many of the volumes with which I have worked; Patricia E. Tucker for her encouragement and typing assistance; Glenn R. Jackson for his assistance with proofing; Fran Lipton for her careful work at Humana Press; and my sister Mary L. Law for her many suggestions and for her optimistic yet extraordinarily practical encouragement.

Others have of course contributed, albeit sometimes unwittingly, to the existence of this book as well as to my interest in the subject. Since their contributions were negative, I shall not mention them by name. Surely, however, some credit should be given to the graduate professor who so gratuitously informed me that he thought fellowships were wasted on women, to those of my fellow graduate students who contended that women in philosophy were usurping a male tradition, and to the department chairman who begrudgingly admitted that an occasional female academician was pretty good—for a woman. Their sometimes dogmatic and one-sided views not only made me painfully aware of prejudices against women, but also developed in me a determination to subject such views to a clear-headed examination.

The idea for this book and an awareness of the need for it grew out of my participation in the Women's Studies Group at Georgia State University, an informal group of scholars, in which I found an intensity of concern and an attitude of mutual support that embodied what for me is the true significance of academe and which sustained me in my completion of this project. In our early discussions of possible women's studies courses, I became aware how little I knew of philosophers' views of woman. I began my research for this anthology when I realized that no such book existed. What I found in the course of my research surprised and delighted me, and I turn the results of my labor over to future readers with the earnest wish that they may find the following positions and arguments as surprising and delightful, as stimulating, as I found them.

Linda A. Bell

Acknowledgments

Plato, *Meno,* trans. W. R. M. Lamb (New York: G. P. Putnam's Sons, 1924).

———, *The Republic,* I, trans. Paul Shorey (New York: G. P. Putnam's Sons, 1930).

———, *Timaeus, The Dialogues of Plato,* Vol. II, trans. B. Jowett (New York: Charles Scribner and Company, 1871).

———, *Laws,* I, trans. R. G. Bury (New York: G. P. Putnam's Sons, 1926).

Xenophon, *Memorabilia and Oeconomicus,* trans. E. C. Marchant (Cambridge: Harvard University Press, 1938), reprinted by permission of the publisher.

Aristotle, *Generation of Animals,* trans. A. L. Peck (Cambridge: Harvard University Press, 1943), reprinted by permission of the publisher.

———, *Historia Animalium,* IX, trans. D'Arcy Wentworth Thompson (Oxford: Oxford University Press, 1949), reprinted by permission of the publisher.

———, *Ethica Nicomachea,* VIII, trans. W. D. Ross (Oxford: Oxford University Press, 1949), reprinted by permission of the publisher.

———, *Politica,* I, trans. Benjamin Jowett (Oxford: Oxford University Press, 1946), reprinted by permission of the publisher.

———, *De Poetica,* trans. Ingram Bywater (Oxford: Oxford University Press, 1946), reprinted by permission of the publisher.

C. Musonius Rufus, "Musonius Rufus, 'The Roman Socrates,' " trans. Cora E. Lutz, *Yale Classical Studies,* Volume Ten, ed. Alfred R. Bellinger (New Haven: Yale University Press, 1947), reprinted by permission of the Department of Classics, Yale University.

Quintus Septimus Florens Tertullian, *The Apparel of Women, Disciplinary, Moral and Ascetical Works,* trans. Rudolph Arbesmann, O.S.A., Sister Emily Joseph Daly, C.S.J., Edwin A. Quain, S.J. (New York: Fathers of the Church, Inc., 1959), reprinted by permission of Sister Emily Joseph Daly, C.S.J., and the Very Reverend Vincent M. Cooke, S. J.

Jerome (Eusebius Hieronymus), Letter XXII, Letter CXXVIII, and *Against Jovinianus, The Principle Works of St. Jerome,* trans. W. H. Fremantle, G. Lewis, and W. G. Martley, *A Select Library of Nicene and Post-Nicene Fathers of the Christian Church,* Vol. VI, ed. Philip Schaff and Henry Wace (New York: The Christian Literature Company, 1893).

Aurelius Augustine, *The City of God,* trans. Marcus Dods (New York: Random House, Inc., 1950), reprinted by permission of T & T Clark Ltd.

———, "Adultrous Marriages," trans. Charles T. Huegelmeyer, *Treatises on Marriage and Other Subjects, Fathers of the Church,* Vol. 27, ed. Roy J. Deferrari (Washington: The Catholic University of America Press, 1955), reprinted by permission of the publisher.

Peter Abelard, "The Seventh Letter Which Is the Reply of Peter to Heloise. Touching the Origin of Nuns," *The Letters of Abelard and Heloise,* trans. C. K. Scott Moncrieff (New York: Alfred A. Knopf, 1926), reprinted by permission of the publisher and Ms. Margaret Storm Jameson whose husband Guy Chapman commissioned the translation and paid for its publication.

Maimonides (Moses ben Maimon), *The Book of Women, The Code of Maimonides,* Book Four, trans. Issac Klein (New Haven: Yale University Press, 1972), reprinted by permission of the publisher.

Thomas Aquinas, The "Summa Theologica," trans. Fathers of the English Dominican Province (New York: Benziger Brothers, 1921), reprinted by permission of the publisher.

Thomas More, Utopia, trans. Paul Turner (Baltimore: Penguin Books Ltd., 1965), copyright (c) 1965 by Paul Turner, reprinted by permission of the publisher.

——, The Correspondence of Sir Thomas More, ed. Elizabeth Frances Rogers (Princeton: Princeton University Press, 1947), copyright (c) 1947 by Princeton University Press, renewed 1974 by Elizabeth Rogers, reprinted by permission of the publisher.

Desiderius Erasmus, In Praise of Folly, trans. anonymous (London: Reeves and Turner, 1876).

——, "The Abbot and the Learned Woman," Twenty Two Select Colloquies out of Erasmus Roterodamus, trans. Sir Roger L'Estrange (London: printed for R. Sare and H. Hindmarsh, 1699).

Luis Vives, Instruction of a Christian Woman and The Learning of Women, Vives and the Renaissance Education of Women, ed. Foster Watson (New York: Longmans, Green and Company, 1912).

Michel Eyguem de Montaigne, "Of Friendship," "Of the Affection of Fathers for their Children," "Of Three Kinds of Association," and "On Some Verses from Virgil," The Complete Essays of Montaigne, trans. Donald M. Frame (Stanford: Stanford University Press, 1958), copyright (c) 1943 by Donald M. Frame, renewed 1971, copyright (c) 1948, 1957, and 1958 by the Board of Trustees of the Leland Stanford Junior University, reprinted by permission of the publisher.

Thomas Hobbes, "Philosophical Elements of a True Citizen," Philosophical Rudiments Concerning Government and Society, The English Works of Thomas Hobbes, Vol. II, ed. Sir William Molesworth (London: John Bohn, 1841).

——, The Elements of Law, ed. Ferdinand Tönnies (Cambridge: Cambridge University Press, 1928), reprinted by permission of the publisher.

Baruch Spinoza, Tractatus Politicus, The Chief Works of Benedict de Spinoza, Vol. I, trans. R. H. M. Elwes (London: George Bell and Sons, 1891).

John Locke, "Essay Concerning the True Original, Extent, and End of Civil Government," Two Treatises of Government (London: C. Baldwin, 1824).

David Hume, A Treatise of Human Nature, ed. L. A. Selby-Bigge (Oxford: Clarendon Press, 1888).

——, "On the Rise and Progress of the Arts and Sciences," "Of Essay Writing," "Of Love and Marriage," and "Of the Study of History," Essays, Moral, Political, and Literary, ed. T. H. Green and T. H. Grose (London: Longmans, Green, and Company, 1875).

Charles-Louis de Secondat, Baron de Montesquieu, Persian Letters, trans. John Davidson (New York: E. P. Dutton and Company, 1891).

——, The Spirit of Laws, trans. Thomas Nugent (New York: The Colonial Press, 1899).

François-Marie Arouet Voltaire, Voltaire's Philosophical Dictionary, Vol. X, trans. William F. Fleming (New York: E. R. DuMont, 1901).

Denis Diderot, "On Women," Dialogues by Denis Diderot, trans. Francis Birrell (Port Washington, New York: Kennikat Press, 1971).

——, "Femme," trans. for this volume by R. Barton Palmer and Irene B. Seay, Encyclopédie, Vol. VI, ed. Diderot and D'Alembert (Paris: Briasson, etc., 1751).

——, Le Bréviaire des jeunes Mariees, trans. for this volume by R. Barton Palmer (Paris: Albert Messein, 1922).

Jean-Jacques Rousseau, "Sur les Femmes," trans. for this volume by Diane L. Fowlkes and Janelle McCammon, Annales de la Societe Jean-Jacques Rousseau, t. 1 (Geneve: A Jullien, 1905).

——, *The Social Contract and Discourses,* An Everyman's Library Edition, trans. G.D.H. Cole (New York: E. P. Dutton and Company, 1950), reprinted by permission of the publisher in the United States, E. P. Dutton, and J. M. Dent & Sons.

——, *Emile,* An Everyman's Library Edition, trans. Barbara Foxley (New York: E. P. Dutton, 1911), reprinted by permission of the publisher in the United States, E. P. Dutton, and J. M. Dent & Sons.

Marie-Jean-Antoine-Nicolas Caritat, Marquis de Condorcet, "On the Admission of Women to the Rights of Citizenship," *The First Essay on the Political Rights of Women,* trans. Alice Drysdale Vickery (Letchworth: Garden City Press, Limited, 1912).

——, *Lettres d'un bourgeois de New-Heaven a un citoyen de Virginie,* trans. for this volume by R. Barton Palmer, *Recherches sur les États-Unis,* Première Partie, Vol. I, ed. M. Mazzei (Paris: A. Colle, 1788).

Mary Wollstonecraft, *A Vindication of the Rights of Woman,* a Norton Critical Edition, ed. Carol H. Poston (New York: W. W. Norton & Company, Inc., 1975), copyright (c) 1975 by W. W. Norton & Company, Inc., reprinted by permission of the publisher.

Immanuel Kant, *The Philosophy of Law: An Exposition of the Fundamental Principles of Jurisprudence as the Science of Right,* trans. W. Hastie (Edinburgh: T & T Clark, 1887, reprinted Clifton, New Jersey: Augustus M. Kelley, 1974).

——, *Observations on the Feeling of the Beautiful and Sublime,* trans. John T. Goldthwait (Berkeley: University of California Press, 1960), reprinted by permission of the publisher.

——, *Anthropology from a Pragmatic Point of View,* ISBN 90-247-1585-7, trans. Mary J. Gregor (The Hague: Martinus Nijoff, 1974), reprinted by permission of the publisher.

J. G. Fichte, *The Science of Rights,* trans. A. E. Kroeger (London: Trübner and Company, 1889).

G. W. F. Hegel, *The Phenomenology of Mind,* trans. J. B. Baillie (New York: The Macmillan Company, 1961), reprinted by permission of George Allen & Unwin Ltd.

——, *Hegel's Philosophy of Right,* trans. T. M. Knox (Oxford: Clarendon Press, 1952), reprinted by permission of Oxford University Press.

Arthur Schopenhauer, "On Women," "Position, or a Man's Place in the Estimation Others," *Essays from the Parega and Paralipomena,* trans. T. Bailey Saunders (London: George Allen & Unwin Ltd., 1890).

——, "Ideas Concerning the Intellect," "Of Jurisprudence and Politics." "Psychological Remarks," *Parega and Paralipomena,* Vol. II, trans. E. F. J. Payne (Oxford: Clarendon Press, 1974), reprinted by permission of Oxford University Press.

——, *The World as Will and Idea,* Vol. III, trans. R. B. Haldane and J. Kemp (London: Kegan Paul, Trench, Trubner and Company, Inc., 1844).

Auguste Comte, *Auguste Comte and Positivism: The Essential Writings,* ed. Gertrud Lenzer (New York: Harper & Row Publishers, Inc., 1975).

John Stuart Mill, *The Subjection of Women* (New York: D. Appleton and Company, 1869).

Frederick Engels, *The Origin of the Family, Private Property and the State,* (Moscow: Foreign Languages Publishing House, 5th Impression), reprinted by permission of International Publishers.

Søren Kierkegaard, *Stages on Life's Way,* trans. and ed. Walter Lowrie (Princeton: Princeton University Press, 1945), copyright 1940 (c) 1968 by Princeton University Press, reprinted by permission of the publishers.

——, *Works of Love,* trans. Howard and Edna Hong (London: Collins Clear-Type Press, 1962), copyright (c) 1962 by Howard Hong, reprinted by permission of Harper & Row Publishers, Inc.

———, *Kierkegaard's Journals and Papers*, Vol. 4, ed. and trans. Howard V. Hong and Edna H. Hong (Bloomington: Indiana University Press, 1975), copyright (c) 1975 by Howard V. Hong, reprinted by permission of the publisher.

Margaret Fuller Ossoli, *Woman in the Nineteenth Century,Woman in the Nineteenth Century, and Kindred Papers Relating to the Sphere, Condition, and Duties of Woman* (Boston: Roberts Brothers, 1875).

Lucretia Mott, "Discourse on Woman," *James and Lucretia Mott: Life and Letters*, ed. Alice Davis Hallowell (Boston and Cambridge : Houghton Mifflin and Company and The Riverside Press, 1884).

Friedrich Nietzsche, "The Greek Woman—Fragment (1871)," *Early Greek Philosophy and Other Essays*, trans. Maximilian A. Mügge, under the general editorship of Oscar Levy (London: T. N. Foulis, 1911), reprinted by permission of George Allen & Unwin Ltd.

———, *Beyond Good and Evil*, trans. Helen Zimmern, under the general editorship of Oscar Levy (New York: reissued Russell & Russell, 1964), reprinted by permission of the publisher and George Allen & Unwin Ltd.

———, *Human, all-too-Human*, Part I, trans. Helen Zimmern, Part II, trans. Paul V. Cohn, under the general editorship of Oscar Levy (London: T. N. Foulis, 1909 and 1911), reprinted by permission of George Allen & Unwin Ltd.

———, *The Joyful Wisdom*, trans. Thomas Common, under the general editorship of Oscar Levy (London: T. N. Foulis, 1910), reprinted by permission of George Allen & Unwin Ltd.

———, *Thus Spake Zarathustra*, trans. Thomas Common, under the general editorship of Oscar Levy (New York: The Macmillan Company, 1923), reprinted by permission of George Allen & Unwin Ltd.

———, *The Twilight of the Idols*, trans. Anthony M. Ludovici, under the general editorship of Oscar Levy (London: T. N. Foulis, 1911), reprinted by permission of George Allen & Unwin Ltd.

———, *The Antichrist*, trans. Anthony M. Ludovici, under the general editorship of Oscar Levy (London: T. N. Foulis, 1911), reprinted by permission of George Allen & Unwin Ltd.

———, *Ecce Homo*, trans. Anthony M. Ludovici, under the general editorship of Oscar Levy (London: T. N. Foulis, 1911), reprinted by permission of George Allen & Unwin Ltd.

———, *The Will to Power*, trans. Anthony M. Ludovici, under the general editorship of Oscar Levy (London: T. N. Foulis, 1909), reprinted by permission of George Allen & Unwin Ltd.

V. I. Lenin, "The Tasks of the Working Women's Movement in the Soviet Republic," *Selected Works* (New York: International Publishers, 1943), reprinted by permission of the publisher.

Josiah Royce, Letter, *The Letters of Josiah Royce*, ed. John Clendenning (Chicago: The University of Chicago Press, 1970), copyright (c) 1970 by the University of Chicago, reprinted by permission of the publisher.

———, *On Certain Limitations of the Thoughtful Public in America, The Basic Writings of Josiah Royce*, Vol. 2, ed. John J. McDermott (Chicago: The University of Chicago Press, 1969), reprinted by permission of David Royce.

William James, *The Principles of Psychology*, Vol. II (New York: Henry Holt and Company, 1904).

———, Review, *The North American Review* 109 (October 1869).

Emily James Putnam, *The Lady: Studies of Certain Significant Phases of Her History* (New York and London: G. P. Putnam's Sons and the Knickerbocker Press, 1910).

Emma Goldman, "Victims of Morality," "The Tragedy of Woman's Emancipation," "The Traffic in Women," "Marriage and Love," *Red Emma Speaks: Selected Writings and Speeches,* ed. Alix Kates Shulman (New York: Random House, 1972), reprinted by permission of Alix Kates Shulman.

Anna Garlin Spencer, *Woman's Share in Social Culture* (New York: reprinted Arno Press Inc., 1972).

Charlotte Perkins Gilman, *Women and Economics,* ed. Carl N. Degler (New York: Harper & Row Publishers, Inc., 1966).

———, *The Home: Its Work and Influence* (New York: McClure, Phillips & Co., 1903).

———, *The Man-Made World* (New York and London: reprinted Johnson Reprint Corporation, 1971), reprinted by permission of The Arthur and Elizabeth Schlesinger Library on the History of Women in America, Radcliffe College.

———, *His Religion and Hers: A Study of the Faith of Our Fathers and the Work of Our Mothers* (Westport, Connecticut: reprinted Hyperion Press, Inc., 1963), reprinted by permission of the Arthur and Elizabeth Schlesinger Library on the History of Women in America, Radcliffe College.

George Santayana, *The Life of Reason,* Book II (New York: Charles Scribner's Sons, 1932), reprinted by permission of the publisher.

Otto Weininger, *Sex and Character,* trans. anonymous (New York: reprinted G. P. Putnam's Sons, 1975).

Bertrand Russell, *Marriage and Morals* (New York: Horace Liveright, 1929), copyright 1929 by Horace Liveright, Inc., renewed 1957 by Bertrand Russell, reprinted by permission of Liveright Publishing Corporation and George Allen & Unwin, Ltd.

Max Scheler, "Zur Idee des Menschen" and "Zum Sinn der Frauenbewegun," trans. for this volume by Thomas Fox, *Vom Umsturz der Werte: Abhandlungen und Aufsätze* (Bern: Francke Verlag, 1955).

C. S. Lewis, Letter, *C. S. Lewis: A Biography* (New York: Harcourt Brace Jovanovich, 1974), reprinted by permission of the publisher.

———, *Mere Christianity* (New York: Macmillan Publishing Company, Inc., 1974), copyright 1943, 1945, 1952 by Macmillan Publishing Company, Inc., copyright renewed, reprinted by permission of the publisher and Collins Publishers.

Simone de Beauvoir, *The Ethics of Ambiguity,* trans. Bernard Frechtman (New York: Philosophical Library, 1948), reprinted by permission of the publisher.

———, *The Second Sex,* trans. H. M. Parshley (New York: Alfred A. Knopf, 1971), copyright (c) 1952 by Alfred A. Knopf, reprinted by permission of the publisher and Jonathan Cape Ltd.

José Ortega y Gasset, *Man and People,* trans. Willard R. Trask (New York: W. W. Norton & Company, Inc., 1957), copyright (c) 1957 by W. W. Norton & Company, Inc., reprinted by permission of the publisher.

———, "The Role of Choice in Love," "Thoughts on Standing Before the Marquesa de Santillana's Portrait," "Landscape with a Deer in the Background," "Portrait of Salome," *On Love,* trans. Toby Talbot (New York: World Publishing Co., 1957), copyright (c) 1957 by Tony Talbot, reprinted by permission of The New American Library, Inc., New York, N.Y.

Julián Marías, *Metaphysical Anthropology,* trans. Frances M. Lopez-Morillas (University Park: The Pennsylvania State University Press, 1971), reprinted by permission of the publisher.

Maryellen MacGuigan, "Is Woman a Question?" *International Philosophical Quarterly* 13 (December 1973), reprinted by permission of the publisher.

Introduction

Why This Book?

What is woman? What do women want? What ought women to do? Are women human?

Such questions have occupied thoughtful people throughout history. People who would never think of asking "what is man?" "what do men want?" "what ought men to do?" "are men human?" have asked these very questions in complete seriousness about women. Only occasionally has anyone challenged the appropriateness of the questions themselves.

The range of answers that has emerged is broad and intriguing. Woman has been variously defined as the weaker sex, a deformed male, the inferior sex, the other, man's helpmate. She has been seen as an enigma, as a temptress, as one who is childlike, confused, or whimsical. She has been viewed both as too good for work and as only good enough for certain kinds of work. She has, on the one hand, been portrayed as an ethereal, almost totally disembodied creature and, on the other, as a creature totally preoccupied with and limited by the functions of her body. She has been seen as capable of being fulfilled only by engaging in "woman's work": childbirth and being the object of a man's love. She has been eulogized as more than human and patronized as less than human. Only rarely has she been regarded simply as human, all too human.

Philosophers, no less than others, have asked these questions about women and have tried to answer them. Even those who question the appropriateness of asking such questions have been forced to address the issues raised by others. With several notable exceptions, however, their statements about women occur within their works in a somewhat offhand way, sometimes as seemingly irrelevant asides, and almost always as incidental to the main topic being discussed. As a result, the statements are relatively inaccessible. To locate them is difficult even for the widely read student of philosophy and all but impossible for the novice.

In the present volume, these passages have been collected and brought together in a form that renders them accessible to everyone. Until fairly recently, many might have responded to such a collection in a bored or quizzical way. Some no doubt would have regarded it as a mere curiosity: why would anyone want to read, much less publish, what has been said about women? Today attitudes are changing. The subject of woman has

1

attracted wide-spread interest. Both men and women are examining their social roles as well as the traditions, myths, folklore, and factual claims within which those roles have been articulated and defined.

This examination, however, is far from complete. Indeed, it is just beginning. If this examination is to challenge traditional attitudes and to lead to truly adequate answers, it will require many critical tools and a far greater awareness of alternatives than has traditionally been the norm. What philosophers have said about women is, then, likely to be especially relevant. Their statements about women vary enormously. Some will likely impress readers as particularly insightful. Others may seem quaint or, given our present assumptions, rather silly. However, even the most outlandish of these statements develop and probe the implications of alternative views of woman, notions that need to be considered seriously whether or not they are ultimately rejected. However limited, one-sided, or fantastic, the views recorded here are nevertheless likely to be more clearly stated, more reflective, and better-argued than are many of the popular views espoused in our society.

Given their range and variety, the statements and arguments about women included in this book are likely to anger some and to offend others. Perhaps such anger and offense will be compounded because they are occasioned by writers and minds whose intellectual products are deeply respected and, in some cases, revered. In spite of (or perhaps because of) the likelihood of anger and offense, a reading of the specific statements embodying these views can help us to see more clearly and to examine with greater sensitivity the myths and the traditions within which we live. They can prompt us to question the folklore and ''facts'' we have been taught. And they can move us to reflect more critically and creatively on the question, What is it to be a woman? and on the correlative question, What is it to be a man?

In order to keep the size of this book within manageable limits, the selections have been limited as much as possible to writings by philosophers. This particular criterion of selectivity was chosen because the philosophical perspectives are those clearly weakest in presently available women's studies textbooks. The selections begin with the work of Plato and end with an excerpt from a very recent book by Julián Marías. Although some attempt has been made to be comprehensive with respect to the range of available positions, no attempt has been made to be exhaustive in the sense of including everything that any philosopher has ever said about women. Much has been omitted because it was repetitious and hence did not add appreciably either to an earlier or better treatment of the same position by another philosopher or to a better treatment of the position by the same philosopher.

To say, however, that the selections in this book have been limited to philosophers is not as clear as it may seem. For the question of who is to be counted as a philosopher is a disturbing one for anyone engaged in collecting opinions. Rather than deciding who is or is not a philosopher on grounds that are themselves philosophical, I have generally employed a more objective and incontestable set of criteria: history, peer recognition, and the individual's educational background. The use of these criteria has, however, had the somewhat unfortunate result of excluding many women who have written on the subject of woman with philosophical astuteness as well as great sensitivity.* Still others have been excluded by the fact that space does not allow the inclusion of recent journal articles.†

The fact that so few women are represented in these pages reflects the position of women vis-à-vis the field of philosophy. Until fairly recently, relatively few women had obtained a philosophical education and even fewer had been regarded by their colleagues as philosophers.‡ In addition, however, the paucity of women included here can be traced to another problem not entirely unrelated to the first. This is the need for effacement that female writers and artists have frequently encountered, namely, the usually unspoken requirement that in order to be accepted and recognized in their respective areas, women adopt the expedient of camouflaging to varying degrees the fact that they are women. Because so many women have had constantly to deny that there are any important differences between themselves and their male colleagues, it becomes unlikely, and possibly even counterproductive, that they would spend much time and energy on questions about the nature, capabilities, and rights of women.

Suggestions for Reading

The selections reprinted here are arranged historically, partly so that they may be read in the context of their philosophical and/or historical settings and partly to give rise in the reader's mind to questions concerning the relation between history and thought. The "newness" of many of the

*One such writer is Dorothy L. Sayers. Two essays from her book *Unpopular Opinions* have recently been reprinted in a little book, *Are Women Human?* Mary McDermott Shideler, ed. (Grand Rapids, Michigan: Eerdmans, 1971).

†Such articles are fairly accessible. Two important collections of recent articles are *Feminism and Philosophy*, edited by Mary Vetterling-Braggain, Frederick A. Elliston, and Jane English (Totowa, New Jersey: Littlefield, Adams, 1977) and the "Women's Liberation" issue of *The Monist* **57** (No. 1): (January 1973). In addition, the following articles go together quite nicely and provide an interesting and important supplement to the present book: J. R. Lucas, "Because You Are a Woman," *Philosophy* **48**:161–171 (April 1973); Susan Haack, "On the Moral Relevance of Sex," *Philosophy* **49**:90–95 (January 1974); Trudy R. Govier, "Woman's Place," *Philosophy* **49**:303–309 (July 1974).

‡As a case in point, it is notable that Simone de Beauvoir is so casually dismissed by many philosophers as merely an "adjunct" to Jean-Paul Sartre, a fact apparently reflected by the failure of *The Encyclopedia of Philosophy* even to include her in the index.

older views and the "oldness" of some of the most recent may well star-
tle readers, thereby helping all of us to shake off the lethargy and mental
inertia that our pervasive and unquestioning faith in the inevitability of
social and intellectual progress seems to generate. Certainly the issues
raised in these selections are far too important to be relegated to the general grab-bag of problems that "time" will somehow resolve.

Many readers, however, may prefer a nonhistorical approach. They
may prefer to read through these selections in a problem-oriented manner,
perhaps even focusing only on certain problems of most pressing concern
to each. As an aid to such readers, a problem-oriented discussion is provided in the last section of this Introduction. For each of the problems, I
have provided a list of recommended readings that not only include the
most important treatments of a particular question, but are also sufficiently comprehensive to give a fair picture of the diversity of answers to
that question. Following the list of recommended readings is a brief
discussion and overview of the answers. Readers who may wish to probe
a particular subject or problem even more thoroughly are referred to the
index.

The specific problems discussed arise naturally from the selections
themselves. They address a wide range of questions including the artistic
capacity of women, their biology, education, and employment, women's
secondary status as reflected in linguistic conventions, women's views of
love and sex, women's role in marriage and the role of marriage in their
lives, women's relation to their children, women's moral capacity, their
political rights and responsibilities, their property rights, their position
vis-à-vis religion, and the function of the women's movement. Although
presently much-debated questions such as abortion and reverse discrimination are not explicitly addressed per se, the subjects dealt with here will
be found to have considerable bearing on these current issues. Throughout these selections, in fact, the reader will frequently discover the philosophical arguments that underlie a great deal of contemporary discussion.

Problems

The Artistic Capacity of Women

Why have women not contributed more substantially to the arts to which
they have long had some access?

MAIN READINGS

Condorcet, *Letters from a Dweller in New Heaven to a Citizen of
Virginia*

Wollstonecraft, *Vindications of the Rights of Woman*
Fichte, *The Science of Rights*
Hegel, *Philosophy of Right*
Schopenhauer, "On Women"
Mill, *The Subjection of Women*
Ossoli, *Woman in the Nineteenth Century*
Nietzsche, *Twilight of the Idols*
            The Will to Power
Spencer, *Woman's Share in Social Culture*
Gilman, *The Man-Made World*
Marías, *Metaphysical Anthropology*

ADDITIONAL READINGS

Rousseau, "On Women"
James, Review

Discussion

Misogynists are fond of pointing to the virtual absence of women's works of art from museums, symphony programs, and books devoted to the history of the arts. They claim that, although artistic pursuits have long been open to women, they have not achieved in these areas, therefore, it must follow that women are inferior to men. Hegel, Schopenhauer, and Nietzsche offer similar explanations for the "fact" of non-achievement by women. Hegel's answer is based on woman's alleged natural place in the universe, while Schopenhauer and Nietzsche base their views on her alleged lack of any artistic sense or susceptibility.

What is important for Ossoli is that women have intellects to be developed, not whether they will contribute to literature or art. Even so, she thinks that "Woman" may have a special genius that inspires rather than creates art. Though women may generally embody more of the feminine element, the masculine and feminine elements pervade every human personality, according to Ossoli; thus, her recognition of a special feminine genius would only lead us to expect fewer artistic achievements by women than by men.

On the other hand, Condorcet suggests that at least part of the explanation for women's lack of achievement is to be found in their submission to men throughout history, adding that few creative geniuses have emerged from other submissive situations such as, for example, monasteries. Wollstonecraft develops a similar argument, emphasizing the role of passive obedience that is trained into women from infancy on. She compares the state of women to that of the wealthy and points to a similar lack of accomplishment in both cases.

Spencer points to the obstacles to intellectual and artistic development posed to a woman by marriage and maternity. Not only is a woman's muse "intermitted" by child-bearing and its duties; but, as she notes, few women have "wives" to care for them and smooth their way. Even second-rate male "geniuses" usually have such assistance in addition to the social approval not granted to a woman who sacrifices the fortunes and well-being of her family to her talent.

For Gilman, the position of woman vis-à-vis art is an inevitable outcome of our "Androcentric Culture." Although women originated the primitive arts along with primitive industry, these were taken over and developed by men while women were made into servants or into idle pets in harems. Women were left with their primitive decorative arts while men developed "Art," frequently imprinting it with a heavily masculinized influence, thus even more successfully barring women from contributing.

Condorcet also suggests that, in fields other than philosophy and the sciences, there is evidence of female genius. Mill wonders whether anything is actually known about what woman can do and be since there is no way to study her apart from her historical subservience to men. (It is this very thesis that is challenged by James.) Apart from this reservation, however, Mill develops an interesting variation of an argument offered earlier by Condorcet, noting that there are few, if any, activities dependent on mental faculties in which women have not achieved a rank at least next to the highest. Thus, although they have been surpassed by some men, some women have accomplished far more than the vast majority of men. Like Mill, Fichte, too, presents the problem of women's non-achievement as an exaggerated problem, contending that women's achievements are notable, although he adds that women are practical and hence unable to go beyond the limits of their feelings. This latter fact, he thinks, explains why women have made remarkable accomplishments in many areas, but not in philosophy and in theoretical aspects of the mathematical sciences.

Toward the end of the selection from Marías, a middle-ground position emerges. Seeing woman's nature as essentially different from man's, Marías argues that women are in effect going against the grain when they try to achieve *within* the forms and categories of what has been and continues to be men's culture, and that it will take time and much creative genius for women to develop a culture that uniquely expresses their nature.

Although not addressing this problem per se, what Rousseau has to say about history is also relevant here: namely, that if women rather than men were to write history, most assuredly their accounts of heroism would differ radically from previous histories (which have been written by men) and would probably recognize the accomplishments of many more women.

Biology of Woman

Is Biology a Destiny?

READINGS

Diderot, "On Women"
Rousseau, *Emile*
Wollstonecraft, *Vindication of the Rights of Woman*
Schopenhauer, "On Women"
Mill, *The Subjection of Women*
Nietzsche, *Beyond Good and Evil*
Gilman, *Women and Economics*
       The Man-Made World
Lewis, Letter to Eddison
de Beauvoir, *The Second Sex*
Ortega, *Man and People*
       On Love ("Portrait of Salome")

Discussion

Many have argued that biology determines a woman's future at least to the extent that her desires, needs, capacity for rationality, and other capabilities are limited accordingly. Those who disagree often point out the difficulty in distinguishing, in human beings at least, those factors that are natural and caused, for example, by hormonal differences, from those that are artificial and produced by education and other forms of social conditioning.

Mill, Gilman, and de Beauvoir argue that biology is no more a destiny for a woman than for a man. Although they agree that there may be certain things that women are precluded from doing because of their sexual constitution or because they may not be able to do them as well as men, both raise questions about the extent of these disabilities and, in particular, raise doubts about how many of them result from education and conditioning rather than from some natural or inherent inferiority.

Rousseau's discussion of woman is especially interesting for what he has to say about the proper method for distinguishing differences owing to sex from other differences: he simply proclaims that similarities between men and women indicate characteristics of the species, whereas *any* differences have to do with the characteristics of sex. In addition, his observation concerning the consequences of sex makes explicit what is probably the underlying assumption common to all those who regard biology as a destiny for a woman, but not for a man. The consequences of sex, Rousseau claims, are entirely different for a woman from those for a man since, whereas "the male is a male only now and again, the female is always a female," with everything reminding her of her sex and her whole life focused around it.

Wollstonecraft, who can be read as an antagonist to Rousseau on most issues concerning women, counters that a woman is and ought to be a woman with her lover; otherwise she is, like a man, a rational creature and needs to develop her understanding. Her excessive regard for her body has been cultivated in her by education, not by nature.

Schopenhauer, Nietzsche, and Ortega see the propagation of the species as the particular and unique natural destiny of women. For Schopenhauer, however, this destiny is more deterministic and inescapable than it is for Ortega. Ortega, true to his existentialist commitments, denies that woman's destiny is purely mechanical and argues that it merely guides, but does not direct, her life. Nietzsche suggests that women are biologically determined and only develop certain "masculine" tastes when something goes awry. For example, he claims, "when a woman has scholarly inclinations there is generally something wrong with her sexual nature." According to Nietzsche, the "first and last function" of women is to bear robust children.

Lewis has been included for his humorous approach to the question. He simply states, in archaic English, the woman's-biology-as-a-destiny view in a pithy, albeit somewhat facetious, way. Finally, although it is not at all clear whether and/or how Diderot answers this question, it is clear that he sees a woman's body as violently shuttling her between the extremes of hysterical ecstasy and miserable servitude.

How and Why Do Women Come to Be?

READINGS

Plato, *Timaeus*
Aristotle, *Generation of Animals*
Aquinas, *The Summa Theologica*
Fichte, *The Science of Rights*
Hegel, *Philosophy of Right*
Kierkegaard, *Stages on Life's Way*
Nietzsche, *The Antichrist*
Gilman, *The Man-Made World*

Discussion

The answers to this question move from discussion of the physical origin of women to the contention that women exist as a rational necessity and finally to parodies of earlier positions.

Plato, Aristotle, and Aquinas each offer different answers regarding the physical origin of women. Plato shows how they come to be in the process of perfecting the generation of animals. Aristotle contends that females are deformed males, coming into being when there is not sufficient heat to produce the superior product. Aquinas argues that, although woman may, physically speaking, be a misbegotten male, nevertheless, religiously speaking, she is not misbegotten since she was created as a helper to man in the work of generation.

Fichte and Hegel claim that the difference between the sexes has a rational necessity. Nature and history are parts of a rational system and, though occasional individuals may diverge, both evince lawfulness and purpose. Hegel and Fichte attempt to demonstrate that—in this natural and historical order—the differences between women and men are rationally intelligible and not merely brute necessities.

In the speech he wrote for Johannes the Seducer, Kierkegaard parodies the satirical "medical" account of love in Plato's *Symposium*. Here, however, the gods curb the power they envy in man by creating woman. This and Nietzsche's account are both at most half serious. It is not the Platonic but the Christian view, however, that Nietzsche mocks when he proclaims that "woman was God's *second* mistake" (the first being God's creation of the animals, who were intended to allay human boredom, but who failed to do so).

In a more serious vein, Gilman argues that women, as we think of them, are made, not born. In no other species can we recognize the feminine as we do among human beings: we can immediately recognize a feminine hand or foot, but not a feminine paw or hoof. For Gilman, the feebleness and clumsiness common to women are the result of the excessive sex-distinction of our "Androcentric Culture"; they, along with women's obsession with love, are man-made and, incidentally, nothing for men to be proud of.

The Education of Women

Are Women Rational?

MAIN READINGS

Aristotle, *Politics*
                Poetics
Vives, *Instruction of a Christian Woman*
Hume, "Of Essay Writing"
Rousseau, *Emile*
Kant, *Observations on the Feeling of the Beautiful and Sublime*
Mill, *The Subjection of Women*
Mott, "Discourse on Woman"
Nietzsche, *Beyond Good and Evil*
                    Human, all-too-Human
Royce, "On Certain Limitations of the Thoughtful Public in America"
            Letter to Abigail Williams May
James, *The Principles of Psychology*
Gilman, *The Home*

Santayana, *The Life of Reason*
Weininger, *Sex and Character*
Russell, *Marriage and Morals*
de Beauvoir, *The Second Sex*
Ortega, *Man and People*
           On Love ("Landscape with a Deer in the Background")
Marías, *Metaphysical Anthropology*

ADDITIONAL READINGS

Aquinas, *The Summa Theologica*
More, Letter to Gonell
Montaigne, "Of the Affection of Fathers for Their Children"
Condorcet, *On the Admission of Women to the Rights of Citizenship*
Fichte, *The Science of Rights*
Schopenhauer, "On Women"
           "Ideas Concerning the Intellect"

Discussion

The rationality of women is a topic that has been widely debated. At the extremes are those who argue, on the one hand, that women are not at all rational and, on the other, that they are, actually or potentially, as rational as men. Between these extremes are a number of different positions, some claiming that women are rational in the same sense that men are, but less reliably so, others that women are rational, but that their rationality differs from that of men.

Only Weininger regards woman as completely irrational, claiming that "mind cannot be predicated of her at all." Ortega comes close to saying the same thing when he argues that the core of a woman's mind is occupied by an irrational power and that she is, therefore, essentially confused.

Most of the other views on this subject consider women to be rational beings, but many see women's rationality as tenuous and capricious. Aristotle, Vives, and Rousseau are the main representatives of this viewpoint, although it is also put forth by Aquinas and Montaigne. Schopenhauer shares this view, noting the weakness of women's reasoning ability: their inability to deal with the remote and the universal.

Gilman, too, sees a marked difference between "a man's brain" and a woman's; for her, though, ". . . the difference is merely that between the world and a house." Operating in the world, "the man adopts one line of business and follows it" while the woman, limited to the home, learns to accommodate "a horde of little things."

Hume praises women's ability to judge "polite writing" and expresses his confidence in the "delicacy" of their taste, but claims that judgment is easily perverted by their "great share" of the "tender and amorous disposition," a tendency that renders suspect their judgment concerning books of gallantry and devotion.

More, Mott, Mill, Royce, Russell, and de Beauvoir see men and women as being equally rational. More regards men's and women's reason as equally suited to education, and Mott and Mill propose that the defects that do presently exist in women's thinking can be corrected: according to Mott, by removing disabilities and restrictions and, for Mill, by education. Arguing against the frequent response, "You think that way because you are a woman," de Beauvoir points out that men are victims of their hormones to the same degree as are women. Rejecting the claim that women, as opposed to men, act on intuition, Royce notes the "overfondness" of intellectual women for abstractions, a fault that, he says, they share with intellectual men. Both Royce and de Beauvoir worry about women being raised to avoid calling attention to themselves or being assertive; both are aware of the effect this has on the use women make of their rational abilities. Russell suggests that women's intellectual timidity, along with any intellectual inferiority that may characterize them, results mainly from the fear of sex, a fear with which they have been raised. Also making no distinction between male and female rationality, Condorcet and Fichte proceed from this assumption to their arguments on the rights of women and on women's sexual impulse, respectively.

There are, in addition, several thinkers who, although allowing that women are rational, contend that women's rationality is totally different from men's. Nietzsche does this in a quite disparaging way. Although admitting that women have intelligence to a high degree—perhaps even higher than that of men—Nietzsche quickly qualifies the compliment. He notes that men do more with their mental capacity and that women's "wisdom" is evinced by the fact that they have always known how to get themselves supported. Nietzsche thus suggests that women's rationality is little more than cleverness. Even her "stupidity in the kitchen" and the "thoughtlessness" with which she manages the household indicate, for Nietzsche, that woman is not a "thinking creature."

James, too, sees a marked difference between the functioning of a woman's brain and that of a man's. A masculine brain can deal with new and complex matter, general principles, and classification, while the feminine brain with its method of direct intuition cannot cope with these.

Kant and Marías also recognize a different type of rationality in women, but do so in a more positive way. According to Kant, women have as much understanding as men have, but the understanding of women is a "beautiful understanding" whereas the understanding of men is a "deep understanding." This means that women's understanding has as its objects "everything closely related to the finer feeling" as opposed to the abstract speculations and "useful but dry" branches of knowledge appropriately studied by those with deep understanding. For Marías, each individual is "situated" in his or her sex and thus will see the world differently and with different forms and categories of rationality. Marías, arguing against the view often expressed by men that women are not rational, proposes that they are equally rational, although they possess two completely different sorts of rationality.*

Finally, there is the point of view of the one who is convinced that women's reasons differ radically from men's, but who is totally unable to grasp how women come to conclusions or make judgments. Santayana seems to be completely mystified with the strange working of women's minds and simply depicts the process as "mysterious and oracular."

How Should Women Be Educated?

MAIN READINGS

Plato, *The Republic*
Musonius, "On the Question Whether Men's Daughters Should Be Educated Similarly to Their Sons"
          "Women Ought to Study Philosophy"
Jerome, "To Gaudentius"
More, Letters
Erasmus, *In Praise of Folly*
          "The Abbott and the Learned Woman"
Vives, *Instruction of a Christian Woman*
        The Learning of Women
Rousseau, "On Women"
          Emile
Wollstonecraft, *Vindication of the Rights of Woman*
Kant, *Observations on the Feeling of the Beautiful and Sublime*
Mill, *The Subjection of Women*
Nietzsche, *Human, All-too-Human*
Putnam, *The Lady*
Gilman, *The Man-Made World*
de Beauvoir, *The Second Sex*

ADDITIONAL READINGS

Hume, "Of the Study of History"
James, *The Principles of Psychology*

Discussion

Since all parties to this discussion assume that women should be educated, the range of opinion here is not as wide as on the previous question. The disagreement concerns only whether men and women should be educated the same way or, if differently, how. On the one side are those who argue that women and men should be educated in the same manner. On

---

*Marías' view of women's rationality is examined critically and perceptively by MacGuigan in her article, included in the Appendix.

the opposite side are representatives of two quite different views: those who contend that either (1) women's rationality or (2) their function requires that they be educated differently. These three views can be found, in a representative way, in Wollstonecraft, Kant, and Rousseau, respectively. The interest of these readings is enhanced by the fact that Rousseau's position and arguments are analyzed and attacked with considerable care by Wollstonecraft.

Plato, More, Wollstonecraft, Mill, Putnam, and Gilman propose that women should be educated in the same way as men. Plato is concerned with developing qualified guardians and rulers for his proposed state, and to that end he advocates a system of education that would educate each capable individual, male or female, to the limits of his or her capability. A historian's report that Plato's own school—the Academy—actually included a couple of women provides an interesting footnote to his theory. More speaks explicitly out of a desire that his children, most of whom were female, all be well-educated. For Wollstonecraft and Mill, extensive social and educational reform is necessitated at least in part by the morally disastrous consequences that result from men's living intimately with intellectual inferiors.

Putnam and Gilman add a unique dimension to this discussion. Both recognize that women's experience has rendered them generally unfit for social life. Unless she is forced to work, a woman leads an individualistic life. Kept in the house, she learns neither through warfare nor in games to act in concert with others. However, both Putnam and Gilman are opposed simply to incorporating girls into the process of education offered to boys. Putnam argues against the coeducational college since the presence of males will introduce the factor of sexual selection: for example, the girl elected to class office may be the one with the longest eyelashes, not the wisest, ablest, or kindest. For Gilman, much of what boys learn in school and in games is too competitive, too "male," for the good of society.

Musonius reflects the Stoic teaching on the education of women and perhaps the fact that some Stoic philosophers were female. He argues that women, too, should be taught philosophy since they as well as men are rational and have a natural inclination toward and capacity for virtue. Against those who fear such study would produce arrogance in women and cause them to neglect their "proper avocations," he points out that the teaching of philosophy "exhorts a woman to be satisfied with [housekeeping] . . . and to work with her own hands."

Because Erasmus treats the question, on the one hand, satirically and, on the other, in the form of a dialog between an abbot and a learned woman (the latter thought to have been modeled after Margaret More Roper, Thomas More's eldest daughter), his answer is more difficult to discern. Yet it is clear that the learned woman wins the intellectual joust with the unscholarly abbot, who is quite unsettled by the thought of women studying Greek and Latin.

James and de Beauvoir also have something to say on this side of the question. James' statement is only a footnote that recites an allegedly irrefutable argument about the propriety of admitting women to the Harvard Medical School. De Beauvoir's treatment of this question is concerned with some of the possible repercussions of raising little girls with the same rewards, expectations, and education as little boys. This is the only way, she claims, to bring about full equality between men and women; political and economic equality are not enough.

On the other side are several rather different supports for educating women differently. Jerome offers advice to a Christian father who is attempting to consecrate his little daughter to a life of virginity. Also from within a Christian framework, Vives argues that women, like men, are reasonable creatures with a wit no less apt, but that their education should suit them for lives as wives and mothers. It should be restricted accordingly. The study of grammar, logic, history, political theory, and mathematics should be reserved for men.

Similarly, Rousseau, in *Emile,* with an eye primarily on the complementary natures of women and men, would provide women with completely different educations, the education of a woman being designed to develop and further this complementariness and thus prepare her for life with a man. He even threatens, rather ominously, that if women were educated like men they would become more like men and, to that extent, lose their influence over men, thus increasing their subordination to them. In his earlier essay "On Women," he argues, somewhat differently, against men's unjust theft of women's freedom and of all their opportunities to manifest their grandeur of soul and love of virtue to the world. Nietzsche sounds more like the later Rousseau when he not only affirms that with several centuries of education women could be made just like men in every but the sexual sense, but also bewails what would, in the meantime, be the result of women's influence on philosophy and politics.

As we have seen, Kant insists that men and women both have understanding, but of very different kinds. Hence, he argues, the education of women must be undertaken with care to preserve and cultivate their unique understanding. Although he recognizes that a woman might succeed in "laborious learning or painful pondering," Kant proposes that her charms would be weakened and that she "might as well even have a beard."

It is unclear to what extent Hume would advocate educating women differently from men, but he does recommend to women the study of history as "best suited both to their sex and education" and as especially important in counterbalancing the false representations of mankind in the romances and novels so popular among women.

Employment

Should the Employment of Women Be Restricted?

READINGS

Plato, *The Republic*
Xenophon, *Economics*
Musonius, ''On the Question Whether Men's Daughters Should Be Educated Similarly to Their Sons''
Jerome, *Against Jovinianus*
More, *Utopia*
Vives, *Instruction of a Christian Woman*
Voltaire, ''Women''
Rousseau, *Emile*
Condorcet, *Letters from a Dweller in New Heaven to a Citizen of Virginia*
Wollstonecraft, *Vindication of the Rights of Woman*
Fichte, *The Science of Rights*
Schopenhauer, ''On Women''
Mill, *The Subjection of Women*
Mott, ''Discourse on Woman''
Nietzsche, ''The Greek Woman''
Lenin, ''The Tasks of the Working Women's Movement in the Soviet Republic''
Spencer, *Woman's Share in Social Culture*
Gilman, *Women and Economics*
Weininger, *Sex and Character*

Discussion

In this set of readings, Plato and Rousseau offer the most extreme contrast. Plato proposes that each individual in the ideal state should do that for which he or she is particularly well-suited and that there is no reason to restrict women from any pursuit, including ruling. Rousseau, in opposition, argues that the roles of mother and wife require certain tastes and feelings that conflict with those required by pursuits outside the home. He maintains that Plato's republic succeeds only by abolishing these roles suited to women and by attempting to transform women into men.

Vives agrees with Rousseau that women should stay at home, since the management of the house is their proper business. His view is that it is not becoming to a woman to rule a school, to ''live'' among men, or to ''speak abroad.'' Furthermore, Vives holds that since women are so easily deceived, they should not teach. Jerome supports this conclusion by appealing to the New Testament admonition against women teaching.

Mott challenges those who base women's subordination and other restrictions on the Old and New Testaments. She argues that a proper reading of scripture shows that women and men were created equal and that

an admonition against women speaking and asking questions in the excited state of the Corinthian church should not be read as a standing injunction against women preaching.

Xenophon discusses a woman's peculiar suitability to "indoor tasks":
her nature is adapted "by God" to such occupations since her body is less
capable of enduring heat and cold, journeys, and campaigns, and since
she has been given a larger share of affection for newborn babies and a
larger share of fear for the purpose of protecting what is stored away.
Musonius gives a somewhat qualified response, claiming that generally
women are more suited to lighter, indoor tasks and men to heavier, outdoor tasks, while recognizing that occasionally there will be men better
suited to the lighter tasks and women to the heavier. Voltaire, too, would
restrict a woman to the home with its lighter labors since the weakness of
her body and its periodic maladies render her unfit for heavy toil.
Schopenhauer agrees with this restriction, but argues that women's minds
as well as their bodies are not suited for great labors. In fact, he contends,
since women are perpetual children themselves, they make excellent
nursemaids.

Nietzsche dismisses Plato's "strange claim" that women are entitled to
"a full share in the rights, knowledge and duties of man." Although he
rejects this as an aberration, he nonetheless goes on to find in the Greek
state itself a proper attitude toward women and their role in the state, a
role analogous to that of sleep in the individual.

Against restricting women to the home, More proposes that everyone
in his utopia, irrespective of sex, is to farm and to be given military training; in addition, each is to be taught a special trade of his own, the
"weaker sex" being given the lighter jobs. Condorcet argues that most
women are on a par with most men, even if most women are weaker and
less creative than a few men, and notes, as does Mill, that it makes no
sense to prohibit anyone from doing what he or she cannot do. Weininger
also argues, on the basis of justice, against forbidding pursuits to a
woman just because they are "unwomanly." In addition, both Condorcet
and Mill raise doubts as to whether we really know what women are capable of doing. Wollstonecraft expresses a similar doubt while advocating
that women pursue various professions and businesses and, through their
ability to support themselves, become truly independent.

Lenin supports the equality of men and women as a way to abolish exploitation. In order to emancipate women and make them really equal
with men, he would free women from the unproductive labor of housework and involve them in productive labor as equals with men, although
not necessarily exactly equal with respect to productivity, amount of labor, working conditions, or the length of their working day.

Gilman challenges those who restrict women to the home and economic dependence because of their maternal duties. Her maternal duties

do not, Gilman argues, restrict a woman's ability to work: her work has always been an important factor in human life, even though it has not affected her economic status.

Recognizing that employment offers an important educational opportunity for both men and women, Spencer discusses some of the practical restrictions on the wage-earning of women. Aware that linking "women and children" in statutes prohibiting industrial exploitation frequently places women in a less competitive situation vis-à-vis men in the work force, Spencer tries to harmonize this concern with that of protecting women as potential mothers by approving legal protections for girls under 21. She also recognizes that the work of women cannot usually proceed in the same uninterrupted way as that of men. Their work in the home, though unrecognized while they are alive, is economically important and, moreover, she argues, their presence is vital for the development of the individuality of children.

Finally, although Fichte does not restrict women to the home, he recommends or presupposes considerable restriction on their employment. He presumes that they will not become teachers, preachers, doctors, and lawyers. In addition, if a woman is a writer, she is to write only for her own sex and only to be useful and helpful to them, not from motives of vanity or ambition.

Language and Woman

Why Have Languages Equated the Male and the Human?

READINGS

Gilman, *The Man-Made World*
Scheler, "Toward an Idea of Man"
de Beauvoir, *The Second Sex*
Ortega, *Man and People*
Marías, *Metaphysical Anthropology*

Discussion

Gilman, Scheler, de Beauvoir, and Marías agree that this linguistic equation between the male and the human reflects the dominance of men. Scheler sees this aspect of language as evidence that men have been so childish as to ignore the depths of the differences between the sexes. de Beauvoir sees language as part of a general pattern of viewing maleness as the normal and the norm, making of woman the abnormal and the deviant—the other. Marías sees this aspect of language not only as taking too much for granted, but also as obscuring the important fact that "man" and "woman" are correlative concepts, each understood in terms of the other.

Gilman discusses the lack of correlative concepts throughout language as indicative of the thoroughgoingness of our "Androcentric Culture." Not only is the male taken as the race type (e.g., lion, lioness), but also *male interests* are identified by men as *human interests*. Gilman supports the latter claim by pointing to newspapers (where there are no "Men's Pages"—sports being assumed of interest to everyone), to written history chronicling wars and the exploits of men, and to literature that deals with the two great subjects of love and war (and love from a masculine point of view at that, presenting the chase and ending with the conquest of the woman by the man). She notes that our culture is so androcentric that we even lack words to describe the problem: we know, for example, how to characterize a society in which there is a disproportionate feminine contribution (effeminate), but we have no word for describing the overly masculinized situation of our male-dominated culture.

Ortega is included in this section, not because he directly confronts and answers the question about sexism and language, but because what he says about the appearance of the woman and her relation to man may shed indirect light on the question. In particular, this reading makes an interesting counterpoint to the selection from de Beauvoir inasmuch as the appearance of another human being is presented from a masculine perspective and, from this perspective, is seen to be radically different only when the other is female.*

Love and Sex

Are There Differences in the Ways That Men and Women View Love and Sex?

READINGS

Montaigne, "On Some Verses of Virgil"
Hume,   "Of Essay Writing"
           "Of Love and Marriage"
Diderot,   *On Women*
           "Woman" ["Woman (Ethics)"]
Rousseau, *A Discourse on the Origin of Inequality*
           Emile
Wollstonecraft, *Vindication of the Rights of Woman*
Fichte, *The Science of Rights*
Schopenhauer, *The World as Will and Representation*
Nietzsche, *Human, All-too-Human*
           The Joyful Wisdom
Mott, "Discourse on Woman"
Goldman,   "The Tragedy of Woman's Emancipation"
           "Marriage and Love"
Gilman, *Women and Economics*

*For a perceptive discussion of Ortega's analysis of the appearance of another, see MacGuigan's article in the Appendix.

de Beauvoir, *The Second Sex*
Ortega, *On Love* ("On the Role of Choice in Love" and "Portrait of
  Salome")

Discussion

One frequently hears that women and men are fundamentally different in
their views of and attitudes toward sex and love. The question is, do they
really differ; and, if so, is the difference natural and inevitable or artificial
and therefore modifiable by changes in education? Only one of these
readings—Hume's "Of Love and Marriage"—suggests that there is no
fundamental difference. The others disagree with this claim, but also disagree among themselves concerning both the differences and their
source(s).

As he recounts and embroiders upon Plato's account of the origin of
love and marriage, Hume suggests that love and sex have the same meaning and importance to women as to men. He does, however, in "Of Essay
Writing," indicate that the disposition of women is far more tender and
amorous than that of men.

Montaigne, Wollstonecraft, Goldman, and Gilman maintain that, although there may indeed be differences in the ways in which men and
women view sex and love, these differences are the result of education
and custom, and hence artificial rather than natural. For Wollstonecraft,
this difference is especially unhealthy for women whose pampered desire
makes them constantly hope to excite love, as a result of which they all
too often become "abject wooers and fond slaves." Goldman sees
women as unemancipated from the "internal tyrants" of public
opinion—ultimately, the prevailing "Property Morality"—that equates
love with marriage and marriage with the dependency and servitude of the
woman. For Gilman, too much emphasis has been placed on sexual
passion by both men and women. However, lacking the man's full use of
other powers and faculties, a woman cannot so easily escape the force of
this "master passion." Pouring her whole life into her love, she is often
injured irretrievably: neglected and abused, but also defenseless, rendered by her passion unable even to testify in court against her abuser.

Against the view that men and women must be opposite in their affections and that such opposition is required for their union into "a perfect
whole," Mott argues that it is rather the union of congenial spirits with
similar affections that perfects the marriage bond. More negatively,
Goldman contends that society separates the two sexes with "an insurmountable wall of superstition, custom, and habit" that renders them
strangers to each other and dooms their unions to failure. Agreeing with
Goldman that society separates the sexes, Gilman claims that it is the economic status of marriage that places the lovers on entirely different social
planes—the woman as houseservant or at least housekeeper to the man—
and thus effectively bars true union.

Although de Beauvoir asserts that women's eroticism and sexual world will never be identical to men's, she, like Montaigne and Wollstonecraft, is quite sensitive to the role of education in influencing a woman's attitude toward sex and love. Her analyses are especially ambitious inasmuch as she brings together and tries to find a common cause—in education— for such diverse phenomena as adolescent girls' platonic crushes, frigidity in women, and the tendency of females generally to idealize love and to seek a "demigod" for a mate.

At the other extreme, although their reasons differ, are Rousseau, Fichte, Schopenhauer, Nietzsche, and Ortega who agree that love and sex are viewed very differently by women and that this difference is rooted in nature, not convention. For Rousseau, the differences are based in part on the natural differences between men and women and in part on an artificially developed moral part of love that involves an emphasis on exclusivity in love and sexual relations. This moral part of love is the result of "social usage," but has been enhanced by women in order to gain some control over their masters. Nietzsche, too, suggests that "the love idolatry" practiced by women is an intelligent device employed to increase their power, but a device by which they more often mystify themselves.

For Fichte, since a man takes the satisfaction of the sexual impulse as an end, it is irrational for women to do this, too. Thus, the sexual impulse appears to women (at least, to morally upright women) in a different form—that of love, ". . . to sacrifice one's self for the sake of another not in consequence of reasoning, but in consequence of a feeling." Whereas a man can continue to overlook his relation to a woman, the woman can never do so since she makes her entire existence dependent upon him.

For Schopenhauer, in love women are by nature inclined to constancy, men to inconstancy, since women are moved by nature to look after their offspring. Beyond this, though, Schopenhauer asserts that both men and women are guided by instinct as they seek mates: qualities sought by both sexes are those that are vitally connected with propagation.

According to Nietzsche, women see love as complete surrender while men, in loving women, want precisely this surrender from them. Ortega suggests a similar difference when he proposes that "a man feels love primarily as a violent desire to be loved, whereas for a woman the primary experience is to feel love itself. . . ." Further differences follow for Ortega from the essential confusion, the irrational core, of women and from the fact that women have less imagination.

Finally, Diderot's treatment emphasizes difference, but does so in a way that makes his position closer to Montaigne's. Love, for Diderot, becomes partly women's way of making themselves hard to get, thereby enhancing their value as possessions in a situation in which men conspire, with the aid of nature, to maintain and increase their power over women.

Marriage

Is Marriage More Central to the Life of a Woman Than to That of a Man?

READINGS

Xenophon, *Economics*
Musonius, "What Is the Chief End of Marriage?"
         "Is Marriage a Handicap for the Pursuit of Philosophy?"
Diderot, "Woman" ["Woman (Ethics)"]
Kant, *Anthropology from a Pragmatic Point of View*
Fichte, *The Science of Rights*
Hegel, *Philosophy of Right*
Schopenhauer, "On Women"
         "Position, or a Man's Place in the Estimation of Others"
Mill, *The Subjection of Women*
Putnam, *The Lady*
Goldman, "The Traffic in Women"
Gilman, *Women and Economics*
Santayana, *The Life of Reason*
Russell, *Marriage and Morals*
de Beauvoir, *The Second Sex*

Discussion

Diderot, Kant, Fichte, Hegel, Schopenhauer, and Santayana answer this question in the affirmative, as do Putman, Goldman, and Gilman, but the latter with qualifications. Xenophon, Musonius, Mill, and de Beauvoir answer in the negative.

With all of his reservations about love and male dominance, Diderot nonetheless in the final analysis sees marriage as the glory of a woman. Kant indicates that marriage is of utmost importance to a woman. He suggests that the possibility of becoming a widow dominates the young wife's relationships with other men and even justifies her coquetry. More extreme is Santayana's view, tracing "the fierce prejudices that prevail about women" to the family, specifically to "a feminine passion that has no mercy for anything that eludes the traditional household, not even for its members' souls."

For Fichte and Hegel, the importance of marriage for women follows from ethical considerations. Fichte sees marriage as the only rational way for a woman to deal with her sexual impulse. It is rational for a man, on the other hand, to seek to satisfy his sexual impulse as an end. Hegel views the family and marriage as far less important to a man since only he has a sphere of ethical activity outside the family. Goldman agrees that traditional morality—she calls it "Property Morality"—makes marriage more important to women than to men since it decrees that only in marriage can a woman lead anything approaching a normal sex life. Those women who defy this property morality become unmarriageable outcasts, in effect forced into a life of prostitution. Both she and Gilman discuss in glowing terms the beauty of the sexual relation once it is freed from the destructive influences of property considerations, the family, and irrelevant economic factors.

For Schopenhauer, women exist for the propagation of the species. In addition, marriage is a woman's only access to all the good things of the earth—which are possessed by men. Mill, Putnam, and Gilman, interestingly enough, also recognize this economic fact. Mill, rejecting the rightfulness of men's ownership of these things, suggests that, with the sexes' natural attraction to one another, each has about the same natural interest in their relationship. de Beauvoir, too, argues that the relation between men and women is most natural and just as important to each. Musonius, with Schopenhauer, sees the procreation of children as an important part of the end of marriage, but Musonius emphasizes the community of life between the husband and wife, who must have common interests and not fix their attention elsewhere. In addition, he argues that marriage is one of the proper concerns of man, to be regarded as a handicap to certain careers no more than being a good citizen is to be so regarded.

Although Xenophon's answer is in agreement with those of Mill and de Beauvoir, his reasoning is very different. For Xenophon, because men and women are peculiarly suited for completely different tasks, they need one another in order to make up for their own deficiencies.

Russell argues against those who for so long have "slobbered" over maternal emotions that supposedly have made marriage so singularly important to women. He maintains that men have no idea how women really feel about children since as long as they were in subjection women dared not be honest about their own emotions.

Finally, Putnam and Gilman challenge the unwarranted interest in marriage that women are encouraged or forced to take. As Putnam observes, women are even raised to be unindividualized: "Like a ready-made garment she should be designed to fit the average man." With Gilman, she worries about male selection and design of women on future generations.

Are Women to Be Subordinate in Marriage?

READINGS

Xenophon, *Economics*
Aristotle, *Nichomachean Ethics*
            Politics

Jerome, *Against Jovinianus*
Aquinas, *The Summa Theologica*
Hobbes, *The Elements of Law*
Locke, *Essay Concerning the True Original, Extent and End of Civil Government*
Hume, "On the Rise and Progress of the Arts and Sciences"
Montesquieu, *Persian Letters*
             The Spirit of Laws
Diderot, "Woman" ("Wise")
       "Letter to his Daughter"
Rousseau, *A Discourse on Political Economy*
         Emile
Kant, *The Philosophy of Law*
     Anthropology from a Pragmatic Point of View
Fichte, *The Science of Rights*
Hegel, *The Phenomenology of Mind*
Schopenhauer, "On Jurisprudence and Politics"
Comte, *The Positive Philosophy*
       System of Positive Philosophy
Mill, *The Subjection of Women*
Engels, *The Origin of the Family, Private Property and the State*
James, Review
Spencer, *Woman's Share in Social Culture*
Gilman, *The Man-Made World*
Russell, *Marriage and Morals*
Lewis, *Mere Christianity*
de Beauvoir, *The Ethics of Ambiguity*
Marías, *Metaphysical Anthropology*

ADDITIONAL READINGS

Tertullian, *The Apparel of Women*
More, *Utopia*
Vives, *The Learning of Women*
Condorcet, *Letters from a Dweller in New Heaven to a Citizen of Virginia*
Kierkegaard, *Works of Love*

Discussion

In these readings, those who argue for the subordination of the woman usually maintain that even in a society of two one must dominate; otherwise disputes cannot be settled. Aristotle argues that by nature man is more fit for command and should rule "in virtue of his superiority," turning over to the woman those matters that befit her. Locke agrees that the rule naturally falls to the man "as the abler and stronger." Hume, too, sees man as endowed by nature with superior strength both of mind and body, a superiority that, in polite societies, he alleviates by the generosity of gallantry. And Montesquieu contends that it is contrary to reason as well as to nature for women to "reign" in families.

Rousseau points to several considerations and argues that, where a preponderant voice is needed, even the smallest factors may and must be weighed and, where the situation is otherwise fairly evenly balanced, these may be decisive. For Rousseau, this preponderance falls to the husband as the result both of the "disadvantages" of women and of the fact that the father must superintend the wife's conduct since he must make sure that the children are his.

As noted in the discussion of Fichte's analysis of love, a woman loves, according to Fichte, in order to satisfy her sexual impulse and, therefore, sacrifices herself to another. In so doing, she submits and even surrenders her personality to her lover. Thus, Fichte offers moral reasons for what he regards as "the most unlimited subjection of the woman to the will of the husband." In a less lofty argument, Schopenhauer sees a more practical reason why women should be subordinate: since they never grow up entirely, they should always be under a man's care.

Although recognizing women as superior to men in feeling and moral goodness, Comte argues that men's superiority in thinking and acting requires them to take command. More and Lewis also believe that the man must be the head in a marriage. More's view of the subordination of the wife is not argued, but provides an interesting counterpoint to his views concerning the education, employment, and military training of women. Lewis argues, first, that not even women could seriously advocate that a woman should be the head in a marriage and, second, that the husband will maintain more just relations with those outside the marriage. He is, of course, discussing the Christian view of marriage and no doubt to some extent presupposes the religious admonition that women are not to have dominion over men, an admonition Vives simply asserts. Kierkegaard, too, proposes that Christianity has never desired equality of rights between men and women. Tertullian and Jerome go a bit further, proposing that women's subjection to their husbands is part of the penalty imposed on women for Eve's participation in the original sin. Aquinas modifies this contention, claiming that even in the state of innocence the rational inferiority of women would make them naturally subject to their rational superiors.

Condorcet, Mill, Engels, Spencer, Gilman, Russell, and de Beauvoir deny the claim that the husband must be dominant. They reject the contention that in any society there must be a ruler. Mill notes that partnerships exist without any one partner being designated by law or by custom as the head. Why, asks Gilman, does a family need "a head" if friendship and love do not? Engels and Russell trace the subordination of women to the attempt to guarantee the fidelity of the wife and the legitimacy of offspring. Unlike Rousseau, however, they do not see this as justification for male dominance. Russell proposes that for "civilized" men and women to be happy in marriage there must be *mutual* adjustment to one another, rather than the onesided adjustment of the wife to the husband: although mutual adjustment admittedly makes marriage more difficult, women's emancipation requires that there be a feeling of complete equality on both sides and no interference with mutual freedom. Spencer argues not only that democracy requires the recognition of marriage as a contract with the consequent legal status of the wife and the possibilities of divorce, but also that a democratic social order must be the outgrowth of a democratic family.

Whereas Condorcet recognizes the great injustice of depriving women of "the advantage of having their own free will," de Beauvoir contends that often the fault lies with the women as well as the men. Women conspire with men, according to de Beauvoir, when they realize the possibility of liberation, but dishonestly resign themselves not to exploit it. Weininger, too, recognizes the responsibility of women for their slavish adoption of men's values and viewpoints, and he urges women to deny their sexual natures and choose their freedom. Even Rousseau, while arguing for the subordination of women, notes that a woman's weakness is often a way of "providing herself beforehand with excuses, with the right to be weak if she chooses."

Xenophon, Hobbes, Diderot, Kant, and James take a middle position. Although agreeing that only one should govern, Hobbes notes that it is *usually* the husband, indicating that this results from convention, not nature or reason. In his discussion of "wife," Diderot doubts whether the husband should always be in the position of authority. Although he apparently would leave the resolution of this problem to the two parties, his advice to his daughter deviates remarkably from this as he urges her to comply with her new husband's every wish. Xenophon proposes that authority properly belongs to whichever is the better.

Kant recognizes a natural equality between the husband and wife, but he nevertheless maintains that this natural equality is not contrary to the husband's legal supremacy, a supremacy required for the sake of harmony in their union and warranted by the superiority of the man. James, too, cannot come down on one side or the other. He is impressed with and unable to answer Mill's arguments against the subjection of women, but at the same time wonders whether American man would want an independent woman and whether, indeed, the dependence of the woman is not necessary for the feelings of security and repose so important to marriage.

Hegel's answer to this question defies any simple categorization. On the one hand, he proposes that the wife is the director and manager of the home. At the same time, this advocacy of an apparent reversal of the more traditional form of subordination is muted by his recognition of the existence of the mediating agency that creates the community and human law, and that in turn must suppress the family, woman, and her spirit of individualism.

What Are a Wife's Duties and Rights, If Any?

READINGS

Maimonides, *The Book of Women*
Montaigne, "Of the Affection of Fathers for Their Children"
Montesquieu, *The Spirit of Laws*
Fichte, *The Science of Rights*
Schopenhauer, "On Women"
                      "Of Jurisprudence and Politics"
Comte, *System of Positive Philosophy*
Engels, *The Origin of the Family, Private Property and the State*
Kierkegaard, *Works of Love*
Mott, "Discourse on Woman"
Goldman, "Marriage and Love"
Gilman, *The Home*

Discussion

Most of these writers presume that the wife is to be subordinate to her husband. Even so, they argue about women's conjugal rights, inheritance rights, and right to divorce their husbands. Kierkegaard's admonition that wives are to be treated as human beings—Christianly speaking, in the category of "neighbor"—is perhaps the least debatable. The selection from Montesquieu is especially illuminating since in it he discusses various laws pertaining to the treatment of women in different types of societies.

Maimonides and Montesquieu propose important rights of a wife, especially pertaining to divorce and repudiation of her husband. Maimonides lists the duties of a wife, but also enumerates her rights, including, for example, conjugal rights on the basis of which she may restrict even the business travels of her husband.

Montaigne, Montesquieu, Schopenhauer, and Mott disagree about whether a wife may properly inherit her husband's estate. Schopenhauer argues that a wife should receive no more than the interest for life on property that was owned by her husband, never the property itself. Since men rather than women make money, it follows, he says, that "women are neither justified in having unconditional possession of it, nor fit persons to be entrusted with its administration." Montesquieu argues that at least there is nothing contrary to nature about wives inheriting estates. Montaigne, too, challenges the alleged natural right of succession by children to their father's estate, a "right" that had been used to deny a woman's right to inherit her husband's estate. Mott argues that justice requires the wife's "inheritance" of the family property that she and her husband have acquired by mutual labor. She also challenges the suspension during marriage of the legal existence of the wife and the surrendering of her property to her husband.

A debate also arises among Schopenhauer, Fichte, Comte, and Engels over monogamy. According to Schopenhauer, the institution of monogamy has placed women in an unnatural and improper position of equality with men. Polygamy would, he says, reduce the artificial "lady" to her true and natural position. Against this, Fichte argues that polygamy is contrary to nature inasmuch as it presupposes that women are merely means to gratify men rather than rational beings like men. Comte, on the other hand, sees monogamy as one of the most precious gifts of the Middle Ages. In this institution, the woman, according to Comte, will be in charge of early education, properly so since she is more spiritual than the man. For Engels, a wife in bourgeois monogamous marriage "differs from the ordinary courtesan only in that she does not hire out her body, like a wage-worker, on piecework, but sells it into slavery once for all." To free women from this servitude and reintroduce them into public industry, Engles proposes the abolition of the individual family as the economic unit of society.

Goldman and Gilman also comment on the wife's servitude in marriage and both urge, with Engels, the abolition of the family as the economic unit of society. Goldman notes that even a middle-class woman cannot properly speak of "her home" since it is guaranteed her only by the grace of her husband. It does not protect her from the drudgery of work, at least of housework. And for the poor who must continue to work outside the home, marriage only increases their work. Gilman, too, comments on this situation, particularly on its economics. For her, it is a dreadful waste of human labor, a waste we would quickly recognize if someone were to suggest furnishing each member of a ship's crew with his own cook/ personal servant. In addition, valuable resources are wasted as each family duplicates "plants" for cooking and cleaning, where, for example, one kitchen could serve twenty families.

For additional discussion of the rights of women in marriage, see above "Marriage: Are Women To Be Subordinate in Marriage."

Maternity

What Are a Woman's Rights and Duties with Respect to Children?

READINGS

Plato, *The Republic*
Hobbes, *Philosophical Elements of a True Citizen*
          The Elements of Law
Montesquieu, *The Spirit of Laws*

Comte, *System of Positive Philosophy*
Engels, *The Origin of the Family, Private Property and the State*
Nietzsche,   *The Joyful Wisdom*
              The Will to Power
Gilman, *The Man-Made World*
Russell, *Marriage and Morals*

Discussion

In *The Republic*, Plato argues that children should be reared and educated by the state; no one, except the rulers, would know the parentage of any of the children. Because the state has a definite interest in producing the best children, it would, therefore, carefully regulate sexual unions. Russell also argues that children redound to the advantage of the state rather than the parents, and thus should be paid for by the state, with the payment going to the mother and with provisions being made by the state so that the mother can return to her previous employment.

Hobbes maintains certain natural rights of maternity. The original dominion over a child belongs to the mother and, in a state of nature, a woman who has a child becomes both mother and lord. Engels recognizes the overthrow of this "mother right" as "the *world-historic defeat of the female sex*" in which women were enslaved and were turned into mere instruments for breeding children. Montesquieu allows such a "mother right" only where there is no marriage; otherwise it is, he says, "a dictate of reason" that "children should follow the station or condition of the father." The father, moreover, is under a natural obligation to nourish and educate his children. Where the father is unknown, this obligation falls to the woman unless she has submitted to public prostitution, in which case she cannot have the convenience of educating her children or, for that matter, any protection from the law.

Comte, Nietzsche, and Gilman emphasize the moral dimensions of maternity. For Comte, maternity extends rather than alters the sphere of a woman's influence. She still serves as the spiritual force in the family, but with maternity she assumes, or would under Comte's positivism, responsibility for the education of the child. Ethically speaking, Nietzsche sees maternity in a more negative light: the child is used by the mother not only as a public apology for her sex life, but also as a part of her conspiracy to use weakness to rule.

For Gilman, the moral responsibilities of motherhood are tremendous and require fundamental changes in our society and in the behavior of men. Men have not shown themselves adequate to the task of selecting the best women as mothers of future generations. Pointing to the females' role in selecting mates in other species, Gilman argues that women would be more adequate to this task in the human species if they were no longer kept ignorant of the reproductive aspect of their existence. This, she thinks, would result in a harsh attitude toward those men who, because of their sexual excesses, infect their innocent wives and offspring with serious and often fatal diseases.

Moral Capacity

Are Women's Virtues Different From Men's?

Is There a General Difference?

READINGS

Plato, *Meno*
Aristotle,   *History of Animals*
             Politics
             Poetics
Musonius, "On the Question Whether Men's Daughters Ought to Be Educated Similarly to Their Sons"
Tertullian, *The Apparel of Women*
Aquinas, *The Summa Theologica*
Diderot, "On Women"
Rousseau, *Emile*
Condorcet, *On the Admission of Women to the Rights of Citizenship*
Wollstonecraft, *Vindication of the Rights of Woman*
Kant, *Observations on the Feeling of the Beautiful and Sublime*
Hegel, *The Phenomenology of Mind*
Schopenhauer,   "On Women"
                "Psychological Remarks"
Kierkegaard, *Stages on Life's Way*
Gilman, *The Home*
Weininger, *Sex and Character*
Lewis, *Mere Christianity*

Discussion

In his dialog, Plato has Meno assert that there are numerous virtues, including a man's virtue and a woman's virtue. Although Socrates professes his displeasure with Meno's introduction of a "swarm" of virtues, many philosophers have taken Meno's point seriously, at least as it pertains to men's and women's virtue. Only Plato (insofar as the character Socrates can legitimately be regarded as his spokesman), Musonius, and Wollstonecraft maintain that there is no specifically "woman's virtue": whatever makes someone virtuous is the same, regardless of the sex of the individual. At the opposite extreme, Kierkegaard has one of the speakers at a banquet seriously question whether women can be properly considered under ethical categories, while Weininger proclaims that women are nonmoral.

Tertullian sees something unqiue about female virtue, at least to the extent that woman, the cause of mankind's fall, bears the greater guilt. Although admitting exceptions, Aquinas sees women's temperament as weak; holding more weakly to reason's judgments, she is more likely to be incontinent.

Kant and Hegel emphasize the difference between women's and men's virtues. Hegel stresses the different functions and spheres of activity of men and women, arguing that a woman as wife is the possessor of divine law, whereas a man moves out of the family into human law. For Kant, this difference follows from the fundamental difference between women and men as the beautiful and the sublime: women's virtue, as opposed to men's will be "beautiful"—women avoid vice only because it is "ugly." He questions whether women are capable of principles, although he admits that these are even "extremely rare" in men.

Diderot, like Kant, sees women as lacking principles of justice, virtue, and vice, but ascribes this to the fact that they lack reflection and hence nothing penetrates deeply into their comprehension. Condorcet notes that women do not possess the sentiment of justice, but, he suggests this follows not from their nature but from the position of subservience in which they have been kept. Lewis ascribes married women's lack of this sentiment to the fact that they are fighting for their own children and husbands against the rest of the world. Schopenhauer connects this lack—"the fundamental fault of the female character''—with woman's defective powers of reasoning and deliberation. He also connects her patience with her mental deficiencies. Although Weininger, too, claims that women have no sense of justice, he argues that they are human beings and should be treated with justice.

Gilman agrees that women differ from men with respect to virtue. Shut up in the home and kept weak, ignorant, and dependent, women lack justice and courage. The home is also a bad environment for the moral education of children and men: children will be affected by their mothers' lack of justice and courage and by the close range at which they are judged, usually too positively, by their mothers and fathers; men will be made selfish by women who wait on them and cater to their individual tastes.

The difference Rousseau proposes hinges on his claim that, to a woman, reputation is as important as actual worth and conduct since she has been placed by nature at the mercy of men's judgment. A man, on the contrary, may defy public opinion as long as he does what is right since he has only himself to consider.

For Aristotle, the difference between male and female virtues follows from the "fact" of male superiority. Not only are the qualities connected with virtues found in their perfection only in man, but also this "natural" aristocracy dictates that the virtues of men and women will differ, for example, courage being shown, in a man, by commanding and, in a woman, by obeying.

Is There a Difference With Respect to Chastity and Sexual Behavior?

READINGS

Musonius, "On Sexual Indulgence"
Jerome, "To Eustochium"
Augustine, "Adultrous Marriages"
Montaigne, "On Some Verses of Virgil"
Hume, *A Treatise of Human Nature*
Montesquieu, *The Spirit of Laws*
Diderot, "On Women"
Rousseau, *Emile*
Wollstonecraft, *Vindication of the Rights of Woman*
Kant, *Anthropology from a Pragmatic Point of View*
Fichte, *The Science of Rights*
Hegel, *Philosophy of Right*
Schopenhauer,   "Position, or a Man's Place in the Estimation of Others"
                        The World as Will and Idea
Kierkegaard, *Stages on Life's Way*
Nietzsche, *The Joyful Wisdom*
Goldman, "Victims of Morality"
Gilman, *Women and Economics*
Russell, *Marriage and Morals*

Discussion

Opinion here ranges from those who see chastity and faithfulness as virtues appropriate only to women to those who require these virtues of both men and women to the claim, in Kierkegaard, that the greatest gift a woman can offer a man is to be unfaithful to him.

Hume, Montesquieu, Diderot, Kant, Fichte, Hegel, and Schopenhauer agree that chastity is much more important to a woman than to a man. Hume contends that chastity and fidelity are imposed on the female sex so that men will be secure in the conviction that the children they labor to maintain and educate are theirs. For Montesquieu, continence in women is a dictate of nature. Violation of chastity indicates that a woman has renounced all virtue; by violating the laws of marriage, she quits the state of her natural dependence.

Diderot proposes that chastity is an intimate and essential part of a woman's honor and gives every indication that this does not hold for a man. Although condemning faithlessness in a husband, Rousseau argues that the faithless wife is worse since she "destroys the family and breaks the bonds of nature"; in giving her husband children not his own she is false both to husband and children. Kant endorses a version of the famous—or infamous—double standard when he notes that, whereas it is "infinitely important" for a man to know whether his wife was continent before marriage, a woman does not even ask about her husband. Kant further proposes that it seems as shameful to a man *not* to respond to a sexual provocation as it appears to a woman to respond too hastily.

Since, according to Fichte, it is rational for women to satisfy their sexual impulses only in marriage, it follows that chastity is a virtue important only to women. For Hegel, a woman loses her honor if she surrenders her body outside marriage. This is not, however, true for a man, since he has a field of activity outside the family.

Schopenhauer connects the importance of female honor—purity in a girl, faithfulness in a wife—with a conspiracy by women to get men to undertake the responsibility for meeting women's needs. Men, needing so little from women, according to Schopenhauer, have no need for this "virtue." With them, faithfulness in marriage is artificial whereas with a woman it is natural since she must "retain the nourisher and protector of the future offspring."

Musonius, Jerome, Augustine, Montaigne, and Russell treat the sexes more nearly equally with respect to chastity and sexual behavior, but here their agreement ends. Jerome and Augustine argue that continence is religiously demanded of both men and women. Jerome sees childbearing as formerly woman's burden resulting from the fall of Adam and Eve, a curse from which she has been freed by Christianity so that she can now religiously commit herself to a life of virginity.

Musonius argues that, if men are superior to women, the former should be expected to exercise more, not less, self-control over their "baser characters." Montaigne proposes that it is "folly" to try to control such a natural and burning desire as the sexual. He maintains, however, that it is not only unnatural but also unfair to hold women but not men to continence. Wollstonecraft, too, deplores the injustice of equating a woman's honor and virtue with her virginity, an equation responsible for much prostitution.

Goldman decries "Property Morality" and its condemnation of woman to "the position of a celibate, a prostitute, or a reckless, incessant breeder of hapless children." Goldman and Gilman comment on the way that society has forced both the prostitute and the "virtuous" woman to sell their sexual services, although they differ on which sells the more cheaply and thus is the "true scab." Gilman, unlike Goldman, praises chastity as a virtue for *both* men and women.

Russell and Goldman agree with Montaigne on the folly of trying to control sexual desire, but probe beyond such folly and unfairness of the double standard to the disastrous results of a required female chastity, not just on the relationships between men and women, but also on women's relationships, even intellectual ones, with the rest of the world.

Even Nietzsche, though not especially concerned with those relationships, sympathizes with the plight of women whose honor depends upon their being educated to be as ignorant as possible of sexual matters, but who are suddenly "hurled as with an awful thunderbolt into reality and knowledge with marriage" and expected to cope with all the contradictions between their present reality and what they have been taught. Nietzsche, like Russell, has little use for the "virtue" of chastity.

Is There a Difference with Respect to Truthfulness?

READINGS

Maimonides, *The Book of Women*
Diderot, "Woman" ["Woman (Ethics)]
Wollstonecraft, *Vindication of the Rights of Woman*
Schopenhauer, "On Women"
                  "On Jurisprudence and Politics"
Kierkegaard, *Journals and Papers*
Nietzsche, *Human, all-too-Human*
Gilman, *The Home*
Weininger, *Sex and Character*
Ortega, *On Love* ("Thoughts on Standing Before the Marquesa de Santillana's Portrait")

Discussion

As might be expected, those who question truthfulness as a virtue for women are generally skeptical about women's truthfulness. Wollstonecraft, however, ascribes their untruthfulness to the fact that women are trained to take a greater interest in the appearance and reputation of virtue than in virtue itself. Nietzsche argues that women are so constituted that truth disgusts them. Weininger sees the problem as women's organic untruthfulness, a fundamental inability to be honest about themselves.

Schopenhauer sees dissimulation as innate in women and even argues that since they tell so many lies their evidence in court should carry proportionately less weight. He traces this untruthfulness not just to the weakness of their powers of reasoning and deliberation, but also to the general weakness of their position in society in contrast to that of men. Maimonides, too, raises doubt about the veracity of women by not regarding them as "qualified" witnesses. One qualified witness is, according to Maimonides, sufficient to counterbalance the opposing testimony of several women.

Diderot also proposes that women's falseness is the result of their weakness, but suggests that, nevertheless, albeit rare, "truthfulness is a virtue to be well admired in women"; in addition, he professes his amazement that, though so poorly educated, women "produce so much virtue and give rise to so little vice." With Diderot, Gilman observes that weakness, helplessness, ignorance, and dependence breed falsehood and evasion. Kierkegaard sees woman as "a born virtuoso in lying," yet he notes that men find this attribute attractive: it is part of her cunning to weaken a man.

Ortega traces the untruthfulness of woman to her desire to keep her inner life secret. Incidentally, he says, women's confusion also has its source in their effort at concealment.

Are Women Capable of Friendship?

READINGS

Montaigne, "Of Friendship"
Wollstonecraft, *Vindication of the Rights of Woman*
Kant, *Anthropology from a Pragmatic Point of View*
Schopenhauer, "On Women"
Nietzsche, *Human, all-too-Human*
               Thus Spake Zarathustra
Santayana, *The Life of Reason*
Weininger, *Sex and Character*
Ortega, *On Love* ("Thoughts on Standing Before the Marquesa de Santillana's Portrait")

Discussion

Montaigne proposes that women are excluded from friendships since their ordinary capacity is inadequate for the communion and fellowship that sustains this bond. Wollstonecraft seems to agree that this is generally the case, but she attributes women's inadequate capacity for friendship to the way they were raised with emphasis upon appearance and "accomplishment," not understanding.

Nietzsche's position is far from clear. He has Zarathustra proclaim that women are "not yet" capable of friendship, but part of the sting is removed from this claim as Zarathustra goes on to ask of men, "who of you are capable of friendship?'' At an earlier point, Nietzsche states that women are capable of entering into friendship with men, although perhaps ''a little physical antipathy'' is required to maintain it.

Weininger also disparages women as friends, claiming that women's friendship is always for the purpose of matchmaking. According to Ortega, since women tend to concealment and secrecy about themselves, friendships between them may be less intimate than those between men.

With Schopenhauer, Santayana, and Kant, it becomes necessary to ask whether the friendship is to be with other women or with men. Where Schopenhauer and Kant see a fundamental rivalry among women, Santayana sees the possibility of friendship—a friendship, based on mutual understanding, rendered impossible between women and men by the great difference between their understandings.

Political Rights and Responsibilities

Should Women Vote and Rule?

READINGS

Plato, *The Republic*
    The Laws
Montaigne, ''Of the Affection of Fathers for Their Children''
    ''Of Three Kinds of Association''
Spinoza, *Tractatus Politicus*
Montesquieu, *The Spirit of Laws*
Voltaire, ''Women''
Diderot, ''Woman'' (''Wife'')
Rousseau, ''On Women''
Condorcet, *On the Admission of Women to the Rights of Citizenship*
    Letters from a Dweller in New Heaven to a Citizen of Virginia
Wollstonecraft, *Vindication of the Rights of Woman*
Kant, *Philosophy of Law*
Fichte, *The Science of Rights*
Hegel, *Philosophy of Right*
Comte, *System of Positive Philosophy*
Mill, *The Subjection of Women*
Ossoli, *Woman in the Nineteenth Century*
Mott, ''Discourse on Woman''
Lenin, ''The Tasks of the Working Women's Movement in the Soviet Republic''
James, Review

Weininger, *Sex and Character*
Spencer, *Woman's Share in Social Culture*
Gilman, *The Man-Made World*

Discussion

Montaigne, Spinoza, Kant, Fichte, Hegel, Comte, and Weininger deny political rights to women. Montaigne would not allow them to rule since, he claims, "no kind of mastery is due to women over men." Spinoza argues that women should be excluded from government because of their weakness; if they were equal to men, there would surely have been an example somewhere of women ruling along with men or over them. Kant proposes that women should be denied the vote along with everyone whose maintenance is arranged by others, including minors, apprentices of tradesmen and merchants, privately employed servants, and resident tutors.

According to Fichte, what makes women ineligible for public office is that they are free and independent only as long as they are unmarried, a condition in which no rational woman can promise to remain. Since her husband is her natural representative in the state, a woman cannot even exercise the suffrage without losing her dignity.

Hegel argues that if women were to rule, the state would be placed in jeopardy inasmuch as women regulate themselves through inclination and opinion. Comte, too, excludes women from political power because they live lives of feeling. Interestingly enough, he excludes philosophers as well and maintains that a philosopher's life of reasoning is a more evident disqualification than a woman's life of feeling.

Weininger proposes that although women are to have equal rights, they should be prohibited, along with children and imbeciles, from taking part in political affairs. Their influence is liable to be harmful to the state since they are unable to distinguish between justice and injustice.

On the other side, Plato argues, in *The Republic,* that women are to be allowed to do whatever their individual capabilities particularly suit them for, even to rule. In *The Laws,* he notes the unfortunate consequences of excluding women from political affairs and from control by law.

Even though Montesquieu maintains that it is contrary to reason for women to rule in families, he proposes that it is perfectly consonant with reason for them to govern empires; in fact, the same property—their weakness—makes it impossible for them to obtain pre-eminence in families and peculiarly well qualifies them for the larger responsibility. Voltaire recognizes that men's ordinary mental and physical superiority over women has allowed them to establish a domination based on strength; but, he notes, where women have been allowed to rule (in hereditary monarchies) they have not, as some claim, allowed themselves to be subdued by their lovers. Rousseau goes further, noting that where women have been allowed to rule, almost all have distinguished themselves by some brilliant deed. Diderot, too, pointing to successful women rulers, argues that there is nothing contradictory about women ruling empires or families.

Noting the ''excesses'' and ''shameful outrages'' that have marked politics under male domination, Mott proposes that women's involvement might improve the situation. She questions, as do Ossoli, Spencer, and Gilman, why women should not aid in making the laws by which they are governed.

Against the argument that men are privately influenced by women and therefore represent them fairly, Ossoli notes the contempt with which men frequently speak of women, of women's rationality, of ''women and children.'' Since few men can rise above the self-centered and patronizing belief that women were made ''for man,'' women can hardly expect men always to do justice to the interests of women.

Spencer argues that democracy requires the recognition of equal rights and opportunities for women. That women cannot fight, she maintains, no more disqualifies them for the suffrage than it should disqualify men over a certain age or under a certain standard of physical strength.

In our overly masculinized ''Androcentric Culture,'' Gilman contends, the idea of governing is connected with bossing, controlling, having authority, fighting, and looting. Thus, it is deemed inappropriate for women to govern. Rather than address the arguments based on this assumption, Gilman challenges the assumption itself as destructive to communal life at a higher stage of industrial and social development.

Condorcet argues that either no human beings have any rights or all do. Since women are on a par with most men in terms of their incapacities and disabilities, these incapacities and disabilities provide no more reason to exclude women from the rights of citizenship than to exclude most men from those rights. Even the recognition that certain domestic duties are natural to women, although perhaps reason enough not to give women preference in elections, cannot be a reason for legal exclusion.

Though apparently in agreement with Condorcet that the care and education of children is women's most important duty as citizens, Wollstonecraft nevertheless recognizes that many women do not marry and many others are forced into marriage by society's treatment of single women. She argues not only that women should be protected by civil law, but also that they should take an active role as citizens.

Mill observes that where women's capacities for government have been tried they have been found adequate. Since it is far worse to exclude an individual who is fit than to allow the possibility that one who is unfit will be chosen, women should not be rendered ineligible to hold public office. Mill challenges those who maintain either that the subjection of women is natural or that it must be justified since women accept it voluntarily. In addition, since no other system has been seriously tried, he refuses to credit the claim that this system has survived the test of experience.

In his review, James seems to side with Mill against arguments that women should be denied political rights because they are naturally subordinate, because they will lose their peculiar grace, or because they would resort to all sorts of "naughtiness" in order to procure votes. Finally, Lenin proclaims the full potential equality of women and men under communism.

Should Women Serve in Armies?

READINGS

Plato, *The Republic*
More, *Utopia*
Voltaire, "Women"
Rousseau, *Emile*
Condorcet, *Letters from a Dweller in New Heaven to a Citizen of Virginia*
Wollstonecraft, *Vindication of the Rights of Woman*
Lenin, "The Tasks of the Working Women's Movement in the Soviet Republic"

Discussion

Plato, More, and Lenin favor imposing on women some army duties. Plato and More would have women, those with sufficient natural ability, appropriately trained to serve alongside men in armies. Lenin does not go quite so far, proposing only that women take an active part in helping the Red Army, working in the midst of war conditions.

Voltaire and Rousseau regard woman as unsuited by her nature for war. Voltaire traces this to her "periodical visitations" where Rousseau connects it with the qualities she requires as a wife and mother, qualities that are incompatible with those required by political affairs and public life in general.

Although Condorcet agrees with the objection that it would be "ridiculous" to choose a woman to command an army, he nonetheless argues against laws that explicitly prohibit this. Even though women are naturally incapable of serving in armies and holding jobs that require hard daily work, he contends, laws excluding them from such positions are pointless at best and harmful at worst. Wollstonecraft argues against Rousseau, suggesting that women's participation in a defensive war might not be so dreadful after all. Whether women participate in war or not, she argues, it does not follow that they are inferior.

Property Rights

Should Women Own Property?

READINGS

Maimonides, *The Book of Women*
Locke, *Essay Concerning the True Original, Extent, and End of Civil Government*
Fichte, *The Science of Rights*
Schopenhauer, "On Women"

Discussion

Locke and Fichte make an interesting contrast since both grant that it is perfectly consonant with natural law that a woman own property. Even a married woman, according to Fichte, has all the rights of any citizen; however, she must, if she is rational, renounce to her husband all her property and all her rights, even though these may revert to her in the event of divorce. On the contrary, Locke sees the absolute sovereignty of the husband and the communality of all property as required not by the ends of marriage, but only by civil law.

Maimonides grants to a husband all the earnings of his wife and anything she finds; but he allows the husband only the usufruct of her estate during her life, even though he is to inherit her estate if she dies.

Schopenhauer would not have women own property or have any right to it. Not only do they not earn it or the money to buy it, according to Schopenhauer, but the weakness of their mental powers precludes their managing it if inherited.

For a discussion of the right of a wife to inherit her husband's property, see above, "Marriage; What Are A Wife's Duties and Rights, If Any?"

Rape

Does a Woman Have Any Rights Against a Rapist?

READINGS

Maimonides, *The Book of Women*

Discussion

Only Maimonides addresses this question, and it should no doubt be noted that he does so in a section entitled "Virgin Maiden." Where force has been used, Maimonides argues, the "violator" must pay not only a fine, but also compensation for the humiliation, pain, and "blemish" that he has caused. The humiliation, pain, and blemish are not the same for all, depending very much on social status, age, and whether the victim has had intercourse before.

Religion

Is Being Female a Religious Handicap?

READINGS

Jerome, "To Eustochium"
Augustine, *The City of God*
        "Adultrous Marriages"
Abelard, "Touching the Origin of Nuns"
Aquinas, *The Summa Theologica*
Montesquieu, *Persian Letters*
Rousseau, *Emile*
Hegel, *The Phenomenology of Mind*
Kierkegaard, *Journals and Papers*
James, Review
Gilman, *The Man-Made World*
       His Religion and Hers
Weininger, *Sex and Character*

Discussion

Jerome, Augustine, Abelard, and Aquinas apparently do not see any particular religious disability in being a woman, although the very fact that they take considerable pain to support their views indicates the extent to which the contrary has been widely held. Abelard, for example, goes to great lengths to refute this contrary claim, extolling to Heloise religious women and their works. Jerome and Augustine indicate that religion makes the same demands of both men and women. Augustine and Aquinas even argue that the image of God is found in women as well as in men and that there will be, after the resurrection, both men and women, not everyone resurrected in the male sex. Aquinas, however, does view Eve's sin as "more grievous" than Adam's; and both Aquinas and Augustine seem to regard women as more closely associated with the flesh and thus further than man from God.

Hegel not only denies that being a woman is a religious handicap, but even proposes that women rather than men are the preservers of divine law. Although disagreeing, James considers the more frequently encountered view that women's patient and submissive suffering makes them morally and religiously superior to men. With a forceful *ad hominen* attack, James questions the sincerity of those who make this claim, doubting that any of them would be willing to exchange their "coarse forbidding masculinities" for the "inestimable privileges" of the submissiveness they extol.

Although not exactly a disability, being a woman is, for Rousseau, a handicap of a lesser sort since women, though capable of a reverent submission to authority in religion, are, like children, incapable of understanding religion. Montesquieu examines a similar claim, but does so satirically from the point of view of Moslems whose religion has erroneously been thought by many, apparently including Montesquieu, to teach that women have no souls. Kierkegaard argues that women are not capable of being truly religious since they are not strong and tough enough and their minds are not able to endure a dialectic.

Weininger argues that women are not religious, that what passes as female mysticism is mere superstition. He does, however, suggest that women might be capable of overcoming themselves, but to do so they would have to deny their existence as women.

Gilman turns the tables as she frequently does in her writings. Being male is, for her, a far more serious religious disability than is being female. Religion generally reflects the over-masculinization of our culture. Even Christianity has, she believes, been perverted by this male influence from the desire to serve, love, and do good into a selfish desire to save one's own soul. A less masculinized religion would not only not blame the evils of the world on women, but would also recognize "that our main duty here is to improve the human race and the world it makes." It would be life- rather than death-based.

The Woman's Movement

Is the Movement a Curse or a Step Forward?

READINGS

Rousseau, *Emile*
Wollstonecraft, *Vindication of the Rights of Woman*
Fichte, *The Science of Rights*
Comte, *System of Positive Philosophy*
Kierkegaard, *Works of Love*
Nietzsche, *Beyond Good and Evil*
       Ecce Homo
       The Will to Power
Ossoli, *Woman in the Nineteenth Century*
Mott, "Discourse on Woman"
Lenin, "The Tasks of the Working Women's Movement in the Soviet Republic"

James, Review
Spencer, *Woman's Share in Social Culture*
Goldman, "The Tragedy of Women's Emancipation"
Gilman, *Women and Economics*
          The Man-Made World
Weininger, *Sex and Character*
Russell, *Marriage and Morals*
Scheler, "On the Meaning of the Women's Movement"
de Beauvoir, *The Second Sex*
Ortega, *Man and People*
Marías, *Metaphysical Anthropology*

Discussion

Fichte, Comte, Kierkegaard, Nietzsche, Weininger, and Ortega oppose the women's movement. Against "some uncalled-for advocates of their cause," Fichte maintains that women are not "treated so badly and unjustly." Against their cries for equal education, he argues that a woman's mind and nature render her incapable of approaching education and culture as a man would. Against their concern for equal rights, he proposes that women's participation in the state via their husbands is what rational women desire and choose of their own volition.

Comte disparages as "visionaries" those who claim political power for women and adds that the claim is made without women's consent. Kierkegaard ridicules the "foolishness" of those who argue, in the name of Christianity, for equal rights for women. Christianity, he retorts, ". . . has never demanded or desired this."

Nietzsche regards the women's movement as contributing to the general "uglifying" of Europe. He not only opposes "the social mishmash" that results from the "equality" of men, but also proposes that the emancipation of woman is an expression of hatred on the part either of women who are "physically botched," i.e., barren, or of men who are, like Henrik Ibsen, "typical old maid(s)." In their march toward emancipation, women have, according to Nietzsche, lost influence in proportion to their increased rights and claims, and their most womanly instincts have increasingly been weakened and deadened.

Weininger engages in what looks like name-calling against women who are held up as admirable examples by advocates of women's rights. It becomes clear, however, that, even though possibly question-begging, it is not necessarily an insult to refer to these women as "sexually intermediate types" since Weininger later urges women to overcome their sexual natures. Consequently, Weininger's opposition to the women's movement is curious: on the one hand, he argues that emancipation is not what women want, while, on the other, he urges women to give up their sexual natures and become truly emancipated.

Goldman expresses her opposition to what the women's movement had become—a concern for women's suffrage and economic equality with men—and, *contra* Weininger, urges women to become truly emancipated by expressing their sexual nature. Women will be emancipated, she argues, when they achieve the most vital right—the right to love and be loved—and when they recognize that being loved is not synonymous with being slaves or subordinate.

Ortega opposes the "equalitarian mania" of those who would deny the essential duality between man and woman and the essential inferiority of woman. In particular, he argues against de Beauvoir and claims that in her book *The Second Sex* de Beauvoir evinces the very confusion that is part of woman's inferiority.

Rousseau appears to be challenging women's rights advocates, at least one of their ways of arguing, when he counters that "it is a poor sort of logic to quote isolated exceptions against laws so firmly established."

On the other side, Wollstonecraft, an early and ardent proponent of women's rights, argues for the education of women and against the gallantry that has treated women as weak and thereby maintained a distinction of sex that is responsible for the neglect of women's understanding. She attributes to this neglect what must be the bane of feminists everywhere, namely, the fact that a considerable amount of opposition to the women's movement comes from women. For Mott, this oppostion results from the disabilities and restrictions that have enervated and mentally paralyzed woman: "like those still more degraded by personal bondage, she hugs her chains."

Ossoli sees the changes demanded by the champions of woman as "signs of the times"—signs of a general movement toward the recognition that "one man cannot be right to hold another in bondage" and that "Man cannot by right lay even well-meant restrictions on Woman." Spencer and Gilman also see the women's movement as part of the general movement of democracy to include those previously subjected or submerged classes of society. Democracy, Spencer argues, requires the recognition of equal rights and opportunities for women. Ironically, she observes, many positions have been opened to women for purely economic reasons, as reflected in the argument presented to a state legislature that two females could be hired to teach "at half the price we now pay one inferior male." Gilman maintains that both democracy and advances in industrialization require the breakdown of the family, i.e., the sex-union as an economic unit. The man-made home is a despotism and cannot adequately prepare a child for life in a democracy. The women's movement is an important step in this breakdown, advancing against the commonly accepted sexual status of women the "unheard of proposition" that "women are persons!"

Lenin notes the poor response in Western Europe to the libertarian movements whose proponents "long, long ago" urged the establishment of legal equality between men and women. Linking this continuation of men's privileges with capitalism, Lenin proclaims that only the Soviet government has freed women from their degraded position vis-à-vis the law. He points to this fact with pride while admitting that the Soviet Union has a long way to go in order to achieve a thoroughgoing emancipation of women. Urging, as does Lenin, the importance of fundamental changes in women's economic condition to free them from dependence and servitude, de Beauvoir gives clear statement to the arguments of the women's movement. Incidentally, de Beauvoir challenges the Soviet government: she argues that it has promised more than it has managed to deliver and that this has happened because true equality can be achieved only if women are raised and educated with the same rewards and expectations as men.

Russell, too, argues for wider implications and aspects of equality than the pioneers of the women's movement had in view, such as sexual freedom for women. With respect to these implications and aspects, Russell sees the revolt still in its infancy, even though almost completed in its political aspects.

Scheler, although arguing in a rather conservative way, defends the women's movement from attack. It is not, he argues, women working that had led to the women's movement, but rather the fact that in present society if women are to compete with men for jobs they must be masculine women. Scheler urges that society be reformed to give importance to female values. If these values were elevated to equal status with male values, there would be, he claims, no problem with women working. Although Marías regards the feminists as habitually either imitating man or rejecting him out of resentment, he nonetheless indicates that these dangers can be avoided and that women may someday be able to "make" a culture that would express their distinctive rationality and creativity.

Finally, James seems generally in favor of the movement even though he proclaims that many or most of the problems and injustices it contends against are not as serious in America as elsewhere.

The Contemporary Outlook

In these selections, philosophers have examined and argued questions and issues that we as readers may initially have taken as settled or as simply too obvious to require further comment. In examining these questions and issues, these philosophers are doing what philosophers have always done, namely, calling into question and making problematic what had previously been taken for granted. Often philosophy's critical tools have been directed outside itself, but frequently it has turned on itself to examine precisely what, in the preceding practice of philosophy, has been accepted and sometimes even regarded as self-evident.

In rendering woman problematic, philosophy has set an important, but difficult, task for itself. First, as Maryellen MacGuigan argues in her essay "Is Woman a Question?" (see the Appendix), philosophers must now examine the conception of the human on the basis of which they have for so long operated. If, as MacGuigan argues, the conception of the human renders dubious the humanity of women, this generally unacceptable implication alone is sufficient warrant for a new examination of this conception.

The task that these readings set for philosophers only begins with an examination of the conception of the human. Serious questions have been raised that must be clarified before they can be investigated further, and this clarification is a job for philosophers even where they may not themselves be equipped to carry out the needed investigations. For example, the question, "Are women rational?" is, as the readings indicate, far from clear. An investigator attempting to settle this question by empirical means, by surveys, tests, experiments, and observations, would do well to wait for further specification of what is to be sought or tested or observed. "Rational" is a word that is laden with values and with norms that are frequently so exacting that few men and women could qualify. To *assume* that men are rational in such a sense and then to *investigate* to determine whether women are is a procedure that obviously will not do; although such an investigation would no doubt find the vast majority of women lacking in rationality, it would, if applied to men, very likely produce similar results.

By their probings, philosophers have broken the ground for the investigation of woman as a subject. Some of the questions raised in these readings require experiments and data that philosophers are not in a position to conduct or to collect. Those equipped to make empirical investigations must carry on this research, examining the past and present, uncovering causes and processes, and discovering how the human mind and psyche work. They can discover what women have contributed to art and literature, how biology affects male and female behavior and attitudes, how the fetus develops into a male or a female. They can establish the effect of education on women and men, the professional and physical capabilities of women, any differences between women's and men's eroticism, and any variant responses of women and men to children. They can discover whether all languages equate the human and the male and what may be the nature of cultures in which such languages develop, whether women are less truthful than men, what sorts of friendships women have with each other and with men, and what leadership women have exerted politically.

Even where scientific tools are required for the investigation of these questions, philosophical tools are needed as well. Philosophical investigation must first clarify many of the questions themselves before they can be empirically or scientifically investigated. In addition, after the empirical investigations have been completed, the critical tools of philosophy are needed in examining the data from the various studies and determining just what they do or do not establish. For example, to discover whether women's eroticism differs from men's, the researchers must beware of her or his own conventional stereotypes, but, even more important, must somehow devise techniques whereby s/he can cut through her or his subjects' habit of seeing themselves and describing their experiences in terms of conventional "wisdom" and stereotypes. Admittedly, this is no easy task. Others, especially those with the ability to examine critically, are needed to keep a watchful eye on such investigations, lest the settled convictions distort the very attempts to question and to examine the facts.

Once such investigations have been carried out to the satisfaction of all parties concerned, philosophical thought once again becomes necessary. It is clearly within the purview of philosophy to examine questions pertaining to rights and duties; what individuals and societies ought to do is an important question in ethics. When the data are in, philosophical questions must then be asked, in particular, what bearing do the data have on questions such as, How should women be educated? What restrictions, if any, should be placed on their activities? What rights and duties should societies give to or demand of women?

If fundamental differences between men's and women's intellects and capabilities either do not exist or are negligible, then it is difficult to see why they should be educated differently and why either sex should be limited to certain activities or denied any political rights and responsibilities. If differences in desires, needs, and attitudes are found to be artifacts of cultural conditioning rather than naturally sex-based, then important implications would follow for societies' structuring of the institution of marriage. If differences are discovered, we must still ask what should be made of these differences. Either way, the data must be philosophically examined from the point of view of wider-ranging and even more fundamental questions concerning justice, fairness, human dignity, and the good of society as a whole.

Many of the questions raised in these readings must be specifically answered by each one of us at some point in our lives. The task before us is a philosophical as well as an existential one. I am certain that every reader will find somewhere among these pages views that make sense and reasons that seem convincing. Each must weigh and analyze, reweigh and reanalyze, such views and reasons, the inconsistencies and contradictions among them—and each must ultimately make some difficult choices if a coherent view is to be developed. Other writers and speakers may supply us with relevant and reasoned arguments and with facts and statistics, but no one save ourselves can make for us the crucial decisions incorporating these arguments and facts into a coherent system that we regard as true and by which we are prepared to live.

Furthermore, each of us confronts the ultimate existential task—that of living. At least to some extent it is up to us to *create* our own truths, especially truths about our femaleness and maleness. What women and men are depends not just on what has been true of women and men, but also on what women and men we make of ourselves. Perhaps Condorcet and Mill were correct in judging that little was known of the capacities of women in particular. If so, then surely much still remains to be learned concerning their capacities. Yet human capacities can only be discovered in the context of effort and accomplishment: we cannot know what our capacities are until we attempt to develop and use them.

Plato

Greek philosopher, 427–347 BC student of Socrates and founder of the Academy in Athens. For his political views, Plato has been accused of advocating totalitarianism; and for his ideas about women, he has been alternatively derided and extolled. Although women of the time were not educated, Plato's school—the Academy—is reported to have included two women among its students.

From *Meno,* a dialog concerning virtue. Socrates has just asked Meno for his account for virtue.

MENO. Why, there is no difficulty, Socrates, in telling. First of all, if you take the virtue of a man, it is easily stated that a man's virtue is this—that he be competent to manage the affairs of his city, and to manage them so as to benefit his friends and harm his enemies, and to take care to avoid suffering harm himself. Or take a woman's virtue: there is no difficulty in describing it as the duty of ordering the house well, looking after the property indoors, and obeying her husband. And the child has another virtue—one for the female, and one for the male; and there is another for elderly men—one, if you like, for freemen, and yet another for slaves. And there are very many other virtues besides, so that one cannot be at a loss to explain what virtue is; for it is according to each activity and age that every one of us, in whatever we do, has his virtue; and the same, I take it, Socrates, will hold also of vice.

SOCRATES. I seem to be in a most lucky way, Meno; for in seeking one virtue I have discovered a whole swarm of virtues there in your keeping. Now, Meno, to follow this figure of a swarm, suppose I should ask you what is the real nature of the bee, and you replied that there are many different kinds of bees, and I rejoined: Do you say it is by being bees that they are of many and various kinds and differ from each other, or does their difference lie not in that, but in something else—for example, in their beauty or size or some other quality? Tell me, what would be your answer to this question?

MENO. Why, this—that they do not differ, as bees, the one from the other.

SOCRATES. And if I went on to say: Well now, there is this that I want you to tell me, Meno: what do you call the quality by which they do not differ, but are all alike? You could find me an answer I presume?

MENO. I could.

SOCRATES. And likewise also with the virtues, however many and various they may be, they all have one common character whereby they are virtues, and on which one would of course be wise to keep an eye when one is giving a definitive answer to the question of what virtue really is. You take my meaning, do you not?

MENO. My impression is that I do; but still I do not yet grasp the meaning of the question as I could wish.

SOCRATES. Is it only the case of virtue, do you think, Meno, that one can say there is one kind belonging to a man, another to a woman, and so on with the rest, or is it just the same too in the case of health and size and strength? Do you consider that there is one health for a man, and another for a woman? Or, wherever we find health, is it of the same character universally, in a man or in anyone else?

MENO. I think that health is the same, both in man and in woman.

SOCRATES. Then is it not so with size and strength also? If a woman is strong, she will be strong by reason of the same form and the same strength; by "the same" I mean that strength does not differ as strength, whether it be in a man or in a woman. Or do you think there is any difference?

MENO. I do not.

SOCRATES. And will virtue, as virtue, differ at all whether it be in a child or in an elderly person, in a woman or in a man?

MENO. I feel somehow, Socrates, that here we cease to be on the same ground as in those other cases.

SOCRATES. Why? Were you not saying that a man's virtue is to manage a state well, and a woman's a house?

MENO. I was.

SOCRATES. And is it possible to manage a state well, or a house, or anything at all, if you do not manage it temperately and justly?

MENO. Surely not.

SOCRATES. Then whoever manages temperately and justly will manage with temperance and justice?

MENO. That must be.

SOCRATES. Then both the woman and the man require the same qualities of justice and temperance, if they are to be good.

From *The Republic,* a discussion of the ideal state.

"Do we expect the females of watch-dogs to join in guarding what the males guard and to hunt with them and share all their pursuits or do we expect the females to stay indoors as being incapacitated by the bearing and the breeding of the whelps while the males toil and have all the care of the flock?" "They have all things in common," he replied, "except that we treat the females as weaker and the males as stronger." "Is it possible, then," said I, "to employ any creature for the same ends as another if you do not assign it the same nurture and education?" "It is not possible." "If, then, we are to use the women for the same things as the men, we must also teach them the same things." "Yes." "Now music together with gymnastic was the training we gave the men." "Yes." "Then we must assign these two arts to the women also and the offices of war and employ them in the same way." "It would seem likely from what you say," he replied. "Perhaps, then," said I, "the contrast with present custom would make much in our proposals look ridiculous if our words are to be realized in fact." "Yes, indeed," he said. "What then," said I, "is the funniest thing you note in them? Is it not obviously the women exercising unclad in the palestra together with the men, not only the young but even the older, like old men in gymnasiums, when, though wrinkled and unpleasant to look at, they still persist in exercising?" "Yes, on my word," he replied, "it would seem ridiculous under present conditions." "Then," said I, "since we have set out to speak our minds, we must not fear all the jibes with which the wits would greet so great a revolution, and the sort of things they would say about gymnastics and culture, and most of all about the bearing of arms and the bestriding of horses." "You're right," he said. "But since we have begun we must go forward to the rough part of our law, after begging these fellows not to mind their own business but to be serious, and reminding them that it is not long since the Greeks thought it disgraceful and ridiculous, as most of the barbarians do now, for men to be seen naked. And when the practice of athletics began, first with the Cretans and then with the Lacedaemonians, it was open to the wits of that time to make fun of these practices, don't you think so?" "I do." "But when, I take it, experience showed that it is better to strip than to veil all things of this sort, then the laughter of the eyes faded away before that which reason revealed to be best, and this made it plain that he talks idly who deems anything else ridiculous but evil, and who tries to raise a laugh by looking to any other pattern of absurdity than that of folly and wrong or sets up any other standard of the beautiful as a mark for his seriousness than the good." "Most assuredly," said he.

"Then is not the first thing that we have to agree upon with regard to these proposals whether they are possible or not? And we must throw open the debate to anyone who wishes either in jest or earnest to raise the question whether female human nature is capable of sharing with the male all tasks or none at all, or some but not others, and under which of these heads this business of war falls. Would not this be that best beginning which would naturally and proverbially lead to the best end?" "Far the best," he said. . . " Come then, consider," said I, "if we can find a way out. We did agree that different natures should have differing pursuits and that the nature of men and women differ. And yet now we affirm that these differing natures should have the same pursuits. That is the indictment." "It is." "What a grand thing, Glaucon," said I, "is the power of the art of contradiction!" "Why so?" "Because," said I, "many appear to me to fall into it even against their wills, and to suppose that they are not wrangling but arguing, owing to their inability to apply the proper divisions and distinctions to the subject under consideration. They pursue purely verbal oppositions, practising eristic, not dialectic on one another." "Yes, this does happen to many," he said; "but does this observation apply to us too at present?" "Absolutely," said I; "at any rate I am afriad that we are unawares slipping into contentiousness." "In what way?" "The principle that natures not the same ought not to share in the same pursuits we are following up most manfully and eristically in the literal and verbal sense; but we did not delay to consider at all what particular kind of diversity and identity of nature we had in mind and with reference to what we were trying to define it when we assigned different pursuits to different natures and the same to the same." "No, we didn't consider that," he said. "Wherefore, by the same token," I said, "we might ask ourselves whether the natures of bald and long-haired men are the same and not, rather, contrary. And, after agreeing that they were opposed, we might, if the bald cobbled, forbid the long-haired to do so, or *vice versa*." "That would be ridiculous," he said. "Would it be so," said I, "for any other reason than that we did not then posit likeness and difference of nature in any and every sense, but were paying heed solely to the kind of diversity and homogeneity that was pertinent to the pursuits themselves? We meant, for example, that a man and a woman who have a physician's mind have the same nature. Don't you think so?" "I do." "But that a man physician and a man carpenter have different natures?" "Certainly, I suppose."

"Similarly, then," said I, "if it appears that the male and the female sex have distinct qualifications for any arts or pursuits, we shall affirm that they ought to be assigned respectively to each. But if it appears that they differ only in just this respect that the female bears and the male begets, we shall say that no proof has yet been produced that the woman differs from the man for our purposes, but we shall continue to think that our guardians and their wives ought to follow the same pursuits.'' ''And rightly,'' said he. ''Then, is it not the next thing to bid our opponent tell us precisely for what art or pursuit concerned with the conduct of a state the woman's nature differs from the man's?'' ''That would be at any rate fair.'' ''Perhaps, then, someone else, too, might say what you were saying a while ago, that it is not easy to find a satisfactory answer on a sudden, but that with time for reflection there is no difficulty.'' ''He might say that.'' ''Shall we, then, beg the raiser of such objections to follow us, if we may perhaps prove able to make it plain to him that there is no pursuit connected with the administration of a state that is peculiar to woman?'' ''By all means.'' ''Come then, we shall say to him, answer our question. Was this the basis of your distinction between the man naturally gifted for anything and the one not so gifted—that the one learned easily, the other with difficulty; that the one with slight instruction could discover much for himself in the matter studied, but the other, after much instruction and drill, could not even remember what he had learned; and that the bodily faculties of the one adequately served his mind, while, for the other, the body was a hindrance? Were there any other points than these by which you distinguish the well endowed man in every subject and the poorly endowed?'' ''No one,'' said he, ''will be able to name any others.'' ''Do you know, then, of anything practiced by mankind in which the masculine sex does not surpass the female on all these points? Must we make a long story of it by alleging weaving and the watching of pancakes and the boiling pot, whereon the sex plumes itself and wherein its defeat will expose it to most laughter?'' ''You are right,'' he said, ''that the one sex is far surpassed by the other in everything, one may say. Many women, it is true, are better than many men in many things, but broadly speaking, it is as you say.'' ''Then there is no pursuit of the administrators of a state that belongs to a woman because she is a woman or to a man because he is a man. But the natural capacities are distributed alike among both creatures, and women naturally share in all pursuits and men in all—yet for all the woman is weaker than the man.'' ''Assuredly.'' ''Shall we, then, assign them all to men and nothing to women?'' ''How could we?'' ''We shall rather, I take it, say that one woman has the nature of a physician and another not, and one is by nature musical, and another unmusical?'' ''Surely.'' ''Can we, then, deny that one woman is naturally athletic and warlike and another unwarlike and averse to gymnastics?'' ''I think not.'' ''And again, one a lover, another a hater, of wisdom? And one high-spirited, and the other lacking spirit?'' ''That also is true.'' ''Then it is likewise true that one woman has the qualities of a guardian and another not. Were not these the natural qualities of the men also whom we selected for guardians?'' ''They were.'' ''The women and the men, then, have the same nature in respect to the guardianship of the state, save in so far as the one is weaker, the other stronger.'' ''Apparently.''

''Women of this kind, then, must be selected to cohabit with men of this kind and to serve with them as guardians since they are capable of it and akin by nature.'' ''By all means.'' ''And to the same natures must we not assign the same pursuits?'' ''The same.'' ''We come round, then, to our previous statement, and agree that it does not run counter to nature to assign music and gymnastics to the wives of the guardians.'' '' By all means.'' ''Our legislation , then, was not impracticable or utopian, since the law we proposed accorded with nature. Rather, the other way of doing things, prevalent to-day, proves, as it seems, unnatural.'' ''Apparently.'' ''The object of our inquiry was the possibility and the desirability of what we were proposing.'' ''It was.'' ''That it is possible has been admitted.'' ''Yes.'' ''The next point to be agreed upon is that it is the best way.'' ''Obviously.'' ''For the production of a guardian, then, education will not be one thing for our men and another for our women, especially since the nature which we hand over to it is the same.'' ''There will be no difference.'' ''How are you minded, now, in this matter?'' ''In what?'' ''In the matter of supposing some men to be better and some worse, or do you think them all alike?'' ''By no means.'' ''In the city, then, that we are founding, which do you think will prove the better men, the guardians receiving the education which we have described or the cobblers educated by the art of cobbling?'' ''An absurd question,'' he said. ''I understand,'' said I; ''and are not these the best of all the citizens?'' ''By far.'' '' And will not these women be the best of all the women?'' ''They, too, by far.'' ''Is there anything better for a state than the generation in it of the best possible women and men?'' ''There is not.'' ''And this, music and gymnastics applied as we described will effect.'' ''Surely.'' ''Then the institution we proposed is not only possible but the best for the state.'' ''That is so.'' ''The women of the guardians, then, must strip, since they will be clothed with virtue as a garment, and must take their part with the men in war and the other duties of civic guardianship and have no other occupation. But in these very duties lighter tasks must be assigned to the women than to the men because of their weakness as a class. But the man who ridicules unclad women, exercising because it is best that they should, 'plucks the unripe fruit' of laughter and does not know, it appears, the end of his laughter nor what he would be at. For the fairest thing that is said or ever will be said is this, that the helpful is fair and the harmful foul.'' ''Assuredly.''

''In this matter, then, of the regulation of women, we may say that we have surmounted one of the waves of our paradox and have not been quite swept away by it in ordaining that our guardians and female guardians must have all pursuits in common, but that in some sort the argument concurs with itself in the assurance that what it proposes is both possible and beneficial." "It is no slight wave that you are thus escaping." "You will not think it a great one," I said, "when you have seen the one that follows." "Say on then and show me," said he. "This," said I, "and all that precedes has for its sequel, in my opinion, the following law." "What?" "That these women shall all be common to all the men, and that none shall cohabit with any privately; and that the children shall be common, and that no parent shall know its own offspring nor any child its parent." "This is a far bigger paradox than the other, and provokes more distrust as to its possibility and its utility." "I presume," said I, "that there would be no debate about its utility, no denial that the community of women and children would be the greatest good, supposing it possible. But I take it that its possibility or the contrary would be the chief topic of contention." "Both," he said, "would be right sharply debated." . . . "Tell me this, Glaucon. I see that you have in your house hunting-dogs and a number of pedigree cocks. Have you ever considered something about their unions and procreations?" "What?" he said. "In the first place," I said, "among these themselves although they are a select breed, do not some prove better than the rest?" "They do." "Do you then breed from all indiscriminately, or are you careful to breed from the best?" "From the best." "And again, do you breed from the youngest or the oldest, or, so far as may be, from those in their prime." "From those in their prime." "And if they are not thus bred, you expect, do you not, that your birds and hounds will greatly degenerate?" "I do," he said. "And what of horses and other animals?" I said; "is it otherwise with them?" "It would be strange if it were," said he. "Gracious," said I, "dear friend, how imperative, then, is our need of the highest skill in our rulers, if the principle holds also for mankind." "Well, it does," he said, "but what of it?" "This," said I, "that they will have to employ many of those drugs of which we were speaking. We thought that an inferior physician sufficed for bodies that do not need drugs but yield to diet and regimen. But when it is necessary to prescribe drugs, we know that a more enterprising and venturesome physician is required." "True; but what is the pertinency?" "This," said I: "it seems likely that our rulers will have to make considerable use of falsehood and deception for the benefit of their subjects. We said, I believe, that the use of that sort of thing was in the category of medicine." "And that was right," he said. "In our marriages, then, and the procreation of children, it seems there will be no slight need of this kind of 'right.' " "How so?" "It follows from our former admissions," I said, "that the best men must cohabit with the best women in as many cases as possible and the worst with the worst in the fewest, and that the offspring of the one must be reared and that of the other not, if the flock is to be as perfect as possible. And the way in which all this is brought to pass must be unknown to any but the rulers, if again, the herd of guardians is to be as free as possible from dissension." "Most true," he said. "We shall, then, have to ordain certain festivals and sacrifices, in which we shall bring together the brides and the bridegrooms, and our poets must compose hymns suitable to the marriages that then take place. But the number of the marriages we will leave to the discretion of the rulers, that they may keep the number of the citizens as nearly as may be the same, taking into account wars and diseases and all such considerations, and that, so far as possible, our city may not grow too great or too small." "Right," he said. "Certain ingenious lots, then, I suppose, must be devised so that the inferior man at each conjugation may blame chance and not the rulers." "Yes, indeed," he said.

"And on the young men, surely, who excel in war and other pursuits we must bestow honors and prizes, and, in particular, the opportunity of more frequent intercourse with the women, which will at the same time be a plausible pretext for having them beget as many of the children as possible." "Right." "And the children thus born will be taken over by the officials appointed for this, men or women or both, since, I take it, the official posts too are common to women and men. The offspring of the good, I suppose, they will take to the pen or crèche, to certain nurses who live apart in a quarter of the city, but the offspring of the inferior, and any of those of the other sort who are born defective, they will properly dispose of in secret, so that no one will know what has become of them." "That is the condition," he said, "of preserving the purity of the guardians' breed." "They will also supervise the nursing of the children, conducting the mothers to the pen when their breasts are full, but employing every device to prevent anyone from recognizing her own infant. And they will provide others who have milk if the mothers are insufficient. But they will take care that the mothers themselves shall not suckle too long, and the trouble of wakeful nights and similar burdens they will devolve upon the nurses, wet and dry." "You are making maternity a soft job for the women of the guardians." "It ought to be," said I, "but let us pursue our design. We said that the offspring should come from parents in their prime." "True." "Do you agree that the period of the prime may be fairly estimated at twenty years for a woman and thirty for a man?" "How do you reckon it?" he said. "The women," I said, "beginning at the age of twenty, shall bear for the state to the age of forty, and the man shall beget for the state from the time he passes his prime in swiftness in running to the age of fifty-five." "That is," he said, "the maturity and prime for both of body and mind." "Then, if anyone older or younger than the prescribed age meddles with procreation for the state, we shall say that his error is an impiety and an injustice, since he is begetting for the city a child whose birth, if it escapes discovery, will not be attended by the sacrifices and the prayers which the priests and priestesses and the entire city prefer at the ceremonial marriages, that ever better offspring may spring from good sires and from fathers helpful to the state sons more helpful still. But this child will be born in darkness and conceived in foul incontinence." "Right," he said. "And the same rule will apply," I said, "if any of those still within the age of procreation goes in to a woman of that age with whom the ruler has not paired him. We shall say that he is imposing on the state a base-born, uncertified, and unhallowed child." "Most rightly," he said. "But when, I take it, the men and the women have passed the age of lawful procreation, we shall leave the men free to form such relations with whomsoever they please, except daughter and mother and their direct descendants and ascendants, and likewise the women, save with son and father, and so on, first admonishing them preferably not even to bring to light anything whatever thus conceived, but if they are unable to prevent a birth to dispose of it on the understanding that we cannot rear such an offspring." "All that sounds reasonable," he said; "but how are they to distinguish one another's fathers and daughters, and the other degrees of kin that you have just mentioned?" "They won't," said I, "except that a man will call all male offspring born in the tenth and in the seventh month after he became a bridegroom his sons, and all female, daughters, and they will call him father. And, similarly, he will call their offspring his grandchildren and they will call his group grandfathers and grandmothers. And all children born in the period in which their fathers and mothers were procreating will regard one another as brothers and sisters. This will suffice for the prohibitions of intercourse of which we just now spoke. But the law will allow brothers and sisters to cohabit if the lot so falls out and the Delphic oracle approves." "Quite right," said he.

From *Timaeus,* concerning the creation of the universe.

Concerning the highest part of the human soul, we should consider that God gave this as a genius to each one, which was to dwell at the extremity of the body, and to raise us like plants, not of an earthly but of a heavenly growth, from earth to our kindred which is in heaven. And this is most true; for the divine power suspended the head and root of us from that place where the generation of the soul first began, and thus made erect the whole body. He, therefore, who is always occupied with the cravings of desire and ambition, and is eagerly striving after them, must have all his opinions mortal, and, as far as man can be, must be all of him mortal, because he has cherished his mortal part. But he who has been earnest in the love of knowledge and true wisdom, and has been trained to think that these are the immortal and divine things of a man, if he attain truth, must of necessity, as far as human nature is capable of attaining immortality, be all immortal, as he is ever serving the divine power; and having the genius residing in him in the most perfect order, he must be preeminently happy. Now there is only one way in which one being can serve another, and this is by giving him his proper nourishment and motion. And the motions which are akin to the divine principle within us are the thoughts and revolutions of the universe. These each man should follow, and correct those corrupted courses of the head which are concerned with generation, and by learning the harmonies and revolutions of the whole, should assimilate the perceiver to the thing perceived, according to his original nature, and by thus assimilating them, attain that final perfection of life, which the gods set before mankind as best, both for the present and the future.

Thus the discussion of the universe which according to our original proposition, was to reach to the origin of man, seems to have an end. A brief mention may be made of the generation of other animals, but there is no need to dwell upon them at length; this would seem to be the best mode of attaining a due proportion. On the subject of animals, then, the following remarks may be offered. Of the men who came into the world, those who are cowards or have led unjust lives may be fairly supposed to change into the nature of women in the second generation. Wherefore also at the time when this took place the gods created in us the desire of generation, contriving in man one animated substance, and in woman another, which they formed respectively in the following manner: The passage for the drink by which liquids pass through the lung under the kidneys and into the bladder, and which receives and emits them by the pressure of the breath, was so fashioned as to penetrate also into the body of the marrow, which passes from the head along the neck and through the back, and which in our previous discussion we have named the seed. And the seed having life, and becoming endowed with respiration, produces, in that part in which it respires, a lively desire of emission, and thus creates in us the love of procreation. Wherefore also in men the organ of generation becoming rebellious and masterful like an animal disobedient to reason, seeks, by the raging of the appetites, to gain absolute sway; and the same is the case with the wombs and other organs of women; the animal within them is desirous of procreating children, and when remaining without fruit long beyond its proper time, gets discontented and angry, and wandering in every direction through the body, closes up the passages of the breath, and, by obstructing respiration, drives them into the utmost difficulty, causing all varieties of disease, until at length the desire and love of the man and the woman, as it were producing and plucking the fruit from the tree, cause the omission of seed into the womb, as into a field, in which they sow animals unseen by reason of their smallness, and formless; these they again separate and mature them within, and after that bring them out into the light, and thus perfect the generation of animals.

Thus were created women and the female sex in general.

From *Laws*, Plato's last dialog, on governing by law.

. . . Listen now, so that we may not spend much time on the matter to no purpose. Everything that takes place in the State, if it participates in order and law, confers all kinds of blessings; but most things that are either without order or badly ordered counteract the effects of the well-ordered. And it is into this plight that the practice we are discussing has fallen. In your case, Clinias and Megillus, public meals for men are, as I said, rightly and admirably established by a divine necessity, but for women this institution is left, quite wrongly, unprescribed by law, nor are public meals for them brought to the light of day; instead of this, the female sex, that very section of humanity which, owing to its frailty, is in other respects most secretive and intriguing, is abandoned to its disorderly condition through the perverse compliance of the lawgiver. Owing to your neglect of that sex, you have had an influx of many consequences that would have been much better than they now are if they had been under legal control. For it is not merely, as one might suppose, a matter affecting one-half of our whole task—this matter of neglecting to regulate women—but in as far as females are inferior in goodness to males, just in so far it affects more than the half. It is better, then, for the welfare of the State to revise and reform this institution, and to regulate all the institutions for both men and women in common. At present, however, the human race is so far from having reached this happy position that a man of discretion must actually avoid all mention of the practice in districts and States where even the existence of public meals is absolutely without any formal recognition. How then shall one attempt, without being laughed at, actually to compel women to take food and drink publicly and exposed to the view of all? The female sex would more readily endure anything rather than this: accustomed as they are to live a retired and private life, women will use every means to resist being led out into the light, and they will prove much too strong for the lawgiver. So that elsewhere, as I said, women would not so much as listen to the mention of the right rule without shrieks of indignation; but in our State perhaps they will. So if we agree that our discourse about the polity as a whole must not—so far as theory goes—prove abortive, I am willing to explain how this institution is good and fitting, if you are equally desirous to listen, but otherwise to leave it alone.

Xenophon

Greek philosopher and historian, c. 430–c. 350 BC, best known for his written recollections of Socrates.

From *Economics,* Ischomachus explains to Socrates how he trained his wife to the household duties.

SOCRATES. Pray tell me, Ischomachus, what was the first lesson you taught her, since I would sooner hear this from your lips than an account of the noblest athletic event or horse race?

ISCHOMACHUS. Well, Socrates, as soon as I found her docile and sufficiently domesticated to carry on conversation, I questioned her to this effect:

"Tell me, dear, have you realized for what reason I took you and your parents gave you to me? For it is obvious to you, I am sure, that we should have had no difficulty in finding someone else to share our beds. But I for myself and your parents for you considered who was the best partner of home and children that we could get. My choice fell on you, and your parents, it appears, chose me as the best they could find. Now if God grants us children, we will then think out how we shall best train them. For one of the blessings in which we shall share is the acquisition of the very best of allies and the very best of support in old age; but at present we share in this our home. For I am paying into the common stock all that I have, and you have put in all that you brought with you. And we are not to reckon up which of us has actually contributed the greater amount, but we should know of a surety that the one who proves the better partner makes the more valuable contribution."

My wife's answer was as follows, Socrates: "How can I possibly help you? What power have I? Nay, all depends on you. My duty, as my mother told me, is to be discreet."

"Yes, of course, dear," I said, "my father said the same to me. But discretion both in a man and a woman, means acting in such a manner that their possessions shall be in the best condition possible, and that as much as possible shall be added to them by fair and honourable means."

"And what do you see that I can possibly do to help in the improvement of our property?" asked my wife.

"Why," said I, "of course you must try to do as well as possible what the gods made you capable of doing and the law sanctions."

"And pray, what is that?" said she.

"Things of no small moment, I fancy," replied I, "unless, indeed, the tasks over which the queen bee in the hive presides are of small moment. For it seems to me, dear, that the gods with great discernment have coupled together male and female, as they are called, chiefly in order that they may form a perfect partnership in mutual service. For, in the first place, that the various species of living creatures may not fail, they are joined in wedlock for the production of children. Secondly, offspring to support them in old age is provided by this union, to human beings, at any rate. Thirdly, human beings live not in the open air, like beasts, but obviously need shelter. Nevertheless, those who mean to win store to fill the covered place, have need of someone to work at the open-air occupations; since plowing, sowing, planting and grazing are all such open-air employments; and these supply the needful food. Then again, as soon as this is stored in the covered place, then there is need of someone to keep it and to work at the things that must be done under cover. Cover is needed for the nursing of the infants; cover is needed for the making of the corn into bread, and likewise for the manufacture of clothes from the wool. And since both the indoor and the outdoor tasks demand labor and attention, God from the first adapted the woman's nature, I think, to the indoor and man's to the outdoor tasks and cares.

"For he made the man's body and mind more capable of enduring cold and heat, and journeys and campaigns; and therefore imposed on him the outdoor tasks. To the woman, since he has made her body less capable of such endurance, I take it that God has assigned the indoor tasks. And knowing that he had created in the woman and had imposed on her the nourishment of the infants, he meted out to her a larger portion of affection for newborn babes than to the man. And since he imposed on the woman the protection of the stores also, knowing that for protection a fearful disposition is no disadvantage, God meted out a larger share of fear to the woman than to the man; and knowing that he who deals with the outdoor tasks will have to be their defender against any wrong-doer, he meted out to him again a larger share of courage. But because both must give and take, he granted to both impartially memory and attention; and so you could not distinguish whether the male or the female sex has the larger share of these. And God also gave to both impartially the power to practice due self-control, and gave authority to whichever is the better—whether it be the man or the woman—to win a larger portion of the good that comes from it. And just because both have not the same aptitudes, they have the more need of each other, and each member of the pair is the more useful to the other, the one being competent where the other is deficient.

"Now since we know, dear, what duties have been assigned to each of us by God, we must endeavour, each of us, to do the duties allotted to us as well as possible. The law, moreover, approves of them, for it joins together man and woman. And as God has made them partners in their children, so the law appoints them partners in the home. And besides, the law declares those tasks to be honorable for each of them wherein God has made the one to excel the other. Thus, to the woman it is more honorable to stay indoors than to abide in the fields, but to the man it is unseemly rather to stay indoors than to attend to the work outside. If a man acts contrary to the nature God has given him, possibly his defiance is detected by the gods and he is punished for neglecting his own work, or meddling with his wife's. I think that the queen bee is busy about just such other tasks appointed by God."

"And pray," said she, "how do the queen bee's tasks resemble those that I have to do?"

"How? she stays in the hive," I answered, "and does not suffer the bees to be idle; but those whose duty it is to work outside she sends forth to their work; and whatever each of them brings in, she knows and receives it, and keeps it till it is wanted. And when the time is come to use it, she portions out the just share to each. She likewise presides over the weaving of the combs in the hive, that they may be well and quickly woven, and cares for the brood of little ones, that it be duly reared up. And when the young bees have been duly reared and are fit for work, she sends them forth to found a colony, with a leader to guide the young adventurers."

"Then shall I too have to do these things?" said my wife.

"Indeed you will," said I; "your duty will be to remain indoors and send out those servants whose work is outside, and superintend those who are to work indoors, and to receive the incomings, and distribute so much of them as must be spent, and watch over so much as is to be kept in store, and take care that the sum laid by for a year be not spent in a month. And when wool is brought to you, you must see that cloaks are made for those that want them. You must see too that the dry corn is in good condition for making food. One of the duties that fall to you, however, will perhaps seem rather thankless: you will have to see that any servant who is ill is cared for."

"Oh no," cried my wife, "it will be delightful, assuming that those who are well cared for are going to feel grateful and be more loyal than before."

"Why, my dear," cried I, delighted with her answer, "what makes the bees so devoted to their leader in the hive, that when she forsakes it, they all follow her, and not one thinks of staying behind? Is it not the result of some such thoughtful acts on her part?"

"It would surprise me," answered my wife, "if the leader's activities did not concern you more than me. For my care of the goods indoors and my management would look rather ridiculous, I fancy, if you did not see that something is gathered in from outside."

"And my ingathering would look ridiculous," I countered, "if there were not someone to keep what is gathered in. Don't you see how they who 'draw water in a leaky jar,' as the saying goes, are pitied, because they seem to labor in vain?"

"Of course," she said, "for they are indeed in a miserable plight if they do that."

"But I assure you, dear, there are other duties peculiar to you that are pleasant to perform. It is delightful to teach spinning to a maid who had no knowledge of it when you received her, and to double her worth to you: to take in hand a girl who is ignorant of housekeeping and service, and after teaching her and making her trustworthy and serviceable to find her worth any amount: to have the power of rewarding the discreet and useful members of your household, and of punishing anyone who turns out to be a rogue. But the pleasantest experience of all is to prove yourself better than I am, to make me your servant; and, so far from having cause to fear that as you grow older you may be less honored in the household, to feel confident that with advancing years, the better partner you prove to me and the better housewife to our children, the greater will be the honor paid to you in our home. For it is not through outward comeliness that the sum of things good and beautiful is increased in the world, but by the daily practice of the virtues."

Aristotle

Greek philosopher, physicist, and biologist, 384–322 BC, student of Plato in the Academy and founder of his own school, the Lyceum, in Athens.

From *Generation of Animals*

. . . Just as it sometimes happens that deformed offspring are produced by deformed parents, and sometimes not, so the offspring produced by a female are sometimes female, sometimes not, but male. The reason is that the female is as it were a deformed male; and the menstrual discharge is semen, though in an impure condition; i.e., it lacks one constituent, and one only, the principle of Soul. . . .[A]n animal is a living body, a body with Soul in it. The female always provides the material, the male provides that which fashions the material into shape; this, in our view, is the specific characteristic of each of the sexes: that is what it means to be male or to be female. Hence, necessity requires that the female should provide the physical part, i.e., a quantity of material, but not that the male should do so, since necessity does not require that the tools should reside in the product that is being made, nor that the agent which uses them should do so. Thus, the physical part, the body, comes from the female, and the Soul from the male, since the Soul is the essence of a particular body. . . .

Now the opinion that the cause of male and female is heat and cold, and that the difference depends upon whether the secretion comes from the right side or from the left, has a modicum of reason in it, because the right side of the body is hotter than the left; hotter semen is semen which has been concocted; the fact that it has been concocted means that it has been set and compacted, and the more compacted semen is, the more fertile it is. All the same, to state the matter in this way is attempting to lay hold of the cause from too great a distance, and we ought to come as closely to grips as we possibly can with the primary causes.

63

We have dealt already elsewhere with the body as a whole and with its several parts, and have stated what each one is, and on account of what cause it is so. But that is not all, for (1) the male and the female are distinguished by a certain ability and inability. Male is that which is able to concoct, to cause to take shape, and to discharge semen possessing the "principle" of the "form"; and by "principle" I do not mean that sort of principle out of which, as out of matter, an offspring is formed belonging to the same kind as its parent, but I mean the *proximate motive principle,* whether it is able to act thus in itself or in something else. Female is that which receives the semen, but is unable to cause semen to take shape or to discharge it. And (2) all concoction works by means of heat. Assuming the truth of these two statements, it follows of necessity that (3) male animals are hotter than female ones, since it is on account of coldness and inability that the female is more abundant in blood in certain regions of the body. . . In human beings, more males are born deformed than females; in other animals, there is no preponderance either way. The reason is that in human beings the male is much hotter in its nature than the female. On that account male embryos tend to move about more than female ones, and owing to their moving about they get broken more, since a young creature can easily be destroyed owing to its weakness. And it is due to this self-same cause that the perfecting of female embryos is inferior to that of male ones (since their uterus is inferior in condition. In other animals, however, the perfecting of female embryos is not inferior to that of male ones: they are not any later in developing than the males, as they *are*) in women, for while still within the mother, the female takes longer to develop than the male does; though once birth has taken place everything reaches its perfection sooner in females than in males–e.g., puberty, maturity, old age—because females are weaker and colder in their nature; and we should look upon the female state as being as it were a deformity, though one that occurs in the ordinary course of nature. While it is within the mother, then, it develops slowly on account of its coldness, since development is a sort of concoction, concoction is effected by heat, and if a thing is hotter its concoction is easy; when, however, it is free from the mother, on account of its weakness it quickly approaches its maturity and old age, since inferior things all reach their end more quickly, and this applies to those which take their shape under the hand of Nature just as much as to the products of the arts and crafts. . . . So that if you reckon up *(a)* that the brain itself has very little heat, *(b)* that the skin surrounding it must of necessity have even less, and *(c)* that the hair, being the furthest off of the three, must have even less still, you will expect persons who are plentiful in semen to go bald at about this time of life. And it is owing to the same cause that it is on the front part of the head only that human beings go bald, and that they are the only animals which do so at all; i.e., they go bald in front because the brain is there, and they alone do so, because they have by far the largest brain of all and the most fluid. Women do not go bald because their nature is similar to that of children: both are incapable of producing seminal secretion. Eunuchs, too, do not go bald, because of their transition into the female state, and the hair that comes at a later stage they fail to grow at all, or if they already have it, they lose it, except for the pubic hair: similarly, women do not have the later hair, though they do grow the pubic hair. This deformity constitutes a change from the male state to the female.

From *History of Animals*

In all genera in which the distinction of male and female is found, Nature makes a similar differentiation in the mental characteristics of the two sexes. This differentiation is the most obvious in the case of human kind and in that of the larger animals and the viviparous quadrupeds. In the case of these latter the female is softer in character, is the sooner tamed, admits more readily of caressing, is more apt in the way of learning; as, for instance, in the Laconian breed of dogs the female is cleverer than the male. Of the Molossian breed of dogs, such as are employed in the chase are pretty much the same as those elsewhere; but the sheep-dogs of this breed are superior to the others in size, and in the courage with which they face the attacks of wild animals.

Dogs that are born of a mixed breed between these two kinds are remarkable for courage and endurance of hard labour.

In all cases, excepting those of the bear and leopard, the female is less spirited than the male; in regard to the two exceptional cases, the superiority in courage rests with the female. With all other animals the female is softer in disposition than the male, is more mischievous, less simple, more impulsive, and more attentive to the nurture of the young; the male, on the other hand, is more spirited than the female, more savage, more simple, and less cunning. The traces of these differentiated characteristics are more or less visible everywhere, but they are especially visible where character is the more developed, and most of all in man.

The fact is, the nature of man is the most rounded off and complete, and consequently in man the qualities or capacities above referred to are found in their perfection. Hence woman is more compassionate than man, more easily moved to tears, at the same time is more jealous, more querulous, more apt to scold and to strike. She is, furthermore, more prone to despondency and less hopeful than the man, more void of shame or self-respect, more false of speech, more deceptive, and of more retentive memory. She is also more wakeful, more shrinking, more difficult to rouse to action, and requires a smaller quantity of nutriment.

As was previously stated, the male is more courageous than the female, and more sympathetic in the way of standing by to help. Even in the case of molluscs, when the cuttle-fish is struck with the trident the male stands by to help the female; but when the male is struck the female runs away.

From *Nicomachean Ethics*

. . . The association of man and wife seems to be aristocratic; for the man rules in accordance with his worth, and in those matters in which a man should rule, but the matters that befit a woman he hands over to her. If the man rules in everything the relation passes over into oligarchy; for in doing so he is not acting in accordance with their respective worth, and not ruling in virtue of his superiority. Sometimes, however, women rule, because they are heiresses; so their rule is not in virtue of excellence but due to wealth and power, as in oligarchies.

From *Politics*

Of household management we have seen that there are three parts—one is the rule of a master over slaves, which has been discussed already, another of a father, and the third of a husband. A husband and father, we saw, rules over wife and children, both free, but the rule differs, the rule over his children being a royal, over his wife a constitutional, rule. For although there may be exceptions to the order of nature, the male is by nature fitter for command than the female, just as the elder and full-grown is superior to the younger and more immature. But in most constitutional states the citizens rule and are ruled by turns, for the idea of a constitutional state implies that the natures of the citizens are equal, and do not differ at all. Nevertheless, when one rules and the other is ruled we endeavor to create a difference of outward forms and names and titles of respect, which may be illustrated by the saying of Amasis about his footpan. The relation of the male to the female is of this kind, but there the inequality is permanent. The rule of a father over his children is royal, for he rules by virtue both of love and of the respect due to age, exercising a kind of royal power. And therefore Homer has appropriately called Zeus 'father of Gods and men,' because he is the king of them all. For a king is the natural superior of his subjects, but he should be of the same kin or kind with them, and such is the relation of elder and younger, of father and son.

Thus it is clear that household management attends more to men than to the acquisition of inanimate things, and to human excellence more than to the excellence of property which we call wealth, and to the virtue of freemen more than to the virtue of slaves. A question may indeed be raised, whether there is any excellence at all in a slave beyond and higher than merely instrumental and ministerial qualities—whether he can have the virtues of temperance, courage, justice, and the like; or whether slaves possess only bodily and ministerial qualities. And, whichever way we answer the question, a difficulty arises; for, if they have virtue, in what will they differ from freemen? On the other hand, since they are men and share in rational principle, it seems absurd to say that they have no virtue. A similar question may be raised about women and children, whether they too have virtues: ought a woman to be temperate and brave and just, and is a child to be called temperate, and intemperate, or not? So in general we may ask about the natural ruler, and the natural subject, whether they have the same or different virtues. For if a noble nature is equally required in both, why should one of them always rule, and the other always be ruled? Nor can we say that this is a question of degree, for the difference between ruler and subject is a difference of kind, which the difference of more and less never is. Yet how strange is the supposition that the one ought, and that the other ought not, to have virtue! For if the ruler is intemperate and unjust, how can he rule well? If the subject, how can he obey well? If he be licentious and cowardly, he will certainly not do his duty. It is evident, therefore, that both of them must have a share of virtue, but varying as natural subjects also vary among themselves. Here the very constitution of the soul has shown us the way; in it one part naturally rules, and the other is subject, and the virtue of the ruler we maintain to be different from that of the subject—the one being the virtue of the rational, and the other of the irrational part. Now, it is obvious that the same principle applies generally, and therefore almost all things rule and are ruled according to nature. But the kind of rule differs—the freeman rules over the slave after another manner from that in which the male rules over the female, or the man over the child; although the parts of the soul are present in all of them, they are present in different degrees. For the slave has no deliberative faculty at all; the woman has, but it is without authority, and the child has, but it is immature. So it must necessarily be supposed to be with the moral virtues also; all should partake of them, but only in such manner and degree as is required by each for the fulfilment of his duty. Hence the ruler ought to have moral virtue in perfection, for his function, taken absolutely, demands a master artificer, and rational principle is such an artificer; the subjects, on the other hand, require only that measure of virtue which is proper to each of them. Clearly, then, moral virtue belongs to all of them; but the temperance of a man and of a woman, or the courage and justice of a man and of a woman, are not, as Socrates maintained, the same; the courage of a man is shown in commanding, of a woman in obeying. And this holds of all other virtues, as will be more clearly seen if we look at them in detail, for those who say generally that virtue consists in a good disposition of the soul, or in doing rightly or the like, only deceive themselves. Far better than such definitions is their mode of speaking, who, like Gorgias, enumerate the virtues. All classes must be deemed to have their special attributes; as the poet says of women,

> 'Silence is a woman's glory'

but this is not equally the glory of man.

From *Poetics,* discussing characterization in a tragedy.

In the Characters there are four points to aim at. First and foremost, that they shall be good. There will be an element of character in the play, if (as has been observed) what a personage says or does reveals a certain moral purpose; and a good element of character, if the purpose so revealed is good. Such goodness is possible in every type of personage, even in a woman or a slave, though the one is perhaps an inferior, and the other a wholly worthless being. The second point is to make them appropriate. The Character before us may be, say, manly; but it is not appropriate in a female Character to be manly, or clever.

C. Musonius Rufus

Roman Stoic philosopher, c. 30–c. 101 AD. Exiled by Nero and Vespasian, Musonius responded without resentment. He has been called "the Roman Socrates" in recognition of features such as his method of questioning and the remarkable harmony of his life with his high moral standards. What remains of his thought is apparently fragments of notes made by one of his pupils. Although some women were included among the Stoic philosophers, unfortunately none of their writings are extant.

That Women Too Should Study Philosophy

When someone asked him* if women too should study philosophy, he began to discourse on the theme that they should, in somewhat the following manner. Women as well as men, he said, have received from the gods the gift of reason, which we use in our dealings with one another and by which we judge whether a thing is good or bad, right or wrong. Likewise the female has the same senses as the male; namely sight, hearing, smell, and the others. Also both have the same parts of the body, and one has nothing more than the other. Moreover, not men alone, but women too, have a natural inclination toward virtue and the capacity for acquiring it, and it is the nature of women no less than men to be pleased by good and just acts and to reject the opposite of these. If this is true, by what reasoning would it ever be appropriate for men to search out and consider how they may lead good lives, which is exactly the study of philosophy but inappropriate for women? Could it be that it is fitting for men to be good, but not for women? Let us examine in detail the qualities which are suitable for a woman who would lead a good life, for it will appear that each one of them would accrue to her most readily from the study of philosophy. In the first place, a woman must be a good housekeeper; that is a careful accountant of all that pertains to the welfare of her house and capable of directing the household slaves. It is my contention that these are the very qualities which would be present particularly in the

*This refers to Musonius [Editor's note].

woman who studies philosophy, since obviously each of them is a part of life, and philosophy is nothing other than knowledge about life, and the philosopher, as Socrates said, quoting Homer, is constantly engaged in investigating precisely this: "Whatsoever of good and of evil is wrought in thy halls." But above all a woman must be chaste and self-controlled; she must, I mean, be pure in respect of unlawful love, exercise restraint in other pleasures, not be a slave to desire, not be contentious, not lavish in expense, nor extravagant in dress. Such are the works of a virtuous woman, and to them I would add yet these: to control her temper, not to be overcome by grief, and to be superior to uncontrolled emotion of every kind. Now these are the things which the teachings of philosophy transmit, and the person who has learned them and practices them would seem to me to have become a well-ordered and seemly character, whether man or woman. Well then, so much for self-control. As for justice, would not the woman who studies philosophy be just, would she not be a blameless life-partner, would she not be a sympathetic help-mate, would she not be an untiring defender of husband and children, and would she not be entirely free of greed and arrogance? And who better than the woman trained in philosophy—and she certainly of necessity if she has really acquired philosophy—would be disposed to look upon doing a wrong as worse than suffering one (as much worse as it is the baser), and to regard being worsted as better than gaining an unjust advantage? Moreover, who better than she would love her children more than life itself? What woman would be more just than such a one? Now as for courage, certainly it is to be expected that the educated woman will be more courageous than the uneducated, and one who has studied philosophy than one who has not; and she will not therefore submit to anything shameful because of fear of death or unwillingness to face hardship, and she will not be intimidated by anyone because he is of noble birth, or powerful, or wealthy, no, not even if he be the tyrant of her city. For in fact she has schooled herself to be high-minded and to think of death not as an evil and life not as a good, and likewise not to shun hardship and never for a moment to seek ease and indolence. So it is that such a woman is likely to be energetic, strong to endure pain, prepared to nourish her children at her own breast, and to serve her husband with her own hands, and willing to do things which some would consider no better than slaves' work. Would not such a woman be a great help to the man who married her, an ornament to her relatives, and a good example for all who know her? Yes, but I assure you, some will say, that women who associate with philosophers are bound to be arrogant for the most part and presumptuous, in that abandoning their own households and turning to the company of men they practice speeches, talk like sophists, and analyze syllogisms, when they ought to be sitting at home spinning. I should not expect the women who study philosophy to shirk their appointed tasks for mere talk any more than men, but I maintain that their discussions should be conducted for the sake of their practical application. For as there is no merit in the science of medicine unless it conduces to the healing of man's body, so if a philosopher has or teaches reason, it is of no use if it does not contribute to the virtue of man's soul. Above all, we ought to examine the doctrine which we think women who study philosophy ought to follow; we ought to see if the study which presents modesty as the greatest good can make them presumptuous, if the study which is a guide to the greatest self-restraint accustoms them to live heedlessly, if what sets forth intemperance as the greatest evil does not teach self-control, if what represents the management of a household as a virtue does not impel them to manage well their homes. Finally, the teachings of philosophy exhort the woman to be content with her lot and to work with her own hands.

Should Daughters Receive the Same Education as Sons?

Once when the question arose as to whether or not sons and daughters ought to be given the same education, he remarked that trainers of horses and dogs make no distinction in the training of the male and the female; for female dogs are taught to hunt just as the males are, and one can see no difference in the training of mares, if they are expected to do a horse's work, and the training of stallions. In the case of man, however, it would seem to be felt necessary to employ some special and exceptional training and education for males over females, as if it were not essential that the same virtues should be present in both alike, in man and woman, or as if it were possible to arrive at the same virtues, not through the same, but through different instruction. And yet that there is not one set of virtues for a man and another for a woman is easy to perceive. In the first place, a man must have understanding and so must a woman, or what pray would be the use of a foolish man or woman? Then it is essential for one no less than the other to live justly, since the man who is not just would not be a good citizen, and the woman would not manage her household well if she did not do it justly; but if she is unjust she will wrong her husband like Eriphyle in the story.* Again, it is recognized as right for a woman in wedlock to be chaste, and so is it likewise for a man; the law, at all events, decrees the same punishment for committing adultery as for being taken in adultery. Gluttony, drunkenness, and other related vices, which are vices of excess and bring disgrace upon those guilty of them, show that self-control is most necessary for every human being, male and female alike; for the only way of escape from wantonness is through self-

---

*Eriphyle and her husband were killed by their son as a result of her acceptance of bribes [Editor's note].

control; there is no other. Perhaps someone may say that courage is a virtue appropriate to men only. That is not so. For a woman too of the right sort must have courage and be wholly free of cowardice, so that she will neither be swayed by hardships nor by fear; othewise, how will she be said to have self-control, if by threat or force she can be constrained to yield to shame? Nay more, it is necessary for women to be able to repel attack, unless indeed they are willing to appear more cowardly than hens and other female birds which fight with creatures much larger than themselves to defend their young. How then should women not need courage? That women have some prowess in arms the race of the Amazons demonstrated when they defeated many tribes in war. If, therefore, something of this courage is lacking in other women, it is due to lack of use and practice rather than because they were not endowed with it. If then men and women are born with the same virtues, the same type of training and education must, of necessity, befit both men and women. For with every animal and plant whatsoever, proper care must be bestowed upon it to produce the excellence appropriate to it. Is it not true that, if it were necessary under like circumstances for a man and a woman to be able to play the flute, and if, furthermore, both had to do so in order to earn a living, we should give them both exactly the same thorough training in flute playing; and similarly if it were necessary for either to play the harp? Well then, if it is necessary for both to be proficient in the virtue which is appropriate to a human being, that is for both to be able to have understanding, and self-control, and courage, and justice, the one no less than the other, shall we not teach them both alike the art by which a human being becomes good? Yes, certainly we must do that and nothing else. "Come now," I suppose someone will say, "do you expect that men should learn spinning the same as women, and that women should take part in gymnastic exercises the same as men?" No, that I should not demand. But I do say that, since in the human race man's constitution is stronger and woman's weaker, tasks should be assigned which are suited to the nature of each; that is the heavier tasks should be given to the stronger and lighter ones to the weaker. Thus spinning and indoor work would be more fitting for women than for men, while gymnastics and outdoor work would be more suitable for men. Occasionally, however, some men might more fittingly handle certain of the lighter tasks and what is generally considered women's work, and again, women might do heavier tasks which seem more appropriate for men whenever conditions of strength, need, or circumstance warranted. For all human tasks, I am inclined to believe, are a common obligation and are common for men and women, and none is necessarily appointed for either one exclusively, but some pursuits are more suited to the nature of one, some to the other, and for this reason some are called men's work and some women's. But whatever things have reference to virtue, these one would properly say are

equally appropriate to the nature of both, inasmuch as we agree that virtues are in no respect more fitting for the one than the other. Hence I hold
it reasonable that the things which have reference to virtue ought to be
taught to male and female alike; and furthermore that straight from infancy they ought to be taught that this is right and that is wrong, and that
is the same for both alike; that this is helpful, that is harmful, that one
must do this, one must not do that. From this training understanding is
developed in those who learn, boys and girls alike, with no difference.
Then they must be inspired with a feeling of shame toward all that is base.
When these two qualities have been created within them, man and woman
are of necessity self-controlled. And most of all the child who is trained
properly, whether boy or girl, must be accustomed to endure hardship,
not to fear death, not to be disheartened in the face of any misfortune; he
must in short be accustomed to every situation which calls for courage.
Now courage, it was demonstrated above, should be present in women
too. Furthermore to shun selfishness and to have high regard for fairness
and, being a human being, to wish to help and to be unwilling to harm
one's fellow men is the noblest lesson, and it makes those who learn it
just. What reason is there why it is more appropriate for a man to learn
this? Certainly if it is fitting for women to be just, it is necessary for both
to learn the same lessons which are in the highest degree appropriate to
the character of each and supremely important. If it happens that a man
knows a little something about a certain skill and a woman not, or again
she knows something and he not, that suggests no difference in the education of either. But about the all-important things let not one know and the
other not, but let them know the same things. If you ask me what doctrine
produces such an education, I shall reply that as without philosophy no
man would be properly educated, so no woman would be. I do not mean
that women should possess technical skill and acuteness in argument. It
would be quite superfluous, since they will use philosophy for the ends of
their life as women. Even in men I do not prize this accomplishment too
highly. I only urge that they should acquire from philosophy goodness in
conduct and nobility of character. Now in very truth philosophy is training in nobility of character and nothing else.

On Sexual Indulgence

Not the least significant part of the life of luxury and self-indulgence lies
also in sexual excess; for example those who lead such a life crave a variety of loves not only lawful but unlawful ones as well, not women alone
but also men; sometimes they pursue one love and sometimes another,
and not being satisfied with those which are available, pursue those which
are rare and inaccessible, and invent shameful intimacies, all of which

constitute a grave indictment of manhood. Men who are not wantons or immoral are bound to consider sexual intercourse justified only when it occurs in marriage and is indulged in for the purpose of begetting children, since that is lawful, but unjust and unlawful when it is mere pleasure-seeking, even in marriage. But of all sexual relations those involving adultery are most unlawful, and no more tolerable are those of men with men, because it is a monstrous thing and contrary to nature. But, furthermore, leaving out of consideration adultery, all intercourse with women which is without lawful character is shameful and is practiced from lack of self-restraint. So no one with any self-control would think of having relations with a courtesan or a free woman apart from marriage, no, nor even with his own maid-servant. The fact that those relationships are not lawful or seemly makes them a disgrace and a reproach to those seeking them; whence it is that no one dares to do any of these things openly, not even if he has all but lost the ability to blush, and those who are not completely degenerate dare to do these things only in hiding and in secret. And yet to attempt to cover up what one is doing is equivalent to a confession of guilt. "That's all very well," you say, "but unlike the adulterer who wrongs the husband of the woman he corrupts, the man who has relations with a courtesan or a woman who has no husband wrongs no one for he does not destroy anyone's hope of children." I continue to maintain that everyone who sins and does wrong, even if it affects none of the people about him, yet immediately reveals himself as a worse and a less honorable person; for the wrong-doer by the very fact of doing wrong is worse and less honorable. Not to mention the injustice of the thing, there must be sheer wantonness in anyone yielding to the temptation of shameful pleasure and like swine rejoicing in his own vileness. In this category belongs the man who has relations with his own slave-maid, a thing which some people consider quite without blame, since every master is held to have it in his power to use his slave as he wishes. In reply to this I have just one thing to say: if it seems neither shameful nor out of place for a master to have relations with his own slave, particularly if she happens to be unmarried, let him consider how he would like it if his wife had relations with a male slave. Would it not seem completely intolerable not only if the woman who had a lawful husband had relations with a slave, but even if a woman without a husband should have? And yet surely one will not expect men to be less moral than women, nor less capable of disciplining their desires, thereby revealing the stronger in judgment inferior to the weaker, the rulers to the ruled. In fact, it behooves men to be much better if they expect to be superior to women, for surely if they appear to be less self-controlled they will also be baser characters. What need is there to say that it is an act of licentiousness and nothing less for a master to have relations with a slave? Everyone knows that.

What Is the Chief End of Marriage?

[That the primary end of marriage is a community of life with a view to the procreation of children.] The husband and wife, he used to say, should come together for the purpose of making a life in common and of procreating children, and furthermore of regarding all things in common between them, and nothing peculiar or private to one or the other, not even their own bodies. The birth of a human being which results from such a union is to be sure something marvelous, but it is not yet enough for the relation of husband and wife, inasmuch as quite apart from marriage it could result from any other sexual union, just as in the case of animals. But in marriage there must be above all perfect companionship and mutual love of husband and wife, both in health and in sickness and under all conditions, since it was with desire for this as well as for having children that both entered upon marriage. Where, then, this love for each other is perfect and the two share it completely, each striving to outdo the other in devotion, the marriage is ideal and worthy of envy, for such a union is beautiful. But where each looks only to his own interests and neglects the other, or, what is worse, when one is so minded and lives in the same house but fixes his attention elsewhere and is not willing to pull together with his yoke-mate nor to agree, then the union is doomed to disaster and though they live together, yet their common interests fare badly; eventually they separate entirely or they remain together and suffer what is worse than loneliness.

Is Marriage a Handicap for the Pursuit of Philosophy?

Again when someone said that marriage and living with a wife seemed to him a handicap to the pursuit of philosophy, Musonius said that it was no handicap to Pythagoras, nor to Socrates, nor to Crates, each of whom lived with a wife, and one could not mention better philosophers than these. Crates, although homeless and completely without property or possessions, was nevertheless married; furthermore, not having a shelter of his own, he spent his days and nights in the public porticoes of Athens together with his wife. How, then, can we, who have a home to start with and some of us even have servants to work for us, venture to say that marriage is a handicap for philosophy? Now the philosopher is indeed the teacher and leader of men in all the things which are appropriate for men according to nature, and marriage, if anything, is manifestly in accord with nature. For, to what other purpose did the creator of mankind first divide our human race into two sexes, male and female, then implant in each a strong desire for association and union with the other, instilling in both a powerful longing each for the other, the male for the female and the female for the male? Is it not then plain that he wished the two to be united and live together, and by their joint efforts to devise a way of life in common, and to produce and rear children together, so that the race might never die? Tell me, then, is it fitting for each man to act for himself alone or to act in the interest of his neighbor also, not only that there may be homes in the city but also that the city may not be deserted and that the common good may best be served? If you say that each one should look out for his own interests alone, you represent man as no different from a wolf or any other of the wildest beasts which are born to live by violence and plunder, sparing nothing from which they may gain some advantage, having no part in a life in common with others, no part in cooperation with others, no share of any notion of justice. If you will agree that man's nature most closely resembles the bee which cannot live alone (for it dies when left alone), but bends its energies to the one common task of his fellows and toils and works together with his neighbors; if this is so, and in addition you recognize that for man evil consists in injustice and cruelty and indifference to a neighbor's trouble, while virtue is brotherly love and goodness and justice and beneficence and concern for the welfare of one's neighbor—with such ideas, I say, it would be each man's duty to take thought for his own city, and to make of his home a rampart for its protection. But the first step toward making his home such a rampart is marriage. Thus whoever destroys human marriage destroys the home, the city, and the whole human race. For it would not last if there were no procreation of children and there would be no just and lawful procreation of children without marriage. That the home or the city does not depend upon women alone or upon men alone, but upon their union with each other is evident. One could find no other association more necessary nor more pleasant than that of men and women. For what man is so devoted to his friend as a loving wife is to her husband? What brother to a brother? What son to his parents? Who is so longed for when absent as a husband by his wife, or a wife by her husband? Whose presence would do more to lighten grief or increase joy or remedy misfortune? To whom is everything judged to be common, body, soul and possessions, except man and wife? For these reasons all men consider the love of man and wife to be the highest form of love; and no reasonable mother or father would expect to entertain a deeper love for his own child than for the one joined to him in marriage. Indeed how much the love of a wife for her husband surpasses the love of parents for their children is clearly illustrated by the familiar story of how Admetus, receiving from the gods the privilege of living twice the time allotted to him if he could get someone else to die in his place, found his parents unwilling to die for him although they were old, but his wedded wife Alcestis, though still very young, readily accepted death in her husband's place.

How great and worthy an estate is marriage is plain from this also, that gods watch over it, great gods, too, in the estimation of men; first Hera (and for this reason we address her as the patroness of wedlock), then Eros, then Aphrodite, for we assume that all of these perform the function of bringing together man and woman for the procreation of children. Where, indeed, does Eros more properly belong than in the lawful union of man and wife? Where Hera? Where Aphrodite? When would one more appropriately pray to these divinities than when entering into marriage? What should we more properly call the work of Aphrodite than the joining of wife and husband? Why, then, should anyone say that such great divinities watch over and guard marriage and the procreation of children, unless these things are the proper concern of man? Why should one say that they are the proper concern of man but not the concern of the philosopher? Can it be because the philosopher is worse than other men? Certainly he ought not to be worse, but better and more just and more truly good. Or could one say that the man who does not take an interest in his city is not worse and more unjust than the man who does, the man who looks out only for his own interests is not worse than the one who looks out for the common good? Or can it be that the man who chooses the single life is more patriotic, more a friend and partner of his fellow-man, than the man who maintains a home and rears children and contributes to the growth of his city, which is exactly what a married man does? It is clear, therfore, that it is fitting for a philosopher to concern himself with marriage and having children. And if this is fitting, how, my young friend, could that argument of yours that marriage is a handicap for a philosopher ever be sound? For manifestly the study of philosophy is nothing else than to search out by reason what is right and proper and by deeds to put it into practice. Such, then, were the words he spoke at that time.

Quintus Septimus Florens Tertullian

African philosopher, Christian theologian, and Church Father, c. 160–c. 220.

From *The Apparel of Women*

If there existed upon earth a faith in proportion to the reward that faith will receive in heaven, no one of you, my beloved sisters, from the time when you came to know the living God and recognized your own state, that is, the condition of being a woman, would have desired a too attractive garb, and much less anything that seemed too ostentatious. I think, rather, that you would have dressed in mourning garments and even neglected your exterior, acting the part of mourning and repentant Eve in order to expiate more fully by all sorts of penitential garb that which woman derives from Eve—the ignominy, I mean, of original sin and the odium of being the cause of the fall of the human race. 'In sorrow and anxiety, you will bring forth, O woman, and you are subject to your husband, and he is your master.' Do you not believe that you are [each] an Eve?

The sentence of God on this sex of yours lives on even in our times and so it is necessary that the guilt should live on, also. You are the one who opened the door to the Devil, you are the one who first plucked the fruit of the forbidden tree, you are the first who deserted the divine law; you are the one who persuaded him whom the Devil was not strong enough to attack. All too easily you destroyed the image of God, man. Because of your desert, that is, death, even the Son of God had to die. And you still think of putting adornments over the skins of animals that cover you? Well, now—if, in the very beginning of the world, the Milesians had invented wool by shearing sheep, and if the Chinese had woven the strands of silk, and the Tyrians had invented dye and the Phrygians embroidery and the Babylonians weaving, if pearls had gleamed and rubies flashed with light, if gold itself had already been brought forth from the bowels of

78

earth by man's greed, and finally, in a mirror had already been capable of giving forth its lying image, do you think that Eve, after she had been expelled from Paradise and was already dead, would have longed for all of these fineries? She would not. Therefore, she ought not to crave them or even to know them now, if she desires to be restored to life again. Those things which she did not have or know when she lived in God, all those things are the trappings appropriate to a woman who was condemned and is dead, arrayed as if to lend splendor to her funeral.

Holy women, let none of you, if she is naturally beautiful, be an occasion of sin; certainly, if even she be so, she must not increase beauty, but try to subdue it. If I were speaking to Gentiles, I would give you a Gentile precept and one that is common to all: you are bound to please no one except your own husbands. And, you will please your husbands in the proportion that you take no pains to please anyone else. Be unconcerned, blessed sisters: no wife is really ugly to her own husband. She was certainly pleasing to him when he chose to marry her, whether it was for her beauty or for her character. Let none of you think that she will necessarily incur the hatred and aversion of her husband if she spends less time in the adornment of her person.

Every husband demands that his wife be chaste; but beauty a Christian husband certainly does not demand, because we Christians are not fascinated by the same things that the Gentiles think to be good. If, on the other hand, the husband be an infidel, he will be suspicious of beauty precisely because of the unfavorable opinion the Gentiles have of us.* For whose sake, then, are you cultivating your beauty? If for a Christian, he does not demand it, and if for an infidel, he does not believe it unless it is artless. Why, then, are you so eager to please either one who is suspicious or one who does not desire it?

To be sure, what I am suggesting is not intended to recommend to you an utterly uncultivated and unkempt appearance; I see no virtue in squalor and filth, but I am talking about the proper way and norm and just measure in the care of the body. We must not go beyond what is desired by those who strive for natural and demure neatness. We must not go beyond what is pleasing to God. For, surely, those women sin against God who anoint their faces with creams, stain their cheeks with rouge, or lengthen their eyebrows with antimony. Obviously, they are not satisfied with the creative skill of God; in their own person, without doubt, they censure and criticize the Maker of all things! Surely they are finding fault when they try to perfect and add to His work, taking these their additions, of course, from a rival artist. . . . To have a painted face, you on whom simplicity in every form is enjoined! To lie in your appearance, you to

*Tertullian here refers to one of the vulgar accusations made against the Christians by the pagans, that of Oedipean intercourse.

whom lying with the tongue is not allowed! To seek for that which is not your own, you who are taught to keep hands off the goods of another! To commit adultery in your appearance, you who should eagerly strive after modesty! Believe me, blessed sisters! How can you keep the commandments of God if you do not keep in your own persons the features which He has bestowed on you?

Of course, I am now merely talking as a man and, jealous of women, I try to deprive them of what is their own! But are there not certain things that are forbidden to us, too, out of regard for the sobriety we should maintain out of fear we owe to God? Now, since, by a defect of nature, there is inborn in men because of women (just as in women because of men) the desire to please, the male sex also has its own peculiar trickeries for enhancing their appearance: for instance, cutting the beard a bit too sharply, trimming it too neatly, shaving around the mouth, arranging and dyeing our hair, darkening the first signs of gray hair, disguising the down on the whole body with some female ointments, smoothing off the rest of the body by means of some gritty powder, then always taking occasion to look in a mirror, gazing anxiously into it. Are not all of these things quite idle and hostile to modesty once we have known God, have put aside the desire to please others and foresworn all lasciviousness? For, where God is there is modesty, where modesty is there is dignity, its assistant and companion. How shall we ever practise modesty if we do not make use of its normal means, that is, dignity? How shall we ever be able to make use of dignity in practising modesty unless we bear a certain seriousness in our countenance, in our dress, and in the appearance of the entire man?

Some women may say: 'I do not need the approval of men. For I do not ask for the testimony of men: it is God who sees my heart.' We all know that, to be sure, but let us recall what the Lord said through the Apostle: 'Let your modesty appear before men.' Why would he have said that unless we should be an example and a witness to those who are evil? Or, what did Christ mean by 'let your works shine before men'? Why did the Lord call us 'the light of the world'? Why did He compare us to a city set on a mountain if we were not to shine in [the midst of] darkness and stand out among those who are sunk down? 'If you hide your light under the measure,' you will necessarily be lost in darkness and run down by many people. It is our good works that make us to be the lights of the world. Moreover, what is good, provided it be true and full, does not love the darkness; it rejoices to be seen and exults in being pointed out by others. It is not enough for Christian modesty merely to be so, but to seem so, too. So great and abundant ought to be your modesty that it may flow out from the mind to the garb, and burst forth from the conscience to the outer appearance, so that even from the outside it may examine, as it were, its own furniture—a furniture that is suited to retain the faith forever. We must, therefore, get rid of such delicacies as tend by their softness and effeminacy to weaken the strength of our faith. Otherwise, I am not so sure that the wrist which is always surrounded by a bracelet will be able to bear the hardness of chains with resignation; I have some doubts that the leg which now rejoices to wear an anklet will be able to bear the tight squeeze of an ankle chain; and I sometimes fear that the neck which is now laden with strings of pearls and emeralds will give no room to the executioner's sword.

Jerome
(Eusebius Hieronymus)

Roman philosopher/theologian and Doctor of the Latin Church, 345–420,
who is best known for his Vulgate Translation of the Bible into Latin and for
his major role in introducing the ascetic life into Western Europe.

From *Letter XXII: To Eustochium.* On the motives and rules which should govern those who devote themselves to a life of virginity.

. . . In those days, as I have said, the virtue of continence was found only in men: Eve still continued to travail with children. But now that a virgin has conceived in the womb and has borne to us a child of which the prophet says that "Government shall be upon his shoulder, and his name shall be called the mighty God, the everlasting Father," now the chain of the curse is broken. Death came through Eve, but life has come through Mary. And thus the gift of virginity has been bestowed most richly upon women, seeing that it has had its beginning from a woman.

From *Letter CXXVIII: To Gaudentius.* Gaudentius had written from Rome to ask Jerome's advice as to the bringing up of his infant daughter; whom after the religious fashion of the day he had dedicated to a life of virginity.

A girl should associate only with girls, she should know nothing of boys and should dread even playing with them. She should never hear an unclean word, and if amid the bustle of the household she should chance to hear one, she should not understand it. Her mother's nod should be to her as much a command as a spoken injunction. She should love her as her parent, obey her as her mistress, and reverence her as her teacher. She is now a child without teeth and without ideas, but, as soon as she is seven years old, a blushing girl knowing what she ought not to say and hesitating as to what she ought, she should until she is grown up commit to memory the psalter and the books of Solomon; the gospels, the apostles and the prophets should be the treasure of her heart. She should not appear in public too freely or too frequently attend crowded churches. All her pleasure should be in her chamber. . . .She must never look at young men or turn her eyes upon curled fops; and the wanton songs of sweet voiced girls which wound the soul through the ears must be kept from her. The more freedom of access such persons possess, the harder is it to avoid them when they come; and what they have once learned themselves they will secretly teach her and will thus contaminate our secluded Danae by the talk of the crowd. Give her for guardian and companion a mistress and a governess, one not given to much wine or in the apostle's words idle and a tattler, but sober, grave, industrious in spinning wool and one whose words will form her childish mind to the practice of virtue. . . .

From *Against Jovinianus.* On the superiority of virginity to the married state.

Among other things, the Corinthians asked in their letter whether after embracing the faith of Christ they ought to be unmarried, and for the sake of continence put away their wives, and whether believing virgins were at liberty to marry. And again, supposing that one of two Gentiles believed on Christ, whether the one that believed should leave the one that believed not? And in case it were allowable to take wives, would the Apostle direct that only Christian wives, or Gentiles also, should be taken? Let us then consider Paul's replies to these inquiries. "Now concerning the things whereof ye wrote: It is good for a man not to touch a woman. But, because of fornications, let each man have his own wife, and let each woman have her own husband. Let the husband render unto the wife her due; and likewise also the wife unto the husband. The wife hath not power over her own body, but the husband: And likewise also the husband hath not power over his own body, but the wife. Defraud ye not one the other, except it be by consent for a season, that ye may give yourselves unto prayer, and may be together again, that Satan tempt you not because of your incontinency. But this I say by way of permission not of commandment. Yet I would that all men were even as I myself. Howbeit each man hath his own gift from God, one after this manner, and another after that. But I say to the unmarried and to widows, it is good for them if they abide even as I. But if they have not continency, let them marry: for it is better to marry than to burn." Let us turn back to the chief point of

the evidence: "It is good," he says, "for a man not to touch a woman."
If it is good not to touch a woman, it is bad to touch one: for there is no
opposite to goodness but badness. But if it be bad and the evil is pardoned, the reason for the concession is to prevent worse evil. But surely a
thing which is only allowed because there may be something worse has
only a slight degree of goodness. . . .

What, I pray you, is the quality of that good thing which hinders
prayer? which does not allow the body of Christ to be received? So long
as I do the husband's part, I fail in continency. The same Apostle in another place commands us to pray always. If we are to pray always, it follows that we must never be in the bondage of wedlock, for as often as I
render my wife her due, I cannot pray. The Apostle Peter had experience
of the bonds of marriage. See how he fashions the Church, and what lesson he teaches Christians: "Ye husbands in like manner dwell with your
wives according to knowledge, giving honor unto the woman, as unto the
weaker vessel, as being also joint heirs of the grace of life; to the end that
your prayers be not hindered." Observe that, as St. Paul before, because
in both cases the spirit is the same, so St. Peter now, says that prayers are
hindered by the performance of marriage duty. When he says "likewise," he challenges the husbands to imitate their wives, because he has
already given them commandment: "beholding your chaste conversation
coupled with fear. Whose adorning let it not be the outward adorning of
plaiting the hair, and of wearing jewels of gold, or of putting on apparel:
but let it be the hidden man of the heart, in the incorruptible apparel of a
meek and quiet spirit, which is in the sight of God of great price." You
see what kind of wedlock he enjoins. Husbands and wives are to dwell
together according to knowledge, so that they may know what God
wishes and desires, and give honor to the weak vessel, woman. If we abstain from intercourse, we give honor to our wives: if we do not abstain, it
is clear that insult is the opposite of honor. He also tells the wives to let
their husbands "see their chaste behavior, and the hidden man of the
heart, in the incorruptible apparel of a meek and quiet spirit." Words
truly worthy of an apostle, and of Christ's rock! He lays down the law for
husbands and wives, condemns outward ornament, while he praises continence, which is the ornament of the inner man, as seen in the incorruptible apparel of a meek and quiet spirit. In effect he says this: Since your
outer man is corrupt, and you have ceased to possess the blessing of incorruption characteristic of virgins, at least imitate the incorruption of the
spirit by subsequent abstinence, and what you cannot show in the body
exhibit in the mind. For these are the riches, and these the ornaments of
your union, which Christ seeks. . . .

But we toil to no purpose. For our opponent urges against us the Apostolic sentence and says, "Adam was first formed, then Eve; and Adam
was not beguiled, but the woman being beguiled hath fallen into trans-

gression: but she shall be saved through the child-bearing, if they continue in faith and love and sanctification with sobriety." Let us consider what led the Apostle to make this declaration: "I desire therefore that the men pray in every place, lifting up holy hands, without wrath and disputing." So in due course he lays down rules of life for the women and says "In like manner that women adorn themselves in modest apparel, with shamefacedness and sobriety; not with braided hair, and gold or pearls or costly raiment; but (which becometh women professing godliness) through good works. Let a woman learn in quietness with all subjection. But I permit not a woman to teach, nor to have dominion over a man, but to be in quietness." And that the lot of a woman might not seem a hard one, reducing her to the condition of a slave to her husband, the Apostle recalls the ancient law and goes back to the first example: that Adam was first made, then the woman out of his rib; and that the Devil could not seduce Adam, but did seduce Eve; and that after displeasing God she was immediately subjected to the man, and began to turn to her husband; and he points out that she who was once tied with the bonds of marriage and was reduced to the condition of Eve, might blot out the old transgression by the procreation of children: provided, however, that she bring up the children themselves in the faith and love of Christ, and in sanctification and chastity. . . . You see how you are mastered by the witness of this passage also, and cannot but be driven to admit that what you thought was on the side of marriage tells in favor of virginity. For if the woman is saved in child-bearing, and the more the children the greater the safety of the mothers, why did he add "if they continue in faith and love and sanctification with chastity"? The woman will then be saved, if she bear not children who will remain virgins: if what she has herself lost, she attains in her children, and makes up for the loss and decay of the root by the excellence of the flower and fruit. . . .

    . . . Woman's love in general is accused of ever being insatiable; put it out, it bursts into flame; give it plenty, it is again in need; it enervates a man's mind, and engrosses all thought except for the passion which it feeds. What we read in the parable which follows is to the same effect: "For three things the earth doth tremble, and for four which it cannot bear: for a servant when he is king: and a fool when he is filled with meat: for an odious woman when she is married to a good husband: and an handmaid that is heir to her mistress." See how a wife is classed with the greatest evils. But if you reply that it is an *odious* wife, I will give you the same answer as before—the mere possibility of such danger is in itself no light matter. For he who marries a wife is uncertain whether he is marrying an odious woman or one worthy of his love. If she be odious, she is intolerable. If worthy of love, her love is compared to the grave, to the parched earth, and to fire. . . .

    Let us read the beginning of Genesis, and we shall find Adam, that is *man,* called both male and female. Having then been created by God good and upright, by our own fault we have fallen to a worse condition; and that which in Paradise had been upright, when we left Paradise was corrupt. If you object that before they sinned there was a distinction in sex between male and female, and that they could without sin have come together, it is uncertain what might have happened. For we cannot know the judgments of God, and anticipate his sentence as we choose. What really happened is plain enough—that they who in Paradise remained in perpetual virginity, when they were expelled from Paradise were joined together. Or if Paradise admits of marriage, and there is no difference between marriage and virginity, what prevented their previous intercourse even in Paradise? They are driven out of Paradise; and what they did not there, they do on earth; so that from the very earliest days of humanity virginity was consecrated by Paradise, and marriage by earth. ''Let thy garments be always white.'' The eternal whiteness of our garments is the purity of virginity. In the morning we sowed our seed, and in the evening let us not cease. Let us who served marriage under the law, serve virginity under the Gospel.

Aurelius Augustine

North African philosopher/theologian and bishop, 354–430, whose dramatic conversion to Christianity is thoroughly described in his autobiographical Confessions, *as are his relations with his mother Monica (a "masculine" faith "in female garb"), his mistress of a decade, and their son.*

From *The City of God*

But we, for our part, have no manner of doubt that to increase and multiply and replenish the earth in virtue of the blessing of God, is a gift of marriage as God instituted it from the beginning before man sinned, when He created them male and female—in other words, two sexes manifestly distinct. And it was this work of God on which His blessing was pronounced. For no sooner had Scripture said, "Male and female created He them," than it immediately continues, "And God blessed them, and God said unto them, Increase, and multiply, and replenish the earth, and subdue it," etc. And though all these things may not unsuitably be interpreted in a spiritual sense, yet "male and female" cannot be understood of two things in one man, as if there were in him one thing which rules, another which is ruled; but it is quite clear that they were created male and female, with bodies of different sexes, for the very purpose of begetting offspring, and so increasing, multiplying, and replenishing the earth; and it is great folly to oppose so plain a fact. It was not of the spirit which commands and the body which obeys, nor of the rational soul which rules and the irrational desire which is ruled, nor of the contemplative virtue which is supreme and the active which is subject, nor of the understanding of the mind and the sense of the body, but plainly of the matrimonial union by which the sexes are mutually bound together, that our Lord, when asked whether it were lawful for any cause to put away one's wife (for on account of the hardness of the hearts of the Israelites Moses permitted a bill of divorcement to be given), answered and said, "Have ye not read that He which made them at the beginning made them male and female, and said, For this cause shall a man leave father and mother, and shall cleave to his wife, and they twain shall be one flesh? Wherefore they are no more twain, but one flesh. What, therefore, God hath joined together, let not man put asunder.'' It is certain, then, that from the first men were created, as we see and know them to be now, of two sexes, male and female, and that they are called one, either on account of the matrimonial union, or on account of the origin of the woman, who was created from the side of the man. And it is by this original example, which God Himself instituted, that the Apostle admonishes all husbands to love their own wives in particular. . . .

In Paradise, then, man lived as he desired so long as he desired what God had commanded. He lived in the enjoyment of God, and was good by God's goodness; he lived without any want, and had it in his power so to live eternally. He had food that he might not hunger, drink that he might not thirst, the tree of life that old age might not waste him. There was in his body no corruption, nor seed of corruption, which could produce in him any unpleasant sensation. He feared no inward disease, no outward accident. Soundest health blessed his body, absolute tranquillity his soul. As in Paradise there was no excessive heat or cold, so its inhabitants were exempt from the vicissitudes of fear and desire. No sadness of any kind was there, nor any foolish joy; true gladness ceaselessly flowed from the presence of God, who was loved "out of a pure heart, and a good conscience, and faith unfeigned.'' The honest love of husband and wife made a sure harmony between them. Body and spirit worked harmoniously together, and the commandment was kept without labor. No languor made their leisure wearisome; no sleepiness interrupted their desire to labor.

In such happy circumstances and general human well-being we should be far from suspecting that offspring could not have been begotten without the disease of lust, but those parts, like all the rest, would be set in motion at the command of the will; and without the seductive stimulus of passion, with calmness of mind and with no corrupting of the integrity of the body, the husband would lie upon the bosom of his wife. Nor ought we not to believe this because it cannot be proved by experiment. But rather, since no wild heat of passion would arouse those parts of the body, but a spontaneous power, according to the need, would be present, thus must we believe that the male semen could have been introduced into the womb of the wife with the integrity of the female genital organ being preserved, just as now, with that same integrity being safe, the menstrual flow of blood can be emitted from the womb of a virgin. To be sure, the seed could be introduced in the same way through which the menses can be emitted. In order that not the groans of labor-pain should relax the female organs for parturition, but rather the impulse of the fully developed fetus, thus not the eager desire of lust, but the normal exercise of the will, should join the male and female for breeding and conception. . . .

There is something similar said in the same divine book of the woman, when God questioned and judged them after their sin, and pronounced sentence on them all—the devil in the form of the serpent, the woman and her husband in their own persons. For when He had said to her, "I will greatly multiply thy sorrow and thy conception; in sorrow shalt thou bring forth children," then He added, "and thy turning shall be to thy husband, and he shall rule over thee." What is said to Cain about his sin, or about the vicious concupiscence of his flesh, is here said of the woman who had sinned; and we are to understand that the husband is to rule his wife as the soul rules the flesh. And therefore, says the apostle, "He that loveth his wife, loveth himself; for no man ever yet hated his own flesh." This flesh, then, is to be healed, because it belongs to ourselves: is not to be abandoned to destruction as if it were alien to our nature. . . .

From the words, "Till we all come to a perfect man, to the measure of the age of the fulness of Christ," and from the words, "Conformed to the image of the Son of God," some conclude that women shall not rise women, but that all shall be men, because God made man only of earth, and woman of the man. For my part, they seem to be wiser who make no doubt that both sexes shall rise. For there shall be no lust, which is now the cause of confusion. For before they sinned, the man and the woman were naked, and were not ashamed. From those bodies, then, vice shall be withdrawn, while nature shall be preserved. And the sex of woman is not a vice, but nature. It shall then indeed be superior to carnal inter-course and child-bearing; nevertheless the female members shall remain adapted not to the old uses, but to a new beauty, which, so far from pro-voking lust, now extinct, shall excite praise to the wisdom and clemency of God, who both made what was not and delivered from corruption what He made. For at the beginning of the human race the woman was made of a rib taken from the side of the man while he slept; for it seemed fit that even then Christ and His Church should be foreshadowed in this event. For that sleep of the man was the death of Christ, whose side, as He hung lifeless upon the cross, was pierced with a spear, and there flowed from it blood and water, and these we know to be the sacraments by which the Church is "built up." For Scripture used this very word, not saying "He formed" or "framed," but "built her up into a woman"; whence also the apostle speaks of the *edification* of the body of Christ, which is the Church. The woman, therefore, is a creature of God even as the man; but by her creation from man unity is commended; and the manner of her creation prefigured, as has been said, Christ and the Church. He, then, who created both sexes will restore both. Jesus Himself also, when asked by the Sadducees, who denied the resurrection, which of the seven broth-ers should have to wife the woman whom all in succession had taken to raise up seed to their brother, as the law enjoined, says, "Ye do err, not knowing the Scriptures nor the power of God." And though it was a fit opportunity for His saying, She about whom you make inquiries shall herself be a man, and not a woman, He said nothing of the kind; but "In the resurrection they neither marry nor are given in marriage, but are as the angels of God in heaven." They shall be equal to the angels in immortality and happiness, not in flesh, nor in resurrection, which the angels did not need, because they could not die. The Lord then denied that there would be in the resurrection, not women, but marriages; and He uttered this denial in circumstances in which the question mooted would have been more easily and speedily solved by denying that the female sex would exist, if this had in truth been foreknown by Him. But, indeed, He even affirmed that the sex should exist by saying, "They shall not be given in marriage," which can only apply to females; "Neither shall they marry," which applies to males. There shall therefore be those who are in this world accustomed to marry and be given in marriage, only they shall there make no such marriages. . . .

From "Adulterous Marriages"

. . . You will remember that I am making these observations about both sexes, but particularly on account of men who think themselves superior to women, lest they deem themselves their equals in the matter of chastity. They should have taken the lead in chastity, so that their wives would follow them as their heads. But, since the law forbids adultery, if weakness of the flesh should be admitted as an excuse for incontinence, an occasion for losing their souls is offered to many under the guise of a false impunity. Women also have flesh, to whom their husbands are unwilling to make some such allowance, as though it were granted them because they are men. Never believe that something is owed the stronger sex as an honor which is detrimental to chastity, since meet honor is owed to virtue and not to vice. On the contrary, when they demand such great chastity on the part of their wives, who assuredly have flesh, so that, when they go on long journeys away from their wives, they wish them to pass their glowing youth, untarnished by any adulterous relations—in fact, a great many women pass their days most virtuously, particularly the women of Syria, whose husbands, absorbed in business affairs, leave them as young men and hardly return to their old wives in their advanced age—by the very fact that they pretend that they are unable to practice continence they prove more clearly that it is not impossible. For, if the weakness of men could not accomplish this, much less could the weaker feminine sex.

Peter Abelard

French philosopher/theologian, 1079–1142, whose attempt to keep his marriage to Heloise a secret led to his emasculation by her relatives, after which both entered monastic life.

From "The Seventh Letter Which Is the Reply of Peter to Heloise. Touching the Origin of Nuns"

And just as the sex of women is feebler, so is their virtue more pleasing to God and more perfect, according to the testimony of the Lord Himself, wherein exhorting the weakness of the Apostles to the crown of strife He says: "My grace is sufficient for thee; for my strength is made perfect in weakness." Who likewise, speaking of the members of His Own Body, which is the Church, through the same Apostle, as though He would specially commend the honor of such weak members, added in the same Epistle, namely the First to the Corinthians: "Nay, much more those members of the body, which seem to be more feeble, are necessary: and those members of the body, which we think to be less honorable, upon these we bestow more abundant honor; and our uncomely parts have more abundant comeliness. For our comely parts have no need: But God hath tempered the body together, having given more abundant honor to that part which lacked: that there should be no schism in the body; but that the members should have the same care one for another."

But who would say that there was so complete a fulfilment by the dispensation of the divine grace in any as in the very infirmity of the womanly sex, which both sin and nature had made contemptible? Examine the different states in this sex, not only virgins and widows, or wives, but also the abominations of harlots, and thou wilt see the grace of Christ to be fuller in them, so that according to the words of the Lord and the Apostle: "The last shall be first, and the first last:" and, "Where sin abounded, grace did much more abound." The benefits of which divine grace, or the honors shown to women, if we seek for them from the first beginning of the world, we shall straightway find that the creation of woman excelled by a certain dignity, inasmuch as she indeed was created in Paradise, but man without. So that women are warned especially to pay heed to this, that Paradise is their native country, and how much more it becomes them to pursue the celibate life of Paradise. Wherefore *Ambrose* in the book, Of Paradise, says: "And God took the man whom he Had made, and set him in Paradise. Thou seest how he who already existed is taken. In Paradise He placed him. Note that the man was made without Paradise, and the woman within. In the inferior place man is found the better and she that was made in the better place is considered inferior."

The Lord also first restored *Eve,* the root of all evil, in *Mary* before He repaired *Adam* in Christ. And as from woman sin, so from woman begins grace, and the privilege of virginity has flowered again. And already in *Anna* and *Mary* the form of their holy profession is shown to widows and virgins before in *John* or the Apostles the examples of monastic religion are set before men. And if, after *Eve,* we consider the virtue of *Deborah,* of *Judith,* of *Esther,* surely we shall blush not a little for the strength of the male sex. For *Deborah,* a Judge of the Lord's people, when the men failed, gave battle, and, their enemies overthrown, and the Lord's people set free, powerfully triumphed. *Judith,* unarmed, with her *Abra,* approached a terrible host, and with his own sword cut off the head of one *Holofernes,* she alone destroyed the whole might of her enemies, and set free a people that was in despair. *Esther,* by the secret suggestion of the Spirit, against even the decree of the law, joined herself in marriage with the gentile king, forestalled the counsel of the most impious *Haman,* and the king's cruel edict, and turned the uttered sentence of the royal deliberation, almost in a moment of time, against the adversary. It is ascribed to great virtue that *David* with a sling and a stone attacked *Goliath* and overthrew him. *Judith,* a widow, proceeded against the hostile army without sling and stone, with no armament soever, to do battle. *Esther* by her word alone set her people free, and the sentence being turned against her enemies they rushed into the snare which they had spread. The memory of which famous deed has earned yearly among the Jews the tribute of a solemn rejoicing. Which no deeds of men, howsoever splendid, have obtained.

Who does not marvel at the incomparable constancy of the mother of seven sons, which, together with their mother, being taken, as the History of the Maccabees relates, the most impious king *Antiochus* vainly endeavored to compel to eat the flesh of swine against the Law? Which mother, forgetting her own nature and heedless of human affection, nor having any but the Lord before her eyes, for as many sons as with her sacred exhortations she sent before her to the Crown, so herself triumphed in as many martyrdoms, consummated lastly by her own. If we search through the whole sequence of the Old Testament, what can we compare to the constancy of this woman? That vehement tempter to the last of Holy *Job,* considering the impotency of human nature to resist death, says: ''Skin for skin, yea, all that a man hath will he give for his life.'' For so do we naturally shrink from all the straits of death that often in defence of one member we offer the other, and in the preservation of this life fear no discomforts. But this woman endured the loss not only of all that she had, but of her own and her sons' lives, rather than incur a single offence against the Law. What is this transgression, I ask, to which she was driven? Was she ever forced to renounce God, or to offer incense to idols? Nothing, I say, was exacted of them, save that they should eat meat which the Law forbade them. . . .

To pass over all other examples, what has been so necessary to our redemption, and to the salvation of the whole world as the female sex which brought forth for us the Savior Himself? The singularity of which honor the woman who first ventured to intrude upon Saint *Hilarion* opposed to his marvelling, saying: ''Wherefore turn away thine eyes? Wherefore shun mine entreaty? Look not upon me as a woman, but as one that is wretched. This sex gave birth to the Savior.'' What glory can be compared to this, which that sex won in the Mother of the Lord? The Redeemer might, had he wished, have assumed His Body from a man, as He chose to form the first woman from a man. But this singular grace of His humility He transferred to the honor of the weaker sex. He could also have been born of another and a more worthy part of the woman's body than are the rest of men, who are born of that same vilest portion wherein they are conceived. But, to the incomparable honor of the weaker body, He far more highly consecrated its genitals by His Birth than He had done those of the male by circumcision.

Maimonides
(Moses Ben Maimon)

Philosopher and codifier of Jewish law, 1135–1204, who settled in Egypt after fleeing Spain to escape religious persecution.

From *The Book of Women,* a codification of Jewish laws pertaining to women.

Treatise I: Marriage

When a man marries a woman, whether virgin or nonvirgin, whether adult or minor, whether a daughter of Israel, a proselyte, or an emancipated bondswoman, he obligates himself to her for ten things, and is in turn entitled to four things from her.

Of the ten, three are found in the Torah: *her food, her raiment, and her conjugal rights* (Exod. 21:10). *Her food* signifies her maintenance; *her raiment,* what the term implies; *her conjugal rights,* sexual intercourse with her, according to the way of the world.

The other seven are of Scribal origin, and all of them are conditions laid down by the court. The first of them is the statutory ketubbah;* the rest are called "conditions contained in the ketubbah." They are the following: to treat her if she falls ill; to ransom her she is captured; to bury her if she dies; to provide for her maintenance out of his estate; to let her dwell in his house after his death for the duration of her widowhood; to let her daughters sired by him receive their maintenance out of his estate after his death, until they become espoused; to let her male children sired by him inherit her ketubbah, in addition to their share with their half-brothers in his estate.

*Written instrument that set down the terms of the marriage contract and represented a lien upon all real estate owned or formerly owned by the husband [Editor's note].

And the four things he is entitled to are all of Scribal origin, namely the following: he is entitled to her earnings, to anything she finds, and to the usufruct of her estate during her lifetime. And should she die in his lifetime, he is her heir, with precedence over anyone else as to her estate. . . .

In a place where it is the custom for a woman not to go out into the street wearing upon her head only a cap, but to wear also a veil that covers her whole body like a cloak, he must include in the garments given to her a veil of the least expensive variety. If he is wealthy, he must give her a veil of better quality according to his wealth, in order that she might wear it to her father's house, to a house of mourning, or to a wedding feast. For every woman is entitled to go to her father's house to visit him, or to a house of mourning or a wedding feast as an act of kindness to her friends and relatives, in order that they in turn might visit her on similar occasions, for she is not in a prison where she cannot come and go.

On the other hand, it is unseemly for a woman to be constantly going out abroad and into the streets, and the husband should prevent his wife from doing this and should not let her go out, except once or twice a month, as the need may arise. Rather, the seemly thing for a woman is to sit in the corner of her house, for so is it written, *All glorious is the king's daughter within the palace* (Ps. 45:14). . . .

The conjugal rights mentioned in the Torah are obligatory upon each man according to his physical powers and his occupation.

How so? For men who are healthy and live in comfortable and pleasurable circumstances, without having to perform work that would weaken their strength, and do nought but eat and drink and sit idly in their houses, the conjugal schedule is every night. For laborers, such as tailors, weavers, masons, and the like, their conjugal schedule is twice a week if their work is in the same city, and once a week if their work is in another city.

For ass-drivers, the schedule is once a week; for camel-drivers, once in thirty days; for sailors, once in six months; for disciples of the wise, once a week, because the study of Torah weakens their strength. It is the practice of the disciples of the wise to have conjugal relations each Friday night.

A wife may restrict her husband in his business journeys to nearby places only, so that he would not otherwise deprive her of her conjugal rights. Hence he may not set out except with her permission.

Similarly, she may prevent him from exchanging an occupation involving a frequent conjugal schedule, for one involving an infrequent schedule, as for example, if an ass-driver seeks to become a camel-driver, or if a camel-driver seeks to become a sailor.

Disciples of the wise, however, may absent themselves for the purpose of studying Torah without their wives' permission for as long as two or three years. Similarly, if a man leading a comfortable and pleasurable life decides to become a disciple of the wise, his wife may not hinder him. . . .

Anything a woman may find and her handiwork belong to her husband. And what is she required to do for him? It all depends on the custom of the country. Where the custom is for wives to weave, she must weave; to embroider, she must embroider; to spin wool or flax, she must spin. If it is not the custom of the women of that town to do all these kinds of work, he cannot compel her to do any of them, except spinning wool only—because flax injures the mouth and the lips—for spinning is a kind of work that is characteristic of women, as it is said, *And all women that were wise-hearted did spin with their hands* (Exod. 35:25).

If she exerts herself to perform more work than is proper for her, the surplus belongs to the husband.

If he has a great deal of money, and even if she herself has many maid-servants, she should not sit idle, without work, because idleness leads to immorality. She should not, however, be compelled to work all day long, but may reduce her work in proportion to their wealth.

If a man makes his wife vow to do no work at all, he must divorce her and pay her her ketubbah, because idleness leads to immorality.

Every wife must likewise wash her husband's face, hands, and feet, pour his cup for him, spread his couch, and wait on him, for example, by handing him water or a vessel, or removing these from before him, and the like. She is not obligated, however, to wait on his father or his son.

The aforementioned kinds of work she herself must perform person-ally. Even if she has many maidservants, these kinds of work may be per-formed for the husband only by his wife.

There are other kinds of work that a wife must perform for her husband when they are poor. These are the following: She must bake bread in the oven—Ezra ordained that a wife should rise early to do her baking, so that bread might be available for the poor—cook food, wash clothes, nurse her child, put fodder before her husband's mount—but not before his cattle—and attend to the grinding of corn. How should she attend to the grinding? By sitting at the flour mill and watching the flour, not by doing the grinding herself; or by driving the beast, so that the mill would not stand idle. If, however, the local custom is for the wives to do their grinding with a hand mill, she must do the grinding herself.

When does this apply? When they are poor. If, however, she has brought him a maidservant, or property sufficient to purchase one maid-servant therewith; or if he himself has a maidservant, or enough money to purchase one maidservant, she need neither attend to the grinding, nor bake, nor launder, nor give fodder to his mount.

If she has brought him two maidservants, or property sufficient to pur-chase two maidservants; or if he himself has two maidservants, or the means to purchase them, she also need not cook, nor nurse her child, but may give it to a maidservant to nurse.

It follows thus that there are five kinds of work that any wife must perform for her husband: she must spin, wash his face, hands, and feet, pour his cup, spread his couch, and wait on him.

And there are also six kinds of work that some wives must, and some need not, perform: attend to the grinding, cook, bake, launder, nurse and give fodder to his mount. . . .

How is the claim respecting defects to be put in? If the defects found in her are such as were of a certainty in her prior to her espousal—for example, an extra finger, or the like—her father must show proof that the husband was aware of them and accepted them, or that the presumption is that he was aware of them. If he cannot bring such proof, she may be dismissed without anything at all of her ketubbah.

If the defects are such as might have developed in her after her espousal, the rule is as follows: If they are discovered after her entrance into her husband's house, the husband must bring proof that she had them before the espousal, and that his acquisition of her was consequently based on a misapprehension. If the defects are discovered while she is still in her father's house, the father must prove that they had developed after the espousal, and that it is therefore the groom's misfortune.

If the husband brings proof that the defects were in her before the espousal, or that she herself had admitted this fact to him, while the father brings proof that the husband had seen them and remained silent, thus showing that he was reconciled to them, or that the presumption is that he was aware of them and was reconciled to them, the husband is liable for her ketubbah.

If after having intercourse with his wife he tarries several days, and then claims that he did not notice this defect until now, no attention need be paid to him, even if the defect is in the folds of her skin or on the sole of her foot, because the presumption is that no man would drink out of a cup without first examining it thoroughly. It is therefore presumed that he was aware of the defect and accepted it.

If a man marries a woman who is then found to have no regular menstrual period, so that she feels the onset of menstruation only as the flow of blood commences, she should not indulge in sexual intercourse without making use of two rags to examine herself therewith, one before intercourse, and the other after. This is in addition to the rag with which the man should wipe himself, as will be explained in the Laws Concerning Forbidden Intercourse.

Even though this is a serious defect, she does not forfeit anything, inasmuch as she does examine herself first before she has intercourse.

If she first examines herself and then has intercourse, and if thereafter, as she and he wipe themselves, blood is found on her rag or on his rag, once this happens three times in succession, she is forbidden to abide with her husband, and must be dismissed without her ketubbah, either the statutory or the supplementary amount, or any of the stipulations attached thereto, inasmuch as she is unfit for sexual intercourse. He must, therefore, dismiss her, and may never remarry her, lest she should be cured later, and it should be found that at the time of the divorce his mind was not set on divorcing her.

She may, however, marry another man, as will be explained in the discussion of menstruation.

When does this apply? If she exhibits these symptoms from the beginning of her marriage, and notices blood after the first intercourse. If, however, this disability occurs after her marriage, it is her husband's misfortune.

Therefore, if he has intercourse with her once and no blood is found, but subsequently she notices blood at every act of intercourse, he must dismiss her and pay her her entire ketubbah, and is forbidden to remarry her forever, as we have explained.

The same applies to a woman who develops defects after her marriage, even if she is stricken with boils; if the husband wishes to retain her, he may do so; if he wishes to dismiss her, he must pay her her ketubbah.

If a man develops defects after his marriage, even such defects as the amputation of his arm or leg, or the blinding of his eye, and if his wife refuses to abide with him, he may not be compelled to dismiss her and pay her her ketubbah; rather, if she consents to abide with him, she may do so; if not, she must be dismissed without her ketubbah, like any other rebellious wife.

If, however, he develops bad breath or nasal odor, or if he turns to collecting canine droppings, hewing copper out of its source, or tanning hides, he must be compelled to dismiss her and pay her her ketubbah. But if she is willing to abide with him, she may do so.

If a man is stricken with boils, he must be compelled to dismiss his wife and pay her her ketubbah. Even if she is willing to abide with him, no attention need be paid to her, and they should be separated against their wishes, because she is bound to aggravate his condition. If, however, she says, "Let me abide with him in the presence of witnesses," so that he would have no intercourse with her, her wish may be honored.

If a woman's husband is afflicted with bad breath or nasal odor, or collects canine droppings, or has a similar defect; and if he dies, and she then becomes subject to levirate marriage with his brother who is afflicted with the same defect, she may say, "From your brother I could take it, but from you I cannot," whereupon he must submit to ḥaliṣah and pay her her ketubbah.

Treatise II: Divorce

If . . . two witnesses come forth at the same time, one saying, "He is dead," and the other saying, "He is not dead," or if two women testify, one saying, "He is dead," and the other saying, "He is not dead," the woman involved may not remarry, and if she does remarry, she must leave her second husband, because her status is in doubt.

If she marries the witness who had testified for her, saying, "It appears clear to me that my first husband is dead," she need not leave her second husband.

If thereupon two witnesses come forth and say, "He is not dead," the wife, even if already remarried, must leave her second husband.

When does this apply? When the single witness on the strength of whose testimony she had remarried carries the same weight as the two who now contradict him; for instance, if she had remarried on the basis of one man's testimony, and then two men came forth and said, "He is not dead," or if she had remarried on the basis of the testimony of a woman, or of her own testimony, and then two women, or two witnesses ineligible to testify on the authority of the Sages, came forth and said, "He is not dead."

If, however, a single qualified witness says, "He is dead," and several women or several ineligible witnesses say, "He is not dead," the opposing witnesses are considered evenly balanced, and therefore, if she then marries the one witness who had testified for her, saying, "I am certain that my first husband is dead," she need not leave her second husband.

If a female witness says, "He is dead," or if the wife herself says, "My husband is dead," and then a qualified witness comes forth and says, "He is not dead," the wife may not remarry. If she has done so already, she must leave her second husband.

If one woman says, "He is not dead," and two other women say, "He is dead," the wife may remarry.

Likewise, if ten women say, "He is not dead," and eleven other women say, "He is dead," the wife may remarry, because the principle that two witnesses are as good as a hundred applies only to qualified witnesses. In the case of disqualified witnesses, the majority prevails, whether on the side of leniency or on the side of stringency.

Treatise IV: Virgin Maiden

The fine of fifty silver shekels constitutes payment for the enjoyment of the intercourse alone. The seducer must also pay, in addition to this fine prescribed by the Torah, compensation for the humiliation and the blemish. The violator must pay, in addition to all these, compensation for the pain, for a woman who submits to intercourse willingly suffers no pain, whereas if she is violated she does suffer pain. Hence it is said of the violated, *because he has pained her* (Deut. 22:29).

It follows therefore that the seducer must pay three kinds of penalties, the fine, compensation for the humiliation, and compensation for the blemish; while the violator must pay four, the fine, compensation for the humiliation, compensation for the pain, and compensation for the blemish.

The fine is the same for all women: whether a man has intercourse with the daughter of a High Priest, or with the daughter of a proselyte, or with the daughter of a bastard, the fine for her is fifty silver shekels.

On the other hand, compensation for the humiliation, for the blemish, and for the pain is not the same for all women, and requires assessment.

How is compensation for the humiliation to be assessed? It all depends on the status of him who has inflicted the humiliation and of her who has been subjected to it, for there is no comparison between him who humiliates an esteemed maiden of distinguished family and him who humiliates a girl of poor and humble family. Nor is there any comparison between one who is humiliated by an important and eminent man and one who is humiliated by an ignoble and utterly worthless man.

The judges must therefore consider the status of the man and of the girl involved, and assess the amount the girl's father and her family would have paid to prevent such a thing from happening to them at the hand of this man, who must then pay the equivalent of such a sum.

Compensation for the blemish is assessed according to the girl's beauty. The judges must therefore consider her as if she were a bondswoman being sold in the market place, and must estimate her value as a nonvirgin as against her value as a virgin. For a man would ordinarily prefer to purchase a virgin bondswoman in order to give her to his slave whom he wishes to benefit and please. The judges must thus determine the amount of her deterioration in value, and the offender must pay accordingly.

Compensation for the pain depends upon the tender age of the girl and the structure of her body, as well as upon the age of the offender and the structure of his body. The judges must thus estimate the amount the father would have paid to prevent his daughter from being hurt by this man, and the latter must pay this amount.

The seducer must pay compensation for the humiliation and the blemish immediately, but need not pay the fine unless he fails to marry the seduced, for it is said, *If her father utterly refuse to give her unto him, he shall pay money* (Exod. 22:16).

The violator, however, must immediately pay all four kinds of penalties, and must then consummate the marriage.

Therefore, if the violated wishes to be divorced, or is widowed, she has no claim to anything whatsoever.

If two men, A and B, have intercourse with the same girl, A in a natural manner and B unnaturally, the rule is as follows: If B was first, he must pay compensation for the humiliation and for the blemish; if he was last, he must pay only for the humiliation, inasmuch as the girl was already blemished. As for A, he must pay the fine and the other penalties, whether he was first or last, but the compensation for the humiliation and for the blemish is not the same for a woman who has never had intercourse before and for a woman who has been subjected to unnatural intercourse.

Thomas Aquinas

Italian philosopher–theologian and Church Father, c. 1224–1274, whose writings, strongly influenced by Aristotle (to whom he refers as "the Philosopher") and therefore controversial when written, came to be regarded as among the most official statements of Catholic doctrine.

From *Summa Theologica*

Question XCII. The Production of Woman

First Article

Whether the Woman Should Have Been Made in the First Production of Things?

We proceed thus to the First Article:

Objection 1. It would seem that the woman should not have been made in the first production of things. For the Philosopher says, that the *female is a misbegotten male.* But nothing misbegotten or defective should have been in the first production of things. Therefore woman should not have been made at that first production.

Obj. 2. Further, subjection and limitation were a result of sin, for to the woman was it said after sin (Gen. iii. 16): *Thou shalt be under the man's power;* and Gregory says that, *Where there is no sin, there is no inequality.* But woman is naturally of less strength and dignity than man; *for the agent is always more honourable than the patient,* as Augustine says. Therefore woman should not have been made in the first production of things before sin.

Obj. 3. Further, occasions of sin should be cut off. But God foresaw that the woman would be an occasion of sin to man. Therefore He should not have made woman.

On the contrary, It is written (Gen. ii. 18): *It is not good for man to be alone; let us make him a helper like to himself.*

I answer that, It was necessary for woman to be made, as the Scripture says, as a *helper* to man; not, indeed, as a helpmate in other works, as some say, since man can be more efficiently helped by another man in other works; but as a helper in the work of generation. This can be made clear if we observe the mode of generation carried out in various living things. Some living things do not possess in themselves the power of generation, but are generated by some other specific agent, such as some plants and animals by the influence of the heavenly bodies, from some fitting matter and not from seed: others possess the active and passive generative power together; as we see in plants which are generated from seed; for the noblest vital function in plants is generation. Wherefore we observe that in these the active power of generation invariably accompanies the passive power. Among perfect animals the active power of generation belongs to the male sex, and the passive power to the female. And as among animals there is a vital operation nobler than generation, to which their life is principally directed; therefore the male sex is not found in continual union with the female in perfect animals, but only at the time of coition; so that we may consider that by this means the male and female are one, as in plants they are always united; although in some cases one of them preponderates, and in some the other. But man is yet further ordered to a still nobler vital action, and that is intellectual operation. Therefore there was greater reason for the distinction of these two forces in man; so that the female should be produced separately from the male; although they are carnally united for generation. Therefore directly after the formation of woman, it was said: *And they shall be two in one flesh* (Gen. ii. 24).

Reply Obj. 1. As regards the individual nature, woman is defective and misbegotten, for the active force in the male seed tends to the production of a perfect likeness in the masculine sex; while the production of woman comes from defect in the active force or from some material indisposition, or even from some external influence; such as that of a south wind, which is moist, as the Philosopher observes. On the other hand, as regards human nature in general, woman is not misbegotten, but is included in nature's intention as directed to the work of generation. Now the general intention of nature depends on God, Who is the universal Author of nature. Therefore, in producing nature, God formed not only the male but also the female.

Reply Obj. 2. Subjection is twofold. One is servile, by virtue of which a superior makes use of a subject for his own benefit; and this kind of subjection began after sin. There is another kind of subjection, which is called economic or civil, whereby the superior makes use of his subjects for their own benefit and good; and this kind of subjection existed even before sin. For good order would have been wanting in the human family if some were not governed by others wiser than themselves. So by such a kind of subjection woman is naturally subject to man, because in man the discretion of reason predominates. Nor is inequality among men excluded by the state of innocence, as we shall prove.

Reply Obj. 3. If God had deprived the world of all those things which proved an occasion of sin, the universe would have been imperfect. Nor was it fitting for the common good to be destroyed in order that individual evil might be avoided; especially as God is so powerful that He can direct any evil to a good end.

Second Article

Whether Woman Should Have Been Made from Man?

We proceed thus to the Second Article:

Objection I. It would seem that woman should not have been made from man. For sex belongs both to man and animals. But in the other animals the female was not made from the male. Therefore neither should it have been so with man.

Obj. 2. Further, things of the same species are of the same matter. But male and female are of the same species. Therefore, as man was made of the slime of the earth, so woman should have been made of the same, and not from man.

Obj. 3. Further, woman was made to be a helpmate to man in the work of generation. But close relationship makes a person unfit for that office; hence near relations are debarred from intermarriage, as is written (Lev. xviii 6). Therefore woman should not have been made from man.

On the contrary, It is written (Ecclus. xvii. 5): *He created of him,* that is, out of man, *a helpmate like to himself,* that is, woman.

I answer that, When all things were first formed, it was more suitable for the woman to be made from the man than (for the female to be from the male) in other animals. First, in order thus to give the first man a certain dignity consisting in this, that as God is the principle of the whole universe, so the first man, in likeness to God, was the principle of the whole human race. Wherefore Paul says that *God made the whole human race from one* (Acts xvii. 26). Secondly, that man might love woman all the more, and cleave to her more closely, knowing her to be fashioned from himself. Hence it is written (Gen. ii. 23, 24): *She was taken out of man, wherefore a man shall leave father and mother, and shall cleave to his wife.* This was most necessary as regards the human race, in which the male and female live together for life; which is not the case with other animals. Thirdly, because, as the Philosopher says, the human male and female are united, not only for generation, as with other animals, but also for the purpose of domestic life, in which each has his or her particular duty, and in which the man is the head of the woman. Wherefore it was suitable for the woman to be made out of man, as out of her principle. Fourthly, there is a sacramental reason for this. For by this is signified that the Church takes her origin from Christ. Wherefore the Apostle says (Eph. v. 32): *This is a great sacrament; but I speak in Christ and in the Church.*

Reply Obj.1 is clear from the foregoing.

Reply Obj. 2. Matter is that from which something is made. Now created nature has a determinate principle; and since it is determined to one thing, it has also a determinate mode of proceeding. Wherefore from determinate matter it produces something in a determinate species. On the other hand, the Divine Power, being infinite, can produce things of the same species out of any matter, such as a man from the slime of the earth, and a woman from a man.

Reply Obj. 3. A certain affinity arises from natural generation, and this is an impediment to matrimony. Woman, however, was not produced from man by natural generation, but by the Divine Power alone. Wherefore Eve is not called the daughter of Adam; and so this argument does not prove.

Third Article

Whether the Woman Was Fittingly Made from the Rib of Man?

We proceed thus to the Third Article:

Objection 1. It would seem that the woman should not have been formed from the rib of man. For the rib was much smaller than the woman's body. Now from a smaller thing a larger thing can be made only— either by addition (and then the woman ought to have been described as made out of that which was added, rather than out of the rib itself), or by rarefaction, because, as Augustine says: *A body cannot increase in bulk except by rarefaction.* But the woman's body is not more rarefied than man's—at least, not in the proportion of a rib to Eve's body. Therefore Eve was not formed from a rib of Adam.

Obj. 2. Further, in those things which were first created there was nothing superfluous. Therefore a rib of Adam belonged to the integrity of his body. So, if a rib was removed, his body remained imperfect; which is unreasonable to suppose.

Obj. 3. Further, a rib cannot be removed from man without pain. But there was no pain before sin. Therefore it was not right for a rib to be taken from the man, that Eve might be made from it.

On the contrary, It is written (Gen. ii. 22): *God built the rib, which He took from Adam, into a woman.*

I answer that, It was right for the woman to be made from a rib of man. First, to signify the social union of man and woman, for the woman should neither *use authority over man,* and so she was not made from his head; nor was it right for her to be subject to man's contempt as his slave, and so she was not made from his feet. Secondly, for the sacramental signification; for from the side of Christ sleeping on the Cross the Sacraments flowed—namely, blood and water—on which the Church was established.

Question XCIII. The Production of the Man

Fourth Article

Whether the Image of God Is Found in Every Man?

We proceed thus to the Fourth Article:

Objection 1. It would seem that the image of God is not found in every man. For the Apostle says that *man is the image of God, but woman is the image of man* (I Cor. xi. 7). Therefore, as woman is an individual of the human species, it is clear that every individual is not an image of God. . . .

Reply Obj. 1. The image of God, in its principal signification, namely the intellectual nature, is found both in man and in woman. Hence after the words, *To the image of God He created him,* it is added, *Male and female He created them* (Gen. i. 27). Moreover it is said *them* in the plural, as Augustine remarks, lest it should be thought that both sexes were united in one individual. But in a secondary sense the image of God is found in man, and not in woman: for man is the beginning and end of woman; as God is the beginning and end of every creature. So when the Apostle had said that *man is the image and glory of God, but woman is the glory of man,* he adds his reason for saying this: *For man is not of woman, but woman of man; and man was not created for woman, but woman for man.*

Question XCIX. The State of the Offspring

Second Article

Whether, in the Primitive State, Women Would Have Been Born?

We proceed thus to the Second Article:

Objection 1. It would seem that in the primitive state woman would not have been born. For the Philosopher says that woman is a *misbegotten male*, as though she were a product outside the purpose of nature. But in that state nothing would have been unnatural in human generation. Therefore in that state women would not have been born.

Obj. 2. Further, every agent produces its like, unless prevented by insufficient power or ineptness of matter: thus a small fire cannot burn green wood. But in generation the active force is in the male. Since, therefore, in the state of innocence man's active force was not subject to defect, nor was there inept matter on the part of the woman, it seems that males would always have been born.

Obj. 3. Further, in the state of innocence generation is ordered to the multiplication of the human race. But the race would have been sufficiently multiplied by the first man and woman, from the fact that they would have lived for ever. Therefore, in the state of innocence, there was no need for women to be born.

On the contrary, nature's process in generation would have been in harmony with the manner in which it was established by God. But God established male and female in human nature, as it is written (Gen. i. and ii.). Therefore also in the state of innocence male and female would have been born.

I answer that, Nothing belonging to the completeness of human nature would have been lacking in the state of innocence. And as different grades belong to the perfection of the universe, so also diversity of sex belongs to the perfection of human nature. Therefore in the state of innocence, both sexes would have been begotten.

Reply Obj. 1. Woman is said to be a *misbegotten male*, as being a product outside the purpose of nature considered in the individual case: but not against the purpose of universal nature, as above explained.

Reply Obj. 2. The generation of woman is not occasioned either by a defect of the active force or by inept matter, as the objection supposes; but sometimes by an extrinsic accidental cause; thus the Philosopher says: *The northern wind favors the generation of males, and the southern wind that of females:* sometimes also by some impression in the soul (of the parents), which may easily have some effect on the body (of the child). Especially was this the case in the state of innocence, when the body was more subject to the soul; so that by the mere will of the parent the sex of the offspring might be diversified.

Reply Obj. 3. The offspring would have been begotten to an animal life, as to the use of food and generation. Hence it was fitting that all should generate, and not only the first parents. From this it seems to follow that males and females would have been in equal number.

Question CLVI. Of Incontinence

First Article

Whether Incontinence Pertains to the Soul or to the Body?

We proceed thus to the First Article:

Objection 1. It seems that incontinence pertains not to the soul, but to the body. For sexual diversity comes not from the soul, but from the body. Now sexual diversity causes diversity of incontinence: for the Philosopher says that *women are not described either as continent or as incontinent.* Therefore incontinence pertains not to the soul, but to the body. . . .

Reply Obj. 1. The human soul is the form of the body, and has certain powers which make use of bodily organs. The operations of these organs conduce somewhat to those operations of the soul which are accomplished without bodily instruments, namely to the acts of the intellect and of the will, in so far as the intellect receives from the senses, and the will is urged by passions of the sensitive appetite. Accordingly, since woman, as regards the body, has a weak temperament, the result is that for the most part, whatever she holds to, she holds to it weakly; although in rare cases the opposite occurs, according to Prov. xxxi. 10, *Who shall find a valiant woman?* And since small and weak things are accounted as though they were not, the Philosopher speaks of women as though they had not the firm judgment of reason, although the contrary happens in some women. Hence he states that we do not describe women as being continent, because they are reckoned to be unstable of reason, and to follow their passions readily.

Question CLXIII. The First Man's Sin

Fourth Article

Whether Adam's Sin Was More Grievous Than Eve's?

We proceed thus to the Fourth Article:

Objection 1. It seems that Adam's sin was more grievous than Eve's. For it is written (I Tim. ii. 14): *Adam was not seduced, but the woman being seduced was in the transgression:* and so it would seem that the woman sinned through ignorance, but the man through assured knowledge. Now the latter is the graver sin, according to Luke xii. 47, 48, *That servant who knew the will of his lord . . . and did not according to his will, shall be beaten with many stripes: but he that knew not, and did things worthy of stripes, shall be beaten with few stripes.* Therefore Adams's sin was more grievous than Eve's.

Obj. 2. Further, Augustine says: *If the man is the head, he should live better, and give an example of good deeds especially to his wife, that she may imitate him.* Now he who ought to do better sins more grievously, if he commit a sin. Therefore Adam sinned more grievously than Eve.

Obj. 3. Further, The sin against the Holy Spirit would seem to be the most grievous. Now Adam, apparently, sinned against the Holy Spirit, because while sinning he relied on God's mercy, and this pertains to the sin of presumption. Therefore it seems that Adam sinned more grievously than Eve.

On the contrary, Punishment corresponds to guilt. Now the woman was more grievously punished than the man, as appears from Gen. iii. Therefore she sinned more grievously than the man.

I answer that, As stated in the foregoing *Article,* the gravity of a sin depends on the species rather than on a circumstance of that sin. Accordingly we must assert that, if we consider the condition attaching to these persons, the man's sin is the more grievous, because he was more perfect than the woman.

As regards the genus itself of the sin, the sin of each is equally described, for each sinned by pride. Hence Augustine says: *Eve in excusing herself betrays disparity of sex, though parity of pride.*

But as regards the species of pride, the woman sinned more grievously, for three reasons. First, because she was more puffed up than the man. For the woman believed in the serpent's persuasive words, namely that God had forbidden them to eat of the tree, lest they should become like to Him, so that in wishing to attain to God's likeness by eating of the forbidden fruit, her pride rose to the height of desiring to obtain something against God's will. On the other hand, the man did not believe this to be true; wherefore he did not wish to attain to God's likeness against God's will: but his pride consisted in wishing to attain thereto by his own power. Secondly, the woman not only herself sinned, but suggested sin to the man; wherefore she sinned against both God and her neighbour. Thirdly, the man's sin was diminished by the fact that, as Augustine says, *he consented to the sin out of a certain friendly good will, on account of which a man sometimes will offend God rather than make an enemy of his friend. That he ought not to have done so is shown by the just issue of the Divine sentence.*

It is therefore evident that the woman's sin was more grievous than the man's.

Reply Obj. 1. The woman was deceived because she was first of all puffed up with pride. Wherefore her ignorance did not excuse, but aggravated her sin, in so far as it was the cause of her being puffed up with still greater pride.

Reply Obj. 2. This argument considers the circumstance of personal condition, on account of which the man's sin was more grievous than the woman's.

Reply Obj. 3. The man's reliance on God's mercy did not reach to contempt of God's justice, wherein consists the sin against the Holy Spirit, but as Augustine says, it was due to the fact that, *having had no experience of God's severity, he thought the sin to be venial,* i.e., easily forgiven.

Question CLXIV. The Punishment of Adam's Sin

Second Article

Whether the Particular Punishments of Our First Parents Are Suitably Appointed in Scripture?

We proceed thus to the Second Article:

Objection 1. It seems that the particular punishments of our first parents are unsuitably appointed in Scripture. For that which would have occurred even without sin should not be described as a punishment for sin. Now seemingly there would have been pain in child-bearing, even had there been no sin: for the disposition of the female sex is such that offspring cannot be born without pain to the bearer. Likewise the subjection of woman to man results from the perfection of the male, and the imperfection of the female sex. Again it belongs to the nature of the earth to bring forth thorns and thistles, and this would have occurred even had there been no sin. Therefore these are unsuitable punishments of the first sin.

Obj. 2. Further, that which pertains to a person's dignity does not, seemingly, pertain to his punishment. But the multiplying of conceptions pertains to a woman's dignity. Therefore it should not be described as the woman's punishment.

Obj. 3. Further, the punishment of our first parents' sin is transmitted to all, as we have stated with regard to death. But all women's conceptions are not multiplied, nor does every man eat bread in the sweat of his face. Therefore these are not suitable punishments of the first sin. . . .

On the contrary, These punishments were appointed by God, Who does all things, *in number, weight, and measure* (Wis. xi. 21).

I answer that, As stated in the foregoing *Article,* on account of their sin, our first parents were deprived of the Divine favor, whereby the integrity of human nature was maintained in them, and by the withdrawal of this favor human nature incurred penal defects. Hence they were punished in two ways. In the first place by being deprived of that which was befitting the state of integrity, namely the place of the earthly paradise: and this is indicated (Gen. iii. 23) where it is stated that *God sent him out of the paradise of pleasure.* And since he was unable, of himself, to return to that state of original innocence, it was fitting that obstacles should be placed against his recovering those things that were befitting his original state, namely food (lest he should take of the tree of life) and place; for *God placed before . . . paradise . . . Cherubim, and a flaming sword.* Secondly, they were punished by having appointed to them things befitting a nature bereft of the aforesaid favor: and this as regards both the body and the soul. With regard to the body, to which pertains the distinction of sex, one punishment was appointed to the woman and another to the man. To the woman punishment was appointed in respect of two things on account of which she is united to the man; and these are the begetting of children, and community of works pertaining to family life. As regards the begetting of children, she was punished in two ways: first in the weariness to which she is subject while carrying the child after conception, and this is indicated in the words (Gen. iii. 16), *I will multiply thy sorrows, and thy conceptions;* secondly, in the pain which she suffers in giving birth, and this is indicated by the words *(ibid.) In sorrow shalt thou bring forth.* As regards family life she was punished by being subject to her husband's authority, and this is conveyed in the words *(ibid.), Thou shalt be under thy husband's power.*

Now, just as it belongs to the woman to be subject to her husband in matters relating to the family life, so it belongs to the husband to provide the necessaries of that life. In this respect he was punished in three ways. First, by the barrenness of the earth, in the words (*verse* 17), *Cursed is the earth in thy work*. Secondly, by the cares of his toil, without which he does not win the fruits of the earth; hence the words (*ibid.*), *With labor and toil shalt thou eat thereof all the days of thy life*. Thirdly, by the obstacles encountered by the tillers of the soil, wherefore it is written (*verse* 18), *Thorns and thistles shall it bring forth to thee*.

Likewise a triple punishment is ascribed to them on the part of the soul. First, by reason of the confusion they experienced at the rebellion of the flesh against the spirit; hence it is written (*verse* 7): *The eyes of them both were opened; and . . . they perceived themselves to be naked*. Secondly, by the reproach for their sin, indicated by the words (*verse* 22), *Behold Adam is become as one of Us*. Thirdly, by the reminder of their coming death, when it was said to him (*verse* 19): *Dust thou art and into dust thou shalt return*. To this also pertains that God made them garments of skin, as a sign of their mortality.

Reply Obj. 1. In the state of innocence, child-bearing would have been painless: for Augustine says: *Just as, in giving birth, the mother was then relieved not by groans of pain, but by the instigations of maturity, so in bearing and conceiving the union of both sexes was one not of lustful desire but of deliberate action*.

The subjection of the woman to her husband is to be understood as inflicted in punishment of the woman, not as to his headship (since even before sin the man was the head and governor of the woman), but as to her having now to obey her husband's will even against her own.

If man had not sinned, the earth would have brought forth thorns and thistles to be the food of animals, but not to punish man, because their growth would bring no labor or punishment for the tiller of the soil, as Augustine says. Alcuin, however, holds that, before sin, the earth brought forth no thorns and thistles whatever: but the former opinion is the better.

Reply Obj. 2. The multiplying of her conceptions was appointed as a punishment to the woman, not on account of the begetting of children, for this would have been the same even before sin, but on account of the numerous sufferings to which the woman is subject, through carrying her offspring after conception. Hence it is expressly stated: *I will multiply thy sorrows, and thy conceptions*.

Reply Obj. 3. These punishments affect all somewhat. For any woman who conceives must needs suffer sorrows and bring forth her child with pain: except the Blessed Virgin, who conceived without corruption, and bore without pain, because her conceiving was not according to the law of nature, transmitted from our first parents. And if a woman neither conceives nor bears, she suffers from the defect of barrenness, which outweighs the aforesaid punishments. Likewise whoever tills the soil must needs eat his bread in the sweat of his brow: while those who do not themselves work on the land, are busied with other labors, for *man is born to labor* (Job v. 7); and thus they eat the bread for which others have labored in the sweat of their brow.

Question CLXV. The Temptation of Adam and Eve

Second Article

Whether the Manner and Order of the First Temptation Was Fitting?

We proceed thus to the Second Article:

Objection 1. It seems that the manner and order of the first temptation was not fitting. For just as in the order of nature the angel was above man, so was the man above the woman. Now sin came upon man through an angel: therefore in like manner it should have come upon the woman through the man; in other words the woman should have been tempted by the man, and not the other way about. . . .

On the contrary, That which is first in any genus should be proportionate to all that follow it in that genus. Now in every kind of sin we find the same order as in the first temptation. For, according to Augustine, it begins with the concupiscence of sin in the sensuality, signified by the serpent; extends to the lower reason, by pleasure, signified by the woman; and reaches to the higher reason by consent in the sin, signified by the man. Therefore the order of the first temptation was fitting.

I answer that, Man is composed of a twofold nature, intellective and sensitive. Hence the devil, in tempting man, made use of a twofold incentive to sin: one on the part of the intellect, by promising the Divine likeness through the acquisition of knowledge which man naturally desires to have; the other on the part of sense. This he did by having recourse to those sensible things, which are most akin to man, partly by tempting the man through the woman who was akin to him in the same species; partly by tempting the woman through the serpent, who was akin to them in the same genus; partly by suggesting to them to eat of the forbidden fruit, which was akin to them in the proximate genus.

Reply Obj. 1. In the act of tempting the devil was by way of principal agent; whereas the woman was employed as an instrument of temptation in bringing about the downfall of the man, both because the woman was weaker than the man, and consequently more liable to be deceived, and because, on account of her union with man, the devil was able to deceive the man especially through her. Now there is no parity between principal agent and instrument, because the principal agent must exceed in power, which is not requisite in the instrumental agent.

Question LXXXI. The Quality after the Resurrection

Third Article

Whether All Will Rise Again of the Male Sex?

We proceed thus to the Third Article:

Objection 1. It would seem that all will rise again of the male sex. For it is written (Ephes. iv. 13) that we shall all meet *unto a perfect man*, etc. Therefore there will be none but the male sex.

Obj. 2. Further, In the world to come all pre-eminence will cease, as a gloss observes on I Cor. xv. 24. Now woman is subject to man in the natural order. Therefore women will rise again not in the female but in the male sex.

Obj. 3. Further, That which is produced incidentally and beside the intention of nature will not rise again, since all error will be removed at the resurrection. Now the female sex is produced beside the intention of nature, through a fault in the formative power of the seed, which is unable to bring the matter of the fetus to the male form: wherefore the Philosopher says that *the female is a misbegotten male*. Therefore the female sex will not rise again.

On the contrary, Augustine says: *Those are wiser, seemingly, who doubt not that both sexes will rise again*.

Further, At the resurrection God will restore man to what He made him at the creation. Now He made woman from the man's rib (Gen. ii. 22). Therefore He will also restore the female sex at the resurrection.

I answer that, Just as, considering the nature of the individual, a different quantity is due to different men, so also, considering the nature of the individual, a different sex is due to different men. Moreover, this same diversity is becoming to the perfection of the species, the different degrees whereof are filled by this very difference of sex and quantity. Wherefore just as men will rise again of various stature, so will they rise again of different sex. And though there be difference of sex there will be no shame in seeing one another, since there will be no lust to invite them to shameful deeds which are the cause of shame.

Reply Obj. 1. When it is said: We shall all meet *Christ unto a perfect man,* this refers not to the male sex but to the strength of soul which will be in all, both men and women.

Reply Obj. 2. Woman is subject to man on account of the frailty of nature, as regards both vigor of soul and strength of body. After the resurrection, however, the difference in those points will be not on account of the difference of sex, but by reason of the difference of merits. Hence the conclusion does not follow.

Reply Obj. 3. Although the begetting of a woman is beside the intention of a particular nature, it is in the intention of universal nature, which requires both sexes for the perfection of the human species. Nor will any defect result from sex as stated above.

Thomas More

English philosopher and political theorist, 1478–1535, who was beheaded for his stand against Henry VIII's break with the Church of Rome.

From *Utopia*. Utopia is a "description" of a fictitious society, probably intended by More as a somewhat tentative outline of a perfect society.

And now for their working conditions. Well, there's one job they all do, irrespective of sex, and that's farming. It's part of every child's education. They learn the principles of agriculture at school, and they're taken for regular outings into the fields near the town, where they not only watch farmwork being done, but also do some themselves, as a form of exercise.

Besides farming which, as I say, is everybody's job, each person is taught a special trade of his own. He may be trained to process wool or flax, or he may become a stonemason, a blacksmith, or a carpenter. Those are the only trades that employ any considerable quantity of labor. They have no tailors or dressmakers, since everyone on the island wears the same sort of clothes—except that they vary slightly according to sex and marital status—and the fashion never changes. These clothes are quite pleasant to look at, they allow free movement of the limbs, they're equally suitable for hot and cold weather—and the great thing is, they're all home-made. So everybody learns one of the other trades I mentioned, and by everybody I mean the women as well as the men—though the weaker sex are given the lighter job, like spinning and weaving, while the men do the heavier ones.

. . . In Utopia they have a six-hour working day—three hours in the morning, then lunch—then a two-hour break—then three more hours in the afternoon, followed by supper. They go to bed at 8 p.m., and sleep for eight hours. All the rest of the twenty-four they're free to do what they like—not to waste their time in idleness or self-indulgence, but to make good use of it in some congenial activity. Most people spend these free periods on further education, for there are public lectures first thing every morning. Attendance is quite voluntary, except for those picked out for academic training, but men and women of all classes go crowding in to hear them—I mean, different people go to different lectures, just as the spirit moves them. However, there's nothing to stop you from spending this extra time on your trade, if you want to. Lots of people do, if they haven't the capacity for intellectual work, and are much admired for such public-spirited behavior. . . .

But let's get back to their social organization. Each household, as I said, comes under the authority of the oldest male. Wives are subordinate to their husbands, children to their parents, and younger people generally to their elders. . . .

At lunch-time and supper-time a bugle is blown, and the whole Sty assembles in the dining hall—except for anyone who's in hospital or ill at home. However, you're quite at liberty to take food home from the market, once the dining halls have been supplied, for everyone knows you wouldn't do it unless you had to. I mean, no one likes eating at home, although there's no rule against it. For one thing, it's considered rather bad form. For another, it seems silly to go to all the trouble of preparing an inferior meal, when there's an absolutely delicious one waiting for you at the dining hall just down the street.

In these dining halls all the rough and dirty work is done by slaves, but the actual business of preparing and cooking the food, and planning the menus, is left entirely to the women of the household on duty—for a different household is responsible for providing the meals every day. The rest of the adults sit at three tables or more, according to their numbers, with the men against the wall and the women on the outside—so that if they suddenly feel sick, as pregnant women do from time to time, they can get up without disturbing anyone else, and retire to the nursery. . . .

Girls aren't allowed to marry until they're eighteen—boys have to wait four years longer. Any boy or girl convicted of premarital intercourse is severely punished, and permanently disqualified from marrying, unless this sentence is remitted by the Mayor. The man and woman in charge of the household in which it happens are also publicly disgraced, for not doing their jobs properly. The Utopians are particularly strict about that kind of thing, because they think very few people would want to get married—which means spending one's whole life with the same person, and putting up with all the inconveniences that this involves—if they weren't carefully prevented from having any sexual intercourse otherwise.

When they're thinking of getting married, they do something that seemed to us quite absurd, though they take it very seriously. The prospective bride, no matter whether she's a spinster or a widow, is exhibited stark naked to the prospective bridegroom by a respectable married woman, and a suitable male chaperon shows the bridegroom naked to the bride. When we implied by our laughter that we thought it a silly system, they promptly turned the joke against *us*.

'What we find so odd,' they said, 'is the silly way these things are arranged in other parts of the world. When you're buying a horse, and there's nothing at stake but a small sum of money, you take every possible precaution. The animal's practically naked already, but you firmly refuse to buy until you've whipped off the saddle and all the rest of the harness, to make sure there aren't any sores underneath. But when you're choosing a wife, an article that for better or worse has got to last you a lifetime, you're unbelievably careless. You don't even bother to take it out of its wrappings. You judge the whole woman from a few square inches of face, which is all you can see of her, and then proceed to marry her—at the risk of finding her most disagreeable, when you see what she's really like. No doubt you needn't worry, if moral character is the only thing that interests you—but we're not all as wise as that, and even those who are sometimes find, when they get married, that a beautiful body can be quite a useful addition to a beautiful soul. Certainly those wrappings may easily conceal enough ugliness to destroy a husband's feelings for his wife, when it's too late for a physical separation. Of course, if she turns ugly after the wedding, he must just resign himself to his fate—but one does need some legal protection against marriage under false pretences!'

In their case, some such precautions are particularly necessary, since unlike all their neighbors they're strictly monogamous. Most married couples are parted only by death, except in the case of adultery or intolerably bad behavior, when the innocent party may get permission from the Council to marry someone else—the guilty party is disgraced and condemned to celibacy for life. But in no circumstances can a man divorce his wife simply because, through no fault of her own, she has deteriorated physically. Quite apart from the cruelty of deserting a person at the very time when she most needs sympathy, they think that, if this sort of thing were allowed, there'd be no security whatever for old age, which not only brings many diseases with it, but is really a disease in itself.

Occasionally, though, divorce by mutual consent is allowed on grounds of incompatibility, when both husband and wife have found alternative partners that seem likely to make them happier. But this requires special permission, which can only be got after a thorough investigation by the Bencheaters and their wives. Even then they're rather reluctant to give it, for they think there's nothing less calculated to strengthen the marriage tie than the prospect of easy divorce.

Adulterers are sentenced to penal servitude of the most unpleasant type. If both offenders are married, their injured partners may, if they like, obtain a divorce and marry one another, or anyone else they choose.

But if they continue to love their undeserving mates, they're allowed to stay married to them, provided they're willing to share their working conditions. In such cases the Mayor is sometimes so touched by the guilty party's remorse and the innocent party's loyalty that he lets them both go free. But a second conviction means capital punishment.

Otherwise there are no fixed penalties prescribed by law—the Council decides in each case what sentence is appropriate. Husbands are responsible for punishing their wives, and parents for punishing their children, unless the offence is so serious that it has to be dealt with by the authorities, in the interests of public morality. . . .

And that brings us to the subject of war. Well, fighting is a thing they absolutely loathe. They say it's a quite subhuman form of activity, although human beings are more addicted to it than any of the lower animals. In fact, the Utopians are practically the only people on earth who fail to see anything glorious in war. Of course, both sexes are given military training at regular intervals, so that they won't be incapable of fighting if they ever have to do it. But they hardly ever go to war, except in self-defense, to repel invaders from friendly territory, or to liberate the victims of dictatorship—which they do in a spirit of humanity, just because they feel sorry for them. . . .

Male priests are allowed to marry—for there's nothing to stop a woman from becoming a priest, although women aren't often chosen for the job, and only elderly widows are eligible. As a matter of fact, clergymen's wives form the cream of Utopian society, for no public figure is respected more than a priest. . . .

At Ending Feasts they fast all day, and go to church in the evening, to thank God for bringing them safely to the end of the year or month in question. Next day, which is of course a Beginning Feast, they meet at church in the morning to pray for happiness and prosperity during the year or month which has just begun. But before going to church at an Ending Feast, wives kneel down at home before their husbands, and children before their parents, to confess all their sins of omission and commission, and ask to be forgiven. This gets rid of any little grudges that may have clouded the domestic atmosphere, so that everyone can attend divine service with an absolutely clear mind.

Letter to William Gonell. More chose Gonell as tutor to his children upon the recommendation of Erasmus. This letter evinces More's practice, in his own home, of Utopian principles of equal instruction for both sexes.

At Court
22 May 1518?

I have received, my dear Gonell, your letter, elegant and full of affection as always. Your devotion to my children I perceive from your letter, your diligence from theirs. Everyone's letter pleased me greatly, but above all that I notice Elizabeth shows a modesty of character in the absence of her mother, which not every girl would show in her mother's presence. Let her understand that such conduct delights me more than all the learning in the world. Though I prefer learning joined with virtue to all the treasures of kings, yet renown for learning, if you take away moral probity, brings nothing else but notorious and noteworthy infamy, especially in a woman. Since erudition in women is a new thing and a reproach to the sloth of men, many will gladly assail it, and impute to learning what is really the fault of nature, thinking from the vices of the learned to get their own ignorance esteemed as virtue. On the other hand, if a woman (and this I desire and hope with you as their teacher for all my daughters) to eminent virtue of mind should add even moderate skill in learning, I think she will gain more real good than if she obtain the riches of Croesus and the beauty of Helen. Not because that learning will be a glory to her, though learning will accompany virtue as a shadow does a body, but because the reward of wisdom is too solid to be lost with riches or to perish with beauty, since it depends on the inner knowledge of what is right, not on the talk of men, than which nothing is more foolish or mischievous.

For as it becomes a good man to avoid infamy, so to lay oneself out for renown is the sign of a man who is not only arrogant, but ridiculous and miserable. A mind must be uneasy which ever wavers between joy and sadness because of other men's opinions. Among all the benefits that learning bestows on men, I think there is none more excellent than that by study we are taught to seek in that very study not praise, but utility. Such has been the teaching of the most learned men, especially of philosophers, who are the guides of human life, although some may have abused learning, like other good things, simply to court empty glory and popular renown.

I have written at length on not pursuing glory, my dear Gonell, because of what you say in your letter, that Margaret's lofty and exalted character of mind should not be debased. In this judgment I quite agree with you; but to me, and, no doubt, to you also, that man would seem to debase a generous character of mind who would accustom it to admire what is vain and low. He, on the contrary, raises it who rises to virtue and true goods, and who looks down with contempt from the contemplation of the sublime, on those shadows of good things which almost all mortals, through ignorance of truth, greedily snatch at as if they were true goods.

Therefore, my dearest Gonell, since I thought we must walk by this road, I have often begged not you only, who, out of your exceptional affection for all my family, would do it of your own accord, nor only my wife, who is sufficiently urged by her truly maternal love for them, which has been proved to me in many ways, but absolutely all my friends, continually to warn my children to avoid as it were the precipices of pride and haughtiness, and to walk in the pleasant meadows of modesty: not to be dazzled at the sight of gold; not to lament the lack of what they erroneously admire in others; not to think more of themselves for gaudy trappings, nor less for the want of them; not to deform the beauty that nature has given them by neglect, nor to try to heighten it by artifice; to put virtue in the first place among goods, learning in the second; and in their studies to esteem most whatever may teach them piety towards God, charity to all, and modesty and Christian humility in themselves. By such means they will receive from God the reward of an innocent life, and in the assured expectation of it will view death without dread, and meanwhile possessing solid joy will neither be puffed up by the empty praise of men, nor dejected by evil tongues. These I consider the real and genuine fruits of learning, and though I admit that all literary men do not possess them, I would maintain that those who give themselves to study with such intent will easily attain their end and become perfect.

Nor do I think that the harvest is much affected whether it is a man or a woman who does the sowing. They both have the name of human being whose nature reason differentiates from that of beasts; both, I say, are equally suited for the knowledge of learning by which reason is cultivated, and, like plowed land, germinates a crop when the seeds of good precepts have been sown. But if the soil of a woman be naturally bad, and apter to bear fern than grain, by which saying many keep women from study, I think, on the contrary, that a woman's wit is the more diligently to be cultivated, so that nature's defect may be redressed by industry. This was the opinion of the ancients, both the wisest and the most saintly. Not to speak of the rest, Jerome and Augustine not only exhorted excellent matrons and honorable virgins to study, but also, in order to assist them, diligently explained the abstruse meanings of the Scriptures, and wrote for tender girls letters replete with so much erudition that nowadays old men who call themselves doctors of sacred literature can scarcely read them correctly, much less understand them. Do you, my learned Gonell, have the kindness to see that my daughters thoroughly learn these works of saintly men. From them they will learn in particular what goal they should set for their studies, and the whole fruit of their endeavors should consist in the testimony of God and a good conscience. Thus they will be inwardly calm and at peace and neither stirred by praise of flatterers nor stung by the follies of unlearned mockers of learning. . . .

From the Court, on the vigil of Pentecost.

Letters: Thomas More To His Most Dear Daughter Margaret (1521?)

There was no reason, my darling daughter, why you should have put off writing me for a single day, because in your great self-distrust you feared that your letters would be such that I could not read them without distaste. Even had they not been perfect, yet the honor of your sex would have gained you pardon from anyone, while to a father even a blemish will seem beautiful in the face of a child. But indeed, my dear Margaret, your letters were so elegant and polished and gave so little cause for you to dread the indulgent judgment of a parent, that you might have despised the censorship of an angry Momus.

You tell me that Nicholas, who is fond of us and so learned in astronomy, has begun again with you the system of the heavenly bodies. I am grateful to him, and I congratulate you on your good fortune; for in the space of one month, with only slight labor, you will thus learn thoroughly these sublime wonders of the Eternal Workman, which so many men of illustrious and almost superhuman intellect have discovered only with hot toil and study, or rather with cold shiverings and nightly vigils in the open air in the course of many ages.

I am, therefore, delighted to read that you have made up your mind to give yourself so diligently to philosophy as to make up by your earnestness in future what you have lost in the past by neglect. My darling Margaret, I indeed have never found you idling—and your unusual learning in almost every kind of literature shows that you have been making active progress—so I take your words as an example of the great modesty that makes you prefer to accuse yourself falsely of sloth rather than to boast truly of your diligence; unless your meaning is that you will give yourself so earnestly to study that your past industry will seem like indolence by comparison. If this is your meaning, my Margaret, and I think it really is, nothing could be more delightful to me, or more fortunate, my sweetest daughter, for you.

Though I earnestly hope that you will devote the rest of your life to medical science and sacred literature, so that you may be well furnished for the whole scope of human life, (which is to have a sound mind in a sound body), and I know that you have already laid the foundations of these studies, and there will be always opportunity to continue the building; yet I am of opinion that you may with great advantage give some years of your yet flourishing youth to humane letters and so-called liberal studies. And this both because youth is more fitted for a struggle with difficulties and because it is uncertain whether you will ever in the future have the benefit of so sedulous, affectionate, and learned a teacher. I need not say that by such studies a good judgment is formed or perfected.

It would be a delight, my dear Margaret, to me to converse long with you on these matters: but I have just been interrupted and called away by the servants, who have brought in supper. I must have regard to others, else to sup is not so sweet as to talk with you.

Farewell, my dearest child, and salute for me my beloved son, your husband. I am extremely glad that he is following the same course of study as yourself. I am ever wont to persuade you to yield in everything to your husband; now, on the contrary, I give you full leave to strive to surpass him in the knowledge of the celestial system. Farewell again. Salute your whole company, but especially your tutor.

(Woodstock?
Autumn 1523)

I cannot put down on paper, indeed I can hardly express in my own mind, the deep pleasure that I received from your most charming letter, my dearest Margaret. As I read it there was with me a young man of the noblest rank and of the widest attainments in literature—one, too, who is as conspicuous for his virtue as he is for his learning, Reginald Pole. He thought your letter nothing short of marvelous, even before he understood how pressed you were for time and distracted by ill health, while you managed to write so long a letter. I could scarce make him believe that you had not been helped by a teacher until he learned truly that there was no teacher at our house, and that it would not be possible to find a man who would not need your help in composing letters rather than be able to give any assistance to you.

Meanwhile, something I once said to you in joke came back to my mind, and I realized how true it was. It was to the effect that you were to be pitied, because the incredulity of men would rob you of the praise you so richly deserved for your laborious vigils, as they would never believe, when they read what you had written, that you had not often availed yourself of another's help: whereas of all the writers you least deserved to be thus suspected. Even when a tiny child you could never endure to be decked out in another's finery. But, my sweetest Margaret, you are all the more deserving of praise on this account. Although you cannot hope for an adequate reward for your labor, yet nevertheless you continue to unite to your singular love of virtue the pursuit of literature and art. Content with the profit and pleasure of your conscience, in your modesty you do not seek for the praise of the public, nor value it overmuch even if you receive it, but because of the great love you bear us, you regard us—your husband and myself—as a sufficiently large circle of readers for all that you write.

In your letter you speak of your imminent confinement. We pray most earnesty that all may go happily and successfully with you. May God and our Blessed Lady grant you happily and safely to increase your family by a little one like to his mother in everything except sex. Yet let it by all means be a girl, if only she will make up for the inferiority of her sex by her zeal to imitate her mother's virtue and learning. Such a girl I should prefer to three boys. Good-bye, my dearest child.

Desiderius Erasmus

Dutch philosopher, classical scholar, and Christian Humanist of the Reformation, 1469–1536, whose biting irony was intended to assist Christian truths in their gentle reformation of church practices, monastic activities, Scholasticism, and popular religion.

From *In Praise of Folly*

But because it seemed expedient that man, who was born for the transaction of business, should have so much wisdom as should fit and capacitate him for the discharge of his duty herein, and yet lest such a measure as is requisite for this purpose might prove too dangerous and fatal, I was advised with for an antidote, who prescribed this infallible receipt of taking a wife, a creature so harmless and silly, and yet so useful and convenient, as might mollify and make pliable the stiffness and morose humor of man. Now that which made Plato doubt under what genus to rank woman, whether among brutes or rational creatures, was only meant to denote the extreme stupidness and Folly of that sex, a sex so unalterably simple, that for any of them to thrust forward, and reach at the name of wise, is but to make themselves the more remarkable fools, such an endeavor, being but a swimming against the stream, nay, the turning the course of nature, the bare attempting whereof is as extravagant as the effecting of it is impossible: for as it is a trite proverb, *That an ape will be an ape, though clad in purple;* so a woman will be a woman, *i.e.*, a fool, whatever disguise she takes up. And yet there is no reason women should take it amiss to be thus charged; for if they do but rightly consider they will find it is to Folly they are beholden for those endowments, wherein they so far surpass and excel man; as first, for their unparalleled beauty, by the charm whereof they tyrannize over the greatest tyrants; for what is it but too great a smatch of wisdom that makes men so tawny and thick-skinned, so rough and prickly-bearded, like an emblem of winter or old age, while women have such dainty smooth cheeks, such a low gentle voice, and so pure a complexion, as if nature had drawn them for a standing pattern of all symmetry and comeliness? Beside, what greater or juster aim and ambition have they than to please their husbands? In order whereunto they garnish themselves with paint, washes, curls, perfumes, and other mysteries of ornament; yet after all they become acceptable to them only for their Folly. Wives are always allowed their humor, yet it is only in exchange for titillation and pleasure, which indeed are but other names for Folly; as none can deny, who consider how a man must hug, and dandle, and kittle, and play a hundred little tricks with his bedfellow when he is disposed to make that use of her that nature designed her for.

The Abbot and the Learned Woman

An Abbot gives a Lady* a Visit; and finding Latin and Greek Books in her Chamber, gives his Reasons against women's meddling with Learning. He professes himself to be a greater Lover of Pleasure, than Wisdom; and makes the Ignorance of Monks, to be the most powerful reason of their Obedience.

Antronius, Magdalia

An. This House methinks is strangely Furnisht.

Ma. Why? Is't not well?

An. I don't know what you call Well; but 'tis not so proper, methinks, for a Woman.

Ma. And why not I pray ye?

An. Why what should a Woman do with so many Books?

Ma. As if you that are an Abbot, and a Courtier, and have liv'd so long in the World, had never seen Books in a Lady's Chamber before.

An. Yes, French ones I have; but here are Greek and Latin.

Ma. Is there no Wisdom then, but in French?

An. But they are well enough, however, for Court Ladies, that have nothing else to do, to pass away their time withall.

Ma. So that you would have only your Court Ladies to be Women of Understanding, and of Pleasure.

An. That's your mistake now, to couple Understanding with Pleasure: For the One is not for a Woman at all; and the Other is only for a Woman of Quality.

Ma. But is it not every Body's business to live well?

An. Beyond all question.

*The "learned woman" in this play is thought to be modeled after Thomas More's daughter Margaret [Editor's note].

Ma. How shall any Man live Comfortably, that does not live Well?

An. Nay rather how shall any Man live Comfortably that does?

Ma. That is to say, you are for a Life that's Easie, let it be never so Wicked.

An. I am of Opinion, I must confess, that a Pleasant Life is a Good Life.

Ma. But what is it that makes one's Life Pleasant. Is it Sense, or Conscience?

An. It is the Sense of Outward Enjoyment.

Ma. Spoken like a Learned Abbot, tho' but a Dull Philosopher. But tell me now, what are those Enjoyments you speak of?

An. Money, Honour, Eating, Drinking, Sleeping; and the Liberty of doing what a Man has a Mind to do.

Ma. But what if God should give you Wisdom, over and above all the rest? Would your Life be ever the Worse for it?

An. Let me know first, what is it that you call Wisdom.

Ma. Wisdom is a knowledge that places the Felicity of Reasonable Nature in the Goods of the Mind, and tells us that a Man is neither the Happier, nor the Better, for the External Advantages of Blood, Honour, or Estate.

An. If that be it, pray'e make the best of your Wisdom.

Ma. But what if I take more delight in a Good Book than you do in a Fox-Chase, A Fuddling-bout, or in the shaking of your Elbow? Will you not allow me then to have a Pleasant Life on't.

An. Every one as they like, but it would not be so to me.

Ma. The question is not what Does, but what Ought to Please you.

An. I should be loth, I do assure you, to have my Monks over Bookish.

Ma. And yet my Husband is never better pleas'd than at his Study. Nor do I see any hurt in't, if your Monks would be so too.

An. Marry hang 'em up as soon; It teaches 'em to Chop Logique, and makes 'em Undutiful. You shall have them expostulating presently, appealing to Peter, and Paul, and Prating out of the Canons and Decretals.

Ma. But I hope you would not have them do anything that Clashes with Peter and Paul tho'?

An. Clash or not clash; I do not much trouble my Head about their Doctrine. But I do naturally hate a Fellow that will have the last Word, and Reply upon his Superior. And betwixt Friends, I do not much care neither to have any of my People wiser than their Master.

Ma. 'Tis but your being Wise yourself, and then there's no fear on't.

An. Alas! I have no time for't.

Ma. How so, I beseech you?

An. I'm so full of Business.

Ma. Have you no time, do you say, to apply your self to Wisdom?

An. No, not a single Minute.

Ma. Pray'e what hinders you; if a body may ask the question.

An. Why, you must know we have devilish long Prayers; and by that time I have lookt over my Charge, my Horses, my Dogs, and made my Court, I have not a Moment left me to spare.

Ma. Is this the mighty Business then that keeps you from looking after Wisdom?

An. We have got a Habit of it; and Custom you know, is a great matter?

Ma. Put the Case now that it were in your power to transform your Self, and all your Monks into any other Animals; and that a body should desire you to turn your Self into a Hunting-Nag, and your whole Flock into a Herd of Swine, would you do't?

An. No, not upon any terms.

Ma. And yet this would secure you from having any of your Disciples wiser than your self.

An. As for my People; I should not much stand upon it what sort of Brutes they were; provided that I might still be a Man myself.

Ma. But can you accompt him for a Man, that neither is Wise, nor has any Inclination so to be?

An. But so long as I have Wit enough for my own Business—

Ma. Why so have the Hogs.

An. You talk like a Philosopher in a Petticoat, methinks.

Ma. And you, methinks, like something that's far from it. But what's your quarrel all this while to the Furniture of this House?

An. A Spinning-wheel, or some Instrument for Good Huswifery were more suitable to your Sex.

Ma. Is it not the Duty then of a Housekeeper to keep her Family in Order, and look to the Education of her Children?

An. 'Tis so.

Ma. And is this Office to be discharg'd without Understanding?

An. I suppose not.

Ma. This Understanding do I gather from my Books.

An. But yet I have above Threescore Monks under my Care, and not so much as one Book in my Lodgings.

Ma. They are well Tutor'd the mean while.

An. Not but that I could endure Books too, provided they be not Latin.

Ma. And why not Latin?

An. 'Tis not a Tongue for a Woman.

Ma. Why what's your Exception to't?

An. 'Tis not a language to keep a Woman Honest.

Ma. Your French Romances, I must confess, are great Provocatives to Modesty.

An. Well, but there's something else in't too.

Ma. Out with it then.

An. If the Women do not understand Latin, they are in less danger of the Priests.

Ma. But so long as you take care that the Priests themselves shall not understand Latin; where's the Danger?

An. 'Tis the Opinion of the Common People however, because it is so Rare a thing for a Woman to understand Latin.

Ma. Why, what do you talk to me of the People? that never did any thing well? Or of Custom? that gives Authority to all Wickedness. We should apply our selves to that which is good, and turn that which was unusual, unpleasant, and perhaps scandalous before, into the Contrary.

An. I hear you.

Ma. Is is not a laudable Quality for a German Lady to speak French?

An. It is so.

Ma. And to what end?

An. That she may be conversation for those that speak French.

Ma. And why may I not as well learn Latin? to fit myself for the Company of so many Wise, and Learned Authors; so many Faithfull Counsellors, and Friends?

An. But 'tis not so well for Women to spend their Brains upon Books, unless they had more to spare.

Ma. What you have to spare I know not; but for my small stock, I had much rather employ it upon honest Studies, than in the Mumbling over of so many Prayers, like a Parrot, by Rote; or the Emptying of so many Dishes, and Beer-glasses till Morning.

An. But much Learning makes a Man mad.

Ma. Your Topers, Drolls, and Buffons, are an Entertainment no doubt to make a body Sober.

An. They make the time pass merrily away.

Ma. But why should so pleasant Company as the Authors I converse with make me Mad then?

An. 'Tis a common saying.

Ma. But yet the Fact itself tells me otherwise; and that Intemperate Feasting, Drinking, Whoring, and Inordinate Watching, is the ready way to Bedlam.

An. For the whole World I would not have a Learned Wife.

Ma. Nor I an Unlearned Husband. Knowledge is such a Blessing, that we are both of us the Dearer one to another for't.

An. But then there's so much Trouble in the getting of it; and we must Die at last too.

Ma. Tell me now by your favor, if you were to march off tomorrow, whether had you rather die a Fool, or a Wise Man?

An. Ay, if I could be a Wise Man without Trouble.

Ma. Why? there's nothing the World to be gotten without it; and when we have gotten what we can (tho' with never so much difficulty), we must leave it behind us in the Conclusion: Wisdom only, and Virtue excepted, which we shall carry the Fruit of into another World.

An. I have often heard that One wise Woman is two Fools.

Ma. Some Fools are of that Opinion. The Woman that is truly Wise does not think herself so; but she that is not so, and yet Thinks herself so, is Twice a Fool.

An. I know not how it is; but to my Fancy, a Packsaddle does as well upon an Ox, as Learning upon a Woman.

Ma. And why not as well as a Mitre upon an Ass? But what do you think of the Virgin Mary?

An. As well as is possible.

Ma. Do you not think that she read Books?

An. Yes; but not such Books as yours.

Ma. What did she read then?

An. The Canonical Hours.

Ma. To what purpose?

An. For the service of the Benedictines.

Ma. Well and do you not find others that spent their time upon godly Books?

An. Yes; but that way is quite out of Fashion.

Ma. And so are Learn'd Abbots too. For 'tis as hard a matter nowadays to find a Scholar amongst them, as it was formerly to find a Blockhead; Nay, Princes themselves in times past were as Eminent for their Erudition, as for their Authority. But 'tis not yet so Rare a thing neither, as you Imagine, to find Learned Women; for I could give you out of Spain, Italy, England, Germany, &c., so many Eminent Instances of our Sex, as if you do not mend your Manners, may come to take Possession of your very Schools, your Pulpits, and your Mitres.

An. God forbid it should ever come to that.

Ma. Nay, do you forbid it; For if you go on at the rate you began, the People will sooner endure Preaching Geese, than Dumb Pastors. The World is come about ye see, and you must either take off the Vizor, or expect that every Man shall put in for his part.

An. How came I to stumble upon this Woman? If you'll find a time to give me a Visit, you may promise yourself a better Entertainment.

Ma. And what shall that be?

An. We'll Dance, Drink, Hunt, Play, Laugh.

Ma. You have put me upon a laughing Pin already.

Luis Vives

Spanish humanist and philosopher, 1492–1540, who advocated the use of the vernacular is teaching, the establishment of public schools, and the education of women.

From *Instruction of a Christian Woman*

Of Her Exercise

. . . Woman's thought in swift, and for the most part, unstable, walking and wandering out from home, and some will slide by reason of it [her] own slipperiness, I wot now how far. Therefore reading were the best, and thereunto I give them counsel specially.

Of the Learning of Maids

Of maids, some be but little meet for learning: likewise as some men be unapt, again some be even born unto it, or at least not unfit for it. Therefore they that be dull are not to be discouraged, and those that be apt, should be heartened and encouraged. I perceive that learned women be suspected of many: as who saith, the subtlety of learning should be a nourishment for the maliciousness of their nature. Verily, I do not allow in a subtle and crafty woman, such learning as should teach her deceit, and teach her no good manners and virtues: not with standing the precepts of living, and the examples of those that have lived well, and had knowledge together of holiness, be the keepers of chastity and pureness, and the copies of virtues, and pricks to prick and to move folks to continue in them. . . . But here, peradventure, a man would ask, what learning should a woman be set unto, and what shall she study? I have told you, the study of wisdom, which doth instruct their manners, and inform their living, and teacheth them the way of good and holy life. As for eloquence, I have no great care, nor a woman needeth it not, but she needeth goodness and wisdom. Nor is it a shame for a woman to hold her peace, but it is a shame for her and abominable, to lack discretion, and to live ill. Nor will I here condemn eloquence, which both Quintilian and St. Jerome following him, say was praised in Cornelia, the mother of Gracchus, and in Hortensia, the daughter of Hortensius. If there may be found any holy and well-learned woman, I had rather have her to teach them; if there be none, let us choose some man, either well aged, or else very good and virtuous, which hath a wife, and that right fair enough, whom he loveth well, and so shall he not desire another. For these things ought to be seen unto, for as much as chastity in bringing up a woman requireth the most diligence, and in a manner altogether. When she shall be taught to read, let those books be taken in hand that may teach good manners. And when she shall learn to write, let not her example be void verses, nor wanton or trifling songs, but some sad sentences prudent and chaste, taken out of holy Scripture, or the sayings of philosophers, which by often writing she may fasten better in her memory. And in learning, as I appoint no end to the man, no more I do to the woman: saving it is meet that the man have knowledge of many and divers things, that may both profit himself and the commonwealth, both with the use and increase of learning. But I would the woman should be altogether in that part of philosophy that taketh upon itself to inform and teach and to amend the dispositions. Finally, let her learn for herself alone and her young children, or her sisters in our Lord. For it neither becometh a woman to rule a school, nor to live amongst men, nor speak abroad, and shake off her demureness and honesty, either all together, or else a great part; which if she be good, it were better to be at home within and unknown to other folks, and in company to hold her tongue demurely, and let few see her, and none at all hear her. The apostle Paul, the vessel of election, informing and teaching the Church of the Corinthians with holy precepts, saith: Let your women hold their tongues in congregations. For they be not allowed to speak but to be subject as the law biddeth. If they would learn any thing, let them ask their husbands at home. And unto his disciple, Timothy, he writeth on this wise: "Let a woman learn in silence with all subjection." But I give no license to a woman to be a teacher, nor to have authority of the man, but to be in silence. For Adam was the first made, and after, Eve, and Adam was not betrayed, the woman was betrayed into the breach of the commandment.

Therefore, because a woman is a frail thing, and of weak discretion, and that may lightly be deceived, which thing our first mother Eve sheweth, whom the Devil caught with a light argument. Therefore a woman should not teach, lest when she hath taken a false opinion and belief of any thing, she spread it into the hearers, by the authority of mastership and lightly bring others into the same error, for the learners commonly do after the teacher with good will.

From "Of the Raiments"

. . . Let her not be clothed with velvet, but with woollen; nor with silk but linen, and that coarse. Let not her raiment shine. Let it not be sluttish. Let it not to be wondered on, nor let it be to be loathed. As for the wearing of gold or silver, pearl or precious stones, I see not what it is good for. . . .

Nor let her not paint nor anoint her face, but wash it, and make it clean; nor dye her hair, but comb it cleanly, nor suffer her head to be full of scurf. Nor let her not delight to wash it in sweet savors, nor to keep it stinking, nor look in a glass to paint herself, or trim her gaily by, but to put away if any foul thing or uncomely be on her head that she could not else see, and then let her array herself thereby, lest anything be in her face to defile her, being else clean and sober.

Finally, that which Socrates bade his scholars, let her think spoken to her, too, that they should look them in a glass, and if they were fair that they should see lest the mind were foul. And if they were foul that with the beauty of the mind they should counterpoise the deformity of body.

Moreover, let an honest maid remember still that beauty hath brought many of them that have had it into great pride, and many of them that have seen it into abominable sin. Wherefore many holy women have labored to seem less fair than they were. . . . A woman shall use no man's raiment, else let her think she hath the man's courage, but take heed to the words of our Lord, saying: A woman shall not put on man's apparel, for to do so is abominable before God. But I trust no woman will do it, except she be past both honesty and shame.

Of the Living Alone of a Virgin

. . . The maid that will do by my counsel shall pass the time with chosen virgins like herself, and in good pastimes, and other whiles with holy reading or communication of such things as she hath read. But let her talk nothing of dancing, or feasting, or pleasures, lest her companions be moved with some false color of delight. Nor let no man be by. And when she is left of her fellows alone in her chamber, let her not be utterly idle, for it is jeopardous to be idle, especially being alone. Nor I would she should suffer her mind to muse; though it be never so good and holy at the beginning. A woman's mind is unstable and abideth not long in one place. It falleth from the good to bad without any labor. And Syrus the poet seemeth not all without a cause to have said: A woman that thinketh alone, thinketh evil. . . .

Of the Virtues of a Woman and Examples of Her Life

. . . Let her apply herself to virtue and be content with a little, and take in worth that she hath, nor seek for other that she hath not, nor for other folks', whereof riseth envy, hate, or curiosity of other folks' matters. The devotion of holy things most agreeth for women. Therefore it is a far worse sight of a woman that abhorreth devotion; she must have much strife with envy, which is both a foolish vice and shameful in women; and yet I wot not how it assaulteth them the most sore, but she that is of good behavior, and hath enough to serve her with, shall have no cause to envy others, nor be curious in any other body's house. And she that is shamefast, sober and reasonable of mind, shall neither be outrageous, angry, nor fall to railing, cruelty, or beastliness. For when it is natural for women to be kind and gentle because they be feeble and need the aid of others, who can be content with outrageous ire and cruelty in a woman. . . .

What the Wife Ought To Do at Home

. . . And because the business and charge within the house lieth upon the woman's hand, I would she should know medicines and salves for such diseases as be common and reign almost daily, and have those medicines ever prepared ready in some closet, wherewith she may help her husband, her little children and her household . . . when any needeth, that she need not oft to send for the physician or buy all things of the apothecaries. I would she should know remedies for such diseases as come often, as the cough, the murre*, and gnawings in the belly, the laske,† costiveness, the worms, the headache, pains in the eyes, for the augue, bones out of joint, and such other things as chance daily by light occasions. Moreover, let her learn to know what manner of diet is good or bad, what meats are wholesome to take, what to eschew, and how long, and of what fashion. And this I would she should learn rather of the experience and use of sad and wise women than of the counsel of any physician dwelling nigh about, and have them diligently written in some little book and not . . . in the great volumes of physic.

From *The Learning of Women*

. . . The Lord doth admit women to the mystery of his religion, in respect of which all other wisdom is but foolishness, and he doth declare

*Murr, severe form of catarrh.
†Lask, diarrhea.

that they were created to know high matters, and to come as well as men unto the beatitude, and therefore they ought and should be instructed and taught, as we men be. And that these are no better, it is our fault, inasmuch as we do not our duties to teach them. If the husband be the woman's head, the mind, the father, the Christ, he ought to execute the office to such a man belonging, and to teach the woman: for Christ is not only a savior and a restorer of his Church, but also a master. The father ought to nourish and to teach his children. And what need is it to reason of the mind and of the head? In the mind is wit, counsel, and reason. In the head are all the senses wherewith we do guide and rule this life, and therefore he doeth not his duty that doth not instruct and teach his wife. And the self-same Socrates doth say that men should be ruled by public and common laws, and women by their own husbands. And Paul forbidding women to speak in the congregation, and commanding that they, if they doubted of anything, should ask their husbands at home, doth bid them to teach their wives. To what effect or purpose should she ask her husband, that he neither will nor can teach her?

. . . There are two principal virtues of a woman, the religion of nature and chastity, although that religion do comprehend all virtues. But we will separately and exactly give the precepts of chastity, for it must be the chastity of the wise virgins, and not of the foolish. She must know that shamefastness is coupled with chastity, and take heed to her good name and fame, that in all places she may be unto the Lord a good savor to the example and quietness of her husband, and how prompt and ready the common sort of people be to judge evil, and with what diligence they do nourish and teach their children. She must learn also to contemn worldly chances, that is, she must be somewhat manly and strong, moderately to bear and suffer both good and evil, lest by the being unmeet to suffer adversity she be constrained either to do or to think wickedly. If she cannot read these things, nor yet by Nature learn them (for there be also such men) her husband must so familiarly and plainly teach her, that she may remember them, and use them when need shall require.

Let her hear those that do read, and speak of such things. If she can read, let her have no books of poetry, nor such trifling books as we have spoken of before, for nature is enough incited to naughtiness, although we put not fire to tow. . . .

. . . But yet if we will or intend privately to teach them any customs, let them be such as shall stir and provoke them to live well and virtuously, and such as be far from all contention and altercation,* whereunto women

*The medieval method of the Disputation, whereby youths were trained in the schools, made the boys keen and subtle dialecticians without arousing within them the love of knowledge. The description given by Vives of the old school methods of disputing, as given in his *de Tradendis Disciplinis,* sufficiently justifies his keenness of desire that, if girls were to be trained in learning, methods inducing "contention and altercation" should not be employed.

are but too much of themselves inclined. Let her read many things to subdue and bring under the affections and to appease and pacify the tempests and unquietness of the mind. A woman hath very great need of this moral part of philosophy, in the which these authors are excellent: Plato, Cicero, Seneca, and Plutarch. And in this thing those writers do help, that declare the notable examples of virtue, worthy to be ensued and followed, as Valerius Maximus, Sabellicus, and in like manner the laudable works of the holy and virtuous men of our religion, and likewise of those, that have followed the worldly wisdom. Aristotle and Xenophon do write, how men should rule and govern their house and family, and of the education and bringing up of children. . . . And as for the knowledge of grammar, logic, histories, the rule of governance of the commonwealth, and the art mathematical, they shall leave it unto men.

The Fruits of a Well-Instructed Woman

A woman well brought up is fruitful and profitable unto her husband, for so shall his house be wisely governed, his children virtuously instructed, the affections less ensued and followed, so that they shall live in tranquillity and virtue. Thou shalt not have her as a servant, nor as a companion of thy prosperity and welfare only, but also as a most faithful secretary of thy cares and thoughts, and in doubtful matters a wise and a hearty counsellor. This is the true society and fellowship of man, not only to participate with him over pains and travails, but also the affections and cares of our mind the which do no less trouble the body, than to plough, to dig, to delve, or to bear any heavy or weighty burden, for if their full and burning hearts should not declare and open themselves, they would none otherwise break than a vessel replenished with fire that hath no vent, for carefulness and thoughts are fire that doth inflame and consume the heart. . . .

Michel Eyguem de Montaigne

French essayist and skeptical philosopher, 1533–1592, who regarded men as vain and immoral and believed that all truth comes to man from God, through grace, not from the use of reason.

From "Of Friendship"

To compare this brotherly affection with affection for women, even though it is the result of our choice—it cannot be done, nor can we put the love of women in the same category. Its ardor, I confess—

> Of us that goddess is not unaware
> Who blends a bitter sweetness with her care
>
> *Catullus*

—is more active, more scorching, and more intense. But it is an impetuous and fickle flame, undulating and variable, a fever flame, subject to fits and lulls, that holds us only by one corner. In friendship it is a general and universal warmth, moderate and even, besides, a constant and settled warmth, all gentleness and smoothness, with nothing bitter and stinging about it. What is more, in love there is nothing but a frantic desire for what flees from us:

> Just as a huntsman will pursue a hare
> O'er hill and dale, in weather cold or fair;
>   The captured hare is worthless in his sight;
> He only hastens after things in flight.
>
> *Ariosto*

As soon as it enters the boundaries of friendship, that is to say harmony of wills, it grows faint and languid. Enjoyment destroys it, as having a fleshly end, subject to satiety. Friendship, on the contrary, is enjoyed according as it is desired; it is bred, nourished, and increased only in enjoyment, since it is spiritual, and the soul grows refined by practice. During

137

the reign of this perfect friendship those fleeting affections once found a place in me, not to speak of my friend, who confesses only too many of them in these verses. Thus these two passions within me came to be known to each other, but to be compared, never; the first keeping its course in proud and lofty flight, and disdainfully watching the other making its way far, far beneath it.

As for marriage, for one thing it is a bargain to which only the entrance is free—its continuance being constrained and forced, depending otherwise than on our will—and a bargain ordinarily made for other ends. For another, there supervene a thousand foreign tangles to unravel, enough to break the thread and trouble the course of a lively affection; whereas in friendship there are no dealings or business except with itself. Besides, to tell the truth, the ordinary capacity of women is inadequate for that communion and fellowship which is the nurse of this sacred bond; nor does their soul seem firm enough to endure the strain of so tight and durable a knot. And indeed, but for that, if such a relationship, free and voluntary, could be built up, in which not only would the souls have this complete enjoyment, but the bodies would also share in the alliance, so that the entire man would be engaged, it is certain that the resulting friendship would be fuller and more complete. But this sex in no instance has yet succeeded in attaining it, and by the common agreement of the ancient schools is excluded from it.

From "Of the Affection of Fathers for Their Children"

It is right to leave the administration of affairs to mothers while the children are not yet of legal age to take over on their own. But the father has brought them up very badly if he cannot hope that at that age they will have more wisdom and ability than his wife, seeing the ordinary weakness of the sex. However, in truth, it would be much more contrary to nature to make mothers dependent on the discretion of their children. They should be given plentiful means to maintain themselves according to the standing of their house and their age, since necessity and indigence are much more unbecoming and hard to bear for them than for men: this should be borne by the children rather than by the mother.

. . . To return to my subject, it seems to me, I know not why, that no kind of mastery is due to women over men except the maternal and natural, unless it is for the punishment of those who, by some feverish humor, have voluntarily submitted themselves to them. But that does not concern old women, of whom we are speaking here. It is the reasonableness of this consideration that has made us create and so readily give force to this law, which no one has ever seen, that deprives women of the succession to our crown; and there is hardly a sovereignty in the world where it is not alleged, as it is here, by some appearance of reason that gives it authority; but fortune has given it more credit in certain places than in others.

It is dangerous to leave the disposal of our succession to women's judgment, according to the choice they will make among the children, which is at all times unfair and capricious. For that disordered appetite and sick taste that they have at the time of their pregnancies they have in their soul at all times. We commonly see them devote themselves to the weakest and most ill-favored, or to those, if they have any, who are still hanging about their necks. For, not having enough force of reason to choose and embrace what deserves it, they most readily let themselves be carried away where the impressions of nature stand most alone; like the animals, who have no knowledge of their young except while they cling to their dugs. . . .

From "Of Three Kinds of Association"

Beauty is the real advantage of the ladies. It is so much their own that ours, though it demands somewhat different characteristics, is at its best only when indistinguishable from theirs, boyish and beardless. They say that at the court of the Grand Turk the youths that serve him on account of their beauty, whose number is infinite, are dismissed, at the latest, at twenty-two. Reason, wisdom, and the offices of friendship are oftener found among men; therefore they govern the affairs of the world.

From "On Some Verses from Virgil"

Women are not wrong at all when they reject the rules of life that have been introduced into the world, inasmuch as it is the men who have made these without them. There is naturally strife and wrangling between them and us: the closest communion we have with them is still tumultuous and tempestuous.

In our author's opinion we treat them inconsiderately in the following way. We have discovered, he says, that they are incomparably more capable and ardent than we in the acts of love—and that priest [Tiresias] of antiquity so testified, who had been once a man and then a woman,

> To him in both aspects was Venus known.
>
> *Ovid*

—and besides, we have learned from their own mouth the proof that was once given in different centuries by an emperor and an empress [Proculus and Messalina] of Rome, master workmen and famous in this task: he indeed deflowered in one night ten captive Sarmatian virgins; but she actually in one night was good for twenty-five encounters, changing company according to her need and liking,

> Her secret parts burning and tense with lust,
> And, tired by men, but far from sated, she withdrew.
>
> *Juvenal*

We know about the dispute that occurred in Catalonia from a woman complaining of the too assiduous efforts of her husband: not so much, in my opinion, that she was bothered by them (for I believe in miracles only in matters of faith), as by way of a pretext to curtail and curb, in the very thing that is the fundamental act of marriage, the authority of husbands over their wives, and to show that the peevishness and malignity of wives extends beyond the nuptial bed and treads underfoot the very graces and sweets of Venus; to which complaint the husband, a truly brutish and perverted man, answered that even on fast days he could not do with less than ten. There intervened that notable sentence of the queen of Aragon, by which, after mature deliberation with her council, this good queen, to give for all time a rule and example of the moderation and modesty required in a just marriage, ordained as the legitimate and necessary limit the number of six a day, relinquishing and giving up much of the need and desire of her sex, in order, she said, to establish an easy and consequently permanent and immutable formula. At which the doctors cry out: "What must the feminine appetite and concupiscence be when their reason, their reformation, and their virtue are set at this rate?" Consider these varying judgments about our sexual needs, and then the fact that Solon, chief of the lawgiving school, assesses conjugal intercourse, in order to keep from failing, at only three times a month. After believing and preaching all this, we have gone and given women continence as their particular share, and upon utmost and extreme penalties.

There is no passion more pressing than this, which we want them alone to resist, not simply as a vice of its own size, but as an abomination and execration, more to be resisted than irreligion and parricide; and meanwhile we give in to it without blame or reproach. Even those of us who have tried to get the better of it have sufficiently admitted what difficulty, or rather impossibility, there was in subduing, weakening, and cooling off the body by material remedies. We, on the contrary, want them to be healthy, vigorous, plump, well-nourished, and chaste at the same time: that is to say, both hot and cold. For marriage, which we say has the function of keeping them from burning, brings them but little cooling off, according to our ways. If they take a husband in whom the vigor of youth is still boiling, he will pride himself on expending it elsewhere:

> Bassus, for shame, or we must go to law:
> I bought your penis at a heavy price;
> You've sold it, Bassus, it is yours no more.
>
> *Martial*

The philosopher Polemon was justly brought to justice by his wife, for sowing in a sterile field the fruit that was due to the genital field. If they take one of those broken-down ones, there they are in full wedlock worse off than virgins or widows. We consider them well provided for because they have a man beside them, as the Romans considered Clodia Laeta, a Vestal, violated because Caligula had approached her, even though it was attested that he had only approached her. But on the contrary, their need is only increased thereby, inasmuch as the contact and company of any male whatever awakens their heat, which would remain quieter in solitude. And for the purpose, it is likely, of rendering their chastity more meritorious by this circumstance and consideration, Boleslaus and Kinge, his wife, the king and queen of Poland, by mutual agreement consecrated it by a vow, while lying together on their very wedding night, and maintained it in the face of marital opportunities.

We train them from childhood to the ways of love. Their grace, their dressing up, their knowledge, their language, all their instruction, has only this end in view. Their governesses imprint in them nothing else but the idea of love, if only by continually depicting it to them in order to disgust them with it. My daughter (she is the only child I have) is at the age at which the laws allow the most ardent of them to marry. She is of a backward constitution, slight and soft, and has been brought up by her mother accordingly, in a retired and private manner: so that she is now only just beginning to grow out of naïveté of childhood.

She was reading a French book in my presence. The word *fouteau* occurred, the name of a familiar tree.* The woman she has to train her stopped her short somewhat roughly and made her skip over that perilous passage. I let her go ahead in order not to disturb their rules, for I do not involve myself at all in directing her: the government of women has a mysterious way of proceeding; we must leave it to them. But if I am not mistaken, the company of twenty lackeys could not have imprinted in her imagination in six months the understanding and use and all the consequences of the sound of those wicked syllables as did this good old woman by her reprimand and interdict:

> The ripened maid delights to learn
> In wanton Ionic dance to turn,
> And fondly dreams, when still a child,
> Of loves incestuous and wild.

*Beech.

Horace

. . . In short, we allure and flesh them by every means; we incessantly heat and excite their imagination; and then we bellyache. Let us confess the truth: there is hardly one of us who is not more afraid of the shame that comes to him for his wife's vices than for his own; who does not take better care (wonderful charity) of his good wife's conscience than of his own; who would not rather be a thief and sacrilegious and have his wife be a murderess and a heretic, than not to have her be more chaste than her husband.

And the women will gladly offer to go to the law courts to seek gain, and to war to seek a reputation, rather than be obliged to keep so difficult a guard in the midst of idleness and pleasures. Don't they see that there is not a merchant, or a lawyer, or a soldier who will not leave his business to run after this other—and the porter and the cobbler, all harassed and worn out as they are with work and hunger? . . .

Iniquitous appraisal of vices! Both we and they are capable of a thousand corruptions more harmful and unnatural than lasciviousness. But we create and weigh vices not according to nature but according to our interest, whereby they assume so many unequal shapes. The severity of our decrees makes women's addiction to this vice more exacerbated and vicious than its nature calls for, and involves it in consequences that are worse than their cause.

I do not know whether the exploits of Caesar and Alexander surpass in hardship the resoluteness of a beautiful young woman brought up in our fashion, in full view of and contact with the world, assailed by so many contrary examples, keeping herself entire in the midst of a thousand continual and powerful solicitations. There is no action more thorny, or more active, than this inaction. I find it much easier to bear a suit of armor all one's life than a virginity; and the vow of virginity is the most noble of all vows, as being the hardest: *The power of the Devil is in the loins,* says Saint Jerome.

Certainly we have resigned to the ladies the most arduous and vigorous of human duties, and we leave them the glory of it. That should serve them as a singular spur to persevere in it. This is a fine occasion for them to defy us and to trample underfoot that vain preeminence in valor and virtue that we claim over them. They will find, if they take note, that they will be not only very esteemed for this but also more loved. A gallant man does not abandon his pursuit for being refused, provided the refusal is dictated by chastity rather than choice. We can swear, threaten, and complain all we like: we lie, we love them the better for it. There is no allurement like a modesty that is not heartless and surly. It is stupidity and baseness to persevere against hatred and contempt, but against a virtuous and constant resolution mingled with a grateful good will, it is the exercise of a noble and generous soul. They may recognize our services up to a certain degree, and honorably make us feel that they do not disdain us.

For that law that commands them to abominate us because we adore them and to hate us because we love them is indeed cruel, if only for its difficulty. Why shall they not hear our offers and requests so long as they keep within the duty of modesty? Why do we go surmissing that they have some more licentious idea within? A queen of our time used to say shrewdly that to refuse to hear these advances was a testimony of weakness and an accusation of one's own facility; and that a lady who had not been tempted could not boast of chastity. . . .

Thus it is folly to try to bridle in women a desire that is so burning and so natural to them. And when I hear them boast of having such a virginal and cold disposition, I laugh at them: they are leaning over too far backward. It is is a toothless and decrepit old woman or a dry and consumptive young one, though it is not altogether credible, at least they have some semblance of truth in saying it. But those who still move and breathe make their position worse in this way, since ill-considered excuses serve as accusation. Like a gentleman, one of my neighbors, who was suspected of impotence,

> Whose member, feebler than a tender beet,
> Never rose even up to middle height.
>
> *Catullus*

who, three or four days after his wedding, to justify himself, went around boldly swearing that he had ridden twenty stages the night before; which was afterward used to convict him of pure ignorance and to annul his marriage. Besides, what these women say has no value, for there is neither continence nor virtue unless there is an urge to the contrary. "It is true," they should say, "but I am not ready to give myself up." The saints themselves talk that way. I mean those women who boast in good earnest of their coldness and insensibility and who, with a straight face, want to be believed. For when it is with an affected countenance, in which the eyes belie their words, and with the jargon of their profession which has its effect in reverse, I think that's fine. I am a great admirer of naturalness and freedom, but there is no help for it: unless it is completely simple and childlike, it is unbecoming to ladies and out of place in these dealings: it promptly slides into shamelessness. Their disguises and their faces deceive only fools. Lying holds an honorable place in love; it is a detour that leads us to truth by the back door. . . .

Likewise whence can come that usurpation of sovereign authority that you assume over those women who grant you favors at their own expense—

> If she gave you furtive favors in the black of night
>
> *Catullus*

—so that you immediately put on the rights, the coldness, and the authority of a husband? It is a free compact; why do you not keep to it as you want to hold them to it? There is no power of prescription in voluntary things. . . .

. . . I say that males and females are cast in the same mold; except for education and custom, the difference is not great. Plato invites both without discrimination to the fellowship of all studies, exercises, functions, warlike and peaceful occupations, in his commonwealth. And the philosopher Antisthenes eliminated any distinction between their virtue and ours. It is much easier to accuse one sex than to excuse the other. It is the old saying: The pot calls the kettle black.

Thomas Hobbes

British philosopher and political theorist, 1588–1679, who developed a contract theory of the state, a contract made necessary by the natural conditions of life that is otherwise " . . . solitary, poor, nasty, brutish, and short . . . ."

From "Philosophical Elements of a True Citizen"

. . . And thus in the state of nature, every woman that bears children becomes both a *mother* and a *lord*. But what some say, that in this case the *father*, by reason of the pre-eminence of sex, and not the *mother* becomes *lord*, signifies nothing. For both, reason shows the contrary; because the inequality of their natural forces is not so great that the man could get the dominion over the woman without war. And custom also contradicts not; for women, namely Amazons, have in former times waged war against their adversaries, and disposed of their children at their own wills. And at this day, in divers places women are invested with the principal authority; neither do their husbands dispose of their children, but themselves; which in truth they do *by the right of nature;* forasmuch as they who have the supreme power are not tied at all (as hath been shewed) to the civil laws. Add also, that in the state of nature it cannot be known who is the *father*, but by the testimony of the *mother;* the child therefore is his whose the mother will have it, and therefore her's. Wherefore original dominion over *children* belongs to the *mother:* and among men no less than other creatures, the birth follows the belly . . . .

From *The Elements of Law*

1. Of three ways by which a man becometh subject to another . . . namely voluntary offer, captivity and birth, the former two have been spoken of under the name of subjects and servants. In the next place, we are to set down the third way of subjection, under the name of children; and by what title one man cometh to have propriety in a child

that proceedeth from the common generation of two (viz.) of male and female. And considering men again dissolved from all covenants one with another, and that . . . every man by the law of nature, hath right or propriety to his own body, the child ought rather to be the propriety of the mother (of whose body it is part, till the time of separation) than the father. For the understanding therefore of the right that a man or woman hath to his or their child, two things are to be considered: first what title the mother or any other originally hath to a child new born; secondly, how the father, or any other man, pretendeth by the mother.

2. For the first: they that have written of this subject have made generation to be a title of dominion over persons, as well as the consent of the persons themselves. And because generation giveth title to two, namely, father and mother, whereas dominion is indivisible, they therefore ascribe dominion over the child to the father only . . . but they shew not, neither can I find out by what coherence, either generation inferreth dominion, or advantage of so much strength, which, for the most part, a man hath more than a woman, should generally and universally entitle the father to a propriety in the child, and take it away from the mother.

3. The title to dominion over a child proceedeth not from the generation, but from the preservation of it; and therefore in the estate of nature, the mother in whose power it is to save or destroy it hath right thereto by that power. . . . And if the mother shall think fit to abandon, or expose her child to death, whatsoever man or woman shall find the child so exposed, shall have the same right which the mother had before; and for the same reason, namely for the power not of generating, but preserving. And though the child thus preserved do in time acquire strength, whereby he might pretend equality with him or her that hath preserved him, yet shall that pretence be thought unreasonable, both because his strength was the gift of him, against whom he pretendeth; and also because it is to be presumed, that he which giveth sustenance to another, whereby to strengthen him, hath received a promise of obedience in consideration thereof. For else it would be wisdom in men, rather to let their children perish, while they are infants, than to live in their danger or subjection, when they are grown.

4. For the pretences which a man may have to dominion over a child by the right of the mother, they be of divers kinds. One by the absolute subjection of the mother: another, by some particular covenant from her, which is less than a covenant of such subjection. By absolute subjection, the master of the mother hath right to her child . . . whether he be the father thereof, or not. And thus the children of the servant are the goods of the master in *perpetuum*.

5. Of covenants that amount not to subjection between a man and woman, there be some which are made for a time and some for life; and where they are for a time, they are covenants of cohabitation, or else of

copulation only. And in this latter case, the children pass by covenants particular. And thus in the copulation of the Amazons with their neighbours, the fathers by covenant had the male children only, the mothers retaining the females.

6. And covenants of cohabitation are either for society of bed, or for society of all things; if for society of bed only, then is the woman called a *concubine*. And here also the child shall be his or hers, as they shall agree particularly by covenant; for although for the most part a concubine is supposed to yield up the right of her children to the father, yet doth not concubinage enforce so much.

7. But if the covenants of cohabitation be for society of all things, it is necessary that but one of them govern and dispose of all that is common to them both; without which (as hath been often said before) society cannot last. And therefore the man to whom for the most part the woman yieldeth the government hath for the most part also the sole right and dominion over the children. And the man is called the husband, and the woman the wife; but because sometimes the government may belong to the wife only, sometimes also the dominion over the children shall be in her only; as in the case of a sovereign queen, there is no reason that her marriage should take from her the dominion over her children. . . .

Baruch Spinoza
(Benedictus de Spinoza)

*Dutch rationalist, moral and political philosopher, 1632–1677, who, al-
though he earned his living by unobtrusively polishing lenses, was expelled
from his synagogue and persecuted for his opinions. His works were banned
as atheistic, and it is only fairly recently that Spinoza has been generally
recognized as the "God-intoxicated Jew" that he was.*

From *Tractatus Politicus*

But, perhaps, someone will ask, whether women are under men's authority by nature or institution? For if it has been by mere institution, then
we had no reason compelling us to exclude women from government. But
if we consult experience itself, we shall find that the origin of it is in their
weakness. For there has never been a case of men and women reigning
together, but wherever on the earth men are found, there we see that men
rule, and women are ruled, and that on this plan, both sexes live in harmony. But on the other hand, the Amazons, who are reported to have
held rule of old, did not suffer men to stop in their country, but reared
only their female children, killing the males to whom they gave birth.*
But if by nature women were equal to men, and were equally distinguished by force of character and ability, in which human power and
therefore human right chiefly consist; surely among nations so many and
different some would be found, where both sexes rule alike, and others,
where men are ruled by women, and so brought up, that they can make
less use of their abilities. And since this is nowhere the case, one may
assert with perfect propriety, that women have not by nature equal right
with men: but that they necessarily give way to men, and that thus it cannot happen, that both sexes should rule alike, much less that men should
be ruled by women. But if we further reflect upon human passions, how

*Justin, *Histories,* ii. 4.

148

men, in fact, generally love women merely from the passion of lust, and esteem their cleverness and wisdom in proportion to the excellence of their beauty, and also how very ill-disposed men are to suffer the women they love to show any sort of favor to others, and other facts of this kind, we shall easily see that men and women cannot rule alike without great hurt to peace. But of this enough.

John Locke

English empiricist and moral and political philospher, 1632–1704, whose social contract theory included a recognition of natural law and inalienable rights.

From "Essay Concerning the True Original, Extent, and End of Civil Government"

God having made man such a creature, that in his own judgment, it was not good for him to be alone, put him under strong obligations of necessity, convenience, and inclination, to drive him into society, as well as fitted him with understanding and language to continue and enjoy it. The first society was between man and wife, which gave beginning to that between parents and children; to which, in time, that between master and servant came to be added: and though all these might, and commonly did meet together, and make up but one family, wherein the master or mistress of it had some sort of rule proper to a family; each of these, or all together, came short of political society, as we shall see, if we consider the different ends, ties, and bounds of each of these.

Conjugal society is made by a voluntary compact between man and woman; and though it consist chiefly in such a communion and right in one another's bodies as is necessary to its chief end, procreation; yet it draws with it mutual support and assistance, and a communion of interests too, as necessary not only to unite their care and affection, but also necessary to their common offspring, who have a right to be nourished and maintained by them, till they are able to provide for themselves.

For the end of conjunction between male and female being not barely procreation, but the continuation of the species; this conjunction betwixt male and female ought to last, even after procreation, so long as is necessary to the nourishment and support of the young ones, who are to be sustained by those that got them, till they are able to shift and provide for themselves. This rule, which the infinite wise Maker hath set to the works of his hands, we find the inferior creatures steadily obey. In those viviparous animals which feed on grass, the conjunction between male and female lasts no longer than the very act of copulation; because the teat of the dam being sufficient to nourish the young, till it be able to feed on grass, the male only begets, but concerns not himself for the female or young, to whose sustenance he can contribute nothing. But in beasts of prey the conjunction lasts longer: because the dam not being able well to subsist herself, and nourish her numerous offspring by her own prey alone, a more laborious, as well as more dangerous way of living, than by feeding on grass; the assistance of the male is necessary to the maintenance of their common family, which cannot subsist till they are able to prey for themselves, but by the joint care of male and female. The same is to be observed in all birds (except some domestic ones, where plenty of food excuses the cock from feeding, and taking care of the young brood), whose young needing food in the nest, the cock and hen continue mates, till the young are able to use their wing, and provide for themselves.

And herein I think lies the chief, if not the only reason, why the male and female in mankind are "tied to a longer conjunction" than other creatures, viz., because the female is capable of conceiving, and de facto is commonly with child again, and brings forth too a new birth, long before the former is out of a dependency for support on his parents help, and able to shift for himself, and has all the assistance that is due to him from his parents: whereby the father, who is bound to take care for those he hath begot, is under an obligation to continue in conjugal society with the same woman longer than other creatures, whose young being able to subsist of themselves before the time of procreation returns again, the conjugal bond dissolves of itself, and they are at liberty, till Hymen at his usual anniversary season summons them again to choose new mates. Wherein one cannot but admire the wisdom of the great Creator, who having given to man foresight, and an ability to lay up for the future, as well as to supply the present necessity, hath made it necessary that society of man and wife should be more lasting than of male and female amongst other creatures; that so their industry might be encouraged, and their interest better united, to make provision and lay up goods for their common issue, which uncertain mixture, or easy and frequent solutions of conjugal society, would mightily disturb.

But though these are ties upon mankind, which make the conjugal bonds more firm and lasting in man, than the other species of animals; yet it would give one reason to inquire, why this compact, where procreation and education are secured, and inheritance taken care for, may not be made determinable, either by consent, or at a certain time, or upon certain conditions, as well as any other voluntary compacts, there being no necessity in the nature of the thing, nor to the ends of it, that it should always be for life; I mean, to such as are under no restraint of any positive law, which ordains all such contracts to be perpetual.

But the husband and wife, though they have but one common concern, yet having different understandings, will unavoidably sometimes have different wills too; it therefore being necessary that the last determination, i.e., the rule, should be placed somewhere; it naturally falls to the man's share, as the abler and the stronger. But this reaching but to the things of their common interest and property, leaves the wife in the full and free possession of what by contract is her peculiar right, and gives the husband no more power over her life than she has over his; the power of the husband being so far from that of an absolute monarch that the wife has in many cases a liberty to separate from him, where natural right or their contract allows it, whether that contract be made by themselves in the state of nature, or by the customs or laws of the country they live in; and the children upon such separation fall to the father's or mother's lot, as such contract does determine.

For all the ends of marriage being to be obtained under politic government, as well as in the state of nature, the civil magistrate doth not abridge the right or power of either naturally necessary to those ends, viz., procreation and mutual support and assistance whilst they are together, but only decides any controversy that may arise between man and wife about them. If it were otherwise, and that absolute sovereignty and power of life and death naturally belonged to the husband and were necessary to the society between man and wife, there could be no matrimony in any of those countries where the husband is allowed no such absolute authority. But the ends of matrimony requiring no such power in the husband, the condition of conjugal society put it not in him, it being not at all necessary to that state. Conjugal society could subsist and attain its ends without it; nay, community of goods, and the power over them, mutual assistance and maintenance, and other things belonging to conjugal society, might be varied and regulated by that contract which unites man and wife in that society, as far as may consist with procreation and the bringing up of children till they could shift for themselves; nothing being necessary to any society that is not necessary to the ends for which it is made.

David Hume

*Scottish empiricist, moral and political philosopher, historian, and econo-
mist, 1711–1776, who, unable to secure an academic appointment and
dominated by a "love of literary fame," suffered severe disappointment as
his major philosophical works "fell dead-born from the press" yet lived to
see them receive the recognition they deserved.*

From *A Treatise of Human Nature*

Of Chastity and Modesty

Whoever considers the length and feebleness of human infancy, with the
concern which both sexes naturally have for their offspring, will easily
perceive that there must be an union of male and female for the education
of the young, and that this union must be of considerable duration. But in
order to induce the men to impose on themselves this restraint, and undergo cheerfully all the fatigues and expenses to which it subjects them,
they must believe that the children are their own, and that their natural
instinct is not directed to a wrong object, when they give a loose to love
and tenderness. . . .

Were a philosopher to examine the matter *a priori*, he wou'd reason
after the following manner. Men are induc'd to labor for the maintenance
and education of their children by the persuasion that they are really their
own; and therefore 'tis reasonable, and even necessary, to give them
some security in this particular. This security cannot consist entirely in
the imposing of severe punishments on any transgressions of conjugal fidelity on the part of the wife; since these public punishments cannot be
inflicted without legal proof, which 'tis difficult to meet with in this subject. What restraint, therefore, shall we impose on women, in order to
counterbalance so strong a temptation as they have to infidelity? There
seems to be no restraint possible, but in the punishment of bad fame or
reputation; a punishment, which has a mighty influence on the human
mind, and at the same time is inflicted by the world upon surmizes, and

conjectures, and proofs, that wou'd never be receiv'd in any court of judi-
cature. In order, therefore, to impose a due restraint on the female sex,
we must attach a peculiar degree of shame to their infidelity, above what
arises merely from its injustice, and must bestow proportionable praises
on their chastity.

But tho' this be a very strong motive to fidelity, our philosopher wou'd
quickly discover, that it wou'd not alone be sufficient to that purpose. All
human creatures, especially of the female sex, are apt to overlook remote
motives in favor of any present temptation: The temptation is here the
strongest imaginable: Its approaches are insensible and seducing: And a
woman easily finds, or flatters herself she shall find, certain means of
securing her reputation, and preventing all the pernicious consequences
of her pleasures. 'Tis necessary, therefore, that, beside the infamy attending such licenses, there shou'd be some preceding backwardness or
dread, which may prevent their first approaches, and may give the female
sex a repugnance to all expressions, and postures, and liberties, that have
an immediate relation to that enjoyment.

Such wou'd be the reasonings of our speculative philosopher: But I am
persuaded, that if he had not a perfect knowledge of human nature, he
wou'd be apt to regard them as mere chimerical speculations, and wou'd
consider the infamy attending infidelity, and backwardness to all its approaches, as principles that were rather to be wish'd than hop'd for in the
world. For what means, wou'd he say, of persuading mankind that the
transgressions of conjugal duty are more infamous than any other kind of
injustice, when 'tis evident they are more excusable, upon account of the
greatness of the temptation? And what possibility of giving a backwardness to the approaches of a pleasure, to which nature has inspir'd so
strong a propensity; and a propensity that 'tis absolutely necessary in the
end to comply with, for the support of the species?

But speculative reasonings, which cost so much pains to philosophers,
are often form'd by the world naturally, and without reflection: As difficulties, which seem unsurmountable in theory, are easily got over in practice. Those, who have an interest in the fidelity of women, naturally disapprove of their infidelity, and all the approaches to it. Those, who have
no interest, are carried along with the stream. Education takes possession
of the ductile minds of the fair sex in their infancy. And when a general
rule of this kind is once establish'd, men are apt to extend it beyond those
principles, from which it first arose. Thus batchelors, however de-
bauch'd, cannot chuse but be shock'd with any instance of lewdness or
impudence in women. And tho' all these maxims have a plain reference
to generation, yet women past child-bearing have no more privilege in
this respect than those who are in the flower of their youth and beauty.
Men have undoubtedly an implicit notion, that all those ideas of modesty
and decency have a regard to generation; since they impose not the same

laws, *with the same force,* on the male sex, where that reason takes not place. The exception is there obvious and extensive, and founded on a remarkable difference, which produces a clear separation and disjunction of ideas. But as the case is not the same with regard to the different ages of women, for this reason, tho' men know, that these notions are founded on the public interest, yet the general rule carries us beyond the original principle, and makes us extend the notions of modesty over the whole sex, from their earliest infancy to their extremest old age and infirmity.

Courage, which is the point of honor among men, derives its merit, in a great measure, from artifice, as well as the chastity of women; tho' it has also some foundation in nature, as we shall see afterwards.

As to the obligations which the male sex lie under with regard to chastity, we may observe that, according to the general notions of the world, they bear nearly the same proportion to the obligations of women as the obligations of the law of nations do to those of the law of nature. 'Tis contrary to the interest of civil society, that men shou'd have an *entire* liberty of indulging their appetites in venereal enjoyment: But as this interest is weaker than in the case of the female sex, the moral obligation arising from it must be proportionably weaker. And to prove this we need only appeal to the practice and sentiments of all nations and ages.

From "Of the Rise and Progress of the Arts and Sciences"

A man is lord in his own family, and his guests are, in a manner, subject to his authority: Hence, he is always the lowest person in the company; attentive to the wants of everyone; and giving himself all the trouble, in order to please, which may not betray too visible an affectation, or impose too much constraint on his guests. Gallantry is nothing but an instance of the same generous attention. As nature has given *man* the superiority above *woman,* by endowing him with greater strength both of mind and body, it is his part to alleviate that superiority, as much as possible, by the generosity of his behavior, and by a studied deference and complaisance for all her inclinations and opinions. Barbarous nations display this superiority, by reducing their females to the most abject slavery; by confining them, by beating them, by selling them, by killing them. But the male sex, among a polite people, discover their authority in a more generous, though not a less evident manner; by civility, by respect, by complaisance, and, in a word, by gallantry. In good company, you need not ask, Who is the master of the feast? The man, who sits in the lowest place, and who is always industrious in helping every one, is certainly the person. We must either condemn all such instances of generosity as foppish and affected, or admit of gallantry among the rest. The ancient Muscovites wedded their wives with a whip, instead of a ring. The same people, in their own houses, took always the precedency above foreigners, even foreign ambassadors. These two instances of their generosity and politeness are much of a piece.

Gallantry is not less compatible with *wisdom* and *prudence,* than with *nature* and *generosity;* and when under proper regulations, contributes more than any other invention, to the *entertainment* and *improvement* of the youth of both sexes. Among every species of animals, nature has founded on the love between the sexes their sweetest and best enjoyment. But the satisfaction of the bodily appetite is not alone sufficient to gratify the mind; and even among brute-creatures, we find, that their play and dalliance, and other expressions of fondness, form the greatest part of the entertainment. In rational beings, we must certainly admit the mind for a considerable share. Were we to rob the feast of all its garniture of reason, discourse, sympathy, friendship, and gaiety, what remains would scarcely be worth acceptance, in the judgment of the truly elegant and luxurious.

What better school for manners, than the company of virtuous women; where the mutual endeavor to please must insensibly polish the mind, where the example of the female softness and modesty must communicate itself to their admirers, and where the delicacy of that sex puts every one on his guard, lest he give offense by any breach of decency.

From "Of Essay Writing"

As 'twou'd be an unpardonable negligence in an Ambassador not to pay his respects to the Sovereign of the State where he is commission'd to reside; so it wou'd be altogether inexcusable in me not to address myself, with a particular respect, to the fair sex, who are the sovereigns of the empire of conversation. I approach them with reverence; and were not my countrymen, the learned, a stubborn independent race of mortals, extremely jealous of their liberty, and unaccustom'd to subjection, I shou'd resign into their fair hands the sovereign authority over the republic of letters. As the case stands, my commission extends no farther, than to desire a league, offensive and defensive, against our common enemies, against the enemies of reason and beauty, people of dull heads and cold hearts. From this moment let us pursue them with the severest vengeance: Let no quarter be given, but to those of sound understandings and delicate affections; and these characters, 'tis to be presum'd, we shall always find inseparable.

To be serious, and to quit the allusion before it be worn thread-bare, I am of opinion, that women, that is, women of sense and education (for to such alone I address myself) are much better judges of all polite writing than men of the same degree of understanding; and that 'tis a vain panic, if they be so far terrify'd with the common ridicule that is levell'd against learned ladies, as utterly to abandon every kind of books and study to our sex. Let the dread of that ridicule have no other effect than to make them conceal their knowledge before fools, who are not worthy it, nor of them. Such will still presume upon the vain title of the male sex to affect a superiority above them: But my fair readers may be assur'd that all men of sense, who know the world, have a great deference for their judgment of such books as ly within the compass of their knowledge, and repose more confidence in the delicacy of their taste, tho' unguided by rules, than in all the dull labors of pedants and commentators. . . .

There is only one subject, on which I am apt to distrust the judgment of females, and that is, concerning books of gallantry and devotion, which they commonly affect as high flown as possible; and most of them seem more delighted with the warmth, than with the justness of the passion. I mention gallantry and devotion as the same subject, because, in reality, they become the same when treated in this manner; and we may observe that they both depend upon the very same complexion. As the fair sex have a great share of the tender and amorous disposition, it perverts their judgment on this occasion, and makes them be easily affected, even by what has no propriety in the expression nor nature in the sentiment.

From "Of Love and Marriage"

I shall tell the women what it is our sex complains of most in the married state; and if they be disposed to satisfy us in this particular, all the other differences will easily be accommodated. If I be not mistaken, 'tis their love of dominion, which is the ground of the quarrel; tho' 'tis very likely, that they will think it an unreasonable love of it in us, which makes us insist so much upon that point. . . .

But to be just, and to lay the blame more equally, I am afraid it is the fault of our sex, if the women be so fond of rule, and that if we did not abuse our authority, they would never think it worth while to dispute it. Tyrants, we know, produce rebels; and all history informs us, that rebels, when they prevail, are apt to become tyrants in their turn. For this reason, I could wish there were no pretensions to authority on either side; but that every thing was carried on with perfect equality, as between two equal members of the same body. And to induce both parties to embrace those amicable sentiments, I shall deliver to them Plato's account of the origin of love and marriage.

Mankind, according to that fanciful philosopher, were not, in their original, divided into male and female, as at present; but each individual person was a compound of both sexes, and was in himself both husband

and wife, melted down into one living creature. This union, no doubt, was very entire, and the parts very well adjusted together, since there resulted a perfect harmony betwixt the male and female, altho' they were obliged to be inseparable companions. And so great were the harmony and happiness flowing from it, that the Androgynes (for so Plato calls them) or men–women, became insolent upon their prosperity, and rebelled against the Gods. To punish them for this temerity, Jupiter could contrive no better expedient than to divorce the male-part from the female, and make two imperfect beings of the compound, which was before so perfect. Hence the origin of men and women, as distinct creatures. But notwithstanding this division, so lively is our remembrance of the happiness which we enjoyed in our primeval state, that we are never at rest in this situation; but each of these halves is continually searching thro' the whole species to find the other half, which was broken from it: And when they meet, they join again with the greatest fondness and sympathy. But it often happens, that they are mistaken in this particular; that they take for their half what no way corresponds to them; and that the parts do not meet nor join in with each other, as is usual in fractures. In this case the union was soon dissolved, and each part is set loose again to hunt for its lost half, joining itself to every one whom it meets, by way of trial, and enjoying no rest till its perfect sympathy with its partner shews, that it has at last been successful in its endeavours.

Were I disposed to carry on this fiction of Plato, which accounts for the mutual love betwixt the sexes in so agreeable a manner, I would do it by the following allegory.

When Jupiter had separated the male from the female, and had quelled their pride and ambition by so severe an operation, he could not but repent him of the cruelty of his vengeance, and take compassion on poor mortals, who were now become incapable of any repose or tranquillity. Such cravings, such anxieties, such necessities arose, as made them curse their creation, and think existence itself a punishment. In vain had they recourse to every other occupation and amusement. In vain did they seek after every pleasure of sense, and every refinement of reason. Nothing could fill that void, which they felt in their hearts, or supply the loss of their partner, who was so fatally separated from them. To remedy this disorder, and to bestow some comfort, at least, on the human race in their forlorn situation, Jupiter sent down Love and Hymen, to collect the broken halves of human kind, and piece them together in the best manner possible. These two deities found such a prompt disposition in mankind to unite again in their primeval state, that they proceeded on their work with wonderful success for some time; till at last, from many unlucky accidents, dissension arose betwixt them. The chief counsellor and favorite of Hymen was Care, who was continually filling his patron's head with prospects of futurity; a settlement, family, children, servants; so that little else was regarded in all the matches *they* made. On the other hand, Love had chosen Pleasure for his favorite, who was as pernicious a counsellor as the other, and would never allow Love to look beyond the present momentary gratification, or the satisfying of the prevailing inclination. These two favorites became, in a little time, irreconcileable enemies, and made it their chief business to undermine each other in all their undertakings. No sooner had Love fixed upon two halves, which he was cementing together, and forming to a close union, but Care insinuates himself, and bringing Hymen along with him, dissolves the union produced by Love, and joins each half to some other half, which he had provided for it. To be revenged of this, Pleasure creeps in upon a pair already joined by Hymen; and calling Love to his assistance, they under hand contrive to join each half by secret links, to halves, which Hymen was wholly unacquainted with. It was not long before this quarrel was felt in its pernicious consequences; and such complaints arose before the throne of Jupiter, that he was obliged to summon the offending parties to appear before him, in order to give an account of their proceedings. After hearing the pleadings on both sides, he ordered an immediate reconcilement betwixt Love and Hymen, as the only expedient for giving happiness to mankind: And that he might be sure this reconcilement should be durable, he laid his strict injunctions on them never to join any halves without consulting their favorites Care and Pleasure, and obtaining the consent of both to the conjunction. Where this order is strictly observed, the Androgyne is perfectly restored, and the human race enjoys the same happiness as in their primeval state. The seam is scarce perceived that joins the two beings; but both of them combine to form one perfect and happy creature.

From "Of the Study of History"

There is nothing which I would recommend more earnestly to my female readers than the study of history, as an occupation, of all others, the best suited both to their sex and education, much more instructive than their ordinary books of amusement, and more entertaining than those serious compositions which are usually to be found in their closets. Among other important truths which they may learn from history, they may be informed of two particulars, the knowledge of which may contribute very much to their quiet and repose; *That* our sex, as well as theirs, are far from being such perfect creatures as they are apt to imagine, and, *That* Love is not the only passion, which governs the male-world, but is often overcome by avarice, ambition, vanity, and a thousand other passions. Whether they be the false representations of mankind in those two particulars, which endear romances and novels so much to the fair sex, I know not; but must confess that I am sorry to see them have such an aversion to matter of fact, and such an appetite for falshood.

Charles-Louis de Secondat, Baron de Montesquieu

French philosopher and political theorist, 1689–1755, who championed freedom, toleration, moderation, and constitutional government.

From *Persian Letters.* This is a satire consisting of letters allegedly written by two Persian visitors to France—Usbek and Rica.

Rica to Ibben, at Smyrna

The King of France [Louis XIV] is the most powerful of European potentates. He has no mines of gold like his neighbor, the King of Spain; but he is much wealthier than that prince, because his riches are drawn from a more inexhaustible source, the vanity of his subjects. He has undertaken and carried on great wars, without any other supplies than those derived from the sale of titles of honor; and it is by a prodigy of human pride that his troops are paid, his towns fortified, and his fleets equipped.

Then again, the king is a great magician, for his dominion extends to the minds of his subjects; he makes them think what he wishes. If he has only a million crowns in his exchequer, and has need of two millions, he has only to persuade them that one crown is worth two, and they believe it.* If he has a costly war on hand, and is short of money, he simply suggests to his subjects that a piece of paper is coin of the realm, and they are straightway convinced of it. He has even succeeded in persuading them that his touch is a sovereign cure for all sorts of diseases, so great is the power and influence he has over their minds.

*The French kings regarded money as a mere symbol, the value of which they could raise or lower at their pleasure. "Kings treat men as they do pieces of money; they give them what value they choose, and people are forced to accept them according to their currency, and not according to their true worth."—LA ROCHEFOUCAULD.

What I have told you of this prince need not astonish you: there is another magician more powerful still, who is master of the king's mind, as absolutely as the king is master of the minds of his subjects. This magician is called the Pope. Sometimes he makes the king believe that three are no more than one; that the bread which he eats is not bread; the wine which he drinks not wine; and a thousand things of a like nature.

And, to keep him in practice, and prevent him from losing the habit of belief, he gives him, now and again, as an exercise, certain articles of faith. Some two years ago he sent him a large document which he called *Constitution,* and wished to enforce belief in all that it contained upon this prince and his subjects under heavy penalties. He succeeded in the case of the king,. . . . * who set the example of immediate submission; but some of his subjects revolted, and declared that they would not believe a single word of what was contained in this document. The women are the prime movers in this rebellion, which divides the court, the kingdom, and every family in the land, because the document prohibits them from reading a book which all the Christians assert is of divine origin: it is, indeed, their Koran. The women, enraged at this affront to their sex, exert all their power against the *Constitution;* and they have brought over to their side all the men who are not anxious about their privilege in the matter. And truly, the Mufti does not reason amiss. By the great Hali! he must have been instructed in the principles of our holy religion, because, since women are inferior creatures compared to us, and may not, according to our prophets, enter into Paradise, why should they meddle with a book which is only designed to teach the way thither? . . .

Usbek to Roxana, at the Seraglio at Ispahan

How happy you are, Roxana,† to be in the delightful country of Persia, and not in these poisoned regions, where shame and virtue are alike unknown! How happy, indeed! In my seraglio you live as in the abode of innocence, inaccessible to the attacks of all mankind; you rejoice in the good fortune which makes it impossible for you to fall; no man has ever sullied you with a lascivious look; your father-in-law himself, even during the license of the festivals, has never beheld your lovely mouth, for you have never neglected to conceal it with a sacred veil. Happy Roxana! In your visits to the country, eunuchs have always walked before you to

*Louis XIV submitted the more readily because he required the Pope's aid to terminate the theological quarrels which had become insufferable to him.

†At the end of these letters, this "happy" Persian wife announces that she has deceived Usbek: that she has hated him and that she is dying, having poisoned herself, thus fully escaping from the slavery from which her mind has always retained its freedom and independence (Editor's note).

deal out death to all those who dared to look at you. As for me, who received you as a gift from heaven to increase my happiness, what trouble did I not have in entering upon the possession of that treasure which you defended with such constancy! How I was mortified, during the first days of our marriage, when you withheld yourself from my sight! How impatient I was, when I did see you! You refused to satisfy my eager longing; on the contrary, you increased it by the obstinate refusals of an alarmed modesty: you failed to distinguish between me and all other men from whom you always conceal yourself. Do you remember that day when I lost you among your slaves, who betrayed me, and baffled me in my search? Or that other time, when, finding your tears powerless, you employed your mother's authority to stay the eagerness of my love? Do you remember when all your resources failed, except those which your courage supplied? Seeing a dagger, you threatened to destroy a husband who loved you, if he continued to demand the sacrifice of what was dearer to you than your husband himself. Two months passed in this combat between love and modesty; and you carried your chaste scruples so far that you did not submit even after you were conquered, but defended to the last gasp a dying virginity. You regarded me as an enemy who had outraged you, and not as a husband who loved you. It was more than three months before you could look at me without blushing; your bashful glance seemed to reproach me for the advantage I had taken. I did not even enjoy a quiet possession; to the best of your ability you robbed me of your charms and graces; and without having received the least favors, I was ravished with the greatest.

If you had been brought up in this country, you would not have been so put about. The women here have lost all reserve: they appear before the men with their faces uncovered, as if they sought their overthrow; they watch for their glances; they accompany them to their mosques, on their promenades, even to their rooms: the service of eunuchs is quite unknown to them. In place of that noble simplicity, that amiable modesty which reigns among you, a brute-like impudence prevails, to which one can never grow accustomed.

Yes, Roxana, were you here, you would feel yourself outraged at the dreadful ignominy in which your sex is plunged; you would fly from this abominable land, sighing for that sweet retreat, where you find innocence and self-security, where no danger makes you afraid; where, in short, you can love me, without fear of ever losing that love which it is your duty to feel for me.

When you heighten the brilliance of your complexion with the loveliest colour, when you perfume your whole body with the most precious essences, when you clothe yourself in your most beautiful garments, when you seek to distinguish yourself from your companions by your gracefulness in the dance, and the sweetness of your song, as you gently dispute with them in beauty, in tenderness, in vivacity, I cannot imagine that you have any other aim than to please me; and, when I see you blushing modestly as your eyes seek mine, as you wind yourself into my heart with soft and flattering words, I cannot, Roxana, suspect your love.

But what am I to think of the women of Europe? The artful composition of their complexion, the ornaments with which they deck themselves, the care they have of their bodies, the desire to please which occupies them continually, are so many stains on their virtue, and affronts to their husbands.

It is not, Roxana, that I believe they carry their encroachment on virtue as far as such conduct might be expected to lead them, or that their debauchery extends to such horrible excess as the absolute violation of their conjugal vow—a thought to make one tremble. There are very few women so abandoned as to go that length: the hearts of all of them are engraved from their birth with an impression of virtue, which education weakens, but cannot destroy. Though they may be lax in the observation of the external duties which modesty requires; yet, when it is a question of the last step, their better nature revolts. And so, when we imprison you so closely, and have you watched by crowds of slaves, when we restrain your desires so forcibly lest they break beyond bounds; it is not because we fear the final deed of infidelity, but because we know that purity cannot be too immaculate, and that the slightest stain would soil it.

I pity you, Roxana. Your long-tried chastity deserves a husband who would never have left you, and who would himself have restrained those desires which without him your virtue must subdue.

Zelis to Usbek, at Paris

Your daughter having attained her seventh year, I have judged it time to remove her to the inner apartments of the seraglio, and not to wait till she should be ten to entrust her to the care of the black eunuchs. It is impossible to deprive a young girl too soon of the liberty of childhood, and to give her a holy upbringing within those walls sacred to modesty.

For I am not of the opinion of those mothers who only sequester their daughters when they are about to bestow them in marriage, who sentence, rather than consecrate them, to the seraglio, and force them to embrace a manner of life which they ought to have taught them to love. Must we expect everything from the compulsion of reason, and leave nothing to the gentle influences of habit?

We are in vain told of the state of subjection in which nature has placed us. It is not enough to make us realize this; we must be made to practice submission, in order that we may be upheld at that critical time when the passions begin to awaken, and that we may learn voluntary subordination.

Were we only attached to you by duty, we might sometimes forget it; or if it were inclination alone that bound us, a more potent feeling might perhaps weaken it. But, when the laws bestow us on one man they withdraw from us all others, and place us as far from them as if a hundred thousand leagues intervened.

Nature, diligent in the service of men, has been no niggard in her dowry of desire; to women also she has not been unkind, and has destined us to be the living instruments of the enjoyment of our masters; she has set us on fire with passion in order that they may live at ease; should they quit their insensibility, she has provided us to restore them to it, without our ever being able to taste the happiness of the condition into which we put them.

Yet, Usbek, do not think that your situation is happier than mine; I have experienced here a thousand pleasures unknown to you. My imagination has labored without ceasing to make me conscious of their worth; I have lived, and you have only languished.

Even in this prison where you keep me I am freer than you. You can only redouble your care in guarding me, that I may rejoice at your uneasiness; and your suspicions, your jealousy, your annoyance, are so many marks of your dependence.

Continue, dear Usbek, to have me watched night and day; take no ordinary precautions; increase my happiness in assuring your own; and know, that I dread nothing except your indifference.

From *The Spirit of Laws*

Of the Condition or State of Women in Different Governments

In monarchies women are subject to very little restraint, because as the distinction of ranks calls them to court, there they assume a spirit of liberty, which is almost the only one tolerated in that place. Each courtier avails himself of their charms and passions, in order to advance his fortune: and as their weakness admits not of pride, but of vanity, luxury constantly attends them.

In despotic governments women do not introduce, but are themselves an object of, luxury. They must be in a state of the most rigorous servitude. Every one follows the spirit of the government, and adopts in his own family the customs he sees elsewhere established. As the laws are very severe and executed on the spot, they are afraid lest the liberty of women should expose them to danger. Their quarrels, indiscretions, repugnancies, jealousies, piques, and that art, in fine, which little souls have of interesting great ones, would be attended there with fatal consequences.

Besides, as princes in those countries make a sport of human nature, they allow themselves a multitude of women; and a thousand considerations oblige them to keep those women in close confinement.

In republics women are free by the laws and restrained by manners; luxury is banished thence, and with it corruption and vice.

In the cities of Greece, where they were not under the restraint of a religion which declares that even amongst men regularity of manners is a part of virtue; where a blind passion triumphed with a boundless insolence, and love appeared only in a shape which we dare not mention, while marriage was considered as nothing more than simple friendship; such were the virtue, simplicity, and chastity of women in those cities, that in this respect hardly any people were ever known to have had a better and wiser polity.

Of Dowries and Nuptial Advantages in Different Constitutions

. . . The community of goods introduced by the French laws between man and wife is extremely well adapted to a monarchical government; because the women are thereby interested in domestic affairs, and compelled, as it were, to take care of their family. It is less so in a republic, where women are possessed of more virtue. But it would be quite absurd in despotic governments, where the women themselves generally constitute a part of the master's property.

As women are in a state that furnishes sufficient inducements to marriage, the advantages which the law gives them over the husband's property are of no service to society. But in a republic they would be extremely prejudicial, because riches are productive of luxury. In despotic governments the profits accruing from marriage ought to be mere subsistence, and no more.

Of Female Administration

It is contrary to reason and nature that women should reign in families, as was customary among the Egyptians; but not that they should govern an empire. In the former case the state of their natural weakness does not permit them to have the pre-eminence; in the latter their very weakness generally gives them more lenity and moderation, qualifications fitter for a good administration than roughness and severity.

Of Domestic Servitude

Slaves are established for the family; but they are not a part of it. Thus I distinguish their servitude from that which the women in some countries suffer, and which I shall properly call domestic servitude. . . .

Nature, which has distinguished men by their reason and bodily strength, has set no other bounds to their power than those of this strength and reason. It has given charms to women, and ordained that their ascendant over man shall end with these charms: but in hot countries, these are found only at the beginning, and never in the progress of life.

Thus the law which permits only one wife is physically conformable to the climate of Europe, and not to that of Asia. This is the reason why Mahommedanism was so easily established in Asia, and with such difficulty extended in Europe; why Christianity is maintained in Europe, and has been destroyed in Asia; and, in fine, why the Mahommedans have made such progress in China, and the Christians so little. Human reasons, however, are subordinate to that Supreme Cause who does whatever He pleases, and renders everything subservient to His will. . . .

Of Polygamy Considered in Itself

With regard to polygamy in general, independently of the circumstances which may render it tolerable, it is not of the least service to mankind, nor to either of the two sexes, whether it be that which abuses or that which is abused. Neither is it of service to the children; for one of its greatest inconveniences is, that the father and mother cannot have the same affection for their offspring; a father cannot love twenty children with the same tenderness as a mother can love two. It is much worse when a wife has many husbands; for then paternal love only is held by this opinion, that a father may believe, if he will, or that others may believe, that certain children belong to him. . . .

May I not say that a plurality of wives leads to that passion which nature disallows? for one depravation always draws on another. I remember that in the revolution which happened at Constantinople, when Sultan Achmet was deposed, history says that the people, having plundered the Kiaya's house, found not a single woman; they tell us that at Algiers, in the greatest part of their seraglios, they have none at all.

Of an Equality of Treatment in Case of Many Wives

From the law which permitted a plurality of wives followed that of an equal behavior to each. Mahomet, who allowed of four, would have everything, as provisions, dress, and conjugal duty, equally divided between them. This law is also in force in the Maldivian isles, where they are at liberty to marry three wives.

The law of Moses even declares that if any one has married his son to a slave, and this son should afterwards espouse a free woman, her food, her raiment, and her duty of marriage shall he not diminish. They might give more to the new wife, but the first was not to have less than she had before.

The Principle on Which the Morals of the East Are Founded

In the case of a multiplicity of wives, the more a family ceases to be united, the more ought the laws to reunite its detached parts in a common center; and the greater the diversity of interests, the more necessary is it for the laws to bring them back to a common interest.

This is more particularly done by confinement. The women should not only be separated from the men by the walls of the house, but they ought also be separated in the same enclosure, in such a manner that each may have a distinct household in the same family. Hence each derives all that relates to the practice of morality, modesty, chastity, reserve, silence, peace, dependence, respect, and love; and, in short, a general direction of her thoughts to that which, in its own nature, is a thing of the greatest importance, a single and entire attachment to her family.

Women have naturally so many duties to fulfill—duties which are peculiarly theirs, that they cannot be sufficiently excluded from everything capable of inspiring other ideas; from everything that goes by the name of amusements; and from everything which we call business.

We find the manners more pure in the several parts of the East, in proportion as the confinement of women is more strictly observed. . . .

Of Domestic Slavery Independently of Polygamy

It is not only a plurality of wives which in certain places of the East requires their confinement, but also the climate itself. Those who consider the horrible crimes, the treachery, the dark villainies, the poisonings, the assassinations, which the liberty of women has occasioned at Goa and in the Portuguese settlements in the Indies, where religion permits only one wife; and who compare them with the innocence and purity of manners of the women of Turkey, Persia, Hindostan, China, and Japan, will clearly see that it is frequently as necessary to separate them from the men, when they have but one, as when they have many.

These are things which ought to be decided by the climate. What purpose would it answer to shut up women in our northern countries, where their manners are naturally good; where all their passions are calm; and where love rules over the heart with so regular and gentle an empire that the least degree of prudence is sufficient to conduct it?

It is a happiness to live in those climates which permit such freedom of converse, where that sex which has most charms seems to embellish society, and where wives, reserving themselves for the pleasures of one, contribute to the amusement of all.

Of Divorce and Repudiation

There is this difference between a divorce and a repudiation, that the former is made by mutual consent, arising from a mutual antipathy; while the latter is formed by the will, and for the advantage of one of the two parties, independently of the will and advantage of the other.

The necessity there is sometimes for women to repudiate, and the difficulty there always is in doing it, render that law very tyrannical which gives this right to men without granting it to women. A husband is the master of the house; he has a thousand ways of confining his wife to her duty, or of bringing her back to it; so that in his hands it seems as if repudiation could be only a fresh abuse of power. But a wife who repudiates only makes use of a dreadful kind of remedy. It is always a great misfortune for her to go in search of a second husband, when she has lost the most part of her attractions with another. One of the advantages attending the charms of youth in the female sex is that in an advanced age the husband is led to complacency and love by the remembrance of past pleasures.

It is then a general rule that in all countries where the laws have given to men the power of repudiating, they ought also to grant it to women. Nay, in climates where women live in domestic slavery, one would think that the law ought to favor women with the right of repudiation, and husbands only with that of divorce.

When wives are confined in a seraglio, the husband ought not to repudiate on account of an opposition of manners; it is the husband's fault if their manners are incompatible.

Repudiation on account of the barrenness of the woman ought never to take place except where there is only one wife: when there are many, this is of no importance to the husband.

Of Marriage

The natural obligation of the father to provide for his children has established marriage, which makes known the person who ought to fulfill this obligation. The people mentioned by Pomponius Mela had no other way of discovering him but by resemblance.

Among civilized nations, the father is that person on whom the laws, by the ceremony of marriage, have fixed this duty, because they find in him the man they want.

Among brutes this is an obligation which the mother can generally perform; but it is much more extensive among men. Their children indeed have reason; but this comes only by low degrees. It is not sufficient to nourish them; we must also direct them; they can already live; but they cannot govern themselves.

Illicit conjunctions contribute but little to the propagation of the species. The father, who is under a natural obligation to nourish and educate his children, is not then fixed; and the mother, with whom the obligation remains, finds a thousand obstacles from shame, remorse, and constraint of her sex and the rigor of laws; and besides, she generally wants the means.

Women who have submitted to public prostitution cannot have the convenience of educating their children: the trouble of education is imcompatible with their station; and they are so corrupt that they can have no protection from the law.

It follows from all this that public continence is naturally connected with the propagation of the species.

Of the Condition of Children

It is a dictate of reason that when there is a marriage, children should follow the station or condition of the father; and that when there is not, they can belong to the mother only.

That the Order of Succession or Inheritance Depends on the Principles of Political or Civil Law, and Not on Those of the Law of Nature

The Voconian law ordained that no woman should be left heiress to an estate, not even if she had an only child. Never was there a law, says St. Augustine, more unjust. A formula of Marculfus treats that custom as impious which deprives daughters of the right of succeeding to the estate of their fathers. Justinian gives the appellation of barbarous to the right which the males had formerly of succeeding in prejudice to the daughters. These notions proceeded from their having considered the right of children to succeed to their father's possessions as a consequence of the law of nature; which it is not.

The law of nature ordains that fathers shall provide for their children; but it does not oblige them to make them their heirs. The division of property, the laws of this division, and the succession after the death of the person who has had this division can be regulated only by the community, and consequently by political or civil laws.

True it is, that a political or civil order frequently demands that children should succeed to their father's estate; but it does not always make this necessary.

That We Ought Not to Regulate by the Principles of the Canon Law Things Which Should Be Regulated by Those of the Civil Law

. . . As the husband may demand a separation by reason of the infidelity of his wife, the wife might formerly demand it, on account of the infidelity of the husband. This custom, contrary to a regulation made in the Roman laws, was introduced into the ecclesiastic court, where nothing was regarded but the maxims of canon law; and indeed, if we consider marriage as a thing merely spiritual, and as relating only to the things of another life, the violation is in both cases the same, but the political and civil laws of almost all nations have, with reason, made a distinction between them. They have required from the women a degree of reserve and continency, which they have not exacted from the men; because in women, a violation of chastity supposes a renunciation of all virtue; because women, by violating the laws of marriage, quit the state of their natural dependence; because nature has marked the infidelity of women with certain signs; and, in fine, because the children of the wife born in adultery necessarily belong and are an expense to the husband, while the children produced by the adultery of the husband are not the wife's, nor are an expense to the wife.

François-Marie Arouet Voltaire

French philosopher, 1694–1778, celebrated in his day for his campaigns against religious fanaticism and for social and judicial reform, best remembered for his satirical attack, in Candide, *on philosophical optimism. The following selection on women is from his famous* Philosophical Dictionary.

From "Women"

Physical and Moral

Woman is in general less strong than man, smaller, and less capable of lasting labor. Her blood is more aqueous; her flesh less firm; her hair longer; her limbs more rounded; her arms less muscular; her mouth smaller; her hips more prominent; and her belly larger. These physical points distinguish women all over the earth, and of all races, from Lapland unto the coast of Guinea, and from America to China. . . .

Women live somewhat longer than men; that is to say, in a generation we count more aged women than aged men. This fact has been observed by all who have taken accurate accounts of births and deaths in Europe; and it is thought that it is the same in Asia, and among the negresses, the copper-colored, and olive-complexioned, as among the white. *Natura est semper sibi consona.**

We have elsewhere adverted to an extract from a Chinese journal, which states, that in the year 1725, the wife of the emperor Yontchin made a distribution among the poor women of China who had passed their seventieth year; and that, in the province of Canton alone, there were 98,222 females aged more than seventy, 40,893 beyond eighty, and 3,453 of about the age of a hundred. Those who advocate final causes say that nature grants them a longer life than men, in order to recompense them for the trouble they take in bringing children into the world and rearing them. It is scarcely to be imagined that nature bestows recom-

---

*Nature is always in harmony with itself [Editor's note].

171

penses, but it is probable that the blood of women being milder, their fibers harden less quickly.

No anatomist or physician has ever been able to trace the secret of conception. Sanchez has curiously remarked: *Mariam et spiritum sanctum emisisse semen in copulatione, et ex semine amborum natum esse Jesum.** This abominable impertinence of the most knowing Sanchez is not adopted at present by any naturalist.

The periodical visitations which weaken females, while they endure the maladies which arise out of their suppression, the times of gestation, the necessity of suckling children, and of watching continually over them, and the delicacy of their organization, render them unfit for the fatigue of war, and the fury of the combat. It is true, as we have already observed, that in almost all times and countries women have been found on whom nature has bestowed extraordinary strength and courage, who combat with men, and undergo prodigious labor; but, after all, these examples are rare. . . .

Physics always govern morals. Women being weaker of body than we are, there is more skill in their fingers, which are more supple than ours. Little able to labor at the heavy work of masonry, carpentering, metalling, or the plow, they are necessarily entrusted with the lighter labors of the interior of the house, and, above all, with the care of children. Leading a more sedentary life, they possess more gentleness of character than men, and are less addicted to the commission of enormous crimes—a fact so undeniable, that in all civilized countries there are always fifty men at least executed to one woman.

Montesquieu, in his "Spirit of Laws," undertaking to speak of the condition of women under divers governments, observes that "among the Greeks women were not regarded as worthy of having any share in genuine love; but that with them love assumed a form which is not to be named." He cites Plutarch as his authority.

This mistake is pardonable only in a wit like Montesquieu, always led away by the rapidity of his ideas, which are often very indistinct. Plutarch, in his chapter on love, introduces many interlocutors; and he himself, in the character of Daphneus, refutes, with great animation, the arguments of Protagenes in favor of the commerce alluded to.

It is in the same dialog that he goes so far as to say, that in the love of woman there is something divine; which love he compares to the sun, that animates nature. He places the highest happiness in conjugal love, and concludes by an eloquent eulogium on the virtue of Epponina. This memorable adventure passed before the eyes of Plutarch, who lived some time

---

*Mary and the Holy Spirit had emitted seed in copulation and that from both their seeds Jesus was born [Editor's note].

in the house of Vespasian. The above heroine, learning that her husband Sabinus, vanquished by the troops of the emperor, was concealed in a deep cavern between Franche-Comté and Champagne, shut herself up with him, attended on him for many years, and bore children in that situation. Being at length taken with her husband, and brought before Vespasian, who was astonished at her greatness of soul, she said to him: "I have lived more happily under ground than thou in the light of the sun, and in the enjoyment of power." Plutarch therefore asserts directly the contrary to that which is attributed to him by Montesquieu, and declares in favor of woman with an enthusiasm which is even affecting.

It is not astonishing, that in every country man has rendered himself the master of woman, dominion being founded on strength. He has ordinarily, too, a superiority both in body and mind. Very learned women are to be found in the same manner as female warriors, but they are seldom or ever inventors.

A social and agreeable spirit usually falls to their lot; and, generally speaking, they are adapted to soften the manners of men. In no republic have they ever been allowed to take the least part in government; they have never reigned in monarchies purely elective; but they may reign in almost all the hereditary kingdoms of Europe—in Spain, Naples, and England, in many states of the North, and in many grand fiefs which are called "feminines."

Custom, entitled the Salic law, has excluded them from the crown of France; but it is not, as Mézeray remarks, in consequence of their unfitness for governing, since they are almost always entrusted with the regency.

It is pretended that Cardinal Mazarin confessed that many women were worthy of governing a kingdom; but he added, that it was always to be feared they would allow themselves to be subdued by lovers who were not capable of governing a dozen pullets. Isabella in Castile, Elizabeth in England, and Maria Theresa in Hungary, have, however, proved the falsity of this pretended bon-mot, attributed to Cardinal Mazarin; and at this moment we behold a legislatrix in the North as much respected as the sovereign of Greece, of Asia Minor, of Syria, and of Egypt, is disesteemed.

It has been for a long time ignorantly assumed, that women are slaves during life among the Mahometans; and that, after their death, they do not enter paradise. These are two great errors, of a kind which popes are continually repeating in regard to Mahometanism. Married women are not at all slaves; and the Sura, or fourth chapter of the Koran, assigns them a dowry. A girl is entitled to inherit one-half as much as her brother; and if there are girls only, they divide among them two-thirds of the inheritance; and the remainder belongs to the relations of the deceased, whose mother also is entitled to a certain share. So little are married women slaves, they are entitled to demand a divorce, which is granted when their complaints are deemed lawful. . . .

Of the Polygamy Allowed by Certain Popes and Reformers

The Abbé Fleury, author of the "Ecclesiastical History," pays more respect to truth in all which concerns the laws and usages of the Church. He avows that Boniface, confessor of Lower Germany, having consulted Pope Gregory, in the year 726, in order to know in what cases a husband might be allowed to have two wives, Gregory replied to him, on the 22nd of November, of the same year, in these words: "If a wife be attacked by a malady which renders her unfit for conjugal intercourse, the husband may marry another; but in that case he must allow his sick wife all necessary support and assistance." This decision appears conformable to reason and policy; and favors population, which is the object of marriage.

But that which appears opposed at once to reason, policy, and nature, is the law which ordains that a woman, separated from her husband both in person and estate, cannot take another husband, nor the husband another wife. It is evident that a race is thereby lost; and if the separated parties are both of a certain temperament, they are necessarily exposed and rendered liable to sins for which the legislators ought to be responsible to God, if—

The decretals of the popes have not always had in view what was suitable to the good of estates, and of individuals. This same decretal of Pope Gregory II., which permits bigamy in certain cases, denies conjugal rights forever to the boys and girls, whom their parents have devoted to the Church in their infancy. This law seems as barbarous as it is unjust; at once annihilating posterity, and forcing the will of men before they even possess a will. It is rendering the children the slaves of a vow which they never made; it is to destroy natural liberty, and to offend God and mankind. . . .

We must distrust authors who relate, that in certain countries women are allowed several husbands. Those who make laws everywhere are born with too much self-love, are too jealous of their authority, and generally possess a temperament too ardent in comparison with that of women, to have instituted a jurisprudence of this nature. That which is opposed to the general course of nature is very rarely true; but it is very common for the more early travellers to mistake an abuse for a law. . . .

End of the Reflections on Polygamy

It appears that power, rather than agreement, makes laws everywhere, but especially in the East. We there beheld the first slaves, the first eunuchs, and the treasury of the prince directly composed of that which is taken from the people.

He who can clothe, support, and amuse a number of women, shuts them up in a menagerie, and commands them despotically. Ben Aboul Kiba, in his "Mirror of the Faithful," relates that one of the viziers of the great Solyman addressed the following discourse to an agent of Charles V.:

"Dog of a Christian!—for whom, however, I have a particular esteem—canst thou reproach me with possessing four wives, according to our holy laws, whilst thou emptiest a dozen barrels a year, and I drink not a single glass of wine? What good dost thou effect by passing more hours at table than I do in bed? I may get four children a year for the service of my august master, whilst thou canst scarcely produce one, and that only the child of a drunkard, whose brain will be obscured by the vapors of the wine which has been drunk by his father. What, moreover, wouldst thou have me do, when two of my wives are in child-bed? Must I not attend to the other two, as my law commands me? What becomes of them? what part dost thou perform, in the latter months of the pregnancy of thy only wife, and during her lyings-in and sexual maladies? Thou either remainest idle, or thou repairest to another woman. Behold thyself between two mortal sins, which will infallibly cause thee to fall headlong from the narrow bridge into the pit of hell. . . .

"What is done in thy country by the trumpeter of day, which thou callest the cock; the honest ram, the leader of the flock; the bull, sovereign of the heifers; has not every one of them his seraglio? It becomes thee, truly, to reproach me with my four wives, whilst our great prophet had eighteen, the Jew David, as many, and the Jew Solomon, seven hundred, all told, with three hundred concubines! Thou perceivest that I am modest. Cease, then, to reproach a sage with luxury, who is content with so moderate a repast. I permit thee to drink; allow me to love. Thou changest thy wines; permit me to change my females. Let every one suffer others to live according to the customs of their country. Thy hat was not made to give laws to my turban; thy ruff and thy curtailed doublets are not to command my doliman. Make an end of thy coffee, and go and caress thy German spouse, since thou art allowed to have no other."

Reply of the German

"Dog of a Mussulman! for whom I retain a profound veneration; before I finish my coffee I will confute all thy arguments. He who possesses four wives, possesses four harpies, always ready to calumniate, to annoy, and to fight one another. Thy house is the den of discord, and none of them can love thee. Each has only a quarter of thy person, and in return can bestow only a quarter of her heart. None of them can serve to render thy life agreeable; they are prisoners who, never having seen anything, have nothing to say; and, knowing only thee, are in consequence thy enemies.

Thou art their absolute master; they therefore hate thee. Thou art obliged to guard them with eunuchs, who whip them when they are too happy. Thou pretendest to compare thyself to a cock, but a cock never has his pullets whipped by a capon. Take animals for thy examples, and copy them as much as thou pleasest; for my part, I love like a man; I would give all my heart, and receive an entire heart in return. I will give an account of this conversation to my wife tonight, and I hope she will be satisfied. As to the wine with which thou reproachest me, if it is an evil to drink it in Arabia, it is a very praiseworthy habit in Germany.—Adieu!''

Denis Diderot

French Encyclopedist, philosopher, satirist, literary writer, and critic,
1713–1784, who edited, with d'Alembert, the famous Encyclopaedia.

From "On Women," A review of a Dissertation on Women by M. Thomas.

Woman has inside her an organ, subject to terrible spasms, which rules
her and rouses up in her phantoms of every sort. In her delirium she goes
back into her past and plunges forward into the future, both states being
all the while present to her. All her extraordinary ideas spring from this
organ, which is peculiar to her sex. A woman who was hysterical in youth
becomes devout in old age: the woman who retains any considerable energy in old age was hysterical in youth. Her head still speaks the language
of the senses, though the senses themselves are mute. Nothing is more
closely related to hysteria than ecstacy, visions, prophecy, revelations,
and fiery poetry. . . .

But one word is sufficient to destroy this fiery imagination, this spirit
one would have thought indomitable. A doctor said to the women of Bor-
deaux, who were tormented by terrible vapors, that they were threatened
with the falling sickness. In an instant they were cured. A doctor shakes
burning iron in the eyes of a troop of epileptic girls. In an instant they are
cured. The magistrates of Miletus announced that the first woman to kill
herself would be exposed, naked, in the public place: and the Milesian
women are reconciled to life. Women are subject to epidemic attacks of
ferocity. The example of one will involve a multitude. Only the first will
be a criminal: the rest are ill. Oh, women, what extraordinary children
you are! With a little pain and sensibility (Fie! M Thomas, why did you
not let yourself go with these two qualities, which are quite familiar to
you?), what pity could you not have inspired in us, by showing us
women, subjected as we are to the infirmities of childhood, more re-
pressed and neglected in their education, abandoned to the same caprices
of fate, with a more mobile soul, more delicate organs, and with none of

that natural or acquired strength which fits us for our destiny: reduced to silence in maturity, subject to a discomfort which urges them to become wives and mothers: then sad, disturbed, melancholy, and, in addition, parents alarmed not only for the health and life of their child, but also for its character: for it is at this critical moment of discomfort that a girl becomes what she will remain all her life, penetrating or stupid, sad or gay, serious or frivolous, good or bad, deceiving or fulfilling her mother's hopes. For many a long year each moon will bring back the same discomfort. The moment has arrived which will free her from parental despotism: her imagination expands before a future full of empty visions: her heart swims in a secret joy. Thou art pleased, unhappy creature, to rejoice: time would unceasingly have weakened the tyranny thou leavest; time will unceasingly increase the tyranny to which thou art passing. A husband is chosen for her. She becomes a mother. Pregnancy is painful to almost all women. It is in suffering, at the peril of their lives, at the price of their charms, and often to the detriment of their health, that women give birth to children. The first home of the child, and the two reservoirs of its nourishment, the organs which particularize its sex, are subject to two incurable maladies. There is, perhaps, no joy comparable to that of the mother who looks on her first-born. But this pleasure is bought very dear. The father hands over the care of the boys to a hireling. The mother remains charged with the guardianship of the girls. Age advances. Beauty passes. The years of desertion, bad temper, and boredom arrive. By discomfort nature persuaded them to be mothers. By a long and dangerous illness she takes away from them the power. What is a woman then? Neglected by her husband, abandoned by her children, a nothing in society, religious observance her one last resource. In almost all countries the cruelty of the civil law is at one against women with the cruelty of nature. They have been treated like imbecile children. In organized countries there is no vexation man cannot safely practise on woman. The only reprisal in her power is followed by a more or less marked contempt, which varies in proportion as society is more or less moral. A savage can practise every sort of vexation on his wife. Woman, unhappy in the town, is unhappier still in the depth of the forest. Listen to the speech of an Indian woman on the banks of the Orinoco, and listen to it, if you can, without emotion. The Jesuit missionary Gumilla reproached her with letting the daughter she had just brought into the world die, by cutting her navelstring too short. "Would to God, Father," she said, "would to God that the moment my mother brought me into the world she had had enough love and compassion to spare her child all I have endured and shall go on enduring till the end of my days. Had my mother suffocated me at birth, I should be dead. But I should not have felt death and should have escaped the unhappiest of conditions. How much have I suffered! and who knows how much remains for me to suffer till my death? Picture to yourself, Father, the pains that lie in store for an Indian woman among the Indians. They accompany us into the fields with bow and arrow. But we, we go there burdened with a child hanging from the breast and with another that we carry in a basket. They go to kill a bird or catch a fish. But we till the earth: and after we have borne the toils of sowing, we bear all the toils of harvest. They return in the evening without any burden, while we bring home roots for them to eat and maize for them to drink. Once home, they go off for conversation with their friends, while we go and look for wood and water to prepare their supper. Having eaten, they go to sleep, while we pass most of the night grinding the maize and preparing them chica. What is the reward of our vigils? They swill their chica, and get drunk; and when drunk they drag us by the hair and trample us underfoot. Oh, Father, would to God my mother had suffocated me at birth. Thou knowest thyself if our complaints be just. I tell thee what thou seest for thyself every day. But our greatest unhappiness thou couldst not know. It is sad for the poor Indian woman to serve her husband like a slave, crushed with labor in the fields, deprived of rest at home. But it is horrible to see him, after twenty years, take another and younger wife, lacking in judgment. He becomes attached to her. She strikes us, she strikes our children, she orders us about, she treats us like servants; and at the slightest murmur that escapes us, the branch of a tree is raised! . . . Oh, Father, how wouldst thou have us tolerate this condition? What can an Indian woman do better than spare her child a slavery a thousand times worse than death? Would to God, Father, I repeat, that my mother had loved me enough to bury me at birth. My heart would have had less for which to suffer, and my eyes for which to weep!''

Woman, how I pity thee! There is only one compensation for your ills. And had I been lawgiver, perhaps you would have received it. Were you freed from all the bonds of slavery, you would have been sacred wherever you had appeared . . . . When we write of women, we must needs dip our pen in the rainbow and throw upon the paper the dust of butterflies' wings. Like the pilgrim's little dog, pearls must fall when we shake our paw. But no pearls fall from the paw of M. Thomas. It is not enough, M. Thomas, to talk and to talk well about women. Make me see them. Hang them up under my eyes like so many thermometers to register the smallest change in manners and customs. Fix, as justly and as impartially as you can, the prerogatives of man and woman. But remember that, owing to her lack of principles and power of reflection, nothing penetrates deeply into the comprehension of women: notions of justice, virtue, vice, goodness, or wickedness, float on the superficies of their soul. Remember that women have clung with all the energy of nature to amour propre and self-interest. More civilized than us externally, they have stayed simple savages within, all more or less Macchiavellian. The symbol of women in general is that of the Apocalypse, on whose front was written *Mystery*.

Where there is a brazen wall for us, for them there is often but a cobweb. We have been asked if women understand friendship. There are women who are men and men who are women, and I admit that I will never make a friend of a man-woman. We have more intellect than women; women more instinct than we. The only thing they are taught is to carry well the fig-leaf they have received from their first ancestress. Everything said and repeated to them eighteen or nineteen years on end comes down to this: "My child, pay attention to your fig-leaf. Your fig-leaf is right; your fig-leaf is wrong"! A declaration is worth practically nothing with a nation prone to gallantry. Man and woman merely see in it a proposal for reciprocal enjoyment. Still, what does this phrase, "I love you," so lightly pronounced, so frivolously interpreted, really mean? It really means "I should be greatly obliged if you would sacrifice to me your innocence and your morals: if you would lose the respect you have for yourself and with which you are treated by others: if you would walk with eyes lowered in society, at least till libertinage has become a habit and you have thrown off modesty: if you would renounce every honest condition; if you would make your parents die of grief and afford me a moment's pleasure." Mothers, read these lines to your daughters. It is a brief commentary on all the flattering speeches which will be made to them. You cannot warn them too early. So much importance has been attached to gallantry that apparently no virtue is left to her who has taken the plunge. It is with her as with the religious humbug and false priest, in whom unbelief is almost the badge of depravity. This great crime once committed, they can be shocked at nothing. We read in books, they in the great book of the world. Thus their ignorance leads them to receive truth promptly when it is offered. No authority holds them in thrall. Truth is always finding, at the door of our heads, a Plato, an Aristotle; an Epicurus, a Zeno standing as sentinels, and armed with pikes to repel her. Women are rarely systematic; they are always guided by the moment. Thomas says nothing of the advantages accruing to men of letters from the society of women. That is ungrateful of him. The soul of women is not more upright than our own, but decency does not permit them to speak with our frankness. So they have invented a delicate warbling by means of which we may say strightforwardly all we want, when we have been whistled into their dovecot. Women either keep silent, or, frequently, give the impression of not daring to say what they do say. We can easily see that Jean-Jacques has wasted a great deal of time at the feet of women, and that Marmontel has passed a great deal of it in their arms. We might easily suspect Thomas and D'Alembert of having been too virtuous. Women accustom us to discuss with charm and clearness the dryest and thorniest subjects. We talk to them unceasingly: we wish them to listen: we are afraid of tiring or boring them. Hence we develop a particular method of explaining ourselves easily which passes from conversation into style.

When women have genius, I think their brand is more original than our own.

From the entry "Woman" in the *Encyclopedia* of Diderot and d'Alembert*

Wife (Natural Law): *Uxor* in Latin, female of the man, considered as such since she is bound to him by the ties of marriage. See then "Marriage" and "Husband."

The Supreme Being, having decided it was not good for man to remain alone, inspired him to join in an intimate relationship with a companion. This relationship was constituted by the voluntary agreement of the two parties. Since such a society has for its principal aim the procreation and raising of the children to be born into it, it requires that both mother and father consecrate all their attention to the nourishing and education of these offspring of their love, until they are able to sustain and guide themselves.

Although husband and wife might have, in the end, the same interests in this relationship, it is, however, essential that one or the other should be in a position of authority. Now the express judicial codes of civilized nations, the laws and customs of Europe award this authority both definitely and unanimously to the male, to the one who, endowed with greater physical and spiritual strength, contributes more to the common good, in secular as well as in religious affairs, with the result that the wife must necessarily be subordinated to her husband and must obey his orders in all domestic matters. This is the opinion of ancient and modern legal experts as well as the formal decision of legislators.

Similarly, the code of Frederick the Great, which appeared in 1750 and which apparently attempted to introduce universal, positive justice, declares that the husband, by nature itself, is the master of the house, the head of the family; and that, since the wife enters the house voluntarily, she is, in a way, under the husband's dominion, from which various prerogatives proceed that favor him. Finally, sacred scripture prescribes that the wife submit to him as her master.

The arguments just alleged in favor of marital power, however, can be answered from a humanistic viewpoint. The nature of this article permits us to state the case strongly.

First of all, it seems: (1) that it would be difficult to demonstrate that the husband's authority comes through nature, because this proposition

---

*Under the article "Woman" Diderot discusses various authoritative views of the female sex, surveying them with humor. A more serious argument follows in the articles "Wife" and "Woman (Ethics)" presented later [Translator's note].

denies the natural equality of men; that from the fact that one is properly in command it does not follow that he actually has the right to do so; (2) the man does not always have greater physical or spiritual strength, greater wisdom, or a greater ability to act properly than a woman; (3) the command of scripture being worded as an injunction indicates that it is only a practical measure. It could be argued that there is no other subordination than that demanded by common law. Consequently nothing prevents the civil law being altered by particular legislative decisions, since both natural law and religion determine nothing to the contrary.

We do not deny that in a society composed of two persons it is necessary for one or the other to have the determining voice; and since ordinarily men are more capable than women to decide matters of detail, it is quite judicious to establish, as a general rule, that the man's voice should prevail as long as the two parties have made no agreement to the contrary, since the general rule proceeds from the human institution and not from natural law. In this way, a wife who does what civil law requires and has purely and simply made her marriage contract is understood to be subject to that civil law.

But if any wife, persuaded that she has more judgment and discretion, or knowing that she by chance or upbringing is superior to the man she marries, stipulates the opposite of what the law provides, to which the husband agrees, should she not have, by the power of natural law, the same power that the husband has by virtue of the laws of princes? The case of a queen, sovereign over herself, who marries a prince of lower rank or, shall we say, one of her subjects, suffices to demonstrate that the authority of a wife over her husband, even in the management of family affairs, is not incompatible with the nature of conjugal union.

In fact, there have been marriages, in the most civilized countries, that submitted the husband to the wife's authority; there has been a princess, heir to a kingdom, who, although marrying, has ruled it alone and reserved for herself the supreme power. Everyone knows the terms of the marriage made between Philip II and Mary, Queen of England; those of Mary, Queen of Scots, and those of Ferdinand and Isabella to govern together the kindom of Castile . . . .

The examples of England and Muscovy demonstrate that women can succeed equally well in a liberal or despotic system; and if it is not against nature or reason that they should rule an empire, it hardly seems more contradictory that they should be mistresses of a family. . . .

At least nothing prevents (because we are not concerned here to take advantage of unique examples to prove too much) nothing prevents, I say, that the authority of the wife in marriage can be established by agreement between two parties of equal social rank, unless the legislature forbids all exceptions despite the freely given consent of those involved.

Marriage is by nature a contract. Consequently, in everything not forbidden by natural law, the terms agreed to by husband and wife determine its reciprocal privileges.

In closing, why cannot the ancient maxim *provisio hominis tollit provisionem legis** be considered in this case, in so far as one authorizes it in the matter of dowries, division of property, and many other cases, where the law prevails only when the parties have not believed it necessary to stipulate differently from that which the law prescribes.

Woman (Ethics): This category touches the soul . . . but does not always elevate it. It gives rise only to agreeable thoughts, which become a moment later disturbing sensations or tender sentiments. And the philosopher intending to contemplate soon becomes only man who desires or a lover who dreams.

A woman has her portrait done. What she lacks to be beautiful is precisely what makes her pretty. She wishes her beauty increased without diminishing her graces; she wishes, all at the same time, for the portrait to be unfaithful and a good likeness. That's just the difficulty faced by anyone who wants to write about women.

This half of the human race, physically comparable to the other, is superior to it in charm if inferior in strength. The roundness of their figures, the finesse of their qualities, the brillance of their color are their distinctive attributes.

In heart and spirit women differ from men no less than they do in size and shape, but upbringing has changed their natural dispositions in many ways. Dissimulation, apparently for them a need, has made their souls so secret, their exceptional qualities so many, so confused with generalities, that the more we observe the less we are sure about.

As with their beauty, so with their spirit; it seems that they allow themselves to be perceived only to be imagined instead. Characters are like colors. There are primary colors, ones that change, an infinitude of shades as you pass from one to another. Women have none other than mixed colors, intermediate or variable, whether upbringing alters their natural shade more than ours or the delicateness of their constitution makes their soul a mirror that accepts everything, reproduces it vividly, but retains nothing.

Who can define women? Everyone speaks of them, but the language is equivocal. She who seems the most indifferent is sometimes the most sensitive; the most indiscreet passes often for the most false. Love or hate determines the prejudiced judgments we make of them. The freest spirit, he who has best studied women, believing to resolve the problems, only manages to pose new ones. There are three things, said such a free spirit,

---

*A man's wish supplants the law [Translators' note].

that I have always loved without understanding at all: painting, music, and women.

If it is true that weakness gives rise to timidity, timidity to finesse, finesse to falseness, one must conclude that truthfulness is a virtue to be well admired in women.

If this same delicateness of constitution that makes a women's imagination more vivid, renders their mind less capable of attention, it can be said that they perceive more quickly, see as well, but do not look as long.

How I should admire virtuous women if they were as fixed in virtue as immoral women are in vice!

A woman's youth, if shorter, is more brilliant than a man's; her old age is longer and more unpleasant.

Women are vengeful. Vengeance that comes from a momentary anger is a proof of moral weakness. The weakest and most timid must be cruel; a general law of nature proportions resentment in every sensitive being to danger.

How could they be discreet? They are curious, and why not? Everything is made a mystery to them; they are called on neither to act nor to advise.

There is less unity among women than among men because women have only one objective in life.

Marked by inequalities, the two sexes nevertheless possess advantages that are nearly equalized. Nature has given to one side power and majesty, reason and courage; but to the other beauty and grace, finesse and emotion. These advantages are not always incompatible. They occasionally balance one another. They sometimes are the same qualities, only present in different degrees. A natural grace or virtue in one sex is a fault or deformity in the other. What is different by nature is sharpened by upbringing. The sculptor's hand is what gives great value to a lump of clay.

For men, who share among themselves the various occupations of civil life, the position for which they are destined decides their education and differentiation from others. For women, however, education is of poor quality and hardly available, rather more neglected than useful. Surprisingly, souls so little cultivated produce so much virtue and give rise to so little vice.

Women who have renounced the world before coming to know it are charged with the moral education of women who must live in it. Thus, many a girl is brought to the altar to take on, through oath, duties of which she knows nothing, and to join with a man she has never seen. More often, she is recalled by her family to receive a second education that overturns all the ideas of the first and that, concerning itself with manners not morals, continually exchanges diamonds, however badly cut and ill-sized, for paste.

Only then, after having spent three quarters of the day before mirror and harpischord, Chloé enters with her mother into the labyrinth that is the world. There her wandering spirit diverges down a thousand detours, detours from which one needs the thread of experience to escape. There, always righteous and silent, with no knowledge of what to esteem or scorn, she does nothing but think. She is afraid to feel, she dares neither see nor listen. Rather, observing everything with as much curiosity as ignorance, she often sees more than there is, hears more than is said, blushes indecently, smiles at the wrong time, and, sure to be equally reproved for what she pretends to know as well as for what she does not, waits, impatient and bored, for a change of name to lead her to independence and pleasure.

One talks of her beauty, a simple and natural way to please without trying, or of her appearance, a system of artificial means to increase the effect of her beauty or take its place (it usually accomplishes neither). Praise of her character or spirit is always taken for proof of ugliness. Her sensibility and reason are apparently only supplements to her beauty. After having groomed Chloé for love, one must forbid her to indulge.

Nature, it seems, has given men the right to rule. Women have had recourse to craft to free themselves. The two sexes have abused each other with their advantages—power and beauty. The two ways to generate unhappiness. Men have increased their natural power by laws they have made. Women have augmented the value of their possession by the difficulty involved in obtaining it. It is not difficult to say where servitude lies today. Whatever may come of it, authority is the goal toward which women tend. The love they give leads them there; that which they take repels them. Attempting to inspire love, trying not to feel it themselves, or, at least, to hide what they feel, is both women's politics and ethics.

This art of pleasing, this desire to please everyone, this fervent wish to please more than one, this silence of the heart, this disordering of the spirit, this continuing lie called coquetry, seems in women to be a primitive characteristic that, born of their natural subordination (unjustly servile), fortified and extended by upbringing, can only be mastered by a rational effort or destroyed by the great heat of emotion. This quality has even been compared to the sacred flame that is never extinguished.

See Chloé enter the world; he who just gave her the right to go along (too filled with love to love his wife, or too ill-favored, too responsive to duty to be loved because of it) appears to give her license to love another. Vain and superficial, less eager to see than to show herself, Chloé hurries to the theater and parties, never missing anything. She has hardly arrived when she is surrounded by men, confident and scornful, without virtue or talent, who seduce women with tricks, take pride in dishonoring them, find pleasure in their despair, who seek every day to increase their conquests by indiscretions, infidelities, and break-ups. They are like bird hunters who make the birds they have captured cry out to lure others to them.

Follow Chloé into the middle of this eager crowd, the flirt come from Crete to the temple of Gnide. She smiles at one, speaks in the ear of another, takes the arm of a third, signals two others to follow her. Does one of them speak to his companion of his love? It's Armide. She leaves him one moment, rejoins him the next, and then leaves him once more. Are they jealous of one another? She's the Celimene of Misanthrope. She reassures them in turn by the evil she speaks of each of his rivals; thus artificially mixing scorn and favor, she revives their temerity by a fevered look, inspiring again their hope with a tender smile. She's the deceptive woman of Archilochus, who holds fire in one hand and water in the other.

But the more women have perfected the art of making those to whom they intend to accord nothing desire, hope for, and pursue them, the more men have multiplied their means of obtaining possession. The art of inspiring desires she does not wish to satisfy has produced in its train the art of feigning emotions she does not feel. Chloé wishes to hide herself only after being seen. Daphnis makes her stop by pretending not to see her. After running through all the winding paths of the game, each finally finds himself in the spot nature intended.

In all hearts there is a hidden principle of union. There is a flame, longtime hidden, that bursts into fire, extends itself despite our efforts to extinguish it, and finally dies against our wishes. There is a seed where enclosed are fear and hope, pain and pleasure, mystery and indiscretion; a seed that contains quarrels and settlements, cries and smiles, tears both bitter and sweet; diffused everywhere, it is more or less ready to develop according to the assistance given or the obstacles placed in its way.

Like a helpless child she protects, Chloé puts love on her knees, plays with his bow, amuses herself with his arrow, clips the ends of his wings, ties his hands with flowers. But she herself is already entrapped by bonds she cannot see, although she feels herself free. While she presses him to her breast, listens to him, smiles, and amuses herself with those who complain to him and those who are afraid, suddenly a bit of involuntary magic makes her squeeze him in her arms and then love is in her heart. She no longer dares to swear that she loves, but begins to think how sweet loving is. All those lovers who follow in her triumphant path she would now dismiss from her with more fervor than she felt in attracting them at first. There is only one of them on whom her eyes ceaselessly glance, from whom they continually turn away. Sometimes it might be said that she hardly notices his presence. Yet there is nothing he has done that she has not seen. When he speaks, she seems not to listen. Yet there is nothing said that is not heard. When she speaks to him? Her voice becomes timid, her features more animated. If she goes to the theater, is he less in view? He is rather the first she sees there, his name always the last she pronounces. If her feelings are unknown, they are so only to her. Everything she has done to hide them has revealed them. All she has done to extinguish them has inflamed them. She is sad, but sadness is one of love's charms. Becoming sensitive she ceases to be a flirt, and seems to have set traps continually only to fall into them herself.

I have read that of all passions love is the most suitable for women. It is at least true that they experience this emotion, the most compassionate element of human nature, to a degree of delicateness and liveliness that very few men can attain. Their souls are apparently made only to feel, they themselves only for the sweet task of loving. To this passion, so natural for them, is opposed the restraint called honor. But it has been said, only too truly, that honor seems to have been imagined only to be sacrificed.

Chloé has pronounced the word. An act fatal to her liberty, she makes her lover the object of all her attention, the goal of all action, the judge of her life. She knows only amusement and boredom, not pain and pleasure. All her days are filled, her hours exciting, full of languishing interludes. Time, always too slow or too fast, still runs on without her realizing it. All these empty names, so dear to her, this sweet commerce of looks and smiles, this silence more eloquent than speech, a thousand memories, plans, and ideas continually come to renew her soul and make it live again. But the last proof of her emotional awakening signals the beginning of her lover's inconstancy. Can the knots of love never be tied on one side without being untied on the other? If there are, among men, some privileged souls in whom love, far from being weakened by pleasure, seems to be strengthened by it, for the most part love to them is a false rejoicing that, preceded by an uncertain desire, is followed by a marked distaste, too often accompanied by hate or scorn. It is said that by the seashore fruits of rare beauty grow that, when touched, dissolve into dust. This is the very image of ephemeral love, such vain folly of the imagination, frail construct of the senses, the weak tribute one pays to beauty. When the source of pleasure is in the heart, it never dries up. Love founded on esteem is inalterable, the charm of life, the prize of virtue.

Occupied only by her lover, Chloé, perceiving he is less tender, suspects that he is unfaithful. She complains, he reassures. He continues to wrong her, she begins to complain once more. Infidelity follows infidelity on one side, reproaches multiply on the other. Quarrels are both frequent and boisterous, misunderstandings drawn out, settlements cold. Meetings become less frequent, conversations shorter, all the tears are bitter. Chloé demands justice from love. What, she asks, has become of the faith of oaths? But it's done. Chloé's deserted, deserted for another, deserted in a flash.

Given over to shame and sorrow, she makes as many oaths to love never again as she made to love always. But, having lived for love, she cannot live for herself. Establishing itself in a soul, love spreads. I do not know what magic alters the source of all other pleasures; but when it takes flight, it leaves all the horror of solitude and the desert. That's no doubt why it is often said to be easier to find a woman never engaged than one engaged only once.

Chloé's despair changes imperceptibly into a languor that makes her days a tissue of boredom. Overcome by the weight of her existence, she does not know what to do with her life, now a dry rock to which she's attached. But old lovers hopefully return, new ones declare themselves. Women arrange dinner parties. She agrees to distract herself, but ends up consoled. She has made a new choice that can hardly prove happier than the first, though it is more voluntary, and that is soon followed by another. She belonged to love, but now she belongs to pleasure. Her senses were a service to her heart, but her spirit now is used by the senses. Art, elsewhere so easy to distinguish from nature, is not here separated from it by more than an imperceptible nuance. Chloé fools herself sometimes. What does it matter if her lover is fooled as well, as long as he's happy. There are lies that come from promiscuity like theatrical fictions, where probability has often more to offer than truth.

Horace paints this picture of society in his time (Ode vi): "A girl hardly leaves behind the innocent games of tender childhood when she pleases herself to learn lascivious dances and all the craft and secrets of love. A wife hardly sits at her husband's table when, with a restless look, she seeks there a lover. Soon she ceases to choose, believing that in darkness all pleasures are legitimate." Soon also Chloé will arrive at this last period of gallantry.* Soon she gives to lust all the appearances of feeling, to complacence all the charms of lust. She dissembles her desires and feigns feelings, makes herself smile, forces the tears to fall. What's in her heart is rarely in her eyes. She has almost nothing on her lips that is in her heart or eyes. What she's done secretly, she tells herself she did not do. What she's been doing she tells herself no one has seen. What the artifice of words cannot justify she has excused by tears. And her caresses ensure it is forgotten.

Wives who act like courtesans have their own ethic. Chloé has made a code for herself that states it is dishonest for a wife, whatever she thinks of her, whatever passion is offered her, to deceive another wife from her social set. It is said also that there are no eternal loves; but one should never form a relationship when its end is foreseen. She has added that between a breakup and a new affair there should be an interval of six

---

*Diderot uses here *galanterie*, a word whose negative and positive connotations are difficult to reproduce in English. To be *galant* is also to be perhaps promiscuous [Translators' note].

months; and she has likewise established that one should never leave a lover without designating his successor.

Chloé finally comes to think that only a solid relationship, or, as she says, a continuous affair, can ruin a woman. She acts accordingly. She has only transient attractions that she calls fancies, which let a suspicion of love develop, but which never give her the time to transform it into certitude. The public sees one love, who vanishes, already replaced by another. I dare say that several lovers present themselves simultaneously. In Chloé's fancies, character is less important than looks, looks even less important than money. She snubs at court those she has sought out in town, denies knowing in town those met in the country, and forgets by evening that morning's privileged fancy so perfectly that she even makes him doubt he was ever favored. In his scorn, he feels exempted from keeping silent about what has been done for him, forgetting in his turn that a woman always has the right to deny that which a man never has the right to say. It's much better to show desire to Chloé than to confess your emotions. Occasionally she permits testaments of love and fidelity; but he who makes them is thought clumsy, he who offers his word certainly perfidious. The only way to become intimate with her, perhaps, is to pardon her infidelity. She fears jealousy more than perjury, importunity more than abandon. She forgives her lovers everything, allows herself everything—except love.

Worse than promiscuous, she believes herself, however, merely a flirt. Thus deluded, at a gaming table, in turn attentive and distracted, she brushes knees with one, gives her hand to another, in the pretense of admiring his lace, and makes suitable talk at the same time with a third. She claims to be without prejudice because she is without principle. She arrogates for herself the title ''honest man'' because she has renounced the one of ''honest woman.'' Most surprising, in all the variety of her fancies, simple pleasure is rarely the excuse.

She bears a famous name and has an easy husband. As long as she has beauty or grace, or at least the pleasant qualities youth bring, the desires of men and the jealousy of wives will take the place of consideration. Her irregular behavior will not exile her from society because it is confirmed by ridicule. Such ridicule finally will come, crueler than dishonor. Chloé ceases to cry, and will not cease to love. She wishes always to appear in public and no one will be seen with her. In such a position, her life is a painful and restless sleep, a profound depression, mixed with anxiety. Her only alternatives become bravado or piety. True piety is the most honest asylum for promiscuous women. But there are few who can pass from the love of men to the love of God. There are few who, weeping from regret, know how to persuade themselves it comes from repentence. There are, to be sure, few who, having been attached to vice, can decide at least to feign virtue.

There are even fewer who can pass from the temple of love to the sanctuary of the Muses, and who are able to hear what they can no longer see. Whatever it may be, Chloé, who set out so often on the wrong path, chasing always some vain pleasure, distancing herself from happiness, errs again in choosing a new route. After having wasted fifteen or twenty years in leering, bantering, smirking, in making intrigues and petty annoyances, after rendering an honest man unhappy, after being given to a fop, after being lent to a crowd of idiots, this fool changes roles, passes from one theater to another, no longer able to play Phyrné, believes it possible to become Aspasie.

I am sure that no woman will recognize herself in the portrait of Chloé; in fact, there have been few whose lives have fallen into such distinct stages.

There is a woman with the spirit to make herself loved but not feared; with the power to make herself esteemed, but not the desire to scorn others; beautiful enough to make her virtue a prize. Equally withdrawn from the shame of loving indiscreetly and from the torment of not loving and from the boredom of living without love, she has so much sympathy for the weaknesses of her sex that the most promiscuous woman pardons her for being faithful. She has so much respect for decorum that the most prudish pardons her for being soft. Leaving to the fools, she's surrounded by flirting, caprice, jealousy, all these small passions, all these trifles that render their lives either vacant or contentious, in the midst of these contagious goings-on, she continually looks to her heart, which is pure, and to her mind, which is sane, rather than to public opinion, that queen of the world, who governs so despotically both fools and the foolish. Happy is the woman who possesses such advantages. Happier still she who possesses the heart of such a woman.

Finally, there is a yet more solid happiness. Its joy is to ignore what the world terms ''pleasure,'' its glory is to live ignored. Confined by the duties of wife and mother, she consecrates her days to the practice of private virtues. Occupied by the management of her family, she rules her husband through his complacence, her children through kindness, her servants by generosity. Her house is the dwelling place of religious sentiment, of filial piety, of conjugal love, of maternal tenderness, of order, of internal peace, of easy sleep, and of health. Economical and homebound, she separates passion from necessity. The poor man at her door is never spurned; a licentious man never comes there. She is reserved and dignified, therefore respected. Her indulgence and sensitivity make her loved; her prudence and determination make others fear her. From her comes a gentle warmth, a pure light that illumines, that enlivens everything it touches. Is it nature or rather reason that has conducted her to the highest rank where I see her?

A Breviary for Young Married Women: An unedited letter of Diderot to his daughter

My daughter, you are about to leave the house of your mother and father to enter your husband's and your own. In giving you away to . . . I have resigned to him all my authority. None remains. A short time ago, I told you what to do, and it was your duty to obey me; now I have only the right to advise. I am going to make use of it.

Your happiness is inseparable from that of your spouse. It must be that you are happy or unhappy through each other. Never lose sight of this, and fear the first disagreement you make for yourselves, since it can be followed by many more.

Comply with your husband's wishes in every way; conform to his reasonable preferences; try to think nothing that you could not tell him, so that he may always be in your heart. Do nothing of which he might not be a witness. Always and in everything behave as though in his presence.

Remember that a young girl who acts like a woman is indecent and that, consequently, a woman who knows how to retain the decent behavior of a young girl has respect for herself and is respected by others.

You cannot show too much esteem for your husband; this is a sure way of putting distance between yourself and women of no morals.

As for your intimate touches of tenderness, reserve them for the privacy of your home; in this way you will avoid ridicule, unpleasant glances, and dishonest propositions.

Look after your health. In the long run good health is the foundation of all your duties; he who loves us the most is the first to feel sorry for us, take care of us, but he finally tires of seeing us constantly suffer. If the sight of illness begins by increasing his interest, it will finish by destroying it.

If you are sweet, compliant, and happy, you will make your home so agreeable to your husband that he will only stay away against his will. You two have a common burden to carry; bear your share courageously. Outside business is his province; domestic affairs are yours. Manage your household economically and intelligently. Your husband's job will be easier if you perform yours with care.

Take stock of yourself every day; never go to bed at night, for any possible reason, without being well aware of what happened during the day.

Reveal the intimate secrets of your home life to no one. Even I wish only to know what is necessary for me to know; and I want everything else to be a complete mystery. Success arouses jealousy, failure only false sympathy. I will always be there at difficult times, and will be all the help you need.

I will deliver no moral injunctions. The suspicion of shady behavior, so common today, will pain me deeply, destroy my respect for you, and drive me from your house and from many others. After being made proud by you, it would kill me to have to be ashamed of you. I expect to hear you mentioned with praise; I could never bear to hear you spoken of with shame. The better known you are, through me as well as through yourself, the more scandalous will be any wrong step.

Be especially careful during the first days of your marriage; a new passion leads one to indiscretions that make themselves noticed and that will become the seeds of an indecency to degenerate into habit. One is honest, but does not appear so. It is very unfortunate that we lose the respect that comes from the exercise of virtue, and, because of the false view we present of ourselves, become confused with those we try not to imitate. We rebel against such injustice, but wrongly. It is just to judge women by appearances and, if there are some of such rigorous standards that they do not have to use them and who would prefer to accord virtue to a libertine rather than remove it from a wise woman, it's a favor they do us.

I love you with all my soul; if you determine to make my affections grow, ask yourself this question: "What would my father think if he saw me, if he heard me, if he knew?" If you do so, you will do well.

You are about to enter the world; be careful with your first steps. Establish your character well. Receive kindly all whom your husband is pleased to introduce to you. He has good sense and judgment, and I expect that he will never open his door to those of doubtful virtue.

Do not judge hastily; but once you discover the truth about someone tell your husband. Do not be overly reticent; it might lead anywhere. Have few, very few friends. Where there are many people, there is much vice. Numerous friends are necessary only to those who are bored and unhappy with themselves.

Judge my happiness with you by the frequency of my visits. The happier I am with you, the more you will see me. Unhappiness to us both if I fear to pass your door!

My child, since I've been in the world I've cried and suffered much. Console me, pity me. I let you go with a pain hardly conceivable. I forgive you for not feeling the same. I stand alone, and, you follow a man you must adore. At the least, instead of speaking with you as I did formerly, when I speak to myself, may I say while wiping away the tears, "She's mine no longer, it's true. But she is happy."

If you plan your first days together carefully, they will be a model to which, for the days to follow, you have only to conform.

Devote the first hours of your morning to your various domestic tasks; they may require the entire morning.

Strengthen your spirit and soul by the reading for which you happily acquired a taste. Do not neglect your talent. It's the only way for you to distinguish yourself, without sacrificing anything essential.

Though you need no master, keep one if it is only to subject you to work. Fear waste, it's a sign of boredom and of distaste for useful occupation. If I visit you several days in a row without finding you in, I will be quite disappointed. If, finding you there, I am fortunate to discover you occupied as I might wish, my heart will be overwhelmed with joy the rest of the day.

I ask you to keep this letter and re-read it at least once a month. This is the last time I will say ''I demand.''

Goodbye, my daughter; goodbye, my dear child. Come to me so that once more I may embrace you. If you have sometimes found me more severe than necessary, I ask forgiveness. Be certain that fathers are certainly cruelly punished by tears, justly or not, which they make their children shed. That you will know one day; then you will forgive me. If you profit from this advice, it will be the most precious gift you could obtain from me.

I bless you ten, a hundred, a thousand times; go, my child, I understand nothing of other fathers. I see that their worry ceases the moment they separate from their children. It seems that mine begins. I found you so happy under my wing! May it be God's wish that the new lover you have chosen for yourself may be as good, as tender, as faithful as I have been.

Jean-Jacques Rousseau

Philosopher, political theorist, essayist, and novelist, 1712–1778, who was born in Geneva but spent much of his life in France and who contrasted the hypocrisy and deceit of contemporary society with the virtue, simplicity, openness, and innocence of the primitive state of the noble savage.

"On Women"*

Another subject at which I marvel is the air of confidence with which we proudly enumerate all the great men that history has celebrated in order to equate them to the few heroines that history has deigned to remember and the fact that we really think that we have gained something from such a comparison. Well, Sirs, let women fantasize and write their own history, and you will see how they rank you and how they will take possession, perhaps on more just grounds, of the preeminent position that you arrogantly usurp from them.

And after all, if we equitably detailed all the beautiful actions that time has unfolded and if we examined the true reasons for those actions, which reasons could possibly have augmented or diminished in number, I do not doubt that we would find the number of actions more nearly in balance, and the scales would remain closer to equilibrium.

Let us consider first the women deprived of their liberty by the tyranny of men who are masters of all things, because the crown, the responsibilities, the occupations, the command of the armies, all is in their hands. They have seized these powers from the earliest time, by what natural right I do not know, that I have never been able to understand quite well,

*Rousseau's essay was found originally in a collection of his early writings owned by Théodore de Saussure and published eventually by Théophile Dufour in Volume I (1905) of the *Annales* of the Jean-Jacques Rousseau Society (Genève: Chez A. Jullien, Éditeur, pp. 202–205; background on the manuscript collection and this period of Rousseau's career as a writer may be found on pp. 179–201). The essay is notable for its treatment of women as wronged victims of society and male historians[Translators' note].

and this seizure certainly would have no other foundation than physical strength. Let us consider also the character of the human spirit that desires only brilliance, that admires virtue only in the midst of grandeur and majesty, but scorns all the most worthy and admirable things that submissive and dependent people can do in their state.

After speculating on all that, let us enter into a detailed comparison [of the actions of men and women] and let us, for example, compare Mithridates with Zenobia, Romulus with Dido, Cato of Utica with Lucretia, one of whom committed suicide after the loss of his liberty and the other after the loss of her honor, the Count of Dunois with Joan of Arc, finally Cornelia, Arria, Artemis, Fulvia, Elizabeth, the Countess of Thököly, and so many heroines of all time with the greatest men. We will find actually that the first ones [heroes] infinitely outnumber the others, but in recompense we will see also in the other sex [female] some models that are perfect in all kinds of civil and moral virtues. If the women had had as much part as we in the management of affairs and in the governing of empires, perhaps they would have done more in the way of heroism and great courage, and greater numbers of women would have been distinguished. Few of those women who had the good luck to rule states and to command armies have remained in the shadows: they are almost all distinguished by some brilliant deed that has won our admiration. We are far from being able to say as much about monarchs who have ruled nations: how many of them are there, as Voltaire says, whose names deserve to be found somewhere in the chronological tables only because they indicated that epoch. I repeat, due allowance being made, the women could have given greater examples of grandeur of soul and of love of virtue, and in larger numbers, than men ever did, if we had not unjustly stolen from them, along with their liberty, all their opportunities for manifesting these traits to the world.

I postpone for another time speaking to you of women who have had a part in the domain of letters and who have enhanced it with their works, which are both ingenious and full of delicacy.

From *A Discourse on the Origin of Inequality*

Let us begin by distinguishing between the physical and moral ingredients in the feeling of love. The physical part of love is that general desire which urges the sexes to union with each other. The moral part is that which determines and fixes this desire exclusively upon one particular object; or at least gives it a greater degree of energy toward the object thus preferred. It is easy to see that the moral part of love is a factitious feeling, born of social usage, and enhanced by the women with much care and cleverness, to establish their empire, and put in power the sex which ought to obey. This feeling, being founded on certain ideas of beauty and merit which a savage is not in a position to acquire, and on comparisons which he is incapable of making, must be for him almost nonexistent; for, as his mind cannot form abstract ideas of proportion and regularity, so his heart is not susceptible of the feelings of love and admiration, which are even insensibly produced by the application of these ideas. He follows solely the character nature has implanted in him, and not tastes which he could never have acquired; so that every woman equally answers his purpose.

From *A Discourse on Political Economy*

In the family, it is clear, for several reasons which lie in its very nature, that the father ought to command. In the first place, the authority ought not to be equally divided between father and mother; the government must be single, and in every division of opinion there must be one preponderant voice to decide. Secondly, however lightly we may regard the disadvantages peculiar to women, yet, as they necessarily occasion intervals of inaction, this is a sufficient reason for excluding them from this supreme authority: for when the balance is perfectly even, a straw is enough to turn the scale. Besides, the husband ought to be able to superintend his wife's conduct, because it is of importance for him to be assured that the children, whom he is obliged to acknowledge and maintain, belong to no one but himself. Thirdly, children should be obedient to their father, at first of necessity, and afterwards from gratitude: after having had their wants satisfied by him during one half of their lives, they ought to consecrate the other half to providing for his. Fourthly, servants owe him their services in exchange for the provision he makes for them, though they may break off the bargain as soon as it ceases to suit them. I say nothing here of slavery, because it is contrary to nature, and cannot be authorized by any right or law.

From *Emile. Emile* is a philosophical novel of human nature and development, written as a guide to the education of the purported writer's son of the same name.

Taste, good or bad, takes its shape especially in the intercourse between the two sexes; the cultivation of taste is a necessary consequence of this form of society. But when enjoyment is easily obtained, and the desire to please becomes lukewarm, taste must degenerate; and this is, in my opinion, one of the best reasons why good taste implies good morals.

Consult the women's opinions in bodily matters, in all that concerns the senses; consult the men in matters of morality and all that concerns the understanding. When women are what they ought to be, they will keep to what they can understand, and their judgment will be right; but since they have set themselves up as judges of literature, since they have begun to criticise books and to make them with might and main, they are altogether astray. Authors who take the advice of bluestockings will always be ill-advised; gallants who consult them about their clothes will always be absurdly dressed. I shall presently have an opportunity of speaking of the real talents of the female sex, the way to cultivate these talents, and the matters in regard to which their decisions should receive attention. . . . We have reached the last act of youth's drama; we are approaching its closing scene.

It is not good that man should be alone. Emile is now a man, and we must give him his promised helpmeet. That helpmeet is Sophy. Where is her dwelling-place, where shall she be found? We must know beforehand what she is, and then we can decide where to look for her. And when she is found, our task is not ended. "Since our young gentleman," says Locke, "is about to marry, it is time to leave him with his mistress." And with these words he ends his book. As I have not the honour of educating "A young gentleman," I shall take care not to follow his example.

Sophy, or Woman

Sophy should be as truly a woman as Emile is a man, i.e., she must possess all those characters of her sex which are required to enable her to play her part in the physical and moral order. Let us inquire to begin with in what respects her sex differs from our own.

But for her sex, a woman is a man; she has the same organs, the same needs, the same faculties. The machine is the same in its construction; its parts, its working, and its appearance are similar. Regard it as you will the difference is only in degree.

Yet where sex is concerned man and woman are unlike; each is the complement of the other; the difficulty in comparing them lies in our inability to decide, in either case, what is a matter of sex, and what is not. General differences present themselves to the comparative anatomist and even to the superficial observer; they seem not to be a matter of sex; yet they are really sex differences, though the connection eludes our observation. How far such differences may extend we cannot tell; all we know for certain is that where man and woman are alike we have to do with the characteristics of the species; where they are unlike, we have to do with the characteristics of sex. Considered from these two standpoints, we find so many instances of likeness and unlikeness that it is perhaps one of the greatest of marvels how nature has contrived to make two beings so like and yet so different.

These resemblances and differences must have an influence on the moral nature; this inference is obvious, and it is confirmed by experience; it shows the vanity of the disputes as to the superiority or the equality of the sexes; as if each sex, pursuing the path marked out for it by nature, were not more perfect in that very divergence than if it more closely resembled the other. A perfect man and a perfect woman should no more be alike in mind than in face, and perfection admits of neither less nor more.

In the union of the sexes each alike contributes to the common end, but in different ways. From this diversity springs the first difference which may be observed between man and woman in their moral relations. The man should be strong and active; the woman should be weak and passive; the one must have both the power and the will; it is enough that the other should offer little resistance.

When this principle is admitted, it follows that woman is specially made for man's delight. If man in his turn ought to be pleasing in her eyes, the necessity is less urgent, his virtue is in his strength, he pleases because he is strong. I grant you this is not the law of love, but it is the law of nature, which is older than love itself.

If woman is made to please and to be in subjection to man, she ought to make herself pleasing in his eyes and not provoke him to anger; her strength is in her charms, by their means she should compel him to discover and use his strength. The surest way of arousing this strength is to make it necessary by resistance. Thus pride comes to the help of desire and each exults in the other's victory. This is the origin of attack and defence, of the boldness of one sex and the timidity of the other, and even of the shame and modesty with which nature has armed the weak for the conquest of the strong.

Who can possibly suppose that nature has prescribed the same advances to the one sex as to the other, or that the first to feel desire should be the first to show it? What strange depravity of judgment! The consequences of the act being so different for the two sexes, is it natural that they should enter upon it with equal boldness? How can any one fail to see that when the share of each is so unequal, if the one were not controlled by modesty as the other is controlled by nature, the result would be the destruction of both, and the human race would perish through the very means ordained for its continuance?

Women so easily stir a man's senses and fan the ashes of a dying passion, that if philosophy ever succeeded in introducing this custom into any unlucky country, especially if it were a warm country where more women are born than men, the men, tyrannized over by the women, would at last become their victims, and would be dragged to their death without the least chance of escape.

Female animals are without this sense of shame, but what of that? Are their desires as boundless as those of women, which are curbed by this shame? The desires of the animals are the result of necessity, and when the need is satisfied, the desire ceases; they no longer make a feint of repulsing the male, they do it in earnest. Their seasons of complaisance are short and soon over. Impulse and restraint are alike the work of nature. But what would take the place of this negative instinct in women if you rob them of their modesty?

The Most High has deigned to do honor to mankind; he has endowed man with boundless passions, together with a law to guide them, so that man may be alike free and self-controlled; though swayed by these passions man is endowed with reason by which to control them. Woman is also endowed with boundless passions; God has given her modesty to restrain them. Moreover, he has given to both a present reward for the right use of their powers, in the delight which springs from that right use of them, i.e., the taste for right conduct established as the law of our behavior. To my mind this is far higher than the instinct of the beasts. . . .

Thus the different constitution of the two sexes leads us to a third conclusion, that the stronger party seems to be master, but is as a matter of fact dependent on the weaker, and that, not by any foolish custom of gallantry, nor yet by the magnanimity of the protector, but by an inexorable law of nature. For nature has endowed woman with a power of stimulating man's passions in excess of man's power of satisfying those passions, and has thus made him dependent on her goodwill, and compelled him in his turn to endeavor to please her, so that she may be willing to yield to his superior strength. Is it weakness which yields to force, or is it voluntary self-surrender? This uncertainty constitutes the chief charm of the man's victory, and the woman is usually cunning enough to leave him in doubt. In this respect the woman's mind exactly resembles her body; far from being ashamed of her weakness, she is proud of it; her soft muscles offer no resistance, she professes that she cannot lift the lightest weight; she would be ashamed to be strong. And why? Not only to gain an appearance of refinement; she is too clever for that; she is providing herself before hand with excuses, with the right to be weak if she chooses.

The consequences of sex are wholly unlike for man and woman. The male is only a male now and again, the female is always a female, or at least all her youth; everything reminds her of her sex; the performance of her functions requires a special constitution. She needs care during pregnancy and freedom from work when her child is born; she must have a quiet, easy life while she nurses her children; their education calls for patience and gentleness, for a zeal and love which nothing can dismay; she forms a bond between father and child, she alone can win the father's love for his children and convince him that they are indeed his own. What loving care is required to preserve a united family! And there should be no question of virtue in all this, it must be a labour of love, without which the human race would be doomed to extinction.

The mutual duties of the two sexes are not, and cannot be, equally binding on both. Women do wrong to complain of the inequality of man-made laws; this inequality is not of man's making, or at any rate it is not the result of mere prejudice, but of reason. She to whom nature has entrusted the care of the children must hold herself responsible for them to their father. No doubt every breach of faith is wrong, and every faithless husband, who robs his wife of the sole reward of the stern duties of her sex, is cruel and unjust; but the faithless wife is worse, she destroys the family and breaks the bonds of nature; when she gives her husband children who are not his own, she is false both to him and them, her crime is not infidelity but treason. To my mind, it is the source of dissension and of crime of every kind. Can any position be more wretched than that of the unhappy father who, when he clasps his child to his breast, is haunted by the suspicion that this is the child of another, the badge of his own dishonor, a thief who is robbing his own children of their inheritance. Under such circumstances the family is little more than a group of secret enemies, armed against each other by a guilty woman, who compels them to pretend to love one another.

Thus it is not enough that a wife should be faithful; her husband, along with his friends and neighbors, must believe in her fidelity; she must be modest, devoted, retiring; she should have the witness not only of a good conscience, but of a good reputation. In a word, if a father must love his children, he must be able to respect their mother. For these reasons it is not enough that the woman should be chaste, she must preserve her reputation and her good name. From these principles there arises not only a moral difference between the sexes, but also a fresh motive for duty and propriety, which prescribes to women in particular the most scrupulous attention to their conduct, their manners, their behavior. Vague assertions as to the equality of the sexes and the similarity of their duties are only empty words; they are no answer to my argument.

It is a poor sort of logic to quote isolated exceptions against laws so firmly established. Women, you say, are not always bearing children. Granted; yet that is their proper business. Because there are a hundred or so of large towns in the world where women live licentiously and have few children, will you maintain that it is their business to have few children? And what would become of your towns if the remote country districts, with their simpler and purer women, did not make up for the barrenness of your fine ladies? There are plenty of country places where women with only four or five children are reckoned unfruitful. In conclusion, although here and there a woman may have few children, what difference does it make? Is it any the less a woman's business to be a mother? And do not the general laws of nature and morality make provision for this state of things?

Even if there were these long intervals, which you assume, between the periods of pregnancy, can a woman suddenly change her way of life without danger? Can she be a nursing mother to-day and a soldier tomorrow? Will she change her tastes and her feelings as a chameleon changes his color? Will she pass at once from the privacy of household duties and indoor occupations to the buffeting of the winds, the toils, the labors, the perils of war? Will she be now timid, now brave, now fragile, now robust? If the young men of Paris find a soldier's life too hard for them, how would a woman put up with it, a woman who has hardly ventured out of doors without a parasol and who has scarcely put a foot to the ground? Will she make a good soldier at an age when even men are retiring from this arduous business?

There are countries, I grant you, where women bear and rear children with little or no difficulty, but in those lands the men go half-naked in all weathers, they strike down the wild beasts, they carry a canoe as easily as a knapsack, they pursue the chase for 700 or 800 leagues, they sleep in the open on the bare ground, they bear incredible fatigues and go many days without food. When women become strong, men become still stronger; when men become soft, women become softer; change both the terms and the ratio remains unaltered.

I am quite aware that Plato, in the *Republic,* assigns the same gymnastics to women and men. Having got rid of the family there is no place for women in his system of government, so he is forced to turn them into men. That great genius has worked out his plans in detail and has provided for every contingency; he has even provided against a difficulty that in all likelihood no one would ever have raised; but he has not succeeded in meeting the real difficulty. I am not speaking of the alleged community of wives which has often been laid to his charge; this assertion only shows that his detractors have never read his works. I refer to that political promiscuity under which the same occupations are assigned to both sexes alike, a scheme which could only lead to intolerable evils; I refer to that subversion of all the tenderest of our natural feelings, which he sacrificed to an artificial sentiment which can only exist by their aid. Will the bonds of convention hold firm without some foundation in nature? Can devotion to the state exist apart from the love of those near and dear to us? Can patriotism thrive except in the soil of that miniature fatherland, the home? Is it not the good son, the good husband, the good father, who makes the good citizen?

When once it is proved that men and women are and ought to be unlike in constitution and in temperament, it follows that their education must be different. Nature teaches us that they should work together, but that each has its own share of the work; the end is the same, but the means are different, as are also the feelings which direct them. We have attempted to paint a natural man, let us try to paint a helpmeet for him.

You must follow nature's guidance if you would walk aright. The native characters of sex should be respected as nature's handiwork. You are always saying, "Women have such and such faults, from which we are free." You are misled by your vanity; what would be faults in you are virtues in them; and things would go worse, if they were without these so-called faults. Take care that they do not degenerate into evil, but beware of destroying them.

On the other hand, women are always exclaiming that we educate them for nothing but vanity and coquetry, that we keep them amused with trifles that we may be their masters; we are responsible, so they say, for the faults we attribute to them. How silly! What have men to do with the education of girls? What is there to hinder their mothers educating them as they please? There are no colleges for girls; so much the better for them! Would God there were none for the boys, their education would be more sensible and more wholesome. Who is it that compels a girl to waste her time on foolish trifles? Are they forced, against their will, to spend half their time over their toilet, following the example set them by you? Who prevents you teaching them, or having them taught, whatever seems good in your eyes? Is it our fault that we are charmed by their beauty and delighted by their airs and graces, if we are attracted and flattered by the arts they learn from you, if we love to see them prettily dressed, if we let them display at leisure the weapons by which we are subjugated? Well then, educate them like men. The more women are like men, the less influence they will have over men, and then men will be masters indeed.

All the faculties common to both sexes are not equally shared between them, but taken as a whole they are fairly divided. Woman is worth more as a woman and less as a man; when she makes a good use of her own rights, she has the best of it; when she tries to usurp our rights, she is our inferior. It is impossible to controvert this, except by quoting exceptions after the usual fashion of the partisans of the fair sex.

To cultivate the masculine virtues in women and to neglect their own is evidently to do them an injury. Women are too clear-sighted to be thus deceived; when they try to usurp our privileges they do not abandon their own; with this result: they are unable to make use of two incompatible things, so they fall below their own level as women, instead of rising to the level of men. If you are a sensible mother you will take my advice. Do not try to make your daughter a good man in defiance of nature. Make her a good woman, and be sure it will be better both for her and us.

Does this mean that she must be brought up in ignorance and kept to housework only? Is she to be man's handmaid or his helpmeet? Will he dispense with her greatest charm, her companionship? To keep her a slave will he prevent her knowing and feeling? Will he make an automaton of her? No, indeed, that is not the teaching of nature, who has given women such a pleasant easy wit. On the contrary, nature means them to think, to will, to love, to cultivate their minds as well as their persons; she puts these weapons in their hands to make up for their lack of strength and to enable them to direct the strength of men. They should learn many things, but only such things as are suitable.

When I consider the special purpose of woman, when I observe her inclinations or reckon up her duties, everything combines to indicate the mode of education she requires. Men and women are made for each other, but their mutual dependence differs in degree; man is dependent on woman through his desires; woman is dependent on man through her desires and also through her needs; he could do without her better than she can do without him. She cannot fulfil her purpose in life without his aid, without his goodwill, without his respect; she is dependent on our feelings, on the price we put upon her virtue, and the opinion we have of her charms and her deserts. Nature herself has decreed that woman, both for herself and her children, should be at the mercy of man's judgment.

Worth alone will not suffice, a woman must be thought worthy; nor beauty, she must be admired; nor virtue, she must be respected. A woman's honor does not depend on her conduct alone, but on her reputation, and no woman who permits herself to be considered vile is really virtuous. A man has no one but himself to consider, and so long as he does right he may defy public opinion; but when a woman does right her tasks is only half finished, and what people think of her matters as much as what she really is. Hence her education must, in this respect, be different from man's education. ''What will people think'' is the grave of a man's virtue and the throne of a woman's.

The children's health depends in the first place on the mother's, and the early education of man is also in a woman's hands; his morals, his passions, his tastes, his pleasures, his happiness itself, depend on her. A woman's education must therefore be planned in relation to man. To be pleasing in his sight, to win his respect and love, to train him in childhood, to tend him in manhood, to counsel and console, to make his life pleasant and happy, these are the duties of woman for all time, and this is what she should be taught while she is young. The further we depart from this principle, the further we shall be from our goal, and all our precepts will fail to secure of happiness or our own. . . .

The exaggeration of feminine delicacy leads to effeminacy in men. Women should not be strong like men but for them, so that their sons may be strong. Convents and boarding-schools, with their plain food and ample opportunities for amusements, races, and games in the open air and in the garden, are better in this respect than the home, where the little girl is fed on delicacies, continually encouraged or reproved, where she is kept sitting in a stuffy room, always under her mother's eye, afraid to stand or

walk or speak or breathe, without a moment's freedom to play or jump or
run or shout, or to be her natural, lively, little self; there is either harmful
indulgence or misguided severity, and no trace of reason. In this fashion
heart and body are alike destroyed. . . .

Boys and girls have many games in common, and this is as it should
be; do they not play together when they are grown up? They have also
special tastes of their own. Boys want movement and noise, drums, tops,
toy-carts; girls prefer things which appeal to the eye, and can be used for
dressing-up—mirrors, jewellery, finery, and specially dolls. The doll is
the girl's special plaything; this shows her instinctive bent towards her
life's work. The art of pleasing finds its physical basis in personal adornment, and this physical side of the art is the only one which the child can
cultivate.

Here is a little girl busy all day with her doll; she is always changing its
clothes, dressing and undressing it, trying new combinations of trim-
mings well or ill matched; her fingers are clumsy, her taste is crude, but
there is no mistaking her bent; in this endless occupation time flies
unheeded, the hours slip away unnoticed, even meals are forgotten. She
is more eager for adornment than for food. "But she is dressing her doll,
not herself," you will say. Just so; she sees her doll, she cannot see herself; she cannot do anything for herself, she has neither the training, nor
the talent, nor the strength; as yet she herself is nothing, she is engrossed
in her doll and her coquetry is devoted to it. This will not always be so; in
due time she will be her own doll.

We have here a very early and clearly-marked bent; you have only to
follow it and train it. What the little girl most clearly desires is to dress
her doll, to make its bows, its tippets, its sashes, and its tuckers; she is
dependent on other people's kindness in all this, and it would be much
pleasanter to be able to do it herself. Here is a motive for her earliest lessons, they are not tasks prescribed, but favors bestowed. Little girls always dislike learning to read and write, but they are always ready to learn
to sew. They think they are grown up, and in imagination they are using
their knowledge for their own adornment. . . .

Whatever may be said by the scornful, good sense belongs to both
sexes alike. Girls are usually more docile than boys, and they should be
subjected to more authority, as I shall show later on, but that is no reason
why they should be required to do things in which they can see neither
rhyme nor reason. The mother's art consists in showing the use of everything they are set to do, and this is all the easier as the girl's intelligence is
more precocious than the boy's. This principle banishes, both for boys
and girls, not only those pursuits which never lead to any appreciable results, not even increasing the charms of those who have pursued them,
but also those studies whose utility is beyond the scholar's present age
and can only be appreciated in later years. If I object to little boys being

made to learn to read, still more do I object to it for little girls until they are able to see the use of reading; we generally think more of our own ideas than theirs in our attempts to convince them of the utility of this art. After all, why should a little girl know how to read and write? Has she a house to manage? Most of them make a bad use of this fatal knowledge, and girls are so full of curiosity that few of them will fail to learn without compulsion. Possibly cyphering should come first; there is nothing so obviously useful, nothing which needs so much practice or gives so much opportunity for error as reckoning. If the little girl does not get the cherries for her lunch without an arithmetical exercise, she will soon learn to count. . . .

Show the sense of the tasks you set your little girls, but keep them busy. Idleness and insubordination are two very dangerous faults, and very hard to cure when once established. Girls should be attentive and industrious, but this is not enough by itself; they should early be accustomed to restraint. This misfortune, if such it be, is inherent in their sex, and they will never escape from it, unless to endure more cruel sufferings. All their life long, they will have to submit to the strictest and most enduring restraints, those of propriety. They must be trained to bear the yoke from the first, so that they may not feel it, to master their own caprices and to submit themselves to the will of others. If they were always eager to be at work, they should sometimes be compelled to do nothing. Their childish faults, unchecked and unheeded, may easily lead to dissipation, frivolity, and inconstancy. To guard against this, teach them above all things self-control. Under our senseless conditions, the life of a good woman is a perpetual struggle against self; it is only fair that woman should bear her share of the ills she has brought upon man.

    . . . A woman's real resource is her wit; not that foolish wit which is so greatly admired in society, a wit which does nothing to make life happier; but that wit which is adapted to her condition, the art of taking advantage of our position and controlling us through our own strength. Words cannot tell how beneficial this is to man, what a charm it gives to the society of men and women, how it checks the petulant child and restrains the brutal husband; without it the home would be a scene of strife; with it, it is the abode of happiness. I know that this power is abused by the sly and the spiteful; but what is there that is not liable to abuse? Do not destroy the means of happiness because the wicked use them to our hurt. . . .

Taste is formed partly by industry and partly by talent, and by its means the mind is unconsciously opened to the idea of beauty of every kind, till at length it attains to those moral ideas which are so closely related to beauty. Perhaps this is one reason why ideas of propriety and modesty are acquired earlier by girls than by boys, for to suppose that this early feeling is due to the teaching of the governesses would show little knowledge of their style of teaching and of the natural development of the human mind. The art of speaking stands first among the pleasing arts; it alone can add fresh charms to those which have been blunted by habit. It is the mind which not only gives life to the body, but renews, so to speak, its youth; the flow of feelings and ideas gives life and variety to the countenance, and the conversation to which it gives rise arouses and sustains attention, and fixes it continuously on one object. I suppose this is why little girls so soon learn to prattle prettily, and why men enjoy listening to them even before the child can understand them; they are watching for the first gleam of intelligence and sentiment.

Women have ready tongues; they talk earlier, more easily, and more pleasantly than men. They are also said to talk more; this may be true, but I am prepared to reckon it to their credit; eyes and mouth are equally busy and for the same cause. A man says what he knows, a woman says what will please; the one needs knowledge, the other taste; utility should be the man's object; the woman speaks to give pleasure. There should be nothing in common but truth. . . .

If boys are incapable of forming any true idea of religion, much more is it beyond the grasp of girls; and for this reason I would speak of it all the sooner to little girls, for if we wait till they are ready for a serious discussion of these deep subjects we should be in danger of never speaking of religion at all. A woman's reason is practical, and therefore she soon arrives at a given conclusion, but she fails to discover it for herself. The social relation of the sexes is a wonderful thing. This relation produces a moral person of which woman is the eye and man the hand, but the two are so dependent on one another that the man teaches the woman what to see, while she teaches him what to do. If women could discover principles and if men had as good heads for detail, they would be mutually independent, they would live in perpetual strife, and there would be an end to all society. But in their mutual harmony each contributes to a common purpose; each follows the other's lead, each commands and each obeys.

As a woman's conduct is controlled by public opinion, so is her religion ruled by authority. The daughter should follow her mother's religion, the wife her husband's. Were that religion false, the docility which leads mother and daughter to submit to nature's laws would blot out the sin of error in the sight of God. Unable to judge for themselves they should accept the judgment of father and husband as that of the church.

While women unaided cannot deduce the rules of their faith, neither can they assign limits to that faith by the evidence of reason; they allow themselves to be driven hither and thither by all sorts of external influences, they are ever above or below the truth. Extreme in everything, they are either altogether reckless or altogether pious; you never find them able to combine virtue and piety. Their natural exaggeration is not wholly to blame; the ill-regulated control exercised over them by men is partly responsible. Loose morals bring religion into contempt; the terrors of remorse make it a tyrant; this is why women have always too much or too little religion. . . .

The reason which teaches a man his duties is not very complex; the reason which teaches a woman hers is even simpler. The obedience and fidelity which she owes to her husband, the tenderness and care due to her children, are such natural and self-evident consequences of her position that she cannot honestly refuse her consent to the inner voice which is her guide, nor fail to discern her duty in her natural inclination.

I would not altogether blame those who would restrict a woman to the labors of her sex and would leave her in profound ignorance of everything else; but that would require a standard of morality at once very simple and very healthy, or a life withdrawn from the world. In great towns, among immoral men, such a woman would be too easily led astray; her virtue would too often be at the mercy of circumstances; in this age of philosophy, virtue must be able to resist temptation; she must know beforehand what she may hear and what she should think of it.

Moreover, in submission to man's judgment she should deserve his esteem; above all she should obtain the esteem of her husband; she should not only make him love her person, she should make him approve her conduct; she should justify his choice before the world, and do honor to her husband through the honor given to the wife. But how can she set about this task if she is ignorant of our institutions, our customs, our notions of propriety, if she knows nothing of the source of man's judgment, nor the passions by which it is swayed? Since she depends both on her own conscience and on public opinion, she must learn to know and reconcile these two laws, and to put her own conscience first only when the two are opposed to each other. She becomes the judge of her own judges, she decides when she should obey and when she should refuse her obedience. She weighs their prejudices before she accepts or rejects them; she learns to trace them to their source, to foresee what they will be, and to turn them in her own favor; she is careful never to give cause for blame if duty allows her to avoid it. This cannot be properly done without cultivating her mind and reason. . . .

The search for abstract and speculative truths, for principles and axioms in science, for all that tends to wide generalization, is beyond a woman's grasp; their studies should be thoroughly practical. It is their business to apply the principles discovered by men, it is their place to make the observations which lead men to discover those principles. A woman's thoughts, beyond the range of her immediate duties, should be directed to the study of men, or the acquirement of that agreeable learning whose sole end is the formation of taste; for the works of genius are beyond her reach, and she has neither the accuracy nor the attention for success in the exact sciences; as for the physical sciences, to decide the relations between living creatures and the laws of nature is the task of that sex which is more active and enterprising, which sees more things, that sex which is possessed of greater strength and is more accustomed to the exercise of that strength. Woman, weak as she is and limited in her range of observation, perceives and judges the forces at her disposal to supplement her weakness, and those forces are the passions of man. Her own mechanism is more powerful than ours; she has many levers which may set the human heart in motion. She must find a way to make us desire what she cannot achieve unaided and what she considers necessary or pleasing; therefore she must have a thorough knowledge of man's mind; not an abstract knowledge of the mind of man in general, but the mind of those men who are about her, the mind of those men who have authority over her, either by law or custom. She must learn to divine their feelings from speech and action, look and gesture. By her own speech and action, look and gesture, she must be able to inspire them with the feelings she desires, without seeming to have any such purpose. The men will have a better philosophy of the human heart, but she will read more accurately in the heart of men. Woman should discover, so to speak, an experimental morality, man should reduce it to a system. Woman has more wit, man more genius; woman observes, man reasons; together they provide the clearest light and the profoundest knowledge which is possible to the unaided human mind; in a word, the surest knowledge of self and of others of which the human race is capable. In this way art may constantly tend to the perfection of the instrument which nature has given us.

. . . In a word, she endures patiently the wrong-doing of others, and she is eager to atone for her own. This amiability is natural to her sex when unspoiled. Woman is made to submit to man and to endure even injustice at his hands. You will never bring young lads to this; their feelings rise in revolt against injustice; nature has not fitted them to put up with it.

Marie-Jean-Antoine-Nicolas Caritat, Marquis de Condorcet

French mathematician, historian, political theorist, and social reformer, 1743–1794, Condorcet was the youngest of the Encyclopedists.

On the Admission of Women to the Rights of Citizenship

Custom may familiarize mankind with the violation of their natural rights to such an extent, that even among those who have lost or been deprived of these rights, no one thinks of reclaiming them, or is even conscious that they have suffered any injustice.

Certain of these violations (of natural right) have escaped the notice of philosophers and legislators, even while concerning themselves zealously to establish the common rights of individuals of the human race, and in this way to lay the foundation of political institutions. For example, have they not all violated the principle of the equality of rights in tranquilly depriving one-half of the human race of the right of taking part in the formation of laws by the exclusion of women from the rights of citizenship? Could there be a stronger proof of the power of habit, even among enlightened men, than to hear invoked the principle of equal rights in favor of perhaps some 300 or 400 men, who had been deprived of it by an absurd prejudice, and forget it when it concerns some 12,000,000 women?

To show that this exclusion is not an act of tyranny, it must be proved either that the natural rights of women are not absolutely the same as those of men, or that women are not capable of exercising these rights.

But the rights of men result simply from the fact that they are rational, sentient beings, susceptible of acquiring ideas of morality, and of reasoning concerning those ideas. Women having, then, the same qualities, have necessarily the same rights. Either no individual of the human species has any true rights, or all have the same; and he or she who votes against the rights of another, whatever may be his or her religion, color, or sex, has by that fact abjured his own.

It would be difficult to prove that women are incapable of exercising the rights of citizenship. Although liable to become mothers of families, and exposed to other passing indispositions, why may they not exercise rights of which it has never been proposed to deprive those persons who periodically suffer from gout, bronchitis, etc.? Admitting for the moment that there exists in men a superiority of mind, which is not the necessary result of a difference of education (which is by no means proved, but which should be, to permit of women being deprived of a natural right without injustice), this inferiority can only consist in two points. It is said that no woman has made any important discovery in science, or has given any proofs of the possession of genius in arts, literature, etc.; but, on the other hand, it is not pretended that the rights of citizenship should be accorded only to men of genius. It is added that no woman has the same extent of knowledge, the same power of reasoning, as certain men; but what results from that? Only this, that with the exception of a limited number of exceptionally enlightened men, equality is absolute between women and the remainder of the men; that this small class apart, inferiority and superiority are equally divided between the two sexes. But since it would be completely absurd to restrict to this superior class the rights of citizenship and the power of being entrusted with public functions, why should women be excluded any more than those men who are inferior to a great number of women? Lastly, shall it be said that there exists in the minds and hearts of women certain qualities which ought to exclude them from the enjoyment of their natural rights? Let us interrogate the facts. Elizabeth of England, Maria Theresa, the two Catherines of Russia—have they not shown that neither in courage nor in strength of mind are women wanting?

Elizabeth possessed all the failings of women. Did these failings work more harm during her reign than resulted from the failings of men during the reign of her father, Henry VIII, or her successor, James I? Have the lovers of certain empresses exercised a more dangerous influence than the mistresses of Louis XIV, of Louis XV, or even of Henry IV?

Will it be maintained that Mistress Macaulay would not have expressed her opinions in the House of Commons better than many representatives of the British nation? In dealing with the question of liberty of conscience, would she not have expressed more elevated principles than those of Pitt, as well as more powerful reasoning. Although as great an enthusiast on behalf of liberty as Mr. Burke could be on behalf of its opposite, would she, while defending the French Constitution, have made use of such absurd and offensive nonsense as that which this celebrated rhetorician made use of in attacking it? Would not the adopted daughter of Montaigne have better defended the rights of citizens in France, in 1614, than the Councillor Courtin, who was a believer in magic and occult powers? Was not the Princesse des Ursins superior to Chamillard?

Could not the Marquise de Chatelet have written equally as well as M. Rouillé? Would Mme. de Lambert have made laws as absurd and as barbarous as those of the "garde des Sceaux," of Armenouville, against Protestants, invaders of domestic privacy, robbers and negroes? In looking back over the list of those who have governed the world, men have scarcely the right to be so very uplifted.

Women are superior to men in the gentle and domestic virtues; they, as well as men, know how to love liberty, although they do not participate in all its advantages; and in republics they have been known to sacrifice themselves for it. They have shown that they possess the virtues of citizens whenever chance or civil disasters have brought them upon a scene from which they have been shut out by the pride and the tyranny of men in all nations.

It has been said that women, in spite of much ability, of much sagacity, and of a power of reasoning carried to a degree equaling that of subtle dialecticians, yet are never governed by what is called "reason."

This observation is not correct. Women are not governed, it is true, by the reason (and experience) of men; they are governed by their own reason (and experience).

Their interests not being the same (as those of men) by the fault of the law, the same things not having the same importance for them as for men, they may, without failing in rational conduct, govern themselves by different principles, and tend towards a different result. It is as reasonable for a woman to concern herself respecting her personal attractions as it was for Demosthenes to cultivate his voice and his gestures.

It is said that women, although superior in some respects to man— more gentle, more sensitive, less subject to those vices which proceed from egotism and hardness of heart—yet do not really possess the sentiment of justice; that they obey rather their feelings than their conscience. This observation is more correct, but it proves nothing; it is not nature, it is education, it is social existence which produces this difference.

Neither the one nor the other has habituated women to the idea of what is just, but only to the idea of what is "honnête" or respectable. Excluded from public affairs, from all those things which are judged of according to rigorous ideas of justice, or according to positive laws, the things with which they are occupied and which are affected by them are precisely those which are regulated by natural feelings of honesty (or, rather, propriety) and of sentiment. It is, then, unjust to allege as an excuse for continuing to refuse to women the enjoyment of all their natural rights motives which have only a kind of reality because women lack the experience which comes from the exercise of these rights.

If reasons such as these are to be admitted against women, it will become necessary to deprive of the rights of citizenship that portion of the people who, devoted to constant labor, can neither acquire knowledge nor exercise their reason; and thus, little by little, only those persons would be permitted to be citizens who had completed a course of legal study. If such principles are admitted, we must, as a natural consequence, renounce the idea of a liberal constitution. The various aristocracies have only had such principles as these for foundation or excuse. The etymology of the word is a sufficient proof of this.

Neither can the subjection of wives to their husbands be alleged against their claims, since it would be possible in the same statute to destroy this tyranny of the civil law. The existence of one injustice can never be accepted as a reason for committing another.

There remain, then, only two objections to discuss. And, in truth, these can only oppose motives of expediency against the admission of women to the right of voting; which motives can never be upheld as a bar to the exercise of true justice. The contrary maxim has only too often served as the pretext and excuse of tyrants; it is in the name of expediency that commerce and industry groan in chains; and that Africa remains afflicted with slavery: it was in the name of public expediency that the Bastille was crowded; that the censorship of the press was instituted; that accused persons were not allowed to communicate with their advisers; that torture was resorted to. Nevertheless, we will discuss these objections, so as to leave nothing without reply.

It is necessary, we are warned, to be on guard against the influence exercised by women over men. We reply at once that this, like any other influence, is much more to be feared when not exercised openly; and that, whatever influence may be peculiar to women, if exercised upon more than one individual at a time, will in so far become proportionately lessened. That since, up to this time, women have not been admitted in any country to absolute equality; since their empire has none the less existed everywhere; and since the more women have been degraded by the laws, the more dangerous has their influence been; it does not appear that this remedy of subjection ought to inspire us with much confidence. Is it not probable, on the contrary, that their special empire would diminish if women had less interest in its preservation; if it ceased to be for them their sole means of defence, and of escape from persecution?

If politeness does not permit to men to maintain their opinions against women in society, this politeness, it may be said, is near akin to pride; we yield a victory of no importance; defeat does not humiliate when it is regarded as voluntary. Is it seriously believed that it would be the same in a public discussion on an important topic? Does politeness forbid the bringing of an action at law against a woman?

But, it will be said, this change will be contrary to general expediency, because it will take women away from those duties which nature has reserved for them. This objection scarcely appears to me well founded. Whatever form of constitution may be established, it is certain that in the present state of civilization among European nations there will never be more than a limited number of citizens required to occupy themselves with public affairs. Women will no more be torn from their homes than agricultural laborers from their plows, or artisans from their workshops. And, among the richer classes, we nowhere see women giving themselves up so persistently to domestic affairs that we should fear to distract their attention; and a really serious occupation or interest would take them less away than the frivolous pleasures to which idleness, a want of object in life, and an inferior education have condemned them.

The principal source of this fear is the idea that every person admitted to exercise the rights of citizenship immediately aspires to govern others. This may be true to a certain extent, at a time when the constitution is being established, but the feeling can scarcely prove durable. And so it is scarcely necessary to believe that because women may become members of national assemblies, they would immediately abandon their children, their homes, and their needles. They would only be the better fitted to educate their children and to rear men. It is natural that a woman should suckle her infant; that she should watch over its early childhood. Detained in her home by these cares, and less muscular than the man, it is also natural that she should lead a more retired, a more domestic life. The woman, therefore, as well as the man in a corresponding class of life, would be under the necessity of performing certain duties at certain times according to circumstances. This may be a motive for not giving her the preference in an election, but it cannot be a reason for legal exclusion. Gallantry would doubtless lose by the change, but domestic customs would be improved by equality in this as in other things.

Up to this time the manners of all nations have been more or less brutal and corrupt. I only know of one exception, and that is in favor of the Americans of the United States, who are spread, few in number, over a wide territory. Up to this time, among all nations, legal inequality has existed between men and women; and it would not be difficult to show that, in these two phenomena, the second is one of the causes of the first, because inequality necessarily introduces corruption, and is the most common cause of it, if even it be not the sole cause.

I now demand that opponents should condescend to refute these propositions by other methods than by pleasantries and declamations; above all, that they should show me any natural difference between men and women which may legitimately serve as foundation for the deprivation of a right.

The equality of rights established between men by our new constitution has brought down upon us eloquent declamations and never-ending pleasantries; but up till now no one has been able to oppose to it one single reason, and this is certainly neither from lack of talent nor lack of zeal. I venture to believe that it will be the same with regard to equality of rights between the two sexes. It is sufficiently curious that, in a great number of countries, women have been judged incapable of all public functions yet worthy of royalty; that in France a woman has been able to be regent, and yet that up to 1776 she could not be a milliner or dressmaker (''marchande des modes'') in Paris, except under cover of her husband's name; and that, lastly, in our elective assemblies they have accorded to rights of property what they have refused to natural right. Many of our noble deputies owe to ladies the honor of sitting among the representatives of the nation. Why, instead of depriving of this right women who were owners of landed estates, was it not extended to all those who possessed property or were heads of households? Why, if it be found absurd to exercise the right of citizenship by proxy, deprive women of this right, rather than leave them the liberty of exercising it in person?

From *Letters from a Dweller in New Heaven to a Citizen of Virginia, On the Uselessness of Sharing Legislative Power among Several Bodies**

. . . I must now make an objection to you. We desire a constitution whose principles would be founded solely on natural human rights, those anterior to social institutions.

We call these rights ''natural'' because they derive from the nature of man himself, that is, because from the moment when he exists as a sensible being, capable of reasoning and of entertaining moral ideas, he is to enjoy these rights by an evident and necessary consequence, rights of which he can never be deprived without injustice. We think that one of these rights is that of voting on matters of common interest, either personally or by means of representatives freely chosen; that a state in which some men, or at least men of property, are deprived of this right ceases to be a free state, that it becomes an aristocracy to some extent, that it is only, like monarchies and aristocracies, a constitution more or less good, depending on whether those who enjoy authority (I do not speak according to reason, but according to the present state of enlightenment) have interests that more or less conform to the general interest; but that it is no longer a true republic. That said, one can state that to the present no such state has actually existed. Is it because they are sensible beings, capable of reason, possessing moral ideas, that men have rights? Women should

---

*Condorcet begins in Letter I with a general discussion of legislation and the principles he believes should underlie it. Letter II concerns itself with the specific composition of a unicameral legislative body, the means it should employ to draw up laws, and the ways in which it should ensure freedom and stability for its citizens. A consideration of voting rights brings Condorcet to an examination of women's role and position in the republic [Translator's note].

therefore enjoy absolutely the same ones; however, in any constitution termed free, women have not exercised the right of citizenship.

Although one would admit the principle (on which M. Delolme has based his admiration for the English constitution) that it is sufficient that the power be in the hands of men who cannot have another interest (personal interest excepted, without doubt) than that of the citizenry at large, one cannot make use of it in this instance. Events have proved that men have, or believe they have, interests quite different from those of women, since everywhere men have made oppressive laws against women, or, at the least, established an enormous inequality between the two sexes. Finally, you will admit without doubt the principle of the English, that one is not legitimately subject to taxes one has not voted on, at least through representatives, and it follows from this principle that every woman has the right to refuse to pay taxes voted by parliament.

I see no real objection to these arguments, at least for widows or unmarried women. As for the rest, it can be said that the exercise of civil rights supposes that a person can act through his own will. I will answer, however, that civil laws which establish such a great inequality between men and women, so that one could suppose women deprived of the advantage of having their own free will, are only a greater injustice. In a society of two persons I can see only a necessary inequality, one that arises from the necessity of determining a deciding voice in the small number of situations that do not permit the interaction of separate wills and that, at the same time, because of necessity, do not permit a synthesis of wills. It is, however, rather difficult to suppose that this deciding voice should, for the totality of these exceptional cases, belong necessarily to one of the two sexes. It would seem more natural for this prerogative to be shared, and to give, sometimes to the man, sometimes to the woman, the deciding vote in those cases where it is most probable that one of the two will conform his will more closely to reason. This idea of establishing more equality between the sexes is not as new as one might believe. The Emperor Julian accorded to women the right to send their husbands a bill of divorce; a right that husbands alone had enjoyed since the first centuries of Rome; and the least gentlemanly perhaps of the Caesars was the most just toward women.

After having established that justice demands that women no longer be excluded from civil rights, however, it remains for me to examine the question of their eligibility for civic office. Any exclusion of this kind leads to two different injustices: one in regard to the electorate whose freedom is circumscribed, the other in regard to those excluded and those who are deprived of a privilege accorded to others. It seems to me then that no such exclusion should be established through law except in the case that reason obviously proves the utility of such a decision; and if one has chosen a good form of election, this situation should arise quite infrequently. I truly believe that, after the exclusion of those condemned by a judgment, as, for instance, those guilty of certain crimes, and of those in domestic service (which can be done without disadvantage), in respect for liberty such limitation should be reserved to the legal acknowledgment of the principle of an incompatibility of situations. I am not speaking of age, which should be that of civil majority, as is required to exercise city rights. One feels that this law of the incompatibility of situations introduces no inequality, properly impedes no choice, since it is not concerned with positions to be denied, but rather with those that are compatible. According to this principle, I believe that women should be legally excluded from no positions. But, one might say, would it not be ridiculous for a woman to command an army or preside over a tribunal? Well! Do you think it necessary to forbid citizens by an explicit law to do anything that might happen, be it a choice or action that seems ridiculous, like choosing a blind man as secretary to a judge, cutting off the nose to spite one's face? Either the electorate will want to choose wisely and have no need of your rules or they will want to choose badly, something your rules won't prevent. It will be either one or the other.

Finally, it is necessary to observe that this proposed change presupposes one in civil law, which would necessitate one in social custom, and another no less important in the education of women, such that the objections that might appear plausible today would have ceased to be so before the new order has been established.

The female constitution renders them hardly capable of going to war and, during part of their lives, certainly denies them positions requiring daily arduous work. Pregnancies, periods of confinement, and nursing all prevent them from exercising these functions. But I don't think that, in any other regard, differences between men and women can be postulated that do not result from the workings of education. Even when it is admitted that inequality in strength, both physical and mental, would be the same as it is today, the only result would be that women of the first order would be equal to men of the second and superior to those of the third, and so on. All talents can be accorded women, save that of creating. Such is the opinion of Voltaire, a man who has been most just toward women and who has known them the best. If only those men capable of creating were admitted to positions, there would be a good many vacant ones, even in the academies. There are many jobs in which the sacrifice of the time of a genius is not something that would be desirable for the public good. Furthermore, this view seems most uncertain to me. By comparing the number of women who have received a regular and careful education with men who have had the same advantages, one will notice the very small number of resulting geniuses; therefore, as you can see, the observation constantly alleged in favor of this view cannot be regarded as a proof. In addition, the restraint in which both the soul and spirit of women are held by social customs, almost from infancy, and particularly from the moment when genius begins to develop, must harm their progress in almost every way. Look how few monks have given any indication of genius, even in those orders where the influence of constraint is least apparent. Moreover, is it truly certain that no woman has given indications of genius? To the present this assertion is true, or so I believe, as far as sciences and philosophy are concerned; but is it for other fields as well? To speak only of French women, is there no genius to be found in the style of Madame de Sévigné? Is there not to be noticed in the novels of Madame de la Fayette and a few others the evidence of a passion and sensibility one would call genius in a dramatic work?

Perhaps you will find this discussion long-wided; but remember that it concerns the rights of half the human race, rights forgotten by all legislators; that it is hardly irrelevant to the liberty of men to indicate the one way of destroying the only objection that can be made to republics, and to demonstrate the real difference between them and states not truly free. Moreover, it is difficult even for a philosopher not to forget himself somewhat when he speaks of women. I am, however, afraid to arouse their indignation should they read this piece. I speak of their rights to equality, not of their dominance; I could be suspected of a secret desire to diminish it; and since Rousseau has merited their good wishes by asserting that they were created only to care for us and are suited only to torment us, I must not hope that they should declare themselves in my favor. But it is good to speak the truth, even to thereby expose oneself to ridicule. I return to the main object of my letter. . . .

Mary Wollstonecraft

British writer and translator, 1759–1797. Although she is not usually considered a philosopher, she regarded herself as one and certainly as doing philosophy. Given her arguments reaffirming the earlier Platonic position on the singular meaning of "virtue" and her concerted attack on Rousseau's depiction of the ideal woman, it is difficult to dispute her view of herself on either count. Her book, Vindication of the Rights of Woman, *was published in 1792 when she was around 33 years old. She died five years later, giving birth to a daughter whose father, William Godwin, she had married shortly before the birth.*

From *Vindication of the Rights of Woman*

The education of women has of late been more attended to than formerly; yet they are still reckoned a frivolous sex, and ridiculed or pitied by the writers who endeavor by satire or instruction to improve them. It is acknowledged that they spend many of the first years of their lives in acquiring a smattering of accomplishments; meanwhile, strength of body and mind are sacrificed to libertine notions of beauty, to the desire of establishing themselves—the only way women can rise in the world—by marriage. And this desire making mere animals of them, when they marry they act as such children may be expected to act—they dress, they paint, and nickname God's creatures.* Surely these weak beings are only fit for a seraglio! Can they be expected to govern a family with judgment, or take care of the poor babes whom they bring into the world?

If, then, it can be fairly deduced from the present conduct of the sex, from the prevalent fondness for pleasure which takes place of ambition and those nobler passions that open and enlarge the soul, that the instruction which women have hitherto received has only tended, with the constitution of civil society, to render them insignificant objects of desire—

---

*Hamlet speaks to Ophelia: "You jig, you amble, and you lisp, and nickname God's creatures, and make your wantonness your ignorance." *Hamlet* III. i. 150.

218

mere propagators of fools!—if it can be proved that in aiming to accomplish them, without cultivating their understandings, they are taken out of their sphere of duties, and made ridiculous and useless when the short-lived bloom of beauty is over,* I presume that *rational* men will excuse me for endeavoring to persuade them to become more masculine and respectable.

Indeed the word masculine is only a bugbear: there is little reason to fear that women will acquire too much courage or fortitude, for their apparent inferiority with respect to bodily strength must render them in some degree dependent on men in the various relations of life; but why should it be increased by prejudices that give a sex to virtue, and confound simple truths with sensual reveries?

Women are, in fact, so much degraded by mistaken notions of female excellence, that I do not mean to add a paradox when I assert that this artificial weakness produces a propensity to tyrannize, and gives birth to cunning, the natural opponent of strength, which leads them to play off those contemptible infantine airs that undermine esteem even whilst they excite desire. Let men become more chaste and modest, and if women do not grow wiser in the same ratio it will be clear that they have weaker understandings. It seems scarcely necessary to say that I now speak of the sex in general. Many individuals have more sense than their male relatives; and, as nothing preponderates where there is a constant struggle for an equilibrium without it has naturally more gravity, some women govern their husbands without degrading themselves, because intellect will always govern.

The Prevailing Opinion of a Sexual Character Discussed

To account for, and excuse the tyranny of man, many ingenious arguments have been brought forward to prove, that the two sexes, in the acquirement of virtue, ought to aim at attaining a very different character; or, to speak explicitly, women are not allowed to have sufficient strength of mind to acquire what really deserves the name of virtue. Yet it should seem, allowing them to have souls, that there is but one way appointed by Providence to lead *mankind* to either virtue or happiness.

If then women are not a swarm of ephemeron triflers, why should they be kept in ignorance under the specious name of innocence? Men complain, and with reason, of the follies and caprices of our sex, when they

*"A lively writer, I cannot recollect his name, asks what business women turned of forty have to do in the world?" [Wollstonecraft's note]. Perhaps Wollstonecraft is referring to a passage in Fanny Burney's popular novel *Evelina* spoken by the licentious Lord Merton: "I don't know what the devil a woman lives for after thirty: she is only in other folks' way" (*Evelina* [London and New York, 1958], p. 253).

do not keenly satirize our headstrong passions and groveling vices. Behold, I should answer, the natural effect of ignorance! The mind will ever be unstable that has only prejudices to rest on, and the current will run with destructive fury when there are no barriers to break its force. Women are told from their infancy, and taught by the example of their mothers, that a little knowledge of human weakness, justly termed cunning, softness of temper, *outward* obedience, and a scrupulous attention to a puerile kind of propriety, will obtain for them the protection of man; and should they be beautiful, everything else is needless, for at least twenty years of their lives. . . .

Men, indeed, appear to me to act in a very unphilosophical manner, when they try to secure the good conduct of women by attempting to keep them always in a state of childhood. Rousseau was more consistent when he wished to stop the progress of reason in both sexes, for if men eat of the tree of knowledge, women will come in for a taste; but, from the imperfect cultivation which their understandings now receive, they only attain a knowledge of evil. . . .

Women are therefore to be considered either as moral beings, or so weak that they must be entirely subjected to the superior faculties of men.

Let us examine this question. Rousseau declares that a woman should never for a moment feel herself independent, that she should be governed by fear to exercise her *natural* cunning, and made a coquettish slave in order to render her a more alluring object of desire, a *sweeter* companion to man, whenever he chose to relax himself. He carries the arguments, which he pretends to draw from the indications of nature, still further, and insinuates that truth and fortitude, the cornerstones of all human virtue, should be cultivated with certain restrictions, because, with respect to the female character, obedience is the grand lesson which ought to be impressed with unrelenting rigor.

What nonsense! When will a great man arise with sufficient strength of mind to puff away the fumes which pride and sensuality have thus spread over the subject? If women are by nature inferior to men, their virtues must be the same in quality, if not in degree, or virtue is a relative idea; consequently their conduct should be founded on the same principles, and have the same aim. . . .

Let it not be concluded that I wish to invert the order of things. I have already granted that, from the constitution of their bodies, men seemed to be designed by Providence to attain a greater degree of virtue.* I speak collectively of the whole sex; but I see not the shadow of a reason to conclude that their virtues should differ in respect to their nature. In fact, how

*Men have more passions to contend with than women: "From the constitution of their bodies" could mean men's difficulty with sexual continence, as well as their superior physical size.

can they, if virtue has only one eternal standard? I must therefore, if I reason consequentially, as strenuously maintain that they have the same simple direction as that there is a God.

It follows then that cunning should not be opposed to wisdom, little cares to great exertions, or insipid softness, varnished over with the name of gentleness, to that fortitude which grand views alone can inspire.

I shall be told that woman would then lose many of her peculiar graces, and the opinion of a well-known poet might be quoted to refute my unqualified assertion. For Pope has said, in the name of the whole male sex*:

> Yet ne'er so sure our passion to create,
> As when she touch'd the brink of all we hate.

In what light this sally places men and women I shall leave to the judicious to determine. Meanwhile, I shall content myself with observing, that I cannot discover why, unless they are mortal, females should always be degraded by being made subservient to love or lust.

To speak disrespectfully of love is, I know, high treason against sentiment and fine feelings; but I wish to speak the simple language of truth, and rather to address the head than the heart. To endeavor to reason love out of the world would be to out-Quixote Cervantes, and equally offend against common sense; but an endeavor to restrain this tumultuous passion, and to prove that it should not be allowed to dethrone superior powers, or to usurp the sceptre which the understanding should ever coolly wield, appears less wild.

Youth is the season for love in both sexes; but in those days of thoughtless enjoyment provision should be made for the more important years of life, when reflection takes place of sensation. But Rousseau, and most of the male writers who have followed his steps, have warmly inculcated that the whole tendency of female education ought to be directed to one point—to render them pleasing.

Let me reason with the supporters of this opinion who have any knowledge of human nature. Do they imagine that marriage can eradicate the habitude of life? The woman who has only been taught to please will soon find that her charms are oblique sunbeams, and that they cannot have much effect on her husband's heart when they are seen every day, when the summer is passed and gone. Will she then have sufficient native energy to look into herself for comfort, and cultivate her dormant faculties? or is it not more rational to expect that she will try to please other men, and, in the emotions raised by the experience of new conquests, endeavor to forget the mortification her love or pride has received? When the hus-

*Alexander Pope, *Moral Essays* II, 51–52.

band ceases to be a lover, and the time will inevitably come, her desire of pleasing will then grow languid, or become a spring of bitterness; and love, perhaps, the most evanescent of all passions, gives place to jealousy or vanity. . . .

As a philosopher, I read with indignation the plausible epithets which men use to soften their insults; and, as a moralist, I ask what is meant by such heterogeneous associations, as fair defects, amiable weaknesses, etc.?* If there be but one criterion of morals, but one archetype for man, women appear to be suspended by destiny, according to the vulgar tale of Mahomet's coffin†; they have neither the unerring instinct of brutes, nor are allowed to fix the eye of reason on a perfect model. They were made to be loved, and must not aim at respect, lest they should be hunted out of society as masculine.

But to view the subject in another point of view. Do passive indolent women make the best wives? Confining our discussion to the present moment of existence, let us see how such weak creatures perform their part? Do the women who, by the attainment of a few superficial accomplishments, have strengthened the prevailing prejudice, merely contribute to the happiness of their husbands? Do they display their charms merely to amuse them? And have women who have early imbibed notions of passive obedience, sufficient character to manage a family or educate children? So far from it, that, after surveying the history of woman, I cannot help agreeing with the severest satirist, considering the sex as the weakest as well as the most oppressed half of the species. What does history disclose but marks of inferiority, and how few women have emancipated themselves from the galling yoke of sovereign man? So few that the exceptions remind me of an ingenious conjecture respecting Newton— that he was probably a being of superior order accidentally caged in a human body.‡ Following the same train of thinking, I have been led to imagine that the few extraordinary women who have rushed in eccentrical directions out of the orbit prescribed to their sex, were *male* spirits, confined by mistake in female frames. But if it be not philosophical to think of sex when the soul is mentioned, the inferiority must depend on the organs; or the heavenly fire, which is to ferment the clay, is not given in equal portions.

But avoiding, as I have hitherto done, any direct comparison of the two sexes collectively, or frankly acknowledging the inferiority of woman,

---

Paradise Lost X. 891–92: "This fair defect/Of nature;" and Pope, *Moral Essays* II. 44: "Fine by defect, and delicately weak."

†Although entirely without foundation, a popular fable existed that Mahomet's coffin hung in the middle of his tomb, suspended by some magic of magnetism.

‡A possible reference to Pope's *Essay on Man* II. 31–34: "Superior beings when of late they saw/A mortal Man unfold all Nature's law,/Admir'd such wisdom in an earthly shape,/and shew'd a Newton as we shew an Ape."

according to the present appearance of things, I shall only insist that men have increased that inferiority till women are almost sunk below the standard of rational creatures. Let their faculties have room to unfold, and their virtues to gain strength, and then determine where the whole sex must stand in the intellectual scale. Yet let it be remembered that for a small number of distinguished women I do not ask a place. . . .

As to the argument respecting the subjection in which the sex has ever been held, it retorts on man. The many have always been enthralled by the few; and monsters, who scarcely have shown any discernment of human excellence, have tyrannized over thousands of their fellow creatures. Why have men of superior endowments submitted to such degradation? For, is it not universally acknowledged that kings, viewed collectively, have ever been inferior, in abilities and virtue, to the same number of men taken from the common mass of mankind—yet have they not, and are they not still treated with a degree of reverence that is an insult to reason? China is not the only country where a living man has been made a God.* *Men* have submitted to superior strength to enjoy with impunity the pleasure of the moment; *women* have only done the same, and therefore till it is proved that the courtier, who servilely resigns the birthright of a man, is not a moral agent, it cannot be demonstrated that woman is essentially inferior to man because she has always been subjugated. . .

The Same Subject Continued

. . . But should it be proved that woman is naturally weaker than man, whence does it follow that it is natural for her to labor to become still weaker than nature intended her to be? Arguments of this cast are an insult to common sense, and savor of passion. The *divine right* of husbands, like the divine right of kings, may, it is to be hoped, in this enlightened age, be contested without danger; and though conviction may not silence many boisterous disputants, yet, when any prevailing prejudice is attacked, the wise will consider, and leave the narrow-minded to rail with thoughtless vehemence at innovation. . . .

I wish to sum up what I have said in a few words, for I here throw down my gauntlet, and deny the existence of sexual virtues, not excepting modesty. For man and woman, truth, if I understand the meaning of the word, must be the same; yet the fanciful female character, so prettily drawn by poets and novelists, demanding the sacrifice of truth and sincerity, virtue becomes a relative idea, having no other foundation than utility, and of that utility men pretend arbitrarily to judge, shaping it to their own convenience.

---

*This could be either a reference to ancestor worship among most Chinese or an allusion to the emperor who is the vice-regent of heaven on earth.

Women, I allow, may have different duties to fulfil; but they are *human* duties, and the principles that should regulate the discharge of them, I sturdily maintain, must be the same.

To become respectable, the exercise of their understanding is necessary, there is no other foundation for independence of character; I mean explicitly to say that they must only bow to the authority of reason, instead of being the *modest* slaves of opinion.

In the superior ranks of life how seldom do we meet with a man of superior abilities, or even common acquirements? The reason appears to me clear, the state they are born in was an unnatural one. The human character has ever been formed by the employments the individual, or class, pursues; and if the faculties are not sharpened by necessity, they must remain obtuse. The argument may fairly be extended to women; for, seldom occupied by serious business, the pursuit of pleasure gives that insignificancy to their character which renders the society of the *great* so insipid. The same want of firmness, produced by a similar cause, forces them both to fly from themselves to noisy pleasures, and artificial passions, till vanity takes place of every social affection, and the characteristics of humanity can scarcely be discerned. Such are the blessings of civil governments, as they are at present organized, that wealth and female softness equally tend to debase mankind, and are produced by the same cause; but allowing women to be rational creatures, they should be incited to acquire virtues which they may call their own, for how can a rational being be ennobled by anything that is not obtained by its *own* exertions? . . .

A king is always a king, and a woman always a woman.* His authority and her sex ever stand between them and rational converse. With a lover, I grant, she should be so,† and her sensibility will naturally lead her to endeavor to excite emotion, not to gratify her vanity, but her heart. This I do not allow to be coquetry; it is the artless impulse of nature. I only exclaim against the sexual desire of conquest when the heart is out of the question. . . .

I lament that women are systematically degraded by receiving the trivial attentions which men think it manly to pay to the sex, when in fact, they are insultingly supporting their own superiority. It is not condescension to bow to an inferior. So ludicrous, in fact, do these ceremonies appear to me that I scarcely am able to govern my muscles when I see a man start with eager and serious solicitude to lift a handkerchief or shut a door, when the *lady* could have done it herself, had she only moved a pace or two.

---

*"And a wit, always a wit, might be added; for the vain fooleries of wits and beauties to obtain attention, and make conquests, are much upon a par" [Wollstonecraft's note].

†"She should be so" means, simply, a "woman" in the generally accepted sense of being incapable of rational converse.

A wild wish has just flown from my heart to my head, and I will not stifle it, though it may excite a horselaugh. I do earnestly wish to see the distinction of sex confounded in society, unless where love animates the behavior. For this distinction is, I am firmly persuaded, the foundation of the weakness of character ascribed to woman; is the cause why the understanding is neglected, whilst accomplishments are acquired with sedulous care; and the same cause accounts for their preferring the graceful before the heroic virtues. . . .

I am fully persuaded that we should hear of none of these infantine airs, if girls were allowed to take sufficient exercise, and not confined in close rooms till their muscles are relaxed, and their powers of digestion destroyed. To carry the remark still further, if fear in girls, instead of being cherished, perhaps, created, were treated in the same manner as cowardice in boys, we should quickly see women with more dignified aspects. It is true, they could not then with equal propriety be termed the sweet flowers that smile in the walk of man; but they would be more respectable members of society, and discharge the important duties of life by the light of their own reason. 'Educate women like men,' says Rousseau, 'and the more they resemble our sex the less power they will have over us.'* This is the very point I aim at. I do not wish them to have power over men; but over themselves. . . .

When I treat of the peculiar duties of women, as I should treat of the peculiar duties of a citizen or father, it will be found that I do not mean to insinuate that they should be taken out of their families, speaking of the majority. 'He that hath wife and children,' says Lord Bacon, 'hath given hostages to fortune; for they are impediments to great enterprises, either of virtue or mischief. Certainly the best works, and of greatest merit for the public, have proceeded from the unmarried or childless men.'† I say the same of women. But the welfare of society is not built on extraordinary exertions; and were it more reasonably organized, there would be still less need of great abilities, or heroic virtues.

In the regulation of a family, in the education of children, understanding, in an unsophisticated sense, is particularly required—strength both of body and mind; yet the men who, by their writings, have most earnestly labored to domesticate women, have endeavored, by arguments dictated by a gross appetite, which satiety had rendered fastidious, to weaken their bodies and cramp their minds. But, if even by these sinister methods they really *persuaded* women, by working on their feelings, to

---

*Emile, p. 327. Rousseau, of course, is not advocating equal education: having made the point that because of their sexual power over men, women are indeed the rulers, he is simply saying that if women were educated as men are, women would lose their sway, presumably an undesirable state of affairs for them.

†Francis Bacon, Essay VIII, "Of Marriage and the Single Life."

stay at home, and fulfil the duties of a mother and mistress of a family, I should cautiously oppose opinions that led women to right conduct, by prevailing on them to make the discharge of such important duties the main business of life, though reason were insulted. Yet, and I appeal to experience, if by neglecting the understanding they be as much, nay, more detached from these domestic employments, than they could be by the most serious intellectual pursuit, though it may be observed, that the mass of mankind will never vigorously pursue an intellectual object,* I may be allowed to infer that reason is absolutely necessary to enable a woman to perform any duty properly, and I must again repeat, that sensibility is not reason. . . .

Another argument that has had great weight with me must, I think, have some force with every considerate benevolent heart. Girls who have been thus weakly educated are often cruelly left by their parents without any provision, and, of course, are dependent on not only the reason, but the bounty of their brothers. These brothers are, to view the fairest side of the question, good sort of men, and give as a favor what children of the same parents had an equal right to. In this equivocal humiliating situation a docile female may remain some time with a tolerable degree of comfort. But when the brother marries—a probable circumstance—from being considered as the mistress of the family, she is viewed with averted looks as an intruder, an unnecessary burden on the benevolence of the master of the house and his new partner.†

Who can recount the misery which many unfortunate beings, whose minds and bodies are equally weak, suffer in such situations—unable to work, and ashamed to beg? The wife, a cold-hearted, narrow-minded woman—and this is not an unfair supposition, for the present mode of education does not tend to enlarge the heart any more than the understanding—is jealous of the little kindness which her husband shows to his relations; and her sensibility not rising to humanity, she is displeased at seeing the property of *her* children lavished on a helpless sister.

These are matters of fact, which have come under my eye again and again. The consequence is obvious; the wife has recourse to cunning to undermine the habitual affection which she is afraid openly to oppose; and neither tears nor caresses are spared till the spy is worked out of her home, and thrown on the world, unprepared for its difficulties; or sent, as a great effort of generosity, or from some regard to propriety, with a small stipend, and an uncultivated mind, into joyless solitude.

---

*The mass of mankind are rather the slaves of their appetites than of their passions [Wollstonecraft's note].

†Wollstonecraft may have in mind the situation of her sister Everina who, before Mary Wollstonecraft helped to make her independent, had been living off their brother Edward.

These two women may be much upon a par with respect to reason and humanity, and, changing situations, might have acted just the same self-ish part; but had they been differently educated, the case would also have been very different. The wife would not have had that sensibility, of which self is the center, and reason might have taught her not to expect, and not even to be flattered by, the affection of her husband, if it led him to violate prior duties. She would wish not to love him merely because he loved her, but on account of his virtues; and the sister might have been able to struggle for herself instead of eating the bitter bread of depend-ence. . . .

Mankind seem to agree that children should be left under the manage-ment of women during their childhood. Now, from all the observation that I have been able to make, women of sensibility are the most unfit for this task, because they will infallibly, carried away by their feelings, spoil a child's temper. The management of the temper, the first, and most im-portant branch of education, requires the sober steady eye of reason; a plan of conduct equally distant from tyranny and indulgence: yet these are the extremes that people of sensibility alternately fall into; always shoot-ing beyond the mark. I have followed this train of reasoning much fur-ther, till I have concluded, that a person of genius is the most improper person to be employed in education, public or private. Minds of this rare species see things too much in masses, and seldom, if ever, have a good temper. That habitual cheerfulness, termed good humor, is, perhaps, as seldom united with great mental powers, as with strong feelings. And those people who follow, with interest and admiration, the flights of gen-ius; or, with cooler approbation suck in the instruction which has been elaborately prepared for them by the profound thinker, ought not to be disgusted, if they find the former choleric, and the latter morose; because liveliness of fancy, and a tenacious comprehension of mind, are scarcely compatible with that pliant urbanity which leads a man, at least, to bend to the opinions and prejudices of others, instead of roughly confronting them. . . .

Still, highly as I respect marriage, as the foundation of almost every social virtue, I cannot avoid feeling the most lively compassion for those unfortunate females who are broken off from society, and by one error torn from all those affections and relationships that improve the heart and mind. It does not frequently even deserve the name of error; for many innocent girls become the dupes of a sincere, affectionate heart, and still more are, as it may emphatically be termed, *ruined* before they know the difference between virtue and vice, and thus prepared by their education for infamy, they become infamous. Asylums and Magdalens* are not the

*Institutions for the reformation of prostitutes.

proper remedies for these abuses. It is justice, not charity, that is wanting in the world!

A woman who has lost her honor imagines that she cannot fall lower, and as for recovering her former station, it is impossible; no exertion can wash this stain away. Losing thus every spur, and having no other means of support, prostitution becomes her only refuge, and the character is quickly depraved by circumstances over which the poor wretch has little power, unless she possesses an uncommon portion of sense and loftiness of spirit. Necessity never makes prostitution the business of men's lives; though numberless are the women who are thus rendered systematically vicious. This, however, arises in a great degree from the state of idleness in which women are educated, who are always taught to look up to man for a maintenance, and to consider their persons as the proper return for his exertions to support them. Meretricious airs, and the whole science of wantonness, have then a more powerful stimulus than either appetite or vanity; and this remark gives force to the prevailing opinion, that with chastity all is lost that is respectable in woman. Her character depends on the observance of one virtue, though the only passion fostered in her heart is love. Nay, the honor of a woman is not made even to depend on her will. . .

Animadversions on Some of the Writers Who Have Rendered Women Objects of Pity, Bordering on Contempt

. . . Rousseau would carry his male aristocracy still further, for he insinuates, that he should not blame those, who contend for leaving woman in a state of the most profound ignorance, if it were not necessary in order to preserve her chastity and justify the man's choice, in the eyes of the world, to give her a little knowledge of men, and the customs produced by human passions; else she might propagate at home without being rendered less voluptuous and innocent by the exercise of her understanding: excepting, indeed, during the first year of marriage, when she might employ it to dress like Sophia. 'Her dress is extremely modest in appearance, and yet very coquettish in fact: she does not make a display of her charms, she conceals them; but in concealing them, she knows how to affect your imagination. Everyone who sees her will say, There is a modest and discreet girl; but while you are near her, your eyes and affections wander all over her person, so that you cannot withdraw them; and you would conclude, that every part of her dress, simple as it seems, was only put in its proper order to be taken to pieces by the imagination.' Is this modesty? Is this a preparation for immortality? Again, What opinion are we to form of a system of education, when the author says of his heroine, 'that with her, doing things well, is but a *secondary* concern; her principal concern is to do them *neatly*.'

Secondary, in fact, are all her virtues and qualities, for, respecting religion, he makes her parents thus address her, accustomed to submission—'Your husband will instruct you in good time.'

After thus cramping a woman's mind, if, in order to keep it fair, he have not made it quite a blank, he advises her to reflect, that a reflecting man may not yawn in her company, when he is tired of caressing her. What has she to reflect about who must obey? and would it not be a refinement on cruelty only to open her mind to make the darkness and misery of her fate *visible*? Yet these are his sensible remarks; how consistent with what I have already been obliged to quote, to give a fair view of the subject, the reader may determine. . . .

I now appeal from the reveries of fancy and refined licentiousness to the good sense of mankind, whether, if the object of education be to prepare women to become chaste wives and sensible mothers, the method so plausibly recommended in the foregoing sketch be the one best calculated to produce those ends? Will it be allowed that the surest way to make a wife chaste is to teach her to practise the wanton arts of a mistress, termed virtuous coquetry, by the sensualist who can no longer relish the artless charms of sincerity, or taste the pleasure arising from a tender intimacy, when confidence is unchecked by suspicion, and rendered interesting by sense?

The man who can be contented to live with a pretty, useful companion, without a mind, has lost in voluptuous gratifications a taste for more refined enjoyments; he has never felt the calm satisfaction that refreshes the parched heart like the silent dew of heaven—of being beloved by one who could understand him. In the society of his wife he is still alone, unless when the man is sunk in the brute. 'The charm of life,' says a grave philosophical reasoner, is 'sympathy; nothing pleases us more than to observe in other men a fellow feeling with all the emotions of our own breast,'*

But according to the tenor of reasoning by which women are kept from the tree of knowledge, the important years of youth, the usefulness of age, and the rational hopes of futurity, are all to be sacrificed to render women an object of desire for a *short* time. Besides, how could Rousseau expect them to be virtuous and constant when reason is neither allowed to be the foundation of their virtue, nor truth the object of their inquiries? . . .

Woman in particular, whose virtue† is built on mutable prejudices, seldom attains to this greatness of mind; so that, becoming the slave of her own feelings, she is easily subjugated by those of others. Thus degraded, her reason, her misty reason! is employed rather to burnish than to snap her chains.

*Adam Smith, *The Theory of Moral Sentiments, op. cit.*, p. 10.
†"I mean to use a word that comprehends more than chastity the sexual virtue" [Wollstonecraft's note].

Indignantly have I heard women argue in the same track as men, and adopt the sentiments that brutalize them, with all the pertinacity of ignorance. . . .

Whilst women avow, and act up to such opinions, their understandings, at least, deserve the contempt and obloquy that men, *who never* insult their persons, have pointedly leveled at the female mind. And it is the sentiments of these polite men, who do not wish to be encumbered with mind, that vain women thoughtlessly adopt. Yet they should know, that insulted reason alone can spread that *sacred* reserve about the person, which renders human affections, for human affections have always some base alloy, as permanent as is consistent with the grand end of existence—the attainment of virtue.

The Baroness de Staël* speaks the same language with more enthusiasm. Her eulogium on Rousseau was accidentally put into my hands, and her sentiments, the sentiments of too many of my sex, may serve as the text for a few comments. 'Though Rousseau,' she observes, 'has endeavored to prevent women from interfering in public affairs, and acting a brilliant part in the theatre of politics; yet in speaking of them, how much has he done it to their satisfaction! If he wished to deprive them of some rights foreign to their sex, how has he forever restored to them all those to which it has a claim! And in attempting to diminish their influence over the deliberations of men, how sacredly has he established the empire they have over their happiness! In aiding them to descend from an usurped throne, he has firmly seated them upon that to which they were destined by nature; and though he be full of indignation against them when they endeavor to resemble men, yet when they come before him with all the *charms, weaknesses, virtues,* and *errors* of their sex, his respect for their *persons* amounts almost to adoration!' True! For never was there a sensualist who paid more fervent adoration at the shrine of beauty. So devout, indeed, was his respect for the person, that excepting the virtue of chastity, for obvious reasons, he only wished to see it embellished by charms, weaknesses, and errors. he was afraid lest the austerity of reason should disturb the soft playfulness of love. The master wished to have a meretricious slave to fondle, entirely dependent on his reason and bounty; he did not want a companion, whom he should be compelled to esteem, or a friend to whom he could confide the care of his children's education, should death deprive them of their father, before he had fulfilled the sacred task. He denies woman reason, shuts her out from knowledge, and turns her aside from truth; yet his pardon is granted, because 'he admits the passion of love.' It would require some ingenuity to show why

*Madame de Staël (born Anne Louise Germaine Necker), daughter of the finance minister of France, was an essayist and novelist. Wollstonecraft's citations are all from Mme. La Baronne de Staël, "Letters sur les Ecrits et le Caractère de J. J. Rousseau," in *Oeuvers Complétes* (Paris, 1820), I, 20–21.

women were to be under such an obligation to him for thus admitting love; when it is clear that he admits it only for the relaxation of men, and to perpetuate the species; but he talked with passion, and that powerful spell worked on the sensibility of a young ecomiast. 'What signifies it,' pursues this rhapsodist, 'to women, that his reason disputes with them the empire, when his heart is devotedly theirs.' It is not empire, but equality, that they should contend for. Yet, if they only wished to lengthen out their sway, they should not entirely trust to their persons, for though beauty may gain a heart, it cannot keep it, even while the beauty is in full bloom, unless the mind lend, at least, some graces.

When women are once sufficiently enlightened to discover their real interest, on a grand scale, they will, I am persuaded, be very ready to resign all the prerogatives of love, that are not mutual, speaking of them as lasting prerogatives, for the calm satisfaction of friendship, and the tender confidence of habitual esteem. Before marriage they will not assume any insolent airs, or afterwards abjectly submit; but endeavoring to act like reasonable creatures, in both situations, they will not be tumbled from a throne to a stool. . .

The Effect Which an Early Association of Ideas Has upon the Character

. . . Love is, in a great degree, an arbitrary passion, and will reign, like some other stalking mischiefs, by its own authority, without deigning to reason; and it may also be easily distinguished from esteem, the foundation of friendship, because it is often excited by evanescent beauties and graces, though, to give an energy to the sentiment, something more solid must deepen their impression and set the imagination to work, to make the most fair—the first good. . . .

Were women more rationally educated, could they take a more comprehensive view of things, they would be contented to love but once in their lives; and after marriage calmly let passion subside into friendship— into that tender intimacy, which is the best refuge from care; yet is built on such pure, still affections, that idle jealousies would not be allowed to disturb the discharge of the sober duties of life, or to engross the thoughts that ought to be otherwise employed. This is a state in which many men live; but few, very few, women. And the difference may easily be accounted for, without recurring to a sexual character. Men, for whom we are told women were made, have too much occupied the thoughts of women; and this association has so entangled love with all their motives of action; and, to harp a little on an old string, having been solely employed either to prepare themselves to excite love, or actually putting their lessons in practice, they cannot live without love. But, when a sense of duty, or fear of shame, obliges them to restrain this pampered desire of pleasing beyond certain lengths, too far for delicacy, it is true, though far from criminality, they obstinately determine to love, I speak of the passion, their husbands to the end of the chapter—and then acting the part which they foolishly exacted from their lovers, they become abject wooers and fond slaves. . . .

Morality Undermined by Sexual Notions of the Importance of a Good Reputation

It has long since occurred to me that advice respecting behavior, and all the various modes of preserving a good reputation, which have been so strenuously inculcated on the female world, were specious poisons, that encrusting morality eat away the substance. And, that this measuring of shadows produced a false calculation, because their length depends so much on the height of the sun, and other adventitious circumstances.

Whence arises the easy fallacious behavior of a courtier? From his situation, undoubtedly: for standing in need of dependents, he is obliged to learn the art of denying without giving offence, and, of evasively feeding hope with the chameleon's food*: thus does politeness sport with truth, and eating away the sincerity and humanity native to man, produce the fine gentleman.

Women likewise acquire from a supposed necessity, an equally artificial mode of behavior. Yet truth is not with impunity to be sported with, for the practiced dissembler, at last become the dupe of his own arts, loses that sagacity, which has been justly termed common sense; namely a quick perception of common truths: which are constantly received as such by the unsophisticated mind, though it might not have had sufficient energy to discover them itself when obscured by local prejudices. The greater number of people take their opinions on trust to avoid the trouble of exercising their own minds, and these indolent beings naturally adhere to the letter rather than the spirit of a law, divine or human. 'Women,' says some author, I cannot recollect who, 'mind not what only Heaven sees.' Why, indeed, should they? it is the eye of man that they have been taught to dread—and if they can lull their Argus† to sleep, they seldom think of Heaven or themselves, because their reputation is safe; and it is reputation, not chastity and all its fair train, that they are employed to keep free from spot, not as a virtue, but to preserve their station in the world. . . .

---

*Because this lizard seemed almost inanimate, it was supposed to live on air.

†According to Greek myth, Zeus fell in love with Io and changed her into a heifer to conceal her from his wife, Hera; Hera set Argus, a monster with a hundred eyes, to guard Io.

Of the Pernicious Effects Which Arise from the Unnatural Distinctions Established in Society

. . . It is vain to expect virtue from women till they are in some degree independent of men; nay, it is vain to expect that strength of natural affection which would make them good wives and mothers. Whilst they are absolutely dependent on their husbands, they will be cunning, mean, and selfish; and the men who can be gratified by the fawning fondness of spaniel-like affection have not much delicacy, for love is not to be bought, in any sense of the words, its silken wings are instantly shrivelled up when anything beside a return in kind is sought. Yet whilst wealth enervates men, and women live, as it were, by their personal charms, how can we expect them to discharge those ennobling duties which equally require exertion and self-denial? Hereditary property sophisticates* the mind, and the unfortunate victims to it—if I may so express myself—swathed from their birth, seldom exert the locomotive faculty of body or mind, and thus viewing everything through one medium, and that a false one, they are unable to discern in what true merit and happiness consist. False, indeed, must be the light when the drapery of situation hides the man, and makes him stalk in masquerade, dragging from one scene of dissipation to another the nerveless limbs that hang with stupid listlessness, and rolling round the vacant eye, which plainly tells us that there is no mind at home. . . .

Women are, in common with men, rendered weak and luxurious by the relaxing pleasures which wealth procures; but added to this they are made slaves to their persons, and must render them alluring that man may lend them his reason to guide their tottering steps aright. Or should they be ambitious, they must govern their tyrants by sinister tricks, for without rights there cannot be any incumbent duties. The laws respecting woman, which I mean to discuss in a future part, make an absurd unit of a man and his wife†; and then, by the easy transition of only considering him as responsible, she is reduced to a mere cipher.

The being who discharges the duties of its station is independent; and speaking of women at large, their first duty is to themselves as rational creatures, and the next, in point of importance, as citizens, is that, which includes so many, of a mother. The rank in life which dispenses with their fulfilling this duty, necessarily degrades them by making them mere dolls. Or should they turn to something more important than merely fitting drapery upon a smooth block, their minds are only occupied by some soft platonic attachment; or the actual management of an intrigue may

---

*Corrupts.

†According to the concept of *couverture* in English common law of the period, a husband and wife were one legal unit, and the responsible legal person was the husband.

keep their thoughts in motion; for when they neglect domestic duties, they have it not in their power to take the field and march and counter-march like soldiers, or wrangle in the senate to keep their faculties from rusting.

I know that, as a proof of the inferiority of the sex, Rousseau has exult-ingly exclaimed, How can they leave the nursery for the camp! And the camp has by some moralists been termed the school of the most heroic virtues; though I think it would puzzle a keen casuist to prove the reasona-bleness of the greater number of wars that have dubbed heroes. I do not mean to consider this question critically; because, having frequently viewed these freaks of ambition as the first natural mode of civilization, when the ground must be torn up, and the woods cleared by fire and sword, I do not choose to call them pests; but surely the present system of war has little connection with virtue of any denomination, being rather the school of *finesse* and effeminacy than of fortitude.

Yet, if defensive war, the only justifiable war, in the present advanced state of society, where virtue can show its face and ripen amidst the rigors which purify the air on the mountain's top, were alone to be adopted as just and glorious, the true heroism of antiquity might again animate fe-male bosoms. But fair and softly, gentle reader, male or female, do not alarm thyself, for though I have compared the character of a modern sol-dier with that of a civilized woman, I am not going to advise them to turn their distaff into a musket, though I sincerely wish to see the bayonet con-verted into a pruning hook. I only recreated an imagination, fatigued by contemplating the vices and follies which all proceed from a feculent stream of wealth that has muddied the pure rills of natural affection, by supposing that society will some time or other be so constituted, that man must necessarily fulfil the duties of a citizen, or be despised, and that while he was employed in any of the departments of civil life, his wife, also an active citizen, should be equally intent to manage her family, edu-cate her children, and assist her neighbors.

But to render her really virtuous and useful, she must not, if she dis-charge her civil duties, want individually the protection of civil laws; she must not be dependent on her husband's bounty for her subsistence during his life, or support after his death; for how can a being be generous who has nothing of its own? or virtuous who is not free? The wife, in the pres-ent state of things, who is faithful to her husband, and neither suckles nor educates her children, scarcely deserves the name of a wife, and has no right to that of a citizen. But take away natural rights, and duties become null. . . .

But what have women to do in society? I may be asked, but to loiter with easy grace; surely you would not condemn them all to suckle fools and chronicle small beer!* No. Women might certainly study the art of

*Othello, II. i. 160.

healing and be physicians as well as nurses. And midwifery, decency seems to allot to them though I am afraid the word midwife, in our dictionaries, will soon give place to *accoucheur,** and one proof of the former delicacy of the sex be effaced from the language.

They might also study politics, and settle their benevolence on the broadest basis; for the reading of history will scarcely be more useful than the perusal of romances, if read as mere biography; if the character of the times, the political improvements, arts, etc., be not observed. In short, if it be not considered as the history of man; and not of particular men, who filled a niche in the temple of fame, and dropped into the black rolling stream of time, that silently sweeps all before it into the shapeless void called—eternity.—For shape, can it be called, 'that shape hath none'?†

Business of various kinds, they might likewise pursue, if they were educated in a more orderly manner, which might save many from common and legal prostitution. Women would not then marry for a support, as men accept of places under Government, and neglect the implied duties; nor would an attempt to earn their own subsistence, a most laudable one! sink them almost to the level of those poor abandoned creatures who live by prostitution. For are not milliners and mantua-makers‡ reckoned the next class? The few employments open to women, so far from being liberal, are menial; and when a superior education enables them to take charge of the education of children as governesses, they are not treated like the tutors of sons, though even clerical tutors are not always treated in a manner calculated to render them respectable in the eyes of their pupils, to say nothing of the private comfort of the individual. But as women educated like gentlewomen are never designed for the humiliating situation which necessity sometimes forces them to fill, these situations are considered in the light of a degradation; and they know little of the human heart, who need to be told, that nothing so painfully sharpens sensibility as such a fall in life.¶

Some of these women might be restrained from marrying by a proper spirit of delicacy, and others may not have had it in their power to escape in this pitiful way from servitude; is not that Government then very defective, and very unmindful of the happiness of one-half of its members, that does not provide for honest, independent women, by encouraging them to fill respectable stations? But in order to render their private virtue a public benefit, they must have a civil existence in the State, married or single; else we shall continually see some worthy woman, whose sensibility has been rendered painfully acute by undeserved contempt, droop like 'the lily broken down by a plowshare.'

*A male physician who presides at childbirth.
†*Paradise Lost* II. 666–667.
‡Dressmakers.
¶Wollstonecraft had spent one year as governess to the older daughters of the Viscount Kingsborough, County Cork, Ireland.

It is a melancholy truth; yet such is the blessed effect of civilization! the most respectable women are the most oppressed; and, unless they have understandings far superior to the common run of understandings, taking in both sexes, they must, from being treated like contemptible beings, become contemptible. How many women thus waste life away the prey of discontent, who might have practiced as physicians, regulated a farm, managed a shop, and stood erect, supported by their own industry, instead of hanging their heads surcharged with the dew of sensibility, that consumes the beauty to which it at first gave lustre; nay, I doubt whether pity and love are so near akin as poets feign, for I have seldom seen much compassion excited by the helplessness of females, unless they were fair; then, perhaps, pity was the soft handmaid of love, or the harbinger of lust. . . .

On National Education

. . . Let men take their choice. Man and woman were made for each other, though not to become one being; and if they will not improve women, they will deprave them.

I speak of the improvement and emancipation of the whole sex, for I know that the behavior of a few women, who, by accident, or following a strong bent of nature, have acquired a portion of knowledge superior to that of the rest of their sex, has often been overbearing; but there have been instances of women who, attaining knowledge, have not discarded modesty, nor have they always pedantically appeared to despise the ignorance which they labored to disperse in their own minds. The exclamations then which any advice respecting female learning commonly produces, especially from pretty women, often arise from envy. When they chance to see that even the luster of their eyes, and the flippant sportiveness of refined coquetry, will not always secure them attention during a whole evening, should a woman of a more cultivated understanding endeavor to give a rational turn to the conversation, the common source of consolation is that such women seldom get husbands. What arts have I not seen silly women use to interrupt by *flirtation*—a very significant word to describe such a maneuver—a rational conversation, which made the men forget that they were pretty women.

But, allowing what is very natural to man, that the possession of rare abilities is really calculated to excite overweening pride, disgusting in both men and women, in what a state of inferiority must the female faculties have rusted when such a small portion of knowledge as those women attained, who have sneeringly been termed learned women, could be singular?—sufficiently so to puff up the possessor, and excite envy in her contemporaries, and some of the other sex. Nay, has not a little rationality exposed many women to the severest censure? I advert to well-known facts, for I have frequently heard women ridiculed, and every little weakness exposed, only because they adopted the advice of some medical men, and deviated from the beaten track in their mode of treating their infants.* I have actually heard this barbarous aversion to innovation carried still further, and a sensible woman stigmatized as an unnatural mother, who has thus been wisely solicitous to preserve the health of the children, when in the midst of her care she has lost one by some of the casualties of infancy, which no prudence can ward off. Her acquaintance have observed that this was the consequence of new-fangled notions—the new-fangled notions of ease and cleanliness. And those who pretending to experience, though they have long adhered to prejudices that have, according to the opinion of the most sagacious physicians, thinned the human race, almost rejoiced at the disaster that gave a kind of sanction to prescription. . . .

Some Instances of the Folly Which the Ignorance of Women Generates with Concluding Reflections on the Moral Improvement That a Revolution in Female Manners Might Naturally Be Expected to Produce

Women are supposed to possess more sensibility, and even humanity, than men, and their strong attachments and instantaneous emotions of compassion are given as proofs; but the clinging affection of ignorance has seldom anything noble in it, and may mostly be resolved into selfishness, as well as the affection of children and brutes. I have known many weak women whose sensibility was entirely engrossed by their husbands; and as for their humanity, it was very faint indeed, or rather it was only a transient emotion of compassion. Humanity does not consist 'in a squeamish ear,' says an eminent orator. 'It belongs to the mind as well as the nerves.'

But this kind of exclusive affection, though it degrades the individual, should not be brought forward as a proof of the inferiority of the sex, because it is the natural consequence of confined views; for even women of superior sense, having their attention turned to little employments, and private plans, rarely rise to heroism, unless when spurred on by love! and love, as an heroic passion, like genius, appears but once in an age. I therefore agree with the moralist who asserts, 'that women have seldom so much generosity as men'†; and that their narrow affections, to which justice and humanity are often sacrificed, render the sex apparently infe-

---

*That is, in suckling their own children rather than giving them to peasant women to nurse.

†Adam Smith, *Theory of Moral Sentiments,* p. 274: "Humanity is the virtue of a woman, generosity of a man. The fair sex, who have commonly much more tenderness than ours, have seldom so much generosity."

rior, especially as they are commonly inspired by men; but I contend that the heart would expand as the understanding gained strength, if women were not depressed from their cradles.

I know that a little sensibility, and great weakness, will produce a strong sexual attachment, and that reason must cement friendship; consequently, I allow that more friendship is to be found in the male than the female world, and that men have a higher sense of justice. The exclusive affections of women seem indeed to resemble Cato's most unjust love for his country. He wished to crush Carthage, not to save Rome, but to promote his vainglory; and, in general, it is to similar principles that humanity is sacrificed, for genuine duties support each other.

Besides, how can women be just or generous, when they are the slaves of injustice? . . .

Asserting the rights which women in common with men ought to contend for, I have not attempted to extenuate their faults; but to prove them to be the natural consequence of their education and station in society. If so, it is reasonable to suppose that they will change their character, and correct their vices and follies, when they are allowed to be free in a physical, moral, and civil sense.*

Let woman share the rights, and she will emulate the virtues of man; for she must grow more perfect when emancipated, or justify the authority that chains such a weak being to her duty. If the latter, it will be expedient to open a fresh trade with Russia for whips: a present which a father should always make his son-in-law on his wedding day, that a husband may keep his whole family in order by the same means; and without any violation of justice reign, wielding this scepter, sole master of his house, because he is the only thing in it who has reason: the divine, indefeasible earthly sovereignty breathed into man by the Master of the universe. Allowing this position, women have not any inherent rights to claim; and, by the same rule, their duties vanish, for rights and duties are inseparable.

*"I had further enlarged on the advantages which might reasonably be expected to result from an improvement in female manners, towards the general reformation of society; but it appeared to me that such reflections would more properly close the last volume" [Wollstonecraft's note].

Immanuel Kant

East Prussian Critical philosopher, 1724–1804. Although his life was uneventful, Kant's writings on metaphysics, epistemology, ethics, esthetics, law, and anthropology brought him recognition and made him the best known professor in Germany—even without his leaving his home town of Königsberg.

From *The Philosophy of Law*

Monogamy and Equality in Marriage.

. . . The relation of the married persons to each other is a relation of *equality* as regards the mutual possession of their persons, as well as of their goods. Consequently marriage is only truly realized in *monogamy;* for in the relation of polygamy the person who is given away on the one side, gains only a part of the one to whom that person is given up, and therefore becomes a mere *res.* But in respect of their goods, they have severally the right to renounce the use of any part of them, although only by a special contract.

. . . The question may be raised as to whether it is not contrary to the equality of married persons when the law says in any way of the husband in relation to the wife, 'he shall be thy master,' so that he is represented as the one who commands, and she as the one who obeys. This, however, cannot be regarded as contrary to the natural equality of a human pair, if such legal supremacy is based only upon the natural superiority of the faculties of the husband compared with the wife, in the effectuation of the common interest of the household; and if the right to command, is based merely upon this fact. For this right may thus be deduced from the very duty of unity and equality in relation to the *end* involved. . . .

The Legislative Power and the Members of the State

The capability of voting by possession of the suffrage properly constitutes the political qualification of a citizen as a member of the state. But this, again, presupposes the independence or self-sufficiency of the individual citizen among the people, as one who is not a mere incidental part of the commonwealth, but a member of it acting of his own will in community with others. The last of the three qualities involved necessarily constitutes the distinction between *active* and *passive* citizenship; although the latter conception appears to stand in contradiction to the definition of a citizen as such. The following examples may serve to remove this difficulty. The apprentice of a merchant or tradesman, a servant who is not in the employ of the state, a minor (*naturaliter vel civiliter*), all women, and, generally, everyone who is compelled to maintain himself not according to his own industry, but as it is arranged by others (the State excepted), are without civil personality, and their existence is only, as it were, incidentally included in the state. The woodcutter whom I employ on my estate; the smith in India who carries his hammer, anvil, and bellows into the houses where he is engaged to work in iron, as distinguished from the european carpenter or smith, who can offer the independent products of his labor as wares for public sale; the resident tutor as distinguished from the schoolmaster; the plowman as distinguished from the farmer and such like, illustrate the distinction in question. In all these cases the former members of the contrast are distinguished from the latter by being mere subsidiaries of the commonwealth and not active independent members of it, because they are of necessity commanded and protected by others, and consequently possess no political self-sufficiency in themselves. Such dependence on the will of others and the consequent inequality are, however, not inconsistent with the freedom and equality of the individuals *as men* helping to constitute the people. Much rather is it the case that it is only under such conditions, that a people can become a state and enter into a civil constitution. But all are not equally qualified to exercise the right of the suffrage under the constitution, and to be full citizens of the state, and not mere passive subjects under its protection. For, although they are entitled to demand to be treated by all the other citizens according to laws of natural freedom and equality, as *passive* parts of the state, it does not follow that they ought themselves to have the right to deal with the state as active members of it, to reorganize it, or to take action by way of introducing certain laws. All they have a right in their circumstances to claim may be no more than that whatever be the mode in which the positive laws are enacted, these laws must not be contrary to the natural laws that demand the freedom of all the people and the equality that is conformable thereto; and it must therefore be made possible for them to raise themselves from this passive condition in the state, to the condition of active citizenship. . . .

From *Observations on the Feeling of the Beautiful and Sublime*

Of the Distinction of the Beautiful and Sublime in the Interrelations of the Two Sexes

He who first conceived of woman under the name of the *fair sex* probably wanted to say something flattering, but he has hit upon it better than even he himself might have believed. For without taking into consideration that her figure in general is finer, her features more delicate and gentler, and her mien more engaging and more expressive of friendliness, pleasantry, and kindness than in the male sex, and not forgetting what one must reckon as a secret magic with which she makes our passion inclined to judgments favorable to her—even so, certain specific traits lie especially in the personality of this sex which distinguish it clearly from ours and chiefly result in making her known by the mark of the beautiful. On the other side, we could make a claim on the title of the *noble sex,* if it were not required of a noble disposition to decline honorific titles and rather to bestow than to receive them. It is not to be understood by this that woman lacks noble qualities, or that the male sex must do without beauty completely. On the contrary, one expects that a person of either sex brings both together, in such a way that all the other merits of a woman should unite solely to enhance the character of the beautiful, which is the proper reference point; and on the other hand, among the masculine qualities the sublime clearly stands out as the criterion of his kind. All judgments of the two sexes must refer to these criteria, those that praise as well as those that blame; all education and instruction must have these before its eyes, and all efforts to advance the moral perfection of the one or the other—unless one wants to disguise the charming distinction that nature has chosen to make between the two sorts of human being. For here it is not enough to keep in mind that we are dealing with human beings; we must also remember that they are not all alike.

Women have a strong inborn feeling for all that is beautiful, elegant, and decorated. Even in childhood they like to be dressed up, and take pleasure when they are adorned. They are cleanly and very delicate in respect to all that provokes disgust. They love pleasantry and can be entertained by trivialities if only these are merry and laughing. Very early they have a modest manner about themselves, know how to give themselves a fine demeanor and be self-possessed—and this at an age when our well-bred male youth is still unruly, clumsy, and confused. They have many sympathetic sensations, goodheartedness, and compassion, prefer the beautiful to the useful, and gladly turn abundance of circumstance into parsimony, in order to support expenditure on adornment and glitter. They have very delicate feelings in regard to the least offense, and are exceedingly precise to notice the most trifling lack of attention and respect toward them. In short, they contain the chief cause in human nature for the contrast of the beautiful qualities with the noble, and they refine even the masculine sex.

I hope the reader will spare me the reckoning of the manly qualities, so far as they are parallel to the feminine, and be content only to consider both in comparison with each other. The fair sex has just as much understanding as the male, but it is a *beautiful understanding*, whereas ours should be a *deep understanding*, an expression that signifies identity with the sublime.

To the beauty of all actions belongs above all the mark that they display facility, and appear to be accomplished without painful toil. On the other hand, strivings and surmounted difficulties arouse admiration and belong to the sublime. Deep meditation and a long-sustained reflection are noble but difficult, and do not well befit a person in whom unconstrained charms should show nothing else than a beautiful nature. Laborious learning or painful pondering, even if a woman should greatly succeed in it, destroy the merits that are proper to her sex, and because of their rarity they can make of her an object of cold admiration; but at the same time they will weaken the charms with which she exercises her great power over the other sex. A woman who has a head full of Greek . . . or carries on fundamental controversies about mechanics . . . might as well even have a beard; for perhaps that would express more obviously the mien of profundity for which she strives. The beautiful understanding selects for its objects everything closely related to the finer feeling, and relinquishes to the diligent, fundamental, and deep understanding abstract speculations or branches of knowledge useful but dry. A woman therefore will learn no geometry; of the principle of sufficient reason or the monads she will know only so much as is needed to perceive the salt in a satire which the insipid grubs of our sex have censured. The fair can leave Descartes his vortices to whirl forever without troubling themselves about them, even though the suave Fontenelle wished to afford them company among the planets and the attraction of their charms loses none of its strength even if they know nothing of . . . the gravitational attraction of matter according to Newton. In history they will not fill their heads with battles, nor in geography with fortresses, for it becomes them just as little to reek of gunpowder as it does the males to reek of musk. . . .

The virtue of a woman is a *beautiful virtue*. That of the male sex should be a *noble virtue*. Women will avoid the wicked not because it is unright, but because it is ugly; and virtuous actions mean to them such as are morally beautiful. Nothing of duty, nothing of compulsion, nothing of obligation! Woman is intolerant of all commands and all morose constraint. They do something only because it pleases them, and the art consists in making only that please them which is good. I hardly believe that the fair sex is capable of principles, and I hope by that not to offend, for these are also extremely rare in the male. But in place of it Providence has put in their breast kind and benevolent sensations, a fine feeling for propriety, and a complaisant soul. One should not at all demand sacrifices and generous self-restraint. A man must never tell his wife if he risks a part of his fortune on behalf of a friend. Why should he fetter her merry talkativeness by burdening her mind with a weighty secret whose keeping lies solely upon him? Even many of her weaknesses are, so to speak, *beautiful faults*. Offense or misfortune moves her tender soul to sadness. A man must never weep other than magnanimous tears. Those he sheds in pain or over circumstances of fortune make him contemptible. *Vanity,* for which one reproaches the fair sex so frequently, so far as it is a fault in that sex, yet is only a beautiful fault. For—not to mention that the men who so gladly flatter a woman would be left in a strait if she were not inclined to take it well—by that they actually enliven their charms. This inclination is an impulse to exhibit pleasantness and good demeanor, to let her merry wit play, to radiate through the changing devices of dress, and to heighten her beauty. Now in this there is not at all any offensiveness toward others, but rather so much courtesy, if it is done with good taste, that to scold against it with peevish rebukes is very ill-bred. A woman who is too inconstant and deceitful is called a coquette; which expression yet has not so harsh a meaning as what, with a changed syllable, is applied to man, so that if we understand each other, it can sometimes indicate a familiar flattery. If vanity is a fault that in a woman much merits excuse, a *haughty bearing* is not only as reproachable in her as in people in general, but completely disfigures the character of her sex. For this quality is exceedingly stupid and ugly, and is set completely in opposition to her captivating, modest charms. Then such a person is in a slippery position. She will suffer herself to be judged sharply and without any pity; for whoever presumes an esteem invites all around him to rebuke. Each disclosure of even the least fault gives everyone a true joy, and the word *coquette* here loses its mitigated meaning. One must always distinguish between vanity and conceit. The first seeks approbation and to some extent honors those on whose account it gives itself the trouble. The second believes itself already in full possession of approbation, and because it never strives to gain any, it wins none.

If a few ingredients of vanity do not deform a woman in the eyes of the male sex, still, the more apparent they are, the more they serve to divide the fair sex among themselves. Then they judge one another very severely, because the one seems to obscure the charms of the other, and in fact, those who make strong presumptions of conquest actually are seldom friends of one another in a true sense.

Nothing is so much set against the beautiful as disgust, just as nothing sinks deeper beneath the sublime than the ridiculous. On this account no insult can be more painful to a man than being called a *fool,* and to a woman, than being called *disgusting*. . . .

In order to remove ourselves as far as possible from these disgusting things, *neatness,* which of course well becomes any person, in the fair sex belongs among the virtues of first rank and can hardly be pushed too high among them, although in a man it sometimes rises to excess and then becomes trifling.

Sensitivity to *shame* is a secrecy of nature addressed to setting bounds to a very intractable inclination, and since it has the voice of nature on its side, seems always to agree with good moral qualities even if it yields to excess. Hence it is most needed, as a supplement to principles, for there is no instance in which inclination is so ready to turn Sophist, subtly to devise complaisant principles, as in this. But at the same time it serves to draw a curtain of mystery before even the most appropriate and necessary purposes of nature, so that a too familiar acquaintance with them might not occasion disgust, or indifference at least, in respect to the final purpose of an impulse onto which the finest and liveliest inclinations of human nature are grafted. This quality is especially peculiar to the fair sex and very becoming to it. . . .

The noble qualities of this sex, which still, as we have already noted, must never disguise the feeling of the beautiful, proclaim themselves by nothing more clearly and surely than by *modesty,* a sort of noble simplicity and innocence in great excellences. Out of it shines a quiet benevolence and respect toward others, linked at the same time with a certain *noble trust* in oneself, and a reasonable self-esteem that is always to be found in a sublime disposition. Since this fine mixture at once captivates by charms and moves by respect, it puts all the remaining shining qualities in security against the mischief of censure and mockery. Persons of this temperament also have a heart for friendship, which in a woman can never be valued highly enough, because it is so rare and moreover must be so exceedingly charming. . . .

Finally age, the great destroyer of beauty, threatens all these charms; and if it proceeds according to the natural order of things, gradually the sublime and noble qualities must take the place of the beautiful, in order to make a person always worthy of a greater respect as she ceases to be attractive. In my opinion, the whole perfection of the fair sex in the bloom of years should consist in the beautiful simplicity that has been brought to its height by a refined feeling toward all that is charming and noble. Gradually, as the claims upon charms diminish, the reading of books and the broadening of insight could refill unnoticed the vacant place of the Graces with the Muses, and the husband should be the first instructor. Nevertheless, when the epoch of growing old, so terrible to every woman, actually approaches, she still belongs to the fair sex, and that sex disfigures itself if in a kind of despair of holding this character longer, it gives way to a surly and irritable mood.

An aged person who attends a gathering with a modest and friendly manner, is sociable in a merry and sensible way, favors with a pleasant demeanor the pleasures of youth in which she herself no longer participates, and, as she looks after everything, manifests contentment and benevolence toward the joys that are going on around her, is yet a finer person that a man of like age and perhaps even more attractive than a girl, although in another sense. Indeed the platonic love might well be somewhat too mystical, which an ancient philosopher asserted when he said of the object of his inclination, ''The Graces reside in her wrinkles, and my soul seems to hover upon my lips when I kiss her withered mouth''; but such claims must then be relinquished. An old man who acts infatuated is a fool, and the like presumptions of the other sex at that age are disgusting. It never is due to nature when we do not appear with a good demeanor, but rather to the fact that we turn her upside down.

In order to keep close to my text, I want to undertake a few reflections on the influence one sex can have upon the other, to beautify or ennoble its feeling. Woman has a superior feeling for the beautiful, so far as it pertains to herself; but for the noble, so far as it is encountered in the male sex. Man on the other hand has a decided feeling for the noble, which belongs to his qualities, but for the beautiful, so far as it is to be found in woman. From this it must follow that the purposes of nature are directed still more to ennoble man, by the sexual inclination, and likewise still more to beautify woman. A woman is embarrassed little that she does not possess certain high insights, that she is timid, and not fit for serious employments, and so forth; she is beautiful and captivates, and that is enough. On the other hand, she demands all these qualities in a man, and the sublimity of her soul shows itself only in that she knows to treasure these noble qualities so far as they are found in him. How else indeed would it be possible that so many grotesque male faces, whatever merits they may possess, could gain such well-bred and fine wives! Man on the other hand is much more delicate in respect to the beautiful charms of woman. By their fine figure, merry naïveté, and charming friendliness he is sufficiently repaid for the lack of book learning and for other deficiencies that he must supply by his own talents. Vanity and fashion can give these natural drives a false direction and make out of many a male a *sweet gentleman*, but out of a woman either a prude or an Amazon; but still nature always seeks to reassert her own order. One can thereby judge what powerful influences the sexual inclination could have especially upon the male sex, to ennoble it, if instead of many dry instructions the moral feeling of woman were seasonably developed to sense properly what belongs to the dignity and the sublime qualities of the other sex, and were thus prepared to look upon the trifling fops with disdain and to yield to no other qualities than the merits. It is also certain that the power of her charms on the whole would gain through that; for it is apparent that their fascination for the most part works only upon nobler souls; the others are not fine enough to sense them. Just as the poet Simonides said, when someone advised him to let the Thessalians hear his beautiful songs: "These fellows are too stupid to be beguiled by such a man as I am." It has been regarded moreover as an effect of association with the fair sex that men's customs have become gentler, their conduct more polite and refined, and their bearing more elegant; but the advantage of this is only incidental.* The principal object is that the man should become more perfect as a man, and the woman as a wife; that is, that the motives of the sexual inclination work according to the hint of nature, still more to ennoble the one and to beautify the qualities of the other. If all comes to the extreme, the man, confident in his merits, will be able to say: "Even if you do not love me, I will constrain you to esteem me," and the woman, secure in the might of her charms will answer: "Even if you do not inwardly admire me, I will still constrain you to love me." In default of such principles one sees men take on femininity in order to please, and woman occasionally (although much more seldom) affect a masculine demeanor in order to stimulate esteem; but whatever one does contrary to nature's will, one always does very poorly.

In matrimonial life the united pair should, as it were, constitute a single moral person, which is animated and governed by the understanding of the man and the taste of the wife. For not only can one credit more insight founded on experience to the former, and more freedom and accuracy in sensation to the latter; but also, the more sublime a disposition is, the more inclined it is to place the greatest purpose of its exertions in the contentment of a beloved object, and likewise the more beautiful it is, the

---

*This advantage itself is really much reduced by the observation that one will have made, that men who are too early and too frequently introduced into company where woman sets the tone generally become somewhat trifling, and in male society they are boring or even contemptible because they have lost the taste for conversation, which must be merry, to be sure, but still of actual content—witty, to be sure, but also useful through its earnest discourse.

more it seeks to requite these exertions by complaisance. In such a relation, then, a dispute over precedence is trifling and, where it occurs, is the surest sign of a coarse or dissimilarly matched taste. If it comes to such a state that the question is of the right of the superior to command, then the case is already utterly corrupted; for where the whole union is in reality erected solely upon inclination, it is already half destroyed as soon as the "duty" begins to make itself heard. The presumption of the woman in this harsh tone is extremely ugly, and of the man is base and contemptible in the highest degree. However, the wise order of things so brings it about that all these niceties and delicacies of feeling have their whole strength only in the beginning, but subsequently gradually become duller through association and domestic concerns, and then degenerate into familiar love. Finally, the great skill consists in still preserving sufficient remainders of those feelings so that indifference and satiety do not put an end to the whole value of the enjoyment on whose account it has solely and alone been worth the trouble to enter such a union. . . .

From *Anthropology from a Pragmatic Point of View*

On the Character of the Sexes

Any machine that is supposed to accomplish just as much as another machine, but with less force, implies *art*. So we can already presuppose that nature's foresight put more art into the makeup of the female than of the male; for it provided the man with greater strength than the woman in order to bring them together into the most intimate *physical* union, which, insofar as they are still *rational* belongs too, it orders to the end most important to it, the preservation of the species. Moreover it provided them, in this capacity of theirs (as rational animals), with social inclinations to stabilize their sexual union in a domestic union.

If a union is to be harmonious and indissoluble, it is not enough for two people to associate as they please; one party must be *subject* to the other and, reciprocally, one must be the *superior* of the other in some way, in order to be able to rule and govern him. For if two people who cannot dispense with each other make *equal* claims, self-love produces nothing but wrangling. As *culture* advances, each party must be superior in his own particular way: the man must be superior to the woman by his physical strength and courage; the woman to the man, however, by her natural talent for gaining mastery over his desire for her. In a still uncivilized state, on the contrary, all superiority is on the man's side. This is why, in anthropology, the proper nature of the female sex is more a study for the philosopher than that of the male sex. In the crude state of nature we can no more recognize her proper nature than we can that of the crab apple and the wild pear, which reveal their diversity only when they are grafted or inoculated; for while civilization does not produce these feminine qualities, it allows them to develop and, under its favoring conditions, become discernible.

We call feminine ways weaknesses, and joke about them. Fools jeer at them, but reasonable men know very well that they are precisely the rudders women use to steer men and use them for their own purposes. Man is easy to scrutinize: woman does not betray her secrets—although (because of her loquacity) she is not very good at keeping other people's. He loves *domestic peace,* and readily submits to her regime, if only so that he will not be prevented from attending to his own business: she does not shrink from *domestic warfare,* which she wages with her tongue; and nature came to her aid here by endowing her with loquacity and emotional eloquence, which disarms the man. He relies on the right of the stronger to command in the house, since he is supposed to defend it against enemies from without: she depends on the right of the weaker to have the male's protection against men, and disarms him by tears of exasperation as she reproaches him with his lack of generosity.

In the crude state of nature it is quite different. There the woman is a domestic animal. The man leads the way with weapons in his hand, and the woman follows him, loaded down with his household belongings. But even where a barbaric civil constitution legalizes polygamy, the favorite woman in the man's prison (called a harem) knows how to gain control over him, and he has no end of trouble to make his life tolerably peaceful, with many women wrangling to be the one (who is to rule over him).

In civil society woman does not give herself up to man's pleasure outside marriage, and indeed *monogamous* marriage. Where civilization has not yet reached the degree of feminine freedom called *gallantry* (where a woman makes no secret of having lovers other than her husband), a man punishes his wife if she threatens him with a rival.* But when gallantry has become the fashion and jealousy ridiculous (as never fails to happen in a period of luxury), the feminine character reveals itself; by man's leave, woman lays claim to freedom over against man and, at the same time, to the conquest of the whole male sex. This inclination, though it

*The old Russian saying that a wife suspects her husband of being unfaithful unless he beats her now and then is usually considered a story. But in Cook's Travels we find that an English sailor in Otahiti saw an Indian punishing his wife by beating her and, wanting to play the gallant, flew at the husband threatening him. The wife immediately turned on the Englishman and asked what it had to do with him: the husband *must* do that!—So too, we find that when a married woman openly practices gallantry and her husband pays no attention to it, but compensates himself for it by drinking, gambling, or chasing other women, she is filled not merely with contempt but also with *hatred* for him; for she knows that he no longer values her at all, and would indifferently abandon his wife to others and let them gnaw the same bone.

indeed stands in ill repute under the name of coquetry, has some real basis of justification. For a young wife is always in danger of becoming a widow, and because of this she scatters her charms over all the men who circumstances might make potential husbands for her, so that, should this situation occur, she would not be wanting for suitors.

Pope believes that the female sex (the cultivated part of it) could be characterized by two things: the inclination to *dominate* and the inclination to *please*. But by the second trait we must understand the inclination to please not at home but in public, where woman can show herself to advantage and distinguish herself. And then the inclination to please dissolves into the inclination to dominate: namely, not to yield to her rivals in pleasing others, but to triumph over them all, where possible, by her taste and charm. But, like inclinations generally, even the inclination to dominate cannot serve to characterize a class of human beings in their conduct toward others. For inclination toward what is advantageous to us is common to all men, and so too is the inclination to dominate insofar as we can. This inclination, accordingly, fails to *characterize* [a class]. The fact that the female sex is constantly feuding with itself while remaining on very good terms with the other sex might rather be considered as its character, were this not merely the natural *result* of women's rivalry among themselves, in which one tries to get the better of others in the favor and devotion of men. For inclination to dominate is woman's real aim, while *pleasing in public,* insofar as it widens the field for her charm, is only the means for giving effect to that inclination.

If we are to succeed in characterizing this sex, we cannot use as our principle what *we make* our end, but only what the end *of nature* was in devising the female sex. And since this end, even though it is to be realized through men's folly, must still be wisdom according to nature's purpose, these conjectural ends of nature can also serve to indicate the principle for characterizing woman—a principle that does not depend on our choice but on a higher purpose for the human race. Nature's ends are: (1) the preservation of the species, (2) the cultivation of society and its refinement by woman.

(1) Nature entrusted to woman's womb its dearest pledge, the species, in the form of the fetus, by which the race is to propagate and perpetuate itself; and in so doing nature was fearful, so to speak, about the preservation of the species, and implanted this fear—fear in the face of *physical* harm and timidity in the face of physical dangers—in woman's nature. Through this weakness woman rightfully demands that man be her protector.

(2) Since nature also wanted to instill the more refined feelings that belong to culture—the feelings, namely, of sociability and decorum—it made woman man's ruler through her modesty and her eloquence in speech and expression. It made her precociously shrewd in claiming gen-

tle and courteous treatment by the male, so that he finds himself imperceptibly fettered by a child through his own generosity and led by it, if not to morality itself, at least to its clothing, the cultivated propriety that is the preparatory training for morality and its recommendation.

Remarks at Random

Woman wants to dominate, man to be dominated (especially before marriage). The gallantry of ancient chivalry has its source in this. Early in life, she becomes confident of pleasing; the young man is always afraid of displeasing, so that he is self-conscious (embarrassed) in the company of ladies. She asserts, merely by virtue of her sex, woman's boast to ward off all man's importunities by the respect she inspires, and the right to demand respect for herself even if she does not deserve it. The woman *refuses,* the man *courts* her; if she yields, it is a favor. Since nature wants her to be sought after, woman cannot be so fastidious in her choice (by taste) as man, whom nature has fashioned more coarsely and who already pleases her if only his physique shows that he has the strength and ability to protect her. For if her ability to fall in love depended on a fussy and refined choice with regard to the beauty of his form, she would have to become the suitor and it would be his role to refuse; and this would reduce to nothing the value of her sex, even in the man's eyes. She must seem to be cold, but the man to be ardent in love. To a man, not to respond to an amorous provocation seems shameful; to respond readily seems shameful to a woman. A woman's desire to play with her charms on every well-bred man is coquetry; a [man's] pose of appearing to be in love with all women is gallantry. Both of these can be a mere affectation that has become the fashion, without any serious consequences—just as [having] a *cavaliere servente* can be an affected freedom of married women, or, in the same way, the *courtesan system* that once existed in Italy. . . . It is said of these courtesans that their well-bred *public* associations contained more refined culture than did mixed gatherings in private houses. Within marriage, the man solicits only *his* wife's desire; the woman, however, the desire of *all* men. A woman *dresses up* only to be seen by her own sex, out of jealousy; she wants to outdo other women in her charm or in the airs she gives herself. A man, on the other hand, dresses up only for the opposite sex—if he can be said to dress up when he goes only so far as not to disgrace his wife by his clothes. Men are lenient in judging feminine faults, but women (in public) judge them very strictly; and young women, if they were allowed to choose whether a male or a female tribunal should pass judgment on their misconduct, would certainly choose the first for their judge. When refined luxury has reached a high level, a wife shows herself virtuous only under constraint and makes no secret of her wish that she were a man, so that she could give her inclinations wider scope and freer play. But no man would want to be a woman.

The woman does not ask whether the man was continent before marriage; but for the man, this question about his wife is of infinite importance. In marriage, women scoff at intolerance (the jealousy of men in general), but it is only a joke of theirs; *single women* judge it more severely. As for the scholarly woman, she uses her *books* in the same way as her *watch,* for example, which she carries so that people will see that she has one, though it is usually not running or not set by the sun.

Feminine and masculine virtue or lack of virtue are very different from each other, more as regards their incentive than their kind. She should be *patient;* he must be *tolerant.* She is *sensitive;* he is *responsive.* Man's economic system consists in *acquiring,* woman's in *saving.* The man is jealous *when he loves;* the woman is jealous even when she does not love, because every admirer gained by other women is one lost to her circle of suitors. The man has taste *on his own:* the woman makes herself the object of *everyone's* taste. "What the world says is true, and what it does, good" is a feminine principle that is hard to unite with character in the strict sense of the term. But there have still been heroic women who, within their own households, maintained creditably a character in keeping with their vocation. Milton's wife urged him to accept the post of Latin Secretary which was offered to him after Cromwell's death, though it was against his principles now to recognize as lawful a regime he had previously declared unlawful. "Ah my dear," he replied; "you and the rest of your sex want to travel in coaches: but I—must be an honorable man." Socrates' wife—and perhaps Job's too—was cornered in the same way by her valiant husband; but masculine virtue upheld itself in his character, without, however, diminishing the merit of the feminine virtue of hers, given the relation in which she was placed.

Pragmatic Consequences

Woman must train and discipline herself in practical matters: man understands nothing of this.

The *young* husband *rules* his wife, even if she is *older* than he. This is based on jealousy: the party who is subject to the other in the sexual relation is apprehensive that the other will violate her right, and so feels compelled to comply with his wishes, to be obliging and attentive in her treatment of him. This is why every experienced wife will advise against marriage with a young man, even with one *the same age* as the woman; for as the years pass, the woman ages earlier than the man; and even if we disregard this inequality, we cannot count positively on the harmony that is based on equality. An intelligent young woman will have a better chance of a happy marriage with a man who is in good health, but appreciably older than she. But a man who has lewdly squandered his *sexual power,* perhaps even before marriage, will be the fool in his own house;

for he can exercise domestic rule only insofar as he does not fail to fulfill any reasonable claim made on him.

Hume notes that women, even old maids, are more annoyed by satires on *marriage* than by gibes against their *sex*. For such gibes can never be serious, whereas satires on the married state could well have serious consequences if they illuminate clearly its difficulties, which bachelors escape. Scepticism about marriage, however, is bound to have bad consequences for the whole female sex; for woman would be degraded to a mere means for satisfying man's desires, while his satisfaction can easily turn into boredom and unfaithfulness. It is by marriage that woman becomes free: man loses his freedom by it.

It is never a woman's concern to spy out the moral qualities in a man *before* the wedding, especially if he is young. She thinks she can improve him: an intelligent woman, she says, can straighten out a badly behaved man. But as a rule she finds herself most lamentably deceived in this judgment. This also applies to those naive people who think that a man's excesses before marriage can be overlooked because, if only he has not exhausted himself, he will now have in his wife adequate provision for his sexual instinct. It does not occur to these good children that sexual debauchery consists precisely in change of pleasure, and that the uniformity of marriage will soon bring him back to his former way of life.*

Who, then, should have supreme command in the household?—for there can be only one person who coordinates all occupations in accordance with one end, which is his. I would say, in the language of gallantry (but not without truth): the woman should *reign* and the man *govern;* for inclination reigns and understanding governs. The husband's behavior must show that his wife's welfare is the thing closest to his heart. But since the man must know best how his affairs stand and how far he can go, he will be like a minister to his monarch who thinks only of amusement. For example, if the monarch undertakes a festival or the building of a palace, the minister will first declare his due compliancy with the order, except that at the moment there is no money in the treasury, or that certain urgent necessities must be settled first, and so on—so that the monarch can do all that he wills, but on one condition: that his minister lets him know what his will is. . . .

---

*It turns out like Voltaire's *Voyage de Scarmentado:* "Finally," he says, "I returned to my fatherland Candia, married there, soon became a cuckold, and found this the most comfortable life of all."

J. G. Fichte

German philosopher and ethical idealist, 1762–1814.

From *The Science of Rights*

Deduction of Marriage

The character of reason is absolute self-activity; pure passivity for the sake of passivity contradicts reason, and utterly cancels it. Hence, it is not against reason that the one sex should propose to itself the satisfaction of its sexual impulse as an end in itself, since it can be satisfied through activity; but it is absolutely against reason that the other sex should propose to itself the satisfaction of its sexual impulse as an end, because in that case it would make a pure passivity its end. Hence, the female sex is either not rational even in its tendencies, which contradicts our presupposition that all men should be rational, or this tendency cannot be developed in that sex in consequence of its peculiar nature, which is a self-contradiction, since it assumes a tendency in nature which nature does not accept; or, finally, that sex can never propose to itself the satisfaction of its sexual impulse as its end. Such an end and rationality utterly cancel each other in that sex.

Nevertheless, the sexual impulse of this female sex, as well as its manifestation and satisfaction, are part of the plan of nature. Hence it is necessary that the sexual impulse should manifest itself in woman under another form; and, in order to be comfortable to reason, it must appear as an impulse to activity; and as a characteristic impulse of nature, it must appear as an activity exclusively appertaining to the female sex.

Since our whole subsequent theory rests upon this proposition, I shall endeavor to place it in its proper light, and to disarm possible misunderstanding of its meaning.

Firstly: we speak here of *nature* and of an *impulse of nature;* that is, of something which a woman will find in herself as something given, original, and not to be explained by any previous act of her own, nor origi-

253

nated by any application of her freedom whatever; something which woman will thus find in herself as soon as its two conditions, reason and activity of the sexual impulse, exist. But we do not at all deny the possibility that woman may not sink below this condition of nature, or may not through freedom elevate herself above it, which elevation, however, is itself not much better than the sinking below it. A woman sinks below nature when she degrades herself to irrationality; in which condition the sexual impulse may manifest itself in consciousness in its true form, and may become a well-considered object of activity. A woman elevates herself above her nature when the satisfaction of the sexual impulse is not an end for her, neither in its coarse form nor in that form which it received in a well-formed female soul; hence, when it is considered by her as means for another end, which she has with free consciousness proposed to herself. Unless this other end is to be an utterly wicked and degrading end—as, for instance, if she should have done it for the purpose of becoming a married woman, and in view of a prospect of a secure income, thus making of her person the means to obtain an enjoyment—we must assume it to be the same end which nature has in view, that is, to have children, and which some such women, indeed, claim to have been their motive. But since she could attain this object with every possible man, and since thus there is no ground to be discovered in her principle why she should have chosen this man and none other for that purpose, we must assume, as, after all, the least degrading motive, that she chose this man because he was the first one she could get, which surely does not evince great personal self-respect. But even apart from this grave circumstance, and admitting for the moment that such an end would justify the resolve to cohabit with a man, the serious question would still remain: Whether the end will be produced by such means, or whether children are really begotten by the resolve to beget them?

We hope this plainness will be pardoned in our endeavor to show up certain dangerous sophistries in all their nakedness, by means of which sophistries many seek to palliate the repudiation of their true destination, and to perpetuate it forever.

Let me characterize this whole relation in an image: The female sex stands one step lower in the arrangement of nature than the male sex; the female sex is the object of a power of the male sex, and no other arrangement was possible if both sexes were to be connected. But at the same time both sexes, as moral beings, ought to be equal. To make this possible, a new faculty, utterly wanting in the male sex, had to be given to the female sex. This faculty is the form in which the sexual impulse appears to woman, whereas to man it appears in its true form. . . .

Woman cannot confess to herself that she gives herself up—and since, in a rational being, everything is only insofar as it arises in consciousness—woman cannot give herself up to the sexual impulse merely to satisfy her own impulse. But since she can give herself up only in obedience to an impulse, this impulse must assume in woman the character of an impulse to satisy the man. Woman becomes, in this act, the means for the end of another, because she cannot be her own end without renouncing her ultimate end—the dignity of reason! This dignity she maintains, although she becomes means, because she voluntarily makes herself means in virtue of a noble natural impulse—*love!*

Love, therefore, is the form in which the sexual impulse appears to woman. But love is to sacrifice one's self for the sake of another not in consequence of a reasoning, but in consequence of a feeling. Mere sexual impulse should never be called love; to do so is a vulgar abuse of language, calculated to cause all that is noble in human nature to be forgotten. In fact, my opinion is that nothing should be called love but what we have just now described. Man *originally* does not feel love, but sexual impulse; and love in man is not an original but a *communicated, derived* impulse, namely, an impulse developed through connection with a loving woman; and has, moreover, quite a different form in man to what it has in woman. Love, the noblest of all natural impulses, is inborn only in woman; and only through woman does it, like many other social impulses, become the common property of mankind. The sexual impulse received this moral form of love in woman, because in its original form it would have canceled all morality in woman. Love is the closest point of union of nature and reason; it is the only link wherein nature connects with reason, and hence it is the most excellent of all that is natural. The Moral Law requires that man should forget himself in the other; but love even sacrifices itself to the other. . . .

The woman who thus surrenders her personality, and yet retains her full dignity in so doing, necessarily gives up to her lover all that she has. For, if she retained the least for her own self, she would thereby confess that it had a higher value for her than her own person; and this undoubtedly would be a lowering of that person. Her own dignity requires that she should give herself up entirely as she is, and lives to her choice and should utterly lose herself in him. The least consequence is, that she should renounce to him all her property and all her rights. Henceforth she has life and activity only under his eyes and in his business. She has ceased to lead the life of an individual; her life has become a part of the life of her lover. (This is aptly characterized by her assuming his name.)

The position of the man, meanwhile, is this: Since he may confess all to himself, and hence finds in himself the whole fullness of humanity, he is able to overlook his whole relation to woman, as woman herself can never overlook it. He, therefore, sees how an originally free being voluntarily submits itself to him with uniimited confidence, and that she makes not only her whole external fate, but also her internal peace of soul and moral character—at least her own faith in it—dependent upon him, since

the faith of woman in herself and in her own innocence and virtue depends upon this, that she may never cease to esteem and love her husband
above all others of his sex.

As the moral impulse of woman manifests itself as love, so in man that
impulse manifests itself as *generosity*. His first wish is to be master; but if
another being surrenders itself to him in perfect confidence, he lays aside
all his power. For to be strong against the vanquished is fit only for the
weak-hearted who cannot oppose force to resistance.

In consequence of this natural generosity, man, in his relation to his
wife, is compelled, first of all, to be worthy of esteem, since her whole
peace of mind depends upon his being held in esteem by her. Nothing so
irrevocably kills the love of the wife as the meanness or infamy of her
husband. Indeed, the female sex will pardon in our sex everything but
cowardice and weakness of character. The ground of this is by no means a
selfish calculation upon our protection; but solely the impossibility to
submit to such men, as woman's destiny nevertheless requires her to submit.

The peace of the wife depends upon her being utterly submitted to her
husband, and having no other will than his own. Now, since he knows
this to be so, his character of manly generosity, which he cannot deny
without denying his own nature and dignity, requires that he should make
it as light as possible for her to do so. This he cannot do by allowing his
wife to rule him; for the pride of her love consists in being and seeming to
be submitted and not knowing otherwise. Men who submit themselves to
the rule of their wives thereby make themselves contemptible in the eyes
of their wives, and destroy all their matrimonial happiness. He can do it
only by attentively discovering her wishes, and causing to be done, as if it
were through his own will, what he knows she would most gladly have
done. It is not to be taken that he thus gratifies her notions and whims
merely in order to have them gratified, but that he has the far higher purpose of thereby making it easier for her to love her husband always above
everything, and of thus retaining her innocence in her own eyes. It cannot
fail but that the wife—whose heart can not be satisfied by an obedience
which calls for no sacrifice on her part—will seek to discover, on her
part, the concealed higher wishes of her husband, in order to satisy them
at some sacrifices. For the greater the sacrifice, the more perfect is the
satisfaction of her heart. Hence arises connubial *tenderness;* that is, tenderness of sentiments, and of the whole relation. Each party wishes to
give up its personality, so that the other one may rule alone. Each finds
content only in the satisfaction of the other; the exchange of hearts and
wills becomes perfect. It is only in connection with a loving woman that
the heart of the man opens to love, to the love which confidingly surrenders and loses itself in the beloved object; it is only in the tie which connects the wife with the husband that she learns generosity and conscious

self-sacrifice; and thus the tie unites them closer every day of their wedded life.

Corollaria

In the union of both sexes, and hence in the realization of man as a *whole,* or as a completed product of nature, but also *only* in this union, is there to be found an *external* impulse to virtue. Man is compelled by his natural impulse of generosity to be noble and venerable, because the fate of a free being which surrendered itself to him in full confidence depends upon his being so. Woman is compelled to observe all her duties by her inborn modesty. She cannot act contrary to reason in any manner, because it would lead her to suspect herself of having acted so in the chief manner, and that she had chosen her husband, not from love—the most insupportable thought to woman—but merely as a means to satisfy her sexual impulse. The man in whom there still lingers generosity, and the woman in whom there still dwells modesty, are open to the utmost degree of culture; but both are on the sure path to all vices when the one becomes mean and the other shameless, as indeed experience invariably shows it to be the case. . . .

Such a union as we have described is called a *marriage*. Marriage is a *complete union* of two persons of both sexes, based upon the sexual impulse, and having its end in itself. . . .

Marriage is a union between *two* persons—*one* man and *one* woman. A woman who has given herself up to one, cannot give herself up to a second, for her whole dignity requires that she should belong only to this one. Again, a man who has to observe the slightest wish of one woman cannot conform to the contradictory wishes of many. Polygamy presupposes that women are not rational beings like men, but merely willess and lawless means to gratify man. Such is, indeed, the doctrine of the religious legislation which tolerates polygamy. This religion has—probably without being clearly conscious of the grounds—drawn one-sided conclusions from the destination of woman to remain passive. Polyandry is utterly against nature, and hence very rare. If it were not a condition of utter brutishness, and if it would presuppose anything, it would have to presuppose that there is no reason and no dignity of reason.

The union of matrimony is in its nature inseparable and eternal, and is necessarily concluded as being eternal. A woman cannot presuppose that she will ever cease to love her husband above all of his sex without abandoning her personal dignity; nor can the husband presuppose that he will every cease to love his wife above all of her sex without abandoning his manly generosity. Both give themselves to each other forever, because they give themselves to each other wholly.

Marriage is, therefore, no invented custom, nor an arbitrary institution, but a relation necessarily and perfectly determined through nature and reason in their union. Perfectly determined, I say, that is, only a marriage such as we have described and absolutely no other union of both sexes for the satisfaction of the sexual impulse is permitted by nature and reason. . . .

Law of Marriage

The conception of marriage involves the most unlimited subjection of the woman to the will of the husband; not from legal, but from moral reasons. She must subject herself for the sake of her own honor. The woman does not belong to herself, but to the man. The state, by recognizing marriage, that is, by recognizing a relation based upon something far higher than itself, abandons all claims to consider the woman as a legal person. The husband supplies her place; her marriage utterly annuls her, so far as the state is concerned, by virtue of her own necessary will, which the state has guaranteed. The husband becomes her guarantee in the eye of the law; or becomes her legal guardian. He lives in all her public life, and she retains for herself only a house life. . . .

The conception of marriage involves that the woman who surrenders her personality shall at the same time surrender the possession of all her property and her exclusive rights in the state. The state, in recognizing the marriage, recognizes and guarantees the possessions of the wife to the husband; that is, *not as against the claims of the wife,* for a law dispute with her is impossible, under our presupposition, but against the claims and attacks of *all other citizens.* The husband becomes, in so far as the state is concerned, the sole proprietor of his previous possessions, and of those which his wife held at the time of her marriage. . . .

The conception of marriage also involves common residence, common labor; in short, living together. To the state both husband and wife appear as only one person; what the one does is as valid as if the other had also done it. All public legal acts are performed only by the husband. . . .

Concerning the Legal Relation of Both Sexes in General to Each Other in the State

Has woman the same rights in the state which man has? This question may appear ridiculous to many. For if the only ground of all legal rights is reason and freedom, how can a distinction exist between two sexes which possess both the same reason and the same freedom?

Nevertheless, it seems that, so long as men have lived, this has been differently held, and the female sex seems not to have been placed on a par with the male sex in the exercise of its rights. Such a universal sentiment must have a ground, to discover which was never a more urgent problem than in our days. If we grant that the female sex, so far as its rights are concerned, has really been thus treated, it by no means suffices to assign as ground a less degree of mental and physical power. For women would reply: "Firstly, you men do not give us the same degree of culture which you extend to your own sex; and secondly, that statement is not even true; for if you will make a list of the men who are the pride of their sex, we can make one of women, who will, justly estimated, be their peers in everything; but finally, even if this inequality were as you state it to be, it would on no account involve such a decided inequality of rights, since there is also among men a great distinction of mental and bodily powers, which does not involve such an oppressive inequality of rights."

Hence, it will be necessary, above all things, to investigate whether women are really treated so badly and unjustly as some of them, and, still more, some uncalled-for advocates of their cause, assert.

The question whether the female sex has really a claim to all the rights of men and of citizens which belong to the male sex could be raised only by persons who doubt whether women are complete human beings. We do not doubt it, as appears sufficiently from the above. But the question may certainly be asked, whether and in how far the female sex *can desire* to exercise all its rights? To facilitate the answering of this question, we shall consider the several conditions of women.

As a rule, woman is either a maid or married. If a maid, she is still under the care of her father, precisely as the unmarried young man. Herein both sexes are perfectly equal. Both become free by marriage, and in regard to their marriage both are equally free; or if there is to be a favor shown, it should be shown to the daughter. For she ought not even to be persuaded to marry, which may be permitted in the case of the son, as we have shown heretofore.

If she is *married,* her whole dignity depends upon her being completely subjected, and seeming to be so subjected, to her husband, Let it be well observed, what my whole theory expresses, but what it is perhaps necessary to repeat once more emphatically—woman is not subjected to her husband in such a manner as to give him a *right of compulsion* over her; she is subjected through her own continuous necessary wish—a wish which is the condition of her morality—to be so subjected. She has the *power* to withdraw her freedom, if she could have the *will* to do so; but that is the very point: she cannot rationally will to be free. Her relation to her husband being publicly known, she must, moreover, will to appear to all whom she knows as utterly subjected to, and utterly lost in, the man of her choice.

Her husband is, therefore, the administrator of all her rights in consequence of her own necessary will; and she wishes those rights asserted and exercised only in so far as *he* wishes it. He is her natural representative in the state and in the whole society. This is her *public* relation to society. She cannot even allow herself to think for a moment that she should exercise herself her rights in the state.

So far as her *private* and *internal* relation in the house is concerned, the *tenderness of the husband necessarily restores to her all and more than she has lost*. The husband will not relinquish her rights, because they are his own; and because, if he did so, he would dishonor himself and his wife before society. The wife has also rights in public affairs, for she is a citizen. I consider it the duty of the husband—in states which give to the citizen a vote on public matters—not to vote without having discussed the subject with his wife, and allowed her to modify his opinion through her own. His vote will then be the result of their common will. The father of a family, who represents not only his own but also the interests of his wife and children, ought indeed to have a greater influence and a more decisive vote in a commonwealth, than the citizen who represents only his own interests. The manner of arranging this is a problem for the science of politics.

Women, therefore, do really exercise the right of suffrage—not immediately, however, in their own person, because they cannot wish to do so without lowering their dignity, but—through the influence which results from the nature of the marriage relation. This is, indeed, proved by the history of all great revolutions. They either emanated from, or at least were led and considerably modified by, women.

Remark

If this must be admitted to be the case, what, then, do women and their advocates really demand? What is it whereof women are deprived, and which must be restored to them? The rights themselves? They are completely possessed of them, as we have shown. It can only be the external show of those rights. They not only want to accomplish, but also to have it known that *they* accomplished it. They not only want their ideas to be carried out, but also to have it publicly known, that *they,* even they, carried them out. They long for celebrity during life, and after death in history.

If this alone is and can be their object in preferring those complaints, then their complaints ought to be unhesitatingly rejected; for they cannot prefer them without renouncing their whole female worth. The fewest, however, who prefer them, do so seriously. Most of them have been persuaded to utter such wonderful words which they cannot *think* without dishonoring themselves, by a few crack-brained men, most of whom have never thought sufficiently high of a woman to make her their companion through life, and who are therefore anxious to remedy the matter by having the whole sex, without exception, immortalized in history.

Even the man who makes glory the chief or but one of the ends of his life, loses the merit of his acts, and sooner or later, also, that very glory.

Women ought to be grateful that their position precludes the very suspicion of such a motive. But what is far more; by such thirst for glory women sacrifice the amiable modesty of their sex, which nothing can more disgust than to be put up for a show. Ambition and vanity are contemptible in a man; but in a woman they are corrupting; for they root out that modesty and self-sacrificing love for her husband upon which her whole dignity rests. A rational and virtuous woman can be proud only of her husband and children; not of herself, for she forgets herself in them. Add to this, that those women who seriously envy men their celebrity, are deceived concerning the true object of their wish. Woman necessarily desires the love of some man, and, in order to attract it, she is anxious to attract the attention of the male sex. This is natural and very proper in an unmarried woman. But those women calculate to increase the charms of their own sex—perhaps not having much confidence in them—by that which attracts the attention of men to men, and seek in celebrity merely a new means of captivating men's hearts. If those women are married, their object is as contemptible as the means are unsuited to accomplish it.

If the husband cannot or refuses to vote, there is no reason why the wife should not appear in his place and cast their common vote, but always as *the vote of the husband.* (She could not cast it as her own without separating herself from her husband.) For the grounded extends no further than the ground; and the ground why the wife could not vote was, because the husband voted for both. If he does not, she can, therefore, vote.

This furnishes us the principle applicable to widows and divorced women, and to maids who are no longer under paternal authority and yet have never been married. All these classes of women are not subjected to a man; hence there is no reason why they should not themselves exercise all civil rights precisely as men do. In a republic they have the right to vote, to appear in court, and to defend their own cause. If from natural bashfulness and modesty they prefer to choose a guardian, they must be permitted to do so, but there is no legal ground why they should be forced to choose one.

Every citizen in the state is to possess property and to administer it according to his will; hence, also, the woman who has no husband. This property need not be absolute property, money or valuables, but may also consist of civil rights or privileges. There is no reason why women should not have these. Woman can own land and carry on agriculture. Or she can carry on an art, or a profession, or some commercial business.

Women are ineligible to public offices for the following simple reasons: public officers are responsible to the State; and hence must be perfectly free, and dependent always only upon their own will; otherwise such a responsibility would be unjust and contradictory. Woman, however, is free and independent only so long as she has no husband. Hence the exclusive condition under which a woman might become eligible to office, would be the promise not to marry. But no rational woman can give such a promise, nor can the state rationally accept it. For woman is destined to love, and love comes to women of itself—does not depend upon her free will. But when she loves, it is her duty to marry, and the state must not form an obstacle to this duty. Now, if a woman, holding a public office, were to marry, two cases are possible. Firstly, she might not subject herself to her husband so far as her official duties were concerned. But this is utterly against female dignity; for she cannot say then, that she has given herself up wholly to the husband. Moreover, where are the strict limits which separate official from private life? Or, secondly, she might subject herself utterly, as nature and morality require, to her husband, even so far as her official duties are concerned. But, in that case, she would cease to be the official, and he would become it. The office would become his by marriage, like the rest of his wife's property and rights. But this the state cannot permit; for it must know the ability and the character of the person upon whom an office is conferred, and cannot accept one chosen merely by love.

This fact, that women are not intended for public offices, has another consequence, which the advocates of woman's rights put forth as a new complaint against our political institutions. For, very naturally, they are not educated for duties they will never have to perform; are sent neither to colleges, nor to universities. Now they cry out, that men neglect their minds, and enviously and cunningly keep them in ignorance, and hold them removed from the sources of enlightening culture. We shall examine this charge carefully.

The learned man by profession studies not merely for himself; *as* student he studies, on the contrary, not at all for himself, but for others. If he wishes to become a preacher, or statesman, or doctor, he studies for the purpose of immediately applying what he has learned; hence he learns at the same time the form, or the manner of applying his science. Or if it is his intention to become a teacher of future students in schools or universities, it is also his intention to communicate again what he now learns, and to increase the stock of his knowledge by discoveries of his own, so that culture may not come to a standstill. Hence he must know *how* to make these discoveries, and how to develop them out of the human soul. But this acquiring a knowledge of the *form* of science is precisely what they, women, cannot make use of since they are to become neither teachers, preachers, doctors, or lawyers.

For their own intellectual culture, men only require the *results* of culture; and these results women learn also in society: in each condition of society the results of the whole culture of that condition. That which they envy us is, therefore, the unessential, the formal, the mere hull. By their position and by our conversation they are saved the trouble of working through this hull, and can receive its contents directly. They could not, indeed, make use of the form at all. Women are not habituated, and cannot be habituated, to look upon the form as means, because they could be accustomed to do so only by making use of the form. Hence they look upon it as an end in itself, as something noble and excellent in itself. This is the reason why really learned women—I do not speak of those who reason purely through their common sense, for these are very estimable—are usually pedantic.

To prevent my being misunderstood, let me explain this further. It cannot be maintained that woman is inferior to man in regard to talents of mind; but it can certainly be maintained that the minds of man and woman have, by nature, a very different character. Man reduces all that is in and for him to clear conceptions, and discovers it only through reasoning—provided, of course, his knowledge is a true conviction, and not a mere historical knowledge. Woman, on the other hand, has a natural sentiment of what is good, true, and proper. Not as if this were given her through mere feeling, for that is impossible; but when it is externally given to her, she has the faculty of judging quickly through her feelings, and without clear insight into the grounds of such judgment, whether it be true and good, or not. It may be said, that man must first make himself rational; whereas, woman is already rational by nature. This is, indeed, clearly to be deduced from the fundamental distinction between woman and man. Her fundamental impulse originally unites with reason, because it would cancel reason unless it did so unite; it becomes a rational impulse. And this is the reason why woman's whole system of feeling is rational, and made to correspond to reason, as it were. Man, on the contrary, must first subordinate all his impulses to reason, through exertion and activity.

Woman, therefore, is especially practical, and not at all speculative in her womanly nature. She cannot and shall not go beyond the limit of her feeling. (This explains the well-known phenomenon, why some women have been known to become distinguished in matters of memory, as languages, and even in mathematics, so far as they can be learned through memory; and some also in matters of invention, in the gentler forms of poetry, in novel writing, and even in the writing of history. But no women are known to have been philosophers, or inventors of new theories in the mathematical science.)

A few words more concerning the passion of women to become authors—a passion which is constantly on the increase among them in these our days.

Literary labor can have only two ends in view: to make known new discoveries in sciences for the examination of the learned, or to communicate that which has already been discovered to the people at large by means of popular representations. We have seen that women cannot make discoveries. Popular writings for women, writings on female education, moral books for the female sex, as such, etc., can certainly be most properly written by women; partly because they know their own sex better than man ever can know it (that is, if they have the gift, also, of rising in part above their sex) and partly because such books are generally more read by women. Even the learned man can extend his knowledge of female character from such writings. Of course, the woman must write as a woman, and must not appear in her writings as a badly disguised man.

I have presupposed, as it will be seen, that a woman will write only for her sex, and only for the purpose of being useful and to alleviate a discovered need of her sex; but on no account for our sex, or from motives of vanity or ambition. Not only would her works have little literary value in the latter case, but the moral character of the authoress would also be greatly injured. Her authorship would be nothing but another means of coquetting. If she is married, she receives, through her literary celebrity, an independence which necessarily weakens and threatens to dissolve her relation to her husband; or, if criticism is unfavorable, she will feel the reproof as an insult to her sex, and will embitter the days of herself and of her husband. . . .

G. W. F. Hegel

German philosopher of absolute idealism, 1770–1831, for whom the real and the rational are identical. His work is especially noted for his dialectical analyses of history and ideas, in which each position is seen as a stage, a partial development on the way to the whole—the absolute.

From *Phenomenology of Mind*

. . . An unmixed intransitive form of relationship, however, holds between brother and sister. They are the same blood, which, however, in them has entered into a condition of stable equilibrium. They therefore stand in no such natural relation as husband and wife, they do not desire one another; nor have they given to one another, nor received from one another, this independence of individual being; they are free individualities with respect to each other. The feminine element, therefore, in the form of the sister, premonizes and foreshadows most completely the nature of ethical life. She does not become conscious of it, and does not actualize it, because the law of the family is her inherent implicit inward nature, which does not lie open to the daylight of consciousness, but remains inner feeling and the divine element exempt from actuality. The feminine life is attached to these household divinities (*Penates*), and sees in them both her universal substance, and her particular individuality, yet so views them that this relation of her individuality to them is at the same time not the natural one of pleasure.

As a daughter, the woman must now see her parents pass away with natural emotion and yet with ethical resignation, for it is only at the cost of this condition that she can come to that individual existence of which she is capable. She thus cannot see her independent existence positively attained in her relation to her parents. The relationships of mother and wife, however, are individualized partly in the form of something natural, which brings pleasure; partly in the form of something negative, which finds simply its own evanescence in those relationships; partly again the individualization is just on that account something contingent which can be replaced by an other particular individuality. In a household of the ethical kind, a woman's relationships are not based on a reference to this particular husband, this particular child, but to a husband, to children *in general*—not to feeling, but to the universal. The distinction between her ethical life (while it determines her particular existence and brings her pleasure) and that of her husband consists just in this, that it has always a directly universal significance for her, and is quite alien to the impulsive condition of mere particular desire. On the other hand, in the husband these two aspects get separated; and since he possesses, as a citizen, the self-conscious power belonging to the universal life, the life of the social whole, he acquires thereby the rights of desire, and keeps himself at the same time in detachment from it. So far, then, as particularity is implicated in this relationship in the case of the wife, her ethical life is not purely ethical; so far, however, as it is ethical, the particularity is a matter of indifference, and the wife is without the moment of knowing herself as *this* particular self in and through an other.

The brother, however, is in the eyes of the sister a being whose nature is unperturbed by desire and is ethically like her own; her recognition in him is pure and unmixed with any sexual relation. The indifference characteristic of particular existence and the ethical contingency thence arising are, therefore, not present in this relationship; instead, the moment of individual selfhood, recognizing and being recognized, can here assert its right, because it is bound up with the balance and equilibrium resulting from their being of the same blood, and from their being related in a way that involves no mutual desire. The loss of a brother is thus irreparable to the sister, and her duty towards him is the highest.

This relationship at the same time is the limit at which the circumscribed life of the family is broken up and passes beyond itself. The brother is the member of the family in whom its spirit becomes individualized, and enabled thereby to turn towards another sphere, towards what is other than and external to itself, and pass over into consciousness of universality. The brother leaves this immediate, rudimentary, and, therefore, strictly speaking, negative ethical life of the family, in order to acquire and produce the concrete ethical order which is conscious of itself.

He passes from the divine law, within whose realm he lived, over to the human law. The sister, however, becomes, or the wife remains, director of the home and the preserver of the divine law. In this way both the sexes overcome their merely natural being, and become ethically significant, as diverse forms dividing between them the different aspects which the ethical substance assumes. Both these universal factors of the ethical world have their specific individuality in naturally distinct self-consciousnesses, for the reason that the spirit at work in the ethical order is the immediate unity of the substance [of ethical life] with self-consciousness—an immediacy which thus appears as the existence of a natural difference, at once as regards its aspect of reality and of difference. It is that aspect which, in the notion of spiritual reality, came to light as "original determinate nature," when we were dealing with the stage of "Individuality which is real to itself." This moment loses the indeterminateness which it still has there, and the contingent diversity of "constitution" and "capacities." It is now the specific opposition of the two sexes, whose natural character acquires at the same time the significance of their respective ethical determinations.

The distinction of the sexes and of their ethical content remains all the same within the unity of the ethical substance, and its process is just the constant development of that substance. The husband is sent forth by the spirit of the family into the life of the community, and finds there his self-conscious reality. Just as the family thereby finds in the community its universal substance and subsistence, conversely the community finds in the family the formal element of its own realization, and in the divine law its power and confirmation. Neither of the two is alone self-complete. Human law as a living and active principle proceeds from the divine, the law holding on earth from that of the nether world, the conscious from the unconscious, mediation from immediacy; and returns too whence it came. The power of the nether world, on the other hand, finds its realization upon earth; it comes through consciousness to have existence and efficacy. . . . .

The ethical realm remains in this way permanently a world without blot or stain, a world untainted by any internal dissension. So, too, its process is an untroubled transition from one of its powers to the other, in such a way that each preserves and produces the other. We see it no doubt divided into two ultimate elements and their realization: but their opposition is rather the confirming and substantiation of one through the other; and where they directly come in contact with each other as actual factors, their mediating common element is the immediate permeation of the one with the other. The one extreme, universal spirit conscious of itself, becomes, through the individuality of man, linked together with its other extreme, its force and its element, with *unconscious* spirit. On the other hand, divine law is individualized, the unconscious spirit of the particular individual finds its existence, in woman, through the mediation of whom the unconscious spirit comes out of its unrealizedness into actuality, and rises out of the state of unknowing and unknown, into the conscious realm of universal spirit. The union of man and woman constitutes the operative mediating agency for the whole, and constitutes the element which, while separated into the extremes of divine and human law, is, at the same time, their immediate union. This union, again, turns both those first mediate connections into one and the same synthesis, and unites into one process the twofold movement in opposite directions—one from reality to unreality, the downward movement of human law, organized into independent members, to the danger and trial of death—the other, from unreality to reality, the upward movement of the law of the nether world to the daylight of conscious existence. Of these movements the former falls to man, the latter to woman. . . .

Human law, then, in its universal mode of existence is the community, in its efficient operation in general is the manhood of the community, in its actual efficient operation is the government. It has its being, its process, and its subsistence by consuming and absorbing into itself the separatist action of the household gods, the individualization into insular independent families which are under the management of womankind, and by keeping them dissolved in the fluent continuum of its own nature. The family at the same time, however, is in general its element, the individual consciousness its universal operative basis. Since the community gets itself subsistence only by breaking in upon family happiness, and dissolving [individual] self-consciousness into the universal, it creates its enemy for itself within its own gates, creates it in what it suppresses, and what is at the same time essential to it—womankind in general. Womankind—the everlasting irony in the life of the community—changes by intrigue the universal purpose of government into a private end, transforms its universal activity into a work of this or that specific individual, and perverts the universal property of the state into a possession and ornament for the family. Woman in this way turns to ridicule the grave wisdom of maturity, which, being dead to all particular aims, to private pleasure, personal satisfaction, and actual activity as well, thinks of, and is concerned for, merely what is universal; she makes this wisdom the laughing-stock of raw and wanton youth, an object of derision and scorn, unworthy of their enthusiasm. She asserts that it is everywhere the force of youth that really counts; she upholds this as of primary significance; extols a son as one who is the lord and master of the mother who has borne him; a brother as one in whom the sister finds man on a level with herself; a youth as one through whom the daughter, freed from her dependence (on the family unity), acquires the satisfaction and the dignity of wifehood.

The community, however, can preserve itself only by suppressing this spirit of individualism; and because the latter is an essential element, the community likewise creates it as well, and creates it, too, by taking up the attitude of seeking to suppress it as a hostile principle. . . .

From *Philosophy of Right*

The difference in the physical characteristics of the two sexes has a rational basis and consequently acquires an intellectual and ethical significance. This significance is determined by the difference into which the ethical substantiality, as the concept, internally sunders itself in order that its vitality may become a concrete unity consequent upon this difference.

Thus one sex is mind in its self-diremption into explicit personal self-subsistence and the knowledge and volition of free universality, i.e., the self-consciousness of conceptual thought and the volition of the objective final end. The other sex is mind maintaining itself in unity as knowledge and volition of the substantive, but knowledge and volition in the form of concrete individuality and feeling. In relation to externality, the former is powerful and active, the latter passive and subjective. It follows that man has his actual substantive life in the state, in learning, and so forth, as well as in labor and struggles with the external world and with himself so that it is only out of his diremption that he fights his way to self-subsistent unity with himself. In the family he has a tranquil intuition of this unity, and there he lives a subjective ethical life on the plane of feeling. Woman, on the other hand, has her substantive destiny in the family, and to be imbued with family piety is her ethical frame of mind.

For this reason, family piety is expounded in Sophocles' *Antigone*—one of the most sublime presentations of this virtue—as principally the law of woman, and as the law of a substantiality at once subjective and on the plane of feeling, the law of the inward life, a life which has not yet attained its full actualization; as the law of the ancient gods, 'the gods of the underworld'; as 'an everlasting law, and no man knows at what time it was first put forth.' This law is there displayed as a law opposed to public law, to the law of the land. This is the supreme opposition in ethics and therefore in tragedy; and it is individualized in the same play in the opposing natures of man and woman. . . .

It must be noticed in connection with sex-relations that a girl in surrendering her body loses her honor. With a man, however, the case is otherwise, because he has a field for ethical activity outside the family. A girl is destined in essence for the marriage tie and for that only; it is therefore demanded of her that her love shall take the form of marriage and that the different moments in love shall attain their true rational relation to each other.

Women are capable of education, but they are not made for activities which demand a universal faculty such as the more advanced sciences, philosophy, and certain forms of artistic production. Women may have happy ideas, taste, and elegance, but they cannot attain to the ideal. The difference between men and women is like that between animals and plants. Men correspond to animals, while women correspond to plants because their development is more placid and the principle that underlies it is the rather vague unity of feeling. When women hold the helm of government, the state is at once in jeopardy, because women regulate their actions not by the demands of universality but by arbitrary inclinations and opinions. Women are educated—who knows how?—as it were by breathing in ideas, by living rather than by acquiring knowledge. The status of manhood, on the other hand, is attained only by the stress of thought and much technical exertion.

Arthur Schopenhauer

*German philosopher of pessimism, 1788–1860, famous for his misogyny,
which many have connected with his bitter and antagonistic relationship
with his mother. Appointed to the post of lecturer at the University of Ber-
lin, he chose to give his lectures at the same hours as Hegel, against whose
popularity he could not successfully compete. After the failure of these lectures, he left academe.*

From "On Women"

You need only look at the way in which she is formed to see that
woman is not meant to undergo great labor, whether of the mind or of the
body. She pays the debt of life not by what she does but by what she
suffers; by the pains of child-bearing and care for the child, and by submission to her husband, to whom she should be a patient and cheering
companion. The keenest sorrows and joys are not for her, nor is she
called upon to display a great deal of strength. The current of her life
should be more gentle, peaceful, and trivial than man's, without being
essentially happier or unhappier.

Women are directly fitted for acting as the nurses and teachers of our
early childhood by the fact that they are themselves childish, frivolous,
and short-sighted; in a word, they are big children all their life long—a
kind of intermediate stage between the child and the full-grown man, who
is man in the strict sense of the word. See how a girl will fondle a child for
days together, dance with it and sing to it; and then think what a man,
with the best will in the world, could do if he were put in her place. . . .

The nobler and more perfect a thing is, the later and slower it is in
arriving at maturity. A man reaches the maturity of his reasoning powers
and mental faculties hardly before the age of twenty-eight; a woman, at
eighteen. And then, too, in the case of woman, it is only reason of a
sort—very niggard in its dimensions. That is why women remain children
their whole life long; never seeing anything but what is quite close to
them, cleaving to the present moment, taking appearance for reality, and
preferring trifles to matters of the first importance. For it is by virtue of

his reasoning faculty that man does not live in the present only, like the brute, but looks about him and considers the past and the future; and this is the origin of prudence as well as of that care and anxiety which so many people exhibit. Both the advantages and the disadvantages which this involves are shared in by the woman to a smaller extent because of her weaker power of reasoning. She may, in fact, be described as intellectually shortsighted, because, while she has an intuitive understanding of what lies quite close to her, her field of vision is narrow and does not reach to what is remote: so that things which are absent or past or to come have much less effect upon women than upon men. This is the reason why women are more often inclined to be extravagant, and sometimes carry their inclination to a length that borders upon madness. In their hearts women think that it is men's business to earn money and theirs to spend it—if possible during their husband's life, but, at any rate, after his death. The very fact that their husband hands them over his earnings for purposes of housekeeping strengthens them in this belief.

However many disadvantages all this may involve, there is at least this to be said in its favor: that the woman lives more in the present than the man, and that, if the present is at all tolerable, she enjoys it more eagerly. This is the source of that cheerfulness which is peculiar to woman, fitting her to amuse man in his hours of recreation, and, in case of need, to console him when he is borne down by the weight of his cares.

It is by no means a bad plan to consult women in matters of difficulty, as the Germans used to do in ancient times; for their way of looking at things is quite different from ours, chiefly in the fact that they like to take the shortest way to their goal, and, in general, manage to fix their eyes upon what lies before them; while we, as a rule, see far beyond it, just because it is in front of our noses. In cases like this, we need to be brought back to the right standpoint, so as to recover the near and simple view.

Then, again, women are decidedly more sober in their judgment than we are, so that they do not see more in things than is really there; whilst, if our passions are aroused, we are apt to see things in an exaggerated way, or imagine what does not exist.

The weakness of their reasoning faculty also explains why it is that women show more sympathy for the unfortunate than men do, and so treat them with more kindness and interest; and why it is that, on the contrary, they are inferior to men in point of justice, and less honorable and conscientious. For it is just because their reasoning power is weak that present circumstances have such a hold over them, and those concrete things which lie directly before their eyes exercise a power which is seldom counteracted to any extent by abstract principles of thought, by fixed rules of conduct, firm resolutions, or, in general, by consideration for the past and the future, or regard for what is absent and remote. Accordingly, they possess the first and main elements that go to make a virtuous character, but they are deficient in those secondary qualities which are often a necessary instrument in the formation of it.*

Hence it will be found that the fundamental fault of the female character is that it has *no sense of justice*. This is mainly due to the fact already mentioned, that women are defective in the powers of reasoning and deliberation; but it is also traceable to the position which nature has assigned to them as the weaker sex. They are dependent, not upon strength, but upon craft; and hence their instinctive capacity for cunning, and their ineradicable tendency to say what is not true. For as lions are provided with claws and teeth, and elephants and boars with tusks, bulls with horns, and the cuttlefish with its cloud of inky fluid, so nature has equipped woman, for her defense and protection, with the arts of dissimulation; and all the power which nature has conferred upon man in the shape of physical strength and reason has been bestowed upon women in this form. Hence dissimulation is innate in woman, and almost as much a quality of the stupid as of the clever. It is as natural for them to make use of it on every occasion as it is for those animals to employ their means of defense when they are attacked; they have a feeling that in doing so they are only within their rights. Therefore a woman who is perfectly truthful and not given to dissimulation is perhaps an impossibility, and for this very reason they are so quick at seeing through dissimulation in others that it is not a wise thing to attempt it with them. But this fundamental defect which I have stated, with all that it entails, gives rise to falsity, faithlessness, treachery, ingratitude, and so on. Perjury in a court of justice is more often committed by women than by men. It may, indeed, be generally questioned whether women ought to be sworn at all. From time to time one finds repeated cases everywhere of ladies who want for nothing, taking things from shop-counters when no one is looking and making off with them.

Nature has appointed that the propagation of the species shall be the business of men who are young, strong, and handsome, so that the race may not degenerate. This is the firm will and purpose of nature in regard to the species, and it finds its expression in the passions of women. There is no law that is older or more powerful than this. Woe, then, to the man who sets up claims and interests that will conflict with it; whatever he may say and do, they will be unmercifully crushed at the first serious encounter. For the innate rule that governs women's conduct, though it is secret and unformulated, nay, unconscious in its working, is this: *We are justified in deceiving those who think they have acquired rights over the*

---

*In this respect they may be compared to an animal organism which contains a liver but no gall-bladder. . . .

species by paying little attention to the individual, that is, to us. The con-
stitution and, therefore, the welfare of the species have been placed in
our hands and committed to our care, through the control we obtain over
the next generation, which proceeds from us; let us discharge our duties
conscientiously. But women have no abstract knowledge of this leading
principle; they are conscious of it only as a concrete fact; and they have
no other method of giving expression to it than the way in which they act
when the opportunity arrives. And then their conscience does not trouble
them so much as we fancy; for in the darkest recesses of their heart they
are aware that, in committing a breach of their duty towards the individual, they have all the better fulfilled their duty towards the species, which
is infinitely greater.

And since women exist in the main solely for the propagation of the
species, and are not destined for anything else, they live, as a rule, more
for the species than for the individual, and in their hearts take the affairs
of the species more seriously than those of the individual. This gives their
whole life and being a certain levity; the general bent of their character is
in a direction fundamentally different from that of man; and it is this
which produces that discord in married life which is so frequent, and almost the normal state.

The natural feeling between men is mere indifference, but between
women it is actual enmity. The reason of this is that trade-jealousy—
odium figulinum—which, in the case of men, does not go beyond the confines of their own particular pursuit, but with women embraces the whole
sex; since they have only one kind of business. Even when they meet in
the street women look at one another like Guelphs and Ghibellines. And it
is a patent fact that when two women make first acquaintance with each
other they behave with more constraint and dissimulation than two men
would show in a like case; and hence it is that an exchange of compli-
ments between two women is a much more ridiculous proceeding than
between two men. Further, whilst a man will, as a general rule, always
preserve a certain amount of consideration and humanity in speaking to
others, even to those who are in a very inferior position, it is intolerable to
see how proudly and disdainfully a fine lady will generally behave towards one who is in a lower social rank (I do not mean a woman who is in
her service), whenever she speaks to her. The reason of this may be that,
with women, differences of rank are much more precarious than with us;
because, while a hundred considerations carry weight in our case, in
theirs there is only one, namely, with which man they have found favor;
as also that they stand in much nearer relations with one another than men
do, in consequence of the one-sided nature of their calling. This makes
them endeavor to lay stress upon differences of rank.

It is only the man whose intellect is clouded by his sexual impulses that
could give the name of *the fair sex* to that undersized, narrow-shouldered,

broad-hipped, and short-legged race: for the whole beauty of the sex is bound up with this impulse. Instead of calling them beautiful, there would be more warrant for describing women as the unesthetic sex. Neither for music, nor for poetry, nor for fine art have they really and truly any sense or susceptibility; it is a mere mockery if they make a pretence of it in order to assist their endeavor to please. Hence, as a result of this, they are incapable of taking a *purely objective interest* in anything; and the reason of it seems to me to be as follows. A man tries to acquire *direct* mastery over things either by understanding them or by forcing them to do his will. But a woman is always and everywhere reduced to obtaining this mastery *indirectly,* namely through a man; and whatever direct mastery she may have is entirely confined to him. And so it lies in woman's nature to look upon everything only as a means for conquering man; and if she takes an interest in anything else it is simulated—a mere roundabout way of gaining her ends by coquetry and feigning what she does not feel. Hence even Rousseau declared: *Women have, in general, no love of any art; they have no proper knowledge of any; and they have no genius. . . .*

And you cannot expect anything else of women if you consider that the most distinguished intellects among the whole sex have never managed to produce a single achievement in the fine arts that is really great, genuine, and original; or given to the world any work of permanent value in any sphere. This is most strikingly shown in regard to painting, where mastery of technique is at least as much within their power as within ours— and hence they are diligent in cultivating it; but still, they have not a single great painting to boast of, just because they are deficient in that objectivity of mind which is so directly indispensable in painting. They never get beyond a subjective point of view. It is quite in keeping with this that ordinary women have no real susceptibility for art at all; for nature proceeds in strict sequence—*non facit saltum.* And Huarte in his book which has been famous for three hundred years denies women the possession of all the higher faculties. The case is not altered by particular and partial exceptions; taken as a whole, women are, and remain, thoroughgoing philistines, and quite incurable. Hence, with that absurd arrangement which allows them to share the rank and title of their husbands, they are a constant stimulus to his ignoble ambitions. And, further, it is just because they are philistines that modern society, where they take the lead and set the tone, is in such a bad way. Napoleon's saying—that *women have no rank*—should be adopted as the right standpoint in determining their position in society; and as regards their other qualities Chamfort makes the very true remark: *They are made to trade with our own weaknesses and our follies, but not with our reason. The sympathies that exist between them and men are skin-deep only, and do not touch the mind or the feelings or the character*. They form the *sexus sequior*—the second sex, inferior in every respect to the first; their infirmities should be treated with consideration; but to show them great reverence is extremely ridiculous, and lowers us in their eyes. When nature made two divisions of the human race, she did not draw the line exactly through the middle. These divisions are polar and opposed to each other, it is true; but the difference between them is not qualitative merely, it is also quantitative. . . .

The laws of marriage prevailing in Europe consider the woman as the equivalent of the man—start, that is to say, from a wrong position. In our part of the world where monogamy is the rule to marry means to halve one's rights and double one's duties. Now, when the laws gave women equal rights with man, they ought to have also endowed her with a masculine intellect. But the fact is that, just in proportion as the honors and privileges which the laws accord to women exceed the amount which nature gives, there is a diminution in the number of women who really participate in these privileges; and all the remainder are deprived of their natural rights by just so much as is given to the others over and above their share. For the institution of monogamy, and the laws of marriage which it entails, bestow upon the woman an unnatural position of privilege, by considering her throughout as the full equivalent of the man, which is by no means the case; and seeing this men who are shrewd and prudent very often scruple to make so great a sacrifice and to acquiesce in so unfair an arrangement.

Consequently, whilst among polygamous nations every woman is provided for, where monogamy prevails the number of married women is limited; and there remains over a large number of women without stay or support, who, in the upper classes, vegetate as useless old maids, and in the lower succumb to hard work for which they are not suited; or else become *filles de joie,* whose life is as destitute of joy as it is of honor. But under the circumstances they become a necessity; and their position is openly recognized as serving the special end of warding off temptation from those women favored by fate, who have found, or may hope to find, husbands. In London alone there are 80,000 prostitutes. What are they but the women, who, under the institution of monogamy, have come off worst? Theirs is a dreadful fate: they are human sacrifices offered up on the altar of monogamy. The women whose wretched position is here described are the inevitable set-off to the European lady with her arrogance and pretension. Polygamy is therefore a real benefit to the female sex if it is taken as a whole. And, from another point of view, there is no true reason why a man whose wife suffers from chronic illness, or remains barren, or has gradually become too old for him, should not take a second. The motives which induce so many people to become converts to

Mormonism* appear to be just those which militate against the unnatural institution of monogamy. . . .

There is no use arguing about polygamy; it must be taken as *de facto* existing everywhere, and the only question is as to how it shall be regulated. Where are there, then, any real monogamists? We all live, at any rate, for a time, and most of us, always, in polygamy. And so, since every man needs many women, there is nothing fairer than to allow him, nay, to make it incumbent upon him, to provide for many women. This will reduce woman to her true and natural position as a subordinate being; and the *lady*—that monster of European civilization and Teutonico-Christian stupidity—will disappear from the world, leaving only *women,* but no more *unhappy women,* of whom Europe is now full. . . .

The first love of a mother for her child is, with the lower animals as with men, of a purely *instinctive* character, and so it ceases when the child is no longer in a physically helpless condition. After that, the first love should give way to one that is based on habit and reason; but this often fails to make its appearance, especially where the mother did not love the father. The love of a father for his child is of a different order, and more likely to last; because it has its foundation in the fact that in the child he recognizes his own inner self; that is to say, his love for it is metaphysical in its origin.

In almost all nations, whether of the ancient or the modern world, even amongst the Hottentots, property is inherited by the male descendants alone; it is only in Europe that a departure has taken place; but not amongst the nobility, however. That the property which has cost men long years of toil and effort, and been won with so much difficulty, should afterwards come into the hands of women, who then, in their lack of reason, squander it in a short time, or otherwise fool it away, is a grievance and a wrong, as serious as it is common, which should be prevented by limiting the right of women to inherit. In my opinion the best arrangement would be that by which women, whether widows or daughters, should never receive anything beyond the interest for life on property secured by mortgage, and in no case the property itself, or the capital, except where all male descendants fail. The people who make money are men, not women; and it follows from this that women are neither justified in having unconditional possession of it, nor fit persons to be entrusted with its administration. . . .

That woman is by nature meant to obey may be seen by the fact that every woman who is placed in the unnatural position of complete independence, immediately attaches herself to some man, by whom she allows herself to be guided and ruled. It is because she needs a lord and master. If she is young, it will be a lover; if she is old, a priest.

*The Mormons have since given up polygamy, and received the American franchise in its stead.

From "Position, or a Man's Place in the Estimation of Others"

In treating of *sexual honor* and the principles on which it rests, a little more attention and analysis are necessary; and what I shall say will support my contention that all honor really sets upon a utilitarian basis. There are two natural divisions of the subject—the honor of women and the honor of men, in either side issuing in a well-understood *esprit de corps*. The former is by far the more important of the two, because the most essential feature in woman's life is her relation to man.

Female honor is the general opinion in regard to a girl that she is pure, and in regard to a wife that she is faithful. The importance of this opinion rests upon the following considerations. Women depend upon men in all the relations of life; men upon women, it might be said, in one only. So an arrangement is made for mutual interdependence—man undertaking responsibility for all woman's needs and also for the children that spring from their union—an arrangement on which is based the welfare of the whole female race. To carry out this plan, women have to band together with a show of *esprit de corps,* and present one undivided front to their common enemy, man—who possesses all the good things of the earth, in virtue of his superior physical and intellectual power—in order to lay siege to and conquer him, and so get possession of him and a share of those good things. To this end the honor of all women depends upon the enforcement of the rule that no woman should give herself to a man except in marriage, in order that every man may be forced, as it were, to surrender and ally himself with a woman; by this arrangement provision is made for the whole of the female race. This is a result, however, which can be obtained only by a strict observance of the rule; and, accordingly, women everywhere show true *esprit de corps* in carefully insisting upon its maintenance. Any girl who commits a breach of the rule betrays the whole female race, because its welfare would be destroyed if every woman were to do likewise; so she is cast out with shame as one who has lost her honor. No woman will have anything more to do with her; she is avoided like the plague. The same doom is awarded to a woman who breaks the marriage tie; for in so doing she is false to the terms upon which the man capitulated; and as her conduct is such as to frighten other men from making a similar surrender, it imperils the welfare of all her sisters. Nay more; this deception and coarse breach of troth is a crime punishable by the loss, not only of personal, but also of civic honor. This is why we minimize the shame of a girl, but not of a wife; because, in the former case, marriage can restore honor, while in the latter, no atonement can be made for the breach of contract.

Once this *esprit de corps* is acknowledged to be the foundation of female honor, and is seen to be a wholesome, nay, a necessary arrangement, as a bottom a matter of prudence and interest, its extreme importance for the welfare of women will be recognized. . . .

The corresponding virtue in men is a product of the one I have been discussing. It is their *esprit de corps,* which demands that, when a man has made that surrender of himself in marriage which is so advantageous to his conqueror, he shall take care that the terms of the treaty are maintained; both in order that the agreement itself may lose none of its force by the permission of any laxity in its observance, and that men, having given up everything, may, at least, be assured of their bargain, namely, exclusive possession. Accordingly, it is part of a man's honor to resent a breach of the marriage tie on the part of his wife, and to punish it, at the very least by separating from her. If he condones the offense, his fellow men cry shame upon him; but the shame in this case is not nearly so foul as that of the woman who has lost her honor; the stain is by no means of so deep a dye—*levioris notae macula*—because a man's relation to woman is subordinate to many other and more important affairs in his life.

From "Ideas Concerning the Intellect"

Craving for knowledge, when directed to the universal, is simply called *desire for knowledge;* but when it is directed to the particular, it is called *inquisitiveness* or *curiosity*. Boys often show a desire for knowledge, little girls mere curiosity, the latter to an astonishing degree and often with tiresome ingenuousness. The tendency to the particular that is characteristic of the female sex and their insusceptibility to the universal are here already in evidence.

From "Of Jurisprudence and Politics"

With rare exceptions, all women are inclined to be extravagant; and so every existing fortune must be protected from their folly, except in those rare cases where they themselves have earned it. For this very reason, I am of the opinion that women never grow up entirely and should always be under the actual care of a man, whether of a father, husband, son, or the state, as is the case in India. Accordingly, they should never be able to dispose arbitrarily of any property that they themselves have not earned. On the other hand, I regard it as unpardonable and pernicious folly to let a mother become even the appointed trustee and administratrix of her children's share of the father's inheritance. In most cases, such a woman will squander on her paramour all that the father of the children has earned out of consideration for them by the labor and industry of his whole life. It will be all the same whether or not she marries the man. . . .

Further, I am of the opinion that in a court of law a woman's evidence. . . should carry less weight than a man's so that, for example, two male witnesses would carry the same weight as three or even four female. For I believe that, taken as a whole, the female sex in a day spouts three times as many lies as does the male, and moreover with a show of plausibility and frankness which is quite beyond the reach of the male. The Mohammedans, of course, go too far in the other direction. A young educated Turk once said to me: 'We regard woman merely as the soil in which the seed is sown; and hence her religion is a matter of indifference. We can marry a Christian without requiring that she be converted.' When I asked him whether dervishes were married, he replied: 'Of course they are; the Prophet was married and they cannot hope to be holier than he'. . . .

From "Psychological Remarks"

Patience, patientia, Geduld, but in particular the Spanish *sufrimiénto,* is so called from *suffering;* consequently, it is passivity, the opposite of the activity of the mind. Where such activity is great, it can hardly be reconciled with patience. It is the inborn virtue of phlegmatic persons and also of the mentally indolent and mentally poor and of women. Nevertheless, the fact that patience is so very useful and necessary betokens a melancholy state of affairs in this world.

From *The World as Will and Idea*

Now that an instinct entirely directed to that which is to be produced lies at the foundation of all sexual love will receive complete confirmation from the fuller analysis of it, which we cannot therefore avoid. First of all we have to remark here that by nature man is inclined to inconstancy in love, woman to constancy. The love of the man sinks perceptibly from the moment it has obtained satisfaction; almost every other woman charms him more than the one he already possesses; he longs for variety. The love of the woman, on the other hand, increases just from that moment. This is a consequence of the aim of nature which is directed to the maintenance, and therefore to the greatest possible increase, of the species. The man can easily beget over a hundred children a year; the woman, on the contrary, with however many men, can yet only bring one child a year into the world (leaving two births out of account). Therefore the man always looks about after other women; the woman, again, sticks firmly to the one man; for nature moves her, instinctively and without reflection, to retain the nourisher and protector of the future offspring. Accordingly faithfulness in marriage is with the man artificial, with the woman it is natural, and thus adultery on the part of the woman is much less pardonable than on the part of the man, both objectively on account of the consequences and also subjectively on account of its unnaturalness.

Auguste Comte

French positivist philosopher, 1798–1857, who developed a science of man in which he attempted to apply the methods of science to the problems of man and that he thought would resolve all social problems caused by industrialization. To this end, he even invented a religion, elaborate in its detail, with a new calendar of saints, festivals, and so on.

From *The Positive Philosophy*

What the ultimate conditions of marriage will be, we cannot know as yet; and if we could, this is not the place to treat of them. It is enough for our purposes to be assured that they will be consonant with the fundamental principle of the institution: the natural subordination of the woman, which has reappeared under all forms of marriage, in all ages, and which the new philosophy will place on its right basis—a knowledge of the individual organism first, and then of the social organism. . . . Sociology will prove that the equality of the sexes, of which so much is said, is incompatible with all social existence, by showing that each sex has special and permanent functions that it must fulfill in the natural economy of the human family, and that concur in a common end by different ways, the welfare that results being in no degree injured by the necessary subordination, since the happiness of every being depends on the wise development of its proper nature.

We have seen that the preponderance of the affective faculties is less marked in man than in the lower animals, and that a certain degree of spontaneous speculative activity is the chief cerebral attribute of humanity, as well as the prime source of the marked character of our social organism. Now, the relative inferiority of woman in this view is incontestable, unfit as she is, in comparison, for the requisite continuousness and intensity of mental labor, either from the intrinsic weakness of her reason or from her more lively moral and physical sensibility, which are hostile to scientific abstraction and concentration. . . . Again, we have seen that, in the affective life of man, the personal instincts overrule the sympathetic or social, which last can, and do, only modify the direction decided by the first, without becoming the habitual moving powers of practical existence. Here again, by a comparative examination, we can estimate the happy social position appropriated to the female sex. It is indisputable that women are, in general, as superior to men in a spontaneous expansion of sympathy and sociality as they are inferior to men in understanding and reason. Their function in the economy of the family, and consequently of society, must therefore be to modify by the excitement of the social instinct the general direction necessarily originated by the cold and rough reason that is distinctive of man. . . .

From *System of Positive Philosophy*

The Influence of Positivism upon Women

The social mission of woman in the positive system follows as a natural consequence from the qualities peculiar to her nature.

In the most essential attribute of the human race, the tendency to place social above personal feeling, she is undoubtedly superior to man. Morally, therefore, and apart from all material considerations, she merits always our loving veneration, as the purest and simplest impersonation of humanity, who can never be adequately represented in any masculine form. But these qualities do not involve the possession of political power, which some visionaries have claimed for women, though without their own consent. In that which is the great object of human life, they are superior to men, but in the various means of attaining that object they are undoubtedly inferior. In all kinds of force, whether physical, intellectual, or practical, it is certain that man surpasses woman, in accordance with the general law prevailing throughout the animal kingdom. Now, practical life is necessarily governed by force rather than by affection, because it requires unremitting and laborious activity. If there were nothing else to do but to love, as in the Christian utopia of a future life in which there are no material wants, woman would be supreme. But we have above everything else to think and to act, in order to carry on the struggle against a rigorous destiny; therefore, man takes the command, notwithstanding his inferiority in goodness. Success in all great undertakings depends more upon energy and talent than upon goodwill, although this last condition reacts strongly upon the others.

Thus, the three elements of our moral constitution do not act in perfect harmony. Force is naturally supreme, and all that women can do is to modify it by affection. Justly conscious of their superiority in strength of feeling, they endeavor to assert their influence in a way that is too often attributed by superficial observers to the mere love of power. But experience always teaches them that in a world where the simplest necessaries of life are scarce and difficult to procure, power must belong to the strongest, not to the most affectionate, even though the latter may deserve it best. With all their efforts they can never do more than modify the harshness with which men exercise their authority. And men submit more readily to this modifying influence, from feeling that in the highest attributes of humanity women are their superiors. They see that their own supremacy is due principally to the material necessities of life, provision for which calls into play the self-regarding rather than the social instincts. Hence we find it the case in every phase of human society that women's life is essentially domestic, public life being confined to men. Civilization, so far from effacing this natural distinction, tends, as I shall afterwards show, to develop it, while remedying its abuses.

Thus the social position of women is in this respect very similar to that of philosophers and of the working classes. And we now see why these three elements should be united. It is their combined action that constitutes the modifying force of society.

Philosophers are excluded from political power by the same fatality as women, although they are apt to think that their intellectual eminence gives them a claim to it. Were our material wants more easily satisfied, the influence of intellect would be less impeded than it is by the practical business of life. But, on this hypothesis, women would have a better claim to govern than philosophers. For the reasoning faculties would have remained almost inert had they not been needed to guide our energies, the constitution of the brain not being such as to favor their spontaneous development, whereas the affective principle is dependent on no such external stimulus for its activity. A life of thought is a more evident disqualification for the government of the world than even a life of feeling, although the self-conceit of philosophers is a greater obstacle to submission than the vanity of women. With all its pretensions, intellectual force is not in itself more moral than material force. Each is but an instrument; the merit depends entirely upon its right employment. The only element of our nature that is in itself moral is love, for love alone tends of itself towards the preponderance of social feeling over self-interest. And since even love cannot govern, what can be the claim of intellect? In practical life precedence must always depend upon superior energy. Reason, even more than feeling, must be restricted to the task of modifying. Philosophers therefore must be excluded from government at least as rigidly as women. It is in vain for intellect to attempt to command; it never can do more than modify. In fact, the morality that it indirectly possesses is due to this impossibility of exercising compulsory power, and would be ruined by the attainment of it, supposing such a dream to be possible. Intellect may do much to amend the natural order of things, but only on the condition of not attempting to subvert it. What it can do is by its power of systematic arrangement to effect the union of all the classes who are likely to exert a beneficial influence on material power. It is with this view that every spiritual power has availed itself of the aid of women, as we see was the case in the Middle Ages. . . .

Spiritual power, as interpreted by positivism, begins with the influence of women in the family; it is afterwards molded into a system by thinkers, while the people are the guarantee for its political efficiency. Although it is the intellectual class that institutes the union, yet its own part in it, as it should never forget, is less direct than that of women, less practical than that of the people. The thinker is socially powerless except insofar as he is supported by feminine sympathy and popular energy.

But, however important the public duties that women will ultimately be called upon to perform, the family is after all their highest and most distinctive sphere of work. It was in allusion to their domestic influence that I spoke of them as the originators of spiritual power. . . .

. . . But in the positive theory of marriage and of the family the principal service to be rendered by woman is one quite unconnected with the function of procreation. It is directly based upon the highest attributes of our nature. . . .

Viewed thus, marriage is the most elementary and yet the most perfect mode of social life. It is the only association in which entire identity of interests is possible. In this union, to the moral completeness of which the language of all civilized nations bears testimony, the noblest aim of human life is realized, as far as it can ever be. For the object of human existence . . . is progress of every kind—progress in morality, that is to say, in the subjection of self-interest to social feeling, holding the first rank. . . .

But independently of the intrinsic value of this sacred union, we have to consider its importance from the social point of view. It is the first stage in our progress towards that which is the final object of moral education—namely, universal love. . . . From personal experience of strong love we rise by degrees to sincere affection for all mankind strong enough to modify conduct, although, as the scope of feeling widens, its energy must decrease. The connection of these two states of feeling is instinctively recognized by all. . . .

The purpose of marriage once clearly understood, it becomes easy to define its conditions. The intervention of society is necessary, but its only object is to confirm and to develop the order of things that exists naturally.

It is essential in the first place to the high purposes for which marriage has been instituted that the union shall be both exclusive and indissoluble. So essential indeed are both conditions that we frequently find them even when the connection is illegal. That anyone should have ventured to propound the doctrine that human happiness is to be secured by levity and inconstancy in love is a fact that nothing but the utter deficiency of social and moral principles can explain. Love cannot be deep unless it remains constant to a fixed object, for the very possibility of change is a temptation to it. . . . Sexual love may become a powerful engine for good, but only on the condition of placing it under rigorous and permanent discipline. . . .

Monogamy, then, is one of the most precious gifts that the Middle Ages has bequeathed to Western Europe. The striking superiority of social life in the West is probably due to it more than to any other cause. Protestant countries have seriously impaired its value by their laws of divorce. But this temporary aberration is alien to the purer feelings of women and of the people, and the mischief done by it is limited to the privileged classes. . . . The mode of resistance to these errors that positivism adopts will render the struggle most useful in hastening the adoption of the true theory of marriage. . . .

To the spirit of anarchy, however, positivism yields nothing. The unity essential to marriage it renders more complete than ever. It develops the principal of monogamy by inculcating, not as a legal institution but as a moral duty, the perpetuity of widowhood. . . . Constant adoration of one whom death has implanted more visibly and deeply on the memory leads all high natures, and philosophic natures especially, to give themselves more unreservedly to the service of humanity, and thus their public life is animated by the ennobling influence of their innermost feelings. Alike from a sense of their own truest happiness and from devotion to public duty, they will be led to this result.

Deep as is the satisfaction in this prolongation of the sacredness of marriage, it may be carried by those who recognize its value yet further. As the death of one did not destroy the bond, so neither should the death of both. Let then those whom death could not divide be laid in the same grave together. . . .

. . . We have examined the position of woman as a wife without supposing her to be a mother. Completing the sociological theory of the subject, we shall find that maternity, while it extends her sphere of moral influence, does not alter its nature.

As a mother, no less than as a wife, her position will be improved by positivism. She will have, almost exclusively, the direction of household education. Public education given subsequently will be, as I have explained in the preceding chapter, little but a systematic development of that which has been previously given at home.

For it is a fundamental principle that education, in the normal condition of society, must be entrusted to the spiritual power, and in the family the spiritual power is represented by woman. . . . That part of education that has the greatest influence on life, what may be called the spontaneous training of the feelings, belongs entirely to the mother. Hence it is, as I have already observed, of the greatest importance to allow the pupil to remain with his family, and to do away with the monastic seclusion of our public schools. . . .

From the relation of mother we return by a natural transition to woman's position as a wife. The mother, though her authority of course tends to decrease, continues to superintend the growth of character until the ordinary age of marriage. Up to that time feminine influence over man has been involuntary on his part. By marriage he enters into a voluntary engagement of subordination to woman for the rest of his life. Thus he completes his moral education. Destined himself for action, he finds his highest happiness in honorable submission to the ennobling influence of one in whom the dominant principle is affection.

The important field of public and private duty thus opened to woman is therefore nothing but a larger and more systematic development of the qualities by which she is characterized. Her mission is so uniform in its nature, and so clearly defined, that there seems hardly room for much uncertainty as to her proper social position. It is a striking instance of the rule that applies universally to all human effort—namely, that the order of things instituted by man ought to be simply a consolidation and improvement of the natural order. . . .

The Religion of Humanity

. . . Women, from their strongly sympathetic nature, were the original source of all moral influence, and they are peculiarly qualified by the passive character of their life to assist the action of the spiritual power in the family. With its most essential function of education they are intimately connected. Private education is entrusted to their sole charge, and public education simply consists in giving a more systematic shape to what the mother has already inculcated in childhood. As wives they assume still more distinctly the spiritual function of counsel, softening by persuasion where the philosopher can only influence by conviction. In social meetings, again, the only mode of public life adapted to their nature, they assist the spiritual power in the formation of public opinion of which it is the systematic organ, by applying the principles that it inculcates to the case of particular actions or persons. In all these matters their influence will be far more effectual when men have done their duty to women by setting them free from the pressure of material necessity, and when women on their side have renounced both power and wealth, as we see so often exemplified among the working classes. . . .

The only cases in which the spiritual power has to interfere specially for the protection of material interests fall under two principles, which are very plainly indicated by the natural order of society. The first principle is that man should support woman; the second, that the active class should support the speculative class. The necessity of both these conditions is evident: without them the affective and speculative functions of humanity cannot be adequately performed. . . . As to the second principle, it is one that has been already admitted by former systems. . . . If temporal and spiritual power are really to be separated, philosophers should have as little to do with wealth as with government. Resembling women in their exclusion from political power, their position as to wealth should be like that of the working classes, proper regard being given to the requirements of their office. By following this course, they may be confident that the purity of their opinions and advice will never be called in question.

These two conditions, then, capitalists, as the normal administrators of the common fund of wealth, will be expected to satisfy. They must, that is, so regulate the distribution of wages that women shall be released from work, and they must see that proper remuneration is given for intellectual labor. To exact the performance of these conditions seems no easy task; yet until they are satisfied, the equilibrium of our social economy will remain unstable. The present holders of a position that is no longer tenable on the imaginary ground of personal right may probably decline to accept these principles. In that case, their functions will pass in one way or another to new organs, until humanity finds servants who will not shirk their fundamental duties, but who will recognize them as the first condition of their tenure of power. . . . Rich men will feel that principles like these, leaving as they do to the individual the merit of voluntary action, are the only method of escaping from the political oppression with which they are now threatened. The free concentration of capital will then be readily accepted as necessary to its social usefulness, for great duties imply great powers.

This, then, is the way in which the priests of humanity may hope to regenerate the material power of wealth and bring the nutritive functions of society into harmony with the other parts of the body politic. The contests for which as yet there are but too many motives will then cease. . . .

John Stuart Mill

English economist, philosopher of logic, and advocate of utilitarianism in ethics, 1806–1873. A great and effective spokesman for the liberal view of man, Mill argued for liberty, claiming that ". . . the sole end for which mankind are warranted, individually or collectively, in interfering with the liberty of any of their number, is self-protection."

From *The Subjection of Women*

Some will object, that a comparison cannot fairly be made between the government of the male sex and the forms of unjust power which I have adduced in illustration of it, since these are arbitrary, and the effect of mere usurpation, while it on the contrary is natural. But was there ever any domination which did not appear natural to those who possessed it?

. . . The subjection of women to men being a universal custom, any departure from it quite naturally appears unnatural. But how entirely, even in this case, the feeling is dependent on custom, appears by ample experience. Nothing so much astonishes the people of distant parts of the world, when they first learn anything about England, as to be told that it is under a queen: the thing seems to them so unnatural as to be almost incredible. To Englishmen this does not seem in the least degree unnatural, because they are used to it; but they do feel it unnatural that women should be soldiers or members of parliament. In the feudal ages, on the contrary, war and politics were not thought unnatural to women, because not unusual; it seemed natural that women of the privileged classes should be of manly character, inferior in nothing but bodily strength to their husbands and fathers. The independence of women seemed rather less unnatural to the Greeks than to other ancients, on account of the fabulous Amazons (whom they believed to be historical), and the partial example afforded by the Spartan women; who, though no less subordinate by law than in other Greek states, were more free in fact, and being trained to bodily exercises in the same manner with men, gave ample proof that they were not naturally disqualified for them. There can be little doubt that Spartan experience suggested to Plato, among many other of his doctrines, that of the social and political equality of the two sexes.

But, it will be said, the rule of men over women differs from all these others in not being a rule of force: it is accepted voluntarily; women make no complaint, and are consenting parties to it. In the first place, a great number of women do not accept it. . . .

All causes, social and natural, combine to make it unlikely that women should be collectively rebellious to the power of men. They are so far in a position different from all other subject classes, that their masters require something more from them than actual service. Men do not want solely the obedience of women, they want their sentiments. All men, except the most brutish, desire to have, in the woman most nearly connected with them, not a forced slave but a willing one, not a slave merely, but a favorite. They have therefore put everything in practice to enslave their minds. The masters of all other slaves rely, for maintaining obedience, on fear; either fear of themselves, or religious fears. The masters of women wanted more than simple obedience, and they turned the whole force of education to effect their purpose. All women are brought up from the very earliest years in the belief that their ideal of character is the very opposite to that of men; not self-will, and government by self-control, but submission, and yielding to the control of others. All the moralities tell them that it is the duty of women, and all the current sentimentalities that it is their nature, to live for others; to make complete abnegation of themselves, and to have no life but in their affections. And by their affections are meant the only ones they are allowed to have—those to the men with whom they are connected, or to the children who constitute an additional and indefeasible tie between them and a man. When we put together three things—first, the natural attraction between opposite sexes; secondly, the wife's entire dependence on the husband, every privilege or pleasure she has being either his gift, or depending entirely on his will; and lastly, that the principal object of human pursuit, consideration, and all objects of social ambition, can in general be sought or obtained by her only through him, it would be a miracle if the object of being attractive to men had not become the polar star of feminine education and formation of character. . . .

The old theory was, that the least possible should be left to the choice of the individual agent; that all he had to do should, as far as practicable, be laid down for him by superior wisdom. Left to himself he was sure to go wrong. The modern conviction, the fruit of a thousand years of experience, is, that things in which the individual is the person directly interested, never go right but as they are left to his own discretion; and that any regulation of them by authority, except to protect the rights of others, is sure to be mischievous. . . .

It is not that all processes are supposed to be equally good, or all persons to be equally qualified for everything; but that freedom of individual choice is now known to be the only thing which procures the adoption of the best processes, and throws each operation into the hands of those who are best qualified for it. Nobody thinks it necessary to make a law that only a strong-armed man shall be a blacksmith. . . .

But if the principle is true, we ought to act as if we believed it, and not to ordain that to be born a girl instead of a boy, any more than to be born black instead of white, or a commoner instead of a nobleman, shall decide the person's position through all life—shall interdict people from all the more elevated social positions, and from all, except a few, respectable occupations. Even were we to admit the utmost that is ever pretended as to the superior fitness of men for all the functions now reserved to them, the same argument applies which forbids a legal qualification for members of Parliament. If only once in a dozen years the conditions of eligibility exclude a fit person, there is a real loss, while the exclusion of thousands of unfit persons is no gain; for if the constitution of the electoral body disposes them to choose unfit persons, there are always plenty of such persons to choose from. In all things of any difficulty and importance, those who can do them well are fewer than the need, even with the most unrestricted latitude of choice: and any limitation of the field of selection deprives society of some chances of being served by the competent, without ever saving it from the incompetent. . . .

Experience cannot possibly have decided between two courses, so long as there has only been experience of one. If it be said that the doctrine of the equality of the sexes rests only on theory, it must be remembered that the contrary doctrine also has only theory to rest upon. All that is proved in its favor by direct experience, is that mankind have been able to exist under it, and to attain the degree of improvement and prosperity which we now see; but whether that prosperity has been attained sooner, or is now greater, than it would have been under the other system, experience does not say. On the other hand, experience does say, that every step in improvement has been so invariably accompanied by a step made in raising the social position of women, that historians and philosophers have been led to adopt their elevation or debasement as on the whole the surest test and most correct measure of the civilization of a people or an age. Through all the progressive period of human history, the condition of women has been approaching nearer to equality with men. This does not of itself prove that the assimilation must go on to complete equality; but it assuredly affords some presumption that such is the case.

Neither does it avail anything to say that the *nature* of the two sexes adapts them to their present functions and position, and renders these appropriate to them. Standing on the ground of common sense and the constitution of the human mind, I deny that any one knows, or can know, the nature of the two sexes, as long as they have only been seen in their present relation to one another. If men have ever been found in society without women, or women without men, or if there had been a society of men and women in which the women were not under the control of the men, something might have been positively known about the mental and moral differences which might be inherent in the nature of each. What is now called the nature of women is an eminently artificial thing—the result of forced repression in some directions, unnatural stimulation in others. . . .

. . . The most favorable case which a man can generally have for studying the character of a woman is that of his own wife: for the opportunities are greater, and the cases of complete sympathy not so unspeakably rare. And in fact, this is the source from which any knowledge worth having on the subject has, I believe, generally come. But most men have not had the opportunity of studying in this way more than a single case: accordingly one can, to an almost laughable degree, infer what a man's wife is like, from his opinions about women in general. To make even this one case yield any result, the woman must be worth knowing, and the man not only a competent judge, but of a character so sympathetic in itself, and so well adapted to hers, that he can either read her mind by sympathetic intuition, or has nothing in himself which makes her shy of disclosing it. Hardly anything, I believe, can be more rare than this conjunction. It often happens that there is the most complete unity of feeling and community of interests as to all external things, yet the one has as little admission into the internal life of the other as if they were common acquaintance. Even with true affection, authority on the one side and subordination on the other prevent perfect confidence. . . . When we further consider that to understand one woman is not necessarily to understand any other woman; that even if he could study many women of one rank, or of one country, he would not thereby understand women of other ranks or countries; and even if he did, they are still only the women of a single period of history; we may safely assert that the knowledge which men can acquire of women, even as they have been and are, without reference to what they might be, is wretchedly imperfect and superficial, and always will be so, until women themselves have told all that they have to tell. . . .

One thing we may be certain of—that what is contrary to women's nature to do, they never will be made to do by simply giving their nature free play. The anxiety of mankind to interfere in behalf of nature, for fear lest nature should not succeed in effecting its purpose, is an altogether unnecessary solicitude. What women by nature cannot do, it is quite superfluous to forbid them from doing. What they can do, but not so well as the men who are their competitors, competition suffices to exclude them from; since nobody asks for protective duties and bounties in favor of women; it is only asked that the present bounties and protective duties in

favor of men should be recalled. If women have a greater natural inclination for some things than for others, there is no need of laws or social
inculcation to make the majority of them do the former in preference to
the latter. Whatever women's sevices are most wanted for, the free play
of competition will hold out the strongest inducements to them to undertake. And, as the words imply, they are most wanted for the things for
which they are most fit; by the apportionment of which to them, the collective faculties of the two sexes can be applied on the whole with the
greatest sum of valuable result.

The general opinion of men is supposed to be that the natural vocation
of a woman is that of a wife and mother. I say, is supposed to be, because, judging from acts—from the whole of the present constitution of
society—one might infer that their opinion was the direct contrary. They
might be supposed to think that the alleged natural vocation of women
was of all things the most repugnant to their nature; insomuch that if they
are free to do anything else—if any other means of living, or occupation
of their time and faculties, is open, which has any chance of appearing
desirable to them—there will not be enough of them who will be willing
to accept the condition said to be natural to them. If this is the real opinion
of men in general, it would be well that it should be spoken out. I should
like to hear somebody openly enunciating the doctrine (it is already implied in much that is written on the subject)—"It is necessary to society
that women should marry and produce children. They will not do so unless they are compelled. Therefore it is necessary to compel them." The
merits of the case would then be clearly defined. It would be exactly that
of the slaveholders of South Carolina and Louisiana. "It is necessary that
cotton and sugar should be grown. White men cannot produce them. Negroes will not, for any wages which we choose to give. *Ergo* they must be
compelled." An illustration still closer to the point is that of impressment. Sailors must absolutely be had to defend the country. It often happens that they will not voluntarily enlist. Therefore there must be the
power of forcing them. How often has this logic been used! and, but for
one flaw in it, without doubt it would have been successful up to this day.
But it is open to the retort—First pay the sailors the honest value of their
labor. When you have made it as well worth their while to serve you, as
to work for other employers, you will have no more difficulty than others
have in obtaining their services. To this there is no logical answer except
"I will not:" and as people are now not only ashamed, but are not desirous, to rob the laborer of his hire, impressment is no longer advocated.
Those who attempt to force women into marriage by closing all other
doors against them, lay themselves open to a similar retort. . . .

But how, it will be asked, can any society exist without government?
In a family, as in a state, some one person must be the ultimate ruler.
Who shall decide when married people differ in opinion? Both cannot
have their way, yet a decision one way or the other must be come to.

It is not true that in all voluntary association between two people, one of them must be absolute master: still less that the law must determine which of them it shall be. The most frequent case of voluntary association, next to marriage, is partnership in business: and it is not found or thought necessary to enact that in every partnership, one partner shall have entire control over the concern, and the others shall be bound to obey his orders. . . .

In the last two centuries, when (which was seldom the case) any reason beyond the mere existence of the fact was thought to be required to justify the disabilities of women, people seldom assigned as a reason their inferior mental capacity; which, in times when there was a real trial of personal faculties (from which all women were not excluded) in the struggles of public life, no one really believed in. The reason given in those days was not women's unfitness, but the interest of society, by which was meant the interest of men: just as the *raison d'état,* meaning the convenience of the government, and the support of existing authority, was deemed a sufficient explanation and excuse for the most flagitious crimes. In the present day, power holds a smoother language, and whomsoever it oppresses, always pretends to do so for their own good: accordingly, when anything is forbidden to women, it is thought necessary to say, and desirable to believe, that they are incapable of doing it, and that they depart from their real path of success and happiness when they aspire to it. But to make this reason plausible (I do not say valid), those by whom it is urged must be prepared to carry it to a much greater length than any one ventures to do in the face of present experience. It is not sufficient to maintain that women on the average are less gifted than men on the average, with certain of the higher mental faculties, or that a smaller number of women than of men are fit for occupations and functions of the highest intellectual character. It is necessary to maintain that no women at all are fit for them, and that the most eminent women are inferior in mental faculties to the most mediocre of the men on whom these functions at present devolve. . . .

Now, the most determined depreciator of women will not venture to deny, that when we add the experience of recent times to that of ages past, women, and not a few merely, but many women, have proved themselves capable of everything, perhaps without a single exception, which is done by men, and of doing it successfully and creditably. The utmost that can be said is that there are many things which none of them have succeeded in doing as well as they have been done by some men—many in which they have not reached the very highest rank. But there are extremely few, dependent only on mental faculties, in which they have not attained the rank next to the highest. . . .

Let us at first make entire abstraction of all psychological considerations tending to show, that any of the mental differences supposed to exist between women and men are but the natural effect of the differences in their education and circumstances, and indicate no radical difference, far less radical inferiority, of nature. Let us consider women only as they already are, or as they are known to have been; and the capacities which they have already practically shown. What they have done, that at least, if nothing else, it is proved that they can do. When we consider how sedulously they are all trained away from, instead of being trained towards, any of the occupations or objects reserved for men, it is evident that I am taking a very humble ground for them, when I rest their case on what they have actually achieved. For, in this case, negative evidence is worth little, while any positive evidence is conclusive. It cannot be inferred to be impossible that a woman should be a Homer, or an Aristotle, or a Michael Angelo, or a Beethoven, because no woman has yet actually produced works comparable to theirs in any of those lines of excellence. This negative fact at most leaves the question uncertain, and open to psychological discussion. But it is quite certain that a woman can be a Queen Elizabeth, or a Deborah, or a Joan of Arc, since this is not inference, but fact. Now it is a curious consideration that the only things which the existing law excludes women from doing are the things which they have proved that they are able to do. There is no law to prevent a woman from having written all the plays of Shakespeare, or composed all the operas of Mozart. But Queen Elizabeth or Queen Victoria, had they not inherited the throne, could not have been intrusted with the smallest of the political duties, of which the former showed herself equal to the greatest.

. . . Exactly where and in proportion as women's capacities for government have been tried, in that proportion have they been found adequate. . . . With equality of experience and of general faculties, a woman usually sees much more than a man of what is immediately before her. Now this sensibility to the present is the main quality on which the capacity for practice, as distinguished from theory, depends. To discover general principles belongs to the speculative faculty: to discern and discriminate the particular cases in which they are and are not applicable constitutes practical talent: and for this, women as they now are have a peculiar aptitude. I admit that there can be no good practice without principles, and that the predominant place which quickness of observation holds among a woman's faculties makes her particularly apt to build over-hasty generalizations upon her own observation; though at the same time no less ready in rectifying those generalizations as her observation takes a wider range. But the corrective to this defect, is access to the experience of the human race; general knowledge—exactly the thing which education can best supply. A woman's mistakes are specifically those of a clever self-educated man, who often sees what men trained in routine do not see, but falls into errors for want of knowing things which have long been known. Of course he has acquired much of the pre-existing knowledge, or he could not have got on at all; but what he knows of it he has picked up in fragments and at random, as women do. . . .

Let us take, then, the only marked case which observation affords of apparent inferiority of women to men, if we except the merely physical one of bodily strength. No production in philosophy, science, or art, entitled to the first rank has been the work of a woman. Is there any mode of accounting for this, without supposing that women are naturally incapable of producing them?

In the first place, we may fairly question whether experience has afforded sufficient grounds for an induction. It is scarcely three generations since women, saving very rare exceptions, have begun to try their capacity in philosophy, science, or art. It is only in the present generation that their attempts have been at all numerous; and they are even now extremely few, everywhere but in England and France. It is a relevant question, whether a mind possessing the requisites of first-rate eminence in speculation or creative art could have been expected, on the mere calculation of chances, to turn up during that lapse of time, among the women whose tastes and personal position admitted of their devoting themselves to these pursuits. In all things which there has yet been time for—in all but the very highest grades in the scale of excellence, especially in the department in which they have been longest engaged, literature (both prose and poetry)—women have done quite as much, have obtained fully as high prizes and as many of them, as could be expected from the length of time and the number of competitors.

. . . The law of servitude in marriage is a monstrous contradiction to all the principles of the modern world, and to all the experience through which those principles have been slowly and painfully worked out. It is the sole case, now that negro slavery has been abolished, in which a human being in the plenitude of every faculty is delivered up to the tender mercies of another human being, in the hope forsooth that this other will use the power solely for the good of the person subjected to it. Marriage is the only actual bondage known to our law. There remain no legal slaves, except the mistress of every house.

It is not, therefore, on this part of the subject, that the question is likely to be asked, *Cui bono?* We may be told that the evil would outweigh the good, but the reality of the good admits of no dispute. In regard, however, to the larger question, the removal of women's disabilities—their recognition as the equals of men in all that belongs to citizenship—the opening to them of all honorable employments, and of the training and education which qualifies for those employments—there are many persons for whom it is not enough that the inequality has no just or legitimate defense: they require to be told what express advantage would be obtained by abolishing it.

To which let me first answer, the advantage of having the most universal and pervading of all human relations regulated by justice instead of injustice. The vast amount of this gain to human nature, it is hardly possible, by any explanation or illustration, to place in a stronger light than it is placed by the bare statement, to any one who attaches a moral meaning to words. All the selfish propensities, the self-worship, the unjust self-preference, which exist among mankind, have their source and root in, and derive their principal nourishment from, the present constitution of the relation between men and women. Think what it is to a boy, to grow up to manhood in the belief that without any merit or any exertion of his own, though he may be the most frivolous and empty or the most ignorant and stolid of mankind, by the mere fact of being born a male he is by right the superior of all and every one of an entire half of the human race: including probably some whose real superiority to himself he has daily or hourly occasion to feel; but even if in his whole conduct he habitually follows a woman's guidance, still, if he is a fool, she thinks that of course she is not, and cannot be, equal in ability and judgment to himself; and if he is not a fool, he does worse—he sees that she is superior to him, and believes that, notwithstanding her superiority, he is entitled to command and she is bound to obey. What must be the effect on his character, of this lesson? And men of the cultivated classes are often not aware how deeply it sinks into the immense majority of male minds.

. . . The relation between husband and wife is very like that between lord and vassal, except that the wife is held to more unlimited obedience than the vassal was. However the vassal's character may have been affected, for better and for worse, by his subordination, who can help seeing that the lord's was affected greatly for the worse? whether he was led to believe that his vassals were really superior to himself, or to feel that he was placed in command over people as good as himself, for no merits or labors of his own, but merely for having, as Figaro says, taken the trouble to be born. The self-worship of the monarch, or of the feudal superior, is matched by the self-worship of the male. Human beings do not grow up from childhood in the possession of unearned distinctions, without pluming themselves upon them.

. . . Whoever has a wife and children has given hostages to Mrs. Grundy. The approbation of that potentate may be a matter of indifference to him, but it is of great importance to his wife. The man himself may be above opinion, or may find sufficient compensation in the opinion of those of his own way of thinking. But to the women connected with him, he can offer no compensation. The almost invariable tendency of the wife to place her influence in the same scale with social consideration, is sometimes made a reproach to women, and represented as a peculiar trait of feebleness and childishness of character in them: surely with great injustice. Society makes the whole life of a woman, in the easy classes, a continued self-sacrifice; it exacts from her an unremitting restraint of the whole of her natural inclinations, and the sole return it makes to her for what often deserves the name of a martyrdom, is consideration. Her consideration is inseparably connected with that of her husband, and after paying the full price for it, she finds that she is to lose it, for no reason of which she can feel the cogency. She has sacrificed her whole life to it, and her husband will not sacrifice to it a whim, a freak, an eccentricity; something not recognized or allowed for by the world, and which the world will agree with her in thinking a folly, if it thinks no worse! The dilemma is hardest upon that very meritorious class of men, who, without possessing talents which qualify them to make a figure among those with whom they agree in opinion, hold their opinion from conviction, and feel bound in honor and conscience to serve it, by making profession of their belief, and giving their time, labor, and means, to anything undertaken in its behalf. The worst case of all is when such men happen to be of a rank and position which of itself neither gives them, nor excludes them from, what is considered the best society; when their admission to it depends mainly on what is thought of them personally—and however unexceptional their breeding and habits, their being identified with opinions and public conduct unacceptable to those who give the tone to society would operate as an effectual exclusion. Many a woman flatters herself (nine times out of ten quite erroneously) that nothing prevents her and her husband from moving in the highest society of her neighborhood—society in which others well known to her, and in the same class of life, mix freely—except that her husband is unfortunately a Dissenter, or has the reputation of mingling in low radical politics. That it is, she thinks, which hinders George from getting a commission or a place, Caroline from making an advantageous match, and prevents her and her husband from obtaining invitations, perhaps honors, which, for aught she sees, they are as well entitled to as some folks. With such an influence in every house, either exerted actively, or operating all the more powerfully for not being asserted, is it any wonder that people in general are kept down in that mediocrity of respectability which is becoming a marked characteristic of modern times?

. . .It is not with impunity that the superior in intellect shuts himself up with an inferior, and elects that inferior for his chosen, and sole completely intimate, associate. Any society which is not improving, is deteriorating: and the more so, the closer and more familiar it is. Even a really superior man almost always begins to deteriorate when he is habitually (as the phrase is) king of his company: and in his most habitual company the husband who has a wife inferior to him is always so. While his self-satisfaction is incessantly ministered to on the one hand, on the other he insensibly imbibes the modes of feeling, and of looking at things, which belong to a more vulgar or a more limited mind than his own. This evil differs from many of those which have hitherto been dwelt on, by being an increasing one. The association of men with women in daily life is much closer and more complete than it ever was before. . . .

Thus far, the benefits which it has appeared that the world would gain by ceasing to make sex a disqualification for privileges and a badge of subjection, are social rather than individual; consisting in an increase of the general fund of thinking and acting power, and an improvement in the general conditions of the association of men with women. But it would be a grievous understatement of the case to omit the most direct benefit of all, the unspeakable gain in private happiness to the liberated half of the species; the difference to them between a life of subjection to the will of others, and a life of rational freedom. . . .

When we consider the positive evil caused to the disqualified half of the human race by their disqualification—first in the loss of the most inspiriting and elevating kind of personal enjoyment, and next in the weariness, disappointment, and profound dissatisfaction with life, which are so often the substitute for it; one feels that among all the lessons which men require for carrying on the struggle against the inevitable imperfections of their lot on earth, there is no lesson which they more need, than not to add to the evils which nature inflicts, by their jealous and prejudiced restrictions on one another. Their vain fears only substitute other and worse evils for those which they are idly apprehensive of: while every restraint on the freedom of conduct of any of their human fellow creatures, (otherwise than by making them responsible for any evil actually caused by it), dries up *pro tanto* the principal fountain of human happiness, and leaves the species less rich, to an inappreciable degree, in all that makes life valuable to the individual human being.

Frederick Engels

German philosopher, 1820–1895, disciple of Karl Marx, with whom he collaborated on many important writings outlining the theory and practice of Communism.

From *The Origin of the Family, Private Property, and the State*

The pairing family, itself too weak and unstable to make an independent household necessary, or even desirable, did not by any means dissolve the communistic household transmitted from earlier times. But the communistic household implies the supremacy of women in the house, just as the exclusive recognition of a natural mother, because of the impossibility of determining the natural father with certainty, signifies high esteem for the women, that is, for the mothers. That woman was the slave of man at the commencement of society is one of the most absurd notions that have come down to us from the period of Enlightenment of the eighteenth century. Woman occupied not only a free but also a highly respected position among all savages and all barbarians of the lower and middle stages and partly even of the upper stage. . . .

I may add, furthermore, that the reports of travellers and missionaries about women among savages and barbarians being burdened with excessive toil in no way conflict with what has been said above. The division of labor between the two sexes is determined by causes entirely different from those that determine the status of women in society. Peoples whose women have to work much harder than we would consider proper often have far more real respect for women than our Europeans have for theirs. The social status of the lady of civilization, surrounded by sham homage and estranged from all real work, is socially infinitely lower than that of the hard-working woman of barbarism, who was regarded among her people as a real lady . . . and was such by the nature of her position. . . .

The overthrow of mother right was the *world-historic defeat of the female sex*. The man seized the reins in the house also, the woman was degraded, enthralled, the slave of the man's lust, a mere instrument for breeding children. This lowered position of women, especially manifest among the Greeks of the Heroic and still more of the Classical Age, has become gradually embellished and dissembled and, in part, clothed in a milder form, but by no means abolished.

The first effect of the sole rule of the men that was now established is shown in the intermediate form of the family which now emerges, the patriarchal family. Its chief attribute is not polygamy—of which more anon—but "the organization of a number of persons, bond and free, into a family, under the paternal power of the head of the family. . . ."

Such a form of the family shows the transition of the pairing family to monogamy. In order to guarantee the fidelity of the wife, that is, the paternity of the children, the woman is placed in the man's absolute power; if he kills her, he is but exercising his right. . . .

Thus, monogamy does not by any means make its appearance in history as the reconciliation of man and woman, still less as the highest form of such a reconciliation. On the contrary, it appears as the subjection of one sex by the other, as the proclamation of a conflict between the sexes entirely unknown hitherto in prehistoric times. In an old unpublished manuscript, the work of Marx and myself in 1846,* I find the following: "The first division of labor is that between man and woman for child breeding." And today I can add: The first class antagonism which appears in history coincides with the development of the antagonism between man and woman in monogamian marriage, and the first class oppression with that of the female sex by the male. . . .

Sex love in the relation of husband and wife is and can become the rule only among the oppressed classes, that is, at the present day, among the proletariat, no matter whether this relationship is officially sanctioned or not. But here all the foundations of classical monogamy are removed. Here, there is a complete absence of all property, for the safeguarding and inheritance of which monogamy and male domination were established. Therefore, there is no stimulus whatever here to assert male domination. What is more, the means, too, are absent; bourgeois law, which protects this domination, exists only for the propertied classes and their dealings with the proletarians. It costs money, and therefore, owing to the worker's poverty has no validity in his attitude towards his wife. Personal and social relations of quite a different sort are the decisive factors here. Moreover, since large-scale industry has transferred the woman from the house to the labor market and the factory, and makes her, often enough, the breadwinner of the family, the last remnants of male domination in the proletarian home have lost all foundation—except, perhaps, for some of that brutality towards women which became firmly rooted with the establishment of monogamy. Thus, the proletarian family is no longer mono-

*The reference is to *Die deutsche Ideologie* [*The German Ideology*].

gamian in the strict sense, even in cases of the most passionate love and strictest faithfulness of the two parties, and despite all spiritual and worldly benedictions which may have been received. The two eternal adjuncts of monogamy—hetaerism and adultery—therefore, play an almost negligible role here; the woman has regained, in fact, the right of separation, and when the man and woman cannot get along they prefer to part. In short, proletarian marriage is monogamian in the etymological sense of the word, but by no means in the historical sense. . . .

In the old communistic household, which embraced numerous couples and their children, the administration of the household, entrusted to the women, was just as much a public, a socially necessary industry as the providing of food by the men. This situation changed with the patriarchal family, and even more with the monogamian individual family. The administration of the household lost its public character. It was no longer the concern of society. It became a *private service*. The wife became the first domestic servant, pushed out of participation in social production. Only modern large-scale industry again threw open to her—and only to the proletarian woman at that—the avenue to social production; but in such a way that, when she fulfils her duties in the private service of her family, she remains excluded from public production and cannot earn anything; and when she wishes to take part in public industry and earn her living independently, she is not in a position to fulfil her family duties. What applies to the woman in the factory applies to her in all the professions, right up to medicine and law. The modern individual family is based on the open or disguised domestic enslavement of the woman; and modern society is a mass composed solely of individual families as its molecules. Today, in the great majority of cases, the man has to be the earner, the breadwinner of the family, at least among the propertied classes, and this gives him a dominating position which requires no special legal privileges. In the family, he is the bourgeois; the wife represents the proletariat. In the industrial world, however the specific character of the economic oppression that weighs down the proletariat stands out in all its sharpness only after all the special legal privileges of the capitalist class have been set aside and the complete juridical equality of both classes is established. The democratic republic does not abolish the antagonism between the two classes; on the contrary, it provides the field on which it is fought out. And, similarly, the peculiar character of man's domination over woman in the modern family, and the necessity, as well as the manner, of establishing real social equality between the two, will be brought out into full relief only when both are completely equal before the law. It will then become evident that the first premise for the emancipation of women is the reintroduction of the entire female sex into public industry; and that this again demands that the quality possessed by the individual family of being the economic unit of society be abolished.

Søren Kierkegaard

Danish philosopher, 1813–1855, "father" of existentialism, who resisted Hegelian rationalism by emphasizing the uniqueness that always places the individual outside any systematic attempt to encompass all reality.

From *Stages on Life's Way.* The following is from an account of a banquet. The subject of the speeches has shifted from love to woman. Constantine is speaking.

"And now for woman, the subject on which I would speak. I too have pondered, and I have fathomed her category; I too have sought, but I have also found, making a peerless discovery which I impart to you herewith. She can only be rightly construed under the category of jest. It is man's part to be absolute, to act absolutely, to give expression to the absolute; woman has her being in relationships. Between two such different beings no genuine reciprocal action can take place. This incongruity is precisely what constitutes jest, and it is with woman jest first came into the world. It follows, however, as a matter of course that man must know how to keep himself under the category of the absolute, for otherwise nothing comes of it, that is to say, there comes of it something only too universal, that man and woman tally with one another, he as a half-man and she as a half-man.

. . . To shoot a woman, to challenge her to a duel, to show contempt for her, only makes the poor man more ridiculous, for woman is the weaker sex. This consideration is brought forward everywhere and brings everything to confusion. If she does something great she is more admired than a man would be, because people did not suppose they might venture to require it of her; if she is deceived, she has all the pathos in her favor, whereas when a man is deceived, people have a little sympathy and a little patience so long as he is present, only to laugh at him when he is gone. . . .

"Forgive me now, dear boon companions if I have spoken too long, and now drain a glass to love and woman. Fair is she and lovely when

302

regarded esthetically—that no one can deny. But since it so often is said, I too will say: one should not remain standing, but 'go further.' So regard her ethically, and the thing becomes a jest. Even Plato and Aristotle take it that woman is an incomplete form, that is, an irrational quantity, which perhaps some time in a better existence might be brought back to the male form. In this life one must take her as she is. What this is will soon appear, for she too is not satisfied with the esthetic sphere, she 'goes further,' she would be emancipated—that she is man enough to say. Let that come to pass, and the jest will be beyond all bounds.''

When Constantine ceased speaking he instantly commanded Victor Eremita to begin. He spoke as follows:

''Plato, as you know, gave thanks to the gods for four things, and the fourth was that he was contemporary with Socrates. An earlier Greek philosopher [Thales of Miletos] had already expressed his gratitude for the first three of them,* so I conclude that they were worth it. But I, alas, supposing I were desirous of expressing my gratitude like those Greeks, cannot very well give thanks for privileges which are denied me, and so I will muster all the powers of my soul to express gratitude for the one boon which was accorded me: that I became a man and not a woman.

''To be a woman is something so strange, so mixed, so complex, that no predicate expresses it, and the many predicates one might use contradict one another so sharply that only a woman can endure it, and, still worse, can enjoy it. The fact that she actually has less significance than man is not what constitutes her misfortune, even if she were to come to know it, for after all this is something that can be endured. No, the misfortune is that, owing to the romantic way in which she is regarded, her life has become meaningless, so that one moment she has the utmost significance and the next moment none whatever, without ever coming to know what her significance really is—yet this is not the whole of her misfortune, for the worst of it is that she can never come to know it because she is a woman. For my part, if I were a woman, I had rather be a woman in the orient where I would be a slave, for to be a slave, neither more nor less, is at any rate something definite, in comparison with being hurrah boys and nothing whatever.

''Even if the life of a woman did not present such contrasts, the distinction which she enjoys and which is rightly assumed to belong to her *qua* woman, a distinction which she does not share with man, already indicates the meaningless of her life. This distinction is that of gallantry. Now gallantry consists quite simply in construing by means of fantastic categories the person towards whom one is gallant. Hence gallantry showed toward a man is an insult, for a man deprecates the application of fantastic categories to him. On the other hand it is a tribute to the fair sex, a dis-

---

*That he had been created a human, not an animal; a man, not a woman; a Greek, not a barbarian.

tinction essentially due to her. Alas, alack! If it were only a single cava-
lier that was gallant, it would not be so serious a matter, after all. But
such is by no means the case. At bottom every man is gallant, he is instinctively gallant. Accordingly, this signifies that nature itself has bestowed this perquisite upon the fair sex. On the other hand, woman instinctively accepts this homage. Once more a misfortune; for if only one
woman here and there were to accept it, a different explanation might be
given. So here again we have the irony of life. If there is to be truth in
gallantry, it must be reciprocal, and gallantry would then be the current
rate quoted on the bourse for the difference between beauty and strength,
cunning and might. But this is not the way of it, gallantry is essentially
woman's due, and the fact that she accepts it instinctively may be explained as an instance of nature's tender care for the weak, for those who
have had a hard deal, to whom an illusion gives more than adequate compensation. But this illusion is precisely the calamity. Not infrequently nature comes to the aid of an ill-favored man by consoling him with the
belief that he is the most beautiful. Thus nature has made good the deficiency, the man possesses in fact even more than he could reasonably desire. But to possess this in a vain conceit, not to be enslaved to wretched-
ness, but to be fooled into a conceit, is in fact a still worse mockery. In
the sense of being ill-favored it cannot be said that woman suffers from
nature's neglect, yet she does suffer in another sense, inasmuch as she
never can free herself from the illusion with which life has consoled her.

"If one will analyze a feminine existence in its entirety so as to bring
out the decisive factors, every feminine existence must make a perfectly
fantastic impression. Woman has turning points in her life of a sort entirely different from those man may be said to have, for her turning points
are in every case ups and downs. In Tieck's romantic dramas one sometimes runs across a character who aforetime was a king in Mesopotamia
and now is a green-grocer in Copenhagen. Precisely as fantastic is every
feminine existence. If you will call the girl Juliana, then her life is as follows: 'aforetime Empress in love's far-reaching realm of exorbitant
speech, and titular Queen of all the exaggerations of tomfoolery—now
Madam Petersen at the corner of Bathhouse Street.' A girl when she is a
child is considered of less account than a boy. When she is a little older
one does not quite know what can be made of her. Finally there comes the
decisive period which makes her a sovereign despot. Man approaches her
adoringly, he is a suitor. Adoringly—for every suitor is an adorer, it is
not the device of an artful deceiver. Even Jack Ketch, when he lays aside
the *fasces* to go a-wooing, even he bows the knee, notwithstanding he has
it in mind at the earliest possible opportunity to play the part of private
executioner at home, which he takes so much for granted that he does not
think of making the excuse that public executions are becoming so rare.
The man of culture behaves in the same way. He kneels, he adores, he
construes the beloved in the most fantastic categories, and thereupon he

very quickly forgets his kneeling posture, and even whilst he knelt he knew full well that it was fantastic. If I were a woman, I had rather be sold by my father to the highest bidder, as in the orient; for a bargain has some sense in it. What a misfortune to be a woman! And yet the misfortune essentially is that when one is a woman one doesn't comprehend this. If she laments, it is not over the former situation but over the latter. If I were a woman, I would first of all decline to be wooed and would resign myself to being the weaker sex, if that is what I am; but I would take heed, as the thing of chiefest concern to a proud person, that one does not go beyond the bounds of truth. This is of small concern to her. Juliana is in the seventh heaven, and Madam Petersen puts up with her fate.

. . . Verily my soul is devoid of envy and is only grateful to the gods; for after all I had rather be a man, and be a little less exalted, and be that in reality, than be a woman, and be an indeterminate quantity, and be made blissful by a vain conceit; I had rather be a concretion which means something than an abstraction which means everything. It is quite true therefore, as I said: through woman ideality came into the world—what would man be without her. Many a man became a genius through a girl, many a man became a hero through a girl, many a man became a poet through a girl, many a man became a saint through a girl—but he didn't become a genius through the girl he got, for through her he became only Privy-Councillor; he didn't become a hero through the girl he got, for through her he only became a general; he didn't become a poet through the girl he got, for through her he only became a father; he didn't become a saint through the girl he got, for he didn't get any, and he wanted only the one he didn't get, just as each of the others became a genius, became a hero, became a poet, through the girl he didn't get.* If the ideality of woman were in itself inspiring, then surely the inspiration must be the woman to whom a man is united for life. But actual existence gives a different account of it. That is to say, in a negative relationship woman makes a man idealistically productive. So understood, she is inspiring, but to assert this directly and without qualification is to be guilty of a paralogism which one would have to be a woman to overlook. Or who has ever heard of anyone becoming a poet through his wife? So long as the man does not have her she is an inspiration. This is the residual truth in the imaginary conceit of poetry and of woman. The fact that he does not possess her denotes perhaps that he is still fighting for her. In this way a girl has inspired many a man and made him a knight. But who has ever heard of anyone becoming valiant through his wife? Or else the fact that he does not possess her means that he cannot get her. In this way a girl

---

*The autobiographical character of this passage hardly needs to be pointed out. S. K. frequently asserts that he became a poet through the girl he didn't get.

has inspired many a man and awakened his idealism, in case she happened to have something worth while to contribute. But a wife who has ever so much to contribute hardly awakens idealism. Or else the fact that he does not possess her means that he is in pursuit of the ideal. He perhaps loves many, and to love many is also an unhappy love affair of a sort, and yet his soul's ideality consists essentially in this striving and yearning, not in the fractions of lovableness which taken all together constitute the *summa summarum* of the contributions of the several individuals. . . .

"So I thank the gods for the fact that I became a man, not a woman; then in the next place I thank the gods that no woman with a lifelong tenure constrains me constantly to think too late.

"What a strange invention marriage is! And what makes it still stranger is the fact that it is regarded as an 'immediate' step. And yet there is no step so decisive, for there is nothing so self-willed and domineering in relation to a human life as is marriage. A thing so decisive as that, one is to do, not reflectively, but 'immediately'! And yet marriage is not a simple thing but something extremely complex and ambiguous. Just as the meat of the turtle savors of all kinds of meat, so has marriage a savor of everything; and as the turtle is a slow-moving beast, so also is marriage. A love affair is a simple thing after all—but marriage! . . .

"If any positive relationship to woman is to be thought of, it must be so thoroughly reflected that by reason of so much reflection it would not become any relationship to her. To be an excellent husband, and yet in secret to seduce every girl; to seem to be a seducer, and yet to cherish secretly within one's heart all the glow of romanticism—that would be something, and in such a case the concession made in the first potency would be obliterated by the second. Man, however, possesses his true ideality only in a reduplication. Every immediate existence must be annihilated, and the annihilation must constantly be insured by a false expression. Such a reduplication woman is unable to grasp, to her it makes man's nature unpronounceable. If a woman could live and move and have her being in such a reduplication, no erotic relationship with her would be thinkable, and her nature being what it notoriously is, the erotic relationship is disturbed by man's nature, which constantly lives and moves in the annihilation of the very thing in which she lives. . . ."

Hardly had Victor finished than the Ladies' Tailor sprang to his feet, upset a bottle of wine standing in front of him and began as follows:

"Well-spoken, dear boon companions, well-spoken, the more I hear you talk, the more I am convinced that you are co-conspirators; I hail you as such, I understand you as such, for conspirators understand one another from afar. And yet what do you know? What is your bit of theory worth to which you give the semblance of experience, your bit of experience which you revamp into a theory? And after all, you now and then believe in her for an instant and are captivated for an instant. No, I know woman on her weak side, that is to say, I know her. I shun no terror in the pursuit of my studies and shun no measures calculated to confirm what I have understood. For I am a madman, and one must be mad in order to understand her, and if one was not mad before, he must be so when he has understood her. As the robber has his haunt near the noisy highway, and the ant-lion his funnel in the loose sand, and the pirate his hiding-place near the roaring sea, so have I my *maison* of fashion in the midst of the human swarm, seductive, irresistible to a woman, as the Venusberg is to man. Here in a *maison* of fashion one learns to know her practically and from the bottom up, without any theoretical fuss. Oh, if fashion meant nothing more than that a woman in the heat of desire were to throw off all her clothes, well, that would be something. But that is not all of it, fashion is not undisguised sensuality, not tolerated debauchery, but a contraband trade in indecency licensed as decorum. As in heathen Prussia a marriageable girl wore a bell which served as a signal to the men, so likewise is the existence of a woman of fashion a perpetual bell-ringing, not for debauchees but for lickerish voluptuaries. It is believed that fortune is a woman—oh, yes, it is changeable, to be sure, but it is changeable in something, for it is able to give much, and to that extent it is not a woman. No it is fashion that is a woman, for fashion is changeable in nonsense, is logically consistent only in becoming more and more crazy. One hour in my *maison* is worth more than a year and a day outside of it, if one wants to learn to know woman. . . .

". . . It requires such prodigious reflection to keep track of a woman's reflection that only a man who sacrifices himself to that task is sufficient for it, and then only in case he has a native gift. A man is fortunate therefore if he never takes up with any woman, in any case she doesn't belong to him, even if she doesn't belong to any other man, she belongs to that phantom which is formed by the unnatural intercourse of feminine reflection with feminine reflection, i.e., fashion. For this reason a woman ought always to swear by fashion, then her oath would have some force, for fashion after all is the one thing she is always thinking about, the one thing she is able to think together with and in everything else. . . .

"You understand me now, you understand why I call you coconspirators, though at a great distance from me. You understand now my interpretation of woman. Everything in life is a matter of fashion, the fear of God is a matter of fashion, and love, and hoop-skirts, and a ring in the nose. So with all my might I will abet the lofty genius who desires to laugh at the most ludicrous of all animals. Since woman has reduced everything to fashion, I by the aid of fashion will prostitute her as she deserves. I give myself no rest, I the Ladies' Tailor; my soul chafes when I think of my task, she must yet come to the point of wearing a ring in her nose. Therefore seek no sweetheart, forego love as you would shun the most dangerous neighborhood, for also your sweetheart would have to come to the point of wearing a ring in her nose."

Thereupon Johannes the Seducer spoke as follows:

"Esteemed boon companions, is Satan plaguing you? You talk like undertakers, your eyes are red with tears and not with wine. You move me almost to tears, for an unfortunate lover is very sadly situated in life. *Hinc illae lacrymae*. Now I am a fortunate lover, and my only desire is to remain such constantly. . . . The man who is twenty years old and does not comprehend that there is a categorical imperative: Enjoy thyself—that man is a fool. And he who does not seize the opportunity is a Wesleyan Methodist. But you are unfortunate lovers, hence you want to remodel woman. God forbid it. I like her as she is, exactly as she is. Even Constantine's notion that she is a jest implies a secret wish. I, on the other hand, am gallant—and why not? Gallantry costs nothing and brings in everything and is the condition of all erotic enjoyment. Gallantry is the Freemasonry of sensuousness and sensuality as between man and woman. It is a primitive language of nature, like love's language in general. It is not made up of sounds but of masked desires which are constantly changing their rôles. I can understand very well that an unfortunate lover is ungallant enough to want to convert his deficit into a bill of exchange on eternity. Yet at the same time I do not understand it, for to me woman possesses abundant intrinsic value. That I will assert of every woman, and it is true, but it is certain also that I am the only one not deceived by this truth. As to whether a deflowered woman is worth less than man is an item not to be found in my price list. I do not pluck broken flowers, I leave that to married men for a decoration at Shrovetide. . . .

"Originally there was one sex, that of the man—so the Greeks report. Gloriously endowed was he, so that he reflected honor upon the gods who created him, so gloriously endowed that the gods were in the position in which a poet sometimes finds himself when he has expended all his forces upon a poetic creation: they became envious of man. Yea, what was worse, they feared him, lest he might bow unwillingly to their yoke. They feared, though it was without reason, that he might cause heaven itself to totter. So then they had conjured up a power they hardly thought themselves capable of curbing. Then there was concern and commotion in the council of the gods. Much had they lavished upon the creation of man, that was magnanimous; now everything must be risked, for everything was at stake, this was self-defense. So thought the gods. And it was impossible to revoke him, as a poet may revoke his thought. By force he could not be compelled, or else the gods themselves might have compelled him, but it was precisely about this they had misgivings. He must then be taken captive and compelled by a power which was weaker than his own and yet stronger, strong enough to compel. What a marvellous power that must be! Necessity, however, teaches the gods to surpass themselves in inventiveness. They sought and pondered and found. This power was woman, the miracle of creation, even in the eyes of the gods a greater miracle than man, a discovery for which the gods in their naîveté could not help patting themselves on the back. What more can be said in honor of her than that she should be able to do what even the gods did not think themselves capable of doing, what more can be said than that she was able? How marvellous she must be to be capable of it! This was a ruse of the gods. Cunningly the enchantress was fashioned; the very instant she had enchanted man she transformed herself and held him captive in all the prolixities of finiteness. This is what the gods wanted. But what can be more delicious, more pleasurable, more enchanting, than this which the gods as they were fighting for their own power devised as the only thing that could decoy man? And verily it is so, for woman is the unique and the most seductive power in heaven and on earth. In this comparison man is something exceedingly imperfect.

"And the ruse of the gods succeeded. However, it did not always succeed. In every generation there were some men, individuals, who became aware of the deception. They perceived her loveliness, it is true, more than did any of the others, but they had an inkling what it was all about. These are what I call erotics, and I reckon myself among them; men call them seducers, woman has no name for them, such a type is for her unmentionable. These erotics are the fortunate ones. They live more luxuriously than the gods, for they eat constantly only that which is more precious than ambrosia and drink what is more delicious than nectar; they dine upon the most seductive fancy which issued from the most artful thought of the gods, they dine constantly upon bait. Oh, luxury beyond compare! Oh, blissful mode of living! They dine constantly upon bait— and are never caught. The other men set to and eat bait as the vulgar eat caviar, and are caught. Only the erotic knows how to appreciate bait, to appreciate it infinitely. Woman divines this, and hence there is a secret understanding between him and her. But he knows also that it is bait, and this is a secret he keeps to himself.

"That nothing more marvellous, nothing more delicious, nothing more seductive can be devised than a woman, the gods vouch for, and the necessity which sharpened their invention; and in turn it vouches for them that they risked their all and in the forming of her nature set heaven and earth in commotion.

"I leave for a moment the myth. The concept of man corresponds exactly to the idea of man. One therefore can think of a single man existing and nothing more than that. On the other hand, the idea of woman is a generality which is not exhaustively exemplified in any single woman. She is not *ebenbürtig** with man but is later, is a part of man, and yet more complete than he. Whether it be that the gods took a part of him while he slept (fearful of awakening him if they took too much), or that

---

*Equal in birth [Editor's note].

they divided him in equal parts so that woman is a half—in any case it is man that was divided. So it is only as a subdivision she is related to man as his mate. She is a deception, but that she is only in her second phase and for him who is deceived. She is finiteness, but in her first phase, she is finiteness raised to the highest power in the delusive infinity of all divine and human illusions. Not yet is the deception—but one more instant and a man is deceived. She is finiteness, and so she is a collective term, to say one woman means many women. This the erotic alone understands, and hence he is so prompt to love many, never being deceived, but sucking up all the voluptuous delights the cunning gods were capable of preparing. Therefore woman cannot be exhaustively expressed by any formula but is an infinity of finitudes. He who is bent upon thinking her idea is like one who gazes into a sea of nebulous shapes which are constantly forming, or like one who is bewildered by looking at the billows with their foaming crests which constantly elude him; for her idea is only a workshop of possibilities, and for the erotic these possibilities are the never-failing source of enthusiasm.

"Thus the gods fashioned her, delicate and ethereal as the mists of a summer's night and yet plump like a ripened fruit, light as a bird in spite of the fact that she carried a world of craving, light because the play of forces is unified at the invisible center of a negative relationship in which she is related to herself, slim of stature, designed with definite proportions and yet to the eye seeming to swell with the wave-lines of beauty, complete and yet as if only now she were finished, cooling, delicious, refreshing as new-fallen snow, blushing with serene transparency, happy as a jest which causes one to forget everything, tranquilizing as the goal whereunto desire tends, satisfying by being herself the incitement of desire. And this is what the gods had counted upon, that man upon catching sight [of her should be amazed as one who gets a sight of himself in the glass, and yet again as if he were familiar with this sight, amazed as one who sees himself reflected in perfection] amazed as one who sees what he never had an inkling of and yet sees, as it appears to him, what must necessarily have occurred to him, what is a necessary part of existence, and yet sees this as the riddle of existence. Precisely this contradiction in his amazement is what elicits his desire, while amazement eggs him on nearer and nearer, so that he cannot desist from looking, cannot cease to seem familiar with this sight, without, however, quite daring to approach, although he cannot cease to desire.

"When the god had thus forecast her form they were fearful lest even they might not be able to express it. But what they feared most was woman herself. They did not dare to let her know how beautiful she was, fearing that she might spoil their ruse if she were cognizant of it. Then was the crown placed upon the work. The gods made her perfect, but then they hid all this from her in the ignorance of innocence and hid it from her once more in the impenetrable mystery of modesty. She was perfect, and

victory was assured. An enticing thing she was, at one moment she en-
ticed by avoiding a man and betaking herself to flight, she was irresistible
for the fact that she herself was resistance. The gods were jubilant. And
indeed no allurement has been discovered in the world equal to woman,
and there is no allurement so absolute as that of innocence, and no temptation so fascinating as that of modesty, and no deception so incomparable as woman. She knows nothing, and yet modesty contains an instinctive presentiment, she is separated from man, and the wall of modesty is a
more decisive separation than the sword of Aladdin. . .—and yet the
erotic, who like Pyramis lays his ear against the separating wall of modesty, has a presentiment, remotely sensed, of all the lust of desire behind
it. . . .

"What rapture it is to relish the deception without being deceived, only
the erotic understands. How blissful it is to be seduced, only woman
knows. I know it from women, though I have never given time to anyone
to explain this to me, but have taken my revenge and served the idea by a
breach as abrupt as death; for a bride and a breach* correspond to one
another as female and male. Woman only knows this, and knows it by
means of her seducer. No married man comprehends such a thing; she
never speaks to him about it. She puts up with her fate, she has a presentiment that thus it must be, that only once can she be seduced. Hence she is
never really angry with her seducer. That is, if he actually did seduce her
and expressed the idea. A broken marriage vow and things like that are of
course galimatias and no seduction. So it is not so great a misfortune for a
woman to be seduced, and she is lucky to be so. A girl who is admirably
seduced may make an admirable wife. If I were not so good at seducing
(though I feel deeply my inferiority in this respect), and if I wanted to be a
married man, I would always choose a seduced woman, so that I might
not have to begin by seducing my wife. Marriage also expresses an idea,
but in relation to this idea that particular thing [i.e., innocence] is a matter
of complete indifference which in relation to my idea is the absolute. A
marriage therefore ought never to be planned to begin as if it were the
beginning of a story of seduction. This much is certain, that for every
woman there is a corresponding seducer. Her good fortune consists in en-
countering precisely him.

"By means of marriage, on the other hand, the gods conquer. Then the
aforetime seduced woman walks through life by the side of her husband,
looks sometimes longingly backward, puts up with her fate until she has
reached life's limit. She dies, but not in the same sense that men die; she
is volatilized and resolved again into the inexplicable element from which
the gods formed her, she vanishes like a dream, like a provisional form
the time for which is past. For what is woman but a dream?—and yet she

*A grim pun. For *en Brud* means a bride and *et Brud*, a breach or break, differentiated
only by the common and the neuter article.

is the highest reality! So it is the erotic understands her and leads her and is led by her at the moment of seduction—outside of time, where she belongs as an illusion. With a husband she becomes temporal, and he through her.

"Oh, marvellous Nature, if I did not admire thee, she would teach me to do so, for she is the *venerabile* of existence. Gloriously hast thou fashioned her, but still more glorious for the fact that thou didst never make one woman like another. In the case of man the essential is the essential and therefore always the same; in the case of woman the accidental is the essential, hence the inexhaustible variety. Brief is her glory, but the pain I quickly forget as if I had not even sensed it, when the same glory is proffered to me again. Yes, I too perceive the uncomeliness which may make its appearance later, but she is not thus with her seducer."

From *Works of Love*

What abominations has the world not seen in the relationship between man and woman—that she, almost like an animal, was a despised creature compared to the male, a creature of another species! What battles there have been to establish women on equal terms with men in the secular world! But Christianity makes only the transformation of infinity and does it, therefore, in all stillness. Outwardly in a way the old remains— for the man shall be the woman's master and she shall be submissive to him, but in inwardness everything is transformed, transformed with the aid of this little question to the woman, whether she has deliberated with her conscience about having this man—for a master, for otherwise she does not get him. Yet the question of conscience about a matter of conscience makes her in inwardness before God absolutely equal with the man. What Christ said about His kingdom, that it is not of this world, holds true of all that is Christian. As a higher order of things it wills to be present everywhere but is not to be grasped; as a friendly spirit it surrounds the lovers everywhere, follows their every step, but cannot be pointed to. In this Christianity wills to be a stranger in life, because it belongs to another world; it is strange in the world, because it is meant to belong to the inner man. Foolish men have foolishly busied themselves in the name of Christianity to make it obvious in the world that women have equal rights with men—Christianity has never demanded or desired this. It has done everything for woman if she Christianly will be satisfied with what is Christian. If she will not, for her loss she gains only a mediocre compensation in the little fragmentary externals she can win by worldly threats. . . .

Without being aware of it himself, a person talks like a pagan about erotic love and friendship, arranges his life paganly in these relationships, and then adds a bit of Christianity by loving his neighbor—that is, some other men. But the person who does not pay attention to the fact that his wife is for him the neighbor, and only then his wife, never comes to love his neighbor, no matter how many people he loves, for he has made an exception of his wife. This exception he will then love either all too intensely throughout his whole life or all too passionately at first and then too coolly. To be sure, one's wife is to be loved differently from the friend and the friend differently from the neighbor, but this is not an essential difference, for the fundamental equality lies in the category *neighbor*. The category *neighbor* is just like the category *human being*. Every one of us is a human being and at the same time the heterogeneous individual which he is by particularity; but being a human being is the fundamental qualification. No one should mistake his distinctiveness to the degree that he cravenly or presumptuously forgets that he is a human being. No one should be preoccupied with the differences so that he cowardly or presumptuously forgets that he is a human being; no man is an exception to being a human being by virtue of his particularising differences. He is rather a human being and then a particular human being. Thus Christianity has nothing against a man loving his wife in a special way, but he must never love her in such a special way that she is an exception to being a neighbor, which every human being is, for then he confuses Christianity—his wife does not become for him his neighbor, and thereby all other men do not become his neighbors, either. If there existed one human being who by virtue of particularising differences was an exception to being a human being, then the concept *human being* would be confused: the exception would not be a human being and other men would not be human beings either.

From *Journals and Papers*

Woman's reflection is almost overpowering to her; this is why it is so dangerous for a woman to reflect. A woman's reflection usually goes like this: if she has won on one point or another, she is so overcome herself that she cannot avoid gazing at her victory—and then she stumbles.

The man is more essentially character; and character consists not so much in winning as in continuing after having won, keeping in character. The woman endures something and counts on the approaching moment when she can take a deep breath. This moment is precisely the danger. Character is essentially continuity.

The Christianity of Our Time

This is why Protestantism has elevated woman so high, more accurately, to first place. Eveything revolves around woman. Charming, but then one can also be sure that everything revolves around chatter, trivialities, and in a refined way, around sexual relations. To some extent woman may be

said to have ennobled social life in that we do not fight any more or drink
and swear as did the old heroes—but refined lust or a carefully concealed,
refined allusion to sexual relations—that is what has ennobled social
life—Christianity!!

Woman . . . is determined to humble man and to make him mediocre.
Existence is also a sovereign and like every sovereign knows very well
how best to maintain its regime—specifically by humbling and breaking
those over whom they rule.

A woman is proficient along this line when a man gets involved with
her too seriously. She contributes the first and the most to his humbling.
Generally it can be assumed that every married man is secretly mortified
because he feels that he has been made a fool of when all this ravishing
talk from the courting days, all this about Julie being the paragon of loveliness and beauty, and getting to possess her is the highest bliss turns out
to be—a false alarm. This is the first knock the husband gets, but this in
itself is not insignificant, because it is hard for a man to admit that he has
been fooled, that both he and Julie must have been crazy. The next
undermining is that the husband and Julie (who incidentally has had the
same experience on her side) agree to keep a stiff upper lip and to hide
things from others; they agree to tell the lie that marriage is the true happiness and that they especially are happy.

When we have settled all this, providence knows that this fellow is
easy to control, that he is one of those who will make no conquests in the
world of ideas. Constantly lying like this is extremely degrading to the
man. It is different for a woman; she is once and for all a born virtuoso in
lying, is really never happy without a little lying, just as it is *a priori*
certain that wherever a woman is there is a little lying. In a sense she is
innocent in this; she cannot help it. It is not possible to get angry about it:
on the contrary, we find it very attractive. She is in the power of a natural
disposition which uses her with extreme cunning to weaken the man.

Thus in the forward march of history—I mean of marriage—there
come along with woman all the follies of finitude, this puttering around
and an egotism peculiar to woman. As wife, as mother—well, here is an
egotism of which the man has no intimation. Society has licensed it under
the name of love—good heavens, no, it is the most powerful egotism in
which woman most certainly does not love herself foremost but through
(egotistically) loving her own she loves herself. From then on ideas, and
every higher infinite striving likewise, whistle in vain for the man—yes,
even if our Lord and his angels tried to move him, it would do no good,
because the egotism of the mother is such an enormous power that she can
hold him fast.

Woman has a dangerous rapport with finitude in a way quite different
from man. She is, as the seducer says, a mystification; there is a moment
in her life when she deceptively appears to be infinitude itself—and that is
when man is captured. And as a wife she is quite simply—finitude.

This is why the Church has laid more emphasis upon the preservation of the woman's virginity than upon the man's and has honored the nun more than the monk, for the woman gives up more than the man when she renounces this life and marriage.

Woman—Man

Woman is personified egotism. Her fervent, burning devotion to man is neither more nor less than her egotism.

But His Honor, Man, has no inkling of this; he considers himself very lucky and feels highly flattered to be the object of such fervent devotion, which always takes the form of submission perhaps because woman has a bad conscience about it, wondering if it is not really egotism; man, however, as mentioned, does not see this but feels enhanced by the devotion of this other I.

Woman herself does not know that it is egotism; she is always a riddle to herself, and by a subtlety of nature the whole mystification of egotism manifesting itself as devotion is concealed from her. If woman could understand what an enormous egotist she is, she would not be that, for in another sense she is too good to be an egotist.

This whole business of man and woman is a very intricate plot or a practical joke intended to destroy man *qua* spirit.

Man is not originally an egotist; not until he is lucky enough to be united with a woman does he become that, and then completely. In contrast to a loose-jointed framework egotism, this union, commonly known as marriage, could be called a stonewall egotism, egotism's proper enterprise.

Having once entered this company enterprise, egotism really begins to hum—and this is also why there are two, a company, in order to have someone to blame and to share the telling of lies (just as in the practical world it is recommended to have an associate who can be blamed for everything).

And it follows as a matter of course that once man enters this company he is essentially lost for everything higher.

This is the reason that Christianity and all more profound views of life take a dim view of the relation to the other sex, for they assume that getting involved with the other sex is the demotion of man.

The Weaker Sex

[She] can wail and scream etc.; this is perhaps why the woman suffers much less than the silent, enclosed man.

In this context one could be tempted to say that woman is the stronger sex, for if it is strength to defend oneself against suffering, then woman defends herself far better than man.

But the main point is this: it is strength to be able to accept suffering, to be able to enter into suffering, to bear up under it; and it is weakness to ward off suffering by every means possible. Woman's weakness lies in the very fact that she immediately has entreaties, tears, and sighs at her disposal to ward off suffering; her weakness is simply her propensity to wail and scream and thus mitigate her suffering. Man's strength is that he has no means of defense, no way to mitigate suffering; therefore his strength—yes, it is a paradox—his strength makes him suffer more than the weaker sex. It is paradoxical, but no more paradoxical than something equally true, that it takes health to become ill; there are sickly people who lack the health to become ill.

Man—Woman—Child Christianity

Basically it is terrible but true, and it expresses the dreadful extent to which it is true—Christianity simply does not exist.

This is the real situation in Christendom, especially in Protestantism.

The men—and that means the miserable weaklings and clods that are called men these days, compared to the Oriental idea of what it is to be a man—men turn away from religion with a certain pride and egotism and say: Religion (Christianity) is something for women and children.

But the truth of the matter is that Christianity as it is found in the New Testament has such prodigious aims that, strictly speaking, it cannot be a religion for women, at most secondhand, and is impossible for children.

As a psychologist I maintain that no woman can endure a dialectical redoubling [Fordoblelse], and everything that is essentially Christian is intrinsically dialectical.

The essentially Christian task requires a man, it takes a man's toughness and strength simply to be able to bear the pressure of the task.

A good which is identified by its hurting, a deliverance which is identified by its making me unhappy, a grace which is identified by suffering, etc.—all this, and everything essentially Christian is like this, no woman can bear, she will lose her mind if she is to be put under the tension of this strenuousness.

As far as children are concerned, it is sheer nonsense that they are supposed to be Christians.

A woman and, above all, a child relate to things directly and breathe the air of directness and immediacy. If something is a good, well, then it must be recognizable by its doing good; there is no use in forcing a woman (I will not even mention the child) into a good that hurts—it would break her.

Just notice why it is that a woman cannot tolerate irony, that as far as her emotions are concerned irony is fatal. Is this not because she cannot bear the dialectical?

Margaret Fuller Ossoli

American philosopher and journalist, 1810–1850, associated with the Boston Transcendentalist circle. She was educated from a very young age in classical and modern languages, literature, and philosophy by a stern father. When her father died, she took over the responsibility of supporting her family. She began by teaching and later moved into journalism, assuming editorship of The Dial, *a Transcendental literary quarterly. She reacted to the narrow education of women in the Boston area with a lecture series— "Conversations."*

From "Woman in the Nineteenth Century"

But to return to the historical progress of this matter. Knowing that there exists in the minds of men a tone of feeling toward women as toward slaves, such as is expressed in the common phrase, "Tell that to women and children"; that the infinite soul can only work through them in already ascertained limits; that the gift of reason, man's highest prerogative, is allotted to them in much lower degree; that they must be kept from mischief and melancholy by being constantly engaged in active labor, which is to be furnished and directed by those better able to think, &c., &c.,—we need not multiply instances, for who can review the experience of last week without recalling words which imply, whether in jest or earnest, these views, or views like these—knowing this, can we wonder that many reformers think that measures are not likely to be taken in behalf of women, unless their wishes could be publicly represented by women?

"That can never be necessary," cry the other side. "All men are privately influenced by women; each has his wife, sister, female friends, and is too much biased by these relations to fail of representing their interests; and, if this is not enough, let them propose and enforce their wishes with the pen. The beauty of home would be destroyed, the delicacy of the sex be violated, the dignity of halls of legislation degraded, by an attempt to introduce them there. Such duties are inconsistent with those of a mother"; and then we have ludicrous pictures of ladies in hysterics at the polls, and senate chambers filled with cradles.

But if, in reply, we admit as truth that woman seems destined by nature rather for the inner circle, we must add that the arrangements of civilized life have not been, as yet, such as to secure it to her. Her circle, if the duller, is not the quieter. If kept from "excitement," she is not from drudgery. Not only the Indian squaw carries the burdens of the camp, but the favorites of Louis XIV accompany him in his journeys, and the washerwoman stands at her tub, and carries home her work at all seasons, and in all states of health. Those who think the physical circumstances of woman would make a part in the affairs of national government unsuitable are by no means those who think it impossible for Negresses to endure fieldwork, even during pregnancy, or for seamstresses to go through their killing labors.

As to the use of the pen, there was quite as much opposition to woman's possessing herself of that help to free agency as there is now to her seizing on the rostrum or the desk; and she is likely to draw, from a permission to plead her cause that way, opposite inferences to what might be wished by those who now grant it.

As to the possibility of her filling with grace and dignity any such position, we should think those who had seen the great actresses, and heard the Quaker preachers of modern times, would not doubt that woman can express publicly the fulness of thought and creation, without losing any of the peculiar beauty of her sex. What can pollute and tarnish is to act thus from any motive except that something needs to be said or done. Woman could take part in the processions, the songs, the dances of old religion; no one fancied her delicacy was impaired by appearing in public for such a cause.

As to her home, she is not likely to leave it more than she now does for balls, theatres, meetings for promoting missions, revival meetings, and others to which she flies, in hope of an animation for her existence commensurate with what she sees enjoyed by men. Governors of ladies'-fairs are no less engrossed by such a charge than the governor of a state by his; presidents of Washingtonian societies no less away from home than presidents of conventions. If men look straitly to it, they will find that, unless their lives are domestic, those of the women will not be. A house is no home unless it contain food and fire for the mind as well as for the body. The female Greek, of our day, is as much in the street as the male to cry, "What news?" We doubt not it was the same in Athens of old. The women, shut out from the marketplace, made up for it at the religious festivals. For human beings are not so constituted that they can live without expansion. If they do not get it in one way, they must in another, or perish.

As to men's representing women fairly at present, while we hear from men who owe to their wives not only all that is comfortable or graceful, but all that is wise, in the arrangement of their lives, the frequent remark, "You cannot reason with a woman,"—when from those of delicacy, no-bleness, and poetic culture, falls the contemptuous phrase "women and children," and that in no light sally of the hour, but in works intended to give a permanent statement of the best experiences—when not one man, in the million, shall I say? no, not in the hundred million, can rise above the belief that woman was made *for Man*—when such traits as these are daily forced upon the attention, can we feel that man will always do just-ice to the interests of woman? Can we think that he takes a sufficiently discerning and religious view of her office and destiny *ever* to do her just-ice, except when prompted by sentiment—accidentally or transiently, that is, for the sentiment will vary according to the relations in which he is placed? The lover, the poet, the artist, are likely to view her nobly. The father and the philosopher have some chance of liberality; the man of the world, the legislator for expediency, none.

Under these circumstances, without attaching importance, in them-selves, to the changes demanded by the champions of woman, we hail them as signs of the times. We would have every arbitrary barrier thrown down. We would have every path laid open to woman as freely as to man. Were this done, and a slight temporary fermentation allowed to subside, we should see crystallizations more pure and of more various beauty. We believe the divine energy would pervade nature to a degree unknown in the history of former ages, and that no discordant collision, but a ravish-ing harmony of the spheres, would ensue.

Yet, then and only then will mankind be ripe for this, when inward and outward freedom for woman as much as for man shall be acknowledged as a *right,* not yielded as a concession. As the friend of the Negro as-sumes that one man cannot by right hold another in bondage, so should the friend of woman assume that man cannot by right lay even well-meant restrictions on woman. If the Negro be a soul, if the woman be a soul, apparelled in flesh, to one master only are they accountable. There is but one law for souls, and, if there is to be an interpreter of it, he must come not as man, or son of man, but as son of God. . . .

Mary Wollstoncraft, like Madame Dudevant (commonly known as George Sand) in our day, was a woman whose existence better proved the need of some new interpretation of woman's rights than anything she wrote. Such beings as these, rich in genius, of most tender sympathies, capable of high virtue and a chastened harmony, ought not to find them-selves, by birth, in a place so narrow, that, in breaking bonds, they be-come outlaws. . . .

Whether much or little has been done, or will be done,—whether women will add to the talent of narration the power of systematizing—whether they will carve marble, as well as draw and paint—is not important. But that it should be acknowledged that they have intellect which needs developing—that they should not be considered complete, if beings of affection and habit alone—is important.

Yet even this acknowledgment, rather conquered by woman than proffered by man, has been sullied by the usual selfishness. Too much is said of women being better educated, that they may become better companions and mothers *for men*. They should be fit for such companionship, and we have mentioned, with satisfaction, instances where it has been established. Earth knows no fairer, holier relation than that of a mother. It is one which, rightly understood, must both promote and require the highest attainments. But a being of infinite scope must not be treated with an exclusive view to any one relation. Give the soul free course, let the organization, both of body and mind, be freely developed, and the being will be fit for any and every relation to which it may be called. The intellect, no more than the sense of hearing, is to be cultivated merely that woman may be a more valuable companion to man, but because the power who gave a power, by its mere existence signifies that it must be brought out toward perfection. . . .

There are two aspects of woman's nature, represented by the ancients as Muse and Minerva. . . .

The especial genius of woman I believe to be electrical in movement, intuitive in function, spiritual in tendency. She excels not so easily in classification, or recreation, as in an instinctive seizure of causes, and a simple breathing out of what she receives, that has the singleness of life, rather than the selecting and energizing of art.

More native is it to her to be the living model of the artist than to set apart from herself any one form in objective reality; more native to inspire and receive the poem, than to create it. In so far as soul is in her completely developed, all soul is the same; but in so far as it is modified in her as woman, it flows, it breathes, it sings, rather than deposits soil, or finishes work; and that which is especially feminine flushes, in blossom, the face of earth, and pervades, like air and water, all this seeming solid globe, daily renewing and purifying its life. Such may be the especially feminine element spoken of as femality. But it is no more the order of nature that it should be incarnated pure in any form, than that the masculine energy should exist unmingled with it in any form.

Male and female represent the two sides of the great radical dualism. But, in fact, they are perpetually passing into one another. Fluid hardens to solid, solid rushes to fluid. There is no wholly masculine man, no purely feminine woman.

History jeers at the attempts of physiologists to bind great original laws by the forms which flow from them. They make a rule; they say from observation what can and cannot be. In vain! Nature provides exceptions to every rule. She sends women to battle, and sets Hercules spinning; she enables women to bear immense burdens, cold, and frost; she enables the man, who feels maternal love, to nourish his infant like a mother. Of late she plays still gayer pranks. Not only she deprives organizations, but organs, of a necessary end. She enables people to read with the top of the head, and see with the pit of the stomach. Presently she will make a female Newton, and a male Syren.

Man partakes of the feminine in the Apollo, woman of the masculine as Minerva . . . .

Every relation, every gradation of nature is incalculably precious, but only to the soul which is poised upon itslf, and to whom no loss, no change, can bring dull discord, for it is in harmony with the central soul.

. . . To be fit for relations in time, souls, whether of man or woman, must be able to do without them in the spirit.

It is therefore that I would have woman lay aside all thought, such as she habitually cherishes, of being taught and led by men. I would have her, like the Indian girl, dedicate herself to the sun, the sun of truth, and go nowhere if his beams did not make clear the path. I would have her free from compromise, from complaisance, from helplessness, because I would have her good enough and strong enough to love one and all beings, from the fulness, not the poverty of being.

Men, as at present instructed, will not help this work, because they also are under the slavery of habit. I have seen with delight their poetic impulses. A sister is the fairest ideal, and how nobly Wordsworth, and even Byron, have written of a sister!

There is no sweeter sight than to see a father with his little daughter. Very vulgar men become refined to the eye when leading a little girl by the hand. At that moment, the right relation between the sexes seems established, and you feel as if the man would aid in the noblest purpose, if you ask him in behalf of his little daughter. Once, two fine figures stood before me, thus. The father of very intellectual aspect, his falcon eye softened by affection as he looked down on his fair child; she the image of himself, only more graceful and brilliant in expression. I was reminded of Southey's Kehama; when, lo, the dream was rudely broken! They were talking of education, and he said,

"I shall not have Maria brought too forward. If she knows too much, she will never find a husband; superior women hardly ever can."

"Surely," said his wife, with a blush, "you wish Maria to be as good and wise as she can, whether it will help her to marriage or not."

"No," he persisted, "I want her to have a sphere and a home, and some one to protect her when I am gone."

It was a trifling incident, but made a deep impression. I felt that the holiest relations fail to instruct the unprepared and perverted mind. If this man, indeed, could have looked at it on the other side, he was the last that would have been willing to have been taken himself for the home and protection he could give, but would have been much more likely to repeat the tale of Alcibiades with his phials.

But men do *not* look at both sides, and women must leave off asking them and being influenced by them, but retire within themselves, and explore the groundwork of life till they find their peculiar secret. Then, when they come forth again, renovated and baptized, they will know how to turn all dross to gold and will be rich and free though they live in a hut, tranquil if in a crowd. Then their sweet singing shall not be from passionate impulse, but the lyrical overflow of a divine rapture, and a new music shall be evolved from this many-chorded world.

Lucretia Mott

American abolitionist and feminist, 1793–1880. As a Quaker minister, she had the opportunity, accorded few women of her time, to develop as an effective public speaker, a talent through which she served the women's movement well.

From "Discourse on Woman"

This lecture was delivered March 17, 1849, with frequent reference to another lecture on the "true and proper position of women," to which Mott had listened "a few days ago" and with which she vehemently disagreed.

In the beginning, man and woman were created equal. "Male and female created he them, and blessed them, and called their name Adam." He gave dominion to both over the lower animals, but not to one over the other.

> *Man o'er woman*
> *He made not lord, such title to himself*
> *Reserving, human left from human free.*

The cause of the subjection of woman to man was early ascribed to disobedience to the command of God. This would seem to show that she was then regarded as not occupying her true and rightful position in society.

The laws given on Mount Sinai for the government of man and woman were equal, and the precepts of Jesus make no distinction. Those who read the Scriptures, and judge for themselves, not resting satisfied with the perverted application of the text, do not find the distinction that theology and ecclesiastical authorities have made in the condition of the sexes. . . .

If these Scriptures were read intelligently, we should not so learn Christ, as to exclude any from a position where they might exert an influence for good to their fellow-beings. The epistle to the Corinthian church, where the supposed apostolic prohibition of woman's preaching is found, contains express directions how woman shall appear when she prayeth or prophesieth. Judge then whether this admonition relative to *speaking* and asking questions, in the excited state of that church, should be regarded as a standing injunction on woman's *preaching,* when that word was not used by the apostle. Where is the Scripture authority for the advice given to the early church, under peculiar circumstances, being binding on the church of the present day? Ecclesiastical history informs us, that for two or three hundred years, female ministers suffered martyrdom, in company with their brethren.

These things are too much lost sight of. They should be known, in order that we may be prepared to meet the assertion, so often made, that woman is stepping out of her appropriate sphere when she shall attempt to instruct public assemblies. The present time particularly demands such investigation. It requires also, that "of yourselves ye should judge what is right," that you should know the ground whereon you stand. This age is notable for its works of mercy and benevolence—for the efforts that are made to reform the inebriate and the degraded, to relieve the oppressed and suffering. Women as well as men are interested in these works of justice and mercy. They are efficient coworkers, their talents are called into profitable exercise, their labors are effective in each department of reform. The blessing to the merciful, to the peacemaker, is equal to man and to woman. It is greatly to be deplored, now that she is increasingly qualified for usefulness, that any view should be presented calculated to retard her labors of love.

Why should not woman seek to be a reformer? If she is to shrink from being such an iconoclast as shall "break the image of man's lower worship," as so long held up to view; if she is to fear to exercise her reason and her noblest powers, lest she should be thought to "attempt to act the man," and not "acknowledge his supremacy"; if she is to be satisfied with the narrow sphere assigned her by man, nor aspire to a higher, lest she should transcend the bounds of female delicacy, truly it is a mournful prospect for woman. We would admit all the difference that our great and beneficent Creator has made, in the relation of man and woman, nor would we seek to disturb this relation; but we deny that the present position of woman is her true sphere of usefulness; nor will she attain to this sphere, until the disabilities and disadvantages, religious, civil, and social, which impede her progress, are removed out of her way. These restrictions have enervated her mind and paralyzed her powers. While man assumes that the present is the original state designed for woman, that the *existing* "differences are not arbitrary nor the result of accident," but grounded in nature, she will not make the necessary effort to obtain her just rights, lest it should subject her to the kind of scorn and contemptuous manner in which she has been spoken of.

So far from her "ambition leading her to attempt to act the man," she needs all the encouragement she can receive, by the removal of obstacles from her path, in order that she may become a "true woman." As it is desirable that man should act a manly and generous part, not "mannish," so let woman be urged to exercise a dignified and womanly bearing, not womanish. Let her cultivate all the graces and proper accomplishments of her sex, but let not these degenerate into a kind of effeminacy, in which she is satisfied to be the mere plaything or toy of society, content with her outward adornings, and with the tone of flattery and fulsome adulation too often addressed to her. True, nature has made a difference in her configuration, her physical strength, her voice—and we ask no change, we are satisfied with nature. But how has neglect and mismanagement increased this difference! It is our duty to develop these natural powers by suitable exercise, so that they may be strengthened "by reason of use." In the ruder state of society, woman is made to bear heavy burdens, while her "lord and master" walks idly by her side. In the civilization to which we have attained, if cultivated and refined woman would bring all her powers into use, she might engage in pursuits which she now shrinks from as beneath her proper vocation. The energies of men need not then be wholly devoted to the counting house and common business of life, in order that women in fashionable society may be supported in their daily promenades and nightly visits to the theatre and ballroom. . . .

In treating upon the affections, the lecturer held out the idea that, as manifested in the sexes, they were opposite, if not somewhat antagonistic, and required a union, as in chemistry, to form a perfect whole. The simile appeared to me far from a correct illustration of the true union. Minds that can assimilate, spirits that are congenial, attract one another. It is the union of similar, not of opposite affections, which are necessary for the perfection of the marriage bond. There seemed a want of proper delicacy in his representing man as being bold in the demonstration of the pure affection of love. In persons of refinement, true love seeks concealment in man as well as in woman. I will not enlarge upon the subject, although it formed so great a part of his lecture. The contrast drawn seemed a fallacy, as has much, very much, that has been presented in the sickly sentimental strains of the poet, from age to age.

The question is often asked, "What does woman want more than she enjoys? What is she seeking to obtain? Of what rights is she deprived? What privileges are withheld from her?" I answer, she asks nothing as favor, but as right; she wants to be acknowledged a moral, responsible being. She is seeking not to be governed by laws, in the making of which she has no voice. She is deprived of almost every right in civil society, and is a cipher in the nation, except in the right of presenting a petition. In religious society her disabilities, as already pointed out, have greatly retarded her progress. Her exclusion from the pulpit or ministry—her duties marked out for her by her equal brother man, subject to creeds, rules, and disciplines made for her by him—this is unworthy of her true dignity. In marriage there is assumed superiority, on the part of the husband, and admitted inferiority, with a promise of obedience, on the part of the wife. This subject calls loudly for examination, in order that the wrong may be redressed. Customs suited to darker ages in eastern countries are not binding upon enlightened society. The solemn covenant of marriage may be entered into without these lordly assumptions and humiliating concessions and promises. . . .

I tread upon delicate ground in alluding to the institutions of religious associations; but the subject is of so much importance that all which relates to the position of woman should be examined, apart from the undue veneration which ancient usage receives.

> Such dupes are men to custom, and so prone
> To reverence what is ancient, and can plead
> A course of long observance for its use,
> That even servitude, the worst of ills,
> Because delivered down from sire to son,
> Is kept and guarded as a sacred thing.

So with woman. She has so long been subject to the disabilities and restrictions with which her progress has been embarrassed, that she has become enervated, her mind to some extent paralyzed; and like those still more degraded by personal bondage, she hugs her chains. Liberty is often presented in its true light, but it is liberty for man, and it is not less a blessing, because oppression has so long darkened the mind that it cannot appreciate it. I would, therefore, urge that woman be placed in such a situation in society, by the recognition of her rights, and have such opportunities for growth and development, as shall raise her from this low, enervated, and paralyzed condition, to a full appreciation of the blessing of entire freedom of mind.

It is with reluctance that I make the demand for the political rights of women, because this claim is so distasteful to the age. Woman shrinks, in the present state of society, from taking any interest in politics. The events of the French Revolution and the claim for woman's rights are held up to her as a warning. But let us not look at the excesses of women alone at that period; but remember that the age was marked with extravagances and wickedness in men as well as women. Indeed, political life abounds with these excesses, and with shameful outrage. Who knows, but that if woman acted her part in governmental affairs, there might be an entire change in the turmoil of political life. It becomes man to speak modestly of his ability to act without her. If woman's judgment were exercised, why might she not aid in making the laws by which she is governed? Lord Brougham remarked that the works of Harriet Martineau upon Political Economy were not excelled by those of any political writer of the present time. The first few chapters of her "Society in America," her views of a republic, and of government generally, furnish evidence of woman's capacity to embrace subjects of universal interest. . . .

May these statements lead you to reflect upon this subject that you may know what woman's condition is in society—what her restrictions are, and seek to remove them. In how many cases in our country the husband and wife begin life together, and by equal industry and united effort accumulate to themselves a comfortable home. In the event of death of the wife, the household remains undisturbed, his farm or his workshop is not broken up, or in any way molested. But when the husband dies, he either gives his wife a *portion* of their joint accumulation, or the law apportions to her a *share*; the homestead is broken up, and she is dispossessed of that which she earned equally with him; for what she lacked in physical strength, she made up in constancy of labor and toil, day and evening. The sons then coming into possession of the property, as has been the custom until of latter time, speak of having to *keep* their mother, when she in reality is aiding to keep them. Where is the justice of this state of things? The change in the law of this State and of New York, in relation to the property of the wife, goes to a limited extent toward the redress of these wrongs, which are far more extensive, and involve much more than I have time this evening to point out.

On no good ground can the legal existence of the wife be suspended during marriage, and her property surrendered to her husband. In the intelligent ranks of society, the wife may not, in point of fact, be so degraded as the law would degrade her; because public sentiment is above the law. Still, while the law stands, she is liable to the disabilities which it composes. Among the ignorant classes of society, woman is made to bear heavy burdens, and is degraded almost to the level of the slave.

There are many instances now in our city, where the wife suffers much from the power of the husband to claim all that she can earn with her own hands. In my intercourse with the poorer class of people, I have known cases of extreme cruelty, from the hard earnings of the wife being thus robbed by the husband, and no redress at law.

Friedrich Nietzsche

German philosopher, 1844–1900. Often interpreted as a misogynist or an anti-Semite, Nietzsche might more properly be said to be a misanthrope, disgusted with the ordinary human being—a member of the herd—who is "human, all-too-human."

From "The Greek Woman"

Of course there is one side of the Platonic conception of woman which stands in abrupt contrast with Hellenic custom: Plato gives to woman a full share in the rights, knowledge, and duties of man, and considers woman only as the weaker sex, in that she will not achieve remarkable success in all things, without however disputing this sex's title to all those things. We must not attach more value to this strange notion than to the expulsion of the artist out of the ideal State; these are sidelines daringly misdrawn, aberrations as it were of the hand otherwise so sure and of the so calmly contemplating eye which at times under the influence of the deceased master becomes dim and dejected; in this mood he exaggerates the master's paradoxes and in the abundance of his love gives himself satisfaction by very eccentrically intensifying the latter's doctrines even to foolhardiness.

The most significant word however that Plato as a Greek could say on the relation of woman to the State, was that so objectionable demand that in the perfect State the *Family was to cease*. At present let us take no account of his abolishing even marriage, in order to carry out this demand fully, and of his substituting solemn nuptials arranged by order of the State, between the bravest men and the noblest women, for the attainment of beautiful offspring. In that principal proposition however he has indicated most distinctly—indeed too distinctly, offensively distinctly—an important preparatory step of the Hellenic Will towards the procreation of the genius. But in the customs of the Hellenic people the claim of the family on man and child was extremely limited: the man lived in the State, the child grew up for the State and was guided by the hand of the State. The Greek Will took care that the need of culture could not be satisfied in the seclusion of a small circle. From the State the individual has to receive everything in order to return everything to the State. Woman accordingly means to the State what *sleep* does to man. In her nature lies the healing power, which replaces that which has been used up, the beneficial rest in which everything immoderate confines itself, the eternal Same, by which the excessive and the surplus regulate themselves. In her the future generation dreams. Woman is more closely related to nature than man and in all her essentials she remains ever herself. Culture is with her always something external, a something which does not touch the kernel that is eternally faithful to Nature, therefore the culture of woman might well appear to the Athenian as something indifferent, yea—if one only wanted to conjure it up in one's mind, as something ridiculous. He who at once feels himself compelled from that to infer the position of women among the Greeks as unworthy and all too cruel, should not indeed take as his criterion the "culture" of modern woman and her claims, against which it is sufficient just to point out the Olympian women together with Penelope, Antigone, Elektra. Of course it is true that these are ideal figures, but who would be able to create such ideals out of the present world?—Further indeed is to be considered *what sons* these women have borne, and what women they must have been to have given birth to such sons! The Hellenic woman as *mother* had to live in obscurity, because the political instinct together with its highest aim demanded it. She *had* to vegetate like a plant, in the narrow circle, as a symbol of the Epicurean wisdom λάθε βιώσας. Again, in more recent times, with the complete disintegration of the principle of the State, she had to step in as helper; the family as a makeshift for the State is her work; and in this sense the *artistic aim* of the State had to abase itself to the level of a *domestic* art. Thereby it has been brought about that the passion of love, as the one realm wholly accessible to women, regulates our art to the very core. Similarly, home education considers itself so to speak as the only natural one and suffers State education only as a questionable infringement upon the right of home education: all this is right as far as the modern State only is concerned.—With that the nature of woman withal remains unaltered, but her *power* is, according to the position which the State takes up with regard to women, a different one. Women have indeed really the power to make good to a certain extent the deficiencies of the State—ever faithful to their nature, which I have compared to sleep. In Greek antiquity they held that position, which the most supreme will of the State assigned to them: for that reason they have been glorified as never since. The goddesses of Greek mythology are their images: the Pythia and the Sibyl, as well as the Socratic Diotima, are the priestesses out of whom divine wisdom speaks. Now one understands why the proud resignation of the Spartan woman at the news of her son's death in battle can be no fable. Woman in relation to the State felt herself in her proper position, therefore she had more *dignity* than woman has ever had since. Plato who through abolishing family and marriage still intensifies the position of woman, feels now so much *reverence* towards them, that oddly enough he is misled by a subsequent statement of their equality with man, to abolish again the order of rank which is their due: the highest triumph of the woman of antiquity, to have seduced even the wisest!

From *Beyond Good and Evil*

84. Woman learns how to hate in proportion as she—forgets how to charm.

85. The same emotions are in man and woman, but in different *tempo*; on that account man and woman never cease to misunderstand each other.

86. In the background of all their personal vanity, women themselves have still their impersonal scorn—for "woman."

114. The immense expectation with regard to sexual love, and the coyness in this expectation, spoils all the perspectives of women at the outset.

115. Where there is neither love nor hatred in the game, woman's play is mediocre.

127. In the eyes of all true women science is hostile to the sense of shame. They feel as if one wished to peep under their skin with it—or worse still! under their dress and finery.

131. The sexes deceive themselves about each other: the reason is that in reality they honor and love only themselves (or their own ideal, to express it more agreeably). Thus man wishes woman to be peaceable: but in fact woman is *essentially* unpeaceable, like the cat, however well she may have assumed the peaceable demeanor.

139. In revenge and in love woman is more barbarous than man.

144. When a woman has scholarly inclinations there is generally something wrong with her sexual nature. Barrenness itself conduces to a certain virility of taste; man, indeed, if I may say so, is "the barren animal."

145. Comparing man and woman generally, one may say that woman would not have the genius for adornment, if she had not the instinct for the *secondary* rôle.

148. To seduce their neighbor to a favorable opinion, and afterwards to believe implicitly in this opinion of their neighbor—who can do this conjuring trick so well as women?

232. Woman* wishes to be independent, and therefore she begins to enlighten men about "woman as she is"—*this* is one of the worst devel-

---

*At the end of the immediately preceding section, Nietzsche requests "permission . . . to utter some truths about 'woman as she is,' provided that it is known at the outset how literally they are merely—*my* truths." [Editor's note].

opments of the general *uglifying* of Europe. For what must these clumsy attempts of feminine scientificality and self-exposure bring to light! Woman has so much cause for shame; in woman there is so much pedantry, superficiality, schoolmasterliness, petty presumption, unbridledness, and indiscretion concealed—study only woman's behavior towards children!—which has really been best restrained and dominated hitherto by the *fear* of man. Alas, if ever the "eternally tedious in woman"—she has plenty of it!—is allowed to venture forth! if she begins radically and on principle to unlearn her wisdom and art—of charming, of playing, of frightening-away-sorrow, of alleviating and taking-easily; if she forgets her delicate aptitude for agreeable desires! Female voices are already raised, which, by Saint Aristophanes! make one afraid:—with medical explicitness it is stated in a threatening manner what woman first and last *requires* from man. Is it not in the very worst taste that woman thus sets herself up to be scientific? Enlightenment hitherto has fortunately been men's affair, men's gift—we remained therewith "among ourselves"; and in the end, in view of all that women write about "woman," we may well have considerable doubt as to whether woman really *desires* enlightenment about herself—and *can* desire it. If woman does not thereby seek a new *ornament* for herself—I believe ornamentation belongs to the eternally feminine?—why, then, she wishes to make herself feared: perhaps she thereby wishes to get the mastery. But she does not *want* truth—what does woman care for truth! From the very first nothing is more foreign, more repugnant, or more hostile to woman than truth—her great art is falsehood, her chief concern is appearance and beauty. Let us confess it, we men: we honor and love *this* very art and *this* very instinct in woman: we who have the hard task, and for our recreation gladly seek the company of beings under whose hands, glances, and delicate follies, our seriousness, our gravity, and profundity appear almost like follies to us. Finally, I ask the question: Did a woman herself ever acknowledge profundity in a woman's mind, or justice in a woman's heart? And is it not true that on the whole "woman" has hitherto been most despised by woman herself, and not at all by us?—We men desire that woman should not continue to compromise herself by enlightening us; just as it was man's care and the consideration for woman, when the church decreed: *mulier taceat in ecclesia.** It was to the benefit of woman when Napoleon gave the too eloquent Madame de Staël to understand: *mulier taceat in politicis!*†—and in my opinion, he is a true friend of woman who calls out to women today: *mulier taceat de muliere!*‡

233. It betrays corruption of the instincts—apart from the fact that it betrays bad taste—when a woman refers to Madame Roland, or Madame

---

*Let woman be silent in church [Editor's note].
†Let woman be silent concerning politics [Editor's note].
‡Let woman be silent concerning woman [Editor's note].

de Staël, or Monsieur George Sand, as though something were proved thereby in *favor* of "woman as she is." Among men, these are the three *comical* women as they are—nothing more!—and just the best involuntary *counterarguments* against feminine emancipation and autonomy.

234. Stupidity in the kitchen; woman as cook; the terrible thoughtlessness with which the feeding of the family and the master of the house is managed! Woman does not understand what food *means,* and she insists on being cook! If woman had been a thinking creature she should certainly, as cook for thousands of years, have discovered the most important physiological facts, and should likewise have got possession of the healing art! Through bad female cooks—through the entire lack of reason in the kitchen—the development of mankind has been longest retarded and most interfered with; even to-day matters are very little better.—A word to High School girls.

237A. Woman has hitherto been treated by men like birds, which, losing their way, have come down among them from an elevation: as something delicate, fragile, wild, strange, sweet, and animating—but as something also which must be cooped up to prevent it flying away.

238. To be mistaken in the fundamental problem of "man and woman," to deny here the profoundest antagonism and the necessity for an eternally hostile tension, to dream here perhaps of equal rights, equal training, equal claims and obligations: that is a *typical* sign of shallow-mindedness; and a thinker who has proved himself shallow at this dangerous spot—shallow in instinct!—may generally be regarded as suspicious, nay more, as betrayed, as discovered; he will probably prove too "short" for all fundamental questions of life, future as well as present, and will be unable to descend into *any* of the depths. On the other hand, a man who has depth of spirit as well as of desires, and has also the depth of benevolence which is capable of severity and harshness, and easily confounded with them, can only think of woman as *Orientals* do: he must conceive of her as a possession, as confinable property, as a being predestined for service and accomplishing her mission therein—he must take his stand in this matter upon the immense rationality of Asia, upon the superiority of the instinct of Asia, as the Greeks did formerly; those best heirs and scholars of Asia—who, as is well known, with their *increasing* culture and amplitude of power, from Homer to the time of Pericles, became gradually *stricter* towards woman, in short, more oriental. *How* necessary, *how* logical, even *how* humanely desirable this was, let us consider for ourselves!

239. The weaker sex has in no previous age been treated with so much respect by men as at present—this belongs to the tendency and fundamental taste of democracy, in the same way as disrespectfulness to old age—what wonder is it that abuse should be immediately made of this respect? They want more, they learn to make claims, the tribute of respect is at last felt to be well-nigh galling; rivalry for rights, indeed actual strife itself, would be preferred: in a word, woman is losing modesty. And let us immediately add that she is also losing taste. She is unlearning to *fear* man: but the woman who "unlearns to fear" sacrifices her most womanly instincts. That woman should venture forward when the fear-inspiring quality in man—or more definitely, the *man* in man—is no longer either desired or fully developed, is reasonable enough and also intelligible enough; what is more difficult to understand is that precisely thereby—woman deteriorates. This is what is happening nowadays: let us not deceive ourselves about it! Wherever the industrial spirit has triumphed over the military and aristocratic spirit, woman strives for the economic and legal independence of a clerk: "woman as clerkess" is inscribed on the portal of the modern society which is in course of formation. While she thus appropriates new rights, aspires to be "master," and inscribes "progress" of woman on her flags and banners, the very opposite realises itself with terrible obviousness: *woman retrogrades.* Since the French Revolution the influence of woman in Europe has *declined* in proportion as she has increased her rights and claims; and the "emancipation of woman," in so far as it is desired and demanded by women themselves (and not only by masculine shallow-pates), thus proves to be a remarkable symptom of the increased weakening and deadening of the most womanly instincts. There is *stupidity* in this movement, an almost masculine stupidity, of which a well-reared woman—who is always a sensible woman—might be heartily ashamed. To lose the intuition as to the ground upon which she can most surely achieve victory; to neglect exercise in the use of her proper weapons; to let-herself-go before man, perhaps even "to the book," where formerly she kept herself in control and in refined, artful humility; to neutralize with her virtuous audacity man's faith in a *veiled,* fundamentally different ideal in woman, something eternally, necessarily feminine; to emphatically and loquaciously dissuade man from the idea that woman must be preserved, cared for, protected, and indulged, like some delicate, strangely wild, and often pleasant domestic animal; the clumsy and indignant collection of everything of the nature of servitude and bondage which the position of woman in the hitherto existing order of society has entailed and still entails (as though slavery were a counter-argument, and not rather a condition of every higher culture, of every elevation of culture): what does all this betoken, if not a disintegration of womanly instincts, a defeminizing? Certainly, there are enough of idiotic friends and corrupters of woman amongst the learned asses of the masculine sex, who advise woman to defeminize herself in this manner, and to imitate all the stupidities from which "man"in Europe, European "manliness," suffers—who would like to lower woman to "general culture," indeed even to newspaper reading and meddling with politics. . . .

From *Human, All-too-Human*

The Perfect Woman—The perfect woman is a higher type of humanity than the perfect man, and also something much rarer. The natural history of animals furnishes grounds in support of this theory.

Friendship and Marriage—The best friend will probably get the best wife, because a good marriage is based on talent for friendship.

Inherited From The Mother—Everyone bears within him an image of woman, inherited from his mother: it determines his attitude towards women as a whole, whether to honor, despise, or remain generally indifferent to them.

Women's Friendships—Women can enter into friendship with a man perfectly well; but in order to maintain it the aid of a little physical antipathy is perhaps required.

An Element Of Love—In all feminine love something of maternal love also comes to light.

The Feminine Intellect—The intellect of women manifests itself as perfect mastery, presence of mind, and utilization of all advantages. They transmit it as a fundamental quality to their children, and the father adds thereto the darker background of the will. His influence determines as it were the rhythm and harmony with which the new life is to be performed; but its melody is derived from the mother. For those who know how to put a thing properly: women have intelligence, men have character and passion. This does not contradict the fact that men actually achieve so much more with their intelligence: they have deeper and more powerful impulses; and it is these which carry their understanding (in itself something passive) to such an extent. Women are often silently surprised at the great respect men pay to their character. When, therefore, in the choice of a partner men seek specially for a being of deep and strong character, and women for a being of intelligence, brilliancy, and presence of mind, it is plain that at bottom men seek for the ideal man, and women for the ideal woman—consequently not for the complement but for the completion of their own excellence.

Hesiod's Opinion Confirmed—It is a sign of women's wisdom that they have almost always known how to get themselves supported, like drones in a beehive. Let us just consider what this meant originally, and why men do not depend upon women for their support. Of a truth it is because masculine vanity and reverence are greater than feminine wisdom; for women have known how to secure for themselves by their subordination the greatest advantage, in fact, the upper hand. Even the care of children may originally have been used by the wisdom of women as an excuse for withdrawing themselves as much as possible from work. And at present they still understand when they are really active (as housekeepers, for instance) how to make a bewildering fuss about it, so that the merit of their activity is usually ten times overestimated by men.

Women In Hatred—In a state of hatred women are more dangerous than men; for one thing, because they are hampered by no regard for fairness when their hostile feelings have been aroused; but let their hatred develop unchecked to its utmost consequences; then also, because they are expert in finding sore spots (which every man and every party possess), and pouncing upon them: for which purpose their dagger-pointed intelligence is of good service (whilst men, hesitating at the sight of wounds, are often generously and conciliatorily inclined).

Love—The love idolatry which women practice is fundamentally and originally an intelligent device, inasmuch as they increase their power by all the idealizings of love and exhibit themselves as so much the more desirable in the eyes of men. But by being accustomed for centuries to this exaggerated appreciation of love, it has come to pass that they have been caught in their own net and have forgotten the origin of the device. They themselves are now still more deceived than the men, and on that account also suffer more from the disillusionment which, almost necessarily, enters into the life of every woman—so far, at any rate, as she has sufficient imagination and intelligence to be able to be deceived and undeceived.

The Emancipation Of Women—Can women be at all just, when they are so accustomed to love and to be immediately biased for or against? For that reason they are also less interested in things and more in individuals: but when they are interested in things they immediately become their partisans, and thereby spoil their pure, innocent effect. Thus there arises a danger, by no means small, in entrusting politics and certain portions of science to them (history, for instance). For what is rarer than a woman who really knows what science is? Indeed the best of them cherish in their breasts a secret scorn for science, as if they were somehow superior to it. Perhaps all this can be changed in time; but meanwhile it is so.

Contradictions In Feminine Minds—Owing to the fact that women are so much more personal than objective, there are tendencies included in the range of their ideas which are logically in contradiction to one another; they are accustomed in turn to become enthusiastically fond just of the representatives of these tendencies and accept their systems in the lump; but in such wise that a dead place originates wherever a new personality afterwards gets the ascendancy. It may happen that the whole philosophy in the mind of an old lady consists of nothing but such dead places.

Who Suffers The More?—After a personal dissension and quarrel between a woman and a man, the latter party suffers chiefly from the idea of having wounded the other, whilst the former suffers chiefly from the idea of not having wounded the other sufficiently; so she subsequently endeavors by tears, sobs, and discomposed mien, to make his heart heavier.

The Future Of Marriage—The noble and liberal-minded women who take as their mission the education and elevation of the female sex, should not overlook one point of view: Marriage regarded in its highest aspect, as the spiritual friendship of two persons of opposite sexes, and accordingly such as is hoped for in future, contracted for the purpose of producing and educating a new generation—such marriage, which only makes use of the sensual, so to speak, as a rare and occasional means to a higher purpose, will, it is to be feared, probably need a natural auxiliary, namely, *concubinage*. For if, on the grounds of his health, the wife is also to serve for the sole satisfaction of the man's sexual needs, a wrong perspective, opposed to the aims indicated, will have most influence in the choice of a wife. The aims referred to: the production of descendants, will be accidental, and their successful education highly improbable. A good wife, who has to be friend, helper, childbearer, mother, family head and manager, and has even perhaps to conduct her own business and affairs separately from those of the husband, cannot at the same time be a concubine; it would, in general, be asking too much of her. In the future, therefore, a state of things might take place the opposite of what existed at Athens in the time of Pericles; the men, whose wives were then little more to them than concubines, turned besides to the Aspasias, because they longed for the charms of a companionship gratifying both to head and heart, such as the grace and intellectual suppleness of women could alone provide. All human institutions, just like marriage, allow only a moderate amount of practical idealizing, failing which coarse remedies immediately become necessary.

The "Storm And Stress" Period Of Women—In the three or four civilized countries of Europe, it is possible, by several centuries of education, to make out of women anything we like—even men, not in a sexual sense, of course, but in every other. Under such influences they will acquire all the masculine virtues and forces, at the same time, of course, they must also have taken all the masculine weaknesses and vices into the bargain: so much, as has been said, we can command. But how shall we endure the intermediate state thereby induced, which may even last two or three centuries, during which feminine follies and injustices, woman's original birthday endowment, will still maintain the ascendancy over all that has been otherwise gained and acquired? This will be the time when indignation will be the peculiar masculine passion; indignation, because all arts and sciences have been overflowed and choked by an unprecedented dilettanteism, philosophy talked to death by brain-bewildering chatter, politics more fantastic and partisan than ever, and society in complete disorganization, because the conservatrices of ancient customs have become ridiculous to themselves, and have endeavored in every way to place themselves outside the pale of custom. If indeed women had their greatest power in custom, where will they have to look in order to reacquire a similar plenitude of power after having renounced custom?

Agreeable Adversaries—The natural inclination of women towards quiet, regular, happily tuned existences and intercourse, the oil-like and calming effect of their influence upon the sea of life, operates unconsciously against the heroic inner impulse of the free spirit. Without knowing it, women act as if they were taking away the stones from the path of the wandering mineralogist in order that he might not strike his foot against them—when he has gone out for the very purpose of striking against them.

Authority And Freedom—However highly women may honor their husbands, they honor still more the powers and ideas recognized by society; they have been accustomed for millennia to go along with their hands folded on their breasts, and their heads bent before everything dominant, disapproving of all resistance to public authority. They therefore unintentionally, and as if from instinct, hang themselves as a drag on the wheels of free-spirited, independent endeavor, and in certain circumstances make their husbands highly impatient, especially when the latter persuade themselves that it is really love which prompts the action of their wives. To disapprove of women's methods and generously to honor the motives that prompt them—that is man's nature and often enough his despair.

Of The Intellect Of Women—The intellectual strength of a woman is best proved by the fact that she offers her own intellect as a sacrifice out of love for a man and his intellect, and that nevertheless in the new domain, which was previously foreign to her nature, a second intellect at once arises as an aftergrowth, to which the man's mind impels her.

Man Promises, Woman Fulfils—By woman, nature shows how far she has hitherto achieved her task of fashioning humanity, by man she shows what she has had to overcome and what she still proposes to do for humanity. The most perfect woman of every age is the holiday task of the Creator on every seventh day of culture, the recreation of the artist from his work.

Souls All Of A Piece—Women and artists think that where we do not contradict them we cannot. Reverence on ten counts and silent disapproval on ten others appears to them an impossible combination, because their souls are all of a piece.

Disgust With Truth—Women are so constituted that all truth (in relation to men, love, children, society, aim of life) disgusts them—and that they try to be revenged on every one who opens their eyes.

How Both Sexes Behave When In The Right—If it is conceded to a woman that she is right, she cannot deny herself the triumph of setting her heel on the neck of the vanquished; she must taste her victory to the full.

On the other hand, man towards man in such a case is ashamed of being right. But then man is accustomed to victory; with woman it is an exception.

Profound Interpretations—He who has interpreted a passage in an author "more profoundly" than was intended, has not interpreted the author but has obscured him. Our metaphysicians are in the same relation, or even in a worse relation, to the text of Nature. For, to apply their profound interpretations, they often alter the text to suit their purpose—or, in other words, corrupt the text. A curious example of the corruption and obscuration of an author's text is furnished by the ideas of Schopenhauer on the pregnancy of women. "The sign of a continuous will to life in time," he says, "is copulation; the sign of the light of knowledge which is associated anew with this will and holds the possibility of a deliverance, and that too in the highest degree of clearness, is the renewed incarnation of the will to life. This incarnation is betokened by pregnancy, which is therefore frank and open, and even proud, whereas copulation hides itself like a criminal." He declares that every woman, if surprised in the sexual act, would be likely to die of shame, but "displays her pregnancy without a trace of shame, nay even with a sort of pride." Now, firstly, this condition cannot easily be displayed more aggressively than it displays itself, and when Schopenhauer gives prominence only to the intentional character of the display, he is fashioning his text to suit the interpretation. Moreover, his statement of the universality of the phenomenon is not true. He speaks of "every woman." Many women, especially the younger, often appear painfully ashamed of their condition, even in the presence of their nearest kinsfolk. And when women of riper years, especially in the humbler classes, do actually appear proud of their condition, it is because they would give us to understand that they are still desirable to their husbands. That a neighbor on seeing them or a passing stranger should say or think "Can it be possible?"—that is an alms always acceptable to the vanity of women of low mental capacity. In the reverse instance, to conclude from Schopenhauer's proposition, the cleverest and most intelligent women would tend more than any to exult openly in their condition. For they have the best prospect of giving birth to an intellectual prodigy, in whom "the will" can once more "negative" itself for the universal good. Stupid women, on the other hand, would have every reason to hide their pregnancy more modestly than anything they hide.—It cannot be said that this view corresponds to reality. Granted, however, that Schopenhauer was right on the general principle that women show more self-satisfaction when pregnant than at any other time, a better explanation than this lies to hand. One might imagine the clucking of a hen even before she lays an egg, saying, "Look! look! I shall lay an egg! I shall lay an egg!"

From *The Joyful Wisdom*

On Female Chastity. There is something quite astonishing and extraordinary in the education of women of the higher class; indeed, there is perhaps nothing more paradoxical. All the world is agreed to educate them with as much ignorance as possible *in eroticis,* and to inspire their soul with a profound shame of such things, and the extremest impatience and horror at the suggestion of them. It is really here only that all the ''honor'' of woman is at stake; what would one not forgive them in other respects! But here they are intended to remain ignorant to the very backbone: they are intended to have neither eyes, ears, words, nor thoughts for this, their ''wickedness''; indeed knowledge here is already evil. And then! To be hurled as with an awful thunderbolt into reality and knowledge with marriage—and indeed by him whom they most love and esteem: to have to encounter love and shame in contradiction, yea, to have to feel rapture, abandonment, duty, sympathy, and fright at the unexpected proximity of God and animal, and whatever else besides! all at once!—There, in fact, a psychic entanglement has been effected which is quite unequaled! Even the sympathetic curiosity of the wisest discerner of men does not suffice to divine how this or that woman gets along with the solution of this enigma and the enigma of this solution; what dreadful, far-reaching suspicions must awaken thereby in the poor unhinged soul; and forsooth, how the ultimate philosophy and scepticism of the woman casts anchor at this point!—Afterwards the same profound silence as before: and often even a silence to herself, a shutting of her eyes to herself.—Young wives on that account make great efforts to appear superficial and thoughtless; the most ingenious of them simulate a kind of impudence.—Wives easily feel their husbands as a questionmark to their honor, and their children as an apology or atonement—they require children, and wish for them in quite another spirit than a husband wishes for them.—In short, one cannot be gentle enough towards women!

No Altruism!—I see in many men an excessive impulse and delight in wanting to be a function; they strive after it, and have the keenest scent for all those positions in which precisely *they* themselves can be functions. Among such persons are those women who transform themselves into just that function of a man that is but weakly developed in him, and then become his purse, or his politics, or his social intercourse. Such beings maintain themselves best when they insert themselves in an alien organism; if they do not succeed they become vexed, irritated, and eat themselves up.

How Each Sex Has its Prejudice about Love. Notwithstanding all the concessions which I am inclined to make to the monogamic prejudice, I will never admit that we should speak of *equal* rights in the love of man and woman: there are no such equal rights. The reason is that man and woman understand something different by the term love—and it belongs to the conditions of love in both sexes that the one sex does *not* presuppose the same feeling, the same conception of "love," in the other sex. What woman understands by love is clear enough: complete surrender (not merely devotion) of soul and body, without any motive, without any reservation, rather with shame and terror at the thought of a devotion restricted by clauses or associated with conditions. In this absence of conditions her love is precisely a *faith*: woman has no other.—Man, when he loves a woman, *wants* precisely this love from her; he is consequently, as regards himself, furthest removed from the prerequisites of feminine love; granted, however, that there should also be men to whom on their side the demand for complete devotion is not unfamiliar—well, they are really—not men. A man who loves like a woman becomes thereby a slave; a woman, however, who loves like a woman becomes thereby a *more perfect* woman. . . . The passion of woman in its unconditional renunciation of its own rights presupposes in fact that there does *not* exist on the other side an equal *pathos,* an equal desire for renunciation: for if both renounced themselves out of love, there would result—well, I don't know what, perhaps a *horror vacui?* Woman wants to be taken and accepted as a possession, she wishes to be merged in the conceptions of "possession" and "possessed"; consequently she wants one who *takes,* who does not offer and give himself away, but who reversely is rather to be made richer in "himself"—by the increase of power, happiness and faith which the woman herself gives to him. Woman gives herself, man takes her. I do not think one will get over this natural contrast by any social contract, or with the very best will to do justice, however desirable it may be to avoid bringing the severe, frightful, enigmatical, and unmoral elements of this antagonism constantly before our eyes. For love, regarded as complete, great, and full, is nature, and as nature, is to all eternity something "unmoral."—*Fidelity* is accordingly included in woman's love, it follows from the definition thereof; with man fidelity *may* readily result in consequence of his love, perhaps as gratitude or idiosyncrasy of taste, and so-called elective affinity, but it does not belong to the *essence* of his love—and indeed so little, that one might almost be entitled to speak of a natural opposition between love and fidelity in man, whose love is just a desire to possess, and *not* a renunciation and giving away; the desire to possess, however, comes to an end every time with the possession. . . . As a matter of fact it is the more subtle and jealous thirst for possession in the man (who is rarely and tardily convinced of having this "possession"), which makes his love continue; in that case it is even possible that the love may increase after the surrender—he does not readily own that a woman has nothing more to "surrender" to him.

From *Thus Spake Zarathustra*

The Friend

Art thou a slave? Then thou canst not be a friend. Art thou a tyrant? Then thou canst not have friends.

Far too long hath there been a slave and a tyrant concealed in woman. On that account woman is not yet capable of friendship: she knoweth only love.

In woman's love there is injustice and blindness to all she doth not love. And even in woman's conscious love, there is still always surprise and lightning and night, along with the light.

As yet woman is not capable of friendship: women are still cats, and birds. Or at the best, cows.

As yet woman is not capable of friendship. But tell me, ye men, who of you are capable of friendship?

Old and Young Women

As I went on my way alone today, at the hour when the sun declineth, there met me an old woman, and she spake thus unto my soul:

"Much hath Zarathustra spoken also to us women, but never spake he unto us concerning woman."

And I answered her: "Concerning woman, one should only talk unto men."

"Talk also unto me of woman," said she; "I am old enough to forget it presently."

And I obliged the old woman and spake thus unto her:

Everything in woman is a riddle, and everything in woman hath one solution—it is called pregnancy.

Man is for woman, a means: the purpose is always the child. But what is woman for man?

Two different things wanteth the true man: danger and diversion. Therefore wanteth he woman, as the most dangerous plaything.

Man shall be trained for war, and woman for the recreation of the warrior: all else is folly.

Too sweet fruits—these the warrior liketh not. Therefore liketh he woman;—bitter is even the sweetest woman.

Better than man doth woman understand children, but man is more childish than woman.

In the true man there is a child hidden: it wanteth to play. Up then, ye women, and discover the child in man!

A plaything let woman be, pure and fine like the precious stone, illumined with the virtues of a world not yet come.

Let the beam of a star shine in your love! Let your hope say: "May I bear the Superman!"

In your love let there be valor! With your love shall ye assail him who inspireth you with fear!

In your love be your honor! Little doth woman understand otherwise about honor. But let this be your honor: always to love more than ye are loved, and never be the second.

Let man fear woman when she loveth: then maketh she every sacrifice, and everything else she regardeth as worthless.

Let man fear woman when she hateth: for man in his innermost soul is merely evil; woman, however, is mean.

Whom hateth woman most?—Thus spake the iron to the loadstone: "I hate thee most, because thou attractest, but art too weak to draw unto thee."

The happiness of man is, "I will." The happiness of woman is, "He will."

"Lo! now hath the world become perfect!"—thus thinketh every woman when she obeyeth with all her love.

Obey, must the woman, and find a depth for her surface. Surface, is woman's soul, a mobile, stormy film on shallow water.

Man's soul, however, is deep, its current gusheth in subterranean caverns: woman surmiseth its force, but comprehendeth it not.

Then answered me the old woman: "Many fine things hath Zarathustra said, especially for those who are young enough for them.

Strange! Zarathustra knoweth little about woman, and yet he is right about them! Doth this happen, because with women nothing is impossible?

And now accept a little truth by way of thanks! I am old enough for it!

Swaddle it up and hold its mouth; otherwise it will scream too loudly, the little truth."

"Give me, woman, thy little truth!" said I. And thus spake the old woman:

"Thou goest to women? Do not forget thy whip!"

Thus spake Zarathustra.

From *The Twilight of the Idols*

13. Man created woman—out of what? Out of a rib of his god—of his "ideal."

20. The perfect woman perpetrates literature as if it were a petty vice: as an experiment, *en passant,* and looking about her all the while to see whether anybody is noticing her, hoping that somebody *is* noticing her.

27. Man thinks woman profound—why? Because he can never fathom her depths. Woman is not even shallow.

28. When woman possesses masculine virtues, she is enough to make you run away. When she possesses no masculine virtues, she herself runs away.

From *The Antichrist*

—Has anybody ever really understood the celebrated story which stands at the beginning of the Bible—concerning God's infernal panic over *science?* . . . Nobody has understood it. This essentially sacerdotal book naturally begins with the great inner difficulty of the priest: *he* knows only one great danger, *consequently* "God" has only one great danger.

The old God, entirely "spirit," a high priest through and through, and wholly perfect, is wandering in a leisurely fashion round his garden; but he is bored. Against boredom even the gods themselves struggle in vain. What does he do? He invents man—man is entertaining. . . . But, behold, even man begins to be bored. God's compassion for the only form of misery which is peculiar to all paradises, exceeds all bounds: so forthwith he creates yet other animals. God's *first* mistake: man did not think animals entertaining—he dominated them, he did not even wish to be an "animal." Consequently God created woman. And boredom did indeed cease from that moment—but many other things ceased as well! Woman was God's *second* mistake.—"Woman in her innermost nature is a serpent, Heva"—every priest knows this: "all evil came into this world through woman"—every priest knows this too. "*Consequently science* also comes from woman." . . . Only through woman did man learn to taste of the tree of knowledge. What had happened? Panic had seized the old God. Man himself had been his *greatest* mistake, he had created a rival for himself, science makes you *equal to God*—it is all up with priests and gods when man becomes scientific!—Moral: science is the most prohibited thing of all—it alone, is forbidden.

From *Ecce Homo*

. . . May I venture to suggest, incidentally, that I know women? This knowledge is part of my Dionysian patrimony. Who knows? maybe I am the first psychologist of the eternally feminine. Women all like me. . . . But that's an old story: save, of course, the abortions among them, the emancipated ones, those who lack the wherewithal to have children. Thank goodness I am not willing to let myself be torn to pieces! the perfect woman tears you to pieces when she loves you: I know these amiable Mænads. . . . Oh! what a dangerous, creeping, subterranean little beast of prey she is! And so agreeable withall! . . . A little woman, pursuing her vengeance, would force open even the iron gates of Fate itself. Woman is incalculably more wicked than man, she is also cleverer. Goodness in a woman is already a sign of *degeneration*. All cases of "beautiful souls" in women may be traced to a faulty physiological condition—but I go no further, lest I should become medicynical. The struggle for equal rights is even a symptom of disease; every doctor knows this. The more womanly a woman is, the more she fights tooth and nail against rights in general: the natural order of things, the eternal war between the sexes, assigns to her by far the foremost rank. Have people had ears to hear my definition of love? It is the only definition worthy of a philosopher. Love, in its means, is war; in its foundation, it is the mortal hatred of the sexes. Have you heard my reply to the question how a woman can be cured, "saved" in fact?—Give her a child! A woman needs children, man is always only a means, thus spake Zarathustra. "The emancipation of women"—this is the instinctive hatred of physiologically botched—that is to say, barren—women for those of their sisters who are well constituted: the fight against "man" is always only a means, a pretext, a piece of strategy. By trying to rise to "Woman *per se*," to "Higher Woman," to the "Ideal Woman," all they wish to do is to lower the general level of women's rank: and there are no more certain means to this end than university education, trousers, and the rights of voting cattle. Truth to tell, the emancipated are the anarchists in the "eternally feminine" world, the physiological mishaps, the most deep-rooted instinct of whom is revenge. A whole species of the most malicious "idealism"—which, by the bye, also manifests itself in men, in Henrik Ibsen for instance, that typical old maid—whose object is to poison the clean conscience, the natural spirit, of sexual love. . . . And in order to leave no doubt in your minds in regard to my opinion, which, on this matter, is as honest as it is severe, I will reveal to you one more clause out of my moral code against vice—with the word "vice" I combat every kind of opposition to nature, or, if you prefer fine words, idealism. The clause reads: "Preaching of chastity is a public incitement to unnatural practices. All depreciation of the sexual life, all the sullying of it by means of the concept 'impure,' is the essential crime against life—is the essential crime agains the Holy Spirit of life."

From *The Will to Power*

Whatever kind of *eccentric ideal* one may have (whether as a "Christian," a "free - spirit," an "immoralist," or a German Imperialist), one should try to avoid insisting upon its being *the* ideal; for, by so doing, it is deprived of all its privileged nature. One should have an ideal as a distinction; one should not propagate it, and thus level one's self down to the rest of mankind.

How is it, that in spite of this obvious fact, the majority of idealists indulge in propaganda for their ideal, just as if they had no right to it unless the *majority* acquiesce therein?—For instance, all those plucky and insignificant girls behave in this way, who claim the right to study Latin and mathematics. What is it urges them to do this? I fear it is the instinct of the herd, and the terror of the herd: they fight for the "emancipation of woman," because they are best able to achieve their own private little distinction by fighting for it under the cover of a *charitable movement,* under the banner bearing the device "For others."

The *cleverness* of idealists consists in their persistently posing as the missionaries and "representatives" of an ideal: they thus "beautify" themselves in the eyes of those who still believe in disinterestedness and heroism. Whereas real heroism consists, *not* in fighting under the banner of self-sacrifice, submission, and disinterestedness, but in *not fighting at all.* . . . "I am thus; I will be thus—and you can go to the devil!". . .

Would any link be missing in the whole chain of science and art, if woman, if woman's work, were excluded from it? Let us acknowledge the exception—it proves the rule—that woman is capable of perfection in everything which does not constitute a work: in letters, in memoirs, in the most intricate handiwork—in short, in everything which is not a craft; and just precisely because in the things mentioned woman perfects herself, because in them she obeys the only artistic impulse in her nature— which is to captivate. . . . But what has woman to do with the passionate indifference of the genuine artist who sees more importance in a breath, in a sound, in the merest trifle, than in himself?—who with all his five fingers gropes for his most secret and hidden treasures?—who attributes no value to anything unless it knows how to take shape (unless it surrenders itself, unless it visualizes itself in some way). Art as it is practiced by artists—do you not understand what it is? is it not an outrage on all our *pudeurs*? . . . Only in this century has woman dared to try her hand at literature ("*Vers la canaille plumière écrivassière,*" to speak with old Mirabeau): woman now writes, she now paints, she is losing her instincts. And to what purpose, if one may put such a question? . . .

Why the weak triumph—On the whole, the sick and the weak have more *sympathy* and are more "humane": the sick and the weak have more intellect, and are more changeable, more variegated, more intellectual—more malicious; the sick alone invented *malice*. (A morbid precocity is often to be observed among rickety, scrofulitic, and tuberculous people.) *Esprit:* the property of older races; Jews, Frenchmen, Chinese. (The anti-Semites do not forgive the Jews for having both intellect—and money. Anti-Semites—another name for "bungled and botched.")

The sick and the weak have always had *fascination* on their side; they are more *interesting* than the healthy: the fool and the saint—the two most interesting kinds of men. . . . Closely related thereto is the "genius." The "great adventurers and criminals" and all great men, the most healthy in particular, have always been *sick* at certain periods of their lives—great disturbances of the emotions, the passion for power, love, revenge, are all accompanied by very profound perturbations. And, as for decadence, every man who does not die prematurely manifests it in almost every respect—he therefore knows from experience the instincts which belong to it: for *half his life* nearly every man is decadent.

And finally, woman! *One-half of mankind is weak,* chronically sick, changeable, shifty—woman requires strength in order to cleave to it; she also requires a religion of the weak which glorifies weakness, love, and modesty as divine: or, better still, she makes the strong weak—she *rules* when she succeeds in overcoming the strong. Woman has always conspired with decadent types—the priests, for instance—against the "mighty," against the "strong," against *men*. Women avail themselves of children for the cult of piety, pity, and love:—the *mother* stands as the symbol of *convincing* altruism. . . .

Finally, *the social mishmash,* which is the result of revolution, of the establishment of equal rights, and of the superstition, the "equality of men." Thus the possessors of the instincts of decline (of resentment, of discontent, of the lust of destruction, of anarchy and Nihilism), as also the instincts of slavery, of cowardice, of craftiness, and of rascality, which are inherent among those classes of society which have long been suppressed, are beginning to get infused into the blood of all ranks. Two or three generations later, the race can no longer be recognized—everything has become *mob*. And thus there results a collective instinct against *selection*, against every kind of *privilege*; and this instinct operates with such power, certainty, hardness, and cruelty that, as a matter of fact, in the end, even the privileged classes have to submit: all those who still wish to hold on to power flatter the mob, work with the mob, and must have the mob on their side—the "geniuses" *above all*. The latter become the *heralds* of those feelings with which the mob can be inspired—the expression of pity, of honor, even for all that suffers, all that is low and despised, and has lived under persecution, becomes predominant (types: Victor Hugo, Richard Wagner).—The rise of the mob signifies once more the rise of old values.

V. I. Lenin

Russian philosopher and revolutionary leader, 1870–1924, who founded Bolshevism.

From "The Tasks of the Working Women's Movement in the Soviet Republic." Speech Delivered at the Fourth Moscow City Non-Party Conference of Women Workers, September 23, 1919.

. . . Comrades, . . . I should like to say a few words about the general tasks of the working women's movement in the Soviet Republic; the tasks connected with the transition to Socialism in general, as well as those which are so persistently forcing their way to the forefront at the present time. Comrades, the question of the position of women was raised by the Soviet government from the very outset. In my opinion, the task of every workers' state that is passing to Socialism will be of a twofold character. The first part of this task is comparatively easy and simple. It is connected with the old laws which placed women in an inferior position as compared with men.

Long long ago, the representatives of all liberation movements in Western Europe not only for decades but for centuries demanded the abolition of these obsolete laws and the establishment of legal equality between men and women. But not a single European democratic state, not one of the most advanced republics, has succeeded in achieving this, because where capitalism exists, where the private ownership of the land, the private ownership of factories and works is preserved, where the power of capital is preserved, men will retain their privileges. We succeeded in achieving this in Russia only because on November 7 (October 25), 1917, the power of the workers was established. From the very outset the Soviet government set itself the aim of existing as the government of the toilers opposed to all exploitation. It set itself the aim of destroying the possibility of the landlords and capitalists exploiting the toilers, of destroying the rule of capital. The aim of the Soviet government was to create the conditions in which the toilers could build their own lives without the private ownership of the land, without the private ownership of the factories and works, without that private ownership which everywhere, all over the world, even where complete political liberty reigns, even in the most democratic republics, actually placed the toilers in conditions of poverty and wage slavery, and placed women in a position of double slavery.

The Soviet government, as the government of the toilers, during the very first months of its existence, brought about a complete revolution in the laws affecting women. Of the laws which placed women in a subordinate position not a trace has been left in the Soviet Republic. I speak precisely of those laws which particularly took advantage of woman's weaker position and put her in an inferior and often in a degrading position; I refer to the divorce laws, the laws concerning children born out of wedlock, the right of a woman to sue the father of her child for maintenance.

It is precisely in this sphere that in bourgeois law, one must say, even in the most advanced countries, advantage is taken of woman's weaker position to make her inferior and to degrade her; and it is precisely in this sphere that the Soviet government has destroyed every trace of the old unjust laws, which were intolerable for the representatives of the toiling masses. And we can now proudly say without the slightest exaggeration that except for Soviet Russia there is not a single country in the world in which there is complete equality between men and women and in which women are not placed in a degraded position, which is particularly felt in everyday family life. This was one of our first and most important tasks.

If you happen to come in contact with parties which are hostile to the Bolsheviks, or if Russian newspapers published in the regions occupied by Kolchak or Denikin happen to fall into your hands, or if you happen to speak with people who share the views of these newspapers, you will often hear accusations to the effect that the Soviet government has violated democracy.

We, the representatives of the Soviet government, the Bolshevik Communists and adherents of Soviet government, are constantly being accused of having violated democracy, and the evidence advanced to prove this is that the Soviet government dispersed the Constituent Assembly. Our usual reply to these charges is: The democracy and the Constituent Assembly which arose under the system of private ownership of land—when people were not equal, when those who owned capital were the masters and the rest worked for them, were their wage slaves—were of no value at all to us. Such democracy served as a screen to conceal slavery even in the most advanced states. We Socialists are adherents of democracy only to the extent that it alleviates the position of the toilers and oppressed. All over the world Socialism pursues the aim of fighting against all exploitation of man by man. We attach real significance to the democracy which serves the exploited, those who are placed in a position of inferiority. If nontoilers are deprived of the franchise, that is real equality. He who does not work shall not eat. In reply to these accusations we say that the question that should be put is: How is democracy carried out in this or that state? We see that equality is proclaimed in all democratic republics, but in civil law, and in the laws governing the position of women in the family, in regard to divorce, we see inequality and the degradation of women at every step. And we say: This is the violation of democracy, and precisely in regard to the oppressed. The Soviet government has applied democracy to a greater extent than even the most advanced countries by refraining from putting into its laws the slightest hint that women are inferior. I repeat, not a single state and not a single legislature has done half of what the Soviet government did for women in the first months of its existence.

Of course, laws are not enough, and we cannot under any circumstances be satisfied merely with what we say in our laws; but we have done all that was expected of us to make women equal with men, and we have a right to be proud of what we have done. The position of women in Soviet Russia is now an ideal position from the point of view of the most advanced states. But we say to ourselves: Of course this is only a beginning.

As long as women are engaged in housework their position is still a restricted one. In order to achieve the complete emancipation of women and to make them really equal with men, we must have social economy, and the participation of women in general productive labor. Then women will occupy the same position as men.

This, of course, does not mean that women must be exactly equal with men in productivity of labor, amount of labor, length of the working day, conditions of labor, etc. But it does mean that women shall not be in an oppressed economic position compared with men. You all know that even with the fullest equality, women are still in an actual position of inferiority because all housework is thrust upon them. Most of this housework is the most unproductive, most barbarous and most arduous work that women perform. This labor is extremely petty and contains nothing that facilitates the development of women.

In pursuit of our Socialist ideals we want to fight for the complete realization of Socialism, and here a wide field of work is opened up for women. We are now seriously preparing to clear the ground for Socialist construction; and the construction of Socialist society will commence only when we, having achieved the complete equality of women, take up our new work together with women who are emancipated from petty, stultifying, unproductive work. This work is sufficient to last us for many, many years. This work cannot produce such quick results and will not create such a striking effect.

We are establishing model institutions, dining rooms and crèches, which will liberate women from housework. And it is precisely the women who must undertake the work of building these institutions. It must be said that at present there are very few institutions in Russia that could help the women to liberate themselves from their state of domestic slavery. Their number is insignificant, and the conditions in which the Soviet Republic is now placed—the military and food conditions about which the other comrades have spoken to you at length—hinder us in this work. Nevertheless, it must be said that the institutions which liberate women from their position of domestic slavery are springing up wherever it is possible for them to do so. We say that the emancipation of the workers must be brought about by the workers themselves, and similarly, the emancipation of women workers must be brought about by the women workers themselves. Women workers themselves should see to the development of such institutions; and their activities in this field will lead to a complete change from the position they formerly occupied in capitalist society.

In order to engage in politics in the old capitalist society, special training was required; that is why women's participation in politics, even in the most advanced and free capitalist countries, is insignificant. Our task is to make politics accessible to every toiling woman. From the moment the private ownership of land and factories was abolished and the power of the landlords and capitalists was overthrown, the tasks of politics became simple, clear and quite accessible to all the toiling masses, and to the toiling women. In capitalist society women are placed in such an inferior position that their participation in politics is insignificant compared with that of men. In order to change this state of affairs the rule of the toilers is required, and when that is achieved the principal tasks of politics will consist of all that which directly concerns the fate of the toilers themselves.

And here the participation of the women workers, not only of Party and class conscious women workers, but also of nonparty and the least class conscious, is necessary. In this respect, the Soviet government opens up a wide field of activity for women workers.

We have experienced very hard times in the struggle against the forces hostile to Soviet Russia which are marching against us. It has been very hard for us to fight in the military field against these forces which are waging war against the rule of the toilers, and in the food field against the profiteers, because the number of people, of toilers, who come forward wholeheartedly to help us by their labor, is not yet sufficiently large. And so the Soviet government prizes nothing so highly as the assistance of the broad masses of nonparty working women. Let them know that in the old bourgeois society a complicated training was required in order to engage in political activity, and that this was inaccessible to women. But the principal aim of political activity in the Soviet Republic is to fight against the landlords and the capitalists, to fight for the abolition of exploitation; and this opens for the women workers in the Soviet Republic a field for political activity which will consist of utilizing their organizing ability to help the men.

We not only need organizational work on a scale affecting millions, we also need organizational work on the smallest scale that woman will also be able to engage in. Women can work amidst war conditions, when it is a matter of helping the army, of carrying on agitation in its ranks. Women must take an active part in this, so that the Red Army may see that it is being cared for and looked after. Women may also work in the food field, in distributing food, in improving mass catering, in developing the dining rooms which have now been opened on such a wide scale in Petrograd.

In these fields of activity the working women acquire real organizational significance. The participation of women is required in the organization of large experimental enterprises and in supervising them so that this shall not be the work of single persons. Without the participation of a large number of toiling women in this work, it cannot be fulfilled. And working women are quite suitable in this field, for such work as supervising the distribution of food and seeing that provisions are more easily obtained. This is work that nonparty working women can easily do, and this work will, in its turn, most of all help firmly to establish Socialist society.

Abolishing the private ownership of land and almost entirely abolishing the private ownership of factories and works, the Soviet government strives to enlist all toilers, not only Party, but also nonparty, not only men, but also women, in the work of economic construction. This work begun by the Soviet government can be advanced only when, instead of hundreds of women, we have millions and millions of women, all over Russia, taking part in it. When that is the case, we are convinced, the work of Socialist construction will be firmly established. Then the toilers will show that they can live and administer without the landlords and capitalists. Then Socialist construction will be so firmly established in Russia that the Soviet Republic will have no cause to fear any external enemies in other countries, or enemies within Russia.

Josiah Royce

American idealist philosopher, 1855–1916, who was born in California and taught at Harvard during what has been called its golden period. Developing a unique blend of Hegelian rationalism and American pragmatism, Royce emphasized the human self as a member of a community of interpretation, ultimately overcoming self-centeredness and evil through loyalty in the Beloved Community.

From a letter to Abigail Williams May

20 Lowell St.
Cambridge, Mass.
Jan. 5, 1886

My Dear Madam:

I always think it a duty, and find it a pleasure, to accept such an invitation as I have received, through yourself and Mrs. Gilman, from the Mass. Society for the University Education of Women; and I shall be glad, accordingly to spend some ten or fifteen minutes at your Annual Meeting in saying a few words about the topic that you suggest. . . .

As I understand your view, then, it would be in accordance with the purposes of your Annual Meeting if I were to read a brief paper there on "The Study of Philosophy in the Higher Education of Women," in which I should frankly set forth both the advantages and the disadvantages that, according to my experience, the young women under my charge have seemed to me to possess in respect of this study. I think, to sum up my view in the briefest form, that the supposed difficulty that women are said to meet in forming abstract ideas, and so in grasping philosophical subtleties, does not exist, in case of young women who chance to be interested in philosophy. The true difficulty, however, which such young women do meet with in their study of philosophy, is rather a moral than an intellectual one: it is a certain fear of standing alone, of being eccentric, of seeming unduly obstinate in thought. This fear makes them, in the long run, too docile followers of a teacher or of an author, and so hinders their freedom of constructive thought. Now eccentricity of thought is, indeed, never the ultimate goal of philosophic study; but it is a necessary stage on the way to real success in thought. And this stage young women are less apt to reach. I wish therefore to suggest this lesson as possibly helpful to young women who may be studying such topics.—If such a statement, made at due length, would be helpful to your meeting, you are welcome to it.—Yr's Truly

Josiah Royce

From *On Certain Limitations of the Thoughtful Public in America*

People often say that men act upon conscious reasoning processes, and women upon intuitions which they refuse to formulate. The assertion is, like most proverbial assertions, inadequate to the wealth of life's facts. Certainly women often enough act with a mysterious swiftness of unconscious wisdom. But so do many of the most effective men. I have, however, often observed that some educated women, some women who enter public life as reformers, and perhaps too many college-bred women, are nowadays troubled with an overfondness both for mere formulas and for abstract arguments about complex practical issues that only a happy instinctive choice and wholesome sentiment can ever successfully decide so long as we remain what we are; namely, frail and ignorant human beings, who see through a glass darkly. The fault of being overfond of abstractions, or of trying to formulate bad reasons for one's instinctive actions, does not characterize the man of business or the successful executive. One does not meet this fault in the market-place. But just this fault does characterize some of our most cultivated and thoughtful people in this country. And among these people I find a good many intellectual women.

William James

American psychologist and pragmatist philosopher, 1842–1910, who supported the "will to believe" in God and in important philosophically disputed but unresolved issues.

From *The Principles of Psychology*

We observe an identical difference between men as a whole and women as a whole. A young woman of twenty reacts with intuitive promptitude and security in all the usual circumstances in which she may be placed.* Her likes and dislikes are formed; her opinions, to a great extent, the same that they will be through life. Her character is, in fact, finished in its essentials. How inferior to her is a boy of twenty in all these respects! His character is still gelatinous, uncertain what shape to assume, 'trying it on' in every direction. Feeling his power, yet ignorant of the manner in which he shall express it, he is, when compared with his sister, a being of no definite contour. But this absence of prompt tendency in his brain to set into particular modes is the very condition which insures that it shall ultimately become so much more efficient than the woman's. The very lack of preappointed trains of thought is the ground on which general principles and heads of classification grow up; and the masculine brain deals with new and complex matter indirectly by means of these, in a manner which the feminine method of direct intuition, admirably and rapidly as it performs within its limits, can vainly hope to cope with.

*Social and domestic circumstances, that is, not material ones. Perceptions of social relations seem very keen in persons whose dealings with the material world are confined to knowing a few useful objects, principally animals, plants, and weapons. Savages and boors are often as tactful and astute socially as trained diplomatists. In general, it is probable that the consciousness of how one stands with other people occupies a relatively larger and larger part of the mind, the lower one goes in the scale of culture. Woman's intuitions, so fine in the sphere of personal relations, are seldom first-rate in the way of mechanics. All boys teach themselves how a clock goes: few girls. Hence Dr. Whately's jest, "Woman is the unreasoning animal, and pokes the fire from on top."

. . . The boys who pull out grasshoppers' legs and butterflies' wings, and disembowel every frog they catch, have no *thought* at all about the matter. The creatures tempt their hands to a fascinating occupation, to which they have to yield. It is with them as with the 'boy-fiend' Jesse Pomeroy, who cut a little girl's throat, 'just to see how she'd act.' The normal provocatives of the impulse are all living beasts, great and small, toward which a contrary habit has not been formed—all human beings in whom we perceive a certain *intent* towards *us,* and a large number of human beings who offend us peremptorily, either by their look, or gait, or by some circumstance in their lives which we dislike. Inhibited by sympathy, and by reflection calling up impulses of an opposite kind, civilized men lose the habit of acting out their pugnacious instincts in a perfectly natural way, and a passing feeling of anger, with its comparatively faint bodily expressions, may be the limit of their physical combativeness. Such a feeling as this may, however, be aroused by a wide range of objects. Inanimate things, combinations of color and sound, bad bills of fare, may in persons who combine fastidious taste with an irascible temperament produce real ebullitions of rage. Though the female sex is often said to have less pugnacity than the male, the difference seems connected more with the extent of the motor consequences of the impulse than with its frequency. Women take offence and get angry, if anything, more easily than men, but their anger is inhibited by fear and other principles of their nature from expressing itself in blows. The hunting instinct proper seems to be decidedly weaker in them than in men. The latter instinct is easily restricted by habit to certain objects, which become legitimate 'game,' while other things are spared. If the hunting instinct be not exercised at all, it may even entirely die out, and a man may enjoy letting a wild creature live, even though he might easily kill it. Such a type is now becoming frequent; but there is no doubt that in the eyes of a child of nature such a personage would seem a sort of moral monster. . . .

A gentleman told me that he had a conclusive argument for opening the Harvard Medical School to women. It was this: "Are not women human?"—which major premise of course had to be granted. "Then are they not entitled to all the rights of humanity?" My friend said that he had never met anyone who could successfully meet this reasoning.

A Review

1. Women's Suffrage; the Reform against Nature, by Horace Bushnell, New York: Scribner, 1869. 2. The Subjection of Women, by John Stuart Mill, New York: Appleton, 1869.

English style is distinguished by the atmosphere of homely splendor, of familiar pomp, of surcharged association, in which its words move. The sentences unroll themselves deliberately, seeming to listen to their own progress, now packing volumes of meaning into a simple word, now yielding to passing suggestions and incorporating into their mass epithets and clauses which writers of other nations would neglect as collateral and exuberant fancies. The secret of this peculiarly English richness of movement has been kept by Dr. Bushnell, perhaps, more steadily than by any other of our contemporary writers. Mr. Mill's sentences, clean, weighted, and going straight to their mark, would, if translated literally, sound as natural and forcible to French, German, or Italian ears as they do to ours. But Dr. Bushnell's, in any tongue but our own, would have an outlandish air. To take an example at random: "Where we touch the limits of reason, they [women] touch the limits of excess; where we are impetuous in a cause, they are uncontrollable in it. We know how, as men, to be moderated in part, by self-moderation, even as ships by their helms in all great storms at sea; for the other part we had women kept in moderation by their element, even as ships in harbor lie swinging by their anchors; but now we get even less of help from these than they do from us." The reef on which the old English style often split came from an excess of this self-listening, and the result was affectation, or, to use the vulgar term, *mouthing*. And Dr. Bushnell with his rich fancy has not steered clear of the reef. A clerical training always tends to make a diffuse writer, and we think that "Women's Suffrage" would have been a more solid book if its author's remarkable powers of *ex*pression had been a little balanced by some cultivation of a correlative power of *re*pression. As it is, he is redundant and careless, not to say often vulgar; as in such phrases as, "the Duchess of Devonshire was a high-life conventional kind of woman."

Dr. Bushnell's thesis is, that although the present status of women is in many respects one of wrongful "abridgment," and although they ought to have facilities for education and occupation opened to them in many hitherto untried ways, society should nevertheless make a resolute stand against admitting them to share in any sort of "government." Preachers they may be, but not pastors or presbyters or bishops; attorneys, but neither advocates nor judges. "Administration" of any kind in which authority is implied lies without their province—most of all, the holding of political office, and the exercise of the suffrage. This weighty conclusion is derived from a conception of the essential nature of woman and of government, expressed in an infinite variety of ways throughout the book. She is not "created" to mingle in any kind of strife, or "to batter the severities of fortune. . . . All government belongs to men . . . . Where agreement is impossible, one of the two clearly must decide, and it must be the man. The woman's law . . . . requires it of her . . . . to submit herself to his fortunes. . . . . If he has no sway force in him . . . . to hold the reins, he is no longer what Nature means when she makes a man." Women are "naturally subject," "subordinate," meant to yield to evil and violence, not to combat them with answering evil and violence. So far so good. If Dr. Bushnell is contented to urge this as an ideal, a matter of inexplicable sentiment, he remains in a strong position. The universal sense of mankind hitherto, and its almost universal sense now, will uphold him. But he is naturally tempted to illustrate the doctrine and enforce it by arguments derived from different orders of considerations, which to our mind are far from making it more imposing; but rather, being unsound themselves, tend to infect it with their own decay, and so undo the authority it possesses in its brute dogmatic form.

The first and chief of these arguments is, that the subordination of women, instead of implying their inferiority, ''gives them, morally considered, the truest and sublimest conditions of ascendancy; . . . . woman has her government as truly as man,'' namely, ''by grace.'' It is to his as the gospel is to the law, ''and accomplishes just what the law, in that it was weak, could not accomplish. . . . . The honors of womanhood lie in gentleness and patience, or it may be the dreadful lot of violence and tyrant cruelty endured.'' Her supreme glory is to be a ''subject nature, ... milder, truer, and closer to the type of God's own dear submissions in the cross of his Son,'' than our ''coarse forbidding masculinities'' will let us attain. This is nothing but the good old Catholic doctrine, invented when people were hopeless of an order to be realized in this world, that suffering is a higher vocation than action. It has done much good in its day—saved many a slave from envy and despair, and consoled sick men in all ages of the world. But there has probably not been an unjust usage in Christendom which has not at some time sought shelter under its wings. No well man or free man ever adopted it for his own use. Protestantism has practically almost abandoned it in its generality. Dr. Bushnell himself probably makes no wider application of it than to the present case. And we have little doubt, if the truth were known, that he would be found loath in his own person to exchange, even if he could, the power which his ''coarse masculinities'' endow him with, for the inestimable privileges of this sort of government by self-sacrifice. Modern civilization, rightly or wrongly, is bent on developing itself along the line of justice, and any defence of woman's position on ascetic principles will fall with little weight on the public ear. One smiles, and thinks of the author's own words, in another part of his book, as one listens to him ''protesting his natural admirations, his zeal to serve and protect, the profuseness of his attentions, and the unstinted tribute of respect and deference he is always wont to render.'' This gallantry makes after all but a poor compensation to women for that restricted moral development which the limitation of the field of their responsibilities imposes on them.

Let us then cancel this particular reasoning in favor of women's abstinence from politics. Dr. Bushnell is immediately ready with another argument. It is that involved in the first of our quotations from him, to the

effect that women now are something, but if allowed to meddle with government they will become less than nothing. The peculiar "grace" of
their nature is so very tender and evanescent that it requires the most carefully adapted medium or "element" to save it from degenerating into
mere repulsiveness. The divinity of which we have just been hearing so
much is, we are surprised to learn, artificial; so that so simple an act as
that of voting will sweep it away and leave not a rack behind. Feminine
beauty we have long known to be but skin deep; it was reserved for Dr.
Bushnell to proclaim emphatically and categorically that the very essence
of what we call the feminine character is of equally epidermic constitution. The portraits he untiringly draws, of women as they will appear after
twenty-five years' enjoyment of the ballot, are almost too harrowing to
quote. Lilies that fester smell far worse than weeds, and accordingly,
whereas the "thunder" that clothes man's neck (our author never wearies
of this "thunder" attribute of masculinity) looks rather well upon *him,*
woman's "look will be sharp, her voice wiry and shrill, her action angu-
lar and abrupt; wiliness, self-asserting boldness, and eagerness for place
and power" will ravage her once fair form. As for her moral state, "the
strange facility of debasement and moral abandonment" which character-
izes her will make her corruptions much worse than ours. Terrible hints
are given, of the naughtinesses to which women will resort in order to
procure votes, and the demoralization which will take place in country
districts, where the voters, male and female, "will be piled in huge wagons to be carried to the polls, and will sometimes on their return encounter a storm that drives them into wayside taverns and other like places for
the night; where"—but enough; the curious reader may find the rest of
the passage on page 149. But the worst of the change in her is, that it is all
to no purpose. The position for which she has abandoned her proper point
of sway is one in which she is sure miserably to miscarry. Throwing away
all she has, to clutch at a shadow, she ends with nothing; and her appearance, "sharp-featured, lank, and dry," will but reflect "the disappointment of an over-instigated nature," conscious of its own ridiculousness.
Unhappy Dr. Bushnell! thus to supersaturate with the bitterness of this
affront all the sweetness of compliment with which he previously smoth-
ered the sex! At their hands, not ours, must he receive his doom. We cannot help noticing, however, as we pass, how common this two-stool line
of argument is in the school to which Dr. Bushnell belongs—first, a vo-
ciferous proclamation of the utter and radical peculiarity of the womanly
nature; then a nervous terror of its being altered from its foundations by a
few outward changes. Mr. Mill's belief in the power of education is timid
in comparison with this.

A chapter entitled "The Report of History" undertakes to show that
wherever women have meddled with political affairs the result has been
disastrous. Some of the examples strike us as unfortunately chosen. Deli-
lah, Herodias, and the mistresses of Louis the Fifteenth would to our

minds serve better as arguments in favor of educating women politically, and giving them the feeling of responsibility. The strongest of all ''women's-rights'' arguments is, that women are frivolous because they are irresponsible.

We have not space to follow the reverend author into further detail. We will just mention, however, the remedy he proposes, for much of the present dissatisfaction. It is, that ''the almost colic stringency'' of women's modesty may be ''relaxed.'' Marriage is her true sphere; and, as three quarters of the men who are bachelors are so from timidity, the women should be allowed without impropriety to encourage them by making matrimonial advances themselves, when feeling prompts it.

On the whole, it does not seem to us that the author has very vividly realized the practical importance of the matter he has undertaken to discuss, or that his essay is a very serious contribution to the literature of the subject. The word ''frivolity'' little consorts with the reverend character; and yet it seems as if manly earnestness ought to dictate some less hollow utterances than these, ought at any rate to lead a writer to feel the facts more truly, and discern where the true *puncta dolorosa* of the disorder lie. We must close upon the note with which we began—style. The little book leaves on one a strong impression that rhetoric—the mere delight of listening to one's self making sweet music—was an important motive in its production. Even in that respect it cannot be considered wholly a success, and it certainly will add nothing in any circle to Dr. Bushnell's reputation either as a thinker or as an advocate.

If Dr. Bushnell's writing advances, tacking and fluttering with the *allure* of an iridescent butterfly, Mr. Mill launches his smashing projectile straight through every intervening obstacle to its goal. Few books were ever written with so few waste sentences. There is, indeed, an air of hot vehemence about it, to which one is not quite accustomed in its author, and which leaves an impression as of a sore subject, long pent up and brooded over in his mind, and published under a sudden passionate determination that, come what may, he will hold his peace no longer. This amount of feeling has led him, we think, in one or two places to press his arguments beyond the point at which, in a subject that he looked at more coolly, he would probably have stopped: as when, for example, he maintains that we are at present all but absolutely ignorant of the true mental characteristics of woman. It even makes him guilty of something like special pleading, as where he attempts to show that we have no good ground for thinking women to be naturally less fitted for original production in music than men. In fact there runs through the whole book a sort of quibble on the expression ''*nature* of women.'' The mainstay of his thesis is that there is nothing fixed in character, but that it may, through the education of a sufficient number of generations, be produced of any quality to meet the demand; yet nevertheless he keeps speaking of woman's present condition as a distorted and ''unnatural'' one. ''Undesirable'' is the only word he can consistently use. His belief in the omnipotence of education leaves him logically free to admit any amount of *present* native diversity in the average mental aptitudes of the sexes, since that would not on his hypothesis be essential or final. As it is, his somewhat nervous anxiety to efface even the present distinction leads him into extremes where numbers—even of those who fully sympathize with his practical aims—will not care to follow, and deprives the book, in adverse eyes, of that wonderful fairness which has always been the secret of Mr. Mill's power to convince.

The "woman question" has hitherto been in the main a practical one. The etiolated and stunted condition of single women on the one hand, and the interests of order in the family on the other, have been the chief points of attack by the reformers, and retort by the conservatives. On purely sentimental grounds no well-organized warfare has as yet been waged, since both parties have not seemed unwilling on the whole to recognize the same standard. We cannot help thinking, accordingly, that the most noteworthy feature of this in all respects noteworthy book is its thorough hostility to the accepted sentimental ideal of the personal intercourse of man and wife.

If we have not misconceived the matter, Mr. Mill's ideal is a new one, to this country as well as to Europe. Much of what he attacks exists here but in feeble form. The legal abuses are in large measure obsolete; the element of brutality which he makes so prominent in the masculine feeling of superiority is foreign; American husbands are as a rule less sensitive about their wives occupying a position of independent publicity than those of whom Mr. Mill writes; and Mrs. Grundy is not the tyrannical reality to American which she is to English matrons. But bating all this, the sentimental kernel of the essay is revolutionary even here. It is true that the author does not force his sentiment into the foreground, and *deduce* from it as frankly as its importance would justify. But it lurks as a hidden premise in all his reasoning, and, incidentally, is abundantly expressed. It is what furnishes that intense contempt for our actual arrangements which gives such a headlong character to his work; and as we just now likened the latter to a projectile, we may liken this feeling to the powder whose explosion supplies the velocity with which it speeds.

A sentimental ideal of this sort is of course too evanescent and subtle to be stated in scientific black-and-white; but we will bring together a number of disconnected passages from the book, and the reader will easily feel out from them what we mean: "If the family in its best forms is, as it is often said to be, a school of sympathy, tenderness, and loving forgetfulness of self, it is still oftener, as respects its chief, a school of wilfulness, overbearingness, unbounded self-indulgence, and a double-dyed and idealized selfishness, of which sacrifice itself is only a particular form—care for the wife and children being only care for them as parts of the man's own interests and belongings, and their individual happiness being immolated in every shape to his smallest preferences. There is nothing which men so easily learn as this self-worship. All privileged persons and all privileged classes have had it. The more we descend in the scale of humanity, the intenser it is. . . . We have had the morality of submission and the morality of chivalry and generosity; the time has come for the morality of justice. . . . . The true virtue of human beings is fitness to live together as equals, ... preferring whenever possible the society of those with whom leading and following can be alternate and reciprocal. . . . . Any sentiment of freedom which can exist in a man, whose nearest and dearest intimacies are with those of whom he is absolute master, is not the genuine or Christian love of freedom, but what the love of freedom generally was in the ancients and in the Middle Ages—an intense feeling of the dignity and importance of his own personality; making him disdain a yoke for himself of which he has no abhorrence whatever in the abstract, but which he is abundantly ready to impose on others for his own interest or glorification. . . . . All the selfish propensities, the self-worship, the unjust self-preference, which exist among mankind have their source and root in, and derive their principal nourishment from, the present constitution of the relation between men and women. . . . . The principle of the modern movement in morals and politics is that conduct, and conduct alone, entitles to respect; that not what men are, but what they do, constitutes their claim to deference. . . . . Intimate society between people radically dissimilar to one another is an idle dream. Unlikeness may attract, but it is likeness which retains; and in proportion to the likeness is the suitability of the individuals to give each other a happy life. . . . It is not with impunity that the superior in intellect shuts himself up with an inferior, and elects it for his sole completely intimate associate. Any society which is not improving is deteriorating, and the more so the closer and more familiar it is. . . . . What marriage may be in the case of two persons of cultivated faculties, identical in opinions and purposes, between whom there exists that best kind of equality—similarity of powers and capacities, with reciprocal superiority in them, so that each can enjoy the luxury of looking up to the other, and can have alternately the pleasure of leading and being led in the path of development—I will not attempt to describe. To those who can conceive it there is no need; to those who cannot it will appear the dream of an enthusiast. But I maintain, with the profoundest conviction, that this, and this only, is the ideal of marriage.''

Now all this is clearly inimical to the conception of a wife as a possession, as a finality. Independence is Mr. Mill's personal ideal, and his notion of love confounds itself with what is generally distinguished as friendship—each party being able to subsist alone, and seeking a mate, not to supply an essential need, but to be enjoyed as a mere ally, or great moral luxury. We think that the ideal of the representative American is opposed to this. However he might shrink from expressing it in naked words, the wife his heart more or less subtly craves is at bottom a dependent being. In the outer world he can only hold good his position by dint of reconquering it afresh every day: life is a struggle where success is only relative, and all sanctity is torn off of him; where failure and humiliation, the exposure of weaknesses, and the unmasking of pretence, are assured incidents: and he accordingly longs for one tranquil spot where he shall be valid absolutely and once for all; where, having been accepted, he is secure from further criticism, and where his good aspirations may be respected no less than if they were accomplished realities. In a word, the elements of security and repose are essential to his ideal; and the question is, Are they easily attainable without some feeling of dependence on the woman's side—without her relying on him to be her mediator with the external world—without his activity overlapping hers and surrounding it on almost every side, so that he makes as it were the atmosphere in which she lives?

Many men will answer No, peremptorily; for instance, Dr. Bushnell, who says: "When a woman has set herself up for a practical dittoship (*sic*) with men, refusing to accept the name of her husband, or have any but a partnership relation with him, she ceases so far to be woman at all. She has no longer the trusting nature; she despises it. She neither idolizes nor idealizes her husband. She has no homages looking up, any more than he in his ranges of force has courtesies to pay her, looking down. He is gruff and she is pungent, and the main sensibility of life is the friction of it." Another class of minds, less dogmatic than this author as to what is *a priori* "natural," will nevertheless make a half-sentimental, half-practical objection to Mr. Mill, somewhat as follows: "Love is now as common as friendship is rare. Mere mutual respect, and sympathy in some end objective to both parties, form but a weak tie in comparison with that flattering interplay of instincts—egotism, since you prefer to call it so, on the one hand, and self-sacrifice on the other. Do you not, then, in attempting to eradicate these latter things, run the risk of sweeping away the main condition that now makes matrimonial affection so cheaply realizable?" Other sceptics still will add: "After all, does not a man's sympathy with his wife differ from his sympathy with his friend in *sphere* rather than quality, as implying a hierarchical arrangement? His sympathy with his wife is in interests purely personal, social ends including the founding of the family, and the minor practical matters of life; but *within that sphere* may there not be the most thorough equality?" It is true Mr. Mill says: "When the two persons both care for great objects, and are a help and encouragement to each other in whatever regards these, the minor matters on which their tastes may differ are not all-important to them; and there is a foundation for solid friendship, of an enduring character, more likely than anything else to make it through the whole of life a greater pleasure to each, to give pleasure to the other, than to receive it.'' (Page 174.) According to this, the most important requisite in an astronomer's wife is that she should have a passion for astronomy. But it may be conscientiously doubted whether in the majority of cases, even where equality was fully believed in by both parties, agreement in the ''minor matters'' would not afford the surest basis for a lifelong harmony; and whether consequently any difference of taste or instinct in the sexes which tends to facilitate such agreement ought not still to be fostered by education.

There is one kind of esthetico-sentimental objection frequently urged against any considerable change in woman's position, that we think has little weight. It is to the effect that what gallantry and chivalry are left among us will disappear. Thus Dr. Bushnell: ''We observe a common-looking man, for example, standing, in a railroad car, that a common-looking woman may sit, and we say inwardly at least, if not audibly, there is yet after all some hope of the world. . . . . These beautiful deferences and homages paid to women are the very best civilizers we have, and we can better afford to spare almost anything else.'' The assumption is that our yielding to women in small matters demands as *quid pro quo* on their part that they refrain from crossing our path in larger affairs; and that if they become our rivals in these latter, we shall no longer scruple to push them to the wall wherever we find them. This leaves altogether out of sight the mere animal potency of sex. An individual man, however his interests may clash with those of an individual woman, will always shrink from appearing personally like a brute in her presence.

We have laid such stress on this sentimental side of Mr. Mill's book, because here, more than anywhere else, a careless reader will be apt to miss its extremely revolutionary purport, and because, as we have already said, we regard it as the soul of the whole. Mr. Mill's sentiment about the marriage relation has for a necessary corollary divorce at will, with all the tremendous changes such divorce must entail upon the relation of children to society. Yet with that strange ''air of suppression'' which critics have complained of in him, he has passed these topics over in utter silence. It may be, he thinks his remedies will go farther when administered in divided doses, and that for the rest—utilitarian that he is—he is biding his time. But there are hosts of readers who feel that in this matter sentimental and practical considerations must go hand in hand, and whom timidity in the latter respect deters from trusting fully their instincts in the former. It were therefore much to be desired that Mr. Mill should publish his whole mind on the subject of divorce and of the family, without delay or reserve.

We shall not touch upon any of the other points the work presents, nor even say what they are; for it ought to be read by every one who cares in the least degree for social questions— and who does not?—in its original form. No one can read it without feeling his thought stimulated and enlarged; numbers of those who are at present sceptical or indifferent will be converted by it; and many will be toughened in their resisting conservatism by the suggestive glimpse it affords of the ultimate tendencies of the democratic flood which is sweeping us along. It may be that Mr. Mill's fervid passion for absolute equality, "justice," and personal independence, as the *summum bonum* for every one, is a personal peculiarity. It may be that he is only more far-seeing than the majority, and that the wiping out of everything *special* in any man's relations to other men—of every moral tie that can possibly be conceived of as varying in varied circumstances, and therefore as artificial—is but the inexorable outcome of the path of progress on which we have entered. If this is so, there can be little doubt that this small volume will be what the Germans call "epoch-making," and that it will hereafter be quoted as a landmark signalizing one distinct step in the progress of the total evolution.

Emily James Putnam

American classics scholar, 1865–1944, and first dean of Barnard College.

From *The Lady*

Every discussion of the status of woman is complicated by the existence of the lady. She overshadows the rest of her sex. The gentleman has never been an analogous phenomenon, for even in countries and times where he has occupied the center of the stage he has done so chiefly by virtue of his qualities as a man. A line of gentlemen always implies a man as its origin, and cannot indeed perpetuate itself for long without at least occasional lapses into manhood. Moreover the gentleman, in the worst sense of the term, is numerically negligible. The lady, on the other hand, has until lately very nearly covered the surface of womanhood. She even occurs in great numbers in societies where the gentleman is an exception; and in societies like the feudal where ladies and gentlemen are usually found in pairs, she soars so far above her mate in the development of the qualities they have in common that he sinks back relatively into the plane of ordinary humanity. She is immediately recognized by everyone when any social spectrum is analyzed. She is an anomaly to which the western nations of this planet have grown accustomed, but which would require a great deal of explanation before a Martian could understand her. Economically she is supported by the toil of others; but while this is equally true of other classes of society, the oddity in her case consists in the acquiescence of those most concerned. The lady herself feels no uneasiness in her equivocal situation, and the toilers who support her do so with enthusiasm. She is not a producer; in most communities productive labor is by consent unladylike. On the other hand she is the heaviest of consumers, and theorists have not been wanting to maintain that the more she spends the better off society is. In aristocratic societies she is required for dynastic reasons to produce offspring, but in democratic societies even this demand is often waived. Under the law she is a privileged character. If it is difficult to hang a gentleman-murderer, it is virtually impossible to hang a lady. Plays like The Doll's House and The Thief show how clearly the lady-forger or burglar should be differentiated from other criminals. Socially she is in general the product and the beneficiary of monogamy; under this system her prestige is created by the existence of great numbers of less happy competitors who present to her the same hopeless problem as the stoker on the liner presents to the saloon-passenger. If the traveller is imaginative, the stoker is a burden on his mind. But after all, how are saloon-passengers to exist if the stoker does not? Similarly the lady reasons about her sisters five decks below. There have been times when the primary social requirement has apparently been waived; it seems difficult, for instance, so to classify the lady as to exclude Aspasia and Louise de la Vallière. Nevertheless the true lady is in theory either a virgin or a lawful wife. Religion has given the lady perhaps her strongest hold. Historically it is the source of much of her prestige, and it has at times helped her to break her taboo and revert to womanhood. Her roots are nourished by its good soil and its bad. Enthusiasm, mysticism, renunciation, find her ready. On the other hand the antisocial forces of religion are embodied in her; she can renounce the world more easily than she can identify herself with it. A lady may become a nun in the strictest and poorest order without altering her view of life, without the moral convulsion, the destruction of false ideas, the birth of character that would be the preliminary steps toward becoming an efficient stenographer. Sentimentally the lady has established herself as the criterion of a community's civilization. Very dear to her is the observance that hedges her about. In some subtle way it is so bound up with her self-respect and with her respect for the man who maintains it, that life would hardly be sweet to her without it. When it is flatly put to her that she cannot become a human being and yet retain her privileges as a noncombatant, she often enough decides for etiquette.

The product of many cross-impulses, exempt apparently in many cases from the action of economic law, of natural law, and of the law of the land, the lady is almost the only picturesque survival in a social order which tends less and less to tolerate the exceptional. Her history is distinct from that of woman though sometimes advancing by means of it, as a railway may help itself from one point to another by leasing an independent line. At all striking periods of social development her status has its significance. In the age-long war between men and women, she is a hostage in the enemy's camp. Her fortunes do not rise and fall with those of women but with those of men.

It follows from the lady's history that she is today, when freed from many of the old restrictions and possessed of a social and financial power undreamed of by her originators, a somewhat dangerous element of society. Her training and experience when not antisocial have been unsocial. Women in general have lived an individualistic life. As soon as the division of early labor sent the man out to fight and kept the woman in the house, the process began which taught men to act in concert while women still acted singly. The man's great adventure of warfare was undertaken shoulder to shoulder with his fellows, while the rumble of the tam-tam thrilled his nerves with the collective motive of the group. The woman's great adventure of maternity had to be faced in cold blood by each woman for herself. The man's exploit resulted in loot to be divided in some manner recognized as equitable, thus teaching him a further lesson in social life. The woman's exploit resulted in placing in her arms a little extension of her ego for which she was fiercely ready to defy every social law. Maternity is on the face of it an unsocial experience. The selfishness that a woman has learned to stifle or to dissemble where she alone is concerned, blooms freely and unashamed on behalf of her offspring. The world at large, which may have made some appeal to the sympathies of the disinterested woman, becomes to the mother chiefly a source of contagious disease and objectionable language. The man's fighting instinct can be readily utilized in the form of sports and games to develop in boys the sense of solidarity; the little girl's doll serves no such social end. The women of the working classes have been saved by their work itself, which has finally carried them out of the house where it kept them so long. In the shop and the factory they have learned what the nursery can never teach. But the lady has had no social training whatever; the noticable weakness of her play at bridge is the tendency to work for her own hand. Being surrounded by soft observance she has not so much as learned the art of temperate debate. With an excellent heart and the best intentions but with her inevitable limitations, the lady seems about to undertake the championship of a view of society to which her very existence is uncongenial.

As the gentleman decays, the lady survives as the strongest evidence of his former predominance. Where he set her, there she stays. One after another the fabrics that supported her have tottered, but she remains, adapting herself to each new set of circumstances as it arises. It is possible that an advancing social sentiment will extinguish her altogether, but she can never be forgotten. . . .

The economic paradox that confronts women in general is especially uncompromising for the lady. In defiance of the axiom that he who works, eats, the lady who works has less to eat than the lady who does not. There is no profession open to her that is nearly as lucrative as marriage, and the more lucrative the marriage the less work it involves. The economic prizes are therefore awarded in such a way as directly to discourage productive activity on the part of the lady. If a brother and sister are equally qualified for, let us say, the practice of medicine, the brother has, besides the scientific motive, the economic motive. The ardent pursuit of his profession will if successful make him a rich man. His sister on the other hand will never earn absolutely as much money as he, and relatively her earnings will be negligible in comparison with her income if she should marry a millionaire. But if she be known to have committed herself to the study of medicine her chance of marrying a millionaire is practically eliminated.

Apart from the crude economic question, the things that most women mean when they speak of "happiness," that is, love and children and the little republic of the home, depend upon the favor of men, and the qualities that win this favor are not in general those that are most useful for other purposes. A girl should not be too intelligent or too good or too highly differentiated in any direction. Like a ready-made garment she should be designed to fit the average man. She should have "just about as much religion as my William likes." The age-long operation of this rule, by which the least strongly individualized women are the most likely to have a chance to transmit their qualities, has given it the air of a natural law. Though the lady has generally yielded it unquestioning obedience, she often dreams of a land like that of the Amazons, where she might be judged on her merits instead of on her charms. Seeing that in the world a woman's social position, her daily food, her chance of children, depend on her exerting sufficient charm to induce some man to assume the responsibility and expense of maintaining her for life, and that the qualities on which this charm depends are sometimes altogether unattainable by a given woman, it is not surprizing that exceptional women are willing to eliminate from their lives the whole question of marriage and motherhood, for the sake of a free develoment irrespective of its bearing on the other sex.

No institution in Europe has ever won for the lady the freedom of development that she enjoyed in the convent in the early days. The modern college for women only feebly reproduces it, since the college for women has arisen at a time when colleges in general are under a cloud. The lady-abbess on the other hand was part of the two great social forces of her time, feudalism and the church. Great spiritual rewards and great worldly prizes were alike within her grasp. She was treated as an equal by the men of her class, as is witnessed by letters we still have from popes and emperors to abbesses. She had the stimulus of competition with men in executive capacity, in scholarship and in artistic production, since her work was freely set before the general public; but she was relieved by the circumstances of her environment of the ceaseless competition in common life of woman with woman for the favor of the individual man. In the cloister of the great days, as on a small scale in the college for women today, women were judged by each other, as men are everywhere judged by each other, for sterling qualities of head and heart and character. The strongest argument against the coeducational college is that the presence of the male brings in the factor of sexual selection, and the girl who is elected to the class-office is not necessarily the ablest or the wisest or the kindest, but the possessor of the longest eyelashes. The lady does not often rise to the point of deciding against sex. The choice is a cruel one, and in the individual case the rewards of the ascetic course are too small and too uncertain. At no other time than the aristocratic period of the cloister have the rewards so preponderated as to carry her over in numbers. In studying this interesting phenomenon we must divest our minds of the conventional picture of the nun. The Little Sister of the Poor is the product of a number of social motives that had not begun to operate when the lady-abbess came into being. In fact her day is almost over when the Poor Clares appear. Her roots lie in a society that is prefeudal, though feudalism played into her hand, and in a psychology that is pre-Christian, though she ruled in the name of Christ.

Emma Goldman

American anarchist, 1869–1940, who founded and edited the journal
Mother Earth. *Skeptical about the suffrage movement, active in the cam-*
paign for birth control, a feminist and rebel, she was deported with other
anarchists to Russia where she became disenchanted with the Soviet experi-
ment.

From "Victims of Morality"

It is Morality which condemns woman to the position of a celibate, a
prostitute, or a reckless, incessant breeder of hapless children.

First, as to the celibate, the famished and withered human plant. When
still a young, beautiful flower, she falls in love with a respectable young
man. But morality decrees that unless he can marry the girl, she must
never know the raptures of love, the ecstasy of passion, which reaches its
culminating expression in the sex embrace. The respectable young man is
willing to marry, but the property morality, the family and social moralities decree that he must first make his pile, must save up enough to establish a home and be able to provide for a family. The young people must
wait, often many long, weary years.

Meanwhile the respectable young man, excited through the daily association and contact with his sweetheart, seeks an outlet for his nature in
return for money. In ninety-nine cases out of a hundred, he will be in-
fected, and when he is materially able to marry, he will infect his wife and
possible offspring. And the young flower, with every fiber aglow with the
fire of life, with all her being crying out for love and passion? She has no
outlet. She develops headaches, insomnia, hysteria; grows embittered,
quarrelsome, and soon becomes a faded, withered, joyless being, a nui-
sance to herself and everyone else. No wonder Stirner preferred the gri-
sette to the maiden grown gray with virtue.

Now, as to the prostitute. In spite of laws, ordinances, persecution, and
prisons; in spite of segregation, registration, vice crusades, and other similar devices, the prostitute is the real specter of our age. She sweeps

across the plains like a fire burning into every nook of life, devastating, destroying.

After all, she is paying back, in a very small measure, the curse and horrors society has strewn in her path. She, weary with the tramp of ages, harassed and driven from pillar to post, at the mercy of all, is yet the Nemesis of modern times, the avenging angel, ruthlessly wielding the sword of fire. For has she not the man in her power? And, through him, the home, the child, the race. Thus she slays, and is herself the most brutally slain.

What has made her? Whence does she come? Morality, the morality which is merciless in its attitude to women. Once she dared to be herself, to be true to her nature, to life, there is no return: the woman is thrust out from the pale and protection of society. The prostitute becomes the victim of morality, even as the withered old maid is its victim. But the prostitute is victimized by still other forces, foremost among them the property morality, which compels woman to sell herself as a sex commodity for a dollar per, out of wedlock, or for fifteen dollars a week, in the sacred fold of matrimony. The latter is no doubt safer, more respected, more recognized, but of the two forms of prostitution the girl of the street is the least hypocritical, the least debased, since her trade lacks the pious mask of hypocrisy; and yet she is hounded, fleeced, outraged, and shunned, by the very powers that have made her: the financier, the priest, the moralist, the judge, the jailor, and the detective, not to forget her sheltered, respectably virtuous sister, who is the most relentless and brutal in her persecution of the prostitute.

Morality and its victim, the mother—what a terrible picture! Is there indeed anything more terrible, more criminal, than our glorified sacred function of motherhood? The woman, physically and mentally unfit to be a mother, yet condemned to breed; the woman, economically taxed to the very last spark of energy, yet forced to breed; the woman, tied to a man she loathes, whose very sight fills her with horror, yet made to breed; the woman, worn and used-up from the process of procreation, yet coerced to breed, more, ever more. What a hideous thing, this much-lauded motherhood! No wonder thousands of women risk mutilation, and prefer even death to this curse of the cruel imposition of the spook of morality. Five thousand are yearly sacrificed upon the altar of this monster, that will not stand for prevention but would cure by abortion. Five thousand soldiers in the battle for their physical and spiritual freedom, and as many thousands more who are crippled and mutilated rather than bring forth life in a society based on decay and destruction.

Is it because the modern woman wants to shirk responsibility, or that she lacks love for her offspring, that she is driven to the most drastic and dangerous means to avoid bearing children? Only shallow, bigoted minds can bring such an accusation. Else they would know that the modern woman has become race-conscious, sensitive to the needs and rights of the child, as the unit of the race, and that therefore the modern woman has a sense of responsibility and humanity, which was quite foreign to her grandmother.

With the economic war raging all around her, with strife, misery, crime, disease, and insanity staring her in the face, with numberless little children ground into gold dust, how can the self- and race-conscious woman become a mother? Morality can not answer this question. It can only dictate, coerce, or condemn—and how many women are strong enough to face this condemnation, to defy the moral dicta? Few, indeed. Hence they fill the factories, the reformatories, the homes for feeble minded, the prisons, the insane asylums, or they die in the attempt to prevent childbirth. Oh, Motherhood, what crimes are committed in thy name! What hosts are laid at your feet, morality, destroyer of life!

Fortunately, the dawn is emerging from the chaos and darkness. Woman is awakening, she is throwing off the nightmare of morality; she will no longer be bound. In her love for the man, she is not concerned in the contents of his pocketbook, but in the wealth of his nature, which alone is the fountain of life and joy. Nor does she need the sanction of the state. Her love is sanction enough for her. Thus she can abandon herself to the man of her choice, as the flowers abandon themselves to dew and light, in freedom, beauty, and ectasy.

Through her reborn consciousness as a unit, a personality, a race builder, she will become a mother only if she desires the child, and if she can give to the child, even before its birth, all that her nature and intellect can yield: harmony, health, comfort, beauty, and, above all, understanding, reverence, and love, which is the only fertile soil for new life, a new being.

Morality has no terrors for her who has risen beyond good and evil. And though morality may continue to devour its victims, it is utterly powerless in the face of the modern spirit, that shines in all its glory upon the brow of man and woman, liberated and unafraid.

From "The Tragedy of Woman's Emancipation"

Liberty and equality for woman! What hopes and aspirations these words awakened when they were first uttered by some of the noblest and bravest souls of those days. The sun in all his light and glory was to rise upon a new world; in this world woman was to be free to direct her own destiny—an aim certainly worthy of the great enthusiasm, courage, perseverance, and ceaseless effort of the tremendous host of pioneer men and women, who staked everything against a world of prejudice and ignorance.

My hopes also move towards that goal, but I ho
of woman, as interpreted and practically applied
that great end. Now, woman is confronte(
emancipating herself from emancipation, if sh
This may sound paradoxical, but is, nevertheic...

What has she achieved through her emancipation? Equ
few states. Has that purified our political life, as many well-mea...
vocates predicted? Certainly not. Incidentally, it is really time that pei
sons with plain, sound judgment should cease to talk about corruption in
politics in a boarding-school tone. Corruption of politics has nothing to
do with the morals, or the laxity of morals, of various political personali-
ties. Its cause is altogether a material one. Politics is the reflex of the
business and industrial world, the mottos of which are: "To take is more
blessed than to give"; "buy cheap and sell dear"; "one soiled hand
washes the other." There is no hope even that woman, with her right to
vote, will ever purify politics.

Emancipation has brought woman economic equality with man; that is,
she can choose her own profession and trade; but as her past and present
physical training has not equipped her with the necessary strength to compete with man, she is often compelled to exhaust all her energy, use up
her vitality, and strain every nerve in order to reach the market value.
Very few ever succeed, for it is a fact that women teachers, doctors, lawyers, architects, and engineers are neither met with the same confidence
as their male colleagues, nor receive equal remuneration. And those that
do reach that enticing equality generally to do so at the expense of their
psychical and physical well-being. As to the great mass of working girls
and women, how much independence is gained if the narrowness and lack
of freedom of the home is exchanged for the narrowness and lack of freedom of the factory, sweat-shop, department store, or office? In addition is
the burden which is laid on many women of looking after a "home, sweet
home"—cold, dreary, disorderly, uninviting—after a day's hard work.
Glorious independence! No wonder that hundreds of girls are so willing
to accept the first offer of marriage, sick and tired of their "independence" behind the counter, at the sewing or typewriting machine. They are
just as ready to marry as girls of the middle class, who long to throw off
the yoke of parental supremacy. A so-called independence which leads
only to earning the merest subsistence is not so enticing, not so ideal, that
one could expect woman to sacrifice everything for it. Our highly praised
independence is, after all, but a slow process of dulling and stifling woman's nature, her love instinct, and her mother instinct.

Nevertheless, the position of the working girl is far more natural and
human than that of her seemingly more fortunate sister in the more cul-
tured professional walks of life—teachers, physicians, lawyers, engi-

, etc., who have to make a dignified, proper appearance, while the
er life is growing empty and dead.

The narrowness of the existing conception of woman's independence
and emancipation; the dread of love for a man who is not her social equal;
the fear that love will rob her of her freedom and independence; the horror
that love or the joy of motherhood will only hinder her in the full exercise
of her profession—all these together make of the emancipated modern
woman a compulsory vestal, before whom life, with its great clarifying
sorrows and its deep, entrancing joys, rolls on without touching or grip-
ping her soul.

Emancipation, as understood by the majority of its adherents and exponents, is of too narrow a scope to permit the boundless love and ectasy
contained in the deep emotion of the true woman, sweetheart, mother, in
freedom.

The tragedy of the self-supporting or economically free woman does
not lie in too many, but in too few experiences. True, she surpasses her
sister of past generations in knowledge of the world and human nature; it
is just because of this that she feels deeply the lack of life's essence,
which alone can enrich the human soul, and without which the majority
of women have become mere professional automatons.

That such a state of affairs was bound to come was foreseen by those
who realized that, in the domain of ethics, there still remained many de-
caying ruins of the time of the undisputed superiority of man; ruins that
are still considered useful. And, what is more important, a goodly number of the emancipated are unable to get along without them. Every
movement that aims at the destruction of existing institutions and the re-
placement thereof with something more advanced, more perfect, has followers who in theory stand for the most radical ideas, but who, nevertheless, in their everyday practice, are like the average Philistine, feigning
respectability and clamoring for the good opinion of their opponents.
There are, for example, Socialists, and even Anarchists, who stand for
the idea that property is robbery, yet who will grow indignant if anyone
owe them the value of a half-dozen pins.

The same Philistine can be found in the movement for woman's emancipation. Yellow journalists and milk-and-water littérateurs have painted
pictures of the emancipated woman that make the hair of the good citizen
and his dull companion stand up on end. Every member of the woman's
rights movement was pictured as a George Sand in her absolute disregard
of morality. Nothing was sacred to her. She had no respect for the ideal
relation between man and woman. In short, emancipation stood only for a
reckless life of lust and sin, regardless of society, religion, and morality.
The exponents of woman's rights were highly indignant at such misrepre-
sentation, and, lacking humor, they exerted all their energy to prove that
they were not at all as bad as they were painted, but the very reverse. Of

course, as long as woman was the slave of man, she could not be good and pure, but now that she was free and independent she would prove how good she could be and that her influence would have a purifying effect on all institutions in society. True, the movement for woman's rights has broken many old fetters, but it has also forged new ones. The great movement of *true* emancipation has not met with a great race of women who could look liberty in the face. Their narrow, puritanical vision banished man, as a disturber and doubtful character, out of their emotional life. Man was not to be tolerated at any price, except perhaps as the father of a child, since a child could not very well come to life without a father. Fortunately, the most rigid Puritans never will be strong enough to kill the innate craving for motherhood. But woman's freedom is closely allied with man's freedom, and many of my so-called emancipated sisters seem to overlook the fact that a child born in freedom needs the love and devotion of each human being about him, man as well as woman. Unfortunately, it is this narrow conception of human relations that has brought about a great tragedy in the lives of the modern man and woman. . . .

A rich intellect and a fine soul are usually considered necessary attributes of a deep and beautiful personality. In the case of the modern woman, these attributes serve as a hindrance to the complete assertion of her being. For over a hundred years the old form of marriage, based on the Bible, ''Till death doth part,'' has been denounced as an institution that stands for the sovereignty of the man over the woman, of her complete submission to his whims and commands, and absolute dependence on his name and support. Time and again it has been conclusively proved that the old matrimonial relation restricted woman to the function of man's servant and the bearer of his children. And yet we find many emancipated women who prefer marriage, with all its deficiencies, to the narrowness of an unmarried life: narrow and unendurable because of the chains of moral and social prejudice that cramp and bind her nature.

The explanation of such inconsistency on the part of many advanced women is to be found in the fact that they never truly understood the meaning of emancipation. They thought that all that was needed was independence from external tyrannies; the internal tyrants, far more harmful to life and growth—ethical and social conventions—were left to take care of themselves; and they have taken care of themselves. They seem to get along as beautifully in the heads and hearts of the most active exponents of woman's emancipation, as in the heads and hearts of our grandmothers.

These internal tyrants, whether they be in the form of public opinion or what will mother say, or brother, father, aunt, or relative of any sort; what will Mrs. Grundy, Mr. Comstock, the employer, the Board of Education say? All these busybodies, moral detectives, jailers of the human spirit, what will they say? Until woman has learned to defy them all, to stand firmly on her own ground and to insist upon her own unrestricted freedom, to listen to the voice of her nature, whether it call for life's greatest treasure, love for a man, or her most glorious privilege, the right to give birth to a child, she cannot call herself emancipated. How many emancipated women are brave enough to acknowledge that the voice of love is calling, wildly beating against their breasts, demanding to be heard, to be satisfied.

From "The Traffic in Women"

Of course, marriage is the goal of every girl, but as thousands of girls cannot marry, our stupid social customs condemn them either to a life of celibacy or prostitution. Human nature asserts itself regardless of all laws, nor is there any plausible reason why nature should adapt itself to a perverted conception of morality.

Society considers the sex experiences of a man as attributes of his general development, while similar experiences in the life of a woman are looked upon as a terrible calamity, a loss of honor and of all that is good and noble in a human being. This double standard of morality has played no little part in the creation and perpetuation of prostitution. It involves the keeping of the young in absolute ignorance on sex matters, which alleged "innocence," together with an overwrought and stifled sex nature, helps to bring about a state of affairs that our Puritans are so anxious to avoid or prevent.

Not that the gratification of sex must needs lead to prostitution; it is the cruel, heartless, criminal persecution of those who dare divert from the beaten track, which is responsible for it.

Girls, mere children, work in crowded, overheated rooms ten to twelve hours daily at a machine, which tends to keep them in a constant overexcited sex state. Many of these girls have no home or comforts of any kind; therefore the street or some place of cheap amusement is the only means of forgetting their daily routine. This naturally brings them into close proximity with the other sex. It is hard to say which of the two factors brings the girl's oversexed condition to a climax, but it is certainly the most natural thing that a climax should result. That is the first step toward prostitution. Nor is the girl to be held responsible for it. On the contrary, it is altogether the fault of society, the fault of our lack of understanding, of our lack of appreciation of life in the making; especially is it the criminal fault of our moralists, who condemn a girl for all eternity, because she has gone from the "path of virtue"; that is, because her first sex experience has taken place without the sanction of the Church.

The girl feels herself a complete outcast, with the doors of home and society closed in her face. Her entire training and tradition is such that the girl herself feels depraved and fallen, and therefore has no ground to stand upon, or any hold that will lift her up, instead of dragging her down. Thus society creates the victims that it afterwards vainly attempts to get rid of. The meanest, most depraved and decrepit man still considers himself too good to take as his wife the woman whose grace he was quite willing to buy, even though he might thereby save her from a life of horror. Nor can she turn to her own sister for help. In her stupidity the latter deems herself too pure and chaste, not realizing that her own position is in many respects even more deplorable than her sister's of the street.

"The wife who married for money, compared with the prostitute," says Havelock Ellis, "is the true scab. She is paid less, gives much more in return in labor and care, and is absolutely bound to her master. The prostitute never signs away the right over her own person, she retains her freedom and personal rights, nor is she always compelled to submit to man's embrace."

From "Marriage and Love"

The popular notion about marriage and love is that they are synonymous, that they spring from the same motives, and cover the same human needs. Like most popular notions this also rests not on actual facts, but on superstition.

Marriage and love have nothing in common; they are as far apart as the poles; are, in fact, antagonistic to each other. No doubt some marriages have been the result of love. Not, however, because love could assert itself only in marriage; much rather is it because few people can completely outgrow a convention. There are today large numbers of men and women to whom marriage is naught but a farce, but who submit to it for the sake of public opinion. At any rate, while it is true that some marriages are based on love, and while it is equally true that in some cases love continues in married life, I maintain that it does so regardless of marriage, and not because of it.

On the other hand, it is utterly false that love results from marriage. On rare occasions one does hear of a miraculous case of a married couple falling in love after marriage, but on close examination it will be found that it is a mere adjustment to the inevitable. Certainly the growing-used to each other is far away from the spontaneity, the intensity, and beauty of love, without which the intimacy of marriage must prove degrading to both the woman and the man.

Marriage is primarily an economic arrangement, an insurance pact. It differs from the ordinary life insurance agreement only in that it is more binding, more exacting. Its returns are insignificantly small compared with the investments. In taking out an insurance policy one pays for it in dollars and cents, always at liberty to discontinue payments. If, however, woman's premium is a husband, she pays for it with her name, her privacy, her self-respect, her very life, "until death doth part." Moreover, the marriage insurance condemns her to life-long dependency, to parasitism, to complete uselessness, individual as well as social. Man, too, pays his toll, but as his sphere is wider, marriage does not limit him as much as woman. He feels his chains more in an economic sense.

Thus Dante's motto over Inferno applies with equal force to marriage: "Ye who enter here leave all hope behind."

That marriage is a failure none but the very stupid will deny. One has but to glance over the statistics of divorce to realize how bitter a failure marriage really is. Nor will the stereotyped Philistine argument that the laxity of divorce laws and the growing looseness of woman account for the fact that: first, every twelfth marriage ends in divorce; second, that since 1870 divorces have increased from 28 to 73 for every hundred thousand population; third, that adultery, since 1867, as ground for divorce, has increased 270.8 per cent; fourth, that desertion increased 369.8 per cent. . . .

Edward Carpenter says that behind every marriage stands the life-long environment of the two sexes; an environment so different from each other that man and woman must remain strangers. Separated by an insurmountable wall of superstition, custom, and habit, marriage has not the potentiality of developing knowledge of, and respect for, each other, without which every union is doomed to failure.

Henrik Ibsen, the hater of all social shams, was probably the first to realize this great truth. Nora leaves her husband, not—as the stupid critic would have it—because she is tired of her responsibilities or feels the need of woman's rights, but because she has come to know that for eight years she had lived with a stranger and borne him children. Can there be anything more humiliating, more degrading than a life-long proximity between two strangers? No need for the woman to know anything of the man, save his income. As to the knowledge of the woman—what is there to know except that she has a pleasing appearance? We have not yet outgrown the theologic myth that woman has no soul, that she is a mere appendix to man, made out of his rib just for the convenience of the gentleman who was so strong that he was afraid of his own shadow. . . .

From infancy, almost, the average girl is told that marriage is her ultimate goal; therefore her training and education must be directed towards that end. Like the mute beast fattened for slaughter, she is prepared for that. Yet, strange to say, she is allowed to know much less about her function as wife and mother than the ordinary artisan of his trade. It is indecent and filthy for a respectable girl to know anything of the marital relation. Oh, for the inconsistency of respectability, that needs the marriage vow to turn something which is filthy into the purest and most sacred arrangement that none dare question or criticize. Yet that is exactly the attitude of the average upholder of marriage. The prospective wife and mother is kept in complete ignorance of her only asset in the competitive field—sex. Thus she enters into life-long relations with a man only to find herself shocked, repelled, outraged beyond measure by the most natural and healthy instinct, sex. It is safe to say that a large percentage of the unhappiness, misery, distress, and physical suffering of matrimony is due to the criminal ignorance in sex matters that is being extolled as a great virtue. Nor is it at all an exaggeration when I say that more than one home has been broken up because of this deplorable fact.

If, however, woman is free and big enough to learn the mystery of sex without the sanction of State or Church, she will stand condemned as utterly unfit to become the wife of a "good" man, his goodness consisting of an empty head and plenty of money. Can there be anything more outrageous than the idea that a healthy, grown woman, full of life and passion, must deny nature's demand, must subdue her most intense craving, undermine her health and break her spirit, must stunt her vision, abstain from the depth and glory of sex experience until a "good" man comes along to take her unto himself as a wife? That is precisely what marriage means. How can such an arrangement end except in failure? This is one, though not the least important, factor of marriage, which differentiates it from love.

Ours is a practical age. The time when Romeo and Juliet risked the wrath of their fathers for love, when Gretchen exposed herself to the gossip of her neighbors for love, is no more. If, on rare occasions, young people allow themselves the luxury of romance, they are taken in care by the elders, drilled and pounded until they become "sensible."

The moral lesson instilled in the girl is not whether the man has aroused her love, but rather is it, "How much?" The important and only God of practical American life: Can the man make a living? Can he support a wife? That is the only thing that justifies marriage. Gradually this saturates every thought of the girl; her dreams are not of moonlight and kisses, of laughter and tears; she dreams of shopping tours and bargain counters. This soul-poverty and sordidness are the elements inherent in the marriage institution. The State and the Church approve of no other ideal, simply because it is the one that necessitates the State and Church control of men and women. . . .

The woman considers her position as worker transitory, to be thrown aside for the first bidder. That is why it is infinitely harder to organize women than men. "Why should I join a union? I am going to get married, to have a home." Has she not been taught from infancy to look upon that as her ultimate calling? She learns soon enough that the home, though not so large a prison as the factory, has more solid doors and bars. It has a keeper so faithful that naught can escape him. The most tragic part, however, is that the home no longer frees her from wage-slavery; it only increases her task.

According to the latest statistics submitted before a Committee "on labor and wages, and congestion of population," ten percent of the wage-workers in New York City alone are married, yet they must continue to work at the most poorly paid labor in the world. Add to this horrible aspect the drudgery of housework, and what remains of the protection and glory of the home? As a matter of fact, even the middle-class girl in marriage can not speak of her home, since it is the man who creates her sphere. It is not important whether the husband is a brute or a darling. What I wish to prove is that marriage guarantees woman a home only by the grace of her husband. There she moves about in *his* home, year after year, until her aspect of life and human affairs becomes as flat, narrow, and drab as her surroundings. Small wonder if she becomes a nag, petty, quarrelsome, gossipy, unbearable, thus driving the man from the house. She could not go, if she wanted to; there is no place to go. Besides, a short period of married life, of complete surrender of all faculties, absolutely incapacitates the average woman for the outside world. She becomes reckless in appearance, clumsy in her movements, dependent in her decisions, cowardly in her judgment, a weight and a bore, which most men grow to hate and despise. Wonderfully inspiring atmosphere for the bearing of life, is it not?

But the child, how is it to be protected, if not for marriage? After all, is not that the most important consideration? The sham, the hypocrisy of it! Marriage protecting the child, yet thousands of children destitute and homeless. Marriage protecting the child, yet orphan asylums and reformatories overcrowded, the Society for the Prevention of Cruelty to Children keeping busy in rescuing the little victims from "loving" parents, to place them under more loving care, the Gerry Society. Oh, the mockery of it!

Anna Garlin Spencer

*American teacher, journalist, minister, and professor of social science, so-
ciology, and ethics, 1851–1931.*

From *Woman's Share in Social Culture*

. . . In spite of their poverty in education, however, the women of the
eighteenth and first half of the nineteenth centuries made some good
showing in letters; and their struggles for professional training and opportunity, especially in the field of medicine, show an heroic temper as well
as a persistent purpose second to no class of men in a similar effort to
obtain rights and chances in the larger life. . . .

In addition to these handicaps must be named the well-known but
scarcely adequately measured interruptions to both study and self-
expression which the women of talent and specialized power have always
experienced. Anyone can see that to write *Uncle Tom's Cabin* on the knee
in the kitchen, with constant calls to cooking and other details of housework to punctuate the paragraphs, was a more difficult achievement than
to write it at leisure in a quiet room. And when her biographer says of an
Italian woman poet, ''during some years her Muse was intermitted,'' we
do not wonder at the fact when he casually mentions her ten children. No
record, however, can even name the women of talent who were so submerged by child-bearing and its duties, and by ''general housework,''
that they had to leave their poems and stories all unwritten. Moreover, the
obstacles to intellectual development and achievement which marriage
and maternity interpose (and which are so important that they demand a
separate study) are not the only ones that must be noted. It is not alone the
fact that women have generally had to spend most of their strength in
caring for others that has handicapped them in individual effort; but also
that they have almost universally had to care wholly for themselves.
Women even now have the burden of the care of their belongings, their
dress, their home life of whatever sort it may be, and the social duties of
the smaller world, even if doing great things in individual work. A successful woman preacher was once asked ''what special obstacles have

you met as a woman in the ministry?'' "Not one," she answered, "except the lack of a minister's wife.'' When we read of Charles Darwin's wife not only relieving him from financial cares but seeing that he had his breakfast in his room, with "nothing to disturb the freshness of his morning," we do not find the explanation of Darwin's genius, but we do see how he was helped to express it. Men geniuses, even of second grade, have usually had at least one woman to smooth their way, and often several women to make sure that little things, often even self-support itself, did not interfere with the development and expression of their talent. On the other hand, the obligation of all the earlier women writers to prepare a useful cookbook in order to buy their way into literature, is a fitting symbol of the compulsion laid upon women, however gifted, to do all the things that women in general accomplish before entering upon their special task. That brave woman who wanted to study medicine so much that not even the heaviest family burdens could deter her from entering the medical school first opened to her sex, but who "first sewed steadily until her entire family was fitted with clothes to last six months," is a not unusual type.*

Added to all this, the woman of talent and of special gifts has had until very lately, and in most countries has still, to go against the massed social pressure of her time in order to devote herself to any particular intellectual task. The expectation of society has long pushed men toward some special work; the expectation of society has until recently been wholly against women's choosing any vocation beside their functional service in the family. This is a far more intense and all-pervading influence in deterring women from success in intellectual work than is usually understood. "Palissy the Potter" is honored with a volume in the series on the *Heroes of Industry*. This is well; for his marked talent, his indomitable purpose pursued in poverty, his choice of inventive rather than of paying work, his final success after intense effort, all mark him as great in his devotion and in his gift to art. We note, however, that his family pay a heavy price for his choices in life; and when his wife objects to his burning up the baby's cradle and the kitchen table in that devouring furnace which has already consumed all their comforts, we are inclined to sympathize with her. She does not feel sure—as indeed how could she?—that Palissy will get the glaze he wants; but she sees clearly that the children are hungry and she cannot feed them. His biographer, however, is clearly of the opinion that men should be sustained in their heroic efforts to solve problems and make inventions; and Palissy himself has that conviction of society concerning the worth and righteousness of man's specialized effort to give tone to his ambition. This it is which makes him feel himself a

---

*Mrs. Thomas, graduated in first class of Women's Medical College of Philadelphia; served as City Physician at Fort Wayne, Ind., eight years.

hero and not merely a selfish man who neglects his family. No book has yet been written in praise of a woman who let her husband and children starve or suffer while she invented even the most useful things, or wrote books, or expressed herself in art, or evolved philosophic systems. On the contrary, the mildest approach on the part of a wife and mother, or even of a daughter or sister, to that intense interest in self-expression which has always characterized genius has been met with social disapproval and until very recent times with ostracism fit only for the criminal. Hence her inner impulsion has needed to be strong indeed to make any woman devote herself to ideas.

In view of these tremendous obstacles, it is fair to assume that when women in the past have achieved even a second or third place in the ranks of genius they have shown far more native ability than men have needed to reach the same eminence. Not excused from the more general duties that constitute the cement of society, most women of talent have had but one hand free with which to work out their ideal conceptions. Denied, at cost of "respectability" itself, any expression of that obstinate egotism which is nature's protection of the genius in his special task, and in the preparation for it, they have had to make secret and painful experiments in self-expression after spending first strength in the commonplace tasks required of all their sex. . . .

The experience of the race shows that we get our most important education not through books but through our work. We are developed by our daily task, or else demoralized by it, as by nothing else. The training of books is recent and superficial for most of the race and only touches the outer and upper edges of the social consciousness. The training by one's necessary work reaches back to the beginnings of social discipline for social ends. It still forms the most vital part of physical, mental and moral training. Hence, the fact that one-third of one-half the race, and that the mother-half that perforce stamps its quality most irrevocably upon offspring, spends from 3 to 10 years in work entered upon without plan, pursued as a mere and often disliked incident on the way from the father's to the husband's home, and therefore accepted with all its evil concomitants of poor wages and bad conditions as *something not to be bettered but to be escaped from as soon as possible,* constitutes a social evil of the first magnitude. Any work not made an education and a discipline becomes inevitably a source of mental or moral injury; and the greatest evils connected with the modern forms of women's labor grow out of the failure to treat the wage-earning of women as a serious and permanent educational opportunity. . . .

With all this in view, let us consider more definitely the social evils bound up with the pathological industrial conditions of women's work.

I. *Prostitution.* It is not true, as a celebrated minister of religion has stated, that "prostitution is solely an economic question." The ancient enemies of human progress, greed and lust, and the ancient draw-backs to human progress,ignorance, laziness, self-indulgence, vanity and lack of moral responsibility, are now, as ever, causes of the social evil. But prostitution is and always has been in part, and often in large part, an economic question. . . .

II. That measure of excessive poverty which is due to physical weakness and disease is intimately connected with the conditions of wage-earning women and girls. All know, and social workers keenly realize, that at least one-third of the "cases" demanding charitable relief have thus to make appeal because of sickness or accident. The connection between this fact and the work conditions of girls of the poorer classes is now so obvious as to constitute matter for study alike by physicians, publicists and philanthropists. All the more important movements toward legally safe-guarding the health and morals of manual workers are now aimed most specifically toward bettering the conditions of "women and children."

. . . We may well be cautious about interfering too partially by law with the work of women of mature age, and with those who have an industrial experience leading them to trade-union organization, through which a more democratic form of protection may reasonably be hoped for. There can be no question, however, that girls under 21 are fit subjects for as much legal protection from industrial exploitation as we can possibly secure and enforce. Further than this, there is no question that to deplete the vitality, to injure the health, to undermine the constitutional vigor of the potential mothers of the race, before they have reached their maturity, is to poison the fountain of life at its very source. . . .

It is said, Of course she can't now; but when we get all women rightly placed in specialties, and there are enough "substitutes" and "assistant" mothers to go around, and they are all well trained and morally dependable, each woman, like each man, will be able to find the home a place of rest and not of work, and there will be no vital difference in vocational experience between men and women. The answer to this is both economic and social; it deals with both the mechanism of living and the sources of life itself.

In the first place, the economic value of the healthy, competent, expert housemother has never yet been properly estimated. "Woman's work" has been despised and, therefore, its value unknown because, and only because, women for long ages have themselves been considered inferior to men and held in law and custom as perpetual minors. Just as the position of disadvantage which Afric-Americans hold in the United States is due, not to the color of their skin, but to the fact that they were once held as slaves, with a Supreme Court decision that they "had no rights which a white man was bound to respect" scourging them like a whip, so the real cause of the disrespect shown toward the housemother's task is due to the fact that the housemother herself has but just emerged to the position of independent personality. All the fine talk about the "sacredness of motherhood" and the "inestimable value of the woman in the home" has but added hypocrisy or *unthinking* compliment to injustice, so long as men were ashamed to be caught tending their own babies, or washing dishes or clothes they had themselves soiled, because such things were "women's work."

. . . The real reason for the lack of appreciation is that men, as they have stepped ahead of women in industrial organization, have been able to choose what they liked best as their share of labor and have left the rest to women; and have called it an "instinct" that made what they did not like to do "women's work." Not only that, but the personal service of individual lives is in itself not enticing; it is often hard and unpleasant. It is only glorified by affection and the need to give the loved one the best one has. Men, having first and most fully attained the position where one can serve the loved one in a chosen single task, instead of by a congeries of general services, have never learned the value of those services. A poet says of a woman: "The charm of her presence was felt when she went." The economic value of the competent housewife is felt only when she dies, and the cost of her hired substitutes shows the manual worker with young children that he "must marry again" because he "can't afford to do without a wife."

Up to date, the family has proved the best and most effective agency for the development of personality. It has so far furnished a breakwater, most vital and helpful, against the nonsocial forces that work against human progress. So far, that breakwater has consisted in large part of exclusive affection, selective and partial love, reserve of intimacy, and a preeminent devotion to the nearest beloved. . . . If children are to gather themselves together "out of the everywhere," it seems necessary that some one should be close at hand, when wanted, to help in the process. It has not so far worked well to have long "hours" or seasons when the child cannot get at anybody to whom it *knows it belongs*. So far, in the organization of the family, the mother has been the person readily at hand when the child's needs, physical or spiritual, have demanded the steadying influence of a companionship on which it felt a rightful claim. This has been thought to be a natural arrangement, because the child is closer to the mother physically than to anyone else in the Universe.

There is a deeper reason, however, underlying that physical relationship which determines the social value of the function of the average mother in this development of the child's personality through constant companionship. Speaking generally, the feminine side of humanity is in the "middle of the road" of life. Biologically, psychologically and sociologically, women are in the central, normal, constructive part of the evolutionary process. On the one side and on the other, men exhibit more geniuses and more feeble-minded, more talented experts and more incompetents who cannot earn a living; more idealistic masters of thought and action and more "cranks" and ne'er-do-wells who shame their mothers. It is because to woman is committed in a peculiar sense this function of bringing to consciousness from the "raw material of evolution," through personal nurture and individual care, this personality of the child, that women are and have always been, and must, it would seem, always be, the practical and teaching half of the race.

In the development of individuality, it seems clear that the most essential thing is that the conserving weight of the middle virtues and the mean of powers should be nearest the child and most constantly at his service. It is later, in the more formal educational processes, that the highly specialized "variations" which men exhibit (and which tend directly toward human progress along particular lines on the one side, and toward human degeneracy on the other side) have their functional use as example or as warning. It would seem, therefore, that no economic readjustment of society in accordance with modern specialization of effort can make it possible for the average mother of several young children to pursue a specialty of work with the same uninterrupted effort that the average man can do. That all women should be educated for self-support at a living wage is a social necessity; that women should be made as valuable now and in the future as they have been in the past as distinct economic factors is unquestionable; that women must reshape many of their activities to suit the general scheme of industry which has created the factory is certain; that women should, for their own best good and for the ends of social progress, keep their hands on some specialty of work, if only in selective interest, through the years when they cannot follow it as the first obligation is clear; that women should hold in mind steadily reëntrance into their chosen vocation when the children are grown, in order that life may mean for them continual flowering of the stalk as well as the past season's scattered blossoms—this is coming to be perceived as the wise plan for all women who would achieve for themselves, as well as help others to achieve, full personality.

. . . The essence of democracy is its assertion that every human being should so respect himself and should be so respected in his own personality that he should have opportunity equal to that of every other human being to "show what he was meant to become." Very slowly has come even partial application of that inner spirit of democracy to women. Class after class of men has emerged from the obscurity of subservience and ignorance and class-registration to the freedom and dignity of individuality, leaving behind their women with their children. As, however, it began to be increasingly perceived that a democratic order of society must be the outgrowth of a democratic family, it began also to be seen that a democratic family must have two "heads" instead of one alone. Thus it came to pass that the most vital element in democratic society, namely, an equal opportunity for education, began to be considered a right of women as of men. At first, as was natural, it was not the right of women as human beings needing self-development for their own purposes of growth that won the opportunity of education; it was rather because the democratic State needed common schools, and women as the natural teachers of the race must go out from the hearthside training of children into the more formal and better organized system of modern education. The first reasons were, therefore, those of social thrift rather than of justice to women, as was shown so obviously in the inauguration of normal schools. As a distinguished gentleman said, when urging an appropriation for a State normal school before a legislative committee (in the fifties of the nineteenth century): "Gentlemen, we have all observed the fine manner in which the best and most cultivated women are educating their own children, and by utilizing this gift of women we may put two females in every school to teach at half the price we now pay one inferior male." On that basis women entered their first educational opportunity above the grammar grades and "female finishing school."

. . . At present we have advanced little beyond the period when the "wife of Thomas Hawkins" was granted by the selectmen of her town, in the seventeenth century, the "right to sell liquors by retayle, considering the necessitie and weak condition of her husband"; and when widows were "approved" by the church trustees to earn a pittance in "sweeping and dusting the meeting house" because they had no "provider." The great city of New York still requires its married women teachers to swear that their husbands are morally, mentally or physically incompetent in order to retain their positions!

. . . The much vaunted "chivalry of men," the proudly assumed "reverence for womanhood" paraded in public addresses on the glory and moral excellence of our present civilization, do not work far down in the social scale. The fact is that because women are the cheapest of laborers and because young women must all work for pay between their school life and their marriage in the case of the poverty-bound, the poorest-paid and many of the hardest and most health-destroying of employments are given them as almost a monopoly. Nature has warned mankind through unnumbered centuries, since the human intelligence has been able to perceive cause and effect, that if we wanted strong nations we must have strong mothers, and if we wanted strong mothers we must safeguard the girls from overwork and all manner of economic evils: but we still turn deaf ears to the warning.

Wherever and whenever the rights of women are recognized as those belonging to all human beings alike, there and then arise problems of marriage and divorce. For there and then marriage becomes a *contract,* and a contract can be broken for the same reasons that a contract may be made, namely, the good of the parties involved. The difficulties inhering in the adjustment of the domestic order to—

> Two heads in council,
> Two beside the hearth,
> Two in the tangled business of the world*

are identical with the difficulties that inhere in democracy as a general social movement. Despotism is easy if you can secure a despot capable of holding his place. All else is a matter of adjustment to justice and right; and all such adjustment is difficult. In the midst of the confusion of ideal and action one thing is sure; namely, that women in the new freedom that has come to them in the last hundred years of Christian civilization will not longer endure the unspeakable indignities and the hopeless suffering which many of them have been compelled to endure in the past. That last outrage upon a chaste wife and a faithful mother, enforced physical union with a husband and father whose touch is pollution and whose heritage to his children is disease and death, will less and less be tolerated by individual or by social morality. In so far as greater freedom in divorce is one effect of the refusal of women to sustain marital relations with unfit men—and it is very largely that today—it is a movement for the benefit and not for the injury of the family. Permanent and legal separation in such cases is now seen by most enlightened people to be both individually just and socially necessary. Whether such separation shall include remarriage of either or both parties is still a moot question in morals. The tendency, however, in all fields of ethical thought is away from "eternal punishment" and in the direction of self-recovery and of trying life experiments over again in the hope of a better outcome. It is likely that marriage and divorce will prove no exception to this hopeful tendency. Moreover, so far as the testimony of actual life is valid as against theories only, the countries where no remarriage is allowed show a lower standard of marital faithfulness, of child-care and of true culture of the moral nature in the relationship of the family group, than is shown in those countries that grant for serious causes absolute divorce with full freedom for remarriage. . . .

Marriage, again, must be held more consciously than it is now as a social arrangement for the benefit of society as a whole. Not in the sense of a mechanical control, that tries stupendous or even ludicrous experiments in artificial production of supermen and superwomen; but marriage as a social arrangement for the benefit of the social whole in the sense that subordinates even love itself, even the passionate longing of the lonely

*Alfred Tennyson, *The Princess.*

heart, to the higher interests of humanity and to the imperious demands of the social conscience.

To help thus in even the smallest degree to reincarnate the old sanctities of the family bond in new forms is a far better service at this time of unrest than, on the one side, to exalt freedom as an end in itself; or, on the other side, to try to revive obsolete forms of subjection of the individual to the domestic autonomy. Above all things socially futile and morally insolent is the attitude of men who attempt to solve alone, without either the judgment or the authority of women, the problems of marriage and divorce! There is nothing which so betrays and emphasizes the evil effect upon the spiritual nature of men of the long subjection of women to masculine control, as the findings of church councils and court decisions and academic discussions, in which men alone participate, as these are related to family life. The monstrous assumption that men can know better than women what women want, or ought to want, or really need, in that marriage relation which means to human beings of the mother-sex a tax upon the whole nature such as men cannot experience, would be impossible to decent and intelligent men were it not for the extreme egotism engendered in all human beings by the possession of unjust power over others.

On the other hand, nothing is more mischievous in a period like our own, when our ideals of democracy have run ahead of our social technique in their administration, than to ignore the claims of society to set metes and bounds by law to the relation of the sexes. To exaggerate the demands of romantic love as above those of the social good, is a mistake of the utmost danger. To assume the anarchistic attitude toward marriage, and to believe that that relationship between men and women which is free of courts and statutes is equal or superior to that which is entered upon soberly and publicly under legal bonds to definitely defined obligations, is a mistake that implies a fatal lack of moral balance.

. . . The mechanism of the vote is devised expressly for the purpose of enabling ''an agreeing majority'' to execute its decisions without an appeal to force, physical or military. That women cannot fight, therefore, or should not do so, is, it is obvious, no more a proper disqualification for the suffrage than would be a rule that men over a certain age or under a certain standard of physical strength should be deprived of their vote. By proxy, and by substitute, and by representative, and by chosen officers, the forceful business of the state is now carried on. Some time, if war is not outlawed for good and all, the nations will be wise and humane enough to choose one pugilist to settle disputes instead of bearing the economic burden of standing armies, great navies and millions of idle men! Some such course will have to be pursued if the common people persist in their aversion to serving as food for cannon or to supporting men who stand idly ready to be such food in case of war. Sensible people cannot much longer mistake the true nature of the actual ''force'' of the modern democratic state.

. The significance of the woman suffrage movement is twofold: it is a response to the general movement of democracy toward the individuation of all members of all previously subjected or submerged classes of society; and it is also a social response to the new demands of citizenship which have followed inevitably the new and varied increase in the functions of government. . . .

There are two arguments, and only two, that can possibly be brought against the application of the general principles of democracy to law-abiding and mentally competent women: one is that women are not human beings; the other that they are a kind of human being so different from men that general principles of right and wrong proved expedient as a basis of action in the development of men do not apply to them.

Few now subscribe to the ancient belief that ''women have neither souls nor minds,'' but are a ''delusion and a snare,'' invented for practical purposes of life, but not to be counted in when the real life of humanity is under consideration. Are then women of such a different sort of humanity that they do not need individual protection of the law, do not require the mental and moral discipline of freedom and personal responsibility for the development of character, are justly and fully provided for through the political arrangements of men, by men and for men, and therefore should be forcibly restrained from complete citizenship? Some, many, seem thus to believe.

The fact that women as a sex, not the favored few of a privileged class but women as a sex, have suffered every form of exploitation at the hands of men and without redress until very recently (an incontestable and easily demonstrated fact, attested by every law book of all Christendom) is sufficient answer to that. The further fact that until women initiated and carried through a great struggle, which although bloodless and pacific on their part, lacked no element of martyrdom, no woman could learn anything but the most elementary scraps of knowledge or develop her vocational power or attain industrial opportunity of any sort commensurate with her needs, is a further proof that women's interests are not fully cared for by men. Women are not so different from men that they can be educated without a chance to go to school, be able to protect themselves against prostitution or ignoble dependence through self-support without the legal right to earn their own living or the legal right to hold and manage their property. Women are not so different from men as to become strong in character without having the discipline of moral responsibility or to become broad-minded and socially serviceable without the opportunity to ''learn by doing'' the duty of a citizen. Men and women are different, but not so unlike that they can become fully developed human beings in circumstances totally different.

Charlotte Perkins Gilman

American lecturer, critic, writer, and journalist, 1860–1935. Strongly in-
fluenced by social Darwinism, she argues against male-dominated
society—which she calls our "Androcentric Culture." Gilman is also
known for two works of fiction, a strongly autobiographical account of a
*woman's madness—*The Yellow Wallpaper—*and a delightful utopian novel*
*depicting an all-female society—*Herland.

From *Women and Economics*

In spite of her supposed segregation to maternal duties, the human female, the world over, works at extramaternal duties for hours enough to
provide her with an independent living, and then is denied independence
on the ground that motherhood prevents her working! . . .

The working power of the mother has always been a prominent factor
in human life. She is the worker *par excellence,* but her work is not such
as to affect her economic status. Her living, all that she gets—food, clothing, ornaments, amusements, luxuries—these bear no relation to her
power to produce wealth, to her services in the house, or to her motherhood. These things bear relation only to the man she marries, the man she
depends on—to how much he has and how much he is willing to give her.
The women whose splendid extravagance dazzles the world, whose economic goods are the greatest, are often neither houseworkers nor
mothers, but simply the women who hold most power over the men who
have the most money. The female of genus homo is economically dependent on the male. He is her food supply. . . .

The degree of feebleness and clumsiness common to women, the comparative inability to stand, walk, run, jump, climb, and perform other
race-functions common to both sexes, is an excessive sex-distinction; and
the ensuing transmission of this relative feebleness to their children, boys
and girls alike, retards human development. Strong, free, active women,
the sturdy, field-working peasant, the burden-bearing savage, are no less
good mothers for their human strength. But our civilized "feminine delicacy," which appears somewhat less delicate when recognized as an ex-

pression of sexuality in excess—makes us no better mothers, but worse. . . .

It is good for the individual and for the race to have developed such a degree of passionate and permanent love as shall best promote the happiness of individuals and the reproduction of species. It is not good for the race or for the individual that this feeling should have become so intense as to override all other human faculties, to make a mock of the accumulated wisdom of the ages, the stored power of the will; to drive the individual—against his own plain conviction—into a union sure to result in evil, or to hold the individual helpless in such an evil union, when made.

Such is the condition of humanity, involving most evil results to its offspring and to its own happiness. And, while in men the immediate dominating force of the passion may be more conspicuous, it is in women that it holds more universal sway. For the man has other powers and faculties in full use, whereby to break loose from the force of this; and the woman, specially modified to sex and denied racial activity, pours her whole life into her love, and, if injured here, she is injured irretrievably. With him it is frequently light and transient, and, when most intense, often most transient. With her it is a deep, all-absorbing force, under the action of which she will renounce all that life offers, take any risk, face any hardships, bear any pain. It is maintained in her in the face of a lifetime of neglect and abuse. The common instance of the police court trials—the woman cruelly abused who will not testify against her husband—shows this. This devotion, carried to such a degree as to lead to the mismating of individuals with its personal and social injury, is an excessive sex-distinction.

But it is in our common social relations that the predominance of sex-distinction in women is made most manifest. The fact that, speaking broadly, women have, from the very beginning, been spoken of expressively enough as "the sex," demonstrates clearly that this is the main impression which they have made upon observers and recorders. Here one need attempt no farther proof than to turn the mind of the reader to an unbroken record of facts and feelings perfectly patent to everyone, but not hitherto looked at as other than perfectly natural and right. So utterly has the status of woman been accepted as a sexual one that it has remained for the woman's movement of the nineteenth century to devote much contention to the claim that women are persons! That women are persons as well as females—an unheard of proposition! . . .

The cruel and absurd injustice of blaming the girl for not getting what she is allowed no effort to obtain seems unaccountable; but it becomes clear when viewed in connection with the sexuo-economic relation. Although marriage is a means of livelihood, it is not honest employment where one can offer one's labor without shame, but a relation where the support is given outright, and enforced by law in return for the functional service of the woman, the "duties of wife and mother." Therefore no honorable woman can ask for it. It is not only that the natural feminine instinct is to retire, as that of the male is to advance, but that, because marriage means support, a woman must not ask a man to support her. It is economic beggary as well as a false attitude from a sex point of view.

. . . The condition of individual economic dependence in which women live resembles that of the savage in the forest. They obtain their economic goods by securing a male through their individual exertions, all competing freely to this end. No combination is possible. The numerous girls at a summer resort, in their attitude toward the scant supply of young men, bear an unconscious resemblance to the emulous savages in a too closely hunted forest. And here may be given an economic reason for the oft-noted bitterness with which the virtuous women regard the vicious. The virtuous woman stands in close ranks with her sisters, refusing to part with herself—her only economic goods—until she is assured of legal marriage, with its lifelong guarantee of support. Under equal proportions of birth in the two sexes, every woman would be tolerably sure of obtaining her demands. But here enters the vicious woman, and offers the same goods—though of inferior quality, to be sure—for a far less price. Every one of such illegitimate competitors lowers the chances of the unmarried women and the income of the married. No wonder those who hold themselves highly should be moved to bitterness at being undersold in this way. It is the hatred of the trade-unionist for "scab labor." . . .

The woman's movement, then, should be hailed by every right-thinking, far-seeing man and woman as the best birth of our century. The banner advanced proclaims "equality before the law," woman's share in political freedom; but the main line of progress is and has been toward economic equality and freedom. While life exists on earth, the economic conditions must underlie and dominate each existing form and its activities; and social life is no exception. A society whose economic unit is a sex-union can no more develope beyond a certain point industrially than a society like the patriarchal, whose political unit was a sex-union, could develop beyond a certain point politically.

When two young people love each other, in the long hours which are never long enough for them to be together in, do they dwell in ecstatic forecast on the duties of housekeeping? They do not. They dwell on the pleasure of having a home, in which they can be "at last alone"; on the opportunity of enjoying each other's society; and, always, on what they will *do* together. To act with those we love—to walk together, work together, read together, paint, write, sing, anything you please, so that it be together—that is what love looks forward to.

Human love, as it rises to an ever higher grade, looks more and more for such companionship. But the economic status of marriage rudely breaks in upon love's young dream. On the economic side, apart from all the sweetness and truth of the sex-relation, the woman in marrying becomes the house-servant, or at least the housekeeper, of the man. Of the world we may say that the intimate personal necessities of the human animal are ministered to by woman. Married lovers do not work together. They may, if they have time, rest together: they may, if they can, play together; but they do not make beds and sweep and cook together, and they do not go down town to the office together. They are economically on entirely different social planes, and these constitute a bar to any higher, truer union than such as we see about us.

Marriage is not perfect unless it is between class equals. There is no equality in class between those who do their share in the world's work in the largest, newest, highest ways and those who do theirs in the smallest, oldest, lowest ways.

From *The Home*

The performance of domestic industries involves, first, an enormous waste of labor. The fact that in nine cases out of ten this labor is unpaid does not alter its wastefulness. If half the men in the world stayed at home to wait on the other half, the loss in productive labor would be that between half and the fraction required to do the work under advanced conditions, say one-twentieth. Any group of men requiring to be cooked for, as a ship's crew, a lumber camp, a company of soldiers, have a proportionate number of cooks. To give each man a private cook would reduce the working strength materially. Our private cooks being women makes no difference in the economic law. We are so accustomed to rate women's labor on a sex-basis, as being her "duty" and not justly commanding any return, that we have quite overlooked this tremendous loss of productive labor.

Then there is the waste of endless repetition of "plant." We pay rent for twenty kitchens where one kitchen would do. . . .

The most truthful nations are the most powerful. The most truthful class is the most powerful. The more truthful sex is the more powerful. Weakness, helplessness, ignorance, dependence, these breed falsehood and evasion; and, in child, servant, and woman, the denizens of the home, we have to combat these tendencies. The standard of sincerity of the father may be taught the son; but the home is not the originator of that standard. In this, as in other virtues, gain made in quite other fields of growth is necessarily transmitted to the home; but fair analysis must discriminate between the effect of religion, of education, of new social demands, and the effect of the home as such.

Courage comes along two main lines—by exposure to danger, and by increase of strength. The home, in its very nature, is intended to shield from danger; it is in origin a hiding place, a shelter for the defenseless. Staying in it is in no way conducive to the growth of courage. Constant shelter, protection, and defense may breed gratitude—must breed cowardice. We expect timidity of "women and children"—the housemates. Yet courage is by no means a sex attribute. Every species of animal that shows courage shows it equally in male and female—or even more in mother than in father. "It is better to meet a she-bear robbed of her whelps than a fool in his folly." This dominant terror—the fool—is contrasted with the female bear—not the male. Belligerence, mere combativeness, is a masculine attribute; but courage is not. . . .

We have made great progress in the sense of justice and fair play; yet we are still greatly lacking in it. What is the contribution of domestic ethics to this mighty virtue? In the home is neither freedom nor equality. There is ownership throughout; the dominant father, the more or less subservient mother, the utterly dependent child; and sometimes that still lower grade—the servant. Love is possible, love deep and reciprocal; loyalty is possible; gratitude is possible; kindness, to ruinous favoritism, is possible; unkindness, to all conspiracy, hate, and rebellion is possible; justice is not possible.

Justice was born outside the home and a long way from it; and it has never even been adopted there.

Justice is wholly social in its nature—extradomestic—even antidomestic. Just men may seek to do justly in their homes, but it is hard work. Intense, personal feeling, close ties of blood, are inimical to the exercise of justice. . . .

There is no perspective—cannot be—in these close quarters. The infant prodigy of talent, praised and petted, brings his production into the cold light of the market, under the myriad facets of the public eye, to the measurement of professional standards—and no most swift return to the home atmosphere can counterbalance the effect of that judgment day. A just estimate of one's self and one's work can only be attained by the widest and most impersonal comparison. The home estimate is essentially personal, essentially narrow. It sometimes errs in underrating a world talent; but nine times out of ten it errs the other way—overrating a home talent. Humility, in the sense of an honest and accurate estimate of one's self, is not a home-made product. A morbid modesty or an unfounded pride often is. The intense self-consciousness, the prominent and sensitive personality developed by home life, we are all familiar with in women. . . .

A man, a healthy, well-placed man, has his position in the world and in the home, and finds happiness in both. He loves his wife, she meets his requirements as a husband, and he expects nothing more of her. His other requirements he meets in other ways. That she cannot give him this, that, and the other form of companionship, exercise, gratification, is no ground of blame; the world outside does that. So the man goes smoothly on, and when the woman is uncertain, capricious, exacting, he lays it to her being a woman, and lets it go at that.

But she, for all field of exertion, has but this house; for all kinds of companionship, this husband. He stands between her and the world, he has elected to represent it to her, to be "all the world" to her. Now, no man that ever lived, no series or combination of husbands that widowhood or polyandry ever achieved can be equivalent to the world. The man needs the wife and has her—needs the world and has it. The woman needs the husband—and has him; needs the world—and there is the husband instead. He stands between her and the world, with the best of intentions, doubtless; but a poor substitute for full human life.

"What else should she want?" he inquires in genuine amazement. "I love her, I am kind to her, I provide a good home for her—she has her children and she has me—what else should she want?"

What else does he want? He has her—the home and the children—does that suffice him? He wants also the human world to move freely in, to act fully in, to live widely in, *and so does she. . . .*

We have called the broader, sounder, better balanced, more fully exercised brain "a man's brain," and the narrower, more emotional and personal one "a woman's brain"; whereas the difference is merely that between the world and the house. . . .

The man adopts one business and follows it. He develops special ability, on long lines, in connection with wide interests—and so grows broader and steadier. The distinction is there, but it is not a distinction of sex. This is why the man forgets to mail the letter. He is used to one consecutive train of thought and action. She, used to a varying zigzag horde of little things, can readily accommodate a few more.

The home-bred brain of the woman continually puzzles and baffles the world-bred brain of the man. . . .

From *The Man-Made World*

We can see at once, glaringly, what would have been the result of giving all human affairs into female hands. Such an extraordinary and deplorable situation would have "feminized" the world. We should have all become "effeminate."

See how in our use of language the case is clearly shown. The adjectives and derivatives based on woman's distinctions are alien and derogatory when applied to human affairs; "effeminate"—too female, connotes contempt, but has no masculine analog; whereas ''emasculate''—not enough male, is a term of reproach, and has no feminine analog. ''Virile''—manly, we oppose to ''puerile''—childish, and the very word ''virtue'' is derived from ''vir''—a man.

Even in the naming of other animals we have taken the male as the race type, and put on a special termination to indicate ''his female,'' as in lion, lioness; leopard, leopardess; while all our human scheme of things rests on the same tacit assumption; man being held the human type; woman a sort of accompaniment and subordinate assistant, merely essential to the making of people.

She has held always the place of a preposition in relation to man. She has been considered above him or below him, before him, behind him, beside him, a wholly relative existence—''Sydney's sister,'' ''Pembroke's mother''—but never by any chance Sydney or Pembroke herself.

Acting on this assumption, all human standards have been based on male characteristics, and when we wish to praise the work of a woman, we say she has ''a masculine mind.''

It is no easy matter to deny or reverse a universal assumption. The human mind has had a good many jolts since it began to think, but after each upheaval it settles down as peacefully as the vine-growers on Vesuvius, accepting the last lava crust as permanent ground.

What we see immediately around us, what we are born into and grow up with, be it mental furniture or physical, we assume to be the order of nature. . . .

Woman's natural work as a female is that of the mother; man's natural work as a male is that of the father; their mutual relation to this end being a source of joy and well-being when rightly held: but human work covers all our life outside of these specialties. Every handicraft, every profession, every science, every art, all normal amusements and recreations, all government, education, religion; the whole living world of human achievement: all this is human.

That one sex should have monopolized all human activities, called them ''man's work,'' and managed them as such, is what is meant by the phrase ''Androcentric Culture.'' . . .

For each man to have one whole woman to cook for and wait upon him is a poor education for democracy. The boy with a servile mother, the man with a servile wife, cannot reach the sense of equal rights we need today. Too constant consideration of the master's tastes makes the master selfish; and the assault upon his heart direct, or through that proverbial side-avenue, the stomach, which the dependent woman needs must make when she wants anything, is bad for the man, as well as for her.

We are slowly forming a nobler type of family; the union of two, based on love and recognized by law, maintained because of its happiness and use. We are even now approaching a tenderness and permanence of love, high pure enduring love; combined with the broad deep-rooted friendliness and comradeship of equals; which promises us more happiness in marriage than we have yet known. It will be good for all the parties concerned—man, woman and child; and promote our general social progress admirably.

If it needs "a head" it will elect a chairman pro tem. Friendship does not need "a head." Love does not need "a head." Why should a family? . . .

We are the only race where the female depends on the male for a livelihood. We are the only race that practices prostitution. From the first harmless-looking but abnormal general relation, follows the well-recognized evil of the second, so long called "a social necessity," and from it, in deadly sequence, comes the "wages of sin"; death not only of the guilty, but of the innocent. It is no light part of our criticism of the Androcentric Culture that a society based on masculine desires alone, has willingly sacrificed such an army of women; and has repaid the sacrifice by the heaviest punishments.

That the unfortunate woman should sicken and die was held to be her just punishment; that man too should bear part penalty was found unavoidable, though much legislation and medical effort has been spent to shield him; but to the further consequences society is but now waking up.

Sheltered by the customs and sanctions of a civilization built and upheld by his own sex, man has brought home to his helpless and innocent family the "wages of sin"—and paid them out most heavily. We are now beginning to learn what a percentage of blindness, of epilepsy, of many horrible forms of illness, idiocy and deformity, of sterility, of babies never born alive, or dying in their cradles; and of the ruined health of wives, their subjection to surgical operation, their wretched lives—is due to this terribly frequent offence. When a more human or less masculine standard of living is at last reached, we shall see these matters in their true light. The present purpose is not to pile up horrors, nor to give technical details; but to point out that this enormous share of disease and degeneracy is directly traceable to our Androcentric Culture.

It is inconceivable that a civilization even half representing women, could so sin against Mother and Child; so poison the current of life at its very springs.

No heavier single charge can be brought against a civilization in which women are dependent upon men than this; that, man, the "natural protector," has not only doomed to misery and ruin so large a number of the protected; blamed and punished in them what he did not blame and punish in himself; then blamed their more fortunate sisters for this cruel judgment; and, above all, brought to the innocent and trusting wife and the helpless child, the penalty of his misdeeds. . . .

Among the many counts in which women have been proven inferior to men in human development is the oft-heard charge that there are no great women artists. Where one or two are proudly exhibited in evidence, they are either pooh-poohed as not very great, or held to be the trifling exceptions which do but prove the rule.

Defenders of women generally make the mistake of overestimating their performances, instead of accepting, and explaining, the visible facts. What are the facts as to the relation of men and women to art? And what, in especial, has been the effect upon art of a solely masculine expression?

When we look for the beginnings of art, we find ourselves in a period of crude decoration of the person and of personal belongings. . . .

Art as a profession, and the Artist as a professional, came later; and by that time women had left the freedom and power of the matriarchate and become slaves in varying degree. The women who were idle pets in harems, or the women who worked hard as servants, were alike cut off from the joy of making things. Where constructive work remained to them, art remained, in its early decorative form. Men, in the proprietary family, restricting the natural industry of women to personal service, cut off their art with their industry, and by so much impoverished the world.

There is no more conspicuously pathetic proof of the aborted development of woman than this commonplace—their lack of a civilized art sense. Not only in the childish and savage display upon their bodies, but in the pitiful products they hang upon the walls of the home, is seen the arrest in normal growth.

After ages of culture, in which men have developed Architecture, Sculpture, Painting, Music, and the Drama, we find women in their primitive environment making flowers of wax, and hair, and worsted, doing mottoes of perforated cardboard, making crazy quilts and mats and "tidies"—as if they lived in a long past age, or belonged to a lower race. . . .

History is, or should be, the story of our racial life. What have men made it? The story of warfare and conquest. . . .

The male naturally fights, and naturally crows, triumphs over his rival, and takes the prize—therefore was he made male. Maleness means war.

Not only so; but as a male, he cares only for male interests. Men, being the sole arbiters of what should be done and said and written, have given us not only a social growth scarred and thwarted from the beginning by continual destruction; but a history which is one unbroken record of courage and red cruelty, of triumph and black shame.

As to what went on that was of real consequence, the great slow steps of the working world, the discoveries and inventions, the real progress of humanity—that was not worth recording, from a masculine point of view. Within this last century, "the woman's century," the century of the great awakening, the rising demand for freedom, political, economic, and domestic, we are beginning to write real history, human history, and not merely masculine history. But that great branch of literature—Hebrew, Greek, Roman, and all down later times, shows beyond all question, the influence of our androcentric culture. . . .

What is the preferred subject matter of fiction?

There are two main branches found everywhere, from the Romaunt of the Rose to the Purplish Magazine—the Story of Adventure, and the Love Story. . . .

It is surely something more than a coincidence that these are the two essential features of masculinity—Desire and Combat—Love and War. . . .

Take human life personally, then. Here is a Human Being, a life, covering some seventy years, involving the changing growth of many faculties; the ever new marvels of youth, the long working time of middle life, the slow ripening of age. Here is the human soul, in the human body, Living. Out of this field of personal life, with all of its emotions, processes, and experiences, fiction arbitrarily selects one emotion, one process, one experience, mainly of one sex.

The "love" of our stories is man's love of woman. If any dare dispute this, and say it treats equally of woman's love for man, I answer, "Then why do the stories stop at marriage?" . . .

Woman's love for man, as currently treated in fiction, is largely a reflex; it is the way he wants her to feel, expects her to feel. Not a fair representation of how she does feel. If "love" is to be selected as the most important thing in life to write about, then the mother's love should be the principal subject. This is the main stream, this is the general underlying, world-lifting force. The "life-force," now so glibly chattered about, finds its fullest expression in motherhood; not in the emotions of an assistant in the preliminary stages.

What has literature, what has fiction to offer concerning mother-love, or even concerning father-love, as compared to this vast volume of excitement about lover-love? Why is the searchlight continually focused upon a two or three years space of life "mid the blank miles round about?" Why indeed, except for the clear reason, that on a starkly masculine basis this is his one period of overwhelming interest and excitement. . . .

The humanizing of woman of itself opens five distinctly fresh fields of fiction: First, the position of the young woman who is called upon to give up her "career"—her humanness—for marriage, and who objects to it. Second, the middle-aged woman who at last discovers that her discontent is social starvation—that it is not more love that she wants, but more business in life: Third, the interrelation of women with women—a thing we could never write about before because we never had it before: except in harems and convents: Fourth, the interaction between mothers and children; this not the eternal "mother and child," wherein the child is always a baby, but the long drama of personal relationship; the love and hope, the patience and power, the lasting joy and triumph, the slow eating disappointment which must never be owned to a living soul—here are grounds for novels that a million mothers and many million children would eagerly read: Fifth, the new attitude of the full-grown woman, who faces the demands of love with the high standards of conscious motherhood. . . .

Now see our attitude toward child's play—under a masculine culture. Regarding women only as a sex, and that sex as manifest from infancy, we make and buy for our little girls toys suitable to this view. Being females—which means mothers, we must needs provide them with babies before they cease to be babies themselves; and we expect their play to consist in an imitation of maternal cares. The doll, the puppet, which interests all children, we have rendered as an eternal baby; and we foist them upon our girl children by ceaseless millions. . . .

Beyond the continuous dolls and their continuous dressing, we provide for our little girls tea sets and kitchen sets, doll's houses, little workboxes—the imitation tools of their narrow trades. For the boy there is a larger choice. We make for them not only the essentially masculine toys of combat—all the enginery of mimic war; but also the models of human things, like boats, railroads, wagons. For them, too, are the comprehensive toys of the centuries, the kite, the top, the ball. As the boy gets old enough to play the games that require skill, he enters the world-lists, and the little sister, left inside, with her everlasting dolls, learns that she is "only a girl," and "mustn't play with boys—boys are so rough!" She has her doll and her tea set. She "plays house." If very active she may jump rope, in solitary enthusiasm, or in combination of from two to four. Her brother is playing games. From this time on he plays the games of the world. The "sporting page" should be called "the Man's Page" as that array of recipes, fashions and cheap advice is called "the Woman's Page."

One of the immediate educational advantages of the boy's position is that he learns "team work." This is not a masculine characteristic, it is a human one; a social power. Women are equally capable of it by nature; but not by education. Tending one's imitation baby is not teamwork; nor is playing house. The little girl is kept forever within the limitations of her mother's "sphere" of action; while the boy learns life, and fancies that new growth is due to his superior sex.

Now there are certain essential distinctions in the sexes, which would manifest themselves to some degree even in normally reared children; as

for instance the little male would be more given to fighting and destroying; the little female more to caring for and constructing things.

"Boys are so destructive!" we say with modest pride—as if it was in
some way a credit to them. But early youth is not the time to display sex
distinction; and they should be discouraged rather than approved. . . .

Play, in the childish sense is an expression of previous habit; and to be
studied in that light. Play in the educational sense should be encouraged
or discouraged to develop desired characteristics. This we know, and
practice; only we do it under androcentric cannons; confining the girl to
the narrow range we consider proper for women, and assisting the boy to
cover life with the expression of masculinity, when we should be helping
both to a more human development.

Our settled conviction that men are people—the people, and that masculine qualities are the main desideratum in life, is what keeps up this
false estimate of the value of our present games. Advocates of football,
for instance, proudly claim that it fits a man for life. Life—from the
wholly male point of view—is a battle, with a prize. To want something
beyond measure, and to fight to get—that is the simple proposition. This
view of life finds its most naive expression in predatory warfare; and still
tends to make predatory warfare of the later and more human processes of
industry. Because they see life in this way they imagine that skill and
practice in the art of fighting, especially in collective fighting, is so valuable in our modern life. This is an archaism which would be laughable if it
were not so dangerous in its effects.

The valuable processes today are those of invention, discovery, all
grades of industry, and, most especially needed, the capacity for honest
service and administration of our immense advantages. These are not
learned on the football field. . . .

It is the inextricable masculinity in our idea of government which so
revolts at the idea of women as voters. "To govern": that means to boss,
to control, to have authority, and that only, to most minds. They cannot
bear to think of the women as having control over even their own affairs;
to control is masculine, they assume. Seeing only self-interest as a natural
impulse, and the ruling powers of the state as a sort of umpire, an authority to preserve the rules of the game while men fight it out forever; they
see in a democracy merely a wider range of self interest, and a wider,
freer field to fight in.

The law dictates the rules, the government enforces them, but the main
business of life, hitherto, has been esteemed as one long fierce struggle;
each man seeking for himself. To deliberately legislate for the service of
all the people, to use the government as the main engine of that service, is
a new process, wholly human, and difficult of development under an
androcentric culture.

Furthermore they put forth those naively androcentric protests—women cannot fight, and in case their laws were resisted by men they could not enforce them—*therefore* they should not vote!

What they do not so plainly say, but very strongly think, is that women should not share the loot which to their minds is so large a part of politics.

Here we may trace clearly the social heredity of male government. . . .

As human beings both male and female stand alike useful and honorable, and should in our governments be alike used and honored; but as creatures of sex, the female is fitter than the male for administration of constructive social interests. The change in government processes which marks our times is a change in principle. Two great movements convulse the world today, the woman's movement and the labor movement. Each regards the other as of less moment than itself. Both are parts of the same world-process. . . .

In this change of systems a government which consisted only of prohibition and commands; of tax collecting and making war; is rapidly giving way to a system which intelligently manages our common interests, which is a growing and improving method of universal service. Here the socialist is perfectly right in his vision of the economic welfare to be assured by the socialization of industry, though that is but part of the new development; and the individualist who opposes socialism, crying loudly for the advantage of "free competition" is but voicing the spirit of the predaceous male.

So with the opposers of the suffrage of women. They represent, whether men or women, the male viewpoint. They see the women only as a female, utterly absorbed in feminine functions, belittled and ignored as her long tutelage has made her; and they see the man as he sees himself, the sole master of human affairs for as long as we have historic record. . . .

Always the antagonist; to the male mind an antagonist is essential to progress, to all achievement. He has planted that root-thought in all the human world; from that old hideous idea of Satan, "The Adversary," down to the competitor in business, or the boy at the head of the class, to be superseded by another.

Therefore, even in science, "the struggle for existence" is the dominant law—to the male mind, with the "survival of the fittest" and "the elimination of the unfit."

Therefore in industry and economics we find always and everywhere the antagonist; the necessity for somebody or something to be overcome—else why make an effort? If you have not the incentive of reward, or the incentive of combat, why work? "Competition is the life of trade."

Thus the Economic Man.

But how about the Economic Woman?

To the androcentric mind she does not exist—women are females, and that's all; their working abilities are limited to personal service.

That it would be possible to develop industry to far greater heights, and to find in social economics a simple and beneficial process for the promotion of human life and prosperity, under any other impulse than these two, Desire and Combat, is hard indeed to recognize—for the "male mind."

From *His Religion and Hers*

Pursuing the evidence of dominant masculinity in the evolution of religions, we find another conspicuous proof—the guileless habit of blaming women for the sin and trouble of the world. One religion after another shows scorn of women, making no provision for their pleasure in heaven, sometimes denying that they have souls at all. That ultramasculine attitude has been maintained even in Christianity, owing to the fundamental mistake of those who arranged its early forms, and who insisted on keeping it connected with the Hebrew religion. This was not surprising, since so many of the early Christians were, still earlier, Hebrews, and naturally wished to preserve their old hopes and promises while facing the dangers and hoping for the rewards of the new faith. . . .

If we look at the great stationary religions of Asia, we see a high development of intellect but a low development of life. Progress, in our sense of improved living conditions, the Orientals do not desire. Life being an evil to be escaped, why indeed should any one waste time trying to make it a little easier? These peoples remain static. They preserve the most ancient customs, do not ask for nor seek anything better than was sustained by their ancestors. The man, proprietor of the woman, makes all the rules which govern her life. He desires a son, for religious reasons, but has small interest in daughters, save to see them married, that they may give some other man a son.

If we accept the postulate that our main duty here is to improve the human race and the world it makes, then all these static religions are to be condemned in so far as they do not tend to improvement. But if our main postulate is that life here is only a necessary evil, a mere stepping stone to life elsewhere, then there is indeed no reason for taking thought for the morrow on earth.

Since such is the main postulate of all the death-based religions, and since those religions are largely responsible for present conditions, we must look more carefully into this main feature of masculine dominance in religious thought.

George Santayana

*American moral, social, and esthetic philosopher and critic, 1863–1952.
He taught at Harvard until he received a small inheritance. After his retire-
ment, he lived in England, Paris, and finally Rome.*

From *The Life of Reason*

The family, too, is largely responsible for the fierce prejudices that prevail about women, about religion, about seemly occupations, about war,
death, and honor. In all these matters men judge in a blind way, inspired
by a feminine passion that has no mercy for anything that eludes the traditional household, not even for its members' souls.

. . . Friends are generally of the same sex, for when men and women
agree, it is only in their conclusions; their reasons are always different. So
that while intellectual harmony between men and women is easily possible, its delightful and magic quality lies precisely in the fact that it does
not arise from mutual understanding, but is a conspiracy of alien essences
and a kissing, as it were, in the dark. As man's body differs from woman's in sex and strength, so his mind differs from hers in quality and function: they can cooperate but can never fuse. The human race, in its intellectual life, is organized like the bees: the masculine soul is a worker,
sexually atrophied, and essentially dedicated to impersonal and universal
arts; the feminine is a queen, infinitely fertile, omnipresent in its brooding
industry, but passive and abounding in intuitions without method and
passions without justice. Friendship with a woman is therefore apt to be
more or less than friendship: less, because there is no intellectual parity;
more, because (even when the relation remains wholly dispassionate, as
in respect to old ladies) there is something mysterious and oracular about
a woman's mind which inspires a certain instinctive deference and puts it
out of the question to judge what she says by masculine standards. She

has a kind of sibylline intuition and the right to be irrationally *à propos*. There is a gallantry of the mind which pervades all conversation with a lady, as there is a natural courtesy toward children and mystics; but such a habit of respectful concession, marking as it does an intellectual alienation as profound as that which separates us from the dumb animals, is radically incompatible with friendship.

Otto Weininger

Viennese philosopher, 1880–1903, whose published doctoral dissertation, a diatribe against women and Jews, brought him instant fame. A Jew himself, he took his own life a few months later, an act praised by anti-Semitic writers as the only reasonable solution to the problems he had had the "wisdom" to recognize.

From *Sex and Character*

. . . A woman's demand for emancipation and her qualification for it are in direct proportion to the amount of maleness in her. The idea of emancipation, however, is many-sided, and its indefiniteness is increased by its association with many practical customs which have nothing to do with the theory of emancipation. By the term emancipation of a woman, I imply neither her mastery at home nor her subjection of her husband. I have not in mind the courage which enables her to go freely by night or by day unaccompanied in public places, or the disregard of social rules which prohibit bachelor women from receiving visits from men, or discussing or listening to discussions of sexual mattters. I exclude from my view the desire for economic independence, the becoming fit for positions in technical schools, universities and conservatories or teachers' institutes. And there may be many other similar movements associated with the word emancipation which I do not intend to deal with. Emancipation, as I mean to discuss it, is not the wish for an outward equality with man, but what is of real importance in the woman question, the deep-seated craving to acquire man's character, to attain his mental and moral freedom, to reach his real interests and his creative power. I maintain that the real female element has neither the desire nor the capacity for emancipation in this sense. All those who are striving for this real emancipation, all women who are truly famous and are of conspicuous mental ability, to the first glance of an expert reveal some of the anatomical characters of the male, some external bodily resemblance to a man. Those so-called "women" who have been held up to admiration in the past and present, by the advocates of woman's rights, as examples of what women can do,

407

have almost invariably been what I have described as sexually intermediate forms. . . .

The further we go in the analysis of woman's claim to esteem the more we must deny her of what is lofty and noble, great and beautiful. As this chapter is about to take the deciding and most extreme step in that direction, I should like to make a few remarks as to my position. The last thing I wish to advocate is the Asiatic standpoint with regard to the treatment of women. Those who have carefully followed my remarks as to the injustice that all forms of sexuality and erotics visit on woman will surely see that this work is not meant to plead for the harem. But it is quite possible to desire the legal equality of men and women without believing in their moral and intellectual equality, just as in condemning to the utmost any harshness in the male treatment of the female sex, one does not overlook the tremendous, cosmic, contrast and organic differences between them. There are no men in whom there is no trace of the transcendent, who are altogether bad; and there is no woman of whom that could truly be said. However degraded a man may be, he is immeasurably above the most superior woman, so much so that comparison and classification of the two are impossible; but even so, no one has any right to denounce or defame woman, however inferior she must be considered. A true adjustment of the claims for legal equality can be undertaken on no other basis than the recognition of a complete, deep seated polar opposition of the sexes. I trust that I may escape confusion of my views as to woman with the superficial doctrine of P. J. Möbius—a doctrine only interesting as a brave reaction against the general tendency. Women are not "physiologically weak-minded," and I cannot share the view that women of conspicuous ability are to be regarded as morbid specimens.

From a moral point of view one should only be glad to recognize in these women (who are always more masculine than the rest) the exact opposite of degeneration, that is to say, it must be acknowledged that they have made a step forward and gained a victory over themselves; from the biological standpoint they are just as little or as much phenomena of degeneration as are womanish men (unethically considered). Intermediate sexual forms are normal, not pathological phenomena, in all classes of organisms, and their appearance is no proof of physical decadence.

Woman is neither high-minded nor low-minded, strong-minded nor weak-minded. She is the opposite of all these. Mind cannot be predicated of her at all; she is mindless. That, however, does not imply weak-mindedness in the ordinary sense of the term, the absence of the capacity to "get her bearings" in ordinary everyday life. Cunning, calculation, "cleverness," are much more usual and constant in the woman than in the man, if there be a personal selfish end in view. A woman is never so stupid as a man can be.

But has woman no meaning at all? Has she no general purpose in the scheme of the world? Has she not a destiny; and, in spite of all her senselessness and emptiness, a significance in the universe?

Has she a mission, or is her existence an accident and an absurdity?

In order to understand her meaning, it is necessary to start from a phenomenon which, although old and well recognized, has never received its proper meed of consideration. It is from nothing more nor less than the deep, her only vital interest, the interest that sexual unions shall take place; the wish that as much of it as possible shall occur, in all cases, places, and times.

. . . After mature consideration of the most varied types of women and with due regard to the special classes besides those which I have discussed, I am of opinion that the only positively general female characteristic is that of matchmaking, that is, her uniform willingness to further the idea of sexual union.

Any definition of the nature of woman which goes no further than to declare that she has the strong instinct for her own union would be too narrow; any definition that would link her instincts to the child or to the husband, or to both, would be too wide. The most general and comprehensive statement of the nature of woman is that it is completely adapted and disposed for the special mission of aiding and abetting the bodily union of the sexes. All women are matchmakers, and this property of the woman to be the advocate of the idea of pairing is the only one which is found in women of all ages, in young girls, in adults, and in the aged. The old woman is no longer interested in her own union, but she devotes herself to the pairing of others. This habit of the old woman is nothing new, it is only the continuance of her enduring instinct surviving the complications that were caused when her personal interests came into conflict with her general desire; it is the now unselfish pursuit of the impersonal idea. . . .

The effort of woman to realize this idea of pairing is so fundamentally opposed to that conception of innocence and purity, the higher virginity which man's erotic nature has demanded from women, that not all his erotic incense would have obscured her real nature but for one factor. I have now to explain this factor which has veiled from man the true nature of woman, and which in itself is one of the deepest problems of woman, I mean her absolute duplicity. Her pairing instinct and her duplicity, the latter so great as to conceal even from woman herself what is the real essence of her nature, must be explained together. . . .

I believe myself that what may be called a psychological sexual traumatism is at the root of hysteria. The typical picture of a hysterical case is not very different from the following: A woman has always accepted the male views on sexual matters; they are in reality totally foreign to her nature, and sometime, by some chance, out of the conflict between what her nature asserts to be true and what she has always accepted as true and believed to be true, there comes what may be called a "wounding of the mind." It is thus possible for the person affected to declare a sexual desire to be an "extraneous body in her consciousness," a sensation which she *thinks* she detests, but which in reality has its origin in her own nature. The tremendous intensity with which she endeavors to suppress the desire (and which only serves to increase it) so that she may the more vehemently and indignantly reject the thought—these are the alternations which are seen in hysteria. And the chronic untruthfulness of woman becomes acute if the woman has ever allowed herself to be imbued with man's ethically negative valuation of sexuality. It is well known that hysterical women manifest the strongest suggestibility with men. Hysteria is the organic crisis of the organic untruthfulness of woman.

I do not deny that there are hysterical men, but these are comparatively few; and since man's psychic possibilities are endless, that of becoming "female" is amongst them, and, therefore, he can be hysterical. There are undoubtedly many untruthful men, but in them the crisis takes a different form, man's untruthfulness being of a different kind and never so hopeless in character as woman's.

This examination into the organic untruthfulness of woman, into her inability to be honest about herself which alone makes it possible for her to think that she thinks what is really totally opposed to her nature, appears to me to offer a satisfactory explanation of those difficulties which the aetiology of hysteria present.

Hysteria shows that untruthfulness, however far it may reach, cannot suppress everything. By education or environment woman adopts a whole system of ideas and valuations which are foreign to her, or, rather, has patiently submitted to have them impressed on her; and it would need a tremendous shock to get rid of this strongly rooted psychical complexity, and to transplant woman to that condition of intellectual helplessness which is so characteristic of hysteria. . . .

But it may be asked, with reason, why all women are not hysterical, since all women are liars? This brings us to a necessary inquiry as to the hysterical constitution. If my theory has been on the right lines, it ought to be able to give an answer in accordance with facts. According to it, the hysterical woman is one who has passively accepted in entirety the masculine and conventional valuations instead of allowing her own mental character its proper play. The woman who is not to be led is the antithesis of the hysterical woman. I must not delay over this point; it really belongs to special female characterology. The hysterical woman is hysterical because she is servile; mentally she is identical with the maidservant. Her opposite (who does not really exist) is the shrewish dame. So that women may be subdivided into the maid who serves, and the woman who commands.*

The servant is born and not made, and there are many women in good circumstances who are "born servants," although they never need to put their rightful position to the test! The servant and the mistress are a sort of "complete woman" when considered as a "whole."†

The consequences of this theory are fully borne out by experience. The Xanthippe is the woman who has the least resemblance to the hysterical type. She vents her spleen (which is really the outcome of unsatisfied sexual desires) on others, whereas the hysterical woman visits hers on herself. The "shrew" detests other women, the "servant" detests herself. The drudge weeps out her woes alone, without really feeling lonely—loneliness is identical with morality, and a condition which implies true duality or manifoldness; the shrew hates to be alone because she must have some one to scold, whilst hysterical women vent their passion on themselves. The shrew lies openly and boldly but without knowing it, because it is her nature to think herself always in the right, and she insults those who contradict her. The servant submits wonderingly to the demands made of her which are so foreign to her nature: the hypocrisy of this pliant acquiescence is apparent in her hysterical attacks when the conflict with her own sexual emotions begins. It is because of this receptivity and susceptibility that hysteria and the hysterical type of woman are so leniently dealt with: it is this type, and not the shrewish type, that will be cited in opposition to my views.‡

Untruthfulness, organic untruthfulness, characterises both types, and accordingly all women. It is quite wrong to say that women lie. That would imply that they sometimes speak the truth. Sincerity, *pro foro interno et externo,* is the virtue of all others of which women are absolutely incapable, which is impossible for them! . . .

The current opinion that woman is religious is equally erroneous. Female mysticism, when it is anything more than mere superstition, is either

---

*We may find the analogy to this in men: there are masculine "servants" who are so by nature, and there is the masculine form of the shrew—e.g., the policeman. It is a noticeable fact that a policeman usually finds his sexual complement in the housemaid.

†A real dame would never dream of asking her husband what she was to do, what she is to give him for dinner, &c.; the hysterical woman, on the contrary, is always lacking in ideas, and wants suggestions from others. This is a rough way of indicating the two types.

‡It is the "yielding type" and not the virago type of woman that men think capable of love. Such a woman's love is only the mental sense of satisfaction aroused by the maleness of some particular man, and, therefore, it is only possible with the hysterical; it has nothing to do with her individual power of loving, and can have nothing to do with it. The bashfulness of woman is also due to her "obsession" by one man; this also causes her neglect of all other men.

thinly veiled sexuality (the identification of the Deity and the lover has been frequently discussed, as, for instance, in Maupassant's "Bel-Ami," or in Hauptmann's "Hannele's Himmelfahrt") as in numberless spiritualists and theosophists, or it is a mere passive and unconscious acceptance of man's religious views which are clung to the more firmly because of woman's natural disinclination for them. The lover is readily transformed into a Savior; very readily (as is well known to be the case with many nuns) the Savior becomes the lover. All the great women visionaries known to history were hysterical; the most famous, Santa Teresa, was not misnamed "the patron saint of hysteria." At any rate, if woman's religiousness were genuine, and if it proceeded from her own nature, she would have done something great in the religious world; but she never has done anything of any importance. I should like to put shortly what I take to be the difference between the masculine and feminine creeds; man's religion consists in a supreme belief in himself, woman's in a supreme belief in other people. . . .

Woman is not a free agent; she is altogether subject to her desire to be under man's influence, herself and all others: she is under the sway of the phallus, and irretrievably succumbs to her destiny, even if it leads to actively developed sexuality. At the most a woman can reach an indistinct feeling of her unfreedom, a cloudy idea of the possibility of controlling her destiny—manifestly only a flickering spark of the free, intelligible subject, the scanty remains of inherited maleness in her, which, by contrast, gives her even this slight comprehension. It is also impossible for a woman to have a clear idea of her destiny, or of the forces within her: it is only he who is free who can discern fate, because he is not chained by necessity; part of his personality, at least, places him in the position of spectator and a combatant outside his own fate and makes him so far superior to it. One of the most conclusive proofs of human freedom is contained in the fact that man has been able to create the idea of causality. Women consider themselves most free when they are most bound; and they are not troubled by the passions, because they are simply the embodiment of them. It is only a man who can talk of the "dira necessitas" within him; it is only he could have created the idea of destiny, because it is only he who, in addition to the empirical, conditioned existence, possesses a free, intelligible ego. . . .

But since every male has a relation to the idea of the highest value, and would be incomplete without it, no male is really ever happy. It is only women who are happy. No man is happy, because he has a relation to freedom, and yet during his earthly life he is always bound in some way. None but a perfectly passive being, such as the absolute female, or a universally active being, like the divine, can be happy. Happiness is the sense of perfect consummation, and this feeling a man can never have; but there are women who fancy themselves perfect. The male always has problems behind him and efforts before him: all problems originate in the past; the future is the sphere for efforts. Time has no objective, no meaning, for woman; no woman questions herself as to the reason of her existence; and yet the sole purpose of time is to give expression to the fact that this life can and must mean something. . . .

The last and absolute proof of the thoroughly negative character of woman's life, of her complete want of a higher existence, is derived from the way in which women commit suicide.

Such suicides are accompanied practically always by thoughts of other people, what they will think, how they will mourn over them, how grieved—or angry—they will be. Every woman is convinced that her unhappiness is undeserved at the time she kills herself; she pities herself exceedingly with the sort of self-compassion which is only a "weeping with others when they weep."

How is it possible for a woman to look upon her unhappiness as personal when she possesses no idea of a destiny? The most appallingly decisive proof of the emptiness and nullity of women is that they never once succeed in knowing the problem of their own lives, and death leaves them ignorant of it, because they are unable to realize the higher life of personality.

I am now ready to answer the question which I put forward as the chief object of this portion of my book, the question as to the significance of the male and female in the universe. Women have no existence and no essence; they are not, they are nothing. Mankind occurs as male or female, as something or nothing. Woman has no share in ontological reality, no relation to the thing-in-itself, which, in the deepest interpretation, is the absolute, is God. Man in his highest form, the genius, has such a relation, and for him the absolute is either the conception of the highest worth of existence, in which case he is a philosopher; or it is the wonderful fairyland of dreams, the kingdom of absolute beauty, and then he is an artist. But both views mean the same. Woman has no relation to the idea, she neither affirms nor denies it; she is neither moral nor antimoral; mathematically speaking, she has no sign; she is purposeless, neither good nor bad, neither angel nor devil, never egoistical (and therefore has often been said to be altruistic); she is as nonmoral as she is nonlogical. But all existence is moral and logical existence. So woman has no existence.

Woman is untruthful. An animal has just as little metaphysical reality as the actual woman, but it cannot speak, and consequently it does not lie. In order to speak the truth one must *be* something; truth is dependent on an existence, and only that can have a relation to an existence which is in itself something. Man desires truth all the time; that is to say, he all along desires only to be something. The cognition-impulse is in the end identical with the desire for immortality. Anyone who objects to a statement without ever having realized it; anyone who gives outward acquiescence without the inner affirmation, such persons, like woman, have no real existence and must of necessity lie. So that woman always lies, even if, objectively, she speaks the truth. . . .

Woman has no limits to her ego which could be broken through, and which she would have to guard.

The chief difference between man's and woman's friendship is referable to this fact. Man's friendship is an attempt to see eye to eye with those who individually and collectively are striving after the same idea; woman's friendship is a combination for the purpose of matchmaking. It is the only kind of intimate and unreserved intercourse possible between women, when they are not merely anxious to meet each other for the purpose of gossiping or discussing every day affairs.*

The emancipation of woman is analogous to the emancipation of Jews and Negroes. Undoubtedly the principal reason why these people have been treated as slaves and inferiors is to be found in their servile dispositions; their desire for freedom is not nearly so strong as that of the Indo-Germans. And even although the whites in America at the present day find it necessary to keep themselves quite aloof from the Negro population because they make such a bad use of their freedom, yet in the war of the Northern States against the Federals, which resulted in the freedom of the slaves, right was entirely on the side of the emancipators.

Although the humanity of Jews, Negroes, and still more of women, is weighed down by many immoral impulses; although in these cases there is so much more to fight against than in the case of Aryan men, still we must try to respect mankind, and to venerate the idea of humanity (by which I do not mean the human community, but the being, man, the soul as part of the spiritual world). No matter how degraded a criminal may be, no one ought to arrogate to himself the functions of the law; no man has the right to lynch such an offender.

The problem of woman and the problem of the Jews are absolutely identical with the problem of slavery, and they must be solved in the same way. No one should be oppressed, even if the oppression is of such a kind as to be unfelt as such. The animals about a house are not "slaves," because they have no freedom in the proper sense of the word which could be taken away.

But woman has a faint idea of her incapacity, a last remnant, however weak, of the free intelligible ego, simply because there is no such thing as an absolute woman. Women are human beings, and must be treated as such, even if they themselves do not wish it. Woman and man have the same rights. That is not to say that women ought to have an equal share in political affairs. From the utilitarian standpoint such a concession, cer-

---

*Men's friendships avoid breaking down their friends' personal reserve. Women expect intimacy from their friends.

tainly at present and probably always, would be most undesirable; in New Zealand, where, on ethical principles, women have been enfranchised, the worst results have followed. As children, imbeciles and criminals would be justly prevented from taking any part in public affairs even if they were numerically equal or in the majority; woman must in the same way be kept from having a share in anything which concerns the public welfare, as it is much to be feared that the mere effect of female influence would be harmful. Just as the results of science do not depend on whether all men accept them or not, so justice and injustice can be dealt out to the woman, although she is unable to distinguish between them, and she need not be afraid that injury will be done her, as justice and not might will be the deciding factor in her treatment. But justice is always the same whether for man or woman. No one has a right to forbid things to a woman because they are ''unwomanly''; neither should any man be so mean as to talk of his unfaithful wife's doings as if they were his affair. Woman must be looked upon as an individual and as if she were a free individual, not as one of a species, not as a sort of creation from the various wants of man's nature; even though woman herself may never prove worthy of such a lofty view.

Thus this book may be considered as the greatest honor ever paid to women. Nothing but the most moral relation towards women should be possible for men; there should be neither sexuality nor love, for both make woman the means to an end, but only the attempt to understand her. Most men theoretically respect women, but practically they thoroughly despise them; according to my ideas this method should be reversed. It is impossible to think highly of women, but it does not follow that we are to despise them for ever. . . .

Men will have to overcome their dislike for masculine women, for that is no more than a mean egoism. If women ever become masculine by becoming logical and ethical, they would no longer be such good material for man's projection; but that is not a sufficient reason for the present method of tying woman down to the needs of her husband and children and forbidding her certain things because they are masculine.

For even if the possibility of morality is incompatible with the idea of the absolute woman, it does not follow that man is to make no effort to save the average woman from further deterioration; much less is he to help to keep woman as she is. In every living woman the presence of what Kant calls ''the germ of good'' must be assumed; it is the remnant of a free state which makes it possible for woman to have a dim notion of her destiny. The theoretical possibility of grafting much more on this ''germ of good'' should never be lost sight of, even although nothing has ever been done, or even if nothing could ever be done in that respect.

The basis and the purpose of the universe is the good, and the whole world exists under a moral law; even to the animals, which are mere phenomena, we assign moral values, holding the elephant, for instance, to be higher than the snake, notwithstanding the fact that we do not make an animal accountable when it kills another. In the case of woman, however, we regard her as responsible if she commits murder, and in this alone is a proof that women are above the animals. If it be the case that womanliness is simply immorality, then woman must cease to be womanly and try to be manly.

I must give warning against the danger of woman trying merely to liken herself outwardly to man, for such a course would simply plunge her more deeply into womanliness. It is only too likely that the efforts to emancipate women will result not in giving her real freedom, in letting her reach free-will, but merely in enlarging the range of her caprices. . . .

A woman who had really given up her sexual self, who wished to be at peace would be no longer "woman." She would have ceased to be "woman," she would have received the inward and spiritual sign as well as the outward form of regeneration.

Can such a thing be?

There is no absolute woman, but even to say "yes" to the above question is like giving one's assent to a miracle. Emancipation will not make woman happier; it will not ensure her salvation, and it is a long road which leads to God. No being in the transition stage between freedom and slavery can be happy. But will woman choose to abandon slavery in order to become unhappy? The question is not merely if it be possible for woman to become moral. It is this: is it possible for woman really to wish to realize the problem of existence, the conception of guilt? Can she really desire freedom? This can happen only by her being penetrated by an ideal, brought to the guiding star. It can happen only if the categorical imperative were to become active in woman; only if woman can place herself in relation to the moral idea, the idea of humanity.

In that way only can there be an emancipation of woman.

Bertrand Russell

British philosopher, mathematician, and social reformer, 1872–1970. Probably best known for his pacificism and for his views on marriage, education, and religion, Russell also made important contributions to both mathematics and philosophy. He received the Nobel Prize for Literature in 1950.

From *Marriage and Morals*

The extreme strength of jealousy in patriarchal societies is due to the fear of falsification of descent. This may be seen in the fact that a man who is tired of his wife and passionately devoted to his mistress will nevertheless be more jealous where his wife is concerned than when he finds a rival to the affections of his mistress. A legitimate child is a continuation of a man's ego, and his affection for the child is a form of egoism. If, on the other hand, the child is not legitimate, the putative father is tricked into lavishing care upon a child with whom he has no biological connection. Hence the discovery of fatherhood led to the subjection of women as the only means of securing their virtue—a subjection first physical and then mental, which reached its height in the Victorian age. Owing to the subjection of women there has in most civilized communities been no genuine companionship between husbands and wives; their relation has been one of condescension on the one side and duty on the other. All the man's serious thoughts and purposes he has kept to himself, since robust thought might lead his wife to betray him. In most civilized communities women have been denied almost all experience of the world and of affairs. They have been kept artifically stupid and therefore uninteresting. From Plato's dialogs one derives an impression that he and his friends regarded men as the only proper objects of serious love. This is not to be wondered at when one considers that all the matters in which they were interested were completely closed to respectable Athenian women. Exactly the same state of affairs prevailed in China until recently, and in Persia in the great days of Persian poetry, and in many other ages and places. Love as a relation between men and women was ruined by the desire to make sure of the legitimacy of children. And not only love, but the whole contribution that women can make to civilization, has been stunted for the same reason. . . .

Let us, however, pause a moment to consider the logical implications of the demand that women should be the equals of men. Men have from time immemorial been allowed in practice, if not in theory, to indulge in illicit sexual relations. It has not been expected of a man that he should be a virgin on entering marriage, and even after marriage, infidelities are not viewed very gravely if they never come to the knowledge of a man's wife and neighbors. The possibility of this system has depended upon prostitution. This institution, however, is one which it is difficult for a modern to defend, and few will suggest that women should acquire the same rights as men through the establishment of a class of male prostitutes for the satisfaction of women who wish, like their husbands, to seem virtuous without being so. Yet it is quite certain that in these days of late marriage only a small percentage of men will remain continent until they can afford to set up house with a woman of their own class. And if unmarried men are not going to be continent, unmarried women, on the ground of equal rights, will claim that they also need not be continent. To the moralists this situation is no doubt regrettable. Every conventional moralist who takes the trouble to think it out will see that he is committed in practice to what is called the double standard, that is to say, the view that sexual virtue is more essential in a woman than in a man. It is all very well to argue that his theoretical ethic demands continence of men also. To this there is the obvious retort that the demand cannot be enforced on the men since it is easy for them to sin secretly. The conventional moralist is thus committed against his will not only to an inequality as between men and women, but also to the view that it is better for a young man to have intercourse with prostitutes than with girls of his own class, in spite of the fact that with the latter, though not with the former, his relations are not mercenary and may be affectionate and altogether delightful. Moralists, of course, do not think out the consequences of advocating a morality which they know will not be obeyed; they think that so long as they do not advocate prostitution they are not responsible for the fact that prostitution is the inevitable outcome of their teaching. This, however, is only another illustration of the well-known fact that the professional moralist in our day is a man of less than average intelligence.

In view of the above circumstances, it is evident that so long as many men for economic reasons find early marriage impossible, while many women cannot marry at all, equality as between men and women demands a relaxation in the traditional standards of feminine virtue. If men are allowed prenuptial intercourse (as in fact they are), women must be allowed it also. And in all countries where there is an excess of women it is an obvious injustice that those women who by arithmetical necessity must remain unmarried should be wholly debarred from sexual experience. Doubtless the pioneers of the women's movement had no such consequences in view, but their modern followers perceive them clearly, and whoever opposes these deductions must face the fact that he or she is not in favour of justice to the female sex.

A very clear-cut issue is raised by this question of the new morality versus the old. If the chastity of girls and the faithfulness of wives is no longer to be demanded, it becomes necessary either to have new methods of safeguarding the family or else to acquiesce in the breakup of the family. It may be suggested that the procreation of children should only occur within marriage, and that all extramarital sexual intercourse should be rendered sterile by the use of contraceptives. In that case husbands might learn to be as tolerant of lovers as Orientals are of eunuchs. The difficulty of such a scheme as yet is that it requires us to place more reliance on the efficacy of contraceptives and the truthfulness of wives than seems rational; this difficulty may, however, be diminished before long. The other alternative compatible with the new morality is the decay of fatherhood as an important social institution, and the taking over of the duties of the father by the State. In particular cases where a man felt sure of his paternity and fond of the child, he might, of course, voluntarily undertake to do what fathers now normally do in the way of financial support for the mother and child; but he would not be obliged to do so by law. Indeed all children would be in the position in which illegitimate children of unknown paternity are now, except that the State, regarding this as the normal case, would take more trouble with their nurture than it does at present.

If, on the other hand, the old morality is to be reestablished, certain things are essential; some of them are already done, but experience shows that these alone are not effective. The first essential is that the education of girls should be such as to make them stupid and superstitious and ignorant; this requisite is already fulfilled in schools over which the churches have any control. The next requisite is a very severe censorship upon all books giving information on sex subjects; this condition also is coming to be fulfilled in England and in America, since the censorship, without change in the law, is being tightened up by the increasing zeal of the police. These conditions, however, since they exist already, are clearly insufficient. The only thing that will suffice is to remove from young women all opportunity of being alone with men: girls must be forbidden to earn their living by work outside the home; they must never be allowed an outing unless accompanied by their mother or an aunt; the regrettable practice of going to dances without a chaperon must be sternly stamped out. It must be illegal for an unmarried woman under fifty to possess a motor-car, and perhaps it would be wise to subject all unmarried women once a month to medical examination by police doctors, and to send to a

penitentiary all such as were found to be not virgins. The use of contraceptives must, of course, be eradicated, and it must be illegal in conversation with unmarried women to throw doubt upon the dogma of eternal
damnation. These measures, if carried out vigorously for a hundred years
or more, may perhaps do something to stem the rising tide of immorality.
I think, however, that in order to avoid the risk of certain abuses, it would
be necessary that all policemen and all medical men should be castrated.
Perhaps it would be wise to carry this policy a step further, in view of the
inherent depravity of the male character. I am inclined to think that moralists would be well advised to advocate that all men should be castrated,
with the exception of ministers of religion.*

. . . Sexual behavior among human beings is not instinctive, so that
the inexperienced bride and bridegroom, who are probably quite unaware
of this fact, find themselves overwhelmed with shame and discomfort. It
is little better when the woman alone is innocent but the man has acquired
his knowledge from prostitutes. Most men do not realize that a process of
wooing is necessary after marriage, and many well-brought-up women do
not realize what harm they do to marriage by remaining reserved and
physically aloof. All this could be put right by better sexual education,
and is in fact very much better with the generation now young than it was
with their parents and grandparents. There used to be a widespread belief
among women that they were morally superior to men on the ground that
they had less pleasure in sex. This attitude made frank companionship
between husbands and wives impossible. It was, of course, in itself quite
unjustifiable, since failure to enjoy sex, so far from being virtuous, is a
mere physiological or psychological deficiency, like a failure to enjoy
food, which also a hundred years ago was expected of elegant females.

Other modern causes of unhappiness in marriage are, however, not so
easily disposed of. I think that uninhibited civilized people, whether men
or women, are generally polygamous in their instincts. They may fall
deeply in love and be for some years entirely absorbed in one person, but
sooner or later sexual familiarity dulls the edge of passion, and then they
begin to look elsewhere for a revival of the old thrill. It is, of course,
possible to control this impulse in the interests of morality, but it is very
difficult to prevent the impulse from existing. With the growth of wom-
en's freedom there has come a much greater opportunity for conjugal infidelity than existed in former times. The opportunity gives rise to the
thought, the thought gives rise to the desire, and in the absence of religious scruples the desire gives rise to the act.

Women's emancipation has in various ways made marriage more difficult. In old days the wife had to adapt herself to the husband, but the

---

*Since reading "Elmer Gantry," I have begun to feel that even this exception is per-
haps not quite wise.

husband did not have to adapt himself to the wife. Nowadays many wives, on grounds of woman's right to her own individuality and her own career, are unwilling to adapt themselves to their husbands beyond a point, while men who still hanker after the old tradition of masculine domination see no reason why they should do all the adapting. This trouble arises especially in connection with infidelity. In old days the husband was occasionally unfaithful, but as a rule his wife did not know of it. If she did, he confessed that he had sinned and made her believe that he was penitent. She, on the other hand, was usually virtuous. If she was not, and the fact came to her husband's knowledge, the marriage broke up. Where, as happens in many modern marriages, mutual faithfulness is not demanded, the instinct of jealousy nevertheless survives, and often proves fatal to the persistence of any deeply rooted intimacy even where no overt quarrels occur. . . .

It is therefore possible for a civilized man and woman to be happy in marriage, although if this is to be the case a number of conditions must be fulfilled. There must be a feeling of complete equality on both sides; there must be no interference with mutual freedom; there must be the most complete physical and mental intimacy; and there must be a certain similarity in regard to standards of values. (It is fatal, for example, if one values only money while the other values only good work.) Given all these conditions, I believe marriage to be the best and most important relation that can exist between two human beings. If it has not often been realized hitherto, that is chiefly because husband and wife have regarded themselves as each other's policeman. If marriage is to achieve its possibilities, husbands and wives must learn to understand that whatever the law may say, in their private lives they must be free.

. . . Now that women are a majority of the electorate, it is not to be supposed that they will submit forever to being kept in the background. Their claims, if recognized, are likely to have a profound effect upon the family. There are two different ways in which married women might acquire economic independence. One is that of remaining employed in the kind of work that they were engaged upon before marriage. This involves giving their children over to the care of others, and would lead to a very great extension of crèches and nursery schools, the logical consequence of which would be the elimination of the mother as well as of the father from all importance in the child's psychology. The other method would be that women with young children should receive a wage from the State on condition of devoting themselves to the care of their children. This method, alone, would, of course, not be adequate, and would need to be supplemented by provisions enabling women to return to ordinary work when their children ceased to be quite young. But it would have the advantage of enabling women to care for their children themselves without degrading dependence upon an individual man. And it would recognize, what in these days is more and more the case, that having a child, which was formerly a mere consequence of sexual gratification, is now a task deliberately undertaken, which, since it redounds to the advantage of the State rather than of the parents, should be paid for by the State, instead of entailing a grave burden upon the father and mother. This last point is being recognized in the advocacy of family allowances, but it is not yet recognized that the payment for children should be made to the mother alone. I think we may assume, however, that working-class feminism will grow to the point where this is recognized, and embodied in the law. . . .

The revolt of women against the domination of men is a movement which in its purely political sense, is practically completed, but in its wider aspects is still in its infancy. Gradually its remoter effects will work themselves out. The emotions which women are supposed to feel are still, as yet, a reflection of the interests and sentiments of men. You will read in the works of male novelists that women find physical pleasure in suckling their young; you can learn by asking any mother of your acquaintance that this is not the case, but until women had votes no man ever thought of doing so. Maternal emotions altogether have been so long slobbered over by men who saw in them subconsciously the means to their own domination that a considerable effort is required to arrive at what women sincerely feel in this respect. Until very recently, all decent women were supposed to desire children, but to hate sex. Even now, many men are shocked by women who frankly state that they do not desire children. Indeed, it is not uncommon for men to take it upon themselves to deliver homilies to such women. So long as women were in subjection, they did not dare to be honest about their own emotions, but professed those which were pleasing to the male. We cannot, therefore, argue from what has been hitherto supposed to be women's normal attitude towards children, for we may find that as women become fully emancipated their emotions turn out to be, in general, quite different from what has hitherto been thought. I think that civilization, at any rate as it has hitherto existed, tends greatly to diminish women's maternal feelings. It is probable that a high civilization will not in future be possible to maintain unless women are paid such sums for the production of children as to make them feel it worthwhile as a moneymaking career. If that were done, it would, of course, be unnecessary that all women, or even a majority, should adopt this profession. It would be one profession among others, and would have to be undertaken with professional thoroughness. These, however, are speculations. The only point in them that seems fairly certain is that feminism in its later developments is likely to have a profound influence in breaking up the patriarchal family, which represents man's triumph over woman in prehistoric times. . . .

For the large class of women who, as things are, must remain permanently unmarried, conventional morality is painful and, in most cases, harmful. I have known, as we all have, unmarried women of strict conventional virtue who deserve the highest admiration from every possible point of view. But I think the general rule is otherwise. A woman who has had no experience of sex and has considered it important to preserve her virtue has been engaged in a negative reaction, tinged with fear, and has therefore, as a rule, become timid, while at the same time instinctive, unconscious jealousy has filled her with disapproval of normal people, and with a desire to punish those who have enjoyed what she has forgone. Intellectual timidity is an especially common concomitant of prolonged virginity. Indeed, I am inclined to think that the intellectual inferiority of women, insofar as it exists, is mainly due to the restraint upon curiosity which the fear of sex leads them to impose. There is no good reason for the unhappiness and waste involved in the lifelong virginity of those women who cannot find an exclusive husband. The present situation, in which this necessarily occurs very frequently, was not contemplated in the earlier days of the institution of marriage, since in those days the numbers of the sexes were approximately equal. Undoubtedly, the existence of a great excess of women in many countries affords a very serious argument in favor of modifications of the conventional moral code.

Marriage, the one conventionally tolerated outlet for sex, itself suffers from the rigidity of the code. The complexes acquired in childhood, the experiences of men with prostitutes, and the attitude of aversion from sex instilled into young ladies in order to preserve their virtue, all militate against happiness in marriage. A well-brought-up girl, if her sexual impulses are strong, will be unable to distinguish, when she is courted, between a serious congeniality with a man and a mere sex attraction. She may easily marry the first man who awakens her sexually, and find out too late that when her sexual hunger is satisfied she has no longer anything in common with him. Everything has been done in the education of the two to make her unduly timid and him unduly sudden in the sexual approach. Neither has the knowledge on sexual matters that each ought to have, and very often initial failures, due to this ignorance, make the marriage ever after sexually unsatisfying to both. Moreover, mental as well as physical companionship is rendered difficult. A woman is not accustomed to free speech on sexual matters. A man is not accustomed to it, except with men and prostitutes. In the most intimate and vital concern of their mutual life, they are shy, awkward, even wholly silent. The wife, perhaps, lies awake unsatisfied and hardly knowing what it is she wants. The man perhaps has the thought, at first fleeting and instantly banished, but gradually becoming more and more insistent, that even prostitutes are more generous in giving than his lawful wife. He is offended by her coldness, at the very moment, perhaps, that she is suffering because he does not know how to rouse her. All this misery results from our policy of silence and decency.

Max Scheler

German phenomenologist, moral and social philosopher, 1874–1928, who, through his studies of sympathy and other states of consciousness, such as resentment, repentance, love, and joy, contributed significantly to ethics, psychology, religion, and sociology.

From "Toward an Idea of Man"

Human Being and Gender

Educated women today—when they are among themselves—have the habit of saying of some other woman: "Oh, yes, she's a 'wonderful human being.'" They deny their sex and take pure humanity as their model. But they forget: not only does the word *Mensch* come from *männisch* (and in many other languages the word for "human being" means "man" at the same time, e.g., *homo, homme*); even the idea of a "human being," supposedly encompassing man and woman, is but a male idea. I do not think this idea would have arisen in a culture dominated by women. Only the man is so "spiritual," so "dualistic," and so—childlike, as to sometimes overlook the depth of the difference we call sexual. To be sure, such a word is needed; but its meaning is not and cannot ever be fully neuter. It is itself almost always the male *or* female idea of precisely that which it is supposed to encompass. Thus those ladies who call themselves "splendid human beings" only show that they are not true females, and—since it is precisely always part of the human *essence* to be either male or female—that they are only diminished "human beings." In times when the difference between sexes was felt to be of positive value, there arose the expression *das Mensch*, its neuter article designed to suggest that the woman in question was no true female and bore "only" "human" traits. A woman who wants to be a "splendid human being" will in fact always only be aping the men. Hence we can also at this point drop the concept of the "all-too-human."

424

From *On the Meaning of the Women's Movement* [1913]

Those circles that view with serious national alarm the considerable fertility decline disclosed by the census statistics and who, unlike the Social Democrats, are incapable of interpreting this altogether as a gratifying sign of improvement in the working classes and their rising standard of living, coincide generally with those groups opposed to the *spirit* at work within the women's movement, in which they perceive an apostasy from the "true calling of woman as housewife and mother." And this attitude seems to have some foundation in that the model woman to which the woman's movement has so far aspired (including the extreme borderline case of the suffragette) in no way suggests the prospect of fertility and a reproduction level suited to the great national purposes of our people. Both those feminine bodily and spiritual qualities that customarily exert an attractive power on the man, insofar as he lets himself be guided not by material considerations but by feminine charms, as well as those other qualities that from the standpoint of biologic suitability offer prospect of sufficiently large, healthy, and early fertility (pelvic width, nursing capacity, etc., erotic allure) appear, apart from a few individuals, to be ever less present insofar as the women in question assume an active role in that movement.

In reply to this it has been pointed out that as they gain economic independence, working women, for whom the women's movement must above all try to speak, will be less compelled in their choice of men to follow material interests and the influence of familial authority usually directed towards these, and, since they are more able to obey the dictates of "their heart," obviously offer prospects for a qualitatively superior coming generation. But this still overlooks various factors. For one thing, the exertions that the woman must make under pressure of the female labor supply and as a result of male competition usually force erotic impulses into the background to such a degree that little guarantee exists for the economically more independent woman "following her heart," but rather, in the choice of a man as well, following exactly the *same* impulses that were strong enough to drive her to economic independence in the first place. The same heightened calculating attitude toward life, which alone within our economic system guarantees a woman sufficient success to attain economic independence, usually expresses itself in the choice of men she habitually uses to obtain the positions she desires. Indeed, in innumerable cases the entrance of women into active economic life is already bound up with the abominable phenomenon of a kind of male patronage, the acceptance of which involves on the woman's side a combination of authority needs and erotic motives guided by interested speculation, and on the man's a mixture of the business requirements of the moment plus the basest sensual motives, working together in a most distressing harmony. When it comes to her decision about entering matrimony, the more calculating woman will then more than ever remain true to the attitude that guided her economically, as already described above. In both cases the masculine material capable of such half-measures and baseness gives little promise for propitious reproduction. Thus neither observation of life nor the conclusions we can draw from statistics speak in favor of the expected outcome. According to the statistics, working women, especially to the degree they have masculine occupations, furnish only a very diminishing portion of children born, both legitimate and illegitimate.

Far more important, however, than this factor is another: namely, that given the quality and quantity of requirements that our industrial system, resting as it does by nature wholly on masculine values and ideals, establishes in the way of female labor, the innately *more virile type* of female individuals appear at the outset to be powerfully *favored* and given a premium. All women whose capacity for continuity of thought and work are little disturbed and distracted by a strongly felt reproductive drive, by passionate feeling, by erotic ideas and fantasies, by pregnancy, child-feeding, by erotic and maternal worries, and who, in keeping with these qualities, also from the outset exhibit less pronounced psychic and physical secondary sexual characters, have a far *greater* prospect (given equal initial property and social class) of getting into the economic labor mechanism of our civilization and, once within it, of perservering there permanently and with economic success. That marriagelessness and childlessness are hereby greatly increased suffers no doubt. Those women *passed over* by that selective force immanent in our industrial system, as well as those female types cast aside as "unsuited" for industrial labor needs, matter little, however, in terms of qualitatively and quantitatively favorable reproduction because, to the same degree they prove "unsuited" for labor needs, thanks to female qualities, they run the danger of sinking into one of the extremely diverse kinds and transitional phases of prostitution, often after their first child. This double tendency of the labor system dominant today acquires to the same degree its real expression and works its damaging results, in that the societies we use for comparison exhibit *industrialistic* character. G. E. Woodruff has rightly emphasized that the strong moralism and prudery of large sections of the American and English female stratum result *not* from any moral *elevation* of women, but largely because the labor requirements of these highly industrialized societies themselves abandon carriers of psyches moved more by love and tenderness to increasing *self-dissolution* through prostitution and the diseases accompanying it, and in this wise tend increasingly to *exclude genetically* the more purely feminine variant.

On the other hand, things which it has been the custom recently to deem increasingly responsible for this phenomenon, the virile type of female (which, by the way, finds considerable expression in the changing trend of women's fashions towards imitation of articles intended for the male figure, as all those well-acquainted with fashion assure us), are in fact far more the *results* than the *causes* of that increasing unfemininity caused by the above-mentioned selective tendency: for example, the work of those leading the political and social women's movement and the "politicization" of woman, as well as the schooling (especially in England) that disassociates the young girl to an increasing degree from the family and awakens her ambition much more strongly than was formerly the case, by adapting the curricula of girls to those of educational institutions for male youth, by means of a type of teacher herself strongly virile. For this very reason it would further be wrong to hope for any essential improvement resulting from a struggle against these mere *symptoms*. The soundness of this explanation is also shown by the fact that the appearance of unfeminine traits in the modern woman, little suited for desirable fertility levels, is not at all a result of woman's economic activity *in general* or rejection of her so-called "natural calling."

Factually it is a completely unfounded historical error to assume that economic or other activity by women beyond the tasks of housewife and mother is in any way a *novel* phenomenon. Disregarding conditions among many primitive peoples, in which woman is quite simply a work animal, women have always, in Germany, for example, been employed most extensively in agriculture; and still today, the statistics tell us, more than half the agricultural labor force in Bavaria, for example, is recruited from the rural female population. In little-industrialized nations or regions, as for example in southern Bavaria, female labor in no way gives rise to that tendency that produces a virile female type. And wherever society's labor needs do not intrinsically lay claim to the specifically "masculine" qualities of stricter rationality, computation, calculation, and a continuity of activity little compatible with the female nature, the increasing economic independence of women can increase chances for desirable fertility levels and reproduction, in that it renders the choice of a mate or lover freer from material considerations and lets women more easily follow their hearts. The way in which that great movement, so differentiated in its individual forms, the so-called "women's movement" (one cause of which, it has often been emphasized, is that the woman follows job opportunities that themselves gravitate more and more out of the home and into the factory), will finally affect national fertility conditions seems above all to depend on the extent to which our cultural and labor system built on specifically *masculine* values, ideals, and capacities, can be altered, through the gradual progress of the movement itself, in the direction of *co*-dominance of specifically *female values* and *ideals*. And on the extent to which this change enables a specifically female labor demand, i.e., a labor demand for *specifically* female strengths, to take shape and overcome the dangerous selective tendency in favor of the virile female type, depicted above, creating in its place another, aimed at making possible and insuring once and for all that the *purer* feminine type be ecomically independent as well.

It is a common error to judge the world-historical meaning of the modern women's movement and its final and lasting import for all human relations in terms of those phenomena that are of necessity linked only to the debut of the *first* female precursors, *their* attitude, and *their* nature and image. That would be just as absurd as having judged the meaning of the English labor movement from the revolutionary disturbances of the Chartists, their destruction of machines, etc., which formed the beginning of that movement, a movement that, we realize today, stands for *maintenance* of capitalist conditions and the capitalist spirit. Indeed, if the drastic example be forgiven, it would be as absurd as viewing a hypothetically successful revolutionary putsch of French royalists against the Republic as a victory of the modern world's "progressive principles," simply because such a putsch would have to rely on support from all sorts of elements whose disposition is more "revolutionary" than "conservative." Every movement, whatever its content and aim, is revolutionary insofar as it turns against older, prevailing conditions and values and, in order to succeed, must needs be *initially* borne and represented by persons and forces of necessity considered "exceptional" and "progressive" in terms of the system's *dominant* values. But this hardly excludes that the content and meaning of the movement in question be exactly *opposite* to the spirit and conscious aims of its first bearers and representatives, nor that *that which* is in fact realized in it be separated and elevated from the *form* of its realization, in the sharpest possible way. And this indeed seems to be the case with the women's movement in every respect, and not merely with regard to its present or eventual relation to the rise and fall in quality and quantity of fertility. The French positivist Auguste Comte long ago correctly drew attention to the two-sideness of the women's movement, and the Jesuits, as indeed to a certain degree the Catholic Church in general (which, unlike Protestantism, has always defended the right of the female principle in all things human and divine), have well-understood the deeper connection between beginning and end. Every definite increase of woman's rights socially, politically, and economically, must of necessity eventually set inner *limits on the impact had by all values and forces* upon which our *present-day material civilization* rests. No change in the female type lying within the limits of historically known variability can indeed ever overcome the fact that woman, as the creature earthier, more vegetative, more unified in all life-experience, and, far more than the man, guided by instinct, feeling, and love, is thus also by nature a *conservative* creature—the guardian of tradition, of custom, of all older forms of thinking and will, and the eternal braking force of a civilization and culture plunging along toward the goals of mere rationality and mere "progress." Despite her greater bodily and psychological plasticity, woman has always preserved a calm and constancy bordering on the miraculous with regard to masculine excesses in history, both those in ideas as well as those of customs and fashion. With the beautiful and peaceful composure of a tree alongside which animals make their intricate leaps, she stands in the ground of her being before the restless drama of male history—ever mindful to hold firm the great simple foundations that our existence as a species has as its own.

Now if indeed the type of female who first gets this movement underway lacks in whatever measure the innate female characteristics named above, this results simply from the fact that in attacking and struggling against these women, our so specifically masculine culture reacts only to *masculine* weapons. But this *initially* necessary mimicry on the part of womankind, through which it at first takes on the protective coloring of its opponent and sends out into battle its comrades of the more virile type, will, however, disappear as the movement acquires extension and power and *succeeds,* whereupon the earlier *weakness* of the female position (which here, as always, forms one precondition of "mimicry") gives way to a stronger position. So long as woman's *personality* in public law and her independent cooperation in the setting of cultural goals are not recognized, and for this reason the values, tasks, and aims that dominate our culture are exclusively masculine, indeed specifically masculine, the woman struggling up within such a system must first of all assume *masculine* traits—this is a wholly self-evident fact. But it is equally self-evident that *if* that movement has at last carried through, and those values, tasks, and goals themselves take on a feminine strain corresponding to the *nature* of the female, then the process of female masculinization with all its evil consequences will have to subside and eventually cease. Indeed, I am of the conviction that in all of history there has been no single peaceful movement that will accomplish such a thoroughgoing change in all human relations as a victorious women's movement. The liberation of the third estate by the French Revolution and the gradual emancipation of the fourth estate in the modern labor movement (in the mere wake of which a major portion of the women's movement, namely the women's labor movement, is presently to be found) will, if viewed in terms of their permanent effects on mankind, disappear into insignificance compared to the women's movement—*if* it is victorious. But the import of this movement in every way will be an enormous infusion of *preservative, accumulative, and sustaining* forces, additional support for all those values above and beyond which the anarchic, revolutionary, splintering spirit of the modern era was accustomed to stride, as over something "obsolete." To be sure, male authority, e.g., over the woman, will be reduced; but the *principle* of authority will gain enormously in every respect, in the state, the church, the community, the school. The content of that particular tradition that demands "obedience of the female" will more and more disappear, but the *principle* of tradition with regard to all other contents conceivable—manners, law, religion, art, science and scholarship, etc.—will gain enormously at the expense of that of "reason." Woman will in a certain sense represent a more rational type; but as for that which modern philosophy has in the past called "reason," the better to exalt its lot of ideas and principles as the final measure of all things human, a tremendous shift in meaning will take place, and the new conception of reason—or whatever is put in place of the word—will absorb within itself the eternal traits of the essence of the female spirit, the constituents of the feminine consciousness.

Georg Simmel has rightly pointed out that all basic concepts of our modern philosophy (here considered as an expression of modern culture), such as "person," "reason," "truth," "the good," etc., bear the singular shortcoming of passing themselves off as "universally human" and thus claiming also to encompass standards for the other half of mankind and that half's noblest powers, but in reality embody only *masculine* values, so that the woman who wants to be "universally human" becomes *eo ipso* "more masculine" in the process. There is still, to be sure, a logical, ethical, and esthetic normativeness that expresses the *nature* itself of mind and of the subject and realm of values in question, and which is thus *one and the same* for both sexes. But this exists only insofar as we ignore completely the subjective dispositions and powers, and the diversity, of those natures for which this normativeness is valid, and in relation to which alone that merely objective and impersonal conformity to law can become the so-called "norm of correct action." The "thinking" of male and female, for example, can be constitutively wholly distinct without in any way injuring the unity of that norm-conformity founded purely in what is thought. The logical "norms" and indeed even the "methods," the correct grasp of which presupposes knowledge of *both* those ideal laws of objects *and* of that constitutive thought-pattern, will thus already of necessity turn out *differently* for each sex, insofar as they are to be "correct." There presently awaits all disciplines of philosophy and psychology the task, still hardly addressed, of seeking out the constituents of the female and male consciousness in all its directions of action, and only then, on the basis of this knowledge, tracing out the fields of mental activity for both sexes. The crude conception of the 18th century, that of Rousseau, for example, that the psychological differences of man and woman are exclusively results of functional bodily and biologic differences between sexes otherwise possessing the same kind of "rational soul," must be eradicated root and branch. The sexual difference is *mentally* just as *primordial* as it is bodily and biologically. The differential sexual psychology that has attained a certain level of development for the lower mental functions (sensitivity, excitability, modes of attention, interest, memory, recollection, imagination) will thus now have to give attention above all to the *higher* and *highest* functions of the culture-shaping mind. Everywhere, precise investigation will show that the sexual distinction here reaches back into the deepest roots of the mind itself, that, e.g., female conceptualization, female judgment, female value-feeling, are constructed utterly differently. The manner in which one's own body is presented to the ego of men and women (e.g., the sense of its distance in both cases) must certainly show an essential and unbridgeable difference. Compared to the way in which the woman constitutively experiences her own body—*how* she feels and knows inside it—the man carries his along with him at such a distance, that it is like a dog on a leash. Yet this is only a metaphor; and what is needed is an exact exploration of all relevant facts, hardly to be initiated here.

I regard as very large the basic obstacle to any knowledge of the correct state of affairs that is here presented, namely that all our intellectual *images* of male and female are themselves in turn built up through male *or* female mental functions—but not through those that would endure and be valid independently of and beyond the sexual difference. The only reason that is not insurmountable is that within concrete individuals both essentially different kinds of mental functions are found together and interpenetrated in the most manifold connections. Success here is likely to result not from accumulation of empirical–statistical studies, incapable of taking into account the characteristic compositeness of male and female in the material studied, but rather only from the *method of reflecting on essence*—performed above all by individuals who either, equipped with a certain balance of both types of functions, are capable of an *overview* of *both* and a comparison, or at least have a certain measure of empathy for the functions of the other sex.

To be sure, this kind of reflection can be finally based only on a philosophic decision as to whether female–male is only an inductive–empirical conceptual distinction, or a *difference in essence* of certain elementary phenomena fixed in the nature of the living being itself that *reach across* the distinction between psychic and physical, and the actual appearance of which on any individualized bearer (person, organ, tissue, cell, cell nucleus, etc.) is then decisive in determining whether it be male or female. However endlessly difficult might be this decision and the isolation of those elementary phenomena for apperception into the superabundance of subject matter, we do not regard the prospects as hopeless. It is already a great step on the way—bringing us at least to the threshold of the problem—to perceive that we are beginning again to see the entire depth of the difference between the sexes, without that premature judgment in which the specific values of one sex were always presupposed. Yes, that and more: both in science and in general culture life, we tend towards the view that this distinction reaches back into the metaphysical roots of all finite living and inspirited existence. In biology, the doctrine regnant up until a decade ago, that the sexual distinction is a relatively late and outward adaptational phenomenon of life and its historical development, is losing its factual support to an ever-increasing degree. Indeed, the old Aristotelian doctrine that everything living is either male or female—even if we cannot ascertain everywhere the distinction—has again found a few adherents in positive biology. The philosophic investigation of differences in essence will have to link up with these biological results. Analogously, in the sphere of human sciences, the older, ready-made line of judgment that, for example, derives the differences between female and male feelings of honor (likewise shame) from mere historical or contemporary economic and political causes (suggestion by the man in the service of his interests), loses currency every day. And the same holds true for the causal explanation of male and female intellectual achievements in history. But men also begin to perceive that this gradual reacquisition of the constitutive differences of male and female are *not* to be played off *against* the women's movement, but on the contrary only speak *for* the wide-reaching cultural significance of that movement. If this difference in feeling, thinking, and achievement goes in fact so deep, if it is indeed a difference in being lying *beyond* all historical variability, then the fear that the women's movement could produce any essential lessening of it is all the more nonsensical. But even the women active in the movement are also increasingly becoming aware that not suppression of specifically feminine moral feelings in favor of adaptation to the masculine moral sensibility, but on the contrary their purest expression, their best formulation and effectuation in public life, is an integrating impulse in the task of the movement itself. And by analogy to this: that the primary basis for justification of the women's movement consists not in proving that woman in history would have been able to achieve just as much as man, but did not only because of "male oppression," but rather in the *inner right* of woman to *reject,* from the depth *of her nature,* any *mere achievement* as the sole and highest standard of value for her being—and for that of human beings in general—and to reduce its power to command general recognition. That is precisely what belongs to the specific special prerogative of the feminine valuation of things, to prefer the values of a person's *whole being* to those of his "achievement" and ability to perform. But insofar as achievement deserves to be accepted as a standard of value, the true consequence of that "oppression" (insofar as it took place) was not that woman failed to achieve what is grand and sublime according to the masculine scheme of things, but that her *specific* powers in *specific* achievements did not sufficiently come into their right.

But let us at this point disregard these latter questions, which might be called those of the "metaphysics of the women's movement," and content ourselves with asking the very obvious and realistic question of how *political* forces would be reshaped through victory of the doctrine of women's suffrage. What effect would it have, for example, if even only all working women of the Bavarian State possessed the right to vote under certain conditions? Hence in this case the whole other (female) half of the agricultural labor force. Or how would political equality for Italian women influence the relation of the papacy to the state and the king? How the relation of France to the Roman See? The journal *Frauenstimmrecht* [Women's Suffrage] (March 1913) points out that the speech of Representative Trimborn in the Prussian Chamber of Deputies on 22 October 1912 has been viewed as a signal for new tactics by Catholic women and taken into practical account. Hedwig Dransfeld, Chairwoman of the Catholic Women's League, noted on this occasion that according to the words of Bishop Dr. Faulhaber, not "the slightest opposition to women's suffrage in and of itself exists" in Catholic dogma, hence its introduction is only a question of suitable opportunity. The journal *Frauenstimmrecht* greeted with ringing words this switch in the Center Party and strongly emphasized the discomfort thus caused the liberal Party: "For nowhere is there so much inborn aversion to woman's participation in politics as in the broad masses of Philistinism where garden-variety Liberalism takes root." This all may be simply the first practical fruit in Germany of the long-prepared insight into the advantages that will in the final analysis accrue to the Catholic Church (as to every conservative cause) from the progress of the women's movement.

Now what has been emphasized so far concerning the meaning of the women's movement is also valid for the specific question about the relationship of the women's movement to *fertility*. All objections that many of our racial biologists have raised against the women's movement from a medical standpoint will be valid precisely until the above-described law of selection granting economic preference to the virile type of woman is nullified. However, it is just this law, based in the very nature of the existing industrial system (this hypervirile system), and not the form taken by a large segment of the present social and political women's movement (however rightly deplored for its own sake by those men), that constitutes the basis for those negative effects of women's labor on female fertility. Hence all exhortative moralizing, as recently practiced by some of those racial biologists, has no effect at all. Moreover, their laments (justified, as far as they go) over the decline of all female characteristics promising healthy fertility (not only a social–biological, but also a racial–biological phenomenon, because of its cumulative hereditary nature) will not become pointless even if women are referred back to their so-called "natural calling"; they will in the final analysis become groundless only through gradual moderation of that selective tendency that is the ultimate cause of the phenomena of which they complain. This moderation, however, is dependent solely on the achievement of social, political, and cultural equality for women, and through this a gradual expansion of woman's codetermination in all goals and tasks of work and culture, so that the labor requirements of our civilization themselves become attuned to the nature of the female and her specific endowments, without whose harmonious cooperation no further tasks can then be undertaken. Then and only then will it be valid to argue that the economically independent woman— who then will no longer *from the very beginning* of necessity have to be of the virile type and constantly develop within herself the powers of this type—also gives promise of better chances for fertility through the *freer* choice of her heart.

A not-inconsiderable significance will in the course of this process accrue to those at present still fully obscure and chaotic strivings that have up to now found most questionable soil in the manifold associations for "Defense of Motherhood and the Rights of Mothers," for "Marriage Reform," and for a so-called "new female ethic." For, however confused these strivings still are at present, they must nonetheless be considered a first beginning for a kind of women's movement standing *in sharpest opposition* to the movement which has hitherto been the center of public attention. This is true if for no other immediate reason than that in this case at least, an effort is made to provide increasing support and higher social esteem for that type of woman the representatives of which, in accordance with the above-described selective tendency of the industrialistic system, stand in most extreme and constant danger of being cast down into prostitution. This is indeed the inner tragedy of this our system: that within it only the unfeminine women (given equal preconditions of wealth and status) can rise up economically to independence on their own powers, while the feminine ones must of necessity end up in a situation that separates them by only one step—according to the social "value judgments" hitherto dominant—from prostitution (and all the more so as the men, too, whom the system raises up economically, are all the less inclined for that very reason to marry a poor girl who awakens love in them, the more calculating they are by nature). Those knowledgeable about this female stratum standing on the " borderline" affirm that its numbers are not only increasing constantly, but also that the human qualities and manners, as well as education and beauty of these girls and women, have improved enormously in recent decades. Given the persistence of the above "tendency," this is hardly miraculous. Now while the older women's movement was directed solely towards the goals of the *economically ascending* woman, the movements just named above seem to express a newly awakened interest for the stratum just mentioned, an interest born of thoroughly healthy and *authentically* feminine instincts. And an interest in particular for that portion of the stratum that, despite high human qualities, and precisely because of its specifically feminine ones, is condemned to sink into the chaos of society, unable to follow those goals that were all the older women's movement propagated.

The specific aims of that new movement need not be entered into here. It has just been too-little realized that, as the aforementioned more authentic and more feminine women's element has sunk—not necessarily into prostitution itself, yet in that direction—a new female *class* has in a certain sense also arisen, just like that new social class of "private white-collar employees" between the laboring strata and the entrepreneurs, a class whose independence of and singularity vis-à-vis the working class were likewise long completely misjudged. In any case it will never do in the long run to deal with this class of women in terms of social value judgments and by finally putting it in a juridical category analogous to prostitution. I entertain the conviction—for causes not to be discussed here—that matrimony by its nature does not suffer divorce, and that continued facilitation of divorce and in general the whole modern juridical fumbling around in an attempt to heal the institution of marriage (in contradistinction to a deeper consciousness of its ethical spirit) can have *in no way*, any favorable effects. It is a *false* method, wanting to heal our present-day relations between the sexes by debasing marriage—the ultimate meaning of which is religious and eternal—through relativizing the conditions upon which it rests. But the conditions described above require all the more that *social judgment* with regard to unmarried mothers and illegitimate children, as well as regard to the moral and legal obligations of the man towards them, take on a wholly different form. It will not do to lump this new stratum of women together with that of prostitution, and it will not do to apportion in so niggardly fashion the moral and legal obligations of the man towards representatives of this stratum, as has been hitherto customary. Help is promised here not by reducing the punishment for abortion, a measure that in very fact *presupposes* the moral and social righteousness of that social ostracism of illegitimate mothers and children, the fear of which forms the principal motive for that terrible crime, but rather a considerable diminution of that ostracism, indeed a certain kind of social and juridical recognition and protection of the *lasting* state of love and the children resulting from it, as well as institution of specific legal guarantees for the women and children in question.

No so-called "new ethic" is required here, but rather the extension of our Christian ethos to take into account that new stratum of women that has not previously existed as a class and therefore did not need to be taken into account. No need to alter principles, but rather to recognize new social *facts*. Both the moral value judgments and the legally and customarily recognized forms of sexual association suffer today from inadequate *differentiation*, while the real forms of this association long since evince a rich differentiation. Our social–moral value judgments and our legal forms are here modeled on a far older state of society, in which a clear middle stratum had not yet elevated itself between matrimony and prostitution. Therefore: not "marriage reform," but rather of form of permanent love relationship and its offspring, with socially recognized but limited claims, subordinated naturally to those of marriage, and juridically expressible, as well as increased welfare and public assistance for illegitimate children.

C. S. Lewis

British novelist, Christian apologist and philosopher, 1898–1963.

From a letter to Eddison. This is a facetious response to Eddison's suggestion that Lewis must be a misogynist.

. . .It is a thing openlie manifeste to all but disards [idiots] and verie goosecaps that feminitee is to itself an imperfection, being placed by the Pythagoreans in the sinister column with matter and mortalitie. Of which we see dailie ensample in that men do gladlie withdraw into their own societie and when they would be either merrie or grave stint not to shutte the dore upon Love herself, whereas we see no woman . . . but will not of good will escape from her sisters and seeke to the conversation of men, as liking by instincte of Nature so to receyve the perfection she lacketh.

From *Mere Christianity_*

And, of course, the promise, made when I am in love and because I am in love, to be true to the beloved as long as I live, commits one to being true even if I cease to be in love. A promise must be about things that I can do, about actions: no one can promise to go on feeling in a certain way. He might as well promise never to have a headache or always to feel hungry. But what, it may be asked, is the use of keeping two people together if they are no longer in love? There are several sound, social reasons; to provide a home for their children, to protect the woman (who has probably sacrificed or damaged her own career by getting married) from being dropped whenever the man is tired of her.

. . . In Christian marriage the man is said to be the "head." Two questions obviously arise here. (1) Why should there be a head at all—why not equality? (2) Why should it be the man?

(1) The need for some head follows from the idea that marriage is permanent. Of course, as long as the husband and wife are agreed, no question of a head need arise; and we may hope that this will be the normal state of affairs in a Christian marriage. But when there is a real disagreement, what is to happen? Talk it over, of course; but I am assuming they have done that and still failed to reach agreement. What do they do next? They cannot decide by a majority vote, for in a council of two there can be no majority. Surely, only one or other of two things can happen: either they must separate and go their own ways or else one or other of them must have a casting vote. If marriage is permanent, one or other party must, in the last resort, have the power of deciding the family policy. You cannot have a permanent association without a constitution.

(2) If there must be a head, why the man? Well, firstly, is there any very serious wish that it should be the woman? As I have said, I am not married myself, but as far as I can see, even a woman who wants to be the head of her own house does not usually admire the same state of things when she finds it going on next door. She is much more likely to say "Poor Mr. X! Why he allows that appalling woman to boss him about the way she does is more than I can imagine." I do not think she is even very flattered if anyone mentions the fact of her own "headship." There must be something unnatural about the rule of wives over husbands, because the wives themselves are half-ashamed of it and despise the husbands whom they rule. But there is also another reason; and here I speak quite frankly as a bachelor, because it is a reason you can see from outside even better than from inside. The relations of the family to the outer world—what might be called its foreign policy—must depend, in the last resort, upon the man, because he always ought to be, and usually is, much more just to the outsiders. A woman is primarily fighting for her own children and husband against the rest of the world. Naturally, almost, in a sense, rightly, their claims override, for her, all other claims. She is the special trustee of their interests. The function of the husband is to see that this natural preference of hers is not given its head. He has the last word in order to protect other people from the intense family patriotism of the wife. If anyone doubts this, let me ask a simple question. If your dog has bitten the child next door, or if your child has hurt the dog next door, which would you sooner have to deal with, the master of that house or the mistress? Or, if you are a married woman, let me ask you this question. Much as you admire your husband, would you not say that his chief failing is his tendency not to stick up for his rights and yours against the neighbors as vigorously as you would like? A bit of an Appeaser?

Simone de Beauvoir

French existentialist philosopher, novelist, and feminist, b. 1908, widely known for her autobiographical works.

From *The Ethics of Ambiguity*

There are beings whose life slips by in an infantile world because, having been kept in a state of servitude and ignorance, they have no means of breaking the ceiling which is stretched over their heads. Like the child, they can exercise their freedom, but only within this universe which has been set up before them, without them. This is the case, for example, of slaves who have not raised themselves to the consciousness of their slavery. The southern planters were not altogether in the wrong in considering the negroes who docilely submitted to their paternalism as "grown-up children." To the extent that they respected the world of the whites the situation of the black slaves was exactly an infantile situation. This is also the situation of women in many civilizations; they can only submit to the laws, the gods, the customs, and the truths created by the males. Even today in western countries, among women who have not had in their work an apprenticeship of freedom, there are still many who take shelter in the shadow of men; they adopt without discussion the opinions and values recognized by their husband or their lover, and that allows them to develop childish qualities which are forbidden to adults because they are based on a feeling of irresponsibility. If what is called women's futility often has so much charm and grace, if it sometimes has a genuinely moving character, it is because it manifests a pure and gratuitous taste for existence, like the games of children; it is the absence of the serious. The unfortunate thing is that in many cases this thoughtlessness, this gaiety, these charming inventions imply a deep complicity with the world of men which they seem so graciously to be contesting, and it is a mistake to be astonished, once the structure which shelters them seems to be in danger, to see sensitive, ingenuous, and lightminded women show themselves harder, more bitter, and even more furious or cruel than their masters. It is then that we discover the difference which distinguishes them from an actual child: the child's situation is imposed upon him, whereas the woman (I mean the western woman of today) chooses it or at least consents to it. Ignorance and error are facts as inescapable as prison walls. The Negro slave of the eighteenth century, the Mohammedan woman enclosed in a harem have no instrument, be it in thought or by astonishment or anger, which permits them to attack the civilization which oppresses them. Their behavior is defined and can be judged only within this given situation, and it is possible that in this situation, limited like every human situation, they realize a perfect assertion of their freedom. But once there appears a possibility of liberation, it is resignation of freedom not to exploit the possibility, a resignation which implies dishonesty and which is a positive fault.

From *The Second Sex*

For a long time I have hesitated to write a book on woman. The subject is irritating, especially to women; and it is not new. Enough ink has been spilled in the quarreling over feminism, now practically over, and perhaps we should say no more about it. It is still talked about, however, for the voluminous nonsense uttered during the last century seems to have done little to illuminate the problem. After all, is there a problem? And if so, what is it? Are there women, really? Most assuredly the theory of the eternal feminine still has its adherents who will whisper in your ear: "Even in Russia women still are *women*"; and other erudite persons—sometimes the very same—say with a sigh: "Woman is losing her way, woman is lost." One wonders if women still exist, if they will always exist, whether or not it is desirable that they should, what place they occupy in this world, what their place should be. "What has become of women?" was asked recently in an ephemeral magazine.

But first we must ask: what is a woman? "*Tota mulier in utero*," says one, "woman is a womb." But in speaking of certain women, connoisseurs declare that they are not women, although they are equipped with a uterus like the rest. All agree in recognizing the fact that females exist in the human species; today as always they make up about one half of humanity. And yet we are told that femininity is in danger; we are exhorted to be women, remain women, become women. It would appear, then, that every female human being is not necessarily a woman; to be so considered she must share in that mysterious and threatened reality known as femininity. Is this attribute something secreted by the ovaries? Or is it a Platonic essence, a product of the philosophic imagination? Is a rustling petticoat enough to bring it down to earth? Although some women try zealously to incarnate this essence, it is hardly patentable. It is frequently described in vague and dazzling terms that seem to have been borrowed from the vocabulary of the seers, and indeed in the times of St. Thomas it was considered an essence as certainly defined as the somniferous virtue of the poppy. . . .

If her functioning as a female is not enough to define woman, if we decline also to explain her through "the eternal feminine," and if nevertheless we admit, provisionally, that women do exist, then we must face the question: what is a woman?

To state the question is, to me, to suggest, at once, a preliminary answer. The fact that I ask it is in itself significant. A man would never get the notion of writing a book on the peculiar situation of the human male. But if I wish to define myself, I must first of all say: "I am a woman"; on this truth must be based all further discussion. A man never begins by presenting himself as an individual of a certain sex; it goes without saying that he is a man. The terms *masculine* and *feminine* are used symmetrically only as a matter of form, as on legal papers. In actuality the relation of the two sexes is not quite like that of two electrical poles, for man represents both the positive and the neutral, as is indicated by the common use of *man* to designate human beings in general; whereas woman represents only the negative, defined by limiting criteria, without reciprocity. In the midst of an abstract discussion it is vexing to hear a man say: "You think thus and so because you are a woman"; but I know that my only defense is to reply: "I think thus and so because it is true," thereby removing my subjective self from the argument. It would be out of the question to reply: "And you think the contrary because you are a man," for it is understood that the fact of being a man is no peculiarity. A man is in the right in being a man; it is the woman who is in the wrong. It amounts to this: just as for the ancients there was an absolute vertical with reference to which the oblique was defined, so there is an absolute human type, the masculine. Woman has ovaries, a uterus; these peculiarities imprison her in her subjectivity, circumscribe her within the limits of her own nature. It is often said that she thinks with her glands. Man superbly ignores the fact that his anatomy also includes glands, such as the testicles, and that they secrete hormones. He thinks of his body as a direct and normal connection with the world, which he believes he apprehends objectively, whereas he regards the body of woman as a hindrance, a prison, weighed down by everything peculiar to it. "The female is a female by virtue of a certain *lack* of qualities," said Aristotle; "we should regard the female nature as afflicted with a natural defectiveness." And St. Thomas for his part pronounced woman to be an "imperfect man," an "incidental" being. This is symbolized in Genesis where Eve is depicted as made from what Bossuet called "a supernumerary bone" of Adam.

Thus humanity is male and man defines woman not in herself but as relative to him; she is not regarded as an autonomous being. Michelet writes: "Woman, the relative being. . . ." And Benda is most positive in his *Rapport d'Uriel*: "The body of man makes sense in itself quite apart from that of woman, whereas the latter seems wanting in significance by itself. . . . Man can think of himself without woman. She cannot think of herself without man." And she is simply what man decrees; thus she is called "the sex," by which is meant that she appears essentially to the male as a sexual being. For him she is sex—absolute sex, no less. She is defined and differentiated with reference to man and not he with reference to her; she is the incidental, the inessential as opposed to the essential. He is the Subject, he is the Absolute—she is the Other. . . .

Man is accustomed to asserting himself; his clients believe in his competence; he can act naturally: he infallibly makes an impression. Woman does not inspire the same feeling of security; she affects a lofty air, she drops it, she makes too much of it. In business, in administrative work, she is precise, fussy, quick to show aggressiveness. As in her studies, she lacks ease, dash, audacity. In the effort to achieve she gets tense. Her activity is a succession of challenges and self-affirmations. This is the great defect that lack of assurance engenders: the subject cannot forget himself. He does not aim gallantly toward some goal: he seeks rather to make good in prescribed ways. In boldly setting out toward ends, one risks disappointments; but one also obtains unhoped-for results; caution condemns to mediocrity.

We rarely encounter in the independent woman a taste for adventure and for experience for its own sake, or a disinterested curiosity; she seeks "to have a career" as other women build a nest of happiness; she remains dominated, surrounded, by the male universe, she lacks the audacity to break through its ceiling, she does not passionately lose herself in her projects. She still regards her life as an immanent enterprise: her aim is not at an objective but, through the objective, at her subjective success. This is a very conspicuous attitude, for example, among American women; they like having a job and proving to themselves that they are capable of handling it properly; but they are not passionately concerned with the *content* of their tasks. Woman similarly has a tendency to attach too much importance to minor setbacks and modest successes; she is turn by turn discouraged or puffed up with vanity. When a success has been anticipated, one takes it calmly; but it becomes an intoxicating triumph when one has been doubtful of obtaining it. This is the excuse when women become addled with importance and plume themselves ostentatiously over their least accomplishments. They are forever looking back to see how far they have come, and that interrupts their progress. By this procedure they can have honorable careers, but not accomplish great things. It must be added that many men are also unable to build any but mediocre careers. It is only in comparison with the best of them that woman—save for very rare exceptions—seems to us to be trailing behind. The reasons I have given are sufficient explanation, and in no way mortgage the future. What woman essentially lacks today for doing great things is forgetfulness of herself; but to forget oneself it is first of all necessary to be firmly assured that now and for the future one has found oneself. Newly come into the world of men, poorly seconded by them, woman is still too busily occupied to search for herself. . . .

A world where men and women would be equal is easy to visualize, for that precisely is what the Soviet Revolution *promised*: women raised and trained exactly like men were to work under the same conditions* and for the same wages. Erotic liberty was to be recognized by custom, but the sexual act was not to be considered a ''service'' to be paid for; woman was to be *obliged* to provide herself with other ways of earning a living; marriage was to be based on a free agreement that the spouses could break at will; maternity was to be voluntary, which meant that contraception and abortion were to be authorized and that, on the other hand, all mothers and their children were to have exactly the same rights, in or out of marriage; pregnancy leaves were to be paid for by the State, which would assume charge of the children, signifying not that they would be *taken away* from their parents, but that they would not be *abandoned* to them.

But is it enough to change laws, institutions, customs, public opinion, and the whole social context, for men and women to become truly equal? ''Women will always be women,'' say the skeptics. Other seers prophesy that in casting off their femininity they will not succeed in changing themselves into men and they will become monsters. This would be to admit that the woman of today is a creation of nature; it must be repeated once more that in human society nothing is natural and that woman, like much else, is a product elaborated by civilization. The intervention of others in her destiny is fundamental: if this action took a different direction, it would produce a quite different result. Woman is determined not by her hormones or by mysterious instincts, but by the manner in which her body and her relation to the world are modified through the action of others than herself. The abyss that separates the adolescent boy and girl has been deliberately opened out between them since earliest childhood; later on, woman could not be other than what she *was made,* and that past was bound to shadow her for life. If we appreciate its influence, we see clearly that her destiny is not predetermined for all eternity. . . .

If the little girl were brought up from the first with the same demands and rewards, the same severity and the same freedom, as her brothers, taking part in the same studies, the same games, promised the same fu-

---

*That certain too laborious occupations were to be closed to women is not in contradiction to this project. Even among men there is an increasing effort to obtain adaptation to profession; their varying physical and mental capacities limit their possibilities of choice; what is asked is that, in any case, no line of sex or caste be drawn.

ture, surrounded with women and men who seemed to her undoubted equals, the meanings of the castration complex and of the Œdipus complex would be profoundly modified. Assuming on the same basis as the father the material and moral responsibility of the couple, the mother would enjoy the same lasting prestige; the child would perceive around her an androgynous world and not a masculine world. Were she emotionally more attracted to her father—which is not even sure—her love for him would be tinged with a will to emulation and not a feeling of powerlessness; she would not be oriented toward passivity. Authorized to test her powers in work and sports, competing actively with the boys, she would not find the absence of the penis—compensated by the promise of a child—enough to give rise to an inferiority complex; correlatively, the boy would not have a superiority complex if it were not instilled into him and if he looked up to women with as much respect as to men.* The little girl would not seek sterile compensation in narcissism and dreaming, she would not take her fate for granted; she would be interested in what she was *doing,* she would throw herself without reserve into undertakings.

I have already pointed out how much easier the transformation of puberty would be if she looked beyond it, like the boys, toward a free adult future: menstruation horrifies her only because it is an abrupt descent into femininity. She would also take her young eroticism in much more tranquil fashion if she did not feel a frightened disgust for her destiny as a whole; coherent sexual information would do much to help her over this crisis. And thanks to coeducational schooling, the august mystery of Man would have no occasion to enter her mind: it would be eliminated by everyday familiarity and open rivalry.

Objections raised against this system always imply respect for sexual taboos; but the effort to inhibit all sex curiosity and pleasure in the child is quite useless; one succeeds only in creating repressions, obsessions, neuroses. The excessive sentimentality, homosexual fervors, and platonic crushes of adolescent girls, with all their train of silliness and frivolity, are much more injurious than a little childish sex play and a few definite sex experiences. It would be beneficial above all for the young girl not to be influenced against taking charge herself of her own existence, for then she would not seek a demigod in the male—merely a comrade, a friend, a partner. Eroticism and love would take on the nature of free transcendence and not that of resignation; she could experience them as a relation between equals. There is no intention, of course, to remove by a stroke of the pen all the difficulties that the child has to overcome in changing into

---

*I knew a little boy of eight who lived with his mother, aunt, and grandmother, all independent and active women, and his weak old half-crippled grandfather. He had a crushing inferiority complex in regard to the feminine sex, although he made efforts to combat it. At school he scorned comrades and teachers because they were miserable males.

an adult; the most intelligent, the most tolerant education could not relieve the child of experiencing things for herself; what could be asked is that obstacles should not be piled gratuitously in her path. Progress is already shown by the fact that "vicious" little girls are no longer cauterized with a red-hot iron. Psychoanalysis has given parents some instruction, but the conditions under which, at the present time, the sexual training and initiation of woman are accomplished are so deplorable that none of the objections advanced against the idea of a radical change could be considered valid. It is not a question of abolishing in woman the contingencies and miseries of the human condition, but of giving her the means for transcending them.

Woman is the victim ·of no mysterious fatality; the peculiarities that identify her as specifically a woman get their importance from the significance placed upon them. They can be surmounted, in the future, when they are regarded in new perspective. Thus, as we have seen, through her erotic experience woman feels—and often detests—the domination of the male; but this is no reason to conclude that her ovaries condemn her to live forever on her knees. Virile aggressiveness seems like a lordly privilege only within a system that in its entirety conspires to affirm masculine sovereignty; and woman *feels* herself profoundly passive in the sexual act only because she already *thinks* of herself as such. Many modern women who lay claim to their dignity as human beings still envisage their erotic life from the standpoint of a tradition of slavery: since it seems to them humiliating to lie beneath the man, to be penetrated by him, they grow tense in frigidity. But if the reality were different, the meaning expressed symbolically in amorous gestures and postures would be different, too: a woman who pays and dominates her lover can, for example, take pride in her superb idleness and consider that she is enslaving the male who is actively exerting himself. And here and now there are many sexually well-balanced couples whose notions of victory and defeat are giving place to the idea of an exchange.

As a matter of fact, man, like woman is flesh, therefore passive, the plaything of his hormones and of the species, the restless prey of his desires. And she, like him, in the midst of the carnal fever, is a consenting, a voluntary gift, an activity; they live out in their several fashions the strange ambiguity of existence made body. In those combats where they think they confront one another, it is really against the self that each one struggles, projecting into the partner that part of the self which is repudiated; instead of living out the ambiguities of their situation, each tries to make the other bear the abjection and tries to reserve the honor for the self. If, however, both should assume the ambiguity with a clear-sighted modesty, correlative of an authentic pride, they would see each other as equals and would live out their erotic drama in amity. The fact that we are human beings is infinitely more important than all the peculiarities that distinguish human beings from one another; it is never the given that confers superiorities: "virtue," as the ancients called it, is defined at the level of "that which depends on us." In both sexes is played out the same drama of the flesh and the spirit, of finitude and transcendence; both are gnawed away by time and laid in wait for by death, they have the same essential need for one another; and they can gain from their liberty the same glory. If they were to taste it, they would no longer be tempted to dispute fallacious privileges, and fraternity between them could then come into existence.

I shall be told that all this is utopian fancy, because woman cannot be "made over" unless society has first made her really the equal of man. Conservatives have never failed in such circumstances to refer to that vicious circle; history, however, does not revolve. If a caste is kept in a state of inferiority, no doubt it remains inferior; but liberty can break the circle. Let the Negroes vote and they become worthy of having the vote: let woman be given responsibilities and she is able to assume them. The fact is that oppressors cannot be expected to make a move of gratuitous generosity; but at one time the revolt of the oppressed, at another time even the very evolution of the privileged caste itself, creates new situations; thus men have been led, in their own interest, to give partial emancipation to women: it remains only for women to continue their ascent, and the successes they are obtaining are an encouragement for them to do so. It seems almost certain that sooner or later they will arrive at complete economic and social equality, which will bring about an inner metamorphosis.

However this may be, there will be some to object that if such a world is possible it is not desirable. When woman is "the same" as her male, life will lose its salt and spice. This argument, also, has lost its novelty: those interested in perpetuating present conditions are always in tears about the marvelous past that is about to disappear, without having so much as a smile for the young future. It is quite true that doing away with the slave trade meant death to the great plantations, magnificent with azaleas and camellias, it meant ruin to the whole refined Southern civilization. The attics of time have received its rare old laces along with the clear pure voices of the Sistine *castrati,* and there is a certain "feminine charm" that is also on the way to the same dusty repository. I agree that he would be a barbarian indeed who failed to appreciate exquisite flowers, rare lace, the crystal-clear voice of the eunuch, and feminine charm.

. . .One can appreciate the beauty of flowers, the charm of women, and appreciate them at their true value; if these treasures cost blood or misery, they must be sacrificed.

But in truth this sacrifice seems to men a peculiarly heavy one; few of them really wish in their hearts for woman to succeed in making it; those among them who hold woman in contempt see in the sacrifice nothing for them to gain, those who cherish her see too much that they would lose. And it is true that the evolution now in progress threatens more than feminine charm alone: in beginning to exist for herself, woman will relinquish the function as double and mediator to which she owes her privileged place in the masculine universe; to man, caught between the silence of nature and the demanding presence of other free beings, a creature who is at once his like and a passive thing seems a great treasure. The guise in which he conceives his companion may be mythical, but the experiences for which she is the source or the pretext are none the less real: there are hardly any more precious, more intimate, more ardent. There is no denying that feminine dependence, inferiority, woe, give women their special character; assuredly woman's autonomy, if it spares men many troubles, will also deny them many conveniences; assuredly there are certain forms of the sexual adventure which will be lost in the world of tomorrow. But this does not mean that love, happiness, poetry, dream, will be banished from it.

Let us not forget that our lack of imagination always depopulates the future; for us it is only an abstraction; each one of us secretly deplores the absence there of the one who was himself. But the humanity of tomorrow will be living in its flesh and in its conscious liberty; that time will be its present and it will in turn prefer it. New relations of flesh and sentiment of which we have no conception will arise between the sexes; already, indeed, there have appeared between men and women friendships, rivalries, complicities, comradeships—chaste or sensual—which past centuries could not have conceived. To mention one point, nothing could seem to me more debatable than the opinion that dooms the new world to uniformity and hence to boredom. I fail to see that this present world is free from bordeom or that liberty ever creates uniformity.

To begin with, there will always be certain differences between man and woman; her eroticism, and therefore her sexual world, have a special form of their own and therefore cannot fail to engender a sensuality, a sensitivity, of a special nature. This means that her relations to her own body, to that of the male, to the child, will never be identical with those the male bears to his own body, to that of the female, and to the child; those who make much of "equality in difference" could not with good grace refuse to grant me the possible existence of differences in equality. Then again, it is institutions that create uniformity. Young and pretty, the slaves of the harem are always the same in the sultan's embrace; Christianity gave eroticism its savor of sin and legend when it endowed the human female with a soul; if society restores her sovereign individuality to woman, it will not thereby destroy the power of love's embrace to move the heart.

It is nonsense to assert that revelry, vice, ecstasy, passion, would become impossible if man and woman were equal in concrete matters; the contradictions that put the flesh in opposition to the spirit, the instant to time, the swoon of immanence to the challenge of transcendence, the absolute of pleasure to the nothingness of forgetting, will never be resolved; in sexuality will always be materialized the tension, the anguish, the joy, the frustration, and the triumph of existence. To emancipate woman is to refuse to confine her to the relations she bears to man, not to deny them to her; let her have her independent existence and she will continue nonetheless to exist for him *also*: mutually recognizing each other as subject, each will yet remain for the other an *other*. The reciprocity of their relations will not do away with the miracles—desire, possession, love, dream, adventure—worked by the division of human beings into two separate categories; and the words that move us—giving, conquering, uniting—will not lose their meaning. On the contrary, when we abolish the slavery of half of humanity, together with the whole system of hypocrisy that it implies, then the "division" of humanity will reveal its genuine significance and the human couple will find its true form.

José Ortega y Gasset

Spanish essayist and existential philosopher, 1883–1955.

From *Man and People*

The appearance of the She is a particular case of the appearance of the Other, and one that shows us the inadequacy of any theory that, like Husserl's, explains the presence of the Other as such by a projection of our inward person on his body. I have pointed out that the expression "alter ego" was not only paradoxical but contradictory and hence improper. *Ego,* strictly, is something that I alone am, and if I refer it to an Other, I have to change its meaning. *Alter ego* has to be understood analogically: there is in the abstract Other *something* that is in him what the *Ego* is in me. The two *Egos,* mine and the analogical one, have in common only certain abstract components, which, being abstract, are unreal. Only the concrete is real. Among these common components is one that, provisionally, was the most important for our study—the capacity to respond to me, to reciprocate. But in the case of a woman, the striking thing is the heterogeneity between my ego and hers, because her response is not the response of an abstract Ego—the abstract Ego does not respond, because it is an abstraction. Her response is already, in itself, from the beginning and with no further ado, feminine, and I am aware of it as such. Husserl's supposition, then, proves clearly invalid; the transposition of my ego, which is irremediably masculine, into a woman's body could only produce an extreme case of a virago, but it is inadequate to explain that prodigious discovery, the appearance of the feminine human being, different from me.

It will be said—and this has led to many mistakes that have been not only theoretical but practical, political (suffragettes, legal equalization of men and women, and so on)—that the woman, since she is a human being, is not "completely different from me." But this error springs from another and far greater one, caused by the fact that no true idea of the relation between the abstract and the concrete has ever reached the generality of mankind. In an object we can isolate one of its components, for example, its color. This operation of isolation, in which we fix our attention on one component of the thing, thus mentally separating it from the other components with which it inseparably exists, is what we call "abstraction." But by abstracting it *from the others* we have destroyed its reality, not only because it does not and cannot exist in isolation—there *is* no color without the surface of particular form and particular dimensions over which it extends—but because its content even as color is different in accordance with this form and these dimensions of the surface. Which means that the other components act on it in turn, giving it its particular character. Similarly, to say that a woman is a being like myself *because* she is capable of responding to me, is to say nothing real, because in these words I ignore and omit the content of her responses, the peculiar *how* of her response. . . .

You will ask: What primary characters do we discern as soon as a woman is present to us, which constitute her elemental femininity for us and produce this paradoxical effect that it is they—even though they are only compresent—that impregnate her body with femininity, that make it a feminine body? There is no room to describe them all here, and it will suffice if I point out three:

(1) The instant we see a woman, we seem to have before us a being whose inward humanity is characterized, in contrast to our own male humanity and that of other men, by being essentially confused. Let us waive the pejorative connotation with which this word is usually understood. Confusion is not a defect in woman, any more than it is a defect in man not to have wings. Even less, in fact—for it makes some sense to wish that man had wings like hawks and angels, but it does not make sense to want woman to stop being "substantially" confused. This would amount to destroying the delight that woman is to man by virtue of her confused being. Man, on the contrary, is made up of clarities. Everything in him is given with clarity. You are to understand, of course, "subjective clarity," not actual, objective clarity concerning the world and his fellow human beings. Perhaps everything that he thinks is sheer nonsense; but within himself, he sees himself clearly. Hence in the masculine inwardness everything normally has strict and definite lines, which makes the human male a being full of rigid angles. Woman, on the other hand, lives in a perpetual twilight; she is never sure whether she loves or not, will do something or not do it, is repentant or unrepentant. In woman there is neither midday nor midnight; she is a creature of twilight. Hence she is constitutionally secret. Not because she does not report what she feels and what befalls her, but because normally she cannot express what she feels and what befalls her. It is a secret for her too. This gives woman the softness of forms which belongs to her "soul" and which for us is the typically feminine. In contrast to man's angles, woman's inwardness seems to have only delicate curves. Confusion, like the cloud, has rounded forms. . . .

(2) Because, in fact, this inwardness that we discover in the feminine

body and which we shall call "woman" presents itself to us from the out-set as a form of humanity inferior to the masculine. This is the second primary characteristic in the appearance of the She. In a time like ours in which, though to a diminishing degree, we suffer under the tyrannical myth of "equality," a time in which we everywhere find the mania of believing that things are better when they are equal, the foregoing state-ment will irritate many people. But irritation is no guarantee of perspicac-ity. In the presence of Woman we men immediately divine a creature who on the level of "humanness" has a vital station somewhat lower than ours. No other being has this twofold condition—being human, and being less so than a man is. This duality is the source of the unparalleled delight that woman is for the masculine man. The aforesaid equalitarian mania has recently resulted in an attempt to minimize what is one of the funda-mental facts in human destiny—the fact of sexual duality. Simone de Beauvoir—a distinguished writer in that capital of graphomania, Paris—has written a very long book on "The Second Sex." This estimable lady finds it intolerable that woman should be considered—and consider herself—constitutively referable to man and hence not centered in herself, as man would seem to be. Mademoiselle de Beauvoir thinks that to consist in "reference to another" is incompatible with the idea of person, which is rooted in "freedom toward oneself." But it is not clear why there must be such incompatibility between being free and consisting in reference to another human being. After all, the amount of reference to woman which constitutes the human male is by no means small. But the human male consists pre-eminently in reference to his profession. Professionality—even in the most primitive of primitive men—is proba-bly the most masculine trait of all, to the point where "doing nothing," having no profession, is felt to be something effeminating in a man. Ma-demoiselle de Beauvoir's book, so prodigal of pages, leaves us with the impression that the writer, very fortunately, confuses things and thus displays in her work the characteristic confusion that assures us of the genuineness of her feminine being. On the other hand, to believe, as fol-lows from her argument, that a woman is more a person when she does not "exist" preoccupied by man but occupied in writing a book on "the second sex," seems to us something decidedly more than simple confu-sion.

The duality of the sexes has as its consequence that men and women are constituted by their reference to one another—and to such a degree that any insufficiency in either men's or women's living in reference to the other sex is something that in every case requires explanation and jus-tification. It is another matter that this reference to the other sex, though constitutive in both, has a preeminent place in woman, while in man its autonomy is reduced by other references. With all the qualifications and reservations that "case histories" would suggest, we may affirm that woman's destiny is "*to be* in view of man." But this formula in no way diminishes her freedom. The human being, as free, is free before and in the face of his destiny. He can accept it or resist it, or, what is the same thing, he can be it or not be it. Our destiny is not only what we have been and now are; it is not only the past, but, coming from the past, it projects itself, in openness, toward the future. This retrospective fatality—what we now are—does not enslave our future, does not inexorably predetermine what we are not yet. Our future being emerges from our freedom, a continuous spring forever flowing out of itself. But freedom presupposes plans of action among which to choose, and these plans can only be created by using the past—our own and others'—as a material that inspires us to new combinations. The past then—our destiny—does not influence us in imperative and mechanical form, but as the guiding thread of our inspirations. We are not inexorably circumscribed in it; rather, at every moment it launches us upon free creation of our future being. Hence the antique formula could not be improved: *Fata ducunt, non trahunt*, "Destiny directs, it does not drag." . . .

All this brief "philosophical" embroidery on past and future, destiny and freedom, comes down to opposing the tendency of certain present-day "philosophers" who invite woman to plan her "future being" by ceasing to be what she has been until now, namely, woman—all in the name of freedom and the idea of the person. Now, what woman has been in the past, her femininity, does not derive from her freedom and person having been negated, either by men or by a biological fatality; on the contrary, it is the result of a series of free creations, of fertile inspirations that have sprung as much from her as from man. For the human being, the zoological duality of the sexes is not—just as the other subhuman conditions are not—something inexorably imposed, but the very opposite—a theme for inspiration. What we call "woman" is not a product of nature but an invention of history, just as art is. This is why the copious pages that Mademoiselle de Beauvoir devotes to the biology of the sexes are so little fertile, so completely beside the point. Only when we are engaged in imagining the origin of man need we keep constantly in mind the facts which the biology of evolution presents to us today—even though we can be certain that tomorrow it will present us others. But once man is man, we enter a world of freedom and creation. Instead of studying woman zoologically, it would be infinitely more fertile to contemplate her as a literary genre or an artistic tradition.

So let us, without a blush that would be pure snobbery, go back to calling woman the "weaker sex" with perfectly quiet consciences. . . .

This patent characteristic of weakness is the basis of woman's inferior vital rank. But, as it could not but be, this inferiority is the source and origin of the peculiar value that woman possesses in reference to man. For by virtue of it, woman makes us happy and *is happy herself, is happy in feeling that she is weak*. Indeed, only a being inferior to man can radically affirm his basic being—not his talents or his triumphs or his achievements, but the elemental condition of his person. The greatest admirer of the gifts that we may have does not corroborate and confirm us as does the woman who falls in love with us. And this is because, in sober truth, only woman knows how to love and is able to love—that is, to disappear in the other.

(3) The confusion of the feminine being appears to us together with its weakness and, in a way, as proceeding from it; but the weakness in its turn becomes compresent to us in the last primary characteristic of the three that I said I would describe.

The feminine ego is so radically different from our male ego that it displays the difference from the very first in something that could not be more elementary—in the fact that its relation to its body is different from the relation in which the masculine ego stands to its body. . . .

The comparative hyperesthesia of woman's organic sensations brings it about that her body exists for her more than man's does for him. Normally, we men forget our brother the body; we are not aware of possessing it except at the chill or burning hour of extreme pain or extreme pleasure. Between our purely psychic I and the outer world, nothing seems to be interposed. Woman, on the contrary, is constantly having her attention claimed by the liveliness of her intracorporeal sensations; she is always aware of her body as interposed between the world and her I, she always carries it before her, at once as a shield of defense and a vulnerable hostage. The consequences are clear: woman's whole psycic life is more involved with her body than man's; in other words, her soul is more corporeal—but, vice versa, her body lives more constantly and closely with her spirit; that is, her body is more permeated with soul. In fact, the feminine person displays a far higher degree of interpenetration between body and spirit than man. In man, comparatively speaking, each normally takes its own course; body and soul know little of each other and are not allied, rather, they act like irreconcilable enemies.

In this observation I believe we can find the cause for an eternal and enigmatic fact which runs through human history from one end to the other, and of which all the explanations so far given have been stupid or superficial—I refer to woman's age-old propensity to adorn and ornament her body. In the light of the idea that I am expounding, nothing could be more natural and at the same time inevitable. Her native physiological structure imposes on woman the habit of noticing, paying attention to her body, which ends by being the closest object in the perspective of her world. And since culture is only sustained reflection on that to which our attention prefers to turn, woman has created the remarkable culture of the body, which, historically, began in adornment, continued in cleanliness, and has ended in courtesy, that inspired feminine invention, which, finally, is the subtle culture of the gesture.

The result of this constant attention that woman devotes to her body is that her body appears to us from the first as impregnated, as wholly filled with soul. This is the foundation for the impression of weakness that her presence creates in us. Because in contrast to the firm and solid appearance of the body, the soul is a little tremulous, the soul is a little weak. In short, the erotic attraction that woman produces in man is not—as the ascetics have always told us in their blindness on these matters—aroused by the feminine body as body; rather, we desire a woman because Her body *is* a soul.

From *On Love*

The Role of Choice in Love

Nine-tenths of that which is attributed to sexuality is the work of our magnificent ability to imagine, which is no longer an instinct, but exactly the opposite: a creation. I merely wish to observe that the notorious disproportion between the sexuality of man and woman, which makes the normally spontaneous woman so conservative in "love," probably coincides with the fact that the human female usually enjoys less imaginative power than the male. Nature, cautiously and foresightedly, wanted it that way, because if the opposite had occurred and the woman were endowed with as much fantasy as the man, licentiousness would have flooded the planet and the human species would have disappeared, volatilized in sensuousness. . . .

Do not repeat, then, so calmly, as if you were saying something clear and simple, that a man falls in love with a woman "physically," and that shock at her character follows subsequently. What actually happens is that some people of both sexes fall in love with a body as such; but such action precisely reveals their specific mode of being. It is the lover possessed of a sensual character who suggests this preference; but it is necessary to add that such lovers are far less frequently encountered than people think. In women this condition is especially rare.

. . . As is well known, the feminine soul is much more integrated than that of the male; that is, the elements of a woman's nature cohere more thoroughly. As a consequence, the disassociation of sexual pleasure and love or ardor is less frequent in her than in the man. In the woman, the one is not aroused without the other. . . .

When the woman is studied from a greater distance and with a calmer eye, with a zoologist's gaze, it is seen with surprise that she tends to the utmost to take her time in whatever engages her, to take root in the custom, idea, or task set before her; in sum, to make a habit out of everything. And the persistent lack of understanding which in this respect exists between the two sexes is consequently touching: the man goes to the woman as to a party or an orgy, to an ectasy which will break the monotony of his existence, and almost always he finds a person who is only happy when engaged in everyday tasks, whether it be darning underwear or going dancing. So true is this that, with great surprise certainly, ethnographers show us that work was invented by women; work, that is, as the compulsory everyday chore, in contrast to enterprise, and such spontaneous activity as sports and adventure. For this reason it is the woman who creates trades: she is the first agriculturist, collector and ceramicist. . . .

Without the first taking notice, the amorous phenomenon cannot take place, although the latter need not necessarily follow. Of course fastening one's attention upon something creates such a favorable atmosphere for the germination of ardor, that it alone is normally equivalent to a beginning of love.

. . . A man famous for his talents possesses, in short, a superior chance of being noticed by a woman. This is sufficiently so that if the woman does not fall in love it is difficult to find an excuse. Such is the case of the great man, who generally enjoys dazzling notoriety. The indifference which the feminine sex feels toward him should, therefore, be multiplied by this important factor. The woman, consciously and not by accident, disdains the great man.

From the point of view of human selection, this fact means that the woman in her sentimental preferences does not collaborate, in the same way as does a man, in the perfection of the species. She tends rather to eliminate the best individuals, speaking from a masculine viewpoint—those who innovate and undertake lofty enterprises—and she manifests a decided enthusiasm for mediocrity. When one has spent a good part of his life with an alert eye, observing the comings and goings of women, it is not easy to harbor any illusion about the standard of her preferences. All the good intentions, which she sometimes shows, of becoming excited about superior men usually fail dismally and, on the other hand, she is seen swimming to her taste, as if in her element, when she circulates among mediocre men.

Thoughts on Standing Before the Marquesa de Santillana's Portrait

So marked is the difference between a man's and a woman's relationship with the public that it produces opposite signs. The more preparations and attentions the woman affects when appearing in public, the greater the distance she establishes between her public and her true personality. In like proportion as the adoration with which a woman surrounds herself increases, the number of males who feel eliminated from the right to her preferences increases and they know that they are doomed to the role of distant spectators. One could say that the purpose of the luxury and elegance, adornment and jewelry which a lady places between herself and others is to conceal her inner self, to make it more mysterious, remote, and inaccessible. The man, on the other hand, publicizes what he most esteems in himself, his most profound pride, those acts and labors into which he has poured the seriousness of his life. The woman possesses a theatrical exterior and a circumspect interior, while in the man it is the interior that is theatrical. The woman goes to the theater; the man carries it inside himself and is the impresario of his own life.

. . . The inner lives of a good number of men do not extend beyond words, and their sentiments are limited to an oral existence. There is in the woman, on the contrary, an instinct of concealment and secrecy: her soul lives as if its back were toward the outside world, hiding its inner passionate fermentation. Gestures of modesty are merely the symbolic form (see Darwin and Piderit) of this inner reserve. It is not actually her body, but rather her reactions to the man's intentions toward her body, which she wishes to defend from his glances. Confusion in a woman most frequently and most intensely arises from the same origin. This emotion is aroused by the fear of being caught off guard in her thoughts and inclinations. The greater our desire to keep something about our inner lives secret, the more exposed we are to confusion. It is usual, for example, for someone telling a lie to become confused, as if he were afraid that another's gaze would see through his mendaciousness and expose its true concealed meaning. The woman lives, however, in perpetual confusion, because she lives in perpetual self-concealment. A girl of fifteen generally has a greater number of secrets than an old man, and a woman of thirty more arcana than a Chief of State.

This possession of a personal, separate, and secret life, this lordship of an inner sanctum in which no one else is permitted to roam, is one of woman's superiorities over man. This is what constitutes a woman's innate "distinction," the tenuous, mystical means for placing a distance between herself and us. This "distinction" is, as Nietzsche saw very well, above all a *"pathos* of distance" between one individual and another. In view of woman's "distinction" friendship between women may be less intimate than between men. One could say that they possess a very clear awareness of where their own incommunicable life begins and where the next person's ends.

The real feminine existence, therefore, flows along masked and concealed, protected from the public by an apparent femininity constructed for the purpose of serving as a mask and plate of armor. I think that every intensely personal life has always had to isolate a fictitious personality, a kind of *dermato-psyche* to hold off and distract the hostile curiosity of inferior people, in order to be able, behind that bulwark, to devote itself freely to being what it is. This mask-personality—the exception in men—turns out to be natural in women.

Landscape with a Deer in the Background

"The more of a man one is, the more is he filled to the brim with rationality. Everything he does and achieves he does and achieves for a reason, especially for a practical reason. A woman's love, that divine surrender of her ultra-inner being which the impassioned woman makes, is perhaps the only thing which is not achieved by reasoning. The core of the feminine mind, no matter how intelligent the woman may be, is occupied by an irrational power. If the male is the rational being, the female is the irrational being. And that is the supreme delight which we find in her! The animal is also irrational, but it is not a person; it is incapable of self-awareness and of responding to us, of being aware of us. There is no room for relating or being intimate with it. The woman offers the man the magic opportunity of relating with another being *without reasoning,* of influencing, dominating, surrendering to another, without any reason entering into it. Believe me: if birds had the minimum personality necessary for being able to respond to us, we would all fall in love with birds and not with women. And, vice versa, if the normal male does not fall in love with another male, it is because he sees that the other man's mind is made up completely of rationality, logic, mathematics, poetry, business, and economy. What, from a masculine point of view, we call absurd and a woman's whim is precisely what attracts us. The world is admirably made by an excellent supervisor, and all of its parts are assembled. . . .

. . . The intelligent man feels a slight revulsion for the very talented woman, unless her over-rationality is compensated for by over-irrationality. The over-rational in a woman smacks of masculinity and, rather than love, he feels friendship and admiration for her.

Portrait of Salome

A serious study, not bogged down in anecdotes or in a casuistry of chance, would reveal to us that the essence of femininity exists in the fact that an individual feels her destiny totally fulfilled when she surrenders herself to another individual. Everything else that the woman does or is has an adjectival and derivative character. In opposition to this marvelous phenomenon, masculinity presents the deep-rooted instinct which impels it to take possession of another person. There exists, therefore, a pre-established harmony between woman and man; for the former, living means surrender; for the latter, living means taking possession; and both destinies, precisely because they are opposites, come to a perfect agreement.

It is an error to assume that the specific man and the specific woman will always conform purely and completely to this pattern; in fact conflict arises when deviations and interferences occur in the deep-rooted in-

stincts of masculinity and femininity. The classification of human beings
into men and women is, obviously, inexact; reality presents innumerable
gradations between both extremes. Biology demonstrates how physical
sexuality hovers indecisively over the embryo to the point that it is possible to subject it experimentally to a change of sex. Each existing individual represents a peculiar equation in which both genders participate, and
nothing is more infrequent than to find someone who is "all man" or "all
woman." What occurs in physical sexuality becomes even more noticeable when we observe psychological sexuality. According to the masculine
and feminine principle, the *Yin* and the *Yang* of Chinese tradition, both
spirits seem to struggle with each other and arrive at different forms of
compromise, which are the various types of man and woman.

Thus, Judith and Salome are two variations of that type of woman
which is most surprising because it is the most contradictory: the woman
of prey.

It would be a vain effort to attempt to speak adequately about either
figure without due length; therefore, I shall limit myself at this time to
presenting a very brief portrayal of Salome.

The growth of a Salome occurs only at the summit of society. In
Palestine she was a pampered, idle princess, and today she could be the
daughter of a banker or an oil king. The decisive factor is that her upbringing, in an atmosphere of potency, erased in her mind the dynamic
line which separates the real from the imaginary. All of her desires were
satisfied, and what was undesirable was eliminated from her environment. . . .

Salome would not have been a woman if she had not felt compelled to
surrender her person to another; but, imaginative and frigid woman that
she was, she surrendered to a vision, a daydream of her own making. In
this manner, her femininity found complete expression in an imaginary
dimension. . . .

For reasons that presently elude us, Salome came one day to believe
that she had found the embodiment of her vision on earth. Perhaps it is
merely a question of a *quid pro quo:* the coincidence of her paradigm with
this man of flesh and bone named John the Baptist was more negative
than anything else. His only resemblance to her ideal was that he was
different from other men. Salome always looks for a man who is so different from other men that he seems almost to belong to an unknown sex;
another sign of deformed femininity. . . .

A man feels love primarily as a violent desire to be loved, whereas for
a woman the primary experience is to feel love itself, the warm flow
which radiates from her being toward her beloved and the impulse toward
him. The need to be loved is felt by her only consequently and secondar-
ily. The normal woman is the opposite of the beast, who pounces on his
prey. She is the prey who pounces on the beast.

Salome, who does not love John the Baptist, nevertheless needs to be loved by him. She needs to take possession of his person, and in order to carry out this masculine desire she will employ all sorts of violence which normally the male uses to impose his will upon the environment. That is why, just as other women carry a lily in their hands, this woman carries a dismembered head in her marble-like fingers. It is her vital prey. With a rhythmic step, a swaying torso, a rooklike Hebrew face, she advances through the legend, and above her rigid head, with glassy eyes, her mien leans forward with the rapacious curve of a goshawk or falcon. . . .

In all events, the tragic flirtation between Salome, the princess, and John the Baptist, the intellectual, is too intricate and drawn-out a story for me to tell now.

Julián Marías

Spanish philosopher, b. 1914, a prominent disciple of Ortega.

From *Metaphysical Anthropology*

The disjunction between man *or* woman affects both man *and* woman, establishing a relationship of *polarity* between them. Each sex co-implicates the other, which is reflected in the biographical fact that each "complicates" the other. We shall say, then, that the sexuate condition is not a "quality" or "attribute" possessed by each man, nor does it consist in the *terms* of the disjunction, but in the disjunction itself, seen alternately from each of its terms. The sexuate condition is not even visible in an isolated life. We see it in each one of us as it is referred to the opposite sex, which means that we see it "from" each one of us rather than "in" ourselves. I cannot understand the reality "woman" without co-implicating the reality "man," *and vice versa,* which means that there is no "second sex," and that this interpretation differs enormously from some recent theories. . . .

Some languages have a word which signifies the human person without distinction, another to signify the male, and still another to designate the woman: . . . *ánthropos, anér,* and *gyné* in Greek: *homo, v ir,* and *mulier* in Latin; *Mensch, Mann,* and *Frau* in German; and in Spanish, certainly, *hombre, varón,* and *mujer.* But the fact is that the word *varón* is not used very much; it is hardly colloquial and, far from being the normal way of referring to the masculine human person, it specifically accentuates the masculine quality. The word "hombre" means both the person in general and the masculine person, as also happens in French—*homme, femme*—in english—"man," "woman"—and in many other languages. This identification of man with the male, obviously taking too much for granted, can have different shadings, and it would be interesting to pursue its semantic evolution in the different languages. It might be a manifestation of the basic social belief that "man" is primarily male and that woman is, at most, a secondary and appended "variant"; but it may be something else: the very clear consciousness of the special feminine condition, which must be recognized with a special word, while male traits are simply incorporated into those of the species.

The Biblical narrative of the creation of Eve, as it is told in Genesis, is revealing: while God creates Adam by breathing life and personality into the dust of which he has molded Adam's body, to create woman he takes one of the sleeping Adam's ribs, and with that already living and human reality, flesh of Adam's flesh and bone of his bone, makes Eve. Woman is even farther from Nature; she implies a higher initial degree of perfection, she is made from man's flesh, and perhaps from his dreams. It will be said that she is "derived," that she begins to exist after man, that she is a "second sex." Is this ture? If we wish to stay within the Biblical narrative, let us not forget the point of departure: the words of the Creator, "It is not good that the man should be alone." It is the proclamation of man's solitude and its unsuitability. If we want to speak of woman's "insufficiency," should we not recall this very plain expression of the insufficiency of man alone?

On the other hand, woman possesses the irreducibility she has as a person. Woman's somatic reality could be derived from Adam's rib, as the psychosomatic reality of children is derived from the germ cells, and therefore the organs, of their parents; but the "I" which each of them represents is, as we said before, absolutely irreducible, to the point that that form of innovation is what the word "creation" means.

All the attributes of human life are found in man and woman, in two different, diametrically opposed, versions. We have tried to describe exactly in what the virile figure of life consists; the pretension in which the fact of being a male—not simply "man"—lies. In other words, what the program or vital project is which happens to man through his disjunction with regard to woman, because he lives face-to-face with woman and is drawn toward her. Now we shall have to turn our attention to the other mode in which human life takes place.

Let us return once more to the face in which the person is presented and made visible, in which the original project is manifested. I have said that beauty is the "meaning" of woman's face. Does this mean that all women are beautiful? Of course not. It means something more important: that they must be beautiful. If they are not, it is not that they do not have beauty, but that beauty is lacking, that they are deprived of it and that they have to try to be beautiful. The woman who does not try to be beautiful does not function as a woman; she has withdrawn from her condition, has given up, has abdicated, has betrayed it—according to circumstances. In the best of cases, we will say that she has sacrificed it. (And then we would have to ask an important question: can that sacrifice be meritorious? Still more: is it licit? Is it possible to sacrifice something that is not a *thing*, but the most fundamental pretension? Would it not be a subtle form of human sacrifice?)

By this time the reader will have observed that when we speak of beauty we do not mean exclusively physical beauty—among other reasons, because the beauty which is called physical is not exclusively so—but personal feminine beauty. Man can also have beauty: perfection of form, harmony of movements, tone of voice, posture, all this has an esthetic dimension, but of a quality different from feminine beauty; and moreover, in man it is secondary, and only appears as such by an effort of abstraction.

The feminine form of beauty is what we call *grace*. The archangel Gabriel's greeting to Mary contains its fullest expression: . . . "Hail, full of grace." But we should not burden this word with all the theology of Grace; [Grace here] is literally "gracious," "graceful." That is why woman is—I mean, once again, that she must be—pleasing, agreeable, and that grace is gratis, a gratuitous gift, an unstable and uncertain, almost a miraculous grace. We must not pass over the impression of "unreality" produced in man by the spectacle of feminine beauty; something surprising, astonishing, which it seems is about to vanish into thin air. And that grace is something winged, light, in contrast to the gravity of the male; gracility means slenderness, slimness, grace, and lightness all in one.

The impression woman gives of fugacity, that improbable, fugitive, fleeting quality, as if she were about to take wing, is the sensorial version of her biographical condition. "The nature of the wing is to raise heavy things on high," said Plato; that is, to raise what is grave, specifically, the gravity of the male. This is why woman's mission is to draw upward—herself and the man attracted to her, captivated by her. It is why woman is not entirely *present:* she scarcely touches the ground, her step is light, she frequently seems startled because she is going to flee—but not because she is a coward, not at all. She dares go very far, and to lead man with her, attracted by his pursuit of her. This is why she is "interesting"; she invites him to overtake her and hold her, to see what her inner being is like. For her reality, instead of showing itself openly, is hidden, concealed, denied, in the form of a superlative degree of interiorness: *intimacy*. Woman's "modesty" is what transpires from her intimacy, it is what reveals and announces her interest.

. . . Those women with none of the attributes of femininity possess them in some corner of their reality, in a faded and deteriorated form, abandoned and covered with dust, perhaps sold or betrayed, and they know that they could be women in some measure, perhaps if someone expected it of them, if someone treated them from out of that diametrical disjunction of which we have spoken so many times in these pages. Sometimes a woman displays grateful surprise when she is unexpectedly treated like one; it seems to recall a forgotten condition, and the latent woman wakens and becomes visible, and for a moment rises triumphant over that which has weighed her down.

The forms of the feminine body are soft, round, tender; they can be energetic, intense, nervous, so long as they do not include harshness or dryness. Woman is stimulating because her function is to set man in motion, to call him; that is why she can be pro-vocative (a word which would be inapplicable to the masculine kind of attractiveness). The fact that initative in love is the province of the male is a social phenomenon and not a natural one—for nothing human is merely natural and not social—but it responds to the respective structure of men and women. When we speak of men's "activity" and women's "passivity," we forget that "moving" is a particularly intense form of activity. For Aristotle, God is "the first unmoving mover," who moves without being moved, and he explains: "like the object of love and desire." The *theós* is the plenary mode of activity, of *enérgeia* with no admixture of passivity whatever.

But there is another very different dimension of the feminine vital project: her stable or stablilizing dimension. The fugitive, evasive, elusive woman, who seems to be always in motion, who draws and incites man and takes him far away and higher up, *stays* somewhere in the end and puts down roots. While man tends to press on, woman, once a certain moment has arrived, prefers to make camp. It is the enveloping, protecting, sheltering condition of woman, symbolized in the hospitable tenderness of her soft and boneless-seeming bodily forms, in her traditional clothing—skirt, veil, shawl—in the tent and in the house.

Is this a desertion, a betrayal of her graceful and fugitive vocation, that of skimming the earth? It can be just the opposite, the fulfillment of the total feminine vocation: that of inwardness, interiorness, intimacy. Woman is the inventor of the interior, of the *chez-soi,* of the hearth where her inner condition is reflected. Woman's "staying" is primarily a "staying home," and that means staying within herself, *absorption with herself.* The great praises of women have been metaphors of enclosure: in the Song of Songs, *hortus conclusus, fons signatus* "a garden enclosed, a fountain sealed." Woman "calls" man, even provokes him, but she draws back and hides herself, encloses herself, and man must knock at her door in the hope that woman will open and let him in, permit him to enter her intimacy.

And from this derives woman's special, unexpected strength, her security, so unlike man's. There is nothing needier or more uncertain than a woman alone—so much so, that her temptation is *to flee from herself,* from her condition as a woman. But when she is fulfilling—in any social or personal form whatever—her contrasting function as a woman, when she is installed in her sexuate feminine condition, she has the security that comes from acceptance of reality. The form which "gravity" acquires in woman is, rather, *tranquillity*; and the strength of this quality clothes woman's image with an exquisite, delicate form of life which is not highly regarded nowadays but which, in the last instance, is the fate of every man and woman: resignation. The structure of human life has one whole side on which, no matter what our projects and hopes, we inexorably emerge into the need for resignation: limitations, illness, old age, separation, death. Woman, by staying within herself, by electing—and that is why she is "elegant"—by waiting, by renouncing, begins, perhaps in her prime, to sketch out the gesture of resignation.

Now we can see very clearly that man and woman are two reciprocal structures. We have been unable to define one without constant reference to the other. The programmatic quality of human life is realized through that polarity; each is the program of the other.

If we imagine the sexuate condition in the situation of man and woman, face to face, looking into each other's eyes, we see that they are not simply together, but that they are "happening" reciprocally, each present in the face and life of the other. Woman leans on man and at the same time envelops him; man sustains her and lets himself be sheltered. Man is an insistent invader, and woman is hospitable. Man is *present,* looking out of his eyes, calling, exercising pressure; the masculine face shows a tension of effort in its structural lines; the male is always doing something, thinking at least. The soft lines of a woman's face indicate a sort of closedness; a woman is always a bit "behind" her face; it is what we most properly call a pretty face, not the face which pleases us by its forms and which we can see as a whole, but the one we have to keep on looking at interminably. The specific beauty of the feminine face is the beauty which spreads and expands, elastically, toward the future; we feel that we must go on looking at that face all our lives, that our "I" is now *the I which must penetrate inside it,* indefinitely. . . .

If we consider the situation in our present-day world of the traits which I have pointed out as essential to man, to woman, and to their mutual presence, we cannot escape a feeling of uneasiness. The most visible and obvious characteristics of our societies present too many differences from what I have just written: leveling off, lessening of polarity, frequent absence of gravity in the man and desire for grace in the woman, uncertainty of the inciting–incitement relationship, and so on. The characterization of the two sexes which I have just made is no longer the reigning one; at least, it is not fully reigning. If one or two traits happened not to agree with the current image, it would not matter: but so many?

It might well be thought either that the sexuate condition is in a serious state of crisis or that my theory is not true. There is a third possibility: since human life is systematic, as soon as a modification is produced this modification carries others with it—and this explains the presence of *too many* divergent traits. On the other hand, in our world the least authentic traits are those which rise to the surface of society—that is, to public notice. Truth . . . is not usually what is most obvious, because ours is a period of deliberate concealment. What is undeniable is that some men

and women do not *want* things to be as I have described them. Fortunately, this desire is not sufficiently strong to change reality, though it is
strong enough to make reality more problematical, more difficult to
achieve. Doubt has very often been cast on woman's rationality. Though
few, or none, would dare to do so today, we must not ignore this historical fact: the older I become the more interested I am in things which,
though not real, are possible; and conversely, in those which, even
though impossible, are necessary. It has been possible to believe that
woman is not rational; to this day there are many people who believe
something different but not entirely unconnected: that she is not reasonable. Man constantly finds that woman is ''illogical.'' On the other hand,
woman does not seem particularly interested in ''being right''—at least in
the sense of the Spanish expression, *tener razón,* ''having reason''—a
sense which, let us not forget, is predominantly masculine, coined in
''man's world.'' It seems, therefore, that woman's relationships with reason are problematical, to say the least. . . .We have seen before that the
sexuate condition affects all of life, from its physical to its mental aspects;
that man and woman are ''installed'' in their sex and project themselves
from it toward reality—toward all reality. If this is true, it is hard to see
why rationality must be an exception. . . .

And then we reach an inevitable conclusion: if human life takes place
in two irreducible and inseparable forms, diametrically opposed and defined by sexuate disjunction, the life of the man and that of the woman,
reason, vital reason, *the reason which is life,* must be affected by that
very disjunction. Reality is constituted in a different form for man and
woman, and concrete reason, that which does not impose an abstract organization on abstract ''realities,'' has to function in two strictly different
forms, masculine and feminine. . . .

Human *doing*—in Ortega's sense, as opposed to more or less inert and
mechanical *activity*—is determined by a *why* and a *wherefore*: they are
the things which simultaneously give reality and intelligibility to what
man does. Now the motives and aims of woman, so far as her projects are
concerned, are different from those of the male, even when male and female activities substantially coincide, and this is the origin of the impression of ''irrationality'' or ''illogicality'' which the woman produces in
the man. He does not understand what she is doing because he usually
does not see *why* and *wherefore* she is doing it, for if he were to do ''the
same'' he would do it for different reasons and with other aims in mind.

Someone will ask why the man does not produce an impression of irrationality or illogicality in the woman, for the difference is mutual, that is,
masculine motives are also ''different'' with respect to woman. Since the
interpretations have usually been worked out—or at least named—by
men, both men and women have usually understood that reason is masculine reason, which is the form of reason that has been talked about, the

kind that has been the object of theory. Moreover, woman has has to anticipate and understand the world of man, for she lives "inside" it, and this has obliged her to foresee man's conduct and comprehend how his reason functions. Hence the special impression of penetration and sharpness produced by woman, even when she is not highly educated. "When man is on the way, woman is already back again," says the Spanish proverb, and it is true: woman has had to imagine man, to place herself in his viewpoint, to divine the structure of his reason, in order to lodge herself in his world and work out her own place in it. This is why woman "manages" man so easily, even the man who is intellectually her superior.

For men and women, things are arranged in different perspectives of interest, valuation, or importance, constituting different configurations of reality, different real worlds. Projects establish this articulation, based on the system of beliefs. These, which are the unexpressed basis of rational operations, their great *assumptions,* also differ. Reason is exercised in the places where it is needed, when action cannot flow spontaneously because there is not an effective belief to regulate conduct or because the conduct that was being employed has failed. Man and woman are not sure of the same things, and therefore they are unsure—and in need of reason—about very different things. And all this is set in motion by the general human pretension: to be happy. Once more, the difference is essential: not only do man and woman need different things to be happy, but they are happy in different senses. A man and a woman do not understand exactly the same thing by "happiness"—and the same would be true if we compared two different peoples or two widely separated epochs.

When man thinks that woman "doesn't know what she wants," and finds her "illogical," probably what is happening is that he does not know what she wants and the woman knows it all too well (and probably hides it). Too well, I have said, for woman's habitual *internal* sureness gives her great security. Accustomed to associating herself with man's strength, to living in his shadow, to counting on him for the more general and abstract things, woman carves out her own internal world, one which is more limited and refined. She usually moves intelligently and confidently in that world; this is why she is overconfident, is convinced that "she knows what she is doing," does not bother to contrast her viewpoint with that of others, and this leads her into error.

The case of the intellectual woman is revealing. She has access to "men's" culture, partakes of theoretical thought, uses the type of reason with which the sciences or politics have been created. At the same time, she continues to be a woman and to operate according to the traditional principles of her sex and the structures of her feminine projects. She is divided, with two frequently contradictory demands, and hence her probable instability and insecurity. Many years will have to pass—or there will have to be a tremendous outburst of feminine genius—before woman will be capable of making "culture" in the objective sense of this term, by putting into play the forms and "categories" of feminine reason. Then we could expect a decisive illumination of many problems which until now have stubbornly resisted solution, and which would perhaps yield to that other form of reason. But if this is to be possible, women will have to avoid two dangerous shoals: imitating man, and rejecting him through resentment—the two things which the "feminists" have habitually done. Women would have to abandon themselves creatively to their own inspiration, and allow their peculiar form of rationality to flow.

Not many men have even a middlingly adequate idea of what a woman is. To form such an idea a man must have a complex interest, and almost all the interests men feel in women are far too simple. Men do many things with women, but rarely think about them. Nor would this be sufficient: if man makes women the "object" of his thought, he will never learn a word about her. Only in the measure in which woman is *lived* as a specific woman can reason work upon her, can she be intelligible. That is why, in the last instance, the man who "deals" with a woman knows more about her than the man who "studies" her, though innumerable essential details still escape him. Were I to be asked for an expression in a nutshell, I would say that it is not a question of thinking about women, but of thinking *with* them. And since thinking means to do what is necessary to know what to hold to, this means in the most literal sense of the word, *living together*. Only when man and woman, each installed in his own sex, project toward each other, and together toward their dual personal vocation, can they become mutually transparent. And only this dual life can set in motion the wholeness of vital reason.

Appendix

From "Is Woman a Question?"

Maryellen MacGuigan

The title of this paper reflects a rather frequent reaction to the notion of investigating woman philosophically: that there is no genuine philosophical question here, or that it is at best a trivial matter. It also reflects the ambiguous situation in which the person who undertakes to discuss the problem of woman may find him/herself. To take woman as a theme of investigation is to affirm, tacitly at least, that woman does present a special problem to the philosopher, over and above the general questions that must be dealt with in the treatment of human reality as such. Yet the conception of woman as a special, and especially problematical, case may well be one of the chief obstacles to the entry of women into the status of fully human persons. If one is convinced that a man is neither more nor less than a human person, and a woman is neither more nor less than a human person, the formulation of a special and peculiar "problem of woman" will appear spurious. At the same time, there is a concrete social problem of woman's role, image, and status; and there are theoretical problems in philosophy, psychology, and the social sciences, all of which seem to bring forth contradictions when they try to establish theories about woman. Clearly, philosophical discussion in this area is called for.

In this paper I shall attempt to show that Western philosophy entertains notions of the human person structured in such a way that some persons are defined as less human than others on the basis of their sex. In this, philosophy has been consistent with the culture as a whole. Traditionally, man and woman have been interpreted as very different, even diametrically opposed, manifestations of humanity; yet philosophical reflection on being human has so far been reflection principally on being human in the male mode. Philosophical statements about "man" tend, explicitly or implicitly, to identify the human being with the male human being, and to relegate the female to the status of a problematical or imperfect being. This masculine bias, as we might call it, does not always show up as a prominent feature of a philosopher's thought. Often, it is discovered more by attending to what is not said than to what is. When philosophers are discussing the various aspects of what it is to be human, in many cases

468

they do not mention women at all; or their references to the female sex are only incidental and marginal. They do not devote much attention to the question of how a woman is to achieve the fulfillment of her humanity, whether in the same way as a man or differently. Nor do they address themselves systematically to the fact that there are two sexes, and to the significance that this fact might have for our attempts to understand what it is to be human. We might suppose that philosophers generally pass over these topics, or give them only brief attention, because they mean their descriptions and analyses to apply to all human beings, regardless of sex. Alas, this happy supposition would be wrong, as we find when we examine what philosophers *do* say about women. It turns out, almost invariably, that whatever has been said about being human does not apply to them. Philosophical views generally echo (and, no doubt, reinforce) the commonly accepted idea that a woman is different from a man in ways that make her incapable of the fullest human development. In short, women are less human than men.

Classical Thinkers

Aristotle is a case in point. His references to women are brief, relatively few, and found mostly in the context of other discussions. Several occur in *On the Generation of Animals,* a work which treats the biological aspect of reproduction in all animals, including the rational species. On the biological level, the female is defined by her deficiency relative to the male: he has the generative power, and she lacks it. Since the male provides the form of the offspring, and the female the matter, the offspring should properly be expected to be male. The female condition is a deformity, occurring when conception takes place under adverse conditions; the existence of females is justified only by the requirements of reproduction.

Women's inferiority extends beyond the biological to the intellectual and moral levels. Although a woman possesses the power of reason, her reasoning is inconclusive. The kind of virtue proper to a woman is that of the subject in the *polis,* but not that of the ruler, while the truly good man needs both kinds. Friendship between husband and wife is a friendship of unequals—and need we ask who is the superior?

Whether Plato is a pro-feminist or an antifeminist is something of a moot point; both interpretations have been argued. In the *Republic* he proposes equal education for women and men, and says that some women would be found fit to be Rulers. Although on the whole women are weaker than men, sex as such does not qualify or disqualify a person for any function in society. However, in the *Symposium* wisdom is for men only: Socrates' speech, which crowns the dialog, concerns the ascent of a man to love of the Good through love of the moral beauty of another man. Although Socrates has learned the true nature of love from the foreign woman, Diotima, there is no suggestion that any real, live Athenian woman could be a participant in the sort of mentor–disciple relationship that he describes. In the *Phaedo*, likewise, the philosopher's last message is for men only; his weeping wife is sent away. In the *Timaeus*, souls who do not live well in the body of a man are threatened with rebirth as a woman; and then, if they do not do better, as an animal. The body is a prison, in Plato's doctrine; but evidently, the female body is a worse prison than the male body.

The thinkers of the Middle Ages do not depart significantly from the Greek view of women. St. Thomas Aquinas, who integrated Aristotle's philosophy into Christian theology, cites him regularly when a question about women arises. In discussing the creation of woman, he interprets the words of *Genesis,* that God made her to be a helper for man, to mean a helper in procreation; because in anything else, a man could be helped better by another man than by a woman. A woman is a deformed man, although this deformity is compatible with the perfection of the universe as a whole. Woman's power of reasoning is less than a man's. Even in the state of innocence, there would have been inequality among humans, because (at least) of differences in sex and age.

What of the modern era? Many philosophers are silent, or as good as as silent, on the subject of women. Silence, as we have seen in the case of Socrates' speech in the *Symposium,* can be significant: does it mean that the philosopher tacitly intends his principles and conclusions to have universal application; or does it mean that he has simply overlooked or discounted the existence of women? Given the very different education, social roles, economic, legal, and political status of women even up to this day, it is plausible to suppose that many thinkers have inadvertently equated human persons and human society with male persons and the ''man's world'' in which they encounter each other. But masculine bias is not always inadvertent. Sometimes it is open and obvious, though not necessarily consistent with the thinker's principles; Rousseau is an example. He offers a doctrine of universal human rights, universal human freedom—only it does not apply to women, who should be educated and trained to be subordinate to men. In *Patriarchal Attitudes,* Eva Figes discusses Rousseau in some detail, pointing out that his position in *The Social Contract* is flagrantly contradicted in his writings on the education of women.

> "To renounce one's liberty is to renounce one's quality as a man, the rights and also the duties of humanity"—but in fact liberty, or perhaps humanity itself is an all-male affair, since he writes of women in *Emile*: "They must be trained to bear the yoke from the first, so that they may not feel it, to master their own caprices and to submit themselves to the will of others." This accords somewhat ill with his diatribes against despotism and his almost mathematical allocation of freedom as part of a popular will. Appar-

ently, woman has no part in the social contract at all, no freedom, no rights.*

Other examples could be added: Kant, Fichte, Hegel, Kierkegaard; the notorious antifeminism of Nietzsche and Schopenhauer is not their idiosyncrasy, but a common attitude. What one finds, over and over, is that philosophical notions of the human being apply properly to men, i.e., male human beings, and imperfectly or not at all to women. Women then appear as problematical beings; sometimes it is difficult to understand how they can be part of the human race or of human society. But if we cannot understand women as human beings in the terms which the philosophers offer us, we must ask whether we understand what men are, or what it is to be human. It is necessary to formulate a notion of the human person which does not contain a built-in bias against women. We are far from having achieved that yet. So thoroughly is our thinking imbued with masculine presuppositions that even philosophers whose avowed intention is to investigate systematically the human significance of sexual differentiation, or to affirm and support the full humanity of both men and women, are not able to overcome them completely. The long persistence of the masculine bias in philosophy will be shown through analysis of the views of [some] twentieth-century thinkers: José Ortega y Gasset . . . and Julián Marías. They have been chosen because each presents a more or less sustained discussion, rather than scattered, passing remarks, and attempts to base his conclusions on philosophical principles. The contradictions and inconsistencies that have their source in the masculine bias† will be pointed out, and the question raised of how to take a more coherent approach.

Ortega y Gasset

Ortega discusses woman briefly in *Man and People,* within the context of the problem of other selves. He believes that Husserl has most accurately formulated this problem, but finds his development of it (in the *Cartesian Meditations*) less successful than his definition. He takes issue with the notion of an analogical projection of my ego on the body of the other as the way in which I become aware of the other *I*. For I experience my body from within, while I see only the exteriority of the other's body. And what reveals the other self to me

. . .is not so much for form of the body as its gestures. The expression that is sorrow or irritation or melancholy, I did not discover in myself but *pri-*

---

*Eva Figes, *Patriarchal Attitudes* (New York: Fawcett), 1971, pp. 98–99.

†I call it "masculine bias" not because it is exhibited by males—it is, but neither exclusively nor universally—but because it consists in taking the masculine as the paradigm of the human, and looking at everything from that (often unconscious) standpoint.

marily in the other and it at once signified inwardness to me—grief, annoyance, melancholy.

But what most clearly reveals Husserl's error, Ortega says, is the fact that the Other who appears to me is sometimes a woman and I (i.e., Ortega) cannot explain the appearance of the She by a projection of my ego upon her body, for in this case the inwardness that is expressed in the body and its gestures is wholly different from mine. Although her body is directly present and her inwardness is only compresent, it is in the inwardness of woman, not in her body, that her difference from man really lies. This inwardness expresses itself in the body, and thus we see it as a feminine body.

> The observation is paradoxical but seems to me undeniable; it is not the feminine body that reveals the "feminine soul" to us, but the feminine "soul" that makes us see its body as feminine.

Ortega points out three primary characters of feminine inwardness. The first is that, in contrast to the humanity of a man, the inward humanity of a woman is essentially confused—which "is not a defect in woman, any more than it is a defect in man not to have wings." Being confused, a woman does not know and cannot express "what she feels and what befalls her," while man is "made up of clarities." He does not have "actual, objective clarity concerning the world and his fellow beings;" however, "within himself, he sees himself clearly." The second primary characteristic is that feminine inwardness is a form of humanity inferior to the masculine.

> In the presence of Woman we men immediately divine a creature who on the level of "humanness" has a vital station somewhat lower than ours. No other being has this twofold condition—being human, and being less so than a man is.

Weakness is the basis of woman's inferior vital rank; "when we see a woman, what we see consists in weakness." Far from displeasing man, woman's confusion, inferiority, and weakness are the source of the delight that she is to him.

Ortega deplores the "equalitarian mania" which has appeared recently. There is, he says (*contra* Simone de Beauvoir), no incompatibility between being free and consisting in reference to another human being. Indeed, "the duality of the sexes has as its consequence that men and women are constituted by their reference to one another." Though the reference to the other sex is constitutive in both, it "has a preeminent place in woman," while a man's chief reference is to his profession. However, the fact that "woman's destiny is to be in view of man" does not diminish her freedom; "the human being, as free, is free before and in the face of his destiny."

The third primary characteristic of woman is that the feminine ego stands in a different relation to its body than the masculine ego to its body; "the feminine body is endowed with a more lively internal sensibility than man's," so that a woman's body "exists for her more than a man's does for him." Woman's psychic life is more involved with her body than is man's. "Her native physiological structure imposes on woman the habit of noticing, paying attention to her body, which ends up being the closest object in the perspective of her world."

In his discussion of woman, Ortega repeats many traditional and widely held views. When his statements are examined in the light of his philosophical principles, however, it appears that some of the distinctions he draws between man and woman make no sense; that he is inconsistent; and that woman is not merely less human than man (whatever sense that notion may have), but cannot be called human at all in his terms. To begin with, he stresses the "paradox" that a woman's inner femininity makes her entire body feminine, rather than the peculiarly feminine parts of her body indicating her mode of being. He conveys the impression that woman is paradoxical in a way that man is not. But whenever I meet another person I encounter the paradox that the bodily gestures and forms signal to me an inwardness other than my own and compresent but in principle inaccessible to me. For it is the compresent inwardness which makes the body flesh, and expressive, so that I experience it as a human body. If the other is a man, it is his masculine inwardness which makes me see his body as masculine. Ortega puts a false stress on the paradox of femininity, and suggests a non-existent difference between women and men.

Moreover, his statements about the primary characters of woman are inconsistent with his theory of human life, as found in the earlier chapters of *Man and People*. He says that woman's inner being is confused, while man's is clear. But he has stated that man (the human person) is essentially confused. By this he means that we find ourselves, without any preparation, living in the midst of an environment or circumstance which presents us with various possibilities among which we have to choose, on our own responsibility. Because there are many possibilities given us, rather than one clear path, "life is a permanent crossroads, a constant perplexity." Here he does not distinguish between inner and outer perplexity, or suggest the possibility of a person being perplexed about the world and at the same clear within himself. At best, one could say that the distinction between man's clarity and woman's confusion is made *ad hoc* and is not justified within the framework of his discussion of life as perplexity; at worst, one might suspect him of contradicting himself. Again, he is not consistent with his own position when he says that "it is not clear why there must be . . . incompatibility between being free and consisting in reference to another human being." For he has already said that we must choose; "man is the only reality that does not simply consist in being but must choose its own being." And only I can choose for myself; no one can do it for me. Life is untransferable; no one can "make his neighbor think for him the thoughts he has to think in order to orient himself in the world . . . and thus find his right line of conduct." But if it is a woman's destiny to live in view of a man, if she is constituted chiefly by reference to a man (who is not constituted chiefly by reference to her), then it would seem that it is a man who decides for her, chooses for her, even—since she is in inner confusion and he possesses inner clarity—thinks for her. Can she be truly free and responsible—in short, be a human being—at all?

Ortega's description of the relation of the feminine ego to its body also presents difficulties. In the earlier chapters he several times refers to the body in such terms as "the closest of all things to . . . the I that is each of us," and points out that my body is the only thing in the world that I know from within. It is not clear that he is justified in making a distinction between man and woman on the score of the closeness of the ego-body relationship.

The incoherence of Ortega's view of woman arises from a limitation of his perspective which is a serious shortcoming both in itself and in the light of his own conception of philosophy. His philosophy is an examination of human life—in the sense of *my* life, personal life—as the radical reality in which all other realities appear to me. In my life I find myself face to face with a world with which I must come to terms. One of the structural laws of "my world" is that it is perspectival. I live my life from a perspective which does not coincide with that of anyone else. Yet when I meet another person, I recognize in him the ability to respond to me, and to initiate actions toward me. The response and the initiative come from a life which is not mine. In my actions I must take account of them, and so I must take account of the other's irreducible perspective. This is what Ortega fails to do in his discussion of woman. He speaks about woman from his own point of view as a man, to other men, as if that point of view were totally adequate. He forgets that a woman lives her life from her own original perspective, and that for her, *he* is the other appearing in her world. That a philosopher should do this is not unusual; but it is a more serious shortcoming in the case of Ortega, for whom philosophy shares the perspectival character of life. . . .

Julián Marías

Julián Marías does not focus his discussion on woman, but on what he calls "the sexuate condition of human life." He places the discussion in the context of "metaphysical anthropology." Marías, like Ortega (whose disciple he is), philosophizes from the perspective of life as radical reality. Metaphysics, or analytical theory of life, deals, with whatever belongs necessarily to human life.

> Human life has a structure which I discover by *analysis* of *my* life. The result of that analysis is a theory which we therefore call analytical . . . and

its contents are the *requisites,* the conditions without which my life is not possible and which must therefore be found in each life.

But we cannot "pass directly from analytic structure to individual, circumstantial, and concrete reality." There is an intermediate level of structure, which Marías calls "empirical structure." The analytical and universal structure of human life is articulated into forms which are discovered empirically. There forms are not merely factual, but structural. They are stable and lasting, though not permanent or invariable. It is a requisite of human life that it be empirically structured. However, no particular empirical structure is necessary. Empirical structure is "the field of *possible variation in history.*" For example, the analytical structure of human life includes senses; but the particular sensorial structure we have is not the only possible one, and in fact, our sensorial structure differs, because of technological developments, from that of the man of a century ago.

The empirical structure of our life is a structure of installations. Life is future-oriented; but I can project myself towards the future only from a manner of being in which I already am. While a situation is concrete and temporary, installation is stable and enduring. It is unitary, but multidimensional. The sexuate condition is one of the radical forms of installation of human life. It "affects all of life, at all times and in all its dimensions." The term does not merely refer to the biological "facts" of sex. "For man, nothing is merely physical, or even biological, but also historical and social. . . . [Being] a "man" or a "woman" is not only a biological matter, but a personal and a social one." The sexuate condition is not a requisite of all human life as such. The sex determination does not appear on the plane of analytical theory, but on the empirical plane. It is different from every other dimension of installation, in that it establishes a relationship of strict disjunction: "man is male *or* female." It both separates and links man and woman, establishing a relationship of mutual reference or coimplication.

> The sexuate condition is not even visible in an isolated life. We see it in each one of us as it is referred to the opposite sex, which means that we see it "from" each one of us rather than "in" ourselves.

Because the sexuate condition is not merely biological, but is interpreted and projected socially, it will have different concrete forms in different times and places. The meaning of the words 'man' and 'woman' will vary from society to society. Their reciprocally opposite function, however, is a stabilizing factor. The fact that a man is a man in contrast to being a woman, and vice versa, means that a schematic function can be derived from the multiplicity of forms of being man or woman. Thus it is possible to study the sexual polarity and the two poles or terms of disjunction. Marías's conception of a relation in which man and woman are defined by their mutual reference seems to preclude any masculinist bias.

However, he does not consistently carry out his conception in his treatment of the sexuate polarity.

The first discrepancy appears when he notes the fact that in many languages, the same word means both the person in general and the male person, with a different word for the female person.

> This identification of man with the male. . . . might be a manifestation of the basic social belief that ''man'' is primarily male and that woman is, at most, a secondary and appended ''variant''; but it may be something else: the very clear consciousness of the special feminine condition, which must be recognized with a special word, while male traits are simply incorporated into those of the species.

This suggests that feminine traits are a modification of, or an addition to, human traits; it seems incompatible with man and woman being defined by their reference to each other. By 'special feminine condition' he apparently means that since being a man and being a woman are two forms of personal life, there are two worlds, that of men and that of women.

> Now since with extremely few exceptions the world has been understood and interpreted as the world of men, within which women possessed or made their private world, ''men's affairs'' have been identified with ''human affairs,'' and the general lines along which *humanity* has been understood have been those which define *virility*.

Women have not been on an equal footing with men in creating the historical, social, political, and cultural world. It is not immediately clear whether Marías means to describe what in fact is the case; what inevitably is so because of the intrinsic character of the sexuate polarity; or what he thinks ought to be. Confusion of this sort recurs throughout his discussion, and is responsible for some of its inconsistency.

The polarity of the sexuate condition introduces an apparent contradiction into the human condition as it is lived by the male. The human condition is one of ''having to do something and not knowing what to hold to''; of insecurity and neediness. But with respect to woman, the man is defined by ''security, knowledge, decision, resources.'' He must aim at personal strength, in order to offer it to woman: ''. . . everything man does to learn, achieve, dominate, gain wealth or security, he does primarily *for* the woman, in reference to her, in order to proffer her that human figure in which the male consists.'' Knowing that life is a burden, man ''must build an island of security . . . [which] we call civilization, science, culture, the State.'' He offers woman the strength he has built, and she, ''of her own will, steps into the shelter of that protection.''

As a man needs strength, a woman needs beauty; not merely physical, but personal feminine beauty, or grace. Grace is ''something winged, light, in contrast to the gravity of the male.'' Woman gives the impression of being about to take wing; and it is her mission to draw man upward. She attracts and sets him in motion; her intimacy, her hidden reality, draw him on. But the feminine vital project also has a stabilizing dimension. In the end, woman stays somewhere and puts down roots, while man presses on. This can be "the fulfillment of the total feminine vocation: that of inwardness, interiorness, intimacy "

Marías notes that the characterization of the two sexes which he has set forth is no longer the reigning one. He attributes this to superficial divergent traits which have risen to the surface of society and are concealing the truth, rather than to a serious crisis of the sexuate condition. His aversion toward modification of the sexuate polarity is curious in view of his evident desire that "feminine reason" should some day come into its own.

He initiates his discussion of reason from the paradox that reason is considered to be essential to and universal in man; yet the rationality of woman has often been questioned. But what is reason? It is "life itself in its function of apprehending reality." A woman's reason and a man's reason confront different realities, and so they must be different. Moreover, life "gives reason" to things; it is by assuming functions in life that things become intelligible.

> But the verb "to live" does not mean exactly the same thing for a man as for a woman. . . . While man moves in the dimension of long-range projects, and in principle has the initiative, woman has traditionally had a smaller world, in which projection is much closer, and has usually had to wait for masculine initiative; that is, she has had to "lodge" her projects within the broader ones of the man.

This is an accurate description of the lives of men and women in Western culture. It implies that in their relation of mutual reference, man and woman are not on even footing. He chooses his project; and, because her project is "lodged" within his, in effect he chooses hers too.

Because their lives are so different, men do not understand women's reason, and so find women unreasonable or illogical. But men do not seem so to women, because "both men and women have usually understood that reason is masculine reason, which is the form of reason that has been talked about, the kind that has been the object of theory." But it is hard to avoid thinking that Marías does consider woman's reason to be less than man's. Lodged in man's world, woman relies on his strength and "counts on him for the more general and abstract things." We have seen that the human condition is "radical, constituent insecurity," in the face of which the human person must create strength. But it seems that man relieves woman of insecurity and of the need to create strength. She depends on his reason to orient herself in the larger reality. Near the beginning of the chapter on masculine and feminine reason, Marías makes a "detour" to discuss the reason of the child. The child is said not to have the use of reason; this means that he needs reason but does not possess it, and so must depend on the reason of others. If woman depends on man's reason, is she not in a position between that of the child and the man? Yet at the same time, he envisions the possibility that some day

> . . .woman will be capable of making "culture" in the objective sense of this term, by putting into play the forms and "categories" of feminine reason. Then we could expect a decisive illumination of many problems which until now stubbornly resisted solution. . .

As long as the sexuate polarity is defined in Marías's terms, women will not become capable of making culture; if they could do so, it would mean that women's life would have changed; and with it, feminine reason.

Concluding Reflections

It seems to me that, of the theories examined here, Marías's most accurately locates the problem of the sexuate condition. His explicit recognition that it is a problem of human life, and not one located peculiarly in woman, goes far toward developing a more satisfactory frame of reference for further philosophical discussion. And his notions of empirical structure and installation allow him to avoid the difficulties which Buytendijk and Stern encounter in attempting to relate masculinity and femininity directly to the essential structures of consciousness. Yet, although he defines the sexuate relationship as one of reciprocal reference, he also defines woman relatively to man in a one-sided way.

For all their differences of analytic method, the . . . theorists hold positions that are obviously similar in several important ways. With the exception of Ortega, whose view is blatantly condescending, all are attempting a positive revaluation of woman as the bearer of the values of interiority and receptiveness. All, including Ortega, cherish these values (however their accounts of them may diverge). However, they all perceive woman as relative to man to a far greater degree and in a more intrinsic way than man is relative to woman. And they seem to discern the characteristics of human existence more clearly in the male person; femininity appears to them as a hindrance to woman's full participation in the human world, for reasons that go beyond mere historical facts. The result of this perception of woman is that they downgrade the very values they are trying to affirm and support, by associating them with persons and characteristics that are less than fully human.

So we see that a masculinist bias persists even in the discussions of philosophers who are attempting to revalue woman and the "womanly" in a positive way. Is this merely a personal aberration on their part; merely a reflection of the difficulty we all have in rooting out of ourselves every vestige of long-held prejudice? I think not. This bias is not just a peculiar shortcoming of these indivdiual philosophers, but is woven into the fabric of Western philosophy. Philosophizing has been the activity of men in a male-centered and sexually segregated culture; the concerns of men have provided its subject matter, the attitudes of men its values, the behavior and activities of men the examples and models for its concepts. In short, in whatever respects they may have differed, the conceptions of the human which Western philosophy has developed have been male-based, and have implicitly equated the human person with the male human person. Everything considered peculiar to women, whether bodily givens, personality traits, or social roles, has been seen as a hindrance to their humanity. In terms of most philosophers' definitions of the human person, women are not persons. Since a denial of the full humanity of women is built into these definitions, they cannot serve as a philosophical groundwork for a reconsideration of women's place in society. They do not provide an adequate basis for women's claim to their rights as persons.

Many people have begun to understand that women both can and must participate fully and on an even footing with men in the building up of the social, cultural, and political world. Such participation implies both the practical and the theoretical recognition of women as human beings, as persons, in as full and true a sense as men. We need, then, to rethink deeply our notions of what it is to be a human being. It is difficult to spell out beforehand all that such a rethinking would involve. However, it must include a serious consideration of the human significance of sexuality. The determination of how this question ought to be formulated would itself be an important phase of the investigation. Reflection on the relationship of personhood to bodily life, and on the relationships between person and person, and between individual and society, would be called for. But what the full ramifications of a new philosophical approach to the "woman question" may be, only time—and the efforts of philosophers—will tell.

INDEX

Abelard, Peter, 40, 91–93

Abortion, *see* Rights: abortion

Abuse, 178–179, 208. *See also* Children: abuse; Marriage: spouse abuse

Academy, 13, 48, 63

Aging, 244–245, 251, 332

Aggressiveness, *see* Feelings: aggressiveness

Androcentric culture, *see* Culture: androcentric culture

Aquinas, Thomas, 8, 10, 24, 30, 40, 102–115, 441, 470

Aristotle, 8, 10, 23, 31, 63–68, 102–103, 105, 107–108, 114, 136, 180, 294, 303, 432, 441, 463, 469–470

Artistic capacity/accomplishments, 4–6, 51–52, 210, 269, 274, 294–295, 319–320, 336, 345, 359, 368, 397, 399

Augustine, Aurelius, 32, 40, 87–90, 106, 109–110, 113–114, 121, 169

Biological differences, 7–8, 197, 430–431, 452, 469

generation of the sexes, 8–9, 15, 56–58, 63–65, 75–76, 84–85, 87, 89, 91–92, 102–108, 115, 157–158, 199, 236, 268–269, 308–309, 319–320, 323, 342–343, 378, 413, 441, 451, 461, 469–470

hormones, 7, 440–441, 443, 445

misbegotten male, 8–9, 63–65, 102–103, 107, 114, 437, 441, 470

nature/nurture controversy, 6–9, 14–16, 19–20, 25, 30, 34, 37–38, 46–47, 50–51, 144, 148, 163, 181–183, 195–197, 201, 210–211, 213, 218–219, 222–223. 233–236, 237–238, 247–248, 288–295, 324–326, 329, 336, 358–360, 394–396, 401–402, 443, 475

role in propagation of species, 8, 20, 22, 28, 32, 42, 54, 57–58, 63–64, 75–77, 85, 87, 103–104, 111, 158, 249, 272–273, 279–280, 300, 328–329, 341, 392, 397, 426, 433–434

sexuality, 7–8, 11, 22, 197–199, 431, 440–441, 447, 449, 451, 453–454, 460, 463–464, 467, 471–475

hysteria, 8, 177, 317, 409–412

love and sexual passion, *see* Feelings: love and sexual passion

menstruation, 38, 88, 97–98, 172, 175, 178, 210, 216, 444

weakness of women, 9, 16, 23–25, 28, 30, 36, 43, 49, 52–53, 60, 64–65, 72, 74, 84, 90–93, 108, 124, 132, 138, 164–165, 171–173, 177–178, 181, 183–184, 190, 195, 199, 201–203, 207, 213, 216, 218–220, 222–223, 225, 233, 247–249, 259, 270, 272, 282, 288, 295, 302, 304–305, 315–316, 321, 325, 327–328, 332, 345–346, 348, 385–386, 391, 394, 403, 452–454, 469, 472, 476

481

Children, 27–29, 48
  abuse, 238, 380, 398
  care and education, 6, 13, 16–17,
      27–28, 30, 32, 37, 55,
      60–61, 65, 70, 82–83, 85,
      97, 128, 136, 138–139,
      150–151, 153, 166, 168–169,
      172, 178–179, 181, 196,
      199–200, 202–203, 213, 218,
      225–227, 230, 234–235, 237,
      270, 280, 285–286, 321, 329,
      331, 334, 367, 380, 381–383,
      385–388, 391, 396–397, 401,
      415, 421–422, 425–427,
      435–444. See also Dolls;
      Games
  inheritance rights, 26, 28, 94,
      169–170, 173, 276. See also
      Rights: inheritance
  legitimacy, 24, 31–32, 54–56,
      153, 169–170, 196, 200,
      299–300, 348, 417–419,
      435–436
  love of, 22, 76, 138–139, 276,
      400, 422
  pregnancy and birth of, 6, 28, 32,
      51, 84, 88–89, 93, 110–112,
      171, 178, 199, 215, 270,
      338–339, 341, 343–344, 346,
      367, 370–372, 375–376, 380,
      422, 426, 443
  rights to, see Rights: to children
Communism, 38, 44, 299–301,
      347–351, 370, 443
Comte, Auguste, 24, 27–28, 36, 42,
      281–287, 428
Condorcet, Marquis de, 5–6, 11, 16,
      24–25, 30, 37–38, 47, 209–217
Coquetry, 21, 185–189, 202, 204,
      220, 224, 228–229, 236, 243,
      249–250, 264, 274
Culture, 42, 249, 329, 453,
      466–467, 476, 478
  androcentric culture, 6, 9, 17–18,
      37, 41, 44, 397–404
  historical writing, 6, 18, 194, 263,
      399–400, 476
  letters, 10, 156–157, 197, 263

  romances, 14, 18, 128, 159, 235,
      400
  sports, 18, 367, 401
  war, 17, 50–51, 145, 288
    attitudes toward, 18, 119, 234,
        389, 402, 405
    stories, 399–400. See also
        Culture: historical writings

d'Alembert, Jean Le Rond, 177,
      181–190
de Beauvoir, Simone, 7, 11, 14,
      17–18, 20, 21, 24–25, 43–44,
      439–448, 451–452, 472
de Staël, Madame, 230, 331–332
Democracy, 25, 37, 42–43, 301,
      332, 347–349, 365, 386,
      389–390, 397
Diderot, Denis, 8, 20, 21, 25, 30,
      31–32, 34, 37, 177–193
Dolls, 204, 367, 401. See also
      Children: care and education
Double standard, see Virtue: double
      standard

Education, 9–14, 126–130, 131–136,
      196–208, 216, 218, 221–232,
      235–238, 262, 269, 289,
      321–322, 344, 383, 390
  art and music, see Artistic
      capacity/accomplishments
  coeducation, 13, 368–369, 444
  equal or complementary, 11–14,
      42–44, 50–53, 71–73,
      116–117, 119–121, 184, 198,
      201–207, 221, 229, 231,
      289–290, 320–322, 336, 356,
      368, 386–387, 427, 443, 467,
      470
  gymnastics, 50, 52, 72, 201, 203,
      225, 288
  history, 14, 159, 235, 242, 335
  household skills, see Employment:
      home
  mathematics, 14, 136, 207, 242,
      345. See also Employment:
      mathematics

philosophy, 3, 13, 69–71, 73, 75–77, 120, 122, 127, 134, 136, 217, 242, 269, 352. *See also* Employment: philosophy

politics, 14, 235. *See also* Rights: political and legal

religion, 82–83, 122, 127, 132, 133, 135, 161. *See also* Employment: religion

sex, 20, 33, 82–83, 133, 141, 184, 339, 376, 378–379, 407, 419–420, 423, 444–445

science and medicine, 14, 122, 134, 207, 217, 242, 262, 269, 281, 335, 355, 381–382. *See also* Employment: medicine; Employment: science

through warfare and games, 13, 16, 72, 203–204, 367, 401–402, 443

Emancipation, *see* Women's movement

Employment, 13, 15–17, 27, 28, 245, 290, 293, 295, 299–301, 319, 347–351, 400, 427, 442, 455, 476

armies, 16, 37, 38, 50, 52–53, 92, 145, 172, 195, 200–201, 216, 234, 288, 320, 351, 366–367, 389, 403

child care, *see* Children: care and education

farming, 16, 116, 172, 179, 236, 427, 433

government, 13, 15, 23, 35–38, 52, 136, 139, 147, 148–149, 165, 173, 195, 201, 210–216, 230, 234, 261–262, 267–269, 283, 288, 290, 294, 317–318, 326, 331, 333, 335, 356–358, 389, 397, 402–403, 469

home, 13, 15–17, 27, 30, 37, 48, 59–62, 69–71, 96, 134, 172, 179, 190–191, 213, 226, 268, 283–284, 300–301, 317–318, 321, 334–335, 349, 366, 373, 380, 381–385, 391, 393–396, 415, 419, 425, 427

cooking, 11, 27, 96–97, 117, 179, 332, 394

household management, 15, 25, 48–49, 61–62, 66–69, 71, 191, 234

spinning and sewing, 60, 62, 72, 96, 116, 128, 204, 320

industry, 300–301, 349, 367, 373, 379–380, 383–387, 426–427, 434

lighter/heavier tasks, 16, 38, 53, 60, 72, 116, 172, 201

mathematics, 6, 136, 263. *See also* Education: mathematics

medicine, 14, 17, 51–52, 235–236, 262, 295, 367–368, 373. *See also* Education: science and medicine

philosophy, 6, 75–77, 263, 319, 336. *See also* Education: philosophy

religion, 16–17, 40, 119, 130, 132, 262, 318, 323–326, 331, 356, 368–369, 381–382, 397, 412. *See also* Education: religion

science, 6, 263, 295, 330, 336, 345. *See also* Education: science and medicine

restrictions on working conditions, 16–17, 349, 384, 415, 443

teaching, 15–16, 43, 85, 132, 262, 373, 387, 397, 407

writing/scholarship, 3, 6, 8, 17, 123, 156–157, 195, 251, 263–264, 318–319, 330–332, 342, 345, 368, 381–382

Engels, Frederick, 24, 27, 28, 229–301

Erasmus, Desiderius, 13, 125–130

Existentialism, 8, 302–316, 328–346, 439–448, 449–459, 460–467

Feelings, 6, 15, 65, 282–283, 330, 450

aggressiveness, 355, 393, 395,
    399, 401–404, 445
compassion, 65, 271, 282, 345
delicacy of, 10, 11, 19, 156–157,
    183, 187, 235, 243
love and sexual passion, 9–11,
    18–21, 24, 32–33, 43, 46,
    57, 73, 75–76, 83–85, 88,
    104, 137, 139–144, 149, 154,
    156–159, 164, 166, 172, 178,
    180, 185, 188–190, 195–199,
    220–222, 227, 230–231, 233,
    236–237, 245–246, 250–251,
    253–257, 261–262, 265–266,
    269, 276, 279, 282–285, 289,
    300, 302–313, 325, 329–330,
    334–335, 339–344, 361–363,
    368, 370–372, 373–374,
    376–380, 389, 392–395, 398,
    400, 404, 410–411, 415,
    417–418, 426, 437, 444–445,
    450, 452–455, 457–459,
    462–463. *See also* Sexual
    relations
shame, *see* Virtue: modesty/shame
Fichte, J. G., 6, 9, 11, 17, 20–21,
    24, 27, 31–33, 36, 39, 42,
    253–264, 471

Gallantry, 43, 142, 155–157, 180,
    188, 199, 213, 224, 248, 250,
    252, 256, 303–304, 308, 357,
    363, 387, 406
Games, 439. *See also* Culture:
    sports; Education: through
    warfare and games
Generation of the sexes, *see*
    Biological differences:
    generation of the sexes
Genius, *see* Rationality: genius
Gilman, Charlotte Perkins, 6–7,
    9–10, 13, 16, 19, 21–22, 24,
    27–28, 30, 32–33, 34, 37, 41,
    43, 391–404
Goldman, Emma, 19, 21–22, 27,
    32–33, 43, 370–380
Gonell, William, 119–121

Hegel, G. W. F., 5, 9, 21, 25,
    30–33, 36, 40, 265–270, 302,
    352, 471
Heloise, 40, 91–93
Hobbes, Thomas, 25, 28, 145–147
Hume, David, 10, 14, 19, 23, 31,
    153–159, 252
Hysteria, *see* Biological differences:
    sexuality: hysteria

Ibsen, Henrik, 42, 344, 365–366,
    378

James, William, 6, 14, 25, 38,
    40–41, 44, 354–364
Jerome (Eusebius Hieronymus),
    14–15, 24, 32, 40, 82–86, 121,
    132, 142

Kant, Immanuel, 11, 13–14, 21, 25,
    30–32, 35–36, 239–252, 471
Kierkegaard, Søren, 9, 24, 26, 29,
    31, 34, 41, 42, 302–316, 471

Language, 17–18, 396–397, 424,
    430, 460–461, 476
Lenin, V. I., 16, 38, 44, 347–351
Lewis, C. S., 8, 24, 30, 437–438
Locke, John, 23, 39, 150–152, 197
Lyceum, 63

MacGuigan, Maryellen, 45, 468–479
Maimonides (Moses ben Maimon),
    26, 34, 39–40, 94–101
Marías, Julián, 6, 11–12, 17, 44,
    460–467, 471, 474–478
Marriage, 6, 19, 21–27, 36, 55,
    75–77, 84–87, 90, 94–99,
    117–119, 138, 150–152,
    157–159, 165, 181, 191–193,
    218, 221–222, 231, 246,
    253–264, 306, 328, 330, 336,
    339, 363, 367, 370–371,
    377–380, 387–389, 392–394,
    397–398, 417, 421, 435–436
divorce/repudiation, *see* Rights:
    divorce/repudiation

head of, 14, 19, 22–27, 30–31, 36, 39, 43, 48, 66, 85, 89, 95, 104–105, 109, 111–112, 117, 119, 135–136, 140, 147, 152, 155, 157, 163–168, 181–182, 190–191, 196, 206–208, 212, 215, 219, 223, 229, 231, 233, 238–239, 247–248, 251–252, 256, 258–261, 270, 281, 286, 289, 291–293, 295–297, 300–301, 312–313, 315, 321, 323–326, 332, 334, 340, 349, 356–357, 360–363, 375, 377, 380, 386–389, 395, 397–398, 407, 420–421, 437–438, 439, 457–459, 474. *See also* Subordination: submissiveness/obedience of women: to men

importance of, 6, 20–22, 37, 59–60, 75, 125, 181, 218, 227, 232, 235, 252, 255–256, 267, 269, 274–275, 277–278, 284, 292, 296–297, 305–307, 311, 314, 328, 333–336, 340–341, 359, 361–362, 367, 370–371, 376, 378–379, 381–382, 388–389, 391–393, 395–398, 400, 418–419, 421, 436, 476–477

marital sexual relations, *see* Sexual relations: marital

monogamy/polygamy, 20, 27, 54, 118, 161–164, 166–168, 174–176, 195, 239, 248, 257, 275–276, 285, 299–301, 366, 420

polyandry, 257

procreation of children, 20, 59–60, 74–75, 87, 150–152, 169, 181, 254, 273, 285, 299–300, 336, 375

selection of mate, 20, 22, 28, 35, 53–56, 59, 97, 117–118, 129, 185, 250–251, 321, 334, 361, 368, 378–379, 392, 423, 425–426, 455, 463

spouse abuse, 19, 166, 178–179, 208, 238, 248, 392, 398

Marx, Karl, 299

Mill, John Stuart, 6, 7, 11, 13, 16, 21–22, 24–25, 37, 47, 288–298, 355–365

Misbegotten male, *see* Biological differences: misbegotten male

Montaigne, Michel de, 10, 19–20, 26, 32–34, 36, 137–144, 210

Montesquieu, Charles de, 23, 26, 28, 31, 36, 41, 160–170, 172–173

More, Thomas, 11, 13, 16, 24, 38, 116–124

Mott, Lucretia, 11, 15–16, 19, 26, 37, 43, 323–327

Musonius Rufus, C., 13, 16, 21–22, 29, 32, 69–77

Nietzsche, Friedrich, 5, 8–9, 11, 14, 16, 20, 28, 33, 34, 42, 328–346, 456, 471

Ortega y Gasset, José, 8, 10, 18, 20, 34–35, 42–43, 449–459, 465, 471–474, 478

Original sin, *see* Virtue: guilt resulting from original sin

Ossoli, Margaret Fuller, 5, 37, 43, 317–322

Plato, 8–9, 13, 15–16, 28–29, 36, 38, 48–58, 125, 157–158, 180, 201, 289, 303, 328, 330, 417, 440, 462, 469–470

Prostitution, *see* Sexual relations: prostitution

Putnam, Emily James, 13, 21–22, 365–369

Rape, *see* Rights: against rapist

Rationality, 8, 9–13, 21, 27, 45, 69, 121, 185, 236–238, 253–254, 269, 274, 293, 360, 407, 430–432, 477

ability to grasp abstractions and principles, 6, 10–12, 14, 36, 179–180, 196–197, 206–208,

211, 224, 226, 232, 242,
246, 263, 269, 271, 273,
278, 281, 283, 294, 320,
331, 335, 352–354, 396, 405,
413, 441, 454, 457, 466–467,
477
attention, 184
cleverness, 11, 65, 68, 205,
219–221, 233, 272, 304, 314,
334, 344, 408
confusion, 10, 20, 34, 43, 136,
229, 315, 335, 412, 450–451,
453, 456–457, 473–474
genius, 5–6, 181, 207–208, 210,
216–217, 227, 237, 305, 319,
328, 346, 382–383, 386, 413,
467
imagination, 20, 177, 184, 454
intuition, 11, 12, 405–406
memory, 65–66, 263
weakness, 10–12, 23–24, 30, 34,
39, 41, 67, 108, 113, 125,
131–133, 139, 182, 204, 208,
210, 216, 219, 225, 239,
270, 281–282, 293, 303, 306,
313, 316–317, 319, 326, 332,
337, 343, 396, 405, 408,
414–415, 423, 427, 465,
469–470
Religion
Adam, *see* Biological differences:
generation of the sexes;
Virtue: guilt resulting from
original sin
Christianity, 14, 24, 26, 32,
40–42, 78–81, 82–93,
102–115, 131–136, 161, 166,
174, 312–316, 323, 344, 357,
361, 378, 404, 428, 433,
436, 437–438, 447, 470
Deborah, 92
education in, *see* Education:
religion
employment in, *see* Employment:
religion
Esther, 92
Eve, *see* Biological differences:
generation of the sexes;

Virtue: guilt resulting from
original sin
Judaism, 92, 94–101, 175, 404
Judith, 92, 458
Islam, 41, 160–164, 166, 173,
175–176, 279, 440
Mary, 82, 92–93, 112, 129, 462
Mormonism, 276
original sin, *see* Virtue: guilt
resulting from original sin
over-masculinization of, 41, 404
Quakers, 323
religious capacity, 27–28, 30,
40–41, 92–93, 106, 119, 135,
206, 265–269, 286, 316, 346,
357, 366, 404–405, 411–412
resurrection of males or females,
40, 89–90, 114–115
Salome, 457–459
submissiveness to religious
authority, 41, 85, 127, 165
Rights/duties, 11, 16, 26–27,
145–147, 209–238, 275, 312,
340
abortion, 371–372, 443
against rapist, 39–40, 99–101
conjugal, 25–26, 83–84, 94–96,
141, 150, 166–167, 174
divorce/repudiation, 26, 39,
87–88, 96–99, 117–118,
151–152, 168, 170, 174, 215,
257, 284–285, 301, 348–349,
363, 378, 387–389, 435, 437,
443
economic, 14, 43, 234, 261, 276,
278, 287, 333, 373, 393,
403–404, 421, 425, 428, 434,
443, 446
inheritance, 26, 39, 94–95,
138–139, 169–170, 173, 226,
276, 278, 300, 327
political and legal, 14, 35–39,
42–44, 50–56, 58, 66–68,
76–77, 161, 164–165, 182,
209–217, 230, 233–234,
240–241, 255, 258–261,
267–269, 282–283, 287,
288–290, 295, 317, 324–326,

333, 344, 347, 349–350,
355–359, 373, 389, 393, 403,
408, 414–415, 426, 428, 433,
446
reverse discrimination, 37, 291
to children, 17, 24, 28, 54, 56,
66, 145–147, 152, 169, 299,
368, 443
to own property, 26, 39, 96, 152,
165, 183, 214, 255, 258,
261, 276, 278, 300, 327, 351
Roper, Margaret More, 13, 120,
122–124, 126
Rousseau, Jean-Jacques, 6–7, 10,
13–14, 15, 20, 24–25, 30,
36–38, 41, 43, 180, 194–208,
217, 218, 220–221, 225,
228–230, 234, 274, 430, 470
Royce, Josiah, 11, 352–353
Russell, Bertrand, 11, 22, 24–25,
28, 32–33, 44, 417–423

Sand, George, 319, 332, 374
Santayana, George, 12, 21, 35,
405–406
Scheler, Max, 17, 44, 424–436
Schopenhauer, Arthur, 5, 8, 10, 16,
20–22, 26–27, 30, 31–32, 33,
35, 39, 270–280, 338, 471
Second sex, 275, 330, 343, 451, 461
Sexual relations, 8, 19–22, 28,
31–33, 43–44, 53–56, 73–74,
140–141, 146–147, 253–257,
269, 313–314, 409, 415, 443,
445, 448
extramarital, see Virtue: chastity/
fidelity
frigidity, 20, 423, 445
marital, 21, 31–33, 74, 83–85, 88,
95, 97–98, 126, 181, 339,
346, 420–421, 423
premarital, 31–33, 117, 251–252,
418. See also Virtue:
continence/virginity
prostitution, 22, 28, 32, 91, 147,
169, 228, 235, 275, 301,
336, 370–371, 376–377,

383–384, 390, 393, 398, 418,
420, 423, 426, 434–435
rape, see Rights: against rapist
venereal disease, 388, 398, 426
virginity, see Virtue: continence/
virginity
Socrates, 29, 48–56, 59–62, 133,
135, 251, 303, 470
Spencer, Anna Garlin, 6, 17, 24–25,
37, 43, 381–390
Spinoza, Baruch, 36, 148–149
Stoics, 13, 69–77
Subordination, 8, 103–104, 145,
195–196
blacks, 414, 439–440. See also
Subordination: slavery
civil subordination of women, see
Rights: political and legal
domestic servitude, 19, 44,
166–168, 179, 301, 348, 350,
381. See also Marriage: head
of
economic dependence, 19, 43–44,
103–104, 190, 226–227,
234–235, 287, 289, 301, 348,
365–367, 374–375, 377–378,
380, 385–387, 391–394, 407,
422, 425
Jews, 345, 407, 414
slavery, 28, 43, 48, 66–69, 74,
100, 103, 106, 117, 155,
162–163, 166, 173, 179, 196,
202, 212, 230, 233, 289,
292, 295, 299, 303, 317,
319, 333, 340–341, 357, 384,
399, 414, 439–440, 445, 448
submissiveness/obedience of
women
to mate, see Marriage: head of
to men, 5–6, 11, 15, 23–25, 28,
30–31, 36–38, 43, 66, 68,
78, 85, 102, 104, 106,
110–111, 114–115, 117,
132, 136, 138–139,
143–144, 146, 163–166,
170, 172, 178–179,
181–182, 185, 194,
198–199, 203–205, 208,

212, 219–220, 222–223,
240, 249–250, 254, 259,
276, 278, 286, 288–289,
296, 298–301, 304–305,
309, 331–334, 337, 342,
346, 348–349, 356–357,
360–361, 368, 377,
384–387, 389–390, 392,
395–399, 407–408, 410,
412, 417, 425, 430,
439–442, 444–445,
447–448, 451, 461, 464,
466, 472–478
to religious authority, *see* Religion:
submissiveness to religious
authority
Suffrage, *see* Rights: political and
legal; Women's Movement

Tertullian, Quintus Septimius
Florens, 24, 30, 78–81

Utilitarianism, 288–298

Virtue, 13, 29–35, 48–49, 58,
67–69, 71–73, 76, 91–93,
134–135, 156, 195, 197–198,
207, 209, 219–235, 238,
241–247, 251, 319, 325,
343–344, 357, 370–372, 390,
408, 415, 432, 446, 469
ambition, 17, 159, 218, 233,
260–261, 264, 426–427
arrogance, 70, 109–110, 121, 236,
243, 273, 395
beauty, 11, 30, 78–81, 84–85, 89,
100, 118, 120–121, 125–126,
133, 139, 149, 163, 183–185,
202, 205, 211, 218–220, 231,
241–247, 273–274, 304,
309–310, 318, 325, 330, 358,
446, 453, 456, 461–462, 476
chastity/fidelity, 24, 31–33, 71,
74, 79, 84–85, 90, 118–119,
131–132, 135, 141–142, 149,
153–155, 161–163, 165, 167,
170, 187–190, 200, 207, 219,
227–228, 230, 232, 234, 248,

251, 272, 277–280, 284–285,
300–301, 308, 311, 315,
339–340, 344, 388, 393,
417–421, 437
competitiveness, 13, 35, 244,
249–250, 273, 277, 379, 393,
403, 425
contentiousness, 127, 135, 248
continence/virginity, 14, 30,
31–33, 39–40, 60–61, 67,
70–71, 73, 74, 82–86, 90,
92, 99–101, 108, 133, 140,
142, 162, 174, 205, 251,
308, 315, 366, 370–371,
375–377, 379, 418–420,
422–423
courage, 30–37, 60, 66–68, 70,
72–73, 92–93, 133, 155, 172,
184, 195, 210, 219, 225,
245, 247, 249, 256, 289,
352, 380, 395, 407, 423, 442
double standard, 31–33, 74, 90,
140–144, 153–155, 170,
199–200, 202, 220–221, 223,
227–228, 250–252, 269,
277–278, 376–377, 418
fear of sex, 11, 423, 444
friendship, 33, 34–35, 48,
137–138, 139, 156, 180, 184,
192, 231, 238, 244, 273,
312–313, 334, 341, 361–362,
400, 405–406, 414, 417, 447,
456, 469
greed, 70
guilt resulting from original sin,
24, 30, 32, 40, 78–79,
83–86, 89, 92, 102, 109–114,
132, 404
importance of reputation, 19, 30,
33, 135, 142, 153–154,
190–191, 200, 203, 205, 220,
224, 232, 251, 277–278, 296,
330, 360, 375, 379, 382–383
jealousy, 65, 134, 189, 222, 248,
251–252, 417
justice, 24, 30, 36–37, 49, 67–68,
70–73, 76, 179, 211,
237–238, 271–272, 296, 324,

331, 335, 361, 395, 405,
415, 438
modesty/shame, 65, 71, 73, 80,
114, 121, 123, 142, 153–155,
180, 198–199, 205, 219, 241,
244, 261, 310–311, 339, 359,
411, 420, 432, 445, 456, 462
patience, 30, 40, 251
rooted in feeling or principle, 30,
36, 211, 225, 229, 237–238,
241–247, 271, 282, 284, 429,
432
selfishness/selflessness, 30, 37, 41,
73, 75–76, 179, 226–227,
233, 237, 255–257, 261, 289,
296–297, 314–315, 342,
360–362, 367, 383, 389, 408
truthfulness, 33–34, 65, 79–80,
99, 143, 159, 180, 183–184,
189, 206, 220, 229, 232,
272, 279, 310, 314, 331,
337, 367, 394, 409–411,
413–414, 419, 456
vanity, 17, 78–79, 133, 159, 164,
202, 222, 224, 227, 243–244,

246, 261, 264, 283, 307,
330, 334, 338, 442
vengeance, 184
Vives, Luis, 10, 14, 15, 24,
131–136
Voltaire, François Marie Arouet, 16,
36, 38, 171–176, 195, 216, 252

War, *see* Employment: in armies;
Culture: war-stories
Weininger, Otto, 10, 16, 25, 30, 33,
35, 36, 41–42, 407–416
Wollstonecraft, Mary, 5, 8, 13, 16,
19–20, 29, 32–34, 37–38, 43,
218–238, 319
Women's Movement, 25, 41–44,
259–260, 262, 282, 303, 319,
330–333, 335, 343–346, 347,
372–376, 390, 392–393,
399–400, 403, 407–408,
414–415, 419–420, 422,
425–436, 449, 451, 467
Work, *see* Employment

Xenophon, 16, 21–22, 25, 59–62,
136